www.wadsworth.com

wadsworth.com is the World Wide Web site for Wadsworth and is your direct source to dozens of online resources.

At *wadsworth.com* you can find out about supplements, demonstration software, and student resources. You can also send e-mail to many of our authors and preview new publications and exciting new technologies.

wadsworth.com
Changing the way the world learns®

Counseling, Treatment, and Intervention Methods with Juvenile and Adult Offenders

Rudolph Alexander, Jr.

College of Social Work
The Ohio State University

Brooks/Cole
Thomson Learning™

Australia • Canada • Mexico • Singapore • Spain • United Kingdom • United States

Executive Editor: Vicki Knight
Acquisitions Editor: Lisa Gebo
Editorial Assistant: Susan Wilson
Marketing Manager: Caroline Concilla
Marketing Assistant: Jessica McFadden
Project Editor: Pam Suwinsky
Print Buyer: Karen Hunt

Production Editor: Carol O'Connell,
   Graphic World Publishing Services
Compositor: Graphic World, Inc.
Cover Designer: Yvo Riezebos
Cover Image: Photodisc
Cover Printer: Webcom Limited
Printer/Binder: Webcom Limited

Printed in Canada

    4   5   6   7   05

For permission to use material from this text,
contact us by
   Web: www.thomsonrights.com
   Fax: 1-800-730-2215
   Phone: 1-800-730-2214

ISBN: 0830-415289

For more information, contact
Wadsworth/Thomson Learning
10 Davis Drive
Belmont, CA 94002-3098
USA
http://www.wadsworth.com

International Headquarters
Thomson Learning
290 Harbor Drive, 2nd Floor
Stamford, CT 06902-7477
USA

UK/Europe/Middle East/South Africa
Thomson Learning
Berkshire House
168-173 High Holborn
London WC1V 7AA
United Kingdom

Asia
Thomson Learning
60 Albert Street #15-01
Albert Complex
Singapore 189969

Canada
Nelson/Thomson Learning
1120 Birchmount Road
Scarborough, Ontario M1K 5G4
Canada

This book is dedicated to my parents, Rudolph Alexander, Sr., and Thelma Jones Alexander. Hindered by social and family restraints that forced them to help care for younger siblings, both of my parents had just grade school educations—one a third-grade education and the other a fourth. However, they instilled in me the importance of education. Later as an adolescent when I encountered a difficult period in my life, they were tirelessly supportive and shepherded me back from my abyss. Through their steadfast support, they made it possible for me to begin a path toward higher education. Without them, this book would not have been ultimately produced. Though both are now gone, they will forever remain in my thoughts and in my heart. This book is dedicated to them.

Contents

❖ ❖ ❖

Preface

⁜ ⁜ ⁜

The idea for this textbook originated from my teaching a course entitled "Social Work Practice in Corrections," within the College of Social Work at Ohio State University. No textbook that I reviewed for this course met my satisfaction. Some textbooks did not discuss juvenile offenders, others slighted female offenders, and virtually all did not discuss the right to treatment or to refuse treatment. For these reasons, I decided to write a text that would cover the areas that I thought should be covered in a textbook on counseling offenders. This textbook, thus, is written for students studying how to counsel, treat, and intervene with various offenders, including students in criminal justice programs, psychology, sociology, human ecology, and social work. It is also written for professionals who work with juvenile and adult offenders in the community or institutions.

Strongly influenced by my background and experiences, this textbook reflects certain philosophical beliefs and assumptions. My academic career began as a criminal justice major, and I received an A.S. Degree in Criminal Justice from Armstrong State College, located in Savannah, Georgia. I continued working toward my Bachelor's Degree when I temporarily discontinued college to accept a position as a wilderness camp counselor for delinquent and emotionally disturbed boys at Hope Center for Youth in Apple Springs, Texas. Later returning to school, I obtained a Bachelor's Degree in Criminology and Corrections from Sam Houston State University in Huntsville, Texas. During that time *Ruiz v. Estelle* had been decided by a federal district court, and the Texas Department of Corrections was held to be massively violating prisoners' rights. I was particularly interested in the part of the ruling that held that prisoners' right to mental health treatment had been violated, and I wanted to know how such a right existed when it was not stated explicitly in the U.S. Constitution.

By that time also, I had become a Family/Youth Worker for Hope Center's main office in Houston, Texas, performing intake interviews and counseling parents of the boys who were in our Wilderness Camp. When I mentioned my intentions to go to graduate school, my advisor at Sam Houston State, who headed the Criminology and Corrections area and who had a Doctoral in Social Work, urged me to seek a social work degree. She stated that a social work degree, combined with a criminal justice degree, would do more for me professionally than two degrees in criminology. I took her advice and enrolled at the School of Social Work at the University of Houston, where I earned a Master's Degree. At the University of Houston, my first field placement, a required component of all social work programs, was in the psychiatric unit of Ben Taub Hospital, increasing my interest in mental health.

Anticipating leaving Texas to enter a Ph.D. program in Social Work at the University of Minnesota and needing to pay off a car loan, I worked as a mental health worker in the adolescent unit of a Psychiatric Hospital in Deer Park, Texas. I worked sixteen hours on Saturdays and sixteen hours on Sundays while maintaining my position as a Family/Youth Worker from Mondays to Fridays. I worked this schedule for nine months until I left Texas for Minnesota.

After getting acclimated to the doctoral program at the University of Minnesota, I worked evenings at a residential home for seriously mentally ill adults for about a year and then took a another position as a mental health worker for seriously mentally ill adults in another group home.

By this time, my ideas, beliefs, and philosophy had been established. While in Minnesota, I was urged by my employer to attend a workshop on dual diagnosis patients. Over 100 mental health professionals in the Twin Cities area were present. Four people led the workshop, and one presenter was extremely good in his presentation. At the end of the workshop, the audience gave them a standing ovation.

I, too, was impressed with the one speaker, but I did not fully endorse the information presented. As an inchoate researcher then, I had begun to believe that sound and rigorous research provides knowledge about what works and what does not work. From previous experiences, I knew that workshop presenters seldom discuss their failures and tend to present their best one or two cases. If a failure is discussed, it is used to discuss how future changes were made that resulted in a success. In criminal justice, clinicians and therapists do likewise, which makes me cautious when someone proclaims to know best how to treat offenders.

My cautiousness also has been strengthened by my belief that sometimes professionals present overly optimistic information. For instance, I heard one administrator of a halfway house for offenders state during a radio interview that the program had an 85% success rate, a dubious claim. From reading the newspaper and listening to the news, I know that there are a lot of failures, and if the experts were correct, offenders would be very scarce. There are a considerable number of experts who state and imply *the* way to treat juveniles, dual diagnosed individuals, sex offenders, and substance abusers. I remain cautious unless I hear or read sound, rigorous research documenting such effectiveness. Further, as a researcher, I also know that even if a research study suggests that a technique, theory, or approach is effective, it does not mean that this is the case for all individuals. A treated group may have a statistically significant lower percentage of arrests or relapses than a control group, but there are still sizable failures in the treated group.

Keeping these views, experiences, and thoughts in mind, readers may understand why this textbook is structured in the manner that it is. For instance, I discuss treatment programs for offenders, beginning with the most sound and rigorous research—studies that used an experimental, quasi-experimental, or multiple-baseline single-subject design. I follow with other researched programs that, while not as rigorous, do provide knowledge. I, then, follow the researched programs with programs that have not been researched. These programs may be effective too, but there is no way to know. While I am cautious regarding unresearched programs, I do not necessarily disbelieve the person writing or describing a program. These programs may be effective too, sounding logical and practicable. Implied in these presentations of researched and unresearched programs is that these descriptions tell criminal justice practitioners how to work with specific offenders. This is especially the case when experimental designs have established effectiveness.

The overall organization of the chapters in this textbook is as follow: It begins with the introduction issues. Then, this book discusses offenders' treatment rights and the constitutional and legal foundation for these rights. This legal discussion is placed here because a number of prisoners choose not to participate in treatment and rehabilitation programs, believing these to be administratively sanctioned mind games. They resist the coercion and just do their time. Presented next are treatment theories, which are followed by a chapter on assessment and diagnosis. Some texts may reverse this order, but I believe that one begins with a theory, and the theory tells a clinician what to assess. If clinicians subscribe to cognitive theory, they would not assess, principally, the client's relationship with his or her parents or assess peer group relations. If the presenting problem is depression and cognitive theory is used, a clinician would not assess concepts that have nothing to do with cognitive theory. Then, the remaining of the text follows, including discussions of individual counseling, group counseling, and counseling interventions with juvenile females, juvenile males, adult females, adult males, and special populations. The rationale for these separations is that the literature shows that adolescent girls are more likely to be sexually abused, and woman offenders are more likely to be abused by a significant other and are more likely to have had responsibility for minor children. At the same time, males are more likely to be violent, and adult males are more likely to be abusive in relationships. All of these issues impact treatment in various ways. Each of these four chapters begins with a brief introduction, the context of counseling, followed by a section called Techniques and Procedures of Treatment, researched programs and unresearched programs.

Two excellent reviewers improved the original manuscript significantly. The author would like to thank Dr. Laura E. Bedard of the School of Criminology and Criminal Justice at Florida State University and Dr. Robert Shearer of the College of Criminal Justice at Sam Houston State University for their helpful criticisms. Much of their suggestions for improvements in the original manuscript were accepted. Any perceived shortcomings, necessitated by page limits and the author's philosophy, should be attributed to the author. Wadsworth and the author would welcome comments and feedback from readers on how this book could be further strengthened.

1

❄ ❄ ❄

Correctional Counseling and Intervention: Introduction and Critical Issues

BACKGROUND OF COUNSELING

❄ INTRODUCTION

America's correctional history, particularly the nineteenth and twentieth centuries, is replete with semantics denoting promises to change criminal offenders. Some involve the influence of religion as suggested by the words *penitentiary* and *refuge*. The invention and naming of the penitentiary suggested that offenders who were allowed to experience penitence would change in a positive direction. Also, *Houses of Refuge* suggested places insulated from evil and bad societal influences. *Houses of Correction* denoted places where offenders might be corrected and returned to society as law-abiding citizens. Similarly, the building of reformatories carried with it the hopes that offenders could be reformed or rehabilitated. Later, many of these institutions were placed in Correction Departments or Departments of Rehabilitation and Correction, suggesting that the mission of these departments was to change offenders.

However, despite the semantics, society's efforts to change or rehabilitate offenders have not obtained the visionary hopes of the people who designed these institutions. Rehabilitating offenders, as determined by whether offenders get into legal trouble after being released, has been found to be difficult to achieve.

In the twentieth century, and especially during the 1960s, crime became more of a political issue. For instance, Senator Barry Goldwater, stressing that crimes had increased during the time the Democrats were in control of the White House, attempted to use crime as a political issue during his failed campaign for president in 1964 against President Lyndon Baines Johnson. In 1968, Richard Nixon, using crimes and perceived liberal rulings regarding criminal defendants from the U.S. Supreme Court as campaign issues, ran on a law-and-order campaign and the need to take a different, harsher approach with criminals (Alexander, 1990). Questions began to be raised regarding whether the country should pursue a policy of rehabilitating offenders or punishing them harshly.

During this period also, criminal justice researchers began to be more interested in whether the criminal justice system could rehabilitate offenders. A little-publicized study of a treatment program in California concluded that there was no empirical evidence that offenders could be rehabilitated (Kassenbaum, Ward, & Wilner, 1971). One of the authors of this study, David Ward, who taught a penology class that the author attended, stated that the concept of rehabilitation was counterproductive for criminal justice policy. According to Professor Ward, rehabilitation suggests to judges that something wonderful was going on in prisons, and, as a result, would lead judges to incarcerating many offenders when these offenders could be better served in the community.

Undoubtedly, the most publicized report regarding whether offenders could be rehabilitated was written by Robert Martinson. This report provided ammunition to lawmakers to abandon, on the record, the concept of rehabilitation. However, treatment professionals countered that many offenders could be rehabilitated, and the country should maintain programs in prisons and community corrections. These proponents contend that Martinson asked the wrong research question. Instead of asking whether treatment was effective, the better question is what type of treatment works best for what type of offenders or crimes. Figure 1.1 provides an illustration of a design that tells what works best for what type of offenders. It can be modified to include female offenders, juvenile offenders, and different types of treatments. The premise of the latter question is that certainly some offenders benefit from treatment.

This book was written with the belief that treatment is effective for some offenders in some circumstances, while acknowledging that changing human behavior is arduous. This first chapter begins by defining rehabilitation and treatment, the Medical Model of treatment, the Martinson Report in which the phrase "nothing works" originated, and the responses to Martinson. Then, it moves to some of the critical issues, such as obstacles to effective treatment, the current treatment focus for offenders, ethical issues in counseling, and training and credentialing for corrections counselors.

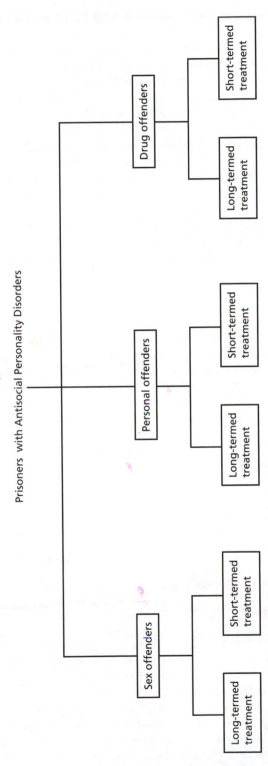

FIGURE 1.1 A Design for Determining What Works Best

Rehabilitation, Treatment, and Mental Health

Rehabilitation is a concept with a variety of meanings. The author has attended community meetings in Ohio with offenders' families, who have lamented the lack of rehabilitation in those prisons. Similarly, prisoners in one Ohio prison echoed the same observations—that prisons are void of rehabilitation. These statements suggest that prisoners and their families have their definition of what rehabilitation is. According to them, rehabilitation is *the availability of programs in prisons*. Related to this definition, participation in programs constitutes being rehabilitated, and the more participation in various programs, the more a prisoner feels that he or she has been rehabilitated. For instance, Joseph Cannon, a thirty-eight-year-old man, had been on Texas death row for twenty-one years. He committed his crime when he was seventeen years old. Since being in prison, Cannon taught himself to read and write. Scheduled to die on April 22, 1998, he stated that he was not optimistic of being spared and that when he died the State of Texas would be killing a different person. As he assessed himself, "I don't know if it has a lot to do with the fact that I'm rehabilitated," referring to the boy he was at the time of the crime and the man nearing execution (Jones, 1998). However, this definition of rehabilitation and being rehabilitated is contrary to the definition held by criminal justice professionals and policy makers.

The Panel on Research on Rehabilitative Techniques (PRRT) defined rehabilitation as "the results of any planned intervention that reduced an offender's further criminal activity, whether that reduction is mediated by personality, behavior, abilities, attitudes, values, or other factors. The effects of maturation and the effects associated with fear or intimidation are excluded, the result of the latter having traditionally been labeled as specific deterrence" (Sechrest, White, & Brown, 1979, pp. 20–21).

This definition by PRRT reflects three major aspects of rehabilitation. First, there must be planned, professional intervention. Impromptu change or reformation is excluded, such as in the case of a prisoner who is about to be executed and prepares for his or her maker, such as Ms. Karla Faye Tucker. Ms. Tucker was a woman who was executed by the State of Texas. Before her death, she, along with her supporters, had professed to have been saved and had accepted Jesus as her personal savior (Katz, 1998). Ms. Tucker's change in attitude does not constitute being rehabilitated, according to the PRRT definition. Second is eclecticism, which means that there is no prior conception of the processes of rehabilitation, such as physiological, psychological, social, or moral hypotheses. Third, the focus is totally on criminal behavior as a measure of rehabilitation, not growth, insight, or happiness.

Rehabilitation may be measured by the seriousness of criminal behavior. In addition, psychological and economic outcomes are intervening variables only for the overall goal of reducing criminal activity. For instance, a program just to find offenders jobs is not a measure of rehabilitation. The job must result in no or less future criminal activity (Sechrest et al., 1979).

Taken together, rehabilitation is achieved through planned interventions by skilled professionals. As a consequence, just serving a sentence in prison cannot result in rehabilitation. Furthermore, because planned activities by professionals in order to change offenders' attitudes, behaviors, and personalities are the heart of rehabilitation, treatment theories are critically important because they form the foundation for directing change efforts. Hence, this linkage explains why a number of treatment theories are presented in Chapter 3 and why subsequent references to treatment theories are discussed in programs for others in the chapters on female juveniles, male juveniles, adult female offenders, and adult male offenders. Simply, sound treatment programs for offenders must be tied to theories.

Rehabilitation is sometimes used interchangeably with treatment. However, treatment, as discussed here, involves two essentially different definitions. First, treatment is indeed used interchangeably with rehabilitation. In prison, treatment consists of diagnosis, classification, a variety of treatment activities, punishment, and prognoses for rehabilitation (Mitford, 1973). There is a no legal right to this treatment. However, there is a legal right to psychological treatment for seriously mentally ill prisoners. In one of the first cases involving the right to mental health treatment, Judge David L. Bazelon, of the Court of Appeals for the District of Columbia, provided a definition of treatment in a psychiatric facility. According to Judge Bazelon,

> [It] includes not only the contacts with a psychiatrist but also activities and contacts with the hospital staff designed to cure or improve the patient. The hospital need not show the treatment will cure or improve but only that there is a bona fide effort to do so. This requires the hospital to show that initial and periodic inquiries are made into the needs and conditions of the patient with a view to providing suitable treatment for him [or her], and that the program provided is suited to his [or her] particular needs. Treatment that has therapeutic value for some may not have such value for others. For example, it may not be assumed that confinement in a hospital is beneficial environmental therapy for all. (*Rouse v. Cameron*, 1966, p. 456)

Although this definition involves a definition of psychiatric or mental health treatment in a psychiatric facility, it has implications for corrections, especially prisons. Some prisoners have a right to mental health treatment. (The rationale for such treatment is discussed in detail in Chapter 2.) For instance, convicted sex offenders are being civilly committed to mental health facilities after the end of their prison sentences. The rationale for this law is that these individuals are dangerous and need treatment for their mental abnormality. Therefore, if a convicted sex offender has been civilly committed to an institution under the guise of treatment, then this prisoner falls within a situation similar to the persons in a psychiatric unit such as Judge Bazelon discussed.

The American Psychiatric Association (1989) defines mental health treatment as it is used in a correctional environment. According to it, "mental health treatment is defined as the use of a variety of mental health therapies, biological as well as psychological, in order to alleviate symptoms of mental disorders which significantly interfere with the inmate's ability to function in the particular criminal justice environment" (1989, p. 10). This definition is consistent with a more recent definition of psychotherapy by the American Psychiatric Association (Committee on the Practice of Psychotherapy, 1996). Revealed in this definition is that mental health treatment is not provided to rehabilitate offenders. This type of treatment is designed to alleviate psychiatric symptoms so that a prisoner or jail detainee can function in his or her environment. A prisoner or jail detainee who is hallucinating has been successfully treated or provided with mental health treatment when his or her hallucinations have been stopped or substantially alleviated by drugs or other mental health therapies.

Finally, Toneatto (1995) proposed a comprehensive set of outcomes based on a model that he developed for persons undergoing drug treatment. The model is called the Regulation of the Cognitive States, which emphasized the importance of cognition in drug use. Treatment based on this model to determine effectiveness examines the extent of substance use following treatment. While total abstinence is highly desirable, a substantial reduction is evidence of effectiveness. Another outcome is a person's ability to self-regulate distressing cognitive experiences without drugs. Ignoring the cognitive aspects will lead to short-term success or a quick relapse. A person will stop using drugs for a while, but as the cognitive states produce more stress, the person will eventually capitulate. Therefore, treatment is geared at a behavioral outcome (i.e., abstinence or reduction) and a cognitive outcome (i.e., acceptance of cognitive states or lessened desire to self-regulate cognitive with drugs) (Toneatto, 1995). Toneatto's model provides a definition of drug treatment: treatment that involves efforts aimed at substantially reducing drug use and helping an individual to deal effectively with cognitive states that facilitate drug use.

Intervention is another term sometimes interchanged with treatment. With a substance-abusing person who is perceived by friends and relatives to have a problem, an intervention is implemented. In this manner, intervention is a planned gathering of friends and relatives to impress strongly upon a substance-abusing individual that he or she has a problem, that people deeply care about him or her, and the individual needs to go into treatment. Often, the substance-abusing person is misled about the reason that he or she is asked to attend a function or go to someone's house. The group, generally, has rehearsed what will be said, who is going to take the lead, and that the group will be unanimous in requesting that the individual get help for his or her substance abuse. In this book, however, intervention means something different. It refers to activities by corrections to change offenders that may or may not involve planned, direct counseling by professionals. For instance, conducting "gang sweeps" by law enforcement officials may be called an intervention and so would a family counseling program by a licensed mental health worker for gang members and their families. Giving parolees stipends or jobs may be an intervention as well as drug counseling. In other words, an intervention is both micro and macro services for offenders.

Additional Clinical Definitions

Psychotherapy is any form of treatment for mental illnesses, behavioral maladaptations, and other emotional problems by a trained person who establishes a professional relationship with a client for the purpose of removing, modifying, or retarding existing symptoms; of attenuating or reversing disturbed patterns of behavior; and of promoting positive personality growth and development (Campbell, 1996).

Spontaneous Remission is the process of a client improving without the benefit of professional therapeutic intervention (Walrond-Skinner, 1986).

Folie à Deux involves two individuals in close association and one imparts a delusional idea which both of them then share (Walrond-Skinner, 1986).

Wounded Healer is a counselor with therapeutic potential who shares his or her psychic pain and vulnerability toward the benefit of the client (Walrond-Skinner, 1986).

Dual Diagnosis is a term to describe an individual who has both a substance abuse problem and a psychiatric disorder (Wilson & Wilson, 1992).

Deterioration is a condition in which the client gets worse after psychotherapy. Among the negative effects of deterioration are worsening of symptoms, the development of new symptoms, a sustained reliance upon therapy or the therapist, and the development of an unrealistic view of the self that leads to disappointment and despair (Walrond-Skinner, 1986).

Adaptation is the capacity of an individual to cope with his or her environment (Moore & Fine, 1990).

The Development of the Medical Model

The medical model posits that criminal behavior is caused by psychological and biological factors. When these factors are identified, successful treatment could be administered (Wolfgang, 1988). Two perspectives exist regarding the development of the medical model. One suggests simply that the medical model was borrowed from the discipline of medicine and the treatment of diseases. Another perspective provides a more in-depth account, linking it to one of the early criminological schools of thought.

For instance, Marshall (1981) links the occurrence of the medical model with the development of positivism. In the eighteenth century, early scientists and philosophers contended that the physical world was characterized by order and regularity; gods and evil spirits were not creating famines, storms, and eclipses because they were angry. In addition, these early scientists and philosophers contended that the social order was not disordered and unexpected. Science had explanations for human behavior. Positivistic empiricism, consisting of observation, experimentation, measurement, and quantification, could explain the physical world and human behavior. As a result, the positivistic approach to understanding criminal behavior developed.

The first school to explain criminal behavior was the classical school, which was founded by Cesare Beccaria. This school assumed that there was good and evil, and people were rational. People also had free will. Moreover, people followed the pleasure principle, which means that they sought the maximum amount of pleasure and avoid pain. Accordingly, people committed crimes essentially because the good, or pleasure, exceeded the bad, or pain.

The positivistic school, on the other hand, rejected the classical school and contended that determinism caused crimes. Cesare Lombroso, the founder of the positivistic school and the professed father of criminology, contended that criminals were born criminogenic, and they could be distinguished by certain physical stigmata. Other positivistic criminologists added social and environmental forces to understand crime and deviance.

As stated by Marshall (1981), "the positivist image of crime is usually referred to as the medical model of deviance. This model portrays crime as attributable primarily to the pathological characteristics of the offender. The medical model views the offender as sick (physically, mentally, or socially). Deviant acts are seen as symptomatic of an underlying pathological disorder" (1981, p. 21). Equally, or more importantly, criminal deviance could be cured.

These views created the idea of individualized treatment. Proponents of this view rejected the nineteenth century's belief that isolation and penitence would reform the offender. Instead, the positivist criminologists contended that no doctor prescribed the same medication for every sick person. A person received medication or treatment based on his or her illness and its causes. Likewise, offenders should not receive the same treatment, and individualized treatment was appropriate.

As stated earlier, the other account of the development of the medical model in corrections simply indicated that it came from medicine. Regardless of the history, everyone agreed that the medical model was officially transported to corrections in 1870 by the National Prison Association. This organization, through its Declaration of Principles, declared that prisoners would be reformed by the application of treatment (Champion, 1998; Marshall, 1981).

The first institution to utilize the medical model, administered by Zebulon Brockway, was the Elmira Reformatory in New York, which was opened in 1876. After an initial period, when difficult inmates from Sing Sing and Auburn prisons were housed at Elmira, Brockway implemented the medical model with more amenable inmates. Brockway referred to Elmira as a "reformatory hospital" and a "college on the hill." According to Pisciotta, "Elmira's indeterminate sentencing model came from the belief that each offender's behavior was determined by a variety of unique environmental, psychological, and/or biological factors. Individualized diagnoses and treatment were, in theory, the key to the Elmira system" (Pisciotta, 1994, p. 18).

In the 1920s, the U.S. Bureau of Prisons adopted the medical model for use with its prisoners (Allen & Simonsen, 1998). It also implemented a classification system, distinguishing which offenders were amenable to reformation (Wilson & Pescor, 1939). Treatment professionals inside prisons would diagnose prisoners, develop treatment plans, and then implement these plans. When the prisoners were determined to be almost well, they would be released on parole. The parole officers would continue treatment, ensuring that the prisoners would remain on the straight and narrow (Allen & Simonsen, 1998).

With respect to juvenile offenders, the concept of rehabilitation manifested itself in the handling of adolescents and the creation of the first juvenile court in 1899. The juvenile justice system followed principles of the medical model. Though the language was different from that used in the adult criminal justice system, the juvenile justice system utilized a semi-indeterminate sentence. Rather than sentencing a juvenile to 1 year to life, juveniles who needed commitment were committed to their majority. For instance, a fifteen-year-old juvenile could be sentenced to his or her majority—21 years of age. In effect, this commitment could be 1 to 6 years. Also, the juvenile justice system, reflecting the influence of social work, used the casework method, consisting of assessment, diagnosis, and treatment (Alexander, 1997).

Certainly, reformers knew early on that changing offenders was difficult. Early statistics showed a high level of recidivism (Alexander, 1997). Also, not every prison system embraced the concept of rehabilitation. While New York built the Elmira Reformatory, it also operated Sing Sing and Auburn penitentiaries, where traditional punishment was the philosophy. Other states operated prison systems in which rehabilitation was not the primary or secondary concern of prison administrators. For instance, in the South, the chain gang emerged in the late nineteenth century and remained for much of the twentieth century; there was no attempt to reform or rehabilitate men on the chain gang. This reality has led some penal historians to argue that the concept of rehabilitation was more of a philosophical statement rather than operating practice (Mitford, 1973). Regardless, the issues of rehabilitation and recidivism were important concepts among many concerned policy makers and criminal justice professionals.

Treatment Research

In 1966, Robert Martinson and several colleagues were hired and charged by the New York State Governor's Special Committee on Criminal Offenders to advise what worked in rehabilitating criminal offenders. In response to this charge, Martinson sought to prepare a comprehensive, worldwide review of rehabilitation programs. While the review was underway, another committee, established to receive funding from the Omnibus Crime Control and Safe Street Act of 1968, assumed supervisory control over Martinson's forthcoming report. This committee, while waiting, decided to proceed with a resurgence of rehabilitation programs in New York. When Martinson's report was completed and presented to the new committee, it was rejected and Martinson was forbidden from publishing it. After the suppressed report was subpoenaed by a lawyer for use as evidence in a case, the 1400-page report was released to the public (Martinson, 1974).

The information reviewed consisted of all rehabilitation studies published in English from 1945 to 1967. Rehabilitation was operationalized as adjustment to prison life, vocational success, educational achievement, personality and attitude change, general adjustment to society, and recidivism. The study had to include a control or comparison group. With these criteria, they found 231 studies (Martinson, 1974).

In Martinson's (1974) first publicized work regarding his controversial study, he reported only the results from his review of recidivism studies. He chose this outcome because recidivism most represented the successfulness of rehabilitation. However, Martinson cautioned that

> the use of even this one measure brings with it enough methodological complications to make a clear reporting of the findings most difficult. The group that are studied, for instance, are exceedingly disparate so that it is hard to tell whether what 'works' for one kind of offender also works for others. In addition, there has been little attempt to replicate studies; therefore one cannot be certain how stable and reliable the various findings are. Just as important, when the various studies use the term 'recidivism rates,' they may in fact be talking about somewhat different measures of offender behavior—i.e., 'failure' measures such as arrest rates or parole violation rates, or 'success' measures such as favorable discharge from parole or probation. (1974, p. 24–25)

Despite the shortcomings, Martinson posed and answered seven questions. With respect to all questions, Martinson's conclusion was that "with few and isolated exceptions, the rehabilitative efforts that have been reported so far have had no appreciative effect on recidivism" (1974, p. 25). It was this conclusion that the new media and politicians emphasized from Martinson's report.

Martinson said more about the methodological shortcomings of the studies he reviewed in his conclusion, but this aspect was ignored. Particularly, he stated that despite excluding some research studies, the studies that were included still had problems. Among the problems were programs' failure to make a rigorous attempt to exclude competing hypotheses, failure to exclude extraneous factors that undermined their measurements, failure to use standard measures of recidivism, failure to use standard follow-up periods, failure to replicate, failure to contemplate system effects, and failure to use interventions based on theory. According to Martinson, "it is just possible that some of our treatment programs are working to some extent, but that our research is so bad that is it incapable of telling" (Martinson, 1974, p. 49).

Martinson's conclusion that nothing works provoked both opponents and proponents of rehabilitation. The opponents used it as an impetus to encourage enactment of more conservative criminal justice policies. Proponents cited the flaws in previous research and asserted that the wrong question was asked. They also stated that newer research and newer research techniques showed that rehabilitation was effective for some groups (Palmer, 1983; Palmer, 1992). Proponents have reviewed Martinson's work and cited the recent history of rehabilitation and the necessity to continue trying to change offenders.

The Responses to Martinson

Sechrest and colleagues (1979) reviewed Martinson's work and basically agreed with his conclusion. However, they were critical of Martinson's acceptance of the adequacy of the treatment given to some offenders. They noted that "many of the intervention tested seem to have been so weak in proportion to the problem involved that it would scarcely have been credible had any effect been found" (1979, p. 32). They posed the question of why would one expect that one hour per week of group therapy with an inadequately trained group leader and unwilling, involuntary prisoners would produce a major behavior change in incarcerated felons, especially considering the powerful effect of the prison background. Sechrest and colleagues stated that some studies that were reported after Martinson's study revealed that some interventions involving work and financial support appeared to show a modest reduction in the severity of criminality. They concluded that "there is not now in the scientific literature any basis for any policy or recommendations regarding rehabilitation of criminal offenders. . . . The magnitude of the task of reforming criminal offenders has been consistently underestimated. It is clear that far more intensive and extensive interventions will be required if rehabilitation is to be possible; even then, there is no guarantee of success" (1979, p. 34).

A stalwart supporter of rehabilitation or intervention (Palmer, 1975; Palmer, 1978; Palmer, 1983), Palmer (1992) traced the policy shifts regarding the philosophy of rehabilitation since the 1960s. According to Palmer's historical account, during the 1960s, optimism was rather high regarding the potential of rehabilitation to positively change offenders. After Martinson's report, far-reaching pessimism spread among policy makers and the public. The country then sought to "get tough" on offenders as a way of changing them, and new prisons and longer sentences became more prevalent. Beginning about 1983, limited confidence in rehabilitation or intervention for some offenders began to sprout again. Certain offenders, such as drug offenders and sex offenders, were causing considerable alarm among policy makers because of their cost to society and concern for the safety of women and children. In the late 1980s, intervention became increasingly more popular as a result of more focused direction supported by stronger research. Specific programs were developed and targeted at these groups. Also, newer, empirically sound research revealed that intervention for juvenile and drug offenders was effective.

Palmer reviewed 32 literature reviews and meta-analyses of studies that were conducted from 1975 to the 1980s. Meta-analysis is "a statistical procedure that allows the data from multiple studies to be combined, thereby increasing the statistical power—the ability to find differences" (Breiling, 1992, p. 1). Most of the programs studied involved institutional- and community-based programs for juvenile offenders. In these studies, comparisons were made between treatment and control or comparison groups. As a rule-of-thumb, Palmer indicated that a large reduction in recidivism was 25% or higher, a moderate reduction was 24% to 10%, a small reduction was less than 10%. Palmer concluded that intervention reduced recidivism and typically these reductions were in the moderate range (Palmer, 1992).

In addition, Lipsey (1992) used meta-analysis to study 443 delinquency treatment studies. He first analyzed the percentages for the outcomes of the 443 studies. Of this total, 285, or 64.3%, favored the treatment group; 131, or 29.6%, favored the control group; and 27, or 6.1%, favored neither the treatment nor the control group. Lipsey found that the mean effect size was equivalent to a 10% reduction in the delinquency of the treated group compared with the control group. Taking into account the unreliability of delinquency recidivism measures and the practice of doubling the effect size to account for this unreliability, Lipsey stated that the true difference between treated and control groups is 20%. In effect, there is, on average, a 20% reduction in delinquency. The programs that had the most impact were structured treatment. In order words, treatment programs that used behavioral techniques, teaching skills, or one of these in combination with other approaches showed the most reduction in delinquency (Lipsey, 1992).

Of course, every offender cannot be changed. Some offenders may be unaffected by correctional treatment. For instance, individuals in the Mafia are not likely to be persuaded by counselors and therapeutic interventions that crime is wrong. Killing, extortion, drug selling, gambling, and prostitution are, in the underworld, acceptable means of making money or facilitating money making. The world in which members of the Mafia live is different from the average citizen. Then, there are others who are not in the Mafia who have similar views, and these individuals, too, are hard to change. But the majority of people who go to prison or break the law have the *potential* to change. Individuals are not born bad or evil. With the exception of a few seriously mentally ill individuals, most individuals know that right and wrong exist. As Sykes and Matza (1991) have stated, most people drift from offending and nonoffending behaviors and neutralize their beliefs in order to commit offending behavior. Because most individuals move from offending and nonoffending, they are capable of engaging in nonoffending or prosocial behaviors. This change can occur as a result of an individual deciding to change a criminal lifestyle. In addition, some offenders can be helped to change a criminal lifestyle with the aid of criminal justice and mental health professionals.

Often, politicians and lay persons quickly condemn offender treatment programs when one or two persons reoffended. If fifty prisoners received treatment and eight reoffended, the public is led to believe that treatment is ineffective. These persons want *all* offenders to not reoffend, which is understandable but not possible. Any significant reduction in a treated group of offenders is worthy of societal efforts, however. If a group of sex offenders have a 74% reoffending rate with no treatment efforts and treatment produces a 41% reoffending rate, wouldn't a reduction of 33% be beneficial to society? We know that if we do nothing but incarcerate, we are going to have a 74% reoffending rate. Thus, the success of a treatment program should be based on whether it can significantly reduce the amount of reoffending if society does nothing but incarcerate. Then, the goal of research and treatment should be how to reduce this reoffending rate even lower.

CRIMINAL JUSTICE CLIENTS AND COUNSELING ENVIRONMENTS

The criminal justice system controls a number of individuals (Champion, 1998), and a number of them need mental health counseling ("Addict Has Chance to Kick Habit," 1997; Alexander, 1996; Armstrong & Altschuler, 1994; Chesney-Lind & Sheldon, 1992; Poe-Yamagata, 1997). As of June 1996, states held 1,019,281 adult prisoners, state jails held 518,492, and the federal government held 93,167 (U.S. Department of Justice, 1997a). Of the totals of state and federal prisoners, 74,730 were female, or about 6.3% (U.S. Department of Justice, 1997a). In 1995, correctional officers comprised 64% of the staff in correctional institutions; administrative, clerical, maintenance, and food service constituted 20%; and professional, technical, and educational staff made up 16% (U.S. Department of Justice, 1997b). In 1996, an estimated 2,851,700 juveniles were arrested. Of this total, 25% were females (Snyder, 1997). For violent index crimes, African American juveniles were more likely to be arrested for homicide and robbery, while white juveniles were more likely to be arrested for forcible rape and aggravated assaults (Snyder, 1997). The settings in which counseling adult and juvenile offenders occur are quite varied, consisting of secure institutions, group homes, probation, parole, and mental health settings. Although the rehabilitation of offenders is the ultimate goal, some environments, such as prisons and jails, have different objectives and goals (Diamant, 1992; Steadman & Veysey, 1997). For instance, the primary goal of jails is to hold individuals for trial and to provide a place for offenders to serve misdemeanor sentences. In addition, some prisons exist only to hold the most dangerous prisoners, such as the federal prison where John Gotti is serving life without parole.

Most adult and juvenile offenders are treated within the community. At the end of 1996, 704,709 adults were on parole (U.S. Department of Justice, 1997). The states with the largest parole populations were Texas with 112,594, California with 97,063, and Pennsylvania with 75,013 (U.S. Department of Justice, 1997d). Nearly 3.2 million adults were on probation during 1996 (U.S. Department of Justice, 1997e). In 1996, about 58,492 adults were in jails (U.S. Department of Justice, 1997a). With respect to juveniles, in 1996, 2,851,700 were arrested in the United States (Snyder, 1997). Most of these juveniles who were adjudicated were put on probation (Sickmund, 1997). In 1995, 69,075 juveniles were in custody in a public institution (Moone, 1997) and 39,671 were held in private juvenile facilities (Office of Juvenile Justice and Delinquency Prevention, 1997a). In sum, a number of adult and juvenile offenders are treated in institutions, but most are treated in the community. Within the community, counseling might be provided by probation or parole officers or counselors employed by mental health agencies and group homes.

CRITICAL ISSUES IN COUNSELING

The Difficulty of Changing Criminal Behavior

Statistics on recidivism and incessant public criticisms regarding offenders' unwillingness to stay out of trouble indicate that changing offenders is difficult. Some politicians and members of the public likely believe that some offenders are evil and bad, and these offenders do not want to change. Conversely, treatment professionals often believe that too little treatment is provided in corrections and only a small group receives treatment (Lipton, Falkin, & Wexler, 1992). Then, there are some professionals who believe that criminal behavior is a natural occurrence in this society (Chambliss, 1997; Hulsman, 1997). Changing offenders' behavior, indeed, is difficult to do, especially en mass because of motivational issues (Krause, 1966). It is difficult for reasons related to offenders factors and criminal justice factors.

Offenders Factors Clinicians agree that offenders constitute reluctant clients or customers. Unlike executives or professionals who have psychiatric problems and willingly seek therapy, offenders do not come to counseling in this manner. Invariably, offenders come to counseling and treatment under the pressure of the legal system or expressed or implied coercion by parole boards. Treating these two groups (i.e., voluntary and involuntary) the same is likely to create frustration for all concerned. Some involuntary clients will never participate fully in counseling, wanting a swift termination as soon as possible. Other involuntary clients may see their reluctance dissipate and come to accept that therapy is beneficial (Brodsky, 1998).

Besides engaging in denial and minimization of their offending behavior, sex offenders in treatment, according to some clinicians, engage in invalidation of therapists. These offenders question and minimize the therapists' credentials, education, training, and experience. They also question the motivation of the therapists, accusing them of being in the business for the money or to experience sex vicariously from hearing sex offenders discuss their offending behavior. Some offenders indirectly threaten therapists in order to intimidate them. For instance, some sex offenders come to group and discuss a dream about killing a therapist or vaguely hinting about a riot and hostage taking. Less frightening, some sex offenders try to seduce therapists psychologically by probing for therapists' vulnerabilities and then addressing them (Allen & Brekke, 1996).

Substance abusers are difficult to treat because they are in the precontemplation stage, as noted by Proshaska, DiClemente, and Norcross (1992). A number of addiction professionals maintain that the treatment process for addiction consists of five stages—precontemplation, contemplation, preparation, action, and maintenance. The precontemplation stage makes treating substance-abusing offenders difficult. In this stage, the offenders have no intention of changing their behavior in the near future. Offenders either are unaware or underaware of a problem. However, others see a problem. When persons in this stage come into counseling, it is primarily from pressure from others, such as spouses, employers, or the courts. As long as the pressure is maintained, a semblance of change may be demonstrated. But when the pressure is off, they revert to their dysfunctional behaviors (Prochaska, Di-Clemente, & Norcross, 1992).

Often, when offender-clients come to treatment, they come with a number of internal barriers and obstacles, making treatment success arduous. First, they tend to have a history of failure. For instance, if the problem is substance abuse, they have likely experienced relapse. Thus, it is incumbent upon treatment professionals to structure success opportunities early in treatment. Second, they have been alienated from other systems, such as social services or law enforcement. Third, they have a sense of hopelessness, that they are in a rut with little chance of getting out of it. Fourth, they are cynical about social services and believe that professionals associated with these agencies are there primarily for employment. Fifth, they come with considerable experiences in manipulating other people and systems. For instance, they have frequently lied to other people to obtain benefits or they have concocted stories to get money from associates. Sixth, they have unrealistic expectations about treatment. They expect problems to be solved expeditiously and are not aware that the treatment process requires their active participation. Seventh, they come with a belief that treatment is for the weak. In this country psychological treatment is utilized mostly by middle- and upper-class whites, with women outnumbering men. Thus, for males in the lower class, treatment is viewed as a process for mentally weak people. Eighth, they come to treatment, especially legally mandated, believing that it is an additional punishment. Thus, if a judge mandates treatment or a parole board requires it, the offender-clients see it as an additional, unfair burden (Aukerman et al., 1994).

In addition, several professionals articulated the reasons why substance-abusing offenders have such a difficult time achieving abstinence. According to them, "offenders tend to be ill-equipped to handle the stressful situations that can bring about relapse, while at the same time they suffer from stresses both more numerous and intense than those affecting the usual patient. Upon release from custody, the offender must immediately assume the unfamiliar task of being responsible for self, while simultaneously attempting to resume family relationships, locate employment, comply with requirements of parole or probation, and resist the temptations presented by drug-using associates or family members. Faced with myriad decisions and often with little positive support, the offender frequently succumbs to drug use to ease feelings of failure, anxiety, confusion, and depression. The cycle of alcohol and other drug abuse and related criminal activity then begins anew (Gorski, Kelley, Haven, & Peters, 1995, p. vii).

Criminal Justice Factors Garrett and MacCormick (1929) wrote that early prisons and reformatories had not considered the psychological effects of penal structures on prisoners. Penal structures resembled animal cages and insinuated that prisoners, as a whole, were a very dangerous group. Only a few prisoners needed to be confined in such a secure manner. After studying male and female prisons and reformatories, Garrett and MacCormick stated that only reformatories for women resembled schools and seemed to recognize the impact of the environment on individuals.

Mitford (1973), and a number of other researchers, have examined the prison environment and organization. Mitford described the tension between the custodial and treatment staff. Custodial staff, who wields more power, tend to see prisoners as devious and cunning, and participation in treatment is part of prisoners' game playing. The tensions between the custodial and treatment staff force some treatment professionals to depart from the prison. The treatment professionals who stay become, in order to coexist with the custodial staff, more punitive in their treatment with prisoners. Treatment such as electric shock, hydrotherapy, drug-facilitated interviews, fever treatment, spinal taps, and insulin treatment became popular (Mitford, 1973). Support for Mitford's assertions can be found in the overuse of medications in prisons and implementation of aversive therapy to prisoners. Even treatment units, such as the Patuxent experiment in Maryland, became places where extreme punishment was implemented under the guise of treatment and rehabilitation (Mitford, 1973).

Other observers have examined the conflict between custodial and treatment staff and the challenges of providing treatment (Tims & Leukefeld, 1992). Josi and Sechrest (1996), as part of a process evaluation, asked treatment and custodial staff their views regarding a substance abuse program, called Amity RighTurn, that was opened within the R. J. Donovan Correctional Center near San Diego, California. They reported that the custodial staff believed that the treatment staff ignored security. In addition, the custodial staff resented the qualifications of the treatment staff, who were mostly recovered addicts. On the other hand, the treatment staff perceived that the custodial staff did not support treatment and wanted it to fail. While the custodial staff believed that workshops with treatment might be helpful, they did not want these workshops to occur during their off-days.

In terms of recommendations for ameliorating this conflict, Josi and Sechrest state that converting to a unit management concept with the correctional officer as part of the treatment team is helpful. However, they point out that some barriers between the custodial and treatment staff will always remain. Programs like Amity rely on former offenders and recovered substance abusers as an important part of their treatment philosophy, and using "untainted" staff would create distance between the offenders and the treatment staff.

Strategies to Address Problems with Correctional Environment and Clients Distressed by the coercive nature of prisons, Marcus-Mendoza, Klein-Saffran, and Lutze (1997) noted that processes and procedures used in boot camps for woman offenders were incompatible with the principles of feminism. Yet they forged a basis for feminist counselors who were employed in a prison environment by insisting that they separate themselves from the power structure to avoid being both therapist and disciplinarian. This delineation requires that a counselor's role and boundaries comprise a crucial dimension of negotiation with prison administrators. Marcus-Mendoza et al. assert that correction counselors can facilitate a helping relationship with prisoners by treating them with respect, advocating for them, and maintaining confidentiality.

Marcus-Mendoza et al. echo other feminists who believe that women should resist oppressive norms and that resistance is healthy and not denial or misconduct. They note that female inmates share many issues with free women—particularly histories of poverty, abuse, domestic violence, and addiction. Yet, they maintain that these issues can be addressed within the parameter of feminist therapy, and they advocate the participation in the prison environment of helping professionals who embrace a feminist philosophy. They observe that "feminist therapists working in boot camp or other prison must aid the clients in identifying and asserting their own needs while their clients are being denied freedom in an environment that demands conformity. In addition, the therapist must find a way to help women identify and express their feeling, including those about their incarceration, in a way that will not be punished. It is incumbent upon the therapist to face these challenges successfully in order to help to counter the negative messages of the boot camp and prison, support the women and foster growth, and help their clients survive the confusion and trauma they are experiencing" (Marcus-Mendoza, 1997, p. 183).

In the probation and parole field, officers experience conflict due to the tension between two primary functions—enforcing the law and helping the offender. Some officers describe these roles as law enforcement or social work. Often, these officers, because of the role conflict, become more punitive and less treatment oriented (Fulton, Stichman, Travis, & Latessa, 1997). To reverse and change this process, an Intensive Supervision Program (ISP) was modified to achieve a more balanced approach by these officers and thus in the end create more of a helping environment for offenders under supervision. The ISP consisted of training on factors related to effective intervention, objectives-based case management, and risk/need assessment. In addition, the officers participated in work groups that aimed to teach program components, policies, and procedures of a prototypical ISP. To evaluate the effectiveness of ISP, an Officer Attitude Survey was implemented. The survey measured, in part, the extent to which officers developed a more balanced approach. The instrument was designed to rate "terms associated with control or assistance tasks and social worker versus law enforcement roles, and to measure the extent to which they buy into strategies aimed at promoting long-term behavioral change versus strategies aimed at short-term offender control" (Fulton et al., 1997, p. 304). The evaluation reveals that officers who had ISP put a stronger emphasis on the rehabilitation function of probation and parole and strategies for offender behavioral change than officers who did not have ISP (Fulton et al., 1997).

Finally, Sapsford (1997), a mental health counselor based in the community, counsels adolescents referred by juvenile authorities. Before she will accept such a referral, Sapsford requires that the juvenile interview her. At the end of the interview, Sapsford asks if the juvenile wants to hire her. If the juveniles say no, the referral is rejected. Though probation officers, knowing of Sapsford's policy, can coerce a juvenile to hire Sapsford, this does reflect the attempt by a counselor to have an offender volunteer for counseling.

Developing a Proper Treatment Program for Offenders

In addition to the methodological weaknesses recorded by Martinson (1974), Palmer (1975), Martin et al. (1981), and Sechrest et al. (1979), another observed weakness is the lack of theory in program development. Researchers have stated that a high number of rehabilitative programs have been developed without any theoretical consideration in many cases, insufficient application of some theories, the claimed use of theory for descriptive purposes with no consideration really given to that theory, and the application of intervention without regard to the type of offender (Empey, 1969; Glaser, 1975; Ross & McKay, 1978; Slaiken, 1973). These deficiencies mean that programs are not designed well, and researchers cannot clearly discern the assumptions, goals, and effectiveness of treatment programs.

Adapting and applying theory can advance the development of knowledge about what works for various offenders. First, use of theory can eliminate what variable or variables are insignificant in offender change. Second, use of theory can help document gaps in knowledge. Third, use of theory can demonstrate how current knowledge may be used in program and experimental research.

Frequently, rehabilitation programs are viewed by treatment professionals in two ways. Either they are panaceas or simplified cured-or-not-cured terms, such as they worked or failed. This conception suggests that behavior is simple rather than a complex phenomenon. Offenders commit a variety of crimes, and an offender may commit different crimes, such as a robbery one week and a sexual assault the next week. Simply, offenders differ with respect to personality, background, motivations, psychological needs, economic needs, and social needs.

A properly developed rehabilitative program must match offender, setting, and intervention. That is, a program designer must consider a number of conditioning variables, such as the type of offenders, timing or the development of the criminal career along with the offender's age, and the optimum amount of treatment to change the offender in a positive direction. In addition, the program designer should consider the legal and ethical factors interposing upon the treatment program. Finally, the program designer should ameliorate the administrative and organizational barriers in order to facilitate implementation of the program as it was developed on paper.

Martin et al. (1981) reviewed a number of theories from a wide range of disciplines. They state that many of these theories were not in competition with each other and might be used to complement each other. Many theories have implications for rehabilitation. Among the theories discussed were cultural deviance, youth subculture, strain, radical, differential association, symbolic interaction, labeling, control, social learning, criminal personality, psychoanalytic, wealth maximization, time allocation, genetics, hormones, structural pathology of the brain, ecological factors, and learning disabilities. As stated previously, these theories have implications for rehabilitation. Some of them also have implementation for individual and group counseling.

Once a theoretically based correctional treatment program has been developed and before an outcome study of its effectiveness is conducted, a process evaluation needs to be performed. The purpose of the process evaluation is to determine whether a program was implemented as planned. Often, a planned program, especially in correction, is modified as a result of institutional and security concerns. These alternations and adjustments need to be documented and evaluated. Failing to do so can impact the validity of the outcome evaluation or obscure that the failure of treatment may have occurred because the program was not implemented as planned. Wolk and Hartman (1996) maintain that five groups need to be assessed in a process evaluation of a prison substance abuse program. These groups are the inmates, treatment staff, prison staff, prison administration, and the parole board. The groups are assessed relative to stages of development of a correctional substance abuse program, consisting of program policy making, evolution, and viability.

CONTEMPORARY COUNSELING FOCUS

During the birth of treatment and rehabilitation in this country, offenders for treatment purposes were basically treated the same. During the reformatory period, a burglar may have received the same sentence as a armed robber, rapist, or murderer—one year to life imprisonment. A similar pattern occurred in the juvenile justice system, where juveniles were committed to the end of their minority regardless of the offense type. A juvenile who killed a peer and a juvenile who stole a bicycle served similar commitments. This practice has changed and so has the focus of intervention.

Two areas are primarily targeted for intervention by criminal justice policy makers. These are sex offenders and drug offenders or offenders with substance abuse backgrounds. No specialized treatment program is available just for murderers, armed robbers, burglars, or check forgers. But there is some specialized attention for sex offenders and drug-involved offenders, with drug-offenders receiving the strongest contemporary attention.

The special attention given to drug abuse is reflected by efforts at the federal level and the leadership and financial resources given to states to develop substance abuse programs for offenders. Congress, moved by the lack of a national policy to combat the cocaine epidemic, created the Office of National Control Policy in 1988. Priority was given to those who use drugs while pregnant, those who use and increase the risk for HIV infection, and those in the criminal justice system. Further, this federal act created an administrative structure consisting of a Director, a Deputy Director for Demand Reduction, and an Associate Director for Supply Reduction, and an Associate Director for State and Local Affairs. The Office of Demand Reduction was charged with providing leadership in prevention and treatment. To this end, a Demand Reduction Working Group was created for treatment, education and prevention, workplace, and international in which a number of federal agencies participated, including the Department of Health and Human Services (Kleber, 1992).

Within the U.S. Department of Health and Human Services, addiction treatment professionals were summoned to develop protocols for the treatment of individuals with substance abuse problems. Thus, a series of manuals have been developed. One was titled Treatment Improvement Protocol (TIP) Series and the other was titled Technical Assistance Publication (TAP) Series. These publications address a number of substance abuse issues and areas and provide directions and guidance to substance abuse counselors in the communities. Another federal initiative was to provide funding for the creation of substance abuse programming in the community and in prisons. Most recently, Vice President Al Gore announced an anti-drug plan that provides drug control initiatives and treatment for prisoners ("Breaking News from the Associate Press," 1999).

Much of this increased focus on substance abuse centers around the introduction of crack cocaine and associated problems with its utilization. Hamid (1990) vividly depicts the effect of crack cocaine. Hamid (1990), using an anthropological framework, explains the impact of crack cocaine on minority communities and why it is associated with violence and other criminal justice problems. Living and working in Harlem as a social worker/crack specialist for social services, Hamid visited a number of locations where crack was consumed and interviewed people using it. He states that unlike the dynamics surrounding the sale and consumption of other drugs, such as marijuana, crack generates it own set of unique dynamics.

First, crack attracts a group of young, immature ethnic males (e.g., African Americans and Hispanics), promising instant fortunes. Second, to do business in crack requires tight control of urban markets and expansion to other markets. Third, controlling the business requires reliable middle people who were not going to siphon profits and the product. This need suggests that younger persons, such as teenagers and preteenagers, were needed as they are easier to control and perhaps cheaper to employ. As evidence of control, force is necessary to differentiate the entrepreneur and his associates from the drug users. Force is also, as a means of control, necessary to make known to competitors, who may be looking to newer markets, that a particular area has been taken and will be defended from outsiders. Control is also necessary in relation to females. Otherwise, the lure of unbridled sex and drugs would quickly and ultimately lead to the demise of the business. Accordingly, females are treated in a misogynistic manner. Fourth, the distribution and marketing of crack requires exploiting users, many of whom are women. For instance, the women users are given some drugs for use of their apartment as a distribution center and a place of other drug users to come and use the product. When the location becomes unprofitable, the crack distributor moves to another drug user. As related by Hamid, one woman took advances of crack for use of her apartment. When the woman's husband vetoed the arrangement, the woman was shot and killed. Fifth, drug users force changes in the family dynamics, forcing often grandmothers to assume guardianship of children. As a result of this abdication of parental responsibility and exploitation of family members, violence sometimes results within the family. Sixth, women users put themselves in positions to be victimized. Addiction causes women to victimize both their male using friends and nonusing friends, incurring retaliation or assault due to the woman's vulnerability. For instance, one woman showed a scar to Hamid resulting from a male friend attempting to "cut her head off " (Hamid, 1990).

The violence that occurred from the introduction of crack has caused the perpetration of other violence in the community. According to Hamid, "the model it so vividly presents—extreme youth in control, adults 'out of control,' women exploited, the short violent life glorified—apparently absorbs whole neighbors faster than crack itself can addict" (1990, p. 68). Yet, Hamid does not see that drug use and distribution are "the work of the alienated, the deviant, the anomic or the diseased, nor yet the pastime of reserve pools of labor" (Hamid, 1990, p. 68). Instead, drug activities accelerated and facilitated existing transformation occurring in the physical appearance of neighborhoods, housing conditions, household composition, relationships among household members, and social integration of the neighbors (Hamid, 1990).

Notwithstanding the reasons for the effects of crack cocaine on minority communities, Congress and state legislatures have passed a number of punitive laws resulting in the incarceration of a significant number of African American males and females. Though treatment is a small part of the national strategy, as exemplified for the funding of some drug treatment programs, the predominant strategy is incarceration, much to the disagreement of many African American professionals and politicians.

Along with the focus on drugs, alcohol use by offenders has been targeted for treatment, too. Hence, we see many references to AOD (Alcohol and Other Drugs) in the TIPs. The current focus on drug-abusing offenders requires a discussion of two concepts—Alcoholics Anonymous (AA) and therapeutic communities—because both are extensively utilized in contemporary counseling of offenders.

Alcoholics Anonymous (AA), founded by Dr. Robert Smith and William Wilson, began on June 10, 1935, as a self-help group for alcoholics. The basic program of AA is reflected by Twelve Steps, which have been practiced since the inception of AA and were formally articulated in 1938 (Makela, 1996). The Twelve Steps as pronounced by Alcoholics Anonymous World Service Incorporation (1957) require individuals to:

1. Admit we were powerless over alcohol - that our lives had become unmanageable.
2. Come to believe that a Power greater than ourselves could restore us to sanity.
3. Make a decision to turn our will and our lives over to the care of God as we understand Him.
4. Make a searching and fearless moral inventory of ourselves.
5. Admit to God, to ourselves and to another human being the exact nature of our wrongs.
6. Be entirely ready to have God remove all these defects of character.
7. Humbly ask Him to remove our shortcomings.
8. Make a list of all persons we had harmed, and become willing to make amends to them all.
9. Make direct amends to such people wherever possible, except when to do so would injure them or others.
10. Continue to take personal inventory and when we are wrong promptly admit it.
11. Seek through prayer and mediation to improve our conscious contact with God as we understand Him, praying only for knowledge of His will for us and the power to carry that out.
12. Having had a spiritual awakening as the result of these steps, we try to carry this message to alcoholics and to practice these principles in all our affairs.

AA has been successful since its inception and has been called "one of the great success stories of our century" by a group of professionals who studied AA in eight societies and was commissioned by the World Health Organization (Makela, 1996, p. 3). Because of its success, AA and its Twelve Steps have served as a model for the treatment of others problems, such as Al-Anon Family Groups, Narcotics Anonymous, Alateen, Gamblers Anonymous, Overeaters Anonymous, Emotions Anonymous, Adult Children of Alcoholics, Debtors Anonymous, Augustine Fellowship Sex & Love Addicts Anonymous, Survivors of Incest Anonymous, Cocaine Anonymous, Nicotine Anonymous, and Co-Dependents Anonymous (Makela, 1996; Nace, 1992). Though successful, AA, because of its religious component, has been legally challenged when prisoners are forced to attend. (This issue is discussed further in Chapter 2.)

A few years after the birth of AA, another new concept emerged. In 1940, Maxwell Jones administered a 100-bed unit of a hospital for soldiers in London suffering from effort syndrome (i.e., becoming unusually fatigued). Then, Britain was being attacked by Germany, and bombs were raining on London. The hospital staff consisted partly of regular civilians pressed to fill the void in health care professionals. Because of the bombing, Britons shared a similar experience of togetherness. For Christmas, the unit was transferred by decoration into a medieval village with the 100 soldiers assuming the staff's functions and discussing the physiological mechanism of effort syndrome. The staff assumed the role of servants, acting as waiters and waitresses. Maxwell Jones attributed this event to the birth of the therapeutic community (Jones, 1979).

In America, the emergence of the therapeutic community sprang from the birth of Synanon, a program for alcoholics and drug addicts in California (Kooyman, 1993; Yablonsky, 1989). Chuck Dederich, an unemployed oil company executive with a history of alcohol abuse and a participant of AA, began holding meetings in his apartment with other persons suffering from alcohol and drug addiction. They would engage in vigorous debate and attacks upon members' world views. Despite the intensity of the meetings, attendance grew. They decided to rent a clubhouse where participants could meet. When one narcotic addict asked for help, he was told that he had to move into the clubhouse. Synanon got its name from an uneducated member who discussed participating in a seminar, which came out as Synanon (Kennard, 1983).

A key aspect of the therapeutic community is that the primary therapist is the community, which consists of peers and recovered substance abusers as role models (Brill, 1960; DeLeon, 1988). Members of Synanon lived in a family-type home and meetings were intense. Some people refer to it as attack therapy. Synanon was viewed as a success, and officials in the criminal justice system began to take notice. Patterned after Synanon, Daytop was started in New York in 1963 and other programs were developed. Currently, a number of therapeutic communities exist that were modeled after Synanon, and some programs have been modified for prisons. One of the most widely publicized therapeutic units in prison is Stay'n Out, which has been extensively researched and found to be effective (Wexler, Falkin, & Lipton, 1990; Wexler & Love, 1994). In Columbus, Ohio, a therapeutic community based on the Synanon and Delancy Street models was developed for offenders. In Chillicote, Ohio, the Ross Correctional Institution created a therapeutic community for prisoners suffering from substance abuse (Alexander, 1998).

In addition to principles from AA and therapeutic communities, other modalities are provided in contemporary drug treatment. DiClemente (1998) explains that substance abuse consists of multiple variables, including classes of drugs such as sedatives, stimulants, and opiates; different sources of drugs such as cocaine, crack, beer, wine, and hard liquor; different routes of use such as oral, nasal, and intravenous; and lastly, individuals from different social classes, gender, race, educational level, and profession. Among the psychosocial and treatment modalities used in substance abuse counseling are group therapy; cognitive-behavioral treatment;

cognitive therapy; couples, family, and social network therapy; behavior-focused treatments; motivational intervention; Twelve Steps approaches; residential treatment; stage-based methods; court-mandated treatment; and relapse prevention and recycling treatment (DiClemente, 1998).

Appropriately linking the type of problem with treatment is called treatment matching. According to DiClemente (1998), there has not been any research matching specific client characteristics to treatment modality. However, some general research has been conducted, which provides some general guidelines.

1. A number of substance-abusing clients have co-occurring alcohol and drug problems, requiring the need to screen for such factors at clinical intake.
2. Individuals in serious withdrawal or who have delirium tremens need supervised detoxification.
3. Individuals with willing significant others do better with some behavioral marital therapy.
4. Individuals with multiple psychosocial problems, such as financial, social, housing, and occupational problems, have better outcomes when these problems are addressed in addition to treatment for drug and alcohol problems.
5. Brief interventions (i.e., 30 to 60 minutes) of discussion and advice appear to produce changes in alcohol and drug use.
6. Neither the intensity of outpatient treatment nor the intensity of inpatient treatment has little relation to outcome for substance-abusing persons.
7. Motivation to change the substance use is an important variable to consider in planning treatment. Persons with low motivation need proactive intervention and intervention that acknowledges the clients' perspectives.
8. A successful outcome may require behavioral and psychosocial intervention in addition to pharmacological treatment, such as nicotine replacements, naltrexone or some other drug that reduces craving for opiates or alcohol, and disulfiram or some other substance that interacts antagonistically with alcohol.

A sound AOD program should take into account several other issues, including treatment matching, risk assessment, need assessment, screening, assessment, and treatment planning. However, these issues will be addressed more fully in Chapter 4.

Ethical Issues in Counseling Offenders

Ethical behavior in criminal justice counseling is critically important and in one sense is more critical than other helping professional fields. Doctor/patient, lawyer/client, clergy/parishoners, professor/student, and therapist/client are different in that violations of ethics may lead to reprimands, loss of professional license, loss of employment, and civil liability (Madden, 1998). Criminal justice counseling professionals have these same sanctions, but they may face a felony criminal conviction when the ethical violation involves sexual misconduct. Since the 1980s, state legislatures have criminalized unethical sexual contact within the correctional environment, which they have not done with other environments. In the academic environment, a professor who has a consensual sexual relationship with an adult student may be fired and/or sued civilly, but he or she is not going to jail. In the legal environment, a lawyer will not go to jail for having consensual sex with a current client. Likewise, a pediatrician who sleeps with the mothers of his patients, which occurred in Ohio, faces medical disciplinary proceedings, but he did not violate any criminal laws (Somerson, 1999). But correctional employees have faced criminal proceedings for sexual activity with prisoners, and some counselors have been criminally sanctioned for this breach.

While overall criminal justice ethics is important, little attention has been paid to it (Kleinig & Smith, 1997; Pepinsky, 1991). But this seems to be changing (Sherman, 1982). Whitehead (1991) examined the issue of the ethics of probation and parole officers, observing that some officers were not doing a very good job and were violating the ethics of the field. Though the issue of ethics in criminal justice counseling and intervention has been a neglected area, the study of ethics has been a field long investigated by individuals. In its purest form, ethics involves the determination of what is right or wrong, good or bad, just or unjust. Ethics also has several connotations, according to Souryal (1992). These connotations consist of (a) a theory that explains an act's quality or appropriateness based on the values encircled in the act; (b) the examination of statements used to support noble behavior or to assail corrupt behavior; (c) the investigation into morality and the exploration for a moral life; and (d) the description of a discernible group that shares similar moral values or characteristics, such as the Protestant work ethics, Christian ethics, and unethical behavior (Souryal, 1992). Although ethics is a concern in all areas of the criminal justice systems, including the legal system, law enforcement, and corrections, the focus here is just on ethical issues involving professionals who provide counseling and intervention. Ethical issues emanate at both the macro level and the micro level.

Macro Ethical Concerns

At the macro level, the issue of informed consent is pertinent, given that working with offenders raises issues of coercion and forced treatment. Informed consent occurs when an individual, given complete and accurate information about what will be done to him or her and the benefits and risks associated with a procedure or process, agrees to a particular action. Informed consent presupposes an individual's autonomy to make decisions, and that autonomy is based on an individual's mental competence (Eth & Robb, 1986). The American Psychological Association speaks to the issue of informed consent in its ethical standards. Psychologists should obtain informed consent before engaging in therapy. Informed consent implies that an individual (a) has the capacity to consent, (b) has been informed of significant information concerning the procedure, (c) *has freely and without undue influence expressed consent* (which may be problematic with involuntary clients such as offenders), and (d) consent has been appropriately documented (American Psychological Association's Ethical Principles of Psychologists and Code of Conduct, 1998). Thus, a fundamental principle in this country is that every person has the right to give consent and refuse consent to treatment (Winick, 1997). With mentally ill individuals and offenders, this principle is minimized. The justification is that some mentally ill persons and offenders are dangerous to themselves and others; as a result, society has the right to force treatment on them. Winick (1997) cautions that offenders, both incarcerated and community-based, are at risk for abuse by the state because medications and mental health treatment are provided for social control purposes, and the U.S. Supreme Court have facilitated involuntarily treatment of offenders.

Offenders are generally coerced into treatment by judges, parole boards, and probation officers, and confusion may exist regarding who the client is (Miller & Miller, 1998; Washton, 1995). Judges may order treatment or give offenders a "choice" of jail or counseling. They are also induced into treatment, such as subtle messages from parole broads that if prisoners want to increase their chances of making parole, these prisoners should participate in treatment programs. Hence, prisoners are not making free choices. Eth and Robb (1986) defined voluntary treatment as one's ability to exercise the free choice to accept treatment without undue influence or coercion. Undue influence may involve excessive reward or questionable techniques.

This issue has raised some thought-provoking questions regarding the ethics of coercing offenders into treatment. First, is it ethical for the justice system to attempt to correct offenders by sentencing them to treatment longer than the punishment for a crime? For instance, a recidivist shoplifter who is an alcoholic might merit 2 or 4 months of jail, but is instead sentenced to 1 year of treatment. Professionals have grappled with the ethics of such sentencing (Chick, 1998). This issue is similar to the argument that was raised about the juvenile justice system. Gerald Gault, a 15-year-old juvenile, was committed (i.e., sentenced) for rehabilitation to the end of his minority for making an obscene telephone call to a woman. If Gault had been an adult, he would have faced 2 months in jail or a $50 fine. Although there were other issues that led the U.S. Supreme Court to rule that Gault was denied due process, the fairness of his length of rehabilitation was commented upon by the Justices (*In re Gault*, 1967).

Another ethical issue is whether the cost of offenders' behavior justifies coerced treatment. At times, we are told how much it costs to keep someone in a maximum security prison or how much it costs to arrest, jail, and try some offenders. But society has a different conception of others' costly behavior. For instance, chronic bronchitis costs society a considerable sum, but smokers are not mandated to treatment (Chick, 1998). Despite these questions, Chick offers no definitive answers regarding the ethics of coerced treatment for offenders.

Chick does, however, note that coerced treatment for offenders with substance abuse problems can be successful. According to Chick (1998), some alcoholics can experience successful treatment if they are provided with clear sanctions by coercing officials for noncompletion of treatment. This coercion is needed to overcome the initial fear and disdain for the treatment process.

With respect to the issue of voluntary and involuntary treatment, Chick indicates that there is little difference between the two groups when the issue of coercion is involved. Employers, for instance, regularly coerce employees into substance abuse treatment programs under the threats of dismissal. Spouses and significant others, under threats of termination of relationships, coerce individuals into relationship counseling or substance abuse counseling. Ridicule and teasing by individuals may coerce a person into treatment for correction of noses, ears, mouth, breasts, or "beer belly." Therefore, not surprising, a comparison of treatment volunteers and nonvolunteers found that a significant number of both groups reported coercion and resentment from that coercion (Chick, 1998).

Correctional treatment, indeed, possesses the potential for abuse and ethical violations on a large scale. The area of involuntary treatment of sex offenders is fraught with ethical, as well as treatment, issues. An increasing number of states, responding to the fervor over recidivist sex offenders, have passed laws to permit the commitment of sex offenders after these sex offenders have served their time in prison. These commitments to mental hospitals or mental health units within a correctional institution are indefinite. These offenders can get out only when they are deemed to be no longer dangerous or no longer have abnormal sexual deviancy.

Though a judge or jury would make this final determination of nondangerousness or a "cured" offender, treating clinicians play a critical role, either in preparing a report or testifying in court. Thus, issues of confidentiality become blurred, and the ethics of procuring information in therapy and relating this information to social control agents is problematic. Though counseling in a prison environment is fraught with ethical issues, a therapist can ensure some general inmates that a limited form of confidentiality can be assured. Threats to self, others, or security are reportable, but other information is confidential. But with sex offenders, this guarantee may not be possible to make. Everything that sex offenders say, think, and do may find its way into a report that determines whether they will continue to be confined. For instance, a sex offender's dream about a puppy might be, depending upon the training of the clinician, a symbol for a child. The therapist might conclude that the offender knows that he cannot discuss children and uses the young of other species, which means that he might be in danger of sexually offending against a child upon release. This interpretation may or may not be correct, but the safer course for the therapist is to err on the side of caution.

Finally, ethical consideration also comes into being in conducting research on treatment efficacy and interventions. As an illustration of the ethical concern, several professionals recruited pregnant adolescents and women to participate in treatment that had a research component. They expressed disappointment when the females balked at participating in a random assignment, which significantly altered their planned study (Farrow, Watts, Krohn, & Olson, 1999). One can only speculate about the extent to which pressure and coercion were applied to potential research participants. While some females refused to participate, other pregnant females did participate.

Incessantly pressured to create effective interventions, clinicians may be researchers and may want to know if a method or technique is effective with different categories of dually diagnosed prisoners, such as offenders diagnosed with antisocial personality disorders or borderline personality disorders and substance abuse. A prisoner may find it difficult to say no to a therapist who asks the prisoner to participate in a research study. A possible solution is for someone other than the therapist to conduct the study. Still, ethical considerations exist as a prisoner can be coerced to participate by receiving additional privileges or financial rewards. Sometimes, prisoners are offered a small sum to participate in studies, but even $5 or $10 is a lot to a prisoner who does not receive funds from family or friends.

On the other hand, intervening with offenders with unproven or ineffective treatment is ethically suspect. It is akin to giving a hungry person a glass of water. Further, an unproved technique may lead to deterioration and psychological pain and suffering. These possibilities also raise ethical concerns.

Micro Ethical Concerns

Though counseling is used to alleviate or eliminate psychological suffering and maladaptive behaviors, counseling can have a deteriorating or negative effect. Such harmful effects occur as the result of actions by a counselor. One way is when a counselor initiates a treatment method that is incompatible with a person's problem. Another way occurs when a counselor persistently uses techniques despite indications that the client is getting worse. Tied to the previous way, a final way occurs when the counselor projects, directly and indirectly, personal attitudes that have an injurious effect upon the individual (Lakin, 1991). For instance, some therapists and counselors have very strong ideologies regarding society and clients' problems, and these professionals force, either intentionally or unintentionally, these beliefs on the clients.

Masters (1994) outlines eight areas involving ethical dilemmas with criminal offenders (Figure 1.2). Among these areas are confidentiality, gratuities, given money and objects to offenders, business relationships with offenders, taking offenders home, distribution of favors for favors, abuse of power, and sexual and romantic relationships. Because a criminal justice counselor has a professional relationship with an offender, the addition of another relationship constitutes a dual relationship (Borys & Pope, 1989), which could negatively affect an individual's counseling. A dual relationship involves different degrees of seriousness for criminal justice counselors. Some dual relationships may lead to professional misconduct, dismissal from employment, and civil and criminal liabilities.

The first seven of Master's areas involve putting a counselor in a compromising situation and may lead to charges of professional misconduct or dismissal from the correctional counselor's employment. For instance, a counselor should not accept gifts from offenders or offenders' families. Accepting such gifts might make the counselor feel obligated to extend more privileges to an offender than other offenders. Also, this form of favoritism could anger other offenders. A counselor should not

1. Confidentiality

2. Gratuities

3. Given money and objects

4. Taking offenders home

5. Giving favors for favors

6. Abuse of power

7. Sexual and romantic relationships

FIGURE 1.2 Ethical Issues

give money to offenders or enter a business relationship with them. In a business relationship, money may be lost or earned. In either event, it affects the counseling relationship. Also, a counselor should not violate an offender's confidentiality unnecessarily and unjustifiably or abuse his or her power. Counselors have a significant amount of power over offenders by possessing sensitive knowledge about them. This information should not be used unethically. Also, probation and parole officers possess significant power over offenders and could affect an offender's freedom.

In all probability, the most serious ethical issue involves a counselor entering a romantic or sexual relationship with an offender. A decade or two ago, such a relationship may have resulted in only a forced resignation or firing. Now, it is much more serious, incurring administrative, civil, and criminal sanctions (Barker, 1993; Borruso, 1991; Cook, 1992a; Duchschere, 1993; Maurer, 1995). These changes in the law occurred as the result of a crackdown on persons in power positions who have professional relationships with others and who sexually exploit those relationships (Cannizaro, 1993; Chacon, 1995; "Ex-Judge Jailed," 1994; Goldberg, 1995; Rankin, 1991; Walston, 1989; "World-wide: A Drill Sergeant," 1996). For instance, teachers who exploit students and therapists who exploit clients are now subject to civil and criminal penalties (Barker, 1993; Borruso, 1991; Maurer, 1995). Also, a licensed social worker who becomes sexually involved with a client can have his or her license revoked and be required to pay the cost of mental health counseling for the victim (Kentucky Revised Statute § 335.150).

In the criminal justice field, correctional officers seem to be the culprits most of the time in sexually abusing offenders (Cook, 1992b; Dowdy, 1996; Grumman, 1995; S. A. Holmes, 1996; Makeig, 1993; McKibben, 1993; Tyson, 1996; Wowk, 1993), and laws have been written directed at them ("Sex Ban Upheld," 1997; Swenson, 1993; Tennessee Code Annotated § 41-21-241.). Some of these cases have resulted from outright rape of female prisoners ("Deputy Is Charged," 1996; Neergaard, 1992), and some have resulted as a result of consensual sex between female prisoners and officers (Deep, 1994). These prisoners, because they are in a vulnerable position and because of the power differential between them and officers, cannot consent to a sexual relationship. Some of these female prisoners seek out sexual encounters with staff members to compromise a staff member and use this relationship to receive contrabands in prison or assistance in escaping (Atkinson, 1996; Holleman, 1995). Regardless of the reasons and circumstances, sexual contact between a staff person and a prisoner is always wrong. The standards and laws that apply to correctional officers also apply to correctional counselors and probation and parole officers (Ellis, 1994).

For instance, a parole officer who worked in Cobb and Carroll Counties Georgia was criminally charged with having a sexual relationship with one of his parolees (Payne, 1995). In a nearby county, a probation officer was arrested and charged with having sex with a female probationer (Plummer, 1995). Also, other professionals who were involved in a counseling relationship with offenders have been criminally sanctioned (Cook, 1992c; Enstad, 1992).

One respected jurist on the Ninth Circuit Court of Appeals stated that no males should be permitted to work in correctional institutions for females as a means of preventing sexual misconduct (*Jordan v. Gardner*, 1993). According to Judge Noonan, "there should not be male guards at a women's prison. There should not be a male superintendent of a women's prison. Our statutes should not be construed to require such mechanical suppression of the recognition that in our culture such a relationship between men in power and women in prison leads to difficulties, temptations, abuse, and finally cruel and unusual punishment" (*Jordan v. Gardner*, 1993, p. 1545). This belief is legally suspect and constitutes the stereotyping of all males, and it will not solve the problem.

While some males in authority have abused their power with offenders, females have the capacity to sexually offend when they, too, are in power positions (Arden-Smith, 1995; Bass, 1995; Davis, 1993; Enstad, 1993; Hardy, 1994; Leonhart, 1995; Liebrum, 1995; Silk, 1995). For instance, both male and female correctional officers have been charged with sexually abusing female prisoners (Applebome, 1992). Also, female correctional officers have been dismissed and charged with becoming sexually involved with both male and female prisoners (Tipton, 1991), and female correctional counselors have been tried for beginning a romantic and sexual relationship with incarcerated juvenile offenders.

The solution is for all criminal justice professionals to exercise sound professional judgment when working with offenders. A counselor, parole officer, or probation officer who is attracted to an offender should maintain professional boundaries at all times. If possible, a counselor should transfer such an offender to another counselor. If not, the criminal justice professional should limit involvement with an offender and never see such an offender alone. Another possibility is for the criminal justice professional to consult an employment assistance counselor, which should be confidential, and seek professional guidance and support. The failure to find an acceptable, ethical strategy could result in a termination of a professional career, financial ruination, and a prison sentence.

In addition, unique ethical issues exist when counseling occurs in substance abuse programs funded wholly or in part with federal funds (Doyle, 1998; Manhal-Baugus, 1996). A series of federal laws mandates confidentiality for substance abuse treatment recipients, including offenders, and requires their informed consent before information may be given to persons outside of treatment. There are some exceptions to the federal law regarding confidentiality, such as sharing information with a qualified service organization, law enforcement when crimes have been committed against treatment staff by a substance abuse client (Doyle, 1998), child abuse, and duty to warn (Manhal-Baugus, 1996).

Qualification and Training for Criminal Justice Counselors

Most states have qualifications and standards for probation and parole officers, institutional social workers, and psychologists. In Texas, the minimum standards for probation officers is (1) to be of good moral character; (2) have a bachelor's degree; (3) have either (a) one year of graduate study in criminology, psychology, sociology, or another field acceptable to the Texas Juvenile Probation Commission or (b) one year of experience in full-time casework, counseling, or community group work; (4) have satisfactory completion of the course of preservice training or instruction required by the Texas Juvenile Probation Commission; (5) have passed the tests or examination required by the Commission, and (6) possess the level of certification required by the Commission (Texas Human Resources Code § 141.061, 1998).

Further, social workers, like psychologists and psychiatrists, have been successful in convincing states to license who can be called a social worker. In Ohio, a person can be licensed as a social work assistant, a social worker, or an independent social worker, and no one can claim such title unless he or she has been licensed by Ohio's Counselor and Social Work Board (Ohio Revised Code Annotated 4757.02, 1998). Presenting oneself to the public as a counselor or social worker without the proper licensure is a crime (Ohio Revised Code Annotated 4757.36, 1998). Likewise, engaging in counseling without a license or calling oneself a Licensed Professional Counselor in Texas is a Class B misdemeanor (Texas Revised Annotated Statute Article 4512, 1998).

While degreed persons may engage in substance abuse counseling, a number of states permit persons who do not have Bachelor's degrees to counsel substance abuse clients. These types of counselors may have a high school education and have received credentialing by the state, provided specific training has been obtained.

The National Association of Alcoholism and Drug Abuse Counselors (NAADAC) offers three levels of certification—National Certified Addiction Counselor, Level I (NCAC I), National Certified Addiction Counselor, Level II (NCAC II), and Master Addiction Counselor (MAC). NCAC I requires current state licensure as a substance abuse counselor; 3 years of full-time or 6,000 hours of supervised experience as a substance abuse counselor; 270 contact hours of education and training in alcoholism and drug abuse or related counseling subjects, which includes 6 hours of ethics training and 6 hours of HIV/AIDS training; and a passing score on the national examination for Level I. NCAC Level II requires a Bachelor's degree from an accredited college or university; current state certification as a substance abuse counselor, 5 years' full time or 10,000 hours of supervised experience as a substance abuse counselor; 450 hours of education and training, which includes 6 hours of ethics training and 6 hours of HIV/AIDS training; and a passing score on the national examination for Level II. The MAC requires current state licensure as a substance abuse counselor or a related healing art, a Master's degree in the healing art, 500 contact hours of specific alcoholism and drug abuse counseling, 3 years supervised experience with two of the years required after receiving the Master's degree, and a passing score on the national examination for the MAC. All three certifications must be renewed every 2 years (NAADCA, 1998).

Training-wise, a variety of programs meets the training needs of substance abuse counselors. As an illustration, the Council for Accreditation of Counseling and Related Education Program (CACREP) assesses the training needs of graduate programs and provides accreditation to them (Morgan, Toloczko, & Comly, 1997). At Pennsylvania State University, the Chemical Dependency Counselor Training Program (CDCTP) assesses the training needs of substance abuse counselors in Pennsylvania and then provides courses to meet those needs.

Carroll (1998) prepared a training manual describing cognitive-behavioral treatment with cocaine-dependent persons for therapists. Reminding therapists that just reading a textbook on surgery does not make a doctor a qualified surgeon, Carroll states that developing skills in cognitive-behavioral treatment requires completion of a didactic seminar and at least two intensely supervised cases. Depending on the experience of the therapist, the didactic seminar lasts from 2 days to 1 week. The seminar comprises a review of cognitive-behavioral theory and techniques, a review of all the topics in the manual, several role-plays, practice exercises, discussion of case examples, and rehearsal strategies for hard cases. In terms of supervised training cases, experienced therapists require one or two cases. The sessions are videotaped for feedback on the therapist's adherence to cognitive-behavioral treatment guidelines and a critique of the therapist's performance. In addition, the supervisor provides 1 hour of supervision for each case (Carroll, 1998). Often these, as well as other programs, are taken by substance abuse counselors to maintain their certifications and licenses.

SUMMARY

This chapter began by discussing historical efforts to rehabilitate offenders. Definitions of rehabilitation, mental health treatment, and intervention were provided. The author observed that there are differences between rehabilitation and mental health treatment, noting that there is a legal right to mental health treatment for seriously mentally ill prisoners, but there is no right to rehabilitation. Then, the author discussed the development of the medical model and the adoption of it and the concept of rehabilitation by the National Prison Association in 1870. Treatment research was discussed, particularly the reports of Robert Martinson and Ted Palmer.

Then, the difficulty of changing offenders was discussed, including offender factors and criminal justice factors. Stressed was the foundation for providing treatment and particularly the grounding of programs in theories. This chapter discussed the current focus of providing treatment to sex offenders and substance-abusing offenders. Ethical considerations, both macro and micro, were discussed. Focus was put upon dual relationships with clients and particularly the legal and professional dangers of a counselor becoming sexually or romatically involved with clients. Finally, this chapter discussed qualification, training, and credentialing for corrections workers.

KEY TERMS

Rehabilitation
Treatment
Mental health
     treatment
Medical model
Recidivism
Dual relationships
Psychotherapy

Spontaneous remission
Dual diagnosis
Wounded healer
Treatment matching
Deterioration
Adaptation
Elmira Reformatory
Positivistic school

Therapeutic community
Alcoholics Anonymous
Substance abuse
     certifications
Synanon

2

✳ ✳ ✳

Legal Issues in
Correctional Treatment

✳ INTRODUCTION

This chapter discusses legal issues in correctional treatment. Knowing the legal parameters of treatment is important for correctional professionals and students who aspire to be counselors in the correctional arena for a number of reasons. Most important, mentally ill prisoners have a constitutional right to mental health treatment (Alexander, 1989), and failure to provide treatment incurs legal liability for institutional workers (*H. C. by Hewett v. Jarrard*, 1986; *O'Connor v. Donaldson*, 1975). Also, the standard for determining a civil rights violation in prison is whether a state official has violated a clearly established right that a reasonable person would know (*Greason v. Kemp*,1990; *Roach v. City of Evansville*, 1997). So, it behooves correctional counselors to know the law regarding clearly established prisoners' rights.

Further, prisoners' rights may not be violated only by the lack of mental health treatment, but also by the right to refuse treatment (Alexander, 1988). As an example, a court was asked to stop a treatment program for sex offenders because it was cruel and unusual punishment. In this program called "drama therapy," the sex offenders, if they wanted to get out of prison early, had to undergo a simulated anal rape while the therapist screamed insults at them. The stated purpose of the treatment program was to instill empathy for sexual assault victims ("Judge Asked to Halt," 1995).

In another example, the Seventh Circuit Court of Appeals ruled that coercing a prisoner to attend a substance abuse counseling program that had a religious content violated a prisoner's First Amendment rights (*Kerr v. Farrey*, 1996). In this case, the prisoner was coerced by threats to increase his security level and by threats to highlight his refusal to participate with the parole board so that the prisoner would not earn parole. So, correctional professionals should be knowledgeable both about prisoners' rights to mental health treatment and about prisoners' rights to refuse mental health treatment.

In addition to avoiding legal liability, professionals and students should know the contours of prisoners' rights regarding counseling and treatment because the courts often determine policy in corrections (Allen & Simonsen, 1995). Courts determine what could and should not be done to prisoners, and correctional treatment staff, as professionals who want to keep abreast of critical policies, should know the law as it relates to treatment.

For instance, the courts have decided whether the U.S. Constitution and various state statutes provide a right to rehabilitation to incarcerated juvenile and adult offenders. The courts have consistently ruled no for adult offenders but inconsistently for juvenile offenders (Alexander, 1995a). Hence, one part of the country has sanctioned a right to treatment for incarcerated juvenile offenders, but other parts of the country have rejected such a right.

Then, there is the issue of sex offenders. A trend has developed in which state legislatures have declared that some sex offenders are mentally ill, requiring them to be treated in a mental health unit following a civil hearing after serving criminal sentences (Alexander, 1995b). Hence, sex offenders who have been legislatively declared to be mentally ill now have a right to treatment while they are confined (*Ohlinger v. Watson*, 1980).

Last, other issues, such as gender differences in treatment programming, have been decided by the courts. A number of courts have ruled inconsistently regarding differences in programming for female and male offenders and female offenders' rights to equal protection of the law (*Keevan v. Smith*, 1996; *Klinger v. Department of Corrections*, 1997; *Women Prisoners of the Dist of Columbia Dept. of Corrections v. District of Columbia*, 1996). For all these reasons, both to protect themselves from liability and to be knowledgeable about correctional treatment policy issues, students and professionals need to know the law regarding treatment issues.

This chapter begins by discussing several important concepts (i.e., rehabilitation, programming, treatment, and habilitation), where prisoners' treatment rights come from, legal concepts and definitions, which inform and determine correctional treatment issues in the courts, the legal test for determining a violation of a prisoner's rights, and the Civil Rights Act of 1871. Then, the author discusses the issue of the right to rehabilitation or treatment for adults, the right to rehabilitation or treatment in juvenile institutions, the right to mental health or psychiatric treatment, the right to habilitation, the right to refuse treatment, involuntary treatment of sex offenders, and gender issues in prison treatment programs.

WHERE DO PRISONERS' TREATMENT RIGHTS COME FROM?

Prisoners rights come from the U.S. Constitution, state Constitutions, and institutional policies (del Carmen, 1992). The courts interpret the Constitution and decide issues that become case law. In presenting these case laws, focus is placed almost totally on federal decisions. There are three reasons for this. First, invariably prisoners file lawsuits under the federal Civil Rights Act. Second, the federal court system has been the most active in delineating prisoners' constitutional rights. Third, the federal judiciary supersedes state judiciaries when issues involve the U.S. Constitution, which prisoners invoke in their lawsuits. The federal judiciary system is depicted in Figure 2.1.

Every state, save Delaware, has several District Courts that are divided by regions, such as the Southern, Middle, and Northern Districts of Georgia. Typically, prisoners begin their legal action by filing a Civil Rights complaint in the U.S. District Court within their region. A decision is rendered, which may or may not be appealed by the prisoner or the prison system. If the decision is appealed by either party, it is appealed to the Court of Appeals for that circuit. There are 11 Circuits, and each contains a number of states. When the Court of Appeals rules, the decision is binding on all the states in that Circuit. Thus, it is possible for one Court of Appeals to rule one way on a legal issue and another Court of Appeals to rule differently, creating different laws in different parts of the country. For instance, the Seventh Circuit Court of Appeals ruled incarcerated juvenile offenders have a right to rehabilitation (*Nelson v. Heyne*, 1974), but the First and Ninth Circuits Court of Appeals ruled that such juveniles do not have a right to rehabilitation (*Gary H. v. Hegstrom*, 1987; *Santana v. Collazo*, 1983).

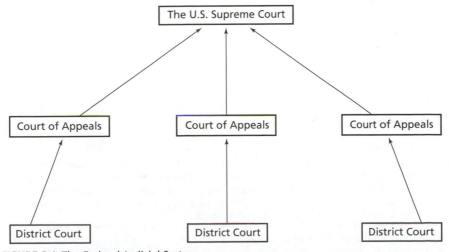

FIGURE 2.1 The Federal Judicial System

The U.S. Supreme Court is the court of final appeal, and decisions from the Courts of Appeals can be taken there. (There are state and military avenues for cases to reach the U.S. Supreme Court, but these avenues are not described here.) However, the U.S. Supreme Court may refuse to hear a case, and generally it refuses to hear more cases than it hears. If the U.S. Supreme Court refuses to hear a case, the decision of the Court of Appeals becomes binding on the parties involved and all the states in that circuit.

Certainly, the federal courts, and especially the U.S. Supreme Court, have become much more conservative in its rulings regarding prisoners' rights within the last decade or so (Alexander, 1993a), and in some instances, state Supreme Courts' rulings have been more favorable to certain prisoners, such as whether mentally ill prisoners on death row can be executed (*Riggins v. Nevada*, 1993). Nonetheless, the overwhelming majority of cases that have established treatment decisions are federal case laws.

CONSTITUTIONAL AMENDMENTS THAT DETERMINE CORRECTIONAL TREATMENT

When the U.S. Constitution was created by the individuals attending the Constitutional Convention in 1787, some of the original 13 states had to be persuaded to ratify it. These states were fearful of providing too much power to the central government. They agreed to accept the new Constitution, provided a Bill of Rights accompanied it. The result of this compromise was the first 10 amendments to the U.S. Constitution (Alexander, 1992a).

The amendments that are implicated in correctional treatment within the Bill of Rights are the First, Eighth, and Fourteenth Amendments. The First and Eighth were passed in 1787, and the Fourteenth Amendment was passed in 1868. See Figure 2.2 for the complete wording of these amendments.

First Amendment

Congress shall make no law respecting an establishment of religion, or prohibiting the free exercise thereof; or abridging the freedom of speech, or of the press, or the right of the people peaceably to assemble, and to petition the Government for a redress of grievances.

Eighth Amendment

Excessive bail shall not be required, nor excessive fines imposed, nor cruel and unusual punishments inflicted.

Fourteenth Amendment

All persons born or naturalized in the United States, and subject to the jurisdiction thereof, are citizens of the United States and the States wherein they reside. No State shall make or enforce any law which shall abridge the privileges or immunities of the citizens of the United States; nor shall any State deprive any person of life, liberty, or property, without due process of law, nor deny to any person within its jurisdiction the equal protection of the laws.

FIGURE 2.2 Significant Amendments

Originally, the first 10 amendments were restrictions on the federal government and did not apply to the states (Alexander, 1992b). Thus, the prohibition in the Eighth Amendment that excessive bail shall not be required nor cruel and unusual punishment inflicted applied only to federal offenders. Because of the social climate in the country, Congress decided to proposed the Fourteenth Amendment. Immediately following slavery, African Americans in the South were being subjected to very brutal treatment and unequal laws. Congress held hearings on the abuses that were occurring. To remedy, in part, the situation, Congress passed the Fourteenth Amendment in 1868.

As one U.S. Senator noted, the Fourteenth Amendment was to prevent an African American citizen from being hanged for a crime for which the white man was not (Berkson, 1975). African American citizens could cite this Amendment to contest unfair laws, trials, sentences, and prison treatment, but little relief was provided by the Fourteenth Amendment as states found ways to get around it.

The Fourteenth Amendment was subsequently interpreted to provide protection to all citizens. For instance, the equal protection clause within this amendment has been invoked to challenge rehabilitative programs in men's correctional institutions, but not women's institutions. A relevant question in this area is whether the Fourteenth Amendment is violated by a state that put an automobile mechanic training program in a men's institution but not in a women's prison.

Bridging the Bill of Rights into the Fourteenth Amendment

In the twentieth century, the U.S. Supreme Court ruled steadily that specific amendments in the Bill of Rights applied to the states by virtue of the Due Process Clause in the Fourteenth Amendment. Hence, the First, Fourth, Fifth, Sixth, and Eighth Amendments applied to the states. More importantly, the First, Eighth, and Fourteenth Amendment specifically had implications for treatment. For instance, Shapiro (1974) argued that forcibly altering a person's thought processes through involuntary medication violates the First Amendment. In addition, other legal scholars have stated that the state cannot alter a person's mind through drugs without sound reasons (*Riggins v. Nevada*, 1992). This view is less settled in law. However, the Eighth and Fourteenth Amendments have direct implications for correctional treatment. Particularly, the Eighth Amendment forbids cruel and unusual punishment and the Fourteenth Amendment provides due process, the right to liberty and property, and equal protection. The following sections explain these important concepts.

Cruel and Unusual Punishment

Historians and Justices on the U.S. Supreme Court have been divided on the origin of the cruel and unusual punishment clause and its meaning. They all agree that it was taken from the English Constitution, but they differ regarding why it was put into the English Constitution. Some individuals contended that it forbids brutal forms of capital punishment, such as drawing and quartering persons (Berkson, 1975). But other individuals contended that it only prohibited punishments not codified by law (*Harmelin v. Michigan*, 1991; Page, 1989).

In 1910, the U.S. Supreme Court began to define what cruel and unusual punishment was. This early attempt to define it came in a case involving a very severe form of punishment given to a federal official for falsifying public records. This person was given 15 years, plus a fine. Also, he was subjected to *cadena temporal*, which meant that he was to serve much of his time chained from his ankle to his waist. He could not have any visitors during his imprisonment, and he was subjected to a lifetime of disabilities. The U.S. Supreme Court held this form of punishment to be cruel and unusual and in violation of the Eighth Amendment. The Court stated that the "Eighth Amendment is progressive and does not prohibit merely the cruel and unusual punishments known in 1689 and 1787, but may acquire wider meaning as public opinion becomes enlightened by humane justice" (*Weems v. United States*, 1910, p. 350).

Later, the Court stated that the Eighth Amendment "must draw its meaning from the evolving standard of decency that marks the progress of a maturing society" (*Trop v. Dulles*, 1959, p. 101). The Court used these perspectives to rule in cases involving capital punishment and prison conditions. Now, the Eighth Amendment is violated whenever the state has inflicted unnecessary and wanton pain on prisoners (*Gregg v. Georgia*, 1976). So, prisoners who are inflicted with unnecessary and wanton pain by the state can claim that their right to be free of cruel and unusual punishment is being violated. This violation can occur in a number of ways, including the deprivation of medical and psychiatric care.

Both *Weems* and *Trop* involved federal cases, so they did not apply to state defendants or prisoners. In 1962, the U.S. Supreme Court applied for the first time the Eighth Amendment prohibition against cruel and unusual punishment to the states. This occurred in the case of a man named Robinson who was convicted in California for being addicted to narcotics. The Court ruled that states cannot criminalize a status, such as an illness, and it was cruel and unusual punishment to do so. The Court reasoned that if states could make addiction, in and of itself, a crime, then the states could make it a crime to be mentally ill or to contract a venereal disease (*Robinson v. California*, 1962).

Robinson's importance was that it applied the Eighth Amendment to the states for the first time regarding the limits to which a state or city could criminalize certain behaviors. Also, the meaning of cruel and unusual punishment, provided by *Weems* and *Trop*, gave guidance to federal judges in applying the Eighth Amendment to state punishments. Laying the groundwork, *Robinson* later was used to carry the protection of the Eighth Amendment inside the prison system, which has had a major impact on the rights of prisoners.

Liberty, Property, Due Process, and Equal Protection

As indicated, states are prohibited from depriving any person of life, liberty, or property without due process of law. The word *liberty* means more than just freedom. According to *Blacks' Law Dictionary* (1990), "the 'liberty' guaranteed and protected by constitutional provisions denotes not only freedom from unauthorized physical restraints, but embraces also the freedom of an individual to use and enjoy his faculties in all lawful ways, acquire useful knowledge, marry, establish a home, and bring up children, worship God according to the dictates of his [or her] own conscience, live and work where he [or she] chooses, engage in any of the common and lawful occupations of life, enter into all contracts which may be proper and essential to carrying out successfully the foregoing purposes, and generally to enjoy those privileges long recognized at common law as essential to the orderly pursuit of happiness by free people" (p. 918). Though this definition discusses free people, prisoners have liberty interests that are protected by the Fourteenth Amendment. This liberty interest involves capricious segregation of prisoners, use of physical restraints, and involuntarily medicating prisoners.

Also, property is broadly defined and may include a job, university tenure, education, or degree (del Carmen, 1992). Whenever a state, through mandatory language of a statute or prison policy, promises to provide a benefit or not to discipline prisoners unless specified rules are violated, the state triggers liberty or property interests that are protected by the Due Process Clause of the Fourteenth Amendment (Reisner, 1985). So, depending upon the language of a state statute or policy, a state's promise to provide rehabilitation to institutionalized juveniles could be property that must be provided.

The right to due process is a frequently cited right. It is the right to have a fair determination of an issue before a person's life, liberty, or property is taken away. At a minimum, it is the right to notice of a complaint, the right to a hearing, the opportunity to present witnesses, the opportunity to cross-examine witnesses, and the right to a neutral tier-of-facts or, in other words, the right to a neutral decision-maker of the issue.

The right to equal protection of the law has varied meanings. Essentially, it requires that similarly situated persons be treated the same. In the prison context, it has been used to contest discriminatory treatment in prisons. So, for example, Muslim prisoners must be treated the same as Christian prisoners. However, a more difficult issue is presented regarding gender issues and equal protection of the law. A number of advocates of female prisoners stated that incarcerated women should not be treated differently than male prisoners, and lawsuits in behalf of female prisoners have been filed (Herbert, 1985).

However, the courts do not view women as similar to men in the same manner as viewing white male prisoners and African American male prisoners. For instance, the Tenth Circuit Court of Appeals has ruled that female correctional officers may participate in strip-searching male prisoners (*Grummett v. Rushen*, 1985; *Michenfelder v. Sumner*, 1988), but this same court has ruled that it is cruel and unusual punishment for male correctional officers to just pat search female prisoners (*Jordan v. Gardner*, 1993). From the perspective of the correctional officers, the Tenth Circuit Court of Appeals stated that female correctional officers would be denied equal protection of the law if they were prohibited from participating in strip searches of male prisoners, but male correctional officers would not be denied equal protection by prohibiting male correctional officers from conducting pat searches of female prisoners. Moreover, one of the Justices stated that the male correctional officers were committing criminal assaults by touching female prisoners (*Jordan v. Gardner*, 1993), but refused to conclude that female correctional officers were committing the same offenses when they touched male prisoners (Alexander, 1994a).

In sum, several amendments to the U.S. Constitution are frequently invoked in correctional treatment. But when prisoners invoke these Amendments and contend that their rights are violated, it does not mean that the courts are going to uphold a prisoner's claim. The courts may agree that a challenge under the Due Process Clause of the Fourteenth Amendment is applicable but may rule in favor of the state. Courts have to balance the prisoners' legal claims against the states' interests. To help balance these interests, the U.S. Supreme Court has articulated a legal test that it called the reasonableness test and has ordered all courts to use it when prisoners contend that their rights have been violated by state officials.

REASONABLENESS TEST

At one time, courts were reluctant to intervene in prisons, taking what many correctional experts called a "hands-off" approach (Alexander, 1994; Crouch & Marquart, 1989; Huff, 1980; Nagel, 1985). When the courts began to listen more to prisoners' claims and decided cases in prisoners' favor, they basically concluded that one or more of the prisoners' constitutional rights were violated. It is unclear what legal standard was being used to decide these cases.

For instance, if a state or federal government passed a law today authorizing involuntary sterilization for all free citizens who were developmentally disabled, the constitutionality of such a law would undoubtedly be decided under a strict scrutiny legal standard. This is the highest standard used in law and is used whenever a person's fundamental rights are at issue. The strict scrutiny standard requires the state to demonstrate that the sterilization law serves a compelling state interest and is narrowly drawn to serve that interest. It cannot be too broad or too narrow. However, this standard has been rejected for the prison environment.

In 1974, the U.S. Supreme Court held that it was unconstitutional for the California prison system to censor mail from attorneys to prisoners. In this case, the Court used the strict scrutiny legal standard. However, the Court decided the case from the perspective of the right of free citizens (i.e., attorneys) to communicate. The Court refused to decide this issue from the perspective of prisoners with use of the strict scrutiny standard (*Procunier v. Martinez*, 1974). When a subsequent court cited *Procunier* as justification for use of strict scrutiny in another case involving a prisoner attempting to write to another prisoner (*Safley v. Turner*, 1985), the U.S. Supreme Court made it very clear that strict scrutiny was inappropriate in a prison environment and a new legal test was to be used in all instances of conflicts when a prison policy allegedly conflicts with prisoners' rights (*Turner v. Safley*, 1987).

The Court stated in *Turner* that prisoners have rights that must be protected. However, the Court stated that administering a prison is a difficult task, and federal judges do not have the expertise to decide what is valid or invalid policy. Therefore, considerable deference should be given to prison administrators. So, a prison policy that conflicts with prisoners' rights is presumed to be valid provided the policy is "reasonably related to legitimate penological interest" (*Turner v. Safley*, 1987, p. 2261). Legitimate penological interests are security and order, deterrence, incapacitation, reformation, and rehabilitation. Whether a prison policy is legitimate is determined by one or more of a four-part test. In deciding whether a prison policy has violated prisoners' right, the courts must determine:

1. Whether there is a valid, rational connection between the prison regulation and the legitimate government interest put forward to justify it.

2. Whether there are alternative means of exercising the rights that remain open to prison inmates.
3. The impact accommodation of the asserted constitutional right will have on guards and other inmates, and on the allocation of prison resources generally.
4. The absence of ready alternatives is evidence of the reasonableness of a prison regulation. (*Turner v. Safley*, 1987, p. 2261)

The reasonableness test is important in correctional treatment because it has been subsequently used to decide whether the state can treat involuntarily with psychotropic drugs a prisoner who suffers from mental illness (*Washington v. Harper*, 1990). It also has been implicated in whether the state can treat an insane death row prisoner involuntarily to restore such a prisoner's sanity so that the prisoner can be executed (*Perry v. Louisiana*, 1990).

Readers now know the critical legal concepts in prison treatment. Also, readers should know what can happen if a correctional official has violated prisoners' constitutional rights. Prisoners can vindicate their rights through a civil rights lawsuit, which can provide a court order enjoining prison officials from further violating prisoners' rights, monetary damages, or imprisonment of the violators. This relief can be provided through a civil rights lawsuit that has its beginning in the period following slavery.

CIVIL RIGHTS ACT OF 1871

As stated earlier, the Fourteenth Amendment was passed primarily to provide relief to African Americans following slavery to protect them from unfair laws by the state. Because many of the persons oppressing African Americans were law enforcement officials and other state officials, Congress passed the Civil Rights Act of 1871 a few years after the Fourteenth Amendment was passed. The Civil Rights Act of 1871 provides that:

> Every person who, under color of any statute, ordinance, regulation, custom or usage, of any State or Territory, subjects, or causes to be subjected, any citizen of the United States or other person within the jurisdiction thereof to the deprivation of any rights, privileges, or immunities secured by the Constitution and laws, shall be liable to the party injured in an action at law, suit in equity, or other proper proceeding for redress. (Title 42 U.S.C., Section 1983, 1871)

The Civil Rights Act of 1871 is frequently used by prisoners to sue prison officials for depriving them of constitutionally protected rights, including treatment rights.

If a counselor purposely violates a prisoner's rights, monetary damages may be awarded. It can also be used by the federal government to imprison people. In the 1960s, it was used against Mississippi law enforcement persons/Klansmen who killed three civil rights workers. It also was used to convict some of the police officers who beat Rodney King. Like the Fourteenth Amendment being interpreted to all persons, the Civil Rights Act now applies to all citizens. It has been used to try an African American juvenile for killing a Jewish scholar in the Crown Heights section of New York. More recently, Congress extended the protection of the Civil

Rights Act to women and hate crimes committed against them. Finally, the criminal aspects of the Civil Rights Act could be used to try a counselor who has applied an unorthodox treatment that caused the death or serious injury to a prisoner.

A final legal principle needs to be discussed when treatment is being forced upon offenders. This principle involves civil commitment and is now being used to commit and treat involuntarily sex offenders who are nearing release from prison.

CRITERIA FOR CIVIL COMMITMENT

Two legal principles exist that justify states incarcerating or imprisoning individuals in an institution. The first is police power. It refers to the right of the state to protect itself both physically and morally. A state's police power provides the basis for all criminal laws. It can be used to protect a community from a person who is mentally ill. The state also has the right to commit individuals under the principle of *parens patriae*. This principle gives the state the right to act as guardian of all persons who are incompetent, such as persons with severe mental illness, persons who are severely developmentally disabled, and children. Care for these groups may be provided in an institutional setting. Children, in many instances, include juvenile offenders, and *parens patriae* has treatment implications.

With respect to persons who are assessed to be mentally disordered, the state may invoke either police power or *parens patriae* or both. To commit civilly an individual who is mentally ill, the person must be both mentally ill and dangerous to self or others (Petrila, Otto, & Poythress, 1994). The absence of either mental illness or dangerousness means that the individual must be released from an institution (*Foucha v. Louisiana*, 1992). Convicted sex offenders serving time in prison are now being civilly committed to mental institutions for forced treatment under the theory that they are mentally ill and dangerous (Alexander, 1995b).

These explanations of various legal concepts and standards provide the basis for courts to rule in a number of areas regarding treatment. Having laid the legal foundations for treatment issues, the author now presents the current state of the law with respect to the right to rehabilitation, the right to treatment, the right to habilitation, and the right to resist involuntary treatment.

THE RIGHT TO REHABILITATION IN ADULT PRISONS

Rotman (1986) wrote a very detailed article proclaiming that criminal offenders have a right to rehabilitation. However, his article was devoid of legal reasoning supporting this contention and was mostly a philosophical argument. The actual legal cases in the literature have provided no support for a right to rehabilitation for adult offenders. In one of the early cases, Smith, a prisoner incarcerated in one of California's prisons, filed a complaint under the Civil Rights Act. He contended that he was addicted to narcotics and the state of California had denied him medical treatment for his addiction and adequate vocational training. The Ninth Circuit Court of Appeals rejected Smith's claim, noting that the Eighth Amendment must draw its meaning from the evolving standard of decency. Accordingly, it could not hold at the present time that the denial of both medical attention for addiction and vocational training to prevent future use after release constituted cruel and unusual punishment (*Smith v. Schneckloth*, 1969).

In two decisions from the state of Alabama, the Fifth Circuit Court of Appeals spoke definitively about the issue of prisoners' rights to rehabilitation. In the first decision, an Alabama prisoner filed a lawsuit alleging that the denial of rehabilitative programs in Alabama prisons constituted cruel and unusual punishment. The Fifth Circuit Court of Appeals conceded that extreme Eighth Amendment violations might support rehabilitative programs, but it was not going to hold that the lack of rehabilitative programs, in and of itself, constituted cruel and unusual punishment (*McCray v. Sullivan*, 1975).

In the second decision two years later, the Fifth Circuit Court of Appeals considered an appeal involving prisoners from Alabama who filed a lawsuit alleging cruel and unusual punishment. The lack of rehabilitative programs was one of many issues raised by the prisoners. In this case, the U.S. Government filed an *amicus curiae* (i.e., friend of the court) brief in behalf of the Alabama prisoners. The Assistant U.S. Attorney General conceded that prisoners do not have a constitutional right to rehabilitation, but the state of Alabama should not permit prisoners' mental, physical, and emotional status to deteriorate. The Fifth Circuit Court of Appeals rebuffed the government's contention, stressing that all people deteriorate and nothing can prevent it. The Fifth Circuit Court of Appeals corrected the government's position and stated that the proper argument was that the state cannot impose conditions that cause deterioration in prisoners (*Newman v. Alabama*, 1977). The Fifth Circuit Court of Appeals said:

> If the State furnishes its prisoners with reasonably adequate food, clothing, shelter, sanitation, medical care, and personal safety, so as to avoid the imposition of cruel and unusual punishment, that ends its obligations under Amendment Eight. The Constitution does not require that prisoners, as individuals or as a group, be provided with any and every amenity which some person may think is needed to avoid mental, physical, and emotional deterioration. (*Newman v. Alabama*, 1977, p. 291)

These decisions seemed to establish firmly that prisoners do not have a constitutional right to rehabilitation. However, one district court in the state of Washington ruled that prisoners have a right to rehabilitation based on the wording of a Washington law. This law indicated that prison administrators were to provide programs and procedures so as to correct, reform, and rehabilitate prisoners. Believing that this wording triggered the protection of the Due Process Clause because it was property, the District Court found for the prisoners. In addition, the District Court stated that the lack of rehabilitative programs contributed to idleness, which contributed to frustration and violence in the prison (*Hoptowit v. Ray*, 1980).

However, the Ninth Circuit Court of Appeals overturned the District Court. The Ninth Circuit Court of Appeals stated that the District Court had overlooked a state decision that held that the word *rehabilitation* in the statute reflected the state interest and the state court's conclusion that the wording did not create any enforceable right by prisoners to rehabilitation. Further, the District Court, according to the Ninth Circuit, had overlooked the growing body of federal decisions that prisoners do not have a constitutional right to rehabilitation (*Hoptowit v. Ray*, 1982).

With respect to adult offenders and the Eighth Amendment prohibition against cruel and unusual punishment, the federal courts have consistently held that prisoners do not have a right to rehabilitation. Also, adult prisoners are being punished for their offending behavior, and the states do not owe them anything above basic care (*Balla v. Idaho State Bd of Corrections*, 1984). However, with respect juvenile offenders' rights to rehabilitation, the courts have not been as definitive, and the issues are more complex.

THE RIGHT TO REHABILITATION IN JUVENILE INSTITUTIONS

Unlike adult correctional institutions, where the emphasis is on punishment, juvenile correctional institutions theoretically are not places where punishment takes place. Only persons who have been lawfully convicted may be punished. Juveniles who have been adjudicated as delinquents are not viewed as being convicted criminals. So, a qualitative difference exists between convicted adult offenders and adjudicated juvenile delinquents (Alexander, 1995a). Yet, criminologists and other social scientists do not agree, and considerable differences of opinion exist regarding juveniles' right to rehabilitation (Becker, 1980; Blasko, 1985; Gardner, 1989; Heugle, 1980; Levine, 1980; Shepherd, 1977).

While the courts have been definitive in their rulings that adult offenders do not have a constitutional right to rehabilitation, the same cannot be said for juvenile offenders. In fact, a number of courts in the 1970s have ruled that juveniles have a constitutional right to rehabilitation (*Morales v. Turman*, 1974; *Nelson v. Heyne*, 1974). This movement to universally establishing that juvenile offenders have a constitutional right to rehabilitation was halted by two decisions in the 1980s (*Gary H. v. Hegstrom*, 1987; *Santana v. Collazo*, 1983). Since then, discussions about juveniles' rights to rehabilitation waned, and the contemporary literature seemed to conclude that such a right does not exist. Recently, Alexander (1995a) reviewed these discussions, rejected the 1980s decisions as not definitive, and has concluded that, indeed, juveniles have a right to rehabilitation, albeit this right is somewhat tenuous.

Early Judicial Rulings

One of the earliest rulings regarding the right to treatment or rehabilitation occurred in Indiana. As a result of a lawsuit, a U.S. District Court found that incarcerated juveniles have a right to rehabilitation based on two U.S. Supreme Court rulings and an Indiana statute. The District Court examined *Kent v. U.S.* (1966) and *In re Winship* (1970) and concluded that the U.S. Supreme Court had endorsed rehabilitation and treatment for juvenile offenders. Also, the U.S. District Court concluded that the Indiana statute promised incarcerated juveniles secure care, guidance, and control. These provisions would be provided for the juveniles' welfare. Considering all three factors, the U.S. District Court ruled that juveniles in Indiana have a right to rehabilitation (*Nelson v. Heyne*, 1972).

The state of Indiana appealed this decision to the Seventh Circuit Court of Appeals, and it upheld the ruling of the lower district court (*Nelson v. Heyne*, 1974).

The effect of the decision by the Seventh Circuit Court of Appeals was that this right existed for all incarcerated juveniles in the Seventh Circuit, which included Illinois and Wisconsin. The state of Indiana asked the U.S. Supreme Court to consider its appeal, but the Court refused to hear the case (*Nelson v. Heyne*, 1974). The U.S. Supreme Court's refusal to hear this case is significant because if the lower federal courts were patently wrong in their decisions, the Court, in all likelihood, would have agreed to hear the case and would have reversed it. Its refusal to hear the case is tacit agreement with the lower courts (Alexander, 1995a).

In another case involving status offenders incarcerated at three New York juvenile institutions, the U.S. District Court for the Southern District of New York ruled that these juveniles' rights to treatment and rehabilitation were being violated. Several legal issues were alleged in this civil rights lawsuit, and the District Court stated that the issue involving the right to treatment was the most difficult. The court stated that "there can be no doubt that the right to treatment, generally, for those held in non-criminal custody (whether based on due process, equal protection or the Eighth Amendment, or a combination of them) has by now been recognized by the Supreme Court, the lower federal courts, and the courts of New York" (*Martarella v. Kelley*, 1972, p. 599).

In Mississippi, a U.S. District Court stated juveniles incarcerated at the Oakley Training School had a right to treatment based on two equally sound theories (*Morgan v. Sproat*, 1977). First, the U.S. Supreme Court ruled that due process required that the actual conditions and programs existing at an institution where a person has been involuntary committed bear a reasonable relationship to that purpose (*Jackson v. Indiana*, 1972). Because "the purpose of incarcerating juveniles in a state training school is treatment and rehabilitation" (p. 1135), due process required the state of Mississippi to provide those activities that served the purpose of treatment and rehabilitation. Second, juveniles were incarcerated under a *parens patriae* philosophy without receiving the full complements of due process rights that were provided to adult offenders. Ordinarily, this deprivation of juveniles' rights would be unlawful. It becomes lawful provided the purpose is to serve a beneficent rather than punitive purpose. The beneficent purpose is to provide rehabilitation so that an individual is returned to society as a better person, and this could only be accomplished by providing rehabilitation. To do less deprives juveniles of their due process rights (*Morgan v. Sproat*, 1977).

In a similar ruling, but one that was more comprehensive, a federal court in Texas ruled that under the theory of *parens patriae* juveniles must be provided with treatment, and the lack of treatment deprives juveniles of due process. At a minimum, the state of Texas must provide the following in order to assure that juveniles' right to treatment was being provided.

1. An individual assessment to serve as the basis for the child's treatment plan; this plan should include a family history, a developmental history, a physical examination, psychological testing, a psychiatric interview, community evaluation, and a language and education analysis evaluation.
2. Social work staff involved in the assessment must be trained at the Master's degree level in social welfare or closely related fields.

3. Social work staff must not have caseloads exceeding 15 cases per week.
4. Psychologists with Master's degrees and properly trained in testing procedures are adequate, but only if a Doctoral-level psychologist is available to supervise their work. A psychiatrist, however, must be available for interviews.
5. For adequate classification, there must be daily contact between caseworker and juvenile, so as to evaluate the juvenile's amenability to guidance and counseling.
6. The Weschler individualized intelligence quotient test, rather than the group Lorge-Thorndike IQ test, must be utilized.
7. The Leiter and Weschler tests, which are standardized for African American and Mexican American youth and designed to reduce discriminatory factors, must be used.
8. Adequate psychological testing should take approximately 15 hours and require the services of one psychologist for every three juveniles classified per week. (*Morales v. Turman*, 1974)

These cases clearly indicated that incarcerated juveniles had a right to rehabilitation and programs designed to serve that end. However, subsequent cases thoroughly rejected all theories that juveniles have a right to rehabilitation.

The first decision to counter juveniles' right to rehabilitation occurred in Puerto Rico. The plaintiffs contended that they were similar to persons civilly committed to mental institutions, who have a constitutional right to treatment based on a quid pro quo theory. *Quid pro quo* means something of value for something of value. Rejecting this contention, the U.S. District Court in Puerto Rico ruled that juveniles have a right to adequate and humane care, but not rehabilitation or treatment. Humane care consisted of food, clothing, and adequate shelter. Depriving juveniles of clothing, heat during the winter, sanitary living condition, or food would violate the U.S. Constitution. However, the lack of services and programming, such as detailed in the Texas case, was not constitutionally required (*Santana v. Collazo*, 1982).

On appeal to the First Circuit Court of Appeals, the lower federal court was upheld. Both Puerto Rico courts reviewed *Jackson v. Indiana* (1972) and concluded that it formed the basis for incarcerating juveniles without rehabilitation. In *Jackson*, the U.S. Supreme Court ruled that the nature of a commitment must bear a reasonable relationship to its purpose. However, they concluded that one of the purposes of the juvenile justice system is to protect the public from juveniles. Therefore, the state does not owe juveniles, under a quid pro quo rationale, treatment or rehabilitation. Furthermore, the decision from the First Circuit Court of Appeals cited a concurring opinion by Chief Justice Warren Burger, who rejected the view that civilly committed persons who are mentally ill have a right to treatment (*Santana v. Collazo*, 1983). A few years later, the Ninth Circuit Court of Appeals adopted the legal rationale presented in *Santana* and stated that juveniles were entitled to just humane treatment (*Gary H. v. Hegstrom*, 1987).

Roth (1985) reviewed many of the decisions regarding juveniles' rights to rehabilitation and discussed the mixed views regarding this issue. Alexander (1995a) also reviewed these issues and subsequent legal decisions that occurred after Roth's article. Alexander (1995a) concluded that the U.S. District Court, the First Circuit Court of Appeals, and the Ninth Circuit Court of Appeals were incorrect in their rulings, and juveniles indeed have a right to rehabilitation as the federal courts found in the 1970s. According to Alexander (1995a), the Puerto Rico courts erred in basing their opinions that civilly committed mentally ill persons do not have a right to treatment on Chief Justice Warren Burger's concurring opinion in *O'Connor v. Donaldson* (1975). *O'Connor* was a unanimous ruling that upheld monetary damages against a superintendent of a mental institution for holding a person committed in Florida who was not being given treatment and who had the capacity to care for himself.

As Alexander (1995a) pointed out, Chief Justice Burger did not write the majority opinion in *O'Connor*, and no other Justices joined him in the view that persons committed on the basis of mental illness to a mental institution do not have a right to treatment. The Chief Justice concurred in the ruling that Donaldson's liberty had been taken away without due process of law, and Donaldson was entitled to damages. Because the issue of the right to treatment came up in a lower court in this case, Chief Justice Burger took it upon himself to attempt to quash the notion that a constitutional right to treatment existed for anyone. The majority felt that the issue of the right to treatment was not properly before the Court, and therefore, the Court did not need to rule on that issue in *O'Connor*. Chief Justice Warren Burger also denounced, in another concurring opinion, the view that severely retarded persons who were civilly committed to an institution have a right to habilitation. Again, he was in the minority, and no other Justice joined him in this view. The majority opinion was that persons civilly committed have a right to training that would permit them from having their liberty interests violated (*Youngberg v. Romeo*, 1982).

The Chief Justice is one Justice out of nine on the U.S. Supreme Court, and his or her vote carries no more weight than any other Justice. At least five Justices are needed to establish constitutional law. Therefore, the First Circuit Court of Appeals in *Santana v. Collazo* (1983) erred in using just Chief Justice Burger's concurring opinion in *O'Connor* as the initial basis for rejecting the comparison between incarcerated juveniles and institutionalized persons with mental illness. Because the Ninth Circuit Court of Appeals based its decision in *Gary H.* totally on the First Circuit decision in *Santana*, the Ninth Circuit also erred in rejecting juveniles' right to rehabilitation.

Although protecting the public may be a goal of the juvenile justice system, it is also a goal of the mental health system. The state has the right under its police power to commit persons who are mentally ill and dangerous. However, protecting the public from persons civilly committed as mentally ill and dangerous is achieved through treatment, not mere institutionalization. Similarly, protecting the public from juvenile offenders can be achieved thorough rehabilitation, and some state statutes specially say so. Accordingly, incarcerated juvenile offenders have a right to rehabilitation (Alexander, 1995a).

How Juveniles Have a Right to Rehabilitation

To understand Alexander's view (1995a), one must begin with the difference between an adult institution and a juvenile institution. Shepherd (1977) and Gardner (1989) have argued that juveniles have a right to punishment, which suggested that juveniles are not punished. In theory, a juvenile who has been adjudicated as delinquent and is in a juvenile correctional institution is not undergoing punishment.

In a like manner, a person who is severely mentally ill is not undergoing punishment when he or she has been civilly committed to a mental institution. Thus, juveniles possess a similar status as civilly incarcerated persons who had been adjudicated as mentally ill and in need of treatment.

As an illustration, Ohio provides that:

> Juvenile delinquency has not been declared a crime in Ohio; indeed, the Juvenile Court law expressly provides that a child is not criminal by reason of a Juvenile Court adjudication, and civil disabilities ordinarily following conviction do not attach. Insofar as children's cases are concerned, the Ohio Juvenile Court Law is neither criminal nor penal in its nature, but is an administrative police regulation of a corrective character. Misdeeds of children are not looked upon in the Juvenile Court as crimes carrying conviction, but as delinquencies which the State endeavors to rectify by placing the child under favorable influences and by the employment of other corrective methods. While the commission of a crime may set the machinery of the Juvenile Court in motion, the accused is not tried in that court for his [or her] crime but for his [or her] incorrigibility. Accordingly, it has been said that the Juvenile Court law vests jurisdiction over the infant, not the crime. (460 Ohio Jur 3d, Family Law 361)

Further, other areas of the Ohio law address the issue of rehabilitation for incarcerated juvenile offenders. For instance, the Ohio legislature stated that the purpose of the juvenile court is "to protect the public interest in removing the consequences of criminal behavior and the taint of criminality from children committing delinquent acts and to substitute therefor a program of supervision, care, and rehabilitation" (460 Ohio Jur. 3d, Family Law 359). The Ohio legislature also stated that the Ohio Department of Youth Services "shall provide treatment and training for children committed to the department and assigned by the department to the various institutions, facilities, and field services of the department (Ohio Revised Code Annotated, Title 51 Public Welfare, Section 5139.13). Finally, the Ohio legislature passed a statute that was entitled "Rehabilitation of Child Committed to Youth Services" and declared that "as a means of correcting the socially harmful tendencies of a child committed to it, the Department of Youth Services may require participation by him [or her] in vocational, physical, educational, and corrective training and activities, and such conduct and modes of life as seem best adapted to rehabilitate him [or her] and fit him [or her] for return to full liberty without danger to the public welfare" (Ohio Revised Code Annotated, Title 51 Public Welfare, Section 5139.070).

Certainly, Ohio, and any other states with similarly worded views regarding juvenile offenders, provides incarcerated juveniles a right to rehabilitation. A state that warehouses a juvenile in an institution with no programming is violating that juvenile's constitutional rights. Such a juvenile could file a civil rights lawsuit, requesting injunctive relief or monetary damages.

However, the state may diminish juveniles' right to rehabilitation by changing its laws and how it handles juvenile offenders. The state can always decide to change its statute to say that juvenile delinquency is a crime, punishable by imprisonment in a youth institution. The state also can abolish the juvenile justice system, extinguishing juveniles' rights to rehabilitation. Because of this possible occurrence, Alexander (1995a) stated that juveniles have a tenuous right to rehabilitation.

However, as long as the law views juveniles not as criminals and promises to rehabilitate them, juveniles have a right to rehabilitation.

THE RIGHT TO HABILITATION

Earlier in this chapter, mention was made of the right to habilitation. This case
involved a man in a Pennsylvania institution who had an IQ of 10 and who had
been committed by his family. He frequently was put in restraints to prevent him
from injuring himself. Having someone in prison like Romeo with an IQ of 10
would be unsettling. However, in some prisons in this country there are probably a
few prisoners like Romeo. Probably unlike Romeo, these prisoners were not born
with this type of developmental disability. But prisoners could acquire this type of
disability. In prison, extreme violence occurs, and there is a strong possibility that a
prisoner has been attacked by another prisoner or prisoners and suffered extreme
brain damage. A common occurrence in traumatic brain injuries is that the injured
persons loses basic skills. They may suffer from memory loss, lose the ability to talk,
or lose the ability to walk. Typically, long hours of therapy are needed to teach lost
skills. When a traumatic brain injury has occurred to prisoners resulting in the loss
of basic living skills, do prisoners have a right to habilitation? The answer appears
to be yes.

In *Romeo*, the U.S. Supreme Court referred to Romeo's liberty rights under the
Fourteenth Amendment. The Court noted that prisoners have liberty interests protected by the Fourteenth Amendment that precluded prison administrators from
putting prisoners in disciplinary units unless the prisoners have violated written institutional policy. Normally, liberty interests are triggered when a state policy says
that a prisoner will not be disciplined unless he or she violates specific rules. As long
as prisoners do not violate these rules, their institutional freedom (i.e., yard time,
the movies, or commissary) cannot be arbitrarily taken away.

The Court stated that if prisoners have liberty interests that are protected by the
Fourteenth Amendment, then an unconvicted person, such as Romeo, must have
the same. So, Romeo was constitutionally entitled to habilitation so that his liberty
interests were protected. He had to be taught skills that would preclude him from
having to be put in restraints. He also had to be taught to bathe, dress, and talk
(*Romeo v. Youngblood*, 1983).

Extrapolating *Romeo* to the prison system, brain-damaged prisoners are legally
entitled to be taught skills that would preserve their liberty. Prisons could not simply transfer a brain-damaged prisoner to a nursing home or mental institution in lieu
of habilitation. Basic skills must be taught as long as the prisoner is in state custody.
The only way to shed this responsibility, perhaps, is to grant the prisoner an emergency parole or executive clemency and allow the family to care for the prisoner.

THE RIGHT TO MENTAL HEALTH
OR PSYCHIATRIC TREATMENT

Looking at the U.S. Constitution, one cannot find an affirmative right to mental health treatment, and these words are not mentioned at all in any of the
amendments (Alexander, 1989). To understand such a right, one must look to the

Eighth Amendment and its prohibition against cruel and unusual punishment (Mayer, 1989). The foundation for prisoners' right to mental health treatment is *Estelle v. Gamble* (1976). In this case, a Texas prisoner brought a lawsuit contending that he had been subjected to cruel and unusual punishment because he was inadequately treated for a back injury. Although this prisoner lost his lawsuit, the U.S. Supreme Court established when a prisoner can make a valid claim of an Eighth Amendment violation based on medical issues.

Justice Marshall, writing for the majority, stated that "in order to state a cognizable claim, a prisoner must allege acts or omissions sufficiently harmful to evidence deliberate indifference to serious medical needs" (*Estelle v. Gamble*, 1976, p. 106). Simply, a prisoner who has a serious medical problem that is being ignored by prison administrators is being inflicted with cruel and unusual punishment. The pain inflicted by a lack of medical treatment serves no legitimate penological interest. Echoing this sentiment with respect to juveniles, the Eleventh Circuit Court of Appeals held, first, that juveniles have the same right to medical treatment that was established in *Estelle v. Gamble*, and a wait of three days to treat an injured juvenile constituted cruel and unusual punishment for which the superintendent was liable (*H.C. by Hewett v. Jarrard*, 1986).

With *Estelle v. Gamble* clearly establishing prisoners' rights to medical treatment, it was quickly extrapolated to psychiatric care. Like Gamble, Bowring, the prisoner involved, did not prevail, but his lawsuit established the parameter for a right to mental health treatment. This prisoner was turned down for parole, in part, because a psychiatric report had indicated that his chances of success on parole were low because of a psychological problem. After getting his rejection for parole, he filed a lawsuit. He contended that because his freedom was being denied because of a psychological problem, the state had a duty to provide mental health treatment to him so that he could make parole. The U.S. District Court rejected the claim without a hearing, but the Fourth Circuit Court of Appeals reversed the District Court's decision and ordered a hearing on Bowring's claim (*Bowring v. Godwin*, 1977).

The Fourth Circuit Court of Appeals did not accept that Bowring had a psychological problem but that a hearing had to be held to determine the extent to which he had a serious medical problem. This hearing was necessary in light of *Estelle v. Gamble* because psychiatric treatment was considered to be medical treatment. Like the U.S. Supreme Court had outlined how a prisoner could make a valid claim of an Eighth Amendment violation because of a medical issue, the Fourth Circuit Court of Appeals did the same with respect to a psychiatric problem. The Fourth Circuit Court of Appeals wrote that:

> A prison inmate is entitled to psychological or psychiatric treatment if a physician or mental health care provider, exercising ordinary skill and care at the time of observation, concludes with reasonable medical certainty (1) that the prisoner's symptoms evidence a serious disease or injury, (2) that such disease or injury is curable or may be substantially alleviated, and (3) that the potential for harm to the prisoners by reason of delay or the denial of care would be substantial. (*Bowring v. Godwin*, 1977, p. 47)

Logically tied to *Estelle*, *Bowring* suggested that prisoners with serious psychiatric problems have their right to be free from cruel and unusual punishment violated when they are allowed to suffer needlessly and painfully. *Bowring* does not mean that counseling must be provided for minor psychological distress. The psychological problem must be serious, such as a prisoner who is suffering from schizophrenia and is causing harm to himself or herself. A prisoner who is suffering from depression would not have a right to counseling for that depression, unless the depression is quite severe and is significantly affecting the prisoner's functioning in the institution.

Numerous mental health professionals have lauded *Bowring,* and federal courts throughout the country have adopted the *Bowring* principles (*Doty v. County of Lassen,* 1994; *Harris v. Thigpen,* 1991; *Greason v. Kemp,* 1990; *Lay v. Norris,* 1989; *Riddle v. Mondragon,* 1996; *Torraco v. Maloney,* 1991; *White v. Napoleon,* 1990). Although some prisoners want and need mental health treatment, some prisoners do not want treatment because treatment means state abuse and a longer period of incarceration. The right to refuse treatment has become a very contentious issue, which the next section discusses.

THE RIGHT TO REFUSE MENTAL HEALTH TREATMENT

Prisoners have a long history of resisting involuntary mental health treatment. At one time, prison administrators transferred sane, but troublesome, prisoners to mental institutions, which meant that these prisoners could not be paroled and were confined longer (Alexander, 1988). These practices were limited by the courts as violations of prisoners' rights. The U.S. Supreme Court held that a prisoner facing involuntary treatment in a mental institution is entitled to due process. In this case, due process required a hearing, the right to present witnesses, the right to notice of the need for treatment, and an impartial person to decide if forced treatment was required (*Vitek v. Jones,* 1979).

In addition, the courts began to scrutinize therapies provided to prisoners. Aversive therapy, legitimately used in psychiatric practice, had become punishment in the prison setting. For instance, an Iowa prisoner contended that he was given a medication that caused him to vomit because of violation of an institutional rule. The prisoner contended that this constituted cruel and unusual punishment, but the state countered that this was aversive therapy. However, the Eighth Circuit Court of Appeals agreed with the prisoner and stated that this was cruel and unusual punishment (*Knecht v. Gillman,* 1973). In California, the Ninth Circuit Court of Appeals made a similar ruling regarding another aversive therapy that gave a prisoner the feeling of being suffocated. It was called treatment by the California prison authorities, but the court held it to be cruel and unusual punishment (*Mackey v. Procunier,* 1973). Neither the Iowa case nor the California case involved prisoners with a recognized diagnosis of mental illness, and the courts properly found these practices unconstitutional.

Of course, some prisoners have universally recognized mental illnesses. The extent to which these prisoners could reject involuntary treatment has not been debated by professionals and advocates as it has been debated regarding free citizens (see Bentley, 1994; Brown, 1984; Poythress & Miller, 1991; Rhoden, 1980; Rosenson, 1994; Shobat, 1985). Alexander (1991) argued that discussions regarding prisoners' rights to refuse psychotropic treatment was slighted because of the qualitative difference between the rights of free citizens and prisoners and because prisoners are a neglected group. More importantly, the United States Supreme Court has permitted the involuntary treatment of prisoners with psychotropic medication. This issue does not involve the Eighth Amendment like *Knecht v. Gillman* (1973) and *Mackey v. Procunier* (1973). Instead, it involved the reasonableness test.

Washington v. Harper

Walter Harper, a prisoner in the state of Washington, was assessed by mental health professionals to be mentally ill. He voluntarily took medication for his illness. After serving a portion of his sentence, he was paroled by the paroling authorities. As a condition of parole, he was required to get psychiatric treatment in the community. In the community, Harper experienced a relapse and was subsequently civilly committed to a mental institution. In the mental institution, he assaulted two nurses. Because these assaults were a violation of his parole, he was returned to prison and placed in a psychiatric unit. Harper briefly took psychotropic medication voluntarily, but he stopped. His refusal caused the prison system to invoke its involuntary medication policy, which was developed to accommodate the due process requirements of *Vitek v. Jones* (1980).

Washington's involuntary medication policy required a panel consisting of a psychiatrist, a psychologist, and the associate superintendent to conduct a hearing. The prisoner had (1) the right to 24 hours' notice of the prison's desire to medicate involuntarily, (2) the right to be present at the hearing, (3) the right to introduce evidence in his or her behalf, (4) the right to cross-examine the prison staff witnesses, (5) the right to assistance by a lay advisor, (6) the right to appeal the decision to the superintendent of the prison, and (7) the right to periodic review subsequent to the initial hearing (*Harper v. the State of Washington*, 1988). These procedures were followed and a decision was made to medicate Harper forcibly. On appeal to the Supreme Court of Washington, the court held that these procedures violated Harper's rights. The court stated that because forcible medication involved a significant bodily intrusion with a medication that had serious side effects, the state had to overcome the strict scrutiny legal test before a judge. This requirement is similar to the rights of a free citizen if the state proposes to perform a lobotomy on a person (*Harper v. the State of Washington*, 1988).

However, the U.S. Supreme Court disagreed. The Court stated that the strict scrutiny test was incompatible with deciding issues in a prison environment and would make it more difficult for prison administrators to manage dangerous prisoners. Instead, the reasonableness test should be used, which the Court had articulated in *Turner v. Safley* (1987). Applying the reasonableness test, the Court ruled that Harper's constitutional right to liberty could be overridden by prison administrators. The Court reasoned that Harper's mental illness made him dangerous to staff and others. Therefore, Harper's limited right to liberty had to yield to the prison legitimate interest in maintaining security and order in the institution. Also, the Court held that providing Harper with a judicial hearing would take scarce resources away from the prison and the cost of accommodating a prisoner's right must be taken into account. In conclusion, the Court stated that the prison psychiatrist knew best how to treat Harper, understood the side effects of the prescribed medication, had an oath to provide medical services only in the patient's medical interest, and, therefore, should not be second-guessed by federal judges (*Washington v. Harper*, 1990).

Later, the U.S. Supreme Court suggested that pretrial detainees who are mentally ill could be medicated involuntarily, provided jails followed the procedures in *Washington v. Harper* (Alexander, 1995c; *Riggins v. Nevada*, 1992).

Riggins involved a mentally ill defendant who was involuntarily medicated to make him competent to be tried. At Riggins' trial, Riggins was convicted and given the death penalty. The Court also remanded a death penalty case to Louisiana involving whether the state of Louisiana could forcibly medicate a mentally ill death row prisoner to make the prisoner sane enough to be executed. In remanding this case, the U.S. Supreme Court instructed the state of Louisiana to use the reasonableness test (*Perry v. Louisiana*, 1990). Both the Supreme Courts of Nevada and Louisiana subsequently ruled that under their state constitutions, these persons could not be executed. The U.S. Supreme Court's ruling in these two cases show that the Court wants the reasonableness test to be used in all prison-related cases involving mental illness.

The application of the reasonableness test to the issue of involuntary medication of prisoners has been applauded and criticized. Prison officials believe such a policy is fair and necessary. However, other professionals believe that it will further the abuse of drugs in prisons to control troublesome prisoners, which some states have long done (Alexander, 1995b). It is not the purpose of this chapter to go into these issues but to state the current law. The involuntary treatment of mentally ill prisoners is controversial. In addition, the involuntary treatment of sex offenders has become controversial as well, and this involves other legal issues.

THE RIGHT TO REFUSE ALCOHOLICS ANONYMOUS OR NARCOTIC ANONYMOUS TREATMENT

Another right to refuse treatment involves prisoners' First Amendment rights and Alcoholics Anonymous (AA) or Narcotic Anonymous (NA) treatment. The First Amendment contains a concept that is referred to as the Establishment Clause. In 1947, the U.S. Supreme Court explained what the Establishment Clause was (*Everson v. Board of Education*, 1947). According to the Court, the Establishment Clause demands that:

> Neither a state nor the federal government can set up a church. Neither can pass laws that aid one religion, aid all religions, or prefer one religion over another. Neither can force nor influence a person to go to or to remain away from church against his [or her] will or force him [or her] to profess a belief or disbelief in any religion. No person can be punished for entertaining or professing religious beliefs or disbelief, for church attendance or nonattendance. No tax in any amount, large or small, can be levied to support any religious activities or institutions, whatever they may be called, or whatever form they may adopt to teach or practice religion. Neither a state nor the federal government can, openly or secretly, participate in the affairs of any religious organizations or groups and vice versa. (*Everson v. Board of Education*, 1947, p. 15-16)

Because AA and NA contain 12-step approaches with emphasis on God, a conflict developed when prison officials have coerced prisoners to participate.

In *Kerr v. Farrey* (1996), the Seventh Circuit Court of Appeals ruled that a Wisconsin prisoner's First Amendment rights were violated because he was coerced into attending an NA program. Kerr, the prisoner, stated that he was told by a prison social worker that attendance at NA was mandatory and Kerr had no choice but to attend. The penalty for not attending would be a transfer from the minimum security prison to a medium security prison. In addition, Kerr's records would indicate his nonattendance so that the parole board would be cognizant of Kerr's refusal to participate in drug treatment. The Seventh Circuit Judges stated that when a prisoner claims that the state is coercing religion on him or her, three questions need to be asked. First, has the state acted? Second, does the action constitute coercion? Third, is the object of the coercion religious or secular? In the Judges' opinion, the answers to the first two questions were yes and the answer to the third question was religious. Therefore, the prison administrators violated Kerr's First Amendment right. However, the Judges granted the prison superintendent and social worker qualified immunity because the right to be free from coercion involving NA was not an established right that a reasonable person would know (*Kerr v. Farrey*, 1996).

A few decisions have been rendered by U.S. District Courts regarding this issue. One court has rejected the challenge made to NA and AA and their religious contents. It used the reasonableness test and concluded that a rational basis existed between forcing prisoners into drug treatment programs and the government interests in reducing drug dependency, reducing recidivism, and increasing security (*Boyd v. Coughlin*, 1996). *Boyd* was decided by a New York District Court several months before *Kerr*. However, the emerging view by a number of courts seems consistent with *Kerr*. Several District Courts suggested that the lack or availability of treatment options affect whether prisoners have legitimate claims based on the Established Clause. A prison system that has only one option, AA or NA, violates prisoners' rights (*Scarpino v. Grosshiem*, 1994; *Warner v. Orange County Dept. of Probation*, 1994), whereas a prison that has several treatment options, in which AA or NA is one, does not violate prisoners' First Amendment rights (*O'Connor v. California*, 1994).

INVOLUNTARY TREATMENT
OF SEX OFFENDERS

In the 1930s, states began to control some sex offenders by civilly committing them to mental institutions. In the 1960s, most states repealed their civil commitment statutes because mental health professionals expressed concern about the appropriateness of mental institutions for relatively minor sex offenders, the causes of sexual deviance, and civil rights concerns. In the late 1980s and 1990s, considerable attention has focused on serious sex offenders, and many states have retrieved civil commitment as a solution (Alexander, 1993b).

Unlike before, a major difference exists in civil commitment in the 1930s and civil commitment in the 1990s. In the 1930s, civil commitment occurred in lieu of imprisonment. But in the 1990s civil commitment occurs after sex offenders have served their sentences in a prison system. In some states, the mental health units where sex offenders are committed are located on the grounds of the prison. In effect, they are moved from one part of the prison to another. The use of civil commitment raises a series of issues, and the courts have grappled with these legal issues.

Mental illness and being a danger to self and others are required for civil commitment to a mental institution. Further, the act of dangerousness must be recent. One of the critical issues is whether sex offenders are mentally ill—a necessary justification for civil commitment. On one hand, some professionals have argued that they are mentally ill (Fujimoto, 1993; Henderson & Kalichman, 1990), but others have argued that they are not (Alexander, 1995b; Erlinder, 1993; LaFond, 1992; Reardon, 1992; Wettstein, 1992). This debate aside, several courts have ruled that sex offenders who are nearing release from prison can be legally committed to mental institutions for an indefinite period (*In re Blodgett*, 1994; *In re Young*, 1993).

How states changed their laws is interesting. The Washington legislature, knowing that its definition of serious mental illness for ordinary citizens would not encompass sex offenders, created a new definition of mental disorder tailored to predatory sex offenders. It defined the sexually violent predator as "any person who has been convicted of or charged with a crime of sexual violence and who suffers from a mental abnormality or personality disorder which makes the person likely to engage in predatory acts of sexual violence." The term *mental abnormality* was defined as "a congenital or acquired condition affecting the emotional or volitional capacity which predisposes the person to the commission of criminal sexual acts in a degree constituting such person a menace to the health and safety of others." *Predatory* was defined as "acts directed towards strangers or individuals with whom a relationship has been established or promoted for the primary purpose of victimization" (Washington Statute, 71.09.060).

The Washington statute was applied to Andre Young and Vance Cunningham. On appeal to the Supreme Court of Washington, the Justices found that both Young and Cunningham met the criteria for civil commitment of mental illness. Justice Durham, writing for the majority, stated that mental abnormality is synonymous with personality disorder as defined in the *Diagnostic and Statistical Manual of Mental Disorders* (DSM-IV). Further, they both suffered from paraphilia. Therefore, Young and Cunningham were mentally ill. With respect to the issue of dangerousness, the Court ruled that Young, who was in prison when he was committed, could not be shown to be dangerous because of his confinement. So, his offense, which led to his criminal sentence, was evidence of his dangerousness. However, Cunningham, who had been released from prison when civil commitment proceedings were initiated against him, had to be shown to have committed a recent act that would be defined as dangerous. Therefore, the Washington court ruled that Young's civil commitment was legal, but Cunningham's was illegal (*In re Young*, 1993).

However, Young's civil commitment has become suspect in federal court. A U.S. District Court has ruled Washington's civil commitment statute for sex offenders unconstitutional. The U.S. District Court ruled that civil commitment constitutes a second punishment. Also, the District Court ruled that the law was unconstitutional because civil commitment required mental illness and Young was not mentally ill. Instead, Young had a personality disorder, which does not constitute mental illness. Finally, the U.S. District Court stated that the civil commitment statute was not law when Young was initially convicted of sexual assault ("Sex Predator Law," 1995).

Minnesota, which did not repeal its statute permitting civil commitment and had maintained it since the 1930s, permitted the civil commitment of sex offenders who evidenced a psychopathic personality disorder. However, the Minnesota Supreme Court refined the original definition. It was subsequently defined as "the existence in any person of such conditions of emotional instability, or impulsiveness of behavior, or lack of customary standards of good judgment, or failure to appreciate the consequences of personal acts, or a combination of any such conditions, as to render such person irresponsible for personal conduct with respect to sexual matters and thereby dangerous to other persons" (*In re Blodgett*, 1994, p. 919).

The Minnesota statute was applied to a prisoner named Blodgett who had a history of sex offenses and who was nearing release from prison. Because a psychologist concluded Blodgett met the definition of a psychopathic personality and was dangerous, Blodgett was committed to a mental institution. On appeal, the Minnesota Justices stated that psychopathic personality disorder was similar to personality disorder in the DSM-III-R. Further, the Justices concluded that Blodgett was dangerous based on his previous behaviors. Like the Washington Justices, the Minnesota Justices held the statute to be constitutional (*In re Blodgett*, 1994). When the U.S. Supreme Court refused to hear the appeal from Blodgett (*Blodgett v. Minnesota*, 1994), civil commitment of sex offenders established law.

In 1997, the U.S. Supreme Court appeared to settle the issue of the constitutionality of civil commitment for sex offenders. Kansas enacted a statute similar to the state of Washington. The Kansas statute permitted civil commitment for persons who had a mental abnormality or personality disorder and were likely to engage in predatory sexual violence. The Supreme Court of Kansas ruled that the conditions of mental abnormality and personality disorder did not satisfy the substantive requirement of mental illness and held the statute unconstitutional. However, the U.S. Supreme Court reversed the Supreme Court of Kansas' decision, holding that mental abnormality or personality disorder was sufficient. One of the additional issues was that civil commitment constituted an additional punishment. The Court rejected this argument. It ruled that the statute was not punitive even if Kansas failed to offer treatment where treatment for a condition was not possible or if treatment was possible was merely an ancillary rather than an overriding concern (*Kansas v. Hendricks*, 1997). The Court seemed to have relegated treatment to a secondary status, but it did not entirely eliminate it. The ruling seems to say that some sex offenders may be civilly committed even if no treatment exists for their problem or treatment was a secondary concern.

GENDER AND EQUAL PROTECTION IN PRISON TREATMENT PROGRAMS

At one time, the most active persons involved in filing lawsuits alleging deprivations of constitutional rights were male prisoners. Within the last couple of decades, female prisoners have become very active in challenging the conditions of their confinement. A difference exists in what male prisoners contended in their lawsuits and what females contended. Typically, male prisoners complained that they were entitled to certain rights based on the U.S. Constitution. However, female prisoners complained that their rights were violated because they were being denied equal protection of the law. Simply, female prisoners use programs provided in male prisons as the norm for what they should have. Initially, female prisoners were prevailing in their lawsuits, but recently they seem to have reached an impasse in this approach (*Keevan v. Smith*, 1996; *Klinger v. Department of Corrections*, 1997; *Glover v. Johnson*, 1996; *Goldyn v. Angelone*, 1994; *Jeldness v. Pearce*, 1994; *Women Prisoners of the Dist. of Columbia Dept. of Corrections v. District of Columbia*, 1996).

In an early case, a U.S. District Court in Michigan found that female prisoners' rights to equal protection of the law were violated because of a lack of parity between the educational and vocational programs at the male and female institutions. The court ordered the state of Michigan to provide comparable programs in the institution for female offenders (*Glover v. Johnson*, 1979). In another case, a female prisoner claimed that her conditions of confinement at a Virginia prison were dissimilar to male prisoners. The state of Virginia attempted to defend itself by noting the differences in the size of the two prisons. The women's prison was much smaller than the men's, which made the provision of programs in women's prisons much more expensive. The court stated that the evidence presented to the court was insufficient to make a decision and another hearing was necessary. Further, the court expressed sympathy for the budgetary pressures on correctional administrators, but such pressures could not be used to maintain an unconstitutional prison system (*Bukhari v. Hutto*, 1980).

Repeating the pronouncement that cost is an unacceptable defense to differences in men and women's prisons, a U.S. District Court in Virginia supported an equal protection challenge to the lack of a boot camp in an institution for females. The state of Virginia contended that limited resources and more pressing problems in male institutions influenced its decision to create a boot camp in the men's prison. In addition to military type drills, the camp included academic education, vocational assessment, and life skills training. The District Court stated that if Virginia's defense was accepted then there would be no programs in women's correctional institutions (*West v. Virginia Dep't of Corrections*, 1994).

However, the cost and equal protection arguments may be in difficulty because of a recent Eighth Circuit Court of Appeals decision. This case originated in Nebraska by women incarcerated at the Nebraska Center for Women (NCW). It was the only correctional institution for women in the state. The population ranged from 90 to 130 inmates of all classifications. In 1988, four women at NCW were in contact with male prisoners at Nebraska State Penitentiary (NSP). The women perceived that major differences existed between the two correctional institutions with respect to programming. They circulated a petition to the superintendent of NCW requesting equal programming. When this approach failed, they filed a lawsuit alleging sex discrimination and requesting monetary damages. The women alleged discrimination based on inequities in employment; economic, educational, vocational, and legal access; medical, dental, and mental health services; recreational services; and visitation.

In deciding these issues, the U.S. District Court stated that three tests were used in deciding equal protection analysis. The three are the strict scrutiny, heightened scrutiny, and rational basis or the reasonableness test described in *Turner v. Safley* (1987). Noting that previous courts have used the heightened scrutiny in cases involving equal protection analysis in prison cases, the District Court concluded that the proper test was heightened scrutiny. Based on it, the U.S. District Court found that female prisoners at NCW were discriminated against in pay for prison jobs, post-secondary education, vocational training, prerelease education, and mental health counseling (*Klinger v. Nebraska Dept. of Correctional Services*, 1993).

However, the Eighth Circuit Court of Appeals reversed the lower District Court's decision because the Eighth Circuit of Appeals had concluded in an earlier case that men and women prisons are dissimilar. In *Timm v. Gunter* (1990), the Eighth Circuit Court of Appeals was presented with a case of male prisoners who contended that they had less privacy at NSP than women had at NCW. Finding against the male prisoners and their equal protection challenge, the Court of Appeals stated that men were different from women prisoners in that men had higher security levels, committed different crimes, had longer lengths of sentences, committed more violence in the institution, attempted to escape more, and possessed more contrabands. Thus, reasoned the court, the Nebraska Department of Corrections could provide less privacy to men than to women prisoners (*Timm v. Gunter*, 1990).

Having established a precedent that male and female prisoners in Nebraska were dissimilar in *Timm*, the Eighth Circuit Court of Appeals reversed the U.S. District Court's finding that the NCW and NSP were similar in *Klinger*. Because an equal protection analysis must find first that groups were similar, the foundation for the U.S. District Court was lacking. Then, the Eighth Circuit Court of Appeals attacked the legal test used by the District Court. Instead of heightened scrutiny, the Circuit stated that the reasonableness test should have been used. The Circuit Court quoted from *Turner* and stated that prison administrators should not be second-guessed when making difficult decisions regarding the allocation of limited resources. Also, the Court stated that all prisoners would be hurt by the District Court decision because "prison officials would be far less willing to experiment and innovate with programs at an individual institution knowing that a federal court would impose liability on the basis of a program comparison. Indeed, inmates would suffer because officials would likely provide each institution with the bare constitutional minimum of programs and services to avoid the threat of equal protection liability" (*Klinger v. Department of Corrections*, 1994, p. 733). If the Eighth Circuit Court of Appeals' decision is followed in *Klinger* by other Circuits and the U.S. Supreme Court, then female prisoners would have a very difficult time procuring a favorable decision in an equal protection case based on inequality in programming in men and women's prisons.

SUMMARY

Initially, the Bill of Rights did not apply to states and was restrictions on only the federal government. Restrictions on states did not occur until Congress passed the Fourteenth Amendment to aid newly freed African Americans following the Civil War. The Fourteenth Amendment prohibited states from depriving persons of life, liberty, and property without due process of law and denying citizens equal protection of the law. A few years later, Congress also passed the Civil Rights Act, which provides civil relief for deprivation of a person's rights and which provides criminal penalties for intentional violation of one's rights. In the twentieth century, the U.S. Supreme Court progressively ruled that the portions of the Bill of Rights were applicable to the states by virtue of the Due Process Clause in the Fourteenth Amendment. As a result, the restrictions enunciated in the First and Eighth Amendments became applicable to the states. Accordingly, prisoners were able to cite these amendments in grounding their civil rights lawsuits. The most significant is the Eighth Amendment, which prohibits the infliction of cruel and unusual punishment upon prisoners.

The Eighth Amendment has been used to establish that prisoners have a right to medical and psychiatric treatment. It has had a limited basis for prisoners' rights to refuse adverse treatment. Moreover, the Fourteenth Amendment has been used to establish due process for prisoners if the states sought to treat them involuntarily in a mental institution. However, prisoners' rights to refuse psychotropic treatment has been effectively diminished with the U.S. Supreme Court announcement of the reasonableness test.

Moreover, sex offenders have been the targets of involuntary treatment through their civil commitment in mental units that sometimes are connected to prisons. They are, in effect, moved from one part of the prison to another. The Washington and Minnesota Supreme Courts have upheld their commitment statutes for sex offenders. However, a federal district court has held that Washington's civil commitment statute is unconstitutional.

Woman prisoners have made gains in the programming that they get by filing lawsuits under the Equal Protection Clause of the Fourteenth Amendment. After some initial successes in the federal district courts, the Eighth Court of Appeals has ruled against woman prisoners in Nebraska. For the first time, a court has used the reasonableness test in an equal protection prison case, which makes it extremely difficult for women to win future cases, provided this decision is followed by other courts.

KEY TERMS

Cruel and unusual punishment	Strict scrutiny	Quid pro quo
Due process	Civil Rights Act of 1871	Habilitation
Equal protection	Standards for civil commitment	Criteria for psychiatric treatment
Liberty	Police power	Criteria for transfer to a mental health facility
Property	Parens patriae	Establishment clause
Reasonableness test		

3

✻✻✻

Treatment Theories

✻ INTRODUCTION

Chapters 5 and 6 discuss individual and group counseling. Each chapter focuses on stages or issues related to each treatment strategy. However, before a counselor can effectively utilize either individual or group counseling, he or she must use a theory or combination of theoretical aspects that explains why behaviors occur and more importantly how to treat these behaviors. If a counselor does not have a theoretical grounding, he or she has no plan in which to do either individual or group counseling. Counseling without a theoretical basis is akin to sailing a ship with no idea where to go or what to do if land is found.

This chapter discusses ten overall theories, with one that has several variations, and techniques derived from these theories. The selection of these theories was based on essentially three criteria—theories that have been found to be empirically effective with offenders, theories that have good potential for corrections, and theories that are currently used in corrections and growing in popularity. As an illustration, cognitive–behavioral theory has strong empirical support, logotherapy has the potential to be useful in corrections, and feminist and afrocentric theories are growing in support. Alcoholics Anonymous (AA), which is extensively used in corrections, was discussed in Chapter 1, but is not discussed here because the author does not consider AA to be a theory. Instead, it is a way of dealing with someone with a substance abuse problem. It does not really explain why alcoholism occurs. Omitted here also are gestalt and client-centered theories. Although these are popular theories with the nonoffender population, they have less utility in corrections. For instance, Gendreau (1996), a Ph.D. psychologist who worked as a clinician and administrator in prisons, avers that the theories that are ineffective with offenders are subcultural, labeling, traditional Freudian psychodynamic, and Rogerian nondirective or client-centered theories.

With these criteria in mind, the major theory focus is on cognitive–behavioral theory because it is the most frequently used theory to treat *drug problems* (Buchanan, 1991; Farabee, Simpson, Dansereau, & Knight, 1995; Denoff, 1987; Fisher, Helfrich, Niedzialkowski, Colburn, & Kaiser, 1995; Goldapple & Montgomery, 1993; Gropper, Liraz, Portowicz, & Schindler, 1995; Hooper, Lockwood, & Inciardi, 1993; Jenson, Wells, Plotnick, Hawkins, & Catalano, 1993; Lovejoy, Rosenblum, Magura, Foote, Handelsman, & Stimmel, 1995; Negreiros, 1994; Nixon, Tivis, & Parsons, 1995; Peyrot, Yen, & Baldassano, 1994; Toneatto, Sobell, Sobell, & Kozlowski, 1995; Trad, 1994; Wells, Peterson, & Gainey, 1994), *sex offenders* (Anderson, Gibeau, & D'Amora, 1995; Annon, 1996; Bingham, Turner, & Piotrowski, 1995; Camp & Thyer, 1993; Finn, 1995; Hall & Nagayama, 1995; Harris, 1995; Knox, 1995; Lee, Proeve, Lancaster, & Jackson, 1996; Hudson, Marshall, Ward, & Johnston, 1995; Morenz & Becker, 1995; Rosen & Leiblum, 1995; Winn, 1996; Witt, Rambus, & Bosley, 1996), and *juvenile offenders* (Lochman, White, Curry, & Rumer 1995; Sheldon, 1995).

Its potency also has been supported by its wide use in the *medical field* (Antony, Meadows, Brown, & Barlow, 1994; Brown & Barlow, 1995; Barratt, Stanford, Kent, & Felthous, 1997; Brok, 1997; Chemtob, 1997; Ellis, 1996; Feske & Chambless, 1995; Friedberg, 1996; Goldstein, 1996; Grabow & Burkhart, 1986; Keefe & Van Horn, 1997; Kuhner, Angermeyer, & Veiel, 1996; Goldston, 1997; Liese & Larson, 1995; Lukins, Davan, & Drummond, 1997; Lutgendorf, Antoni, Ironson, Klimas, Kumar, Starr, McCabe, Cleven, Fletcher, & Schneiderman 1997; Marcotte, 1997; Newman, Kenardy, Herman, Taylor, & Barr, 1997; Overholser, 1996; Robertson & Taylor, 1985; Shapiro, 1997; Thompson, 1996).

Justifying this special focus, Mackenzie (1997) conducted a review of the literature on treatment of criminal offenders and found that cognitive–behavioral therapy was the most successful. However, despite the effectiveness of cognitive–behavioral theory, other theories will also be presented as well. As was stated in Chapter 1, an important question is not whether offenders can be rehabilitated or changed, but what works best for whom? While cognitive–behavioral theory is effective, other theories may have some success with some offenders.

In the discussions of these theories, one feature of this chapter is to point out the extent to which the theories discussed are applicable for individual and group counseling. For instance, cognitive–behavioral approaches can be used in group and individual counseling, but other theories, such as social bonding, which has been used to prevent juvenile delinquency, are geared more toward group and family treatment principles. So, the applicability of each theory for individual and group counseling will be pointed out at the end of this chapter.

In this chapter, the author uses the terms *theory* and *therapy* somewhat interchangeably to describe a theoretical perspective, such as behavioral therapy and behavioral theory. In discussing a particular therapy, the author describes the theoretical basis for the approach. Also, when the author discusses a theory, the author describes the treatment principles derived therefrom.

The theories that are discussed are cognitive–behavioral theory, including a feminist version, behavior theory, behavioral modification, psychoanalytic theory, logotherapy, afrocentric theory, feminist theory, social bonding theory, system theory, and reality therapy. In discussing each theory, its relevance to counseling offenders is described.

COGNITIVE–BEHAVIORAL THEORY AND THERAPY

Cognitive theory is most associated with Albert Ellis and Aaron Beck (Kuehlwein, 1993). They were the first cognitive clinicians to include behavioral techniques in their practices (Beck & Freeman, 1990). Ellis, however, has developed his own cognitive therapy, which he called rational emotive therapy. Presently, cognitive therapy is mostly associated with Aaron Beck (Freeman, 1983). However, variations of cognitive therapy exist, such as Arnold Lazarus' mutimodal therapy, Donald Meichenbaum's cognitive–behavioral modification, and Maxie Maultsby's rational behavior therapy (Freeman, 1983). In addition, Emery (1993) has championed radical cognitive therapy, and Bricker, Young, and Flanagan (1993) have created schema-focused cognitive therapy.

These cognitive therapies have essentially the same foundation with some minor twists. Although the most popular term is cognitive–behavioral therapy, this is essentially cognitive therapy with behavioral treatment techniques, so some clinicians may refer to themselves as cognitive therapists, and other clinicians may refer to themselves as cognitive–behavioral therapists. Both follow the same cognitive principles and use similar treatment techniques (Kroese, 1997).

Cognitive–behavioral therapy is grounded in the proposition that behavior is modifiable through the systematic use of empirically supported learning principles (Smith, 1990). Combining elements from behavioral and dynamically oriented principles, cognitive therapy is "a relatively short-term form of psychotherapy which is active and directive, and in which the therapist and patient work collaboratively. The goal of therapy is to help patients uncover their dysfunctional and irrational thinking and behavior and build more adaptive and functional techniques for responding both inter- and intrapersonally" (Freeman, 1983, p. 2). It is not necessarily conducted to cure a client, but to help a client to develop effective coping strategies for problems in life and work. Clients who know their dysfunctional and irrational belief systems possess the tools to better address future life problems (Freeman, 1983).

Theoretical Constructs

According to Kroese (1997), counseling professionals came to realize that the use of principles from learning theory was insufficient in treating psychological problems. Research developments had indicated the importance of cognitive factors in maintaining behavior, such as beliefs, expectancies, self-statements, and problem solving (Kendall & Braswell, 1985). These cognitive factors are important in functional as well as in dysfunctional behaviors.

As reported by Freeman (1983), all people seem to have the ability to distort reality. For people whose distortions are major, they may lose touch with reality, such as persons with diagnoses of schizophrenia. For people whose distortions are less severe, they may not be disturbed enough for a diagnosis of major mental illness, but they have a dysfunction in their cognitive processing. The distortions are kindled by schemata, which refers to underlying assumptions that may begin in childhood (Freeman, 1983).

Beck distinguished among schema, rules, and basic beliefs. He stated that schema represented the cognitive structures that coordinate experiences and behaviors. Belief and rules involve the content of the schema, and, as a result, determine the content of one's thinking, affect, and behavior. Automatic thoughts, for instance, are the products of the schema (Beck & Freeman, 1990). As stated by another Beck (1995), the daughter of Aaron Beck, the automatic thoughts occur in the manner as illustrated in Figure 3.1. Freeman (1983) asserted that dysfunctional, underlying assumptions are analogous to irrational belief systems or rules for living. They become a substrate where cognitive distortions emanate. When an external stimulus impinges on a schema, the stimulus activates a distortion that may be of several types. Some examples of distortions are

1. *All or Nothing Thinking.* This type of thinking is reflected by the tendency to assess one's performance or personal qualities in extreme polarity. There is no in-between or gray area. This type of thinking forces a person to be perfect or feel totally worthless. For instance, a student with this mind-set who wants a grade of A for a course but receives a B+ feels that he or she is a total failure. Life and people are not totally one way or totally another, which makes this type of thinking illogical. Life is neither all superb nor all the pits. People are not God or the devil. There is a mixture in all, or most, people.

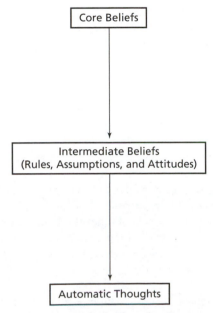

FIGURE 3.1 An Illustration of How Automatic Thoughts Occur

2. *Overgeneralization.* This type of thinking refers to the process of a person thinking that a single negative experience will occur repeatedly. For instance, a person who has just learned to drive an automobile takes and fails the license examination and dejectedly concludes that he or she will never pass the examination or learn to parallel park.

3. *Selective Negative Focus.* This refers to an individual who focuses on a few negative events exclusively and ignores that these few negative events occurred among a number of positive events. For example, a student may write a research paper and receive extensive positive feedback throughout the paper. While 90% of the paper contains very positive comments regarding a student's analyses, interpretations, and foresight but 10% of the comments implored the student to think further about some content, the student chooses to focus only on the 10%, concluding that the professor was too critical and unfair.

4. *Disqualifying the Positive.* This involves a person rejecting or dismissing positive events. For example, a person may state that no one cares about him or her, although significant others have demonstrated caring behaviors. When confronted with this contradiction, the person dismisses the significant others' behaviors as not counting because they are friends or relatives.

5. *Arbitrary Inference.* This refers to a person drawing a negative or arbitrary conclusion without justification. There are two types. One is mind-reading, where an individual assumes that others think negatively but does not check it out. This individual may respond by withdrawing or counter attacking. The other type is negative prediction. The individual imagines something bad is about to happen without cause, such as predicting that he or she is depressed and will always be that way. Another illustration is a prisoner who believes that, when released from confinement, no one will employ him or her.

6. *Magnification or Minimization.* This refers to the process of magnifying or minimizing events. Generally, an individual magnifies his or her imperfections or minimizes positives. When magnification and minimization are employed, the individual feels inferior to others.

7. *Emotional Reasoning.* This refers to an individual interpreting his or her emotions as fact. For instance, a person may say "I feel guilty, therefore I am bad."

8. *Should Statements.* These refer to command statements, such as "I must do this," or "I should do this." These types of statements, when not done, cause an individual to feel guilty, pressured, or resentful.

9. *Labeling and Mislabeling.* These refer to an individual giving himself or herself a negative label based on perceived imperfections. Examples are "I'm a loser," not "I lost out on this opportunity this time." "I'm a failure," rather than "I made a mistake." Labeling is an extreme type of over-generalization.

10. *Personalization.* This refers to attributing a negative event to oneself without justification. For example, a person takes the blame for something when there is no connection between the behavior and an outcome. An illustration is a therapist taking responsibility for a client returning to an abusive spouse (Freeman, 1983).

While these distortions may have some functional benefits at times, they often are negative and lead to dysfunctional behaviors (Freeman, 1983). Some of these distortions also contribute to maladaptive thoughts. Beck (1976) defines these thoughts as ideations that impede a person's ability to contend with life experiences, needlessly interrupting internal harmony, and causing inappropriate or extreme emotional reactions that are unpleasant and painful.

These concepts and principles from cognitive–behavioral theory provide a number of techniques that can be used in treatment.

Therapeutic Techniques

Cognitive therapists have utilized a variety of treatment strategies with different types of clients. For instance, Wessler (1993) has reported that cognitive therapy is appropriate for treating individuals with personality disorders, which exist in large numbers in correctional institutions (Fishbein, 1994; Hodgins & Cote, 1993; Jordan, Schlenger, & Caddell, 1997; Maden, Swinton, & Gunn, 1994; Shaw, Herkon, & Greer, 1995; Stevens, 1994; Wolf, Friedlander, Addad, & Silfan, 1993), and with individuals with bipolar disorders (Basco & Rush, 1996). For younger offenders, such as adolescents, cognitive therapy has been said to be appropriate for conduct disorders (DiGiuseppe, 1988); however, some of the techniques need to be modified because of differences between adults and adolescents (Kendall & Braswell, 1985).

As stated, differences exist between adult and juvenile offenders. So, treatment for each group would be different. For the most part, treatment with adults is aimed at correcting cognitive errors (i.e., cognitive distortions), such as irrational beliefs, unwholesome cognitive processes, and flawed self-talk. In other words, adults' cognitive errors illustrate illogical interpretations of the environment, very high and somewhat unrealistic expectations for self, and erroneous perceptions of everyday life problems. Adults' thought processes are operating, but these processes produce faulty outcomes (Kendall & Braswell, 1985).

By contrast, children's cognitive problems typically occur as a result of cognitive absences (i.e., cognitive deficiencies). Problem children do not possess or use cognitive skills that would permit them to function satisfactorily in their environment. Children do not engage in the type of information processing that control behavior and solve problems appropriately. The type of children suitable for cognitive–behavioral therapy are impulsive, not self-controlled, attention-disordered, isolated, withdrawn, and depressed (Kendall & Braswell, 1985).

Because adults and children differ in terms of cognitive development, some strategies that are appropriate for adults will not be understood by children (Meichenbaum & Camera, 1982). As an illustration, confronting irrational beliefs in adults would be understood as scolding by a child. The child would not understand what the counselor's purpose is (e.g., a change in philosophy) (Kendall & Braswell, 1985).

Treatment for adolescents is geared at a number of areas, such as training in social perspective taking, social problem-solving, self-instruction, discerning correctly physiological arousal and affective state, relaxation techniques to control physiological arousal, and moral reasoning (Lochman et al., 1995).

For adults, a number of specific treatment strategies exist for intervening from a cognitive–behavioral framework. Two of the most commonly used approaches are for the therapist to penetrate and explore maladaptive cognitive processes and confront maladaptive beliefs and thoughts. When maladaptive cognitions are identified, the counselor uses cognitive therapy to confront these cognitions by helping the client to examine the evidence, consider alternative explanations, and consider the consequences. Appropriate questions for the client are (1) what is the evidence that this belief is true; (2) what is another way of explaining this belief; and (3) assume the belief is true and then consider how bad is it (Francis & Hart, 1992).

A plethora of specific techniques are available to achieve these two ends. For instance, Glantz and McCourt (1983), illustrating how to treat individuals with alcohol problems, asserted that some cognitive strategies used to test the reality of individuals are questioning the evidence, reattribution, fantasizing consequences, understanding idiosyncratic meaning, developing options and alternatives, and decatastrophizing. Along with these, some of the behavioral treatment strategies are graded task assignments, activity scheduling for mastery and pleasure, in vivo work, and collecting evidence (Glantz & McCourt, 1983).

Beck and colleagues (1993) provided some additional strategies for treating individuals with alcohol and drug problems. Cognitive techniques for drug users include an advantage-disadvantage analysis. According to Beck and colleagues (1993), drug offenders hold beliefs that minimize the disadvantages and maximize the advantages. The advantages-disadvantages technique is designed to challenge these beliefs. In this method, the offender is asked to list in a 2 × 2 matrix, the advantages and disadvantage of quitting drugs and not quitting. See Figure 3.2.

Another strategy is the identification and modification of drug-related beliefs, such as drugs relax me, my life is difficult and drugs cannot make it much worse, and everyone does drugs. For some of these or similar statements, the "downward arrow"

	Quitting Drugs	Not Quitting
Advantages	More money Happier family Reduced chance of prison	Keep bad friends Retain cool image
Disadvantages	Reduced sexual pleasures Rejection by old friends	Pressure to get money Getting bad drugs Being burned by dealers Target for snitchers Imprisonment

FIGURE 3.2 An Analytic Technique to Show Clients the Advantages and Disadvantages of Quitting and Not Quitting Drugs

approach might be used. Some individuals tend to have fatalistic thoughts about themselves, life, and the future. Statements that illustrate these thoughts are "I can't do anything right," "my life is going to crumble," "I'll fall apart without drugs." The downward arrow technique is called downward because of the way it is depicted on paper.

Downward Technique

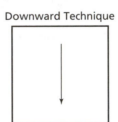

A revised illustration of Beck and colleagues' (1993) downward technique follows.

Counselor: Joseph, you seem to have a strong reaction against the idea of staying away from alcohol at your upcoming party. "What is your concern about being sober at the party?"

Client: I would not be fun if I don't drink.

Counselor: Suppose you are correct and you are not fun, "what would be the implications?"

Client: People wouldn't want to be around me.

Counselor: If people didn't hang around you, "what would that mean?" [Downward]

Client: They don't like me.

Counselor: Assume this is all true, "what would the consequences be?" [Downward]

Client: My career would be jeopardized.

Counselor: If your career were threatened, "what would be the ultimate consequences?" [Downward]

Client: I could lose my job, family, and house.

Counselor: And all these things would happen by not drinking at a party?

The purpose of the downward technique is to show the client how illogical his or her thoughts are (Beck et al., 1993, p 141).

One of the critical issues for prisoners is the attribution of blame to others for their problems and the belief that they have little control over their lives (Goodstein, MacKenzie, & Shotland, 1984; Griffith, 1984; Pugh, 1993). Beck and colleagues (1993) noted that people who drank alcohol often attributed their drinking to external factors, such as a spouse, children, or employment pressures. A key task of the counselor is to help the alcoholic person to attribute his or her use more toward internal factors, where the individual has more control, rather than to external factors. Caution, however, should be exercised in utilizing this technique because the person may believe the counselor is being judgmental and accusatory. If the client feels this way, the counseling relationship is likely to sour. The Socratic method, employed by a skilled and experienced clinician, is excellent in accomplishing this objective. An example by Beck and colleagues (1993) follows that illustrates this skill.

> **Counselor:** William, you report that you are back drinking again. What are your beliefs?
>
> **Client:** It's because of my wife, who has been nagging me a lot lately. I could stay off the bottle if she cut me some slack at home.
>
> **Counselor:** So, you believe your wife is causing you to drink?
>
> **Client:** Yes, she is a big part of the reasons, but there are other minor reasons.
>
> **Counselor:** Tell me more about the intricacies in this issue. Specifically, what role does your wife have and what role do your beliefs and actions have.
>
> **Client:** She nags me nonstop and I begin thinking that I can't have a peaceful evening and I'm trapped by her.
>
> **Counselor:** And then what?
>
> **Client:** And then I think, I should get drunk and forget about the bind that I am in.
>
> **Counselor:** Let me see if I hear you right. When you think about your marital situation, you conclude there is only one course of action and that is to get shit-face drunk. Am I correct?
>
> **Client:** Yes.
>
> **Counselor:** Is it fair to conclude that you decide to drink instead of choosing another method of dealing with the issues with your wife.
>
> **Client:** Yes, I guess it is my decision to drink, but it is easier to blame the wife.
>
> **Counselor:** Although blaming your wife is easier, does blaming her assist you in achieving your goal to deal effectively with your drinking problem?
>
> **Client:** No.
>
> **Counselor:** What would help?
>
> **Client:** Assuming charge of my life and decisions, no matter what my wife does.
>
> **Counselor:** Sure, it is not easy, but it is a noble goal.

This technique is appropriate for offenders and is often used in the justice system. The latter parts of this dialogue are similar to reality therapy, which is discussed later in the book. However, Beck's method is softer and tries to get the person to come up with the answers. Often, in reality therapy, offenders are told not to blame others and told to take responsibility for their actions. Offenders may blame their drug use on an inability to get a job and the frustrations that go with repeated rejections when seeking employment. Beck's technique may be used to help the offtender to explore the choice to use drugs rather than being compelled by environmental forces.

The next section focuses on treating several groups that make up a significant proportion of offenders in the criminal justice system with cognitive–behavioral therapy.

Aggressive Youths Theorizing about the causes of aggression in adolescents and using a cognitive–behavioral framework, Lochman and colleagues (1995) stated that aggression in youth occurs as a result of idiosyncratic perceptions that determine the arousal the youth experiences and his or her decision regarding how to react. Pictorially, this explanation is viewed as shown in Figure 3.3.

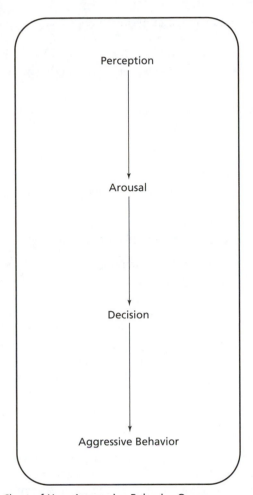

FIGURE 3.3 A Flow Chart of How Aggressive Behavior Occurs

Lochman and associates (1995) offered this explanation to account for the be-havior of institutionalized delinquent boys.

This model of aggression in youth provides a number of strategies for interven-tion. These include strategies aimed at social perspective-taking, social problem-solving training, self-instruction training, accurate awareness of physiological arousal, and moral reasoning training (Lochman et al., 1995). In addition, treat-ment strategies have been used that included extinction, time-out, arousal reduc-tion, and environmental manipulation (Brown & Prout, 1989).

The model depicted by Lochman and colleagues supports the understanding and treatment of adolescent anger. Adolescents frequently become angry because of their illogical beliefs. Beliefs that lead to anger are "the world should be fair," "I must have things go my way," "I ought to be able to do what I want," and "I have to have respect." When these rules are not adhered to by other individuals, many adolescents become angry. Anger is unhealthy when it is accompanied by rage, bit-terness, and hate. Healthy anger is moderate and accompanied by disappointment, displeasure, and irritation. Wilde (1996) used cognitive, behavioral, and emotive techniques to treat unhealthy anger in adolescents.

Cognitively, the justification for anger is explored. Wilde used a simple approach, which is illustrated by the following example of a youth who is upset with another youth.

Youth: He has no right to tell me no.
Counselor: Why not?
Youth: He just shouldn't have.
Counselor: Why?
Youth: It's not righteous.
Counselor: Why can't he act that way though? Why can't he simply be not righteous.
Youth: Because I don't dig it.
Counselor: But why do you have to like the way he responded?

In this example, the underlying assumption is that "a person should do what I want." The counselor is attempting to challenge the youth's belief in this regard.

Behaviorally, a counselor could address a youth's anger with reinforcement for controlled behavior and perhaps the rubber band technique, whereby an adolescent who is becoming angry pops his or her wrist with a rubber band. Emotively, an adolescent's anger can be altered by imagery techniques. The adolescents can imagine the good or positive experiences with the person with whom the adolescent is angry. Another technique is rational role reversal, which involves an adolescent and counselor switching roles. The counselor explains why others should do what the counselor wants, and the adolescent attempts to explain why the counselor's explanations are irrational (Wilde, 1996).

Lochman and Wells (1996) described a program called the Anger Coping Program, which was developed to treat cognitive distortions and deficiencies in aggressive students. It was developed for a group approach and presented in about 18 sessions. In Session 1, the leaders addressed the group structure and purpose. During Sessions 2 and 3, self-instruction training is implemented. In Sessions 4 and 5, the counselors instructed the group in perspective-taking. In Session 6, the counselor taught the group about physiological arousal. In Session 7, the group members and leaders engaged in goal setting. In Sessions 8 through 18, the group engaged in problem solving.

During Session 1, the group leaders instituted a behavior management system with points for in-group and out-of-group behavior, which were tied to the adolescents' goals. During the self-instruction tasks, the group leaders helped the adolescents identify circumstances that lead to intense emotions and helped the adolescents learn restraining self-instructions, such as "Stop!" "Think!" and "What can I do?" in order to check their automatic aggressive responses. Perspective-taking was introduced to the group through the presentation of pictures of ambiguous situations that were then used to stimulate group discussions. For instance, a picture might be presented of a frowning adolescent, and the group might be asked what they would think if the person in the picture was present and looking at them in that manner. Likely, some students would say that the adolescent doesn't like them and wanted to fight. Then, the leaders could inject other reasons for the adolescent's frown and solicit views on an appropriate response. Emphasis was put on attending to friendly or civil cues and how to recognize aroused cues in themselves and others. This activity provides an opportunity to get into problem solving. Specifically, students were presented with the basic problem-solving steps, consisting of problem identification, choices, and consequences. They were further provided with repeated modeling and role-playing of problem solving. To aid the process of inculcating the group experience and the treatment process, the students were allowed to videotape themselves and a problem-solving session (Lochman & Wells, 1996).

Substance Abusers Beck, Wright, Newman, and Liese (1993) theorized regarding the cognitive processes involving persons who have substance abuse problems. These individuals possess characteristics that made them susceptible to substance abuse. Among these characteristics are a general exaggerated sensitivity to unpleasing feelings, inadequate motivation to control behavior, impulsivity, excitement seeking and low tolerance for boredom, low tolerance for frustration, inadequate prosocial alternative for acquiring pleasurable feelings, and a sense of despair in obtaining this end. A cognitive approach seeks to weaken the urge to use by eroding the beliefs that support use and increasing individuals' capacity to control and modify their dysfunctional behavior.

Toneatto (1995) developed a model that was called the Regulation of the Cognitive State (RCS) to treat drug and alcohol abuse. The hypothesis that supported RCS was that "abusive consumption of psychoactive substance is maintained by the rapid modification of undesirable cognitive states subsequent to such consumption" (Toneatto, 1995, p. 93). These cognitive states refer to thoughts, perceptions, sensations, memories, imagery, and emotions. An additional cognitive state is called *metacognition*, and it is a person's beliefs about these other cognitive states. Drugs and alcohol can affect these cognitive states and reinforce them in the following manner: the alteration of biological arousal, cognitive process and content, and appreciation of cognitive states.

According to persons who abuse substances, they report that certain feelings, emotions, and beliefs are responsible for their use and relapse. These feelings, emotions, and beliefs are unsettling, painful, and unpleasant. Whenever a person uses drugs or alcohol, "these cognitive processes are modified such that the resultant cognitive content becomes more tolerable (e.g., judging a situation to be less unpleasant, less disturbed about marital stress) and increasing the probability of engaging in inhibited behaviors (e.g., increased assertiveness following drug-induced enhancements of self-esteem)" (p. 94).

The task of the counselor, working under the RCS model, is to shepherd clients to exposure to averted cognitive states. This means assisting clients to

1. Become more cognizant of the parameters of their cognitive states. This means developing an awareness of thoughts, feelings, memories, perceptions, and sensations regardless of whether these cognitive states are desirable, uncomfortable, disturbing, or pleasurable.
2. Correctly comprehend the nature of cognition. This means that the counselor accepts that these cognitions are real to clients but underscores that these

subjective experiences are extremely temporary, unstable, difficult to control, and mostly harmless, while conceding that some experiences may be unpleasant.

3. Learn to separate cognitive events from an individual's metacognition and act on the event, not an individual's interpretation about the event.

4. Learn to recognize the contents of awareness that are related to substance abuse. This means recognizing which cognition state, together with environmental factors, leads to substance abuse. For instance, if a person realizes that he or she is more likely to use when depressed and alone or depressed and with a certain person, these realizations would be underscored in the person's mind.

5. Learn to deal with unpleasant states of awareness without changing them with drugs and alcohol. This can be done by learning that these unpleasant states can be altered without drugs and alcohol, once a person truly understands them. Also, a person can avoid modifying these states with substances by understanding that these states are not events that should be viewed as dangerous or frightening and require overcoming with drugs and alcohol.

Barrett and Meyer (1993) indicated that alcoholism is a disease that steadily gets worse and, if not treated, can lead to death. It consists of four factors–biological, psychological, sociological, and spiritual–and all four must be treated. Unlike depressed persons who view themselves as helpless and powerless, alcoholic persons present the opposite. They are optimistic and positive about their health and circumstances. For instance, medical tests that show no current liver damage is viewed as evidence of good health and psychological tests that do not show permanent brain dysfunction also are viewed positively. The alcoholic person, showing his or her power, attempts to demonstrate self-assuredness. An alcoholic tries to show others that he or she is in charge. On a treatment unit, they attempt to show that they are in control of their lives.

A Feminist Version of Cognitive–Behavioral Therapy

Feminist counselors indicate that cognitive–behavioral therapy is consistent with feminist theory (Fodor, 1988; Stere, 1986; Worell & Remer, 1992), but some feminist counselors believe that cognitive–behavioral therapy should be revised before using it to counsel women (Fodor, 1988; Worell & Remer, 1992). Fodor (1988), for instance, endorsed the view that some individuals have irrational beliefs. Some of these beliefs that are customary for women are: (a) a woman must be loved by everyone for everything she does; (b) a woman's needs are secondary to others' needs; (c) when difficulties arise, it is better for a woman to avoid these difficulties than to face them; (d) a woman needs a strong, significant other to lean on or take care of her; and (e) a woman does not have control over her emotions (Fodor, 1988).

Fodor (1988) provided some examples for how to dispute these irrational beliefs.

Belief 1: Outer pressures cause emotional distress, and I have little control over my feelings. As an example, when my husband threatens to leave me, I become extremely anxious.

Disputation 1: No person can make me feel anxious, and how I see a situation determines whether I become anxious. I can learn to contain and alter my emotions.

Belief 2: These people must be right about their assessment of my marriage because they sound extremely knowledgeable, and they are nearly unanimous.

Disputation 2: How can these people know what is best for me or the extent of my pain? What will I really lose by divorcing my husband? If my marriage ends, how does this make me a failure as a woman or as a person? How does anyone know that I will not be able to appeal to another man? Even if I don't find anyone else, what evidence is there that I can't be happy as a single woman and take care of myself?

Belief 3: It would be terrible if I hurt another person's feelings. It was inconsiderate of me to cancel the dinner date with my in-laws. I must be a wretched daughter-in-law.

Disputation 3: How can taking care of my mental health be terrible and why are my in-laws' feelings more important than mine? Furthermore, how can putting myself first make me a bad person or hurt someone else?

Belief 4: I must be loved by everyone, especially by people who are important to me. If I were not, it would be awful. Simply, it is very bad to be called a bitch, hag, or witch.

Disputation 4: Why is it disastrous to be called a hag, a witch, or a bitch? How does calling me names make me a worthless woman?

Worell and Remer (1992) endorsed cognitive–behavioral therapy with women, but they believed that some modifications were needed because some concepts (i.e., distortion, irrationality, and faulty thinking) suggested that women were pathological. This view is contrary to feminist theory because it accepts women's feelings as real. The feminist therapist relabels the pathological concept, focuses on feelings, and integrates social role theory. Worell and Remer discuss a case example of how a feminist therapist would relabel the above referred cognitive–behavioral concepts. In their case example, a 37-year-old woman, following the breakup of her marriage, was depressed and suicidal. She was convinced that she was a failure as a woman, no other man would want her, and if she were lucky enough to find another man, she would be too old to have children.

Instead of convincing the woman of the irrationality of her thoughts, the feminist therapist urge the woman to ponder the societal messages about a woman's proper role (i.e., a good woman gets a husband and has children), the mandates for a blissful marriage (i.e., a good wife maintains and preserves her marriage), the stereotypes about single women (i.e., single women have sexual hang-ups, are closet lesbians, and are counting the ticks from her biological clock), and the fears about living alone (i.e., a woman is vulnerable without a man).

Feminist counseling focuses on feelings of hopelessness, fearfulness, sadness, and anxiety. Moreover, a safe environment is provided for a woman to display her anger, debunking the view that a woman should suppress her anger. Social role theory is used in a broad sense to reflect how roles, expectations, and power differences affect women's lives. Social role theory also provides additional concepts relevant to women, such as role conflict, role strain, and role overload. In sum, social role theory permits a feminist therapist to understand a woman's behavior against the backdrop of gender socialization. Accordingly, the feminist therapist sees a woman's unique behavior in a comprehensive context, such as power imbalances, patriarchy, sexism, and discrimination. Instead of using terms like *deficit behavior*, the feminist counselor uses the terms *over* or *under socialization*, and instead of remediating deficient behavior, the feminist counselor uses resocialization or construction of an environment (Worell & Remer, 1992).

BEHAVIORAL THEORIES

Like the comparisons between cognitive–behavioral theory and rational emotive behavior theory, behavioral therapy has been discussed in conjunction with behavioral modification (Martin & Pear, 1992). That is, some behaviorists use the terms *behavior therapy* and *behavioral modification* interchangeably. Other behaviorists differentiate the two terms. Those behaviorists who differentiate the two approaches state that behavioral therapy emphasizes counter-conditioning methods, whereas behavior modification emphasizes operant procedures.

Counter-conditioning refers to the interchanging of one type of response for another response based on learning principles. For example, anxiety may be interchanged for relaxation. On the other hand, operant procedures refer to the principle that behaviors can be modified by their consequences. For example, a person who is mentally ill can be influenced to make a bed in exchange for rewards (Rimm & Masters, 1979). Given these two differences, the following sections discuss behavior and behavior modification theories. Behavioral modification is very popular with offenders in institutions and group homes (Rimm & Masters, 1979; Sundel & Sundel, 1993), and to a lesser extent, behavior therapy also is used with offender populations (i.e., the substitution of criminal and delinquent behavior for social and responsible behavior).

A criminal case in Ohio illustrates clearly the type of offender who is suitable for behavior therapy and behavior modification. In Ironton, Ohio, an explosion occurred at a fireworks store, killing nine people. The person accused of igniting some fireworks inside the store that caused it to explode was a 25-year-old man who was severely brain damaged. Todd Hall, the accused, was involved in a skateboard accident when he was 15 years old, causing severe brain damage. Doctors had to remove parts of his temporal and frontal lobes, the portion that helps control behavior and impulsivity. Hall, during an early court appearance, screamed loudly that he did not do anything and was uncontrollable in court. He was evaluated to determine whether he was competent to be tried. On the hospital unit, Hall demonstrated significant behavioral problems. He had conflicts with peers and staff. On the unit, he violated hospital rules, such as spitting, cursing, inappropriate touching, and inappropriate affection with others. Hall was found incompetent to be tried, and he was committed to a mental institution that housed offenders (Price, 1997).

Behavior Therapy

As stated earlier, the principle of counter-conditioning is credited with providing the roots for behavior therapy. An analogous way of stating this principle is that behavior therapy sprang from Pavlovian conditioning, named after Ivan Pavlov. Pavlov was a physiologist who was interested in studying glands and the endocrine system. In one experiment, a tube was implanted in a dog's gland to measure the amount of secretion as the dog ate. Because the dog had to be held by Pavlov, Pavlov's assistant fed the dog. As the dog ate, the dog salivated copiously and Pavlov was able to measure the dog's secretion. In the course of conducting this experiment over several days, they both noticed a strange phenomenon. They noticed that when the assistant came into the room, the dog would begin to salivate before the food was made available. Simply, the mere presence of the assistant caused the dog to salivate. The dog's response caused Pavlov to investigate this unexpected phenomenon further.

From his further investigations, Pavlov developed the concept of respondent conditioning. He gave the dog meat powder for several meals, which caused the dog to salivate, as expected. Then, he began to ring a bell every time he gave the dog the meals. Later, Pavlov just rang the bell without giving the dog any food, and as expected, the dog salivated. As Pavlov concluded, the dog's salivating to the bell occurred because the bell had been paired with the food, and the salivation response to the bell was then contingent upon previous pairings of the bell and the food (Malott, Whaley, & Malott, 1993).

Pavlov named the concepts gleaned from his experiments with the dog. The food given to the dog was called the *unconditional stimulus (US)*. The salivation response that was produced without prior conditioning was called *unconditioned response (UR)*. The ringing of the bell was called the *conditional stimulus*. The salivation in response to the bell alone was called the *conditioned response*. Finally, *conditioning* was defined as the pairing of the conditioned stimulus (i.e., the ringing of the bell) with unconditioned stimulus (i.e., the food) (Malott, Whaley, & Malott, 1993).

Although lay people may not appreciate the importance of Pavlov's work, it has tremendous importance to the understanding of behavior. A dog's salivation is analogous to people's emotional responses. Both the dog's salivation and people's emotional responses are produced by the physiological system. Just as the dog's salivation is automatic, so are emotional responses. A number of researchers contend that emotional behaviors occur as the result of respondent or Pavlovian conditioning. They have found that, for example, "the consistent pairing of fear-producing stimuli with other stimuli may bring about fear reactions to these other stimuli, the ones that didn't originally produce fear responses" (Malott, Whaley, & Malott, 1993, p. 327).

Other researchers have extended Pavlov's work to verbal behavior by demonstrating that it responded to the same principles as animal and human motor behavior. These researchers found that verbal conditioning follows operant conditioning and that reinforcement, under some conditions, shaped verbal behavior. Additional studies showed that the amount of change in verbal conditioning was affected by the social setting, previous experience with the investigator, expectancy, variation in the meaning of reinforcing stimuli, and other interpersonal variables (Krasner, 1982).

Behavior therapy concentrates on the environmental cues that serve as reinforcers and verbal behaviors that may serve as response classes. Reinforcers may be food, cigarettes, smiles, toys, tokens, head nods, and compliments. Behavior therapy has been used to treat such behavior as smoking, drug addiction, and overeating (Rose, 1977).

Behavior Therapy Techniques Kaplan (1986) reviewed a series of traditional operant condition techniques that were used in behavioral therapy. The techniques are continuous reinforcement, intermittent reinforcement, differential reinforcement of other behavior, differential reinforcement of incompatible behavior, differential reinforcement of high and low rates of behavior, the good behavioral game, shaping, forward and backward chaining, instructional control, graduated guidance, prompting and fading, reinforced practice, extinction, negative practice, stimulus satiation, graduated extinction and habituation, punishment, and behavioral contracting. Many of these techniques are appropriate for offenders who have developmental problems, such as offenders who have mental retardation, mental illness, or just organic impairment. Kaplan reviewed a list of techniques, which are elaborated on below.

Continuous reinforcement involves the continuous implementation of a stimulus following a response. This technique is used early in the learning of a new behavior, but behavior reinforced in this manner is more likely to be terminated by an individual than other techniques. For instance, an uncaring person who holds a door open for a person whose hands are full and is told "thank you, that was very nice of you," may stop after someone else whose hands are full says nothing.

Intermittent reinforcement involves the predetermined administration of a stimulus at a variable schedule. This procedure may be used in treatment near termination and to wean an individual from continuous reinforcement.

Differential reinforcement of other behavior is the administration of a stimulus after a predetermined time period has passed in which a behavior has not occurred. This procedure is generally used in conjunction with other reinforcements. Most behaviorists state that the interval should not be longer than one hour, but there is no limit to the minimum length of the interval. The nature of the problem would determine the minimum amount of time lapse before the administration of the stimulus.

Differential reinforcement of incompatible behavior is the elimination of a stimulus that is maintaining an inappropriate behavior, and a behavior that is incompatible with the inappropriate behavior is reinforced. The clinician must make sure that the old behavior is properly extinguished, that the new behavior is truly incompatible, and that the new behavior is timely reinforced.

Differential reinforcement of high and low rates of behavior is a technique in which a behavior has been specified as high and/or low. The aim is to reinforce an individual if a number of tasks are done during a specified interval. It has been used to decrease the frequency of maladaptive behavior and increase work behavior in settings where a high rate of behaviors are primary treatment goals.

The good behavior game is a technique based on a variable-interval schedule with a number of reinforcement processes and cueing procedures. As an illustration, an individual is reinforced according to variable schedule determined by the clinician. A bell is rung during this schedule, and a clinician immediately looks at the individual. If the individual is on task, he or she is rewarded. This technique is often used in schools and sheltered workshop settings in which a goal of treatment is consistent, on-task activities.

Shaping refers to a series of reinforcement in order to move an individual to a complex, terminal behavior. It has been called successive approximations. Simply, it refers to the continuous reinforcement of a person to a desired end.

The individual is reinforced for incremental tasks, such as being reinforced for putting on one shoe untied, then two shoes untied, and then tying one shoe, and finally tying both shoes. Though it is effective, shaping is time-consuming. It also may seem impractical for a typical offender population. However, there may be some prisoners who are brain damaged and may lose basic, caring skills.

Forward and backward chaining is somewhat similar to shaping. It differs in that there is a primary goal of teaching a complex behavior and several lesser objectives. A clinician can start at the beginning of the chain and work forward or start at the end of the chain and work backward. For example, the overall goal might be to assist an individual in getting up and started in the morning. The chain may consist of ordinal behavior (i.e., low to high), such as brushing one's teeth, dressing, tying one's shoes, and walking. The clinician may begin with motivating the individual to brush his or her teeth and end with walking to breakfast. If the end of the chain is dressing, the clinician may begin there and work backward with brushing one's teeth last. The goal is to use reinforcements to get the individual up and moving in the morning.

Instructional control is simply providing feedback to an individual on his or her behavior and the correctness or appropriateness of it. While most individuals respond to instructions, some individuals, whether because they are mentally handicapped or have not imbibed appropriate habits well, do not. Teaching a person to comply with commands is important before a clinician is able to modify inappropriate behavior.

Graduated guidance is a technique that is useful for persons who are severely hearing impaired, visually impaired, or someone without adequate control of his or her behavior. It involves physically helping a person with a response. As the client needs less help, the clinician withdraws the manual assistance and perhaps shadows the person, ready to offer help when the response is ill-directed.

Prompting and fading is a type of guidance in which a clinician either verbally or physically helps a person to perform a behavior. Usually, the clinician has initially assessed that this individual will not or cannot perform a task. Fading is the gradual decreasing of prompting.

Reinforced practice is an opportunity for an individual to practice a new behavior repeatedly. Every time the individual practices the newly learned behavior correctly, reinforcement is provided. This technique is useful when a person does not have the opportunity to practice a new behavior in his or her environment. So, the clinician should provide a number of opportunities for the person to practice.

Extinction is the cessation of the contingent relationship between a response and its reinforcements. When achieved, a progressive decrease occurs in the rate, force, duration, and typography of a response. A clinician should be aware that there might be an increase in other inappropriate behavior as a behavior is being extinguished and should consider very carefully the appropriateness of the behavior to be extinguished.

Negative practice is a technique in which an individual speedily and incessantly engages in a behavior whenever the individual has engaged in this behavior. For instance, an individual may have a habit in a therapeutic community of scratching himself or herself in the pubic region. Assuming, or determining, that there is no medical reason for this behavior, the person is instructed to scratch incessantly as fast as he or she can. Caution should be exercised in using this technique. It should not be used if there is a probability of injury. It also should be in conjunction with other techniques, such as differential reinforcement of other behavior or differential reinforcement of incompatible behavior.

Stimulus satiation is a procedure in which the clinician, having learned the stimulus for a client's behavior, repeatedly exposes the stimulus to the individual. The purpose is to satiate the client with the stimulus with the goal of making it unattractive. This procedure, too, should be used with caution because it might exacerbate the undesired behavior.

Graduated extinction or habituation is a technique designed to help a person to overcome avoidance or other fearful behavior. This is done by gradually reexposing an individual to a fear-evoking stimulus. The introduction of fearevoking stimulus must be done slowly so as not to introduce too much anxiety at one time.

Punishment is a temporary and immediate removal of an individual from a situation when an individual has engaged in a prohibited behavior. This may be a form of requiring a person to take time-out, return to a dormitory or room, or sit in a chair away from a group. Punishment may also be imposed by the use of aversive stimuli, such as a clinician verbally and physically (e.g., shaking one's head or frowning) conveying that a client's behavior is inappropriate.

Behavioral contracting is a signed agreement between the clinician and client specifying the desired behavior and the reinforcers to be given for the desired behavior. An advantage of contracting is the necessity of being concrete and specific. Also, the contract may be revised to create a new understanding as behavior is achieved.

Behavioral Modification

Key in understanding behavioral modification is that it sprang from the principle of operant conditioning. Simply, an *operant* is a response that affects a consequent. Another important concept is reinforcement. A *reinforcement* is "an environmental event or stimulus consequence (C) that is contingent upon the particular response (R) and whose occurrence increases the probability that the response will occur again" (Kanfer & Phillips, 1970, p. 250). Any response, whether it occurs very frequently or very infrequently, is susceptible to the reinforcement principle. A response may be caused by any of four contingent reinforcing consequences. These are positive stimuli, both presented or removed. For instance, a piece of candy may be given to a child for desired behavior. At the same time, a piece of candy may be taken away, which affects the child's response too. In addition, a negative stimulus can also be presented or removed. Both types of consequences can be stopped after presentation, and this fact yields six reinforcing operations—positive reinforcement, punishment, response cost, negative reinforcement, extinction, and avoidance. Further, anything that decreases a behavior is punishment, and anything that increases a behavior is a reinforcer (Rimm & Masters, 1979). See Table 3.1.

Table 3.1 Reinforcement and Punishment Procedures

Operations	Positive Consequences	Negative Consequences
Contingent Presentation	**Positive Reinforcement** A delinquent youth uses socially appropriate language A counselor praises the youth	**Punishment** A delinquent child uses profanity The counselor chides the youth
Contingent Removal	**Response Cost** A delinquent youth injects profanity in a conversation The counselor does not attend after initially attending	**Negative Reinforcement** A delinquent youth apologizes for language The counselor stops chiding the youth
Contingent Stopped After Administration	**Extinction** A delinquent youth screams and hollers The counselor ignores the youth	**Avoidance** A delinquent youth stopped cursing when first requested The counselor withholds the chiding

Adapted from Kanfer and Phillips *Learning Foundations of Behavior Therapy* (New York: John Wiley & Sons, 1970).

The delinquent behaviors depicted in Table 3.1 are the responses that are affected by the stimuli, which is the range of the counselor's behaviors.

This theory provides a technique that is called contingency management. Contingency is the pairing of a reward for desired behavior. The reward is contingent upon performing a specific behavior. So, contingency management is a system of rewards and punishment. As an illustration, Dettweiler, Acker, Guthrie, and Gregory (1972) described a token economy for children in an institution in Victoria, British Columbia, which was developed to modify inappropriately disruptive and violent behavior of children in the institution. The system developed involved a token economy with rewards and punishments. In addition, there was a level system consisting of level 1, which was the lowest, and level 5, which was the highest.

In this system, there were two types of points awarded—academic and behavioral. Each staff person carried a sheet with each child's name and place upon which points could be recorded. Positive points were awarded for appropriate interaction with peers and adults, punctuality, working on an appropriate activity, compliance, and institutionally acceptable behavior. Negative points were subtracted from each child's total for physical and verbal assaults, noncompliance, and other rule-breaking behavior. Academic points were based on academic achievement and the performance of school tasks, and behavioral points were based on normal institutional activity outside of school.

Color-coded tokens were given for performing a specific activity. For instance, a yellow token was given to each child for getting up at the appropriate time, getting dressed, making his bed, and washing his face and hands. This yellow token would allow him into the cafeteria. After eating breakfast, the child would be given a green token, which permitted him to return to his living area to brush his teeth. Upon brushing his teeth, the child would be given a red token, and this token allowed him admittance to school. One of the rewards of going to school was that it began with physical activities, and participation in these exercises provided an opportunity to earn an exceedingly high amount of points.

A child at level 1 was supervised constantly and spent his points on meals and other necessities. As the child moved from the lower levels to the higher levels, he was given more freedom; however, with more freedom came more responsibility and consequences for misbehavior. So, negative points were more potent at level 5 than at level 1. Also, a child at level 4 had to earn at least 200 academic points each week to remain at level 4. Toward the end of level 4, the child would be phased off of the point system. At level 5, the child would attend public school and might work at an evening job in the community.

Social Skills Training Related to behavior modification but which may flow from other theories, social skill training is an intervention that has been applied to persons within the mental health field, such as persons diagnosed with schizophrenia and persons within the correctional system. For anyone who evidences inadequate social functioning, social skills training is an appropriate corrective strategy. Social skills training addresses a broad repertoire of interpersonal dimensions, including assertiveness, friendliness, warmth, initiating and maintaining conversations, and demonstrating empathy. Each of these factors requires a set of verbal and nonverbal response elements. For instance, assertiveness requires that an individual speak in an audible voice and make eye contact. In sum, social skills may be grouped in three broad categories—expressive elements, receptive elements, and interactive balance (Morrison, 1985). Morrison depicts elements of the social skills, accordingly.

Elements of Social Skills

Expressive Elements	Receptive Elements (Social Perception)	Interactive Mode
Speech content	Attention	Response timing
Paralinguistic elements	Decoding	Turn talking
Voice	Knowledge of context factors	Social
Pace	and cultural mores	reinforcement
Pitch		
Tone		
Nonverbal behavior		
Proxemics		
Kinesics		
"Eye contact"		
Facial expression		

PSYCHOANALYTIC THEORY

Freud has been credited with the development of psychoanalytic theory. Freud retrospectively formulated psychoanalytic theory to explain therapeutic issues that he had observed in his practice (Allan, 1979). At first, Freud espoused a topographical model of the mind consisting of an unconscious, a conscious, and a preconscious. The unconscious constituted a person's desires, fantasies, and wishes, and these aspects were unknown to the individual and involved primarily a sexual or aggressive nature. The conscious involved thoughts and feelings of which the person was cognizant. The preconscious involved ideas that were subconscious but could be made conscious by focusing. In further refining his theory, Freud overlaid on his topographical model a structural component of the mind that he called the *id*, *ego*, and *superego*.

The *id* constitutes the unconscious aspect of the psyche and is dictated to by primary urges or instinctual drives. The id is controlled by the pleasure principle, which is pursued to reduce tension. The *ego* is a higher order structure that guides and controls. It controls conscious perceptions, arbitrating between the organism and the environment and assisting in adaptation. If the ego constrains, it uses unconscious defense mechanisms (i.e., repression, denial, projection, negation, displacement, interjection, reaction formation, isolation, undoing, rationalization, intellectualization, and sublimation). (See Chapter 5 for an explanation of these mechanisms). The ego is controlled by the reality principle, which acquires objects for the careful gratification of the id. The ego is logical, rational, and realistic. The *superego* is concerned with right and wrong. It is the inserted parental authority. All three (i.e., id, ego, and the superego) contribute to a person's intrapsychic functioning and determine normal and abnormal psychological functioning.

One of the key principles of psychoanalytic theory is psychic determination, which means that everything that happens regarding a person's mental functioning occurs because of a purpose. Nothing happens by chance and "everything a person feels, thinks, and fantasizes, dreams, and does has a psychological motive" (Strean, 1996, p. 523). In assessing behaviors, a counselor should include assessment of a person's unconscious wishes, fantasies, defenses, and ethical rules. According to Freud, the human personality consists of several intermeshing factors, consisting of the topographical, structural, genetic, dynamics, economic, interpersonal, and cultural. In combination, they represent a metapsychological approach. All are needed to understand fully an individual. This approach is used in counseling by a counselor who endorses a psychoanalytic framework for his or her practice.

For instance, the recognition of the unconscious is critical in helping a counselor assess an individual's presenting problems. Psychoanalytic practitioners contend that an incessant marital complaint represents an unconscious wish of the complaining spouse. The man who incessantly complains that his wife is cold and unresponsive unconsciously prefers such a woman. A different woman would repel him. In a similar manner, parents who complain about the behaviors of their children unconsciously desire and support such behavior. In fact, the parents reinforce the behavior that they claim they despise (Hearn, 1979). Finally, a car theft by juveniles has been assessed to occur because of deficiencies in juveniles' psychic; however, this perspective has been strongly rejected and ridiculed by persons outside the counseling profession (Smith & Berlin, 1988). Kaplan and Sadock (1998) contend that some individuals are inappropriate for psychoanalytic treatment. Among them are persons with poor impulse control, inability to tolerate anxiety and frustration, and antisocial personality disorders. In addition, persons who engage in concrete thinking, are not psychologically minded, and are extremely dishonest are inappropriate for psychoanalytic treatment. Though Kaplan and Sadock do not specifically indicate that offenders are inappropriate for psychoanalytic treatment, it is obvious that psychoanalytic theory is not suited for many offenders, both adults and juveniles. While there has been limited endorsement of psychoanalytic theory with offenders since Aichorn's (1935) work, most counselors use some aspects of psychoanalytic theory with offenders, such as the use of defense mechanisms to understand an individual's behavior and to assess an individual's ego.

LOGOTHERAPY

Viktor E. Frankl, a practicing psychiatrist, developed logotherapy when he was imprisoned in Auschwitz, one of Germany's concentration camps. Logotherapy is a combination of a German word, *logo*, which translates for *meaning*, and *therapy*. Essentially, logotherapy constitutes meaning therapy. As a prisoner in Auschwitz, Frankl came to realize that a person must have, or find, meaning in his or her life. This "will to meaning" is for human beings their primary motivational force. When Frankl's completed manuscript was confiscated by the Germans when Frankl entered Auschwitz, he began writing a new manuscript on bits of paper. He knew, as other psychiatrists have since learned, that "those who knew that there was a task waiting for them to fulfill were most apt to survive" (Frankl, 1963, p. 165).

For every person, meaning is unique and specific to this person and can be fulfilled only by this person. The meaning of life differs from individual to individual, day to day, and from hour to hour. There is no general meaning of life. It is a specific meaning of an individual's life at a given moment. It is akin to knowing that there is no such thing as the best chess move. The best chess move depends upon a player's strategy and the opponent's moves.

According to Frankl, logotherapy's assignment is assisting an individual in finding meaning in his or her life. A common problem of many persons, especially depressed and neurotic persons, is feelings of total or ultimate meaninglessness of their lives. These persons have an existential vacuum. As an illustration, a recent story involving Kirk Douglas, the actor, indicated that Mr. Douglas was searching for meaning in his life and turned to Judaism (Rothman, 1997). Furthermore, in the fictional but realistic television series involving a prison in New York, McManus, director of a treatment unit, told one prisoner serving life without parole that this prisoner's life still could have meaning even if this prisoner died in prison (Levinson, 1997).

Lantz (1997), who has written extensively on logotherapy, wrote that it involve five elements—human meeting, dynamic reflection, existential reflection, therapeutic directives, and tribalization. *Human meeting* refers to the committed presence of an individual to other persons and a willingness to appreciate the potentials of other persons in spite of difficulty, demand, or unpleasantness. Other terms for this concept are *integrity, commitment,* and *loyalty.* The therapist must be willing to make a commitment of human meeting to the person seeking help. *Dynamic reflection* refers to the breaking down and solving of problems. It seeks to clarify problems through verification and objectification. *Existential reflection* refers to the process of gaining a richer and wider discovery and understanding of the meaning of life and meaning potential. Existential reflection aids in awareness and discovery through participation, encounter, and concrete involvement. *Therapeutic directives* are task assignments given to a client to assist the client in learning the meaning of life and meaning potential. *Tribalization*, also called *network intervention* or *social system development*, refers to a treatment strategy that helps clients to increase meaning potential and acquiring resources. The use of tribalization means that the counselor appreciates that a major reason for clients not learning their meaning in life comes from the physical, social, political, economic, and cultural environments.

After Frankl survived Auschwitz and resumed his psychiatric practice, many of the clients he saw suffered from neurosis and depression. His most frequently used techniques were de-reflection and paradoxical intention. De-reflection involves helping a person to focus on a proper target instead of a peripheral issue, which a number of people do. Paradoxical intention involves instructing a person to do the opposite of the person's problem. For instance, one client was suicidal because of writer's cramp. In trying to write neatly and legibly, the client's hand would cramp. So, the therapist advised the client to write with the worse possible scrawl. When the client tried, he wrote neatly. In another example, a client who could not sleep was advised not to try to sleep and to stay up as long as possible. Frankl acknowledged that paradoxial intention is no panacea, but it is a useful tool in treating obsessive, compulsive, and phobic conditions where the underlying cause is anticipatory anxiety (Frankl, 1963).

While logotherapy may seem geared more toward middle-class clients, it has applicability for the prison environment. For instance, Scarnati (1992) described an eclectic treatment approach for dangerous prisoners within the Ohio Department of Mental Health, which included psychoanalysis, logotherapy, and group psychotherapy. The setting was used, in addition, for medical students to help them acquire empathy through personal contact with prisoners (i.e., human meeting) and learn about stresses in prisons. Logotherapy also has been used to help individuals with drug problems find meaning in life (Wolf, Katz, & Nachson, 1995).

Whiddon (1983) discussed the use of logotherapy in a Mississippi prison. Its use was justified on the conjecture that criminal behavior has numerous causes, and one of these causes may include the absence of meaning. To test this hypothesis, Whiddon advertised in the prison newspaper for volunteers to participate in a new treatment program. Initially, no one among the 1,734 prisoners responded. So, in a subsequent newspaper issue, the prisoners were promised additional visiting privileges for their participation. Forty-three prisoners then volunteered, but seventeen were excluded because of security problems. Of the twenty-six remaining prisoners three were paroled and three quit, leaving twenty participants for the group.

Whiddon's primary purpose was to test the effectiveness of logotherapy. He used a quasi-experimental design, using two comparison groups of prisoners. One was a no-treatment comparison group, and the other group consisted of prisoners in a religious group. To measure meaning in life, Whiddon used the Purpose-in-Life scale and administered it at the beginning of the group and at the end. This scale had a range of 70 to 116. The group met for three hours a session, three nights per week for twenty-four weeks.

For the actual logotherapy program, Whiddon used a program developed by Crumbaugh (1973). It consisted of five stages that were provided during the twenty-four-week period. The stages were (1) the provision of psychoeducational training in the ideals of logotherapy; (2) the growth of self-awareness; (3) the reconfigurating of self-esteem and self image; (4) the moving toward values and their social impli-cations; and (5) the development of personal meaning, goals, and the implications for future behavior. The first stage consisted of four weeks of discussions regarding the logotherapy and theories regarding criminal behaviors. During the second stage, which consisted of five weeks, exercises were conducted that helped the prisoners to develop awareness of themselves. The third stage consisted of four weeks and contained a series of exercises geared toward increasing the prisoners' self-esteem and self-image. The fourth stage consisted of five weeks and involved the shifting of attention from self to attention toward other life values. Discussion topics involved value clarification and societal expectations. The final stage lasted five weeks and consisted of encouraging the prisoners to use the increased understanding of their values and themselves in order to recognize their lives' meaning and purpose.

The results of the Purpose-in-Life scale revealed that the scores for the prisoners increased from eighty-one at pretest to ninety-six at posttest, a gain of fifteen points. One comparison group that received no treatment showed a three-point increase, and the group that had the religious instruction had a decrease of three points. Other positive changes were that the treatment group had no disciplinary reports during the period, and group cohesion developed to the point that the members re-quested that they be permitted to live together on the same unit. For 18 months, the group lived together on a self-governing unit with no disciplinary reports.

Logotherapy has applicability for prisons because of recent sentencing changes in a number of states. Because of the "get tough" on criminals movement, a number of states have passed sentences that provide life without parole. These prisoners are not likely to get out and are likely to die in prison. These prisoners may need to find meaning in their lives. Logotherapy may seem like a luxury, but it may be a tool for prisoners where rehabilitation is not an option. Prisoners who are serving life with-out parole can become very difficult to handle because they have nothing to lose, and a system may not have enough administrative cells to contain them. So, it be-hooves the prison system to have other treatment techniques available for a group, such as lifers and other long-termed offenders.

AFROCENTRIC THEORY

African American social scientists have been concerned with the dominance and influence of theories and concepts developed by white social and political sci-entists in examining social problems and providing a basis for American social and political structures. African American social scientists were concerned because they believed that this white, or Eurocentric, perspective denigrates and diminishes per-spectives and expressions from people of color. As a consequence, African Ameri-can social scientists sought to construct a conceptual paradigm that affirmed the history, tradition, and visions of African Americans. Because African American scholars position Africa as the center of their conceptual framework, they have been called Afrocentrists (Schiele, 1997).

Vital to understanding the Afrocentric perspective is the accentuation on world-view. Worldview involves a racial or ethnic group's cosmology, ontology, and epis-temology. Therefore, there is a Eurocentric worldview and Afrocentric worldview. The foundation of Afrocentric worldview is found in traditional African culture and practices of historical African groups, such as Ashanti, Twe, Nubians, Kemites, and Dogon. Afrocentric theorists refer to the values and mores of these groups before the pillage of the African Continent by the European and Arab slave traders. As stressed by Schiele (1997), "the Afrocentric worldview is a set of philosophical assumptions that are believed to have emanated from common cultural themes of traditional Africa and which are thought to be helpful in not only liberating people of African descent but also for facilitating positive human and societal transformation for all" (p. 23). Afrocentric values are in direct opposition to Eurocentric worldview and values of individualism, materialism, and fragmentation. Thus, Afrocentric values are communality, spiritualism, and wholeness (Schiele, 1997).

According to King (1994), the Afrocentric worldview situates Africa and African culture and history at the core of African Americans' struggle to deal with problems emanating from institutional slavery, segregation, and racism. The African worldview underscores six principles consisting of interconnectedness; harmony; balance; affective epistemology; authenticity, spontaneity, and naturalness; and cultural awareness. Moreover, the Nguzo Saba furnishes an etho that elaborates upon these seven principles. Nguzo Saba consists of Umoja, Kujichagulia, Ujima, Ujammaa, Nia, Kuumba, and Imani (King, 1994).

Myers (1988) extrapolated a psychology tailored for African Americans from the Afrocentric worldview that she described as optimal "because it is structured to yield maximally positive experience in a holistic way" (p. 4). See Table 3.2. Specifically extended to counseling, Myers (1988) proposed a therapeutic process that she called *Belief Systems Analysis (BSA)*, which aims to assist individuals in acquiring an optimal conceptual system and experiences. In a way, BSA is a form of cognitive therapy in that it involves the process of knowing, and knowing involves both awareness and judgment. As a holistic therapy, the cognitive aspect is not disconnected from the affective, the behavioral, the optimal, the unconscious, the cultural, the metaphysical, and the feminine. BSA differs from other cognitive therapy in that BSA is based on an Afrocentric model of psychological functioning, and it provides the conceptual system of the worldview (Afrocentric) that the counselor hopes the client develops.

BSA begins with an analysis of a client's current belief system and an assessment of the amount of change the client wants. The counselor can determine a client's current belief system by examining the presenting problems and the assumptions or conceptual framework that produced the client's problems. A comprehensive understanding of the client's assumptions or conceptual framework would involve an examination of the client's personal history, goals, and consciousness. According to Myers (1988), "an underlying premise is that ultimately everyone seeks everlasting peace and happiness, but many are limited by their abilities to attain it in terms of their level of consciousness (undergirded by their conceptual system). Difficulties arise from not knowing that an optimal state is now achievable, not knowing how to achieve it, and not understanding the requisite structures for its sustenance" (p. 72).

The counselor using BSA provides alternatives that are favorable to spiritual growth. Then, the individual is in a better position to choose and take responsibility for his or her choices. As the foundation for all knowledge, self-knowledge must be acquired first, and the urge for self-knowledge must come from within the client. As the process of acquiring self-knowledge is initiated, it is heuristic or self-correcting. As stated by Myers, "as one comes to know more about his/her true identity in the Afrocentric paradigm, as God manifesting, and comes to rely on that inner knowledge, the therapy becomes more supportive, reinforcing, and clarifying, less didactic" (p. 72).

Table 3.2 Linda Myers' Conceptual Systems

Assumptions	Optimal	Sub-Optimal
Ontology (Nature of Reality)	Spiritual (known in an extrasensory fashion) and Material (known through the five senses) as one	Material With Possible Spiritual Aspect That Is Separate and Secondary
Epistemology (Nature of Knowledge)	Self-Knowledge Known Through Symbolic Imagery and Rhythm	External Knowledge Known Through Counting and Measuring
Axiology (Nature of Value)	Highest Value in Positive Interpersonal Relationships between wo/man	Highest Values in Objects or Acquisition
Logic (Reason)	Diunital–Union of Opposites	Dichotomous–Either/Or
Process	Ntuology–All Sets are Interrelated Through Human and Spiritual Network	Technology–All Sets are Repeatable and Reproducible
Identity	Extended Self, Multidimensional	Individual Form
Self-Worth	Intrinsic in Being	Based on External Criteria or Materialism
Values Guiding Behavior	Spiritualism, Oneness With Nature, Communalism	Materialism, Competition, Individualism
Sense of Well-Being	Positively Consistent Despite Appearances Due to Relationships With Source	In Constant Flux and Struggle
Life-Space	Infinite and Unlimited (Spirit Manifesting)	Finite and Limited (Beginning with Birth and Ending with Death)
Perspective	Holistic/Oneness	Segmented, Fragmented (Duality)
Peace, Happiness Orientation	External	Temporal (Temporary)
Stress, Anxiety Orientation	Carefree	Continual Confrontation
Love Orientation	Unconditional (See Beyond to Truth)	Conditional (Focus on Appearance)
Close Interpersonal Relationships	Manifestation of Sharing Spiritual Union	Manifestation of Material Attraction
Group Orientation	Unity Though Ideology	Unity Through Common Goals or Specific Aim
Aesthetic orientation	Tied to Ethics and Character	External, Superficial

From *Understanding an Afrocentric World View: Introduction to an Optimal Psychology* by Linda Myers (Dubuque, IA: Kendall/Hunt Publishing Company, 1993, p. 98). © 1993 by Kendall/Hunt Publishing Company. Used with permission.

The evidence of the internalization of knowledge by clients will be manifested in several ways. One way is through changes in self-esteem. Particularly, the client stops grounding his or her self-worth on external factors and stops being concerned about what other people think. Another way in which knowledge has been manifested is through changes in mental health and resourcefulness. Particularly, the client refrains from being governed by the appearances of circumstances and permits these circumstances to justify his or her feelings. Moreover, the client is empowered to explicate reality himself or herself. Last, changes are manifested in prosperity and self-determination. Particularly, the client allows infinite spirit as direct and supply source, depends on faith or positive belief, does as directed, and is patient.

The outcome of creating one's belief system in line with the optimal conceptual system is the understanding of one's being as a manifestation of an infinite positive power. BSA, like other cognitive therapies,

> "emphasizes rational thinking, but unlike others, utilizes a transcendent system of reasoning (diunital logic), rooted in a specific cultural and historical context. . . . However in this regard, it is imperative that the active ingredients of BSA be translated into the language and belief structure of the client. This task may require that the therapist not use words such as transcendence, but to convey meanings in the terms the client can comprehend and more readily assimilate. Both client and therapist are encouraged to be open and honest in exploring and articulating the nature and processes of their beliefs and how their beliefs affect themselves and each other. As with all therapists, the individual client may want total change, minimal change, or no change at all. BSA can outline for the client what life would be like incorporating the worldview alternative defined as optimal. The client need not, however, be exposed to the whole paradigm at once. A group setting can be ideal for BSA, providing the additional benefit of a support group" (Myers, 1988, pp. 72-73).

Elements of an Afrocentric perspective have been incorporated in programs for African American offenders. King (1994) averred that African American adolescents and adults need Afrocentric programs because of several deficits. Particularly, they lack a positive social and cultural identify from their African and African American experiences; they lack a culturally relevant belief system that will aid them in surviving and thriving in a hostile and racist society; they lack a sense of compassion and respect for other African Americans, with lesser compassion for other African American males; they lack nurturing and social support needed to deal with seemingly hopeless situations; and they lack the social competencies needed to carry out social and cultural responsibilities.

Specific programs are discussed in the latter part of this textbook. See Chapter 8 for a description of a program for African American adolescent male offenders, Chapter 9 for a program for African American woman offenders, and Chapter 10 for a program for African American adult male offenders.

FEMINIST THEORY

At first, feminist philosophy demanded a comprehensive examination of all environmental factors that oppress women. With this framework as a background, the feminist therapist would use whatever treatment theory that he or she embraced (Dutton-Douglas & Walker, 1988). Later, feminist theory emerged as an independent explanation for women's condition and problems. It is rooted in a presumption of health, not illness. It sees women's maladaptive behavior not as resulting from sickness but from oppression (Rosewater, 1988). From this viewpoint, feminist theory has applicability for female offenders (Chesney-Lind, 1995; Russell, 1984).

Feminist theory has evolved to the point that there is not one feminist theory, but a series of feminist theories or perspectives (Dutton-Douglas & Walker, 1988). Fundamentally, feminist theory refers to "a body of knowledge which offers critical explanations of women's subordination. . . . It also tends to operate at some level of abstraction, using analytical categories that move beyond the merely descriptive or anecdotal, and at some level of generalisation [sic] moving beyond the individual case. . . . Typically, feminist theory offers some kind of analysis and explanation of how and why women have less power than men, and how this imbalance could be challenged and transformed" (Stacey, 1993, p. 50).

As an illustration of the application of feminist theory, Abbott (1995) explained women and substance abuse. Abbott linked the role of inequality in society, differential power between the genders, and the effect of this system on women's self-esteem and their susceptibility to substance abuse. Particularly, men, namely white men, possess a highly disproportionate share of societal power, and they determine what is valuable, important, not valuable, and unimportant. Because women are made to feel worthless, a condition is established in which they seek a need to feel complete and in control. Using substances is a way of compensating for their sense of powerlessness and frustration. A feminist understanding proposes that "by using alcohol and other drugs, women seek a paradoxical solution. They initially feel power over the decision to use a substance and seize the opportunity to control their intake of that substance to help them escape their social plight. In the process, as dependence on and tolerance of the substance develop, women are once again controlled by an external force, becoming powerless against it" (Abbott, 1995, p. 262).

Another example of the use of feminist theory is the challenging of the traditional perspective of human development. Conarton and Silverman (1988) challenged Erik Erickson's five stages of human development and the appropriateness of this conceptualization for women. Instead, they theorized that women undergo eight phases: bonding, orientation toward others, cultural adaptation, awakening and separation, the development of the feminine, empowerment, spiritual development, and integration. Conarton and Silverman did not see these phases as stages in which women systematically pass through. Instead, they saw these phases as cyclical and explained that women reexperience these phases throughout their lives. Building on Conarton and Silverman's work, Wastell (1996) proposed a specific counseling focus for each stage (Table 3.3).

Nes and Iadicola (1989) identified three models of feminism and their implications for practice. The models are liberal, radical, and socialist. Liberal feminism maintains that men and women possess a similar capacity to achieve. However, this capacity for women has been impeded by the social conditions impinging on women. Some inequality among individuals, however, is expected because of differences in motivation and potential. So, inequality that appears to approximate a bell-shaped curve, irrespective of gender, is natural. However, should such

Table 3.3 Developmental Stages and Counseling Focus for Women

Focus	Counseling Focus
Bonding	Counseling will need to focus on the importance of bonding, empathy, and attachment for female development.
Orientation Toward Others	Counseling may need to examine the extent to which the woman fosters unnecessary dependence and develops the skill of self-nurturance.
Cultural Adaptation	The rediscovery of their voice and the valuing of such attributes as intuition and feeling. The focus in counseling is on reclaiming what has been denied.
Awakening and Separation	This phase is the adult experience of separation anxiety as well as social rejection in the form of family and counselors' attitudes. Counseling must enable the woman to move through this transition.
Development of the Feminine	Counseling must assist women to "sit with themselves." They must deal with feelings of selfishness, guilt, and anxiety as they enact a new life that reflects their values, not those of a male-dominated society.
Empowerment	Women need to be enabled to trust their intuitive judgment and assisted to enact their goals by methods they feel are appropriate.
Spiritual Development	A process of mourning must be followed, and the women need to be supported in the exploration of their innermost selves. This may involve "body" work that brings together diverse aspects of the self.
Integration	This is a very difficult phase and only occurs during mid to later life. Counseling must support women in the exploration of these insights and the plans that will bring new and different involvement in living.

From C. A. Wastell: Feminist Developmental Theory: Implications for Counseling. *Journal of Counseling & Development,* 74:577, 1996. © ACA. Reprinted with permission.

distribution be skewed towards males, then a problem exists that needs to be rooted out. For adherents of the liberal perspective, the issue is not male oppression but the denial of equal opportunity and full liberty for women. Women can prosper socially and economically within the current patriarchal system. Men's attitudes and behaviors are what needs to change, not men's nature. The change that women need to make is to be more competitive, assertive, individualistic, and self-directed.

Radical feminism views men's and women's natures as being different. Proponents of this perspective believe that women's nature is superior to men's, and that men should be more like women instead of vice versa. The social order mirrors males' nature and need to dominate and control. Patriarchy was once based on biological factors. Now, it rests upon ideology, law, and violence against women. The need of men to dominate and control women gratifies men's ego. Male children come into a society that teaches them to oppress females. Radical feminists seek the total destruction of patriarchy and seek a new social order based on women's values.

Social feminism involves varied viewpoints. All viewpoints, however, agree that women are oppressed by men. The source of the oppression is the subject of different views. Some based the oppression on class and others on sex. Then,

Table 3.4 A Comparison of Liberal, Radical, and Socialist Feminist Perspectives

Subject	Liberal Feminist	Radical Feminist	Socialist Feminist
Problem Identification	Identify individual deficits, particularly those rooted in sex-role socialization; identify problems of opportunity structures, especially those rooted in sexism; identify the interplay between individual deficits and opportunity structures; and identify existence of social-institutional supports.	Identify linkages between individual's problems and oppressive social relations that are rooted in patriarchy; identify social and institutional arrangements that promote traditional sex roles and authoritarian-hierarchical (patriarchal) relationships; and examine personality attributes that are outcomes of patriarchal sex roles socialization.	Identify impact of institution processes and belief systems that are manifestation of patriarchy and class systems; identify problems in terms of the contradictions that arise within and between the two systems and examine personality attributes that are outcomes of systems of domination.
Assessment	Occurs on four levels (1) assess the degree and manifestation of the individual's deficits, (2) assess the degree and impact of problems of blockages in opportunity structures, (3) enumerate and assign priorites to the interplay between the individual's deficits and opportunity structures, and (4) assess the availability of social-institutional supports.	Assess primary and secondary relationships in terms of the degree to which they are characteristic of patriarchy; assess the impact of those patriarchal institutional processes on the individual; and assess the impact of patriarchal sex-gender role socialization on personality development.	Same as in radical feminism, and in addition; assess the impact of class, race, and the general socioeconomic condition of the client; and examine issues of alienation, self-fulfillment, and locus of control as they relate to systems of domination.

Treatment Strategies	Traditional therapies employed; use of individual psychotherapy, group treatment to deal with personal pathologies, and some family therapy; casework and outreach employed for addressing person-in-environment system, attempting to tap resources within survival and emotional needs; use of advocacy to ensure against discrimination of clients based on sex especially, but also race, age, and the like; creation of client-centered support groups.	Consciousness-raising for women and men (elimination of psychology of oppressed and oppressor); support and self-help groups for women; some conventional forms of therapy used (emphasis on women helping women); and constructive outlets sought for emotional and intellectual responses and application of consciousness-raising and therapy through politicization and mobilization of women around women's issues.	Consciousness-raising to enable individuals to interpret the impact of classism, sexism, and other forms of oppression upon their relationships; use of support self-help and advocacy groups aimed at meeting basic needs and changing the systems of domination; coalition building and empowering individuals and groups, showing ways to meet needs outside the parameters of systems of domination; and encouraging clients toward political action.
Treatment Goals	To correct the individual's deficits; to open up problematic opportunity structures; and to establish support groups to aid clients' fulfillment and validation of choices.	To create individual and collective awareness that personal problems have their roots in patriarchy (make the personal political); to reintegrate masculine and feminine personality attributes to create a personality marked by sex role transcendence; to promote change in primary and secondary relationships that are characterized by patriarchy (return control over one's life); to mobilize and politicize women to effect change in the larger social system (eliminate patriarchy); to eliminate blockages that stem from patriarchal sex role socialization; to create alternative communities for women; and to promote sisterhood.	Same as in radical feminism, and also: to raise political consciousness, showing the linkages between class and patriarchy to end the personality of oppression and to end the systems of oppression themselves; to encourage organizing, coalition-building, empowering individuals and groups to enable them to make changes in conditions of their existence that have been limited by systems of domination; to enable individuals to meet physical and species needs in such a way that an individual's potentials can be realized without expense to others.

Reprinted, with permission, from J.A. Nes & P. Iadicola: Toward a Definition of Feminist Social Work: A Comparison of Liberal, Radical, and Socialist Models. *Social Work*, 34:31, 1996.
© National Association of Social Workers, Inc.

there are some that see variations of both. Nonetheless, one is class oppression that is based on the production of things, and the second is sex oppression that is based on the production of human beings. Another important concept in social feminism is that of human nature. Human nature is based on human needs. Humans have physical or natural needs like all animals (i.e., food, clothing, water, sex, and shelter). Humans also have needs that are specific to their species, such as the ability to think, create, and imagine. Women are restricted in terms of their human needs. Men control and exploit the two spheres of production and reproduction—the workplace and home. According to social feminists, "the primary factor that perpetuates sex inequality . . . is that the modes of production and reproduction and the articulation of these two modes from the foundation of the social order" (Nes & Iadicola, 1989, p. 15). Therefore, a key strategy is to raise women's consciousness so that they would know that their physical and species needs for nurturance, love, and companionship can be realized in a dominance-less and submission-less relationship (Nes & Iadicols, 1989). Given these three perspectives of feminism, Nes and Iadicola (1989) illustrate how each is used in treatment, including problem identification, assessment, treatment strategies, and treatment goals. See Table 3.4.

Other feminist counselors have examined the application of feminist theory to specific problems that women have. For instance, Rosewater (1988) stated that women tend to have problems with depression, substance abuse, anxiety disorders, and victimization from violence. Wallace (1995) also indicated that Latino and African American women have more problems than other women with the criminal justice and child welfare systems because of their drug problems. Given these problems, one objective of treatment is to help women achieve autonomy or become self-actualized. Feminist counselors understand this state to be one in which a woman nurtures herself and does not allow the needs of others to exceed her needs, manages multiple roles effectively, and creates an identity that is centralized in oneself. Feminist counselors can help women who are beginning a new life by a divergence of treatment methods. Feminist counselors should help women undergoing change in six domains—emotional, legal, economic, parenting, community, and psychological. The goal is to help women create functional role performance and identify.

Abbott (1995) has articulated other goals for treatment for women. These goals are to

❖ Challenge axioms that biology, gender, and race determine destiny and reframe the axiom so as to include the disease model.
❖ Eliminate false dichotomies and dichotomized thinking.
❖ Promote programs that are sensitive to all groups.
❖ Encourage empowerment for all oppressed groups.
❖ Support policies that facilitate treatment.

SOCIAL BONDING THEORY

Travis Hirschi (1969) developed a theory to explain conforming behavior by adolescents and in the process indirectly explain delinquent behavior. Hirschi contended that adolescents conform to societal rules because they are bonded to society, and this bond consists of attachment, commitment, involvement, and belief. Attachment concerns family, friends, and community. Commitment involves family career, success, future, and goals. Involvement consists of school activities, sport teams, community organizations, religious groups, and social clubs. Belief refers to the honesty, morality, fairness, patriotism, and responsibility (Siegel & Senna, 1997). So, strong attachment, commitment, involvement, and belief insulate adolescents from delinquency. Conversely, adolescents who have weak or nonexistent attachments, commitments, involvement, and beliefs are more likely to be delinquent.

Hirschi (1995) explained the elements of the bond to society. Before presenting a definition of attachment, Hirschi discussed the nature of adhering to norms and the connection of adhering to norms to attachment. An early sociologist stated that individuals are moral beings to the extent that they are social beings. Hirschi interpreted this contention to mean that individuals are moral beings to the extent that they have internalized the norms of society. *Norms*, by definition, mean that individuals adhere to the rules established by the group. So, if someone violates a norm, it means that this individual is acting contrary to the expectations of others. It also means that an individual who violates a norm is insensitive to the wishes of others and is free to deviate. The core of an individual internalizing norms rests with the degree to which the individual is attached to others. Hirschi approached attachment in this manner in order to avoid previous problems that theoreticians have had in operationalizing attachment. It does not suggest that a person's internal control or superego dissipates and reoccurs magically.

For instance, a married man has more restraints than a single man. If the married man is divorced, he doesn't lose his conscience and reacquires it when he remarries. In Hirschi's explanation, a married man's attachment is stronger when he has obligations for others and others are dependent upon him. In short, attachment is the degree to which a person is obligated to others and others are dependent upon him or her.

Commitment concerns the extent to which a person is willing to invest time, energy, and himself or herself in a particular activity. This activity could be getting an education, building up a business, or acquiring a reputation for honesty or virtue. The concept of commitment presupposes that society is organized in a manner so that the interests of individuals would be jeopardized by committing criminal acts. This includes not only what one has but what one hopes to acquire. Hence, ambitions and aspirations perform a significant role in generating conformity. An individual commits to a conventional line of action and as a result becomes committed to conformity (Hirschi, 1995).

Involvement in conventional activities is a much-utilized concept in any control theory. Simply, a person who is involved in conventional activities has less opportunity to engage in deviant acts. Individuals who are involved in conventional activities are consumed by work, deadlines, appointments, plans, and tasks. By engaging in these conventional activities, these individuals do not have time to engage in deviant acts. Many individuals owe their upright statuses to a lack of opportunities to do differently. Time and energy are limited. This is the reason why some delinquency prevention programs accentuate adolescents' involvement in sports and recreational activities. Similarly, youths who were skirting trouble were, at one time, encouraged to join the Army (Hirschi, 1995).

Beliefs involve views held by individuals that influence participating in behaviors. The beliefs that unleash an individual to commit deviant acts are unmotivated. That is, an individual does not need to construct beliefs that support criminal acts. However, there are variations in beliefs. People vary in the extent to which they should conform to societal rules. There is a negative relationship between the extent to which someone believes that he or she should obey rules and the extent of engagement in deviant acts. For instance, societal rules forbid juveniles from possessing or consuming alcohol. The less a juvenile believes in this rule, the more likely he or she is actually going to consume alcohol (Hirschi, 1995).

The application of social bonding theory as a treatment intervention has been illustrated by school officials in South Carolina. The program was called Positive Action Through Holistic Education (PATHE), and its purpose was to prevent and reduce juvenile delinquency in several middle and high schools. PATHE sought to reduce delinquency by elevating students' conformity to society. Particularly, PATHE endeavors to strengthen students' commitment to school, success experiences in school, attachment to conforming members of the schools, and participation in school activities. By bolstering student's social competence, belonging, and usefulness, PATHE intended to promote the development of students positively or in a positive direction and away from delinquency (Siegel & Senna, 1991).

SYSTEM THEORY

Miller (1955) was the first person to articulate clearly a definition of general system theory. According to him, general system theory is a number of related definitions, assumptions, and postulates about all types of systems. These systems involve atomic particles, atoms, molecules, crystals, viruses, cells, organs, individuals, small groups, societies, planets, solar systems, and galaxies. Hearn (1979) took general system theory and reformulated it as system theory to explain the areas that concern social work, such as working with individuals, groups, organizations, and communities. Figure 3.4 illustrates the interrelation of the individual, family, and community. Each is a complete system, but each is also interrelated or connected to other systems.

Drawing from general system theory, Hearn explained the concepts that are important for understanding system theory. First, some systems are living and some are not. For instance, an individual constitutes a living system, but a planet is not. A system has an environment, which is everything external to a system. Systems have various degrees of entropy, which is the amount of disorganization in a system. Systems strive to maintain a condition known as a steady state or homoeostasis. Viewed in this manner, a system, when it has been disrupted, seeks to return to the state that existed before the disruption. Another important concept is that of *equifinality*, which refers to obtaining the same results from different initial conditions. For instance, skilled counselors may be developed from a person with an undergraduate degree in criminal justice and several years of experience, a person with a Master's degree in social work, a person with a Master's degree in counseling, or a person with Ph.D. in clinical psychology. The end is a skilled counselor, and there are a number of ways of reaching this end.

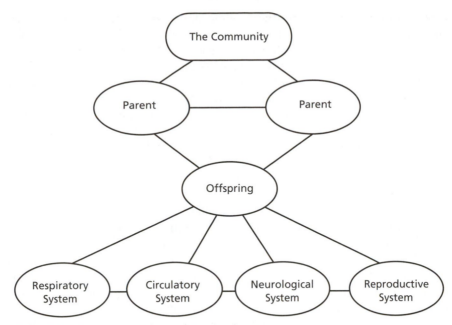

FIGURE 3.4 A Condensed Version of System Theory

A system may be opened or closed and, as a result, provide inputs or outputs. System theorist, taking from the field of physics, transported the concept of *holon*, which is a component that is simultaneously a whole and a part. Related to this principle is that every system, except for the smallest system, has subsystems. Another important concept is that of the *focal system*. It is the system that is of primary interest at the moment. According to Hearn, "a family may be identified as a focal system. If viewed as a holon, attention must be given both to its members and to its significant environments, such as schools, community, work organization, other families and the neighborhood. Merely to look at the interactions among family members (the family as a whole) ignores the functions of the family as part" (p. 336).

Hearn then distinguished between opened and closed systems. An opened system interchanges energy and information with its environment. An opened system, compared to a closed system, is self-regulatory. Opened systems operate as functional processes. This means that all parts of a system perform harmoniously so as to maintain the system in a steady state. Opened systems facilitate *feedback,* which is defined as a feature that adjusts future conduct by past performance, and feedback helps maintain a system's steady state.

Hearn summarized the system concepts that are used in assessing and intervening with various systems. The most prevalently adopted concepts are boundary definition and maintenance, feedback, open system, entropy, input-throughout-output, steady state, equifinality, interdependence, homeostasis, wholeness/holism, interrelatedness, holon, and synergy and environment.

As related above, a family is a system, and system theory has been used to provide a theoretical basis for family therapy. Because of the importance of treating some juvenile offenders within the family context (Fraser, Hawkins, & Howard, 1988; Lord & Barnes, 1996) and because some offenders are ordered into treatment along with their families (Michaels & Green, 1979; Sutphen, Thyer, & Kurtz, 1995), the following section describes family system theory and its use in treatment.

A contemporary family consists of many arrangements. These arrangements consist of nuclear family (i.e., a family that consists of only parents and unmarried children), single-parent families (i.e., a family of one parent and one or more children), a common-law relationship (i.e., a man and a woman who live together with or without children), a reconstituted family (i.e., a husband and wife with children from a previous marriage by one of the spouses), a blended family (i.e., a husband and wife who are not married with children from one or both of the spouses), an extended family (i.e., parents, unmarried children, and other relatives, such as uncles, aunts, and grandparents), a consanguine family (i.e., a family organized around blood relatives, such as several sisters or brothers living together), a conjugal family (i.e., a family consisting of just a husband and wife), and same-sex couples with or without children.

Each family, regardless of its type, provides various instrumental and expressive functions for each member, such as socialization, safety, procreation, care, and social support. According to Anreae (1996), "the family system represents a subsystem of the larger community of which the following assumptions may be made" (p. 606): (a) the whole is greater than the sum of its part; (b) modifying one system will lead to changes in other systems; (c) over a period of time, families organize and evolve; (d) for the most part, families are opened systems, they receive information and exchange it with other family members and with outside systems, the degree of openness of a family differs according to circumstances and the life of the family;

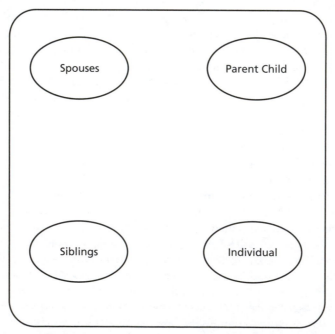

FIGURE 3.5 Systems Focus

(e) individual dysfunction emanates from an active emotional system. Often, a symptom in one member diverts attention from another part of the system.

A nuclear family system involves four major subsystems, including (1) spouses or couples; (2) parent-child; (3) siblings; and (4) the individual (Andreae, 1996). A counselor would have four different systems in which to intervene, shown in Figure 3.5. As an illustration, take an adolescent who has been adjudicated delinquent for sexual molestation of a relative and has been ordered into treatment, along with the adolescent's family. Following an assessment, a counselor could focus on just the adolescent, the siblings, the parents, one parent and the adolescent, or the family as a whole.

REALITY THERAPY

Glasser contended that individuals who exhibit various problems share two common characteristics. A man who claims to be Jesus Christ, a woman with incapacitating migraine headaches, a disruptive student in class, a bus driver who acts irrationally by driving a bus with passengers sixty miles in the opposite direction from a planned route, and a juvenile in reform school all are unable to fill their needs. The severity of their problems is negatively associated with the degree to which an individual meets his or her needs. In other words, the less a person is able to fulfill his or her needs, the more severe is the problem the person has.

A second common characteristic is that they all deny the reality around them. For instance, offenders break the law while denying the rules of society. Substance abusers use chemicals to obliterate the inadequacies they feel. However, using substances would not need to happen provided they had learned to behave differently with respect to their problems. Some individuals choose suicide rather than face the reality that they could solve the problems that made them suicidal. According to Glasser, "therapy will be successful when they [the above individuals] are able to give up denying the world and recognize that reality not only exists but that they must fulfill their needs within its framework. A therapy that leads all patients toward reality, toward grappling successfully with the tangible or intangible aspects of the real world, might accurately be called a therapy toward reality, or simply Reality Therapy" (Glasser, 1965, p. 6).

Reality therapy involves more than just helping an individual to face reality. Somehow, an individual must learn to fulfill his or her needs. Filling one's needs requires that an individual be involved with at least one other person. At all times, a person must have at least one other individual, or preferably individuals, who are about that person and vice versa. If a person does not have this critical individual or individuals, he or she will not be able to fulfill basic needs. This relationship may be as a parent is to a child or a teacher to a student; however, it does not need to be this intimate or physically close. A distant relationship is suitable as long as each knows of the other and equally cares. The only requirement is that this other person or persons must be in touch with reality and able to fulfill their needs (Glasser, 1965).

What are these needs? All humans have the same physiological and psychological needs. Psychiatry is concerned primarily with two psychological needs. These are "the need to love and be loved and the need to feel that we are worthwhile to ourselves and to others" (Glasser, 1965, p. 9). The aim of reality therapy is to help individuals fulfill these two needs. Although all individuals have these two needs, they vary in the extent to which they can fulfill these needs. In all society, individuals exist in which their psychological needs are not satisfied. They are unable to love or be loved, and they have no, or little, sense of worth to themselves or others. In different ways, these individuals present themselves to the helping profession and social control agencies. These social control agencies, because of the problematic behaviors exemplified by the lack of being able to fulfill these two needs, place some individuals in psychiatric or correctional institutions (Glasser, 1965).

Learning to fulfill one's needs is an ongoing process because of changes in one's condition and environment. Learning to fulfill one's needs must start in infancy and continue to late adulthood or death. If individuals do not learn to love in childhood, they will seek unrealistic means as adults to fulfill their needs. For instance, a person who has lost a significant other must find a way to fulfill his or her needs for love. If this person does not fulfill this need adequately, problems will result, such as depression or promiscuity (Glasser, 1965).

To feel worthwhile, an individual must sustain a satisfactory standard of behavior. To do so, an individual must learn to correct himself or herself when wrongs are done, and to acknowledge when rights are done. If an individual does not evaluate his or her behavior, or, having made an evaluation, does nothing to correct negative behavior, he or she will not fulfill the need to feel worthwhile. When individuals do not fulfill one or both needs, they feel pain or discomfort (Glasser, 1965).

Responsibility, another important concept in reality therapy, is the ability to fulfill one's needs in a manner that does not interfere with others from fulfilling their needs. A responsible individual can give and receive love. If a woman falls in love with a man and conveys her love to him, he, as a responsible person, should reciprocate that love or tell her sensitively that he does not feel that way and probably would never feel that way. However, if he uses her love to take advantage of her, then he is not a responsible person. In addition, a responsible person does that which gives him or her a feeling of self-worth and a feeling that he or she is worthwhile to others. A responsible person does what he or she promises to another person both to show respect for that person and to acquire or maintain self-respect. An irresponsible person may or may not do what he or she promises. It depends on how he or she feels, the amount of effort required, and what is in it for him or her. This person gains neither respect for himself or herself nor respect for others. Eventually, the irresponsible person will suffer or cause others to suffer. Reality therapy concerns those who have lost or have not learned to be responsible, such as persons in mental hospitals and prisons (Glasser, 1965).

According to Glasser (1965), reality therapy involves three separate but interrelated procedures. The first is involvement between the reality therapist and the client. The therapist must become involved with the client so that the client begins to face reality and to see how unpractical the dysfunctional behavior is. Second, the therapist must reject the dysfunctional behavior, while accepting the client and maintaining involvement with the client. Third, the therapist must teach appropriate ways for the client to meet his or her needs functionally (Glasser, 1965).

Involvement between a counselor and client in reality therapy is difficult because some clients, such as offenders, do not want counseling or some, such as patients in a mental institution, do not know they are in counseling. Compounding this difficulty is the necessity of getting involved with a person in a relatively short period of time. Glasser attempts to define this involvement by describing the qualities that the reality therapist counselor must have (Glasser, 1965).

The reality therapist must be a very responsible person, showing toughness, humaneness, sensitivity, and interest. Also, the therapist must be able to fulfill his or her own needs and evidence a willingness to discuss some of his or her own personal struggles. This will show the client that, though difficult, behaving responsibly is possible. The reality therapist must have the capacity to have his or her values tested by the client and to endure extreme criticism by the client. This shows the client that even during an intense attack a person still can act responsibly.

The reality therapist must reject irresponsible behavior but always accept the client. This requirement involves politely rejecting a client's pleas for sympathy and justification for inappropriate and irresponsible behaviors. Thus, a reality therapist must be strong—strong in his or her personal life and strong in his or her refusal to accept the client's excuses for inappropriate behavior. Glasser illustrated this principle of rejecting irresponsible behavior while accepting the client by retelling the story of "The Miracle Worker." In this story, Helen Keller, visually and hearing impaired, ate by walking around the dinner table and taking food from others' plates. Ann Sullivan refused to allow Helen to eat from her plate and rejected the family's pleas to have pity on Helen. Ann Sullivan insisted that Helen learned responsible table manners. Ann Sullivan accepted Helen Keller as a person but rejected her table manners and other irresponsible behaviors (Glasser, 1965).

When the client acknowledges that his or her behaviors are irresponsible, the last stage of reality therapy begins. In fact, no readily discernible change in treatment occurs. Relearning is merged into the whole process. The client must depend on the counselor's knowledge and experience in learning appropriate behaviors. As stated by Glasser (1965), "when the young delinquent learns the value of working and experiences the good feelings that accompany responsible action, therapy is approaching an end. It is only a matter of time until the patient, with his [or her] newly acquired responsible behavior, begins to fulfill his [or her] needs. He [or she] finds new relationships, more satisfying involvement, and needs the therapist less" (p. 33).

Glasser (1965) described his use of reality therapy for seriously delinquent females at the Ventura School for Girls in California. Because of the emphasis on offenders taking responsibility for the behaviors, other criminal justice professionals have endorsed reality therapy as appropriate for offenders and preferable to other psychotherapies (Cavior & Schmidt, 1978; Reed & Tachman, 1979). For instance, Czajkoski (1976) wrote that reality therapy was appropriate for corrections because most offenders are lacking in educational skills, unsophisticated, and inarticulate. As a result, they are unable to deal with psychotherapies that rely on good verbal abilities and the aptitude to comprehend abstractions and symbolic behaviors. Reality therapy has been used with drug abusers because of its emphasis on personal responsibility, rejection of mental illness as an excuse for acting out behavior, involvement, problem solving, love, and the growth of self-worth (Bassin, 1976a; Bassin, 1976b; Bratter, 1976). It had been adopted by the Florida Division of Youth Service (Bassin, 1976a), and when the rehabilitation was a philosophy of the Federal Bureau of Prisons, reality therapy was the preferred treatment approach.

Currently, reality therapy, along with other treatment modalities, has been stated to be highly appropriate for sex offenders (Marsh & Walsh, 1995). It has been used with juvenile delinquents in a wilderness environment (Clagett, 1992a). Internationally, reality therapy has been used with drug addicted persons in India (Surati, 1989) and adult felons in Israel (Cohen & Sordo, 1984).

APPLICABILITY OF AFOREMENTIONED THEORIES TO INDIVIDUAL AND GROUP COUNSELING

Rose (1977) stated that "almost all problems amenable to individual therapy also can be dealt with in a group since the majority of such problems have interactive components" (p. 3). Rose's statement suggests that individuals are social beings and, as such, they interact with others. This conclusion is the basis for sociological thinking, which indicates that behavior is social in nature. However, some theories are applicable for some treatment approaches, and some theories are more applicable for a particular approach.

According to cognitive theorists, cognitive–behavioral therapy can be used in individual or group counseling (Courchaine & Dowd, 1994; Kaplan & Sadock, 1991; Kaminer & Bukstein, 1992; Michelson, 1987; Prinz, 1995). Ludgate, Wright, Bowers, and Camp (1993) discussed the use of individual counseling with inpatients. They noted that the complete range of techniques used in cognitive therapy are available for inpatients in individual counseling, including guided discovery (Socratic questioning), identification of cognitive errors, recognition and change of automatic thoughts, schema modification, activity scheduling, graded-task assignments, and homework. However, they cautioned that some adaptation must be done for inpatients, especially those in hospitals for depression or anxiety disorders.

Schrodt (1993) stated that assessments must be done before treating adolescents in individual counseling. A number of assessment tools are available to help in assessing intellectual functioning, learning disabilities, attention span, level of cognitive maturity, personality characteristics, impulse control, and reality testing. If no standardized tests are utilized, a professional assessment should be made at least of the adolescent's cognitive abilities. With adolescents, the common dysfunctions are their attitudes that adults pester them, a fierce need for approval from peers, and a lack of commitment to anything except sex, drugs, and music. In addition, adolescents have a farfetched belief about their ability to be independent, which makes collaboration with a counselor difficult. Accordingly, a number of standard objectives should be established, which includes the creation of a collaborate relationship, keeping a problem-oriented approach, the identification of negative automatic thoughts and their relationship to dysphoric mood and maladaptive behavior, recognition of cognitive errors, experimentation with distorted automatic thoughts and underlying assumptions, alteration of self-defeating cognitive style and substituting them with practical and adaptive viewpoint, improvement of the adolescent's sense of self-efficacy by developing social skills and problem-solving competencies, development of strategies to prevent relapse, and a plan of therapeutic self-help tasks between individual sessions (Schrodt, 1993).

In terms of group counseling, a number of issues exist that must be recognized by the cognitive–behavioral group counselor. These include the group selection, length and frequency of group sessions, location and setting, therapist staffing, here-and-now focus, and pace of the group stages. Some individuals may not be appropriate for the group, such as persons with organic brain syndromes; persons with acute psychosis; and persons with extreme, disruptive personality disorders. Among the techniques found to be beneficial in groups are tasks that help to identify automatic thoughts, graded-task assignments, rehearsal, and listing advantages and disadvantages or alternatives for dysfunctional behaviors (Freeman, Schrodt, Gilson, & Ludgate, 1993).

Pure psychoanalytic theory or therapy, the uncovering of tensions among the id, ego, and superego, is more applicable for individual counseling. But most of the other theories discussed in this chapter are suitable for individual or group counseling as Rose suggested. For instance, reality therapy is appropriate for group or individual counseling. Clagett (1992b) discussed the functions of reality therapy in a group setting in a wilderness program for delinquent boys in Apple Springs, Texas.

The author had the pleasure of working as a counselor in the program discussed by Clagett. All the counselors were trained in use of reality therapy and instructed to use this modality in working with the boys. The wilderness program was developed to use reality therapy within a group setting. It used the dynamics of the group, such as group pressure, to help lead the boys toward responsible behaviors. At the same time, counselors had numerous opportunities to counsel boys on a one-on-one basis, such as walking with a boy from a campsite to the main office or transporting a boy to a doctor in a nearby town. Repeatedly, the boy would be urged to take responsibility for his behavior; not to blame others, such as parents; and to collaborate on a plan for responsible behaviors in the future.

Another manner in viewing the issue of the applicability of specific theories for individual and group counseling is to perceive the issue as involving micro or macro intervention strategies. A micro intervention strategy means that intervention is geared toward the individual and a macro intervention strategy is geared more toward a societal intervention. Perceived from this perspective, social bonding theory is geared more toward a macro intervention strategy rather than a micro strategy. For instance, a school system, to prevent juvenile delinquency among its students, may employ social bonding theory and its concepts to intervene with the entire student body. Emphasis would be put on strengthening students' bonds to society by increasing their commitment, involvement, belief, and attachment to the conventional social order.

Table 3.5 depicts each of the theories or therapies and whether it is most appropriate for individual, group, or equally suitable for individual or group counseling. Exceptions, of course, may be taken for some of the designations, such as system theory, which could be the basis for individual or group counseling. However, system theory seems more appropriate for family counseling. Other arguments may be made for other designations, but this table is only a guideline.

Table 3.5 Suitability of Theories to Counseling Modality

Individual	Group	Individual & Group
Psychoanalytic	Social Bonding	Cognitive–Behavioral
Behavioral	System theory	Rational Emotive
		Radical Cognitive
		Feminist
		Behavioral Modification
		Logotherapy
		Reality Therapy

SUMMARY

This chapter discussed ten theories that provide treatment techniques for counseling offenders. Considerable attention was given to cognitive–behavioral therapy, which included a feminist version of cognitive–behavioral therapy. This theory essentially emphasizes the importance of individuals' cognition in creating and maintaining dysfunctional behavior. Numerous examples were provided to illustrate various cognitive techniques used to treat irrational or counterproductive behavior. The feminist version of cognitive–behavioral therapy disdains the use of pejorative words, such as irrational behaviors, because they suggest that women are crazy. This chapter then discussed behavior therapy and behavior modification, discussing the roots of each and techniques that may be used from each therapy. A brief discussion was provided of psychoanalytic therapy and its contributions to counseling in general. Logotherapy was discussed and its applicability for long-term prisoners highlighted. Afrocentric theory was described, which included a discussion of the Afrocentric worldview. This chapter provided a discussion of feminist theory, three perspectives of feminist theory, and its use in assessing and treating women's problems. Next was discussed social bonding theory and how this theory may be used to prevent juvenile delinquency. System theory was described and its use in providing a framework for family therapy. Reality therapy was described and its use in corrections noted. Finally, this chapter discussed whether a particular theory was most appropriate for individual counseling, group counseling, or equally or individual and group counseling.

KEY TERMS

Beliefs

Automatic thoughts

Cognitive distortions

Stimulus

Cognition

RCS model

Reinforcement

Contingency

Behavior therapy
    techniques

Social skills training

Will to meaning

Belief system analysis

Developmental stages
    and counseling focus

Steady state

Boundary

Focal system

4

❊ ❊ ❊

Screening, Assessment, and Diagnosis in Correctional Treatment

❊ INTRODUCTION

Logically comparing the need for assessment for a medical problem, Crowe and Reeves (1994) parallel that need with the need for assessment for individuals with alcohol and drug problems. For instance, in a medical situation, two individuals may go to a doctor complaining of pain in their elbows. Obviously, this pain could be caused by a number of medical conditions, such as a broken bone, an infected wound, arthritis, cancer of the bone marrow, cardiovascular disease, and so on. Detailed questions would need to be asked by the doctor, such as how and when the pain started, how badly it hurts, how long the pain has existed, the exact location of the pain, and other physical symptoms. Tests will need to be conducted, and perhaps a referral to a specialist will be needed. When all the information is gathered, a diagnosis is made and a treatment plan is devised. Each person may have a different treatment plan because the cause of the pain may be different. One may get a pre-scription for Tylenol, and the other may get an arm cast (Crowe & Reeves, 1994).

In substance abuse cases, screening, assessment, and diagnosis are also important to develop the most appropriate treatment plan (Crowe & Reeves, 1994). Likewise, the same is true for offenders who present different problems, such as substance abuse, mental disorders, developmental disability, violence, or sexual offending. Screening and assessment are needed to determine the cause of the offending and the most appropriate treatment needs.

Subscribing to this view, twenty members of the House of Representatives of Ohio introduced a bill requiring both the Ohio Department of Rehabilitation and Correction and the Ohio Department of Youth Services to maintain Multifactored Assessment Programs (MAP) for covered inmates and felony delinquents, begin-ning one year after the offender begins his or her sentence. All inmates would be covered unless they have death sentences. The objectives of MAP are to promote, to the extent practicable, the rehabilitation of covered inmates and to provide, to the extent practicable, each covered inmate with an opportunity to acquire an ed-ucation, vocational training, employment skills, social skills, psychological or psy-chiatric care, and substance abuse education or treatment. The primary objective is to permit the inmate to live as a productive, socially adjusted, physically and men-tally healthy, and law-abiding citizen when the inmate is released from confinement (Ohio Legislative Service Commission, 1999).

To achieve this goal, conducting a multifactored assessment is mandated. It con-sists of four types of evaluation: (1) an evaluation of the general intelligence of the inmate, the educational level, vocational training, employment history, and the need for additional educational, vocational training, or employment skills in order to help the offender become a productive, socially adjusted, physically and mentally healthy, and law-abiding citizen upon release from confinement; (2) a sociological, psychological, and psychiatric evaluation of the inmate, including, but not limited to, an evaluation of the inmate's adaptive behavior, a determination of the inmate's need to receive social skills training or psychological or psychiatric treatment, and a determination as to whether the inmate is a developmentally disabled person, a mentally retarded person, a person who is at least moderately mentally retarded, or a person who has a mental illness; (3) an evaluation of other aspects of the inmate's physical and mental health that are not covered by the evaluation described above. Such an evaluation would include whether an inmate is deaf, hard of hearing, or-thopedically handicapped, speech handicapped, visually impaired, or drug depen-dent; (4) any other evaluation that either the director of the department of rehabilitation and correction or the director of the department of youth services would consider necessary to achieve the objectives of the Multifactored Assessment Plan (Ohio Legislative Service Commission, 1999).

CRIMINAL JUSTICE INTERVIEWING

To gather some of the information for these various assessments, basic inter-viewing of offenders needs to be conducted. For criminal justice clients, Shearer (1993) recounts seven primary interviewing skills: empathy, speed and pacing, summarization, concreteness, immediacy, confrontation, and assertion. Shearer acknowledges that these seven skills do not represent the total number of skills needed in criminal justice interviewing, but they represent the foundation skills that criminal justice practitioners can build on thorough staff training and development.

Empathy is the most important of the seven skills in an interviewing training model. It consists of accurately conveying to a client the interviewer's understanding of the client's feelings, experience, and behavior. This means that the interviewer is empathic with what the criminal justice client is saying, not with the client's crime, personality, or identity.

Speed and pacing involve controlling an interview to avoid participants taking ritualized turns in speaking. Shearer states that often an undesired pattern of conversing between two individuals occurs, which resembles a Ping-Pong game. One person speaks, then the other person speaks, then back to the first speaker, then the second person speaks, and then back to the first person, and so on. The problem with such an exchange is that it prevents natural silence from occurring. Permitting silence is an important part of not only interviewing but also counseling. Silence is not bad. A skillful interview does not have to be filled with nonstop questions and answers. A good criminal justice interview permits silence. Shearer, using an x to represent the criminal justice client, a y to represent the criminal justice interviewer, and a *straight line* to indicate silence, depicts a pattern reflective of a controlled interview.

XY_____XXYX
XYXXX_____XX_____XX_____YXYX

By contrast, a poor interview is reflective by the following:

XYXYXYXYXYXYXYXYXYXYXYXYXYXYXYXYXYXYXYXYXYXYXYXYXYXY

Summarization, appropriately and timely made, reinforces empathy and controls the speed and pace of an interview. A *summary* is simply the emphasizing of key points and aspects of a client's information. It is offered to the client to confirm or correct. As an illustration, the criminal justice interviewer may say, "What I hear you saying is that you didn't start using drugs until after your car accident and before your wife left you and took the children. Is that correct?"

Concreteness consists of conducting an interview that elicits precise, exact, and specific information. A client saying that he or she is "doing fairly well" is too vague and inadequate of information to document or relate to professional colleagues. An interviewer should ask open-ended questions that start with *what, when, how, how much, where,* and *how often* to elicit concrete information. For instance, a criminal justice interviewer will ask what you mean by "doing fairly well."

Immediacy involves the criminal justice interviewer being aware of himself or herself as well as the relationship between the interviewer and the criminal justice client. Shearer asserts that

immediacy skills are used when an interview situation needs to stay in the here-and-now, or present moment experiencing. Immediacy is particularly necessary when an interviewee persists in talking about past or future feelings or experiences. Specifically, they dwell on what they have accomplished or are going to accomplish with few references to the present. Immediacy is also called for when interviewers see that they or the interviewee has *nonverbalized* thoughts and feelings about what is taking place in the interview that are getting in the way. (Shearer, 1993, p. 117)

Confrontation is a skill needed in criminal justice interviews because frequently offenders are inconsistent, incongruent, dishonest, guarded, and untruthful. Confrontation is needed to point out discrepancies in the offender's information, and it is needed when an offender engages in denial, distortions, lying, unawareness, baiting, evasions, and games and tricks. Confrontation is critical in highlighting these aforementioned problems. Though it is needed, confrontation should be used cautiously and skillfully because some offenders are aggressive. For instance, it may not be wise to call an offender a liar or state that he or she is not telling the truth. Instead, the criminal justice interviewer can calmly invite the client to explain or give a reason for the discrepancy between the offender's information and other information. It is quite possible too that an offender's version of an event is true and law enforcement is incorrect.

Assertion skills represent the last resort in an interview. They do not represent facilitative skills, such as the previously described six skills. Instead, assertion skills involve the necessity to assert and define the criminal justice interviewer's adherence to personal and professional goals, responsibilities, and limitations. With involuntary clients, such as offenders, assertion skills are important. An interviewer may need to convey firmness and directness with offenders. Not doing so may lead some offenders to perceive the interviewers as gullible, easy, and manipulable. However, demonstrating assertion does not mean being aggressive or flaunting one's professional power.

MOTIVATIONAL INTERVIEWING

Shearer provides the basics of criminal justice interviewing. However, interviewing substance abuse offenders requires motivating them and increasing their readiness to change (Gavin, Sobell, & Sobell, 1998; Isenhart & Krevelen, 1998). This type of process is called *motivational interviewing* and is defined as a directive, individual-focused counseling style that is designed to help an addictive person or offender examine and eliminate ambivalence about making behavioral change (Rollnick & Morgan, 1995). Underlying motivational interviewing are several core principles. First, a counselor should demonstrate empathy with the offender. This is accomplished by listening to the client nonjudgmentally and displaying that the offender's perspective is understood. Second, the counselor should highlight discrepancies between the offender's stated goals and current behavior. Third, the counselor should avoid arguing with the offender. Fourth, the counselor should lessen resistance by reframing the offender's hostile statements. Fifth, the counselor should support self-efficacy on the offender's part because it is a foundation for a positive outcome (Miller & Rollnick, 1991).

DIAGNOSTIC GUIDES

Making a professional diagnosis, as the above medical example involving pain in the elbow illustrates, follows interviewing and assessing a person's problems and situation. A universal guide for making mental health diagnoses is the *Diagnostic and Statistical Manual of Mental Disorders*, 4th Edition (DSM-IV) (1994). This source and related sources are discussed next because the assessment discussion includes many concepts and diagnoses from the DSM-IV. For instance, dual diagnosis involves a mental disorder, such as antisocial personality disorder and substance abuse disorder. Before discussing assessing such a dual diagnosis, a description should precede that describes what these diagnoses are and the different types. Readers should keep in mind that a diagnosis follows the assessment; however, a clinician may make a tentative diagnosis and use the assessment to confirm or disconfirm the diagnosis.

Diagnostic and Statistical Manual of Mental Disorders

Realizing the need for a classification system for mental disorders, the American Psychiatric Association in 1952 published its first volume, the DSM-I, to provide clinicians with an assessment guide and universal nomenclature for research purposes (American Psychiatric Association, 1994). Later, in a cautionary statement, the American Psychiatric Association warned readers that the purpose of the DSM-IV is "to provide descriptions of diagnostic categories in order to enable clinicians and investigators to diagnose, communicate about, study, and treat people with various mental disorders" (American Psychiatric Association, 1994, p. xxvii).

While some lay persons may believe that offenders are mentally ill or have mental disorders, this conclusion may or may not be warranted. The DSM-IV has defined what a mental disorder is and is not. Particularly, each mental disorder in the DSM-IV is "a clinically significant behavioral or psychological syndrome or pattern that occurs in an individual and that is associated with present distress (e.g., a painful symptom) or disability (i.e., impairment in one or more important areas of functioning) or with a significantly increased risk of suffering death, pain, disability, or an important loss of freedom" (American Psychiatric Association, 1994, p. xxi). However, the syndrome or pattern cannot be a cultural or normal response to an incident, such as the death of parent or child. But whatever the initial source of an individual's distress, when seen by a mental health professional, the individual must show current manifestations of a behavioral, biological, or psychological functioning (American Psychiatric Association, 1994).

Equally important, deviant behavior or conflicts between an individual and society, such as the refusal to pay taxes, do not constitute having a mental disorder unless the source of such behavior occurs as a result of psychological, biological, or behavioral dysfunction. Given this definition, an offender who steals may not have a mental disorder, but another offender who steals may. Critical to this determination is the expertise of the mental health professional. Although the criteria for diagnoses are quite clear, the DSM-IV should not be used in a cookbook fashion. It is a supplemental tool to aid clinicians in their judgments. In effect, a particular individual may not quite meet all the criteria for a diagnosis, but the clinician, using his or her experience, training, and judgment, can be justified in applying such a diagnosis (American Psychiatric Association, 1994).

Assessments and diagnoses may be made within a multiaxial system. *Axis I* involves Clinical Disorders and Other Conditions That May Be a Focus of Clinical Attention, *Axis II* involves Personality Disorders and Mental Retardation, *Axis III* involves General Medical Conditions, *Axis IV* involves Psychosocial and Environmental Problems, and *Axis V* involves Global Assessment of Functioning. Each axis refers to a different domain that may assist a clinician in planning treatment and prediction outcome. It is a beneficial manner of organizing and communicating clinical information, for encapsulating the complexity of clinical problems, and for picturing the heterogeneity of individuals with the same diagnosis (Hales, Yudofsky & Talbott, 1994).

In the offender population, a number of mental disorders are present more than other mental disorders, such as substance-related disorders, which are quite abundant, and sleep disorders, which may be rarer. Other disorders found in corrections are schizophrenia and other psychotic disorders, mood disorders, anxiety disorders, and mental retardation. For the older offender population, dementia may be an issue. Within the juvenile population, one might find childhood disorders, such as attention-deficit/hyperactivity disorder, but conduct disorder and oppositional defiant disorder are probably the most prevalent. Each diagnosis may be designated as mild, moderate, or severe. The disorders listed below reflect several of the most common disorders found in offenders (reprinted with permission from the *Diagnostic and Statistical Manual of Mental Disorders, Fourth Edition*. Copyright 1994 American Psychiatric Association). Among juvenile offenders two disorders are presented—conduct disorder and oppositional defiant disorder

Conduct Disorder

A. A repetitive and persistent pattern of behavior in which the basic rights of others or major age-appropriate societal norms or rules are violated, as manifested by the presence of three (or more) of the following criteria in the past twelve months, with at least one criterion present in the past six months.

Aggression to People and Animals
1. Often bullies, threatens, or intimidates others
2. Often initiates physical fights
3. Has used a weapon that can cause serious physical harm to others (e.g., a bat, brick, broken bottle, knife, gun)
4. Has been physically cruel to people
5. Has been physically cruel to animals
6. Has stolen while confronting a victim (e.g., mugging, purse-snatching, extortion, armed robbery)
7. Has forced someone into sexual activity

Destruction of Property
1. Has deliberately engaged in firesetting with the intention of causing serious damage
2. Has deliberately destroyed others' property (other than by fire setting)

Deceitfulness or Theft
1. Has broken into someone else's house, building, or car
2. Often lies to obtain goods or favors or to avoid obligations (i.e., "cons" others)
3. Has stolen items of nontrivial values without confronting a victim (e.g., shoplifting, but without breaking and entering, forgery)

Serious Violations of Rules
1. Often stays out at night despite parental prohibitions, beginning before age thirteen years
2. Has run away from home overnight at least twice while living in parental or parental surrogate home (or once without returning for a lengthy period)

3. Is often truant from school, beginning before age thirteen years
B. The disturbance in behavior causes clinically significant impairment in social, academic, or occupational functioning.
C. If the individual is age eighteen years or older, criteria are not met for antisocial personality disorder.

Depending upon the age of the first onset, one of two types is distinguished. If at least one criterion occurred prior to age ten years, it is childhood-onset type. If none of the characteristics occurred prior to age ten years, then it is adolescent-onset type.

Oppositional Defiant Disorder A diagnosis of oppositional defiant disorder requires that an adolescent show:

A. A pattern of negativistic, hostile, and defiant behavior lasting at least six months, during which four (or more) of the following are present:
   1. Often loses temper
   2. Often argues with adults
   3. Often actively defies or refuses to comply with adults' requests or rules
   4. Often deliberately annoys people
   5. Often blames others for his or her mistakes or misbehavior
   6. Is often touchy or easily annoyed by others
   7. Is often angry and resentful
   8. Is often spiteful or vindictive

A clinician should accept that a criterion is met if an adolescent seems to engage in a behavior more than adolescents of comparable age and developmental level.

B. The disturbance in behavior causes significant impairment in social, academic, or occupational functioning.
C. The behaviors do not occur exclusively during the course of a psychotic or mood disorder.
D. Criteria are not met for conduct disorder and, if individual is age eighteen years or older, criteria are not met for antisocial personality disorder.

Substance abuse may be diagnosed in juvenile and adult offenders. Among the substance-related disorders are alcohol-related disorders, amphetamine-related disorders, caffeine-related disorders, cannabis-related disorders, cocaine-related disorders, hallucinogen-related disorders, inhalant-related disorders, nicotine-related disorders, opioid-induced disorders, and phencyclidine-related disorders. Because of the presence of substance abuse in the offender population, the factors related to substance abuse and dependence, according to the DSM-IV, are presented. A diagnosis of substance abuse requires that an individual manifest the following:

A. A maladaptive pattern of substance use leading to clinically significant impairment or distress, as manifested by one (or more) of the following occurring within a twelve-month period:

1. Recurrent substance use resulting in a failure to fulfill major role obligations at work, school, or home (e.g., repeated absence or poor work performance related to substance use; substance-related absences, suspensions, or expulsion from school; neglect of children or household)
2. Recurrent substance use in situations in which it is physically hazardous (e.g. driving an automobile or operating a machine when impaired by substance use)
3. Recurrent substance-related legal problems (e.g., arrests for substance-related disorderly conduct)
4. Continued substance use despite having persistent or recurrent social or interpersonal problems caused or exacerbated by the effects of the substance (e.g., arguments with spouse about consequences of intoxication, physical fights)

B. The symptoms have never met the criteria for substance dependence for this class of substance (American Psychiatric Association, 1994).

For a diagnosis of substance dependence, a person must manifest a maladaptive pattern of substance use, leading to clinically significant impairment or distress, as manifested by three (or more) of the following, occurring at any time in the same twelve-month period:

A. Tolerance, as defined by either of the following:
   1. A need for markedly increased amounts of the substance to achieve intoxication or desired effect
   2. Markedly diminished effect with continued use of the same amount of the substance
B. Withdrawal, as manifested by either of the following:
   a. The characteristic withdrawal syndrome for the substance occurs (refer to criteria A and B of the criteria sets for withdrawal from the specific substance).
   b. The same (or closely related) substance is taken to relieve or avoid withdrawal symptoms.
   c. The substance is often taken in larger amounts or over a longer period than was intended.
   d. There is a persistent desire or unsuccessful efforts to cut down or control substance use.
   e. A great deal of time is spent in activities necessary to obtain the substance (e.g., visiting multiple doctors or driving long distances, use the substance (e.g., chain-smoking), or recover from its effects.
   f. Important social, occupational, or recreational activities are given up or reduced because of substance use.
   g. The substance is continued despite knowledge of having a persistent or recurrent physical or psychological problem that is likely to have been caused or exacerbated by the substance (e.g., current cocaine use despite recognition of cocaine-induced depression, or continued drinking despite recognition that an ulcer was made worse by alcohol consumption) (American Psychiatric Association, 1994).

Criminal justice policy-makers, here and abroad, have documented the high proportion of offenders with substance abuse disorders (Brochu, Guyon, & Desjardins, 1999; Bureau of Justice Statistics, 1997). The Ross Correctional Institution in Chillicothe, Ohio, developed a long-term residential substance abuse program for offenders, and it assessed the extent and frequency of all the categories of substance abuse described above (Alexander, 1998).

Another category that is quite prevalent in the adult correctional population is personality disorders. Among the diagnoses are paranoid personality disorder, schizoid personality disorder, schizotypal personality disorder, antisocial personality disorder, borderline personality disorder, histrionic personality disorder, narcissistic personality disorders, avoidant personality disorder, dependent personality disorder, obsessive-compulsive personality disorder, and personality disorder not otherwise specified. Within this group, antisocial personality disorders probably are the most prevalent in correction (Meloy, 1996). For instance, one study found that 65% of prisoners in a prison methadone program had diagnosis of antisocial personality disorder (Darke, Kaye, & Findlay-Jones, 1998), and another study found that 66% of a cohort of prisoners had antisocial personality disorder (Hodgins & Cote, 1993).

The criteria for antisocial personality disorder are

A. There is a pervasive pattern of disregard for and violation of the rights of others occurring since age fifteen years, as indicated by three (or more) of the following:
   1. Failure to conform to social norms with respect to lawful behaviors as indicated by repeatedly performing acts that are grounds for arrest
   2. Deceitfulness, as indicated by repeated lying, uses of aliases, or conning others for personal profit or pleasure
   3. Impulsivity or failure to plan ahead
   4. Irritability and aggressiveness, as indicated by repeated physical fights or assaults
   5. Reckless disregard or safety of self or others
   6. Consistent irresponsibility, as indicate by repeated failure to sustain consistent work behavior or honor financial obligations
   7. Lack of remorse, as indicated by being indifferent to or rationalizing having hurt, mistreated, or stolen from others
B. The individual is at least age eighteen years.
C. There is evidence of conduct disorder with onset before age fifteen years.
D. The occurrence of antisocial behavior is not exclusively during the course of schizophrenia or a manic episode.

Psychopathy

A concept that is sometimes interchanged with antisocial personality disorder, but is not correct, is psychopathy. According to Hare (1996), *psychopathy* is "a socially devastating disorder defined by a constellation of affective, interpersonal, behavioral characteristics, including egocentricity; impulsivity; irresponsibility; shallow emotions; lack of empathy, guilt, or remorse; pathological lying; manipulativeness; and the persistent violation of social norms and expectations" (p. 25). About 25% of prisoners are psychopaths, and these offenders tend to commit the most heinous crimes (Hare,

Strachan, & Forth, 1993). However, psychopaths are not found only in the criminal population, they also represent mercenaries, corrupt politicians, unethical lawyers, terrorists, cult leaders, black marketeers, and radical political activists (Hare, 1996).

Antisocial personality disorder focuses on behaviors, and psychopathy focuses on personality traits. Psychopathy is a psychological construct that consists of two factors. Factor 1 concerns affective/interpersonal aspects, and Factor 2 concerns impulsive, antisocial, unstable lifestyle, or social deviance. Most individuals with a diagnosis of antisocial personality disorder do not meet the criteria for psychopathy, whereas most individuals with a diagnosis of psychopathy meet the criteria for antisocial personality disorder. Factor 2 correlates with antisocial personality disorder but Factor 1 does not.

Assessment of psychopathy is important because it has been strongly linked to recidivism and treatment outcome. Referring to the latter, treatment has been found to make some psychopaths worse (Hare, 1996; Rice, 1997). To assess it, Hare developed the Psychopathy Checklist (PCL), which has been revised (PCL-R). This revised version is a twenty-item clinical rating scale involving a semistructured interview and information from case files. It has strong validity and high reliability. Each item is rated on a three-point scale, 0 to 2. Thus, the range of scores is 0 to 40. For research purposes, a score of 30 or more is considered to be an indication of psychopathy, but some researchers have used 25 as the cutoff score. Meloy (1988) groups the psychopathy scale into Mild Psychopathic Disturbance from 10-19, Moderate Psychopathic Disturbance from 20-29, and Severe Psychopathic Disturbance from 30-40. The PCL-R has been further modified to measure psychopathy in children, and it correlates well with adolescents who have been diagnosed as having conduct disorders (Frick, O'Brien, Wootton, & McBurnett, 1994).

Structured Clinical Interview for the DSM-IV (SCID)

Williams (1994) presents the use of the Structured Clinical Interview for the DSM-IV (SCID). The SCID is a schedule to help a clinician gather information to make Axis I and Axis II diagnoses. The clinician begins with the current illness and past instances of psychopathology. Then, the clinician explores whether the individual has had specific symptoms to rule in and out specific disorders. SCID has multiple versions for different settings and purposes. One version may be used for psychiatric inpatients, another for psychiatric outpatients, and another for persons not identified as psychiatric patients who are in the community. One version is used in the diagnosis of personality disorders; however, a supplemental questionnaire is given to the individual to complete prior to the interview.

Training Guides for the DSM-IV

A number of sources are available for clinicians working with persons with mental disorders. Reid and Wise (1995) have written a training guide for the DSM-IV. Among the areas covered are the Multiaxial Classification System, the Diagnostic Process, and Axis I through Axis V. Admonitions to clinicians not to use the DSM-IV as a cookbook suggest that the DSM-IV is "a dry book that cannot begin to capture the complexity of dealing with human lives and problems" (Frances & Ross, 1996, p. xi). For this reason, clinicians have developed casebooks based on the DSM-IV. Francis and Ross describe the process of differential diagnosis and indicate that that the process consists of the evaluation of six steps.

First, the clinician should rule out substance-related etiology because substance abuse may produce symptoms of psychopathology. This requires that a careful history be taken and may involve medical testing to determine whether substances are present in the body. If a substance is determined to be in the body, the clinician must determine the nature of the relationship between the symptom and the substance. Important is the temporal sequence of the substance and symptoms. Among the questions that need to be asked is whether the substance abuse occurred before the symptoms or vice versa.

Second, the clinician should rule out medical conditions. Just as substance abuse can produce psychopathology, a medical condition may also. Determining whether there is a medical basis for psychopathology can be difficult because some medical conditions, such as Parkinson disease, produce similar symptoms. General medical conditions, by their effect on the central nervous system, can cause psychiatric symptoms. They can also cause symptoms such as depression or anxiety.

Third, a clinician must determine the specific primary disorder that is present. Once an etiology related to substance use and medical condition is ruled out, a clinician must determine which primary disorder best describes the presenting symptoms. To aid in this process, the clinician can utilize the exclusionary criteria in the DSM-IV and the Decision Tree in Appendix A of the DSM-IV.

Fourth, a clinician who determines that an individual's symptoms do not meet the criteria for any of the specific diagnoses in the DSM-IV should consider a diagnosis of Not Otherwise Specified or Adjustment Disorder. An adjustment disorder can be given for symptoms that are a maladaptive response to a psychosocial stressor. When no stressor can explain the symptom, then the Not Otherwise Specific Category is appropriate.

Fifth, a clinician should establish the boundary with no mental disorder. Many conditions are close to normal behavior. In order for a mental disorder to exist, the clinician must assess the symptoms to cause clinically significant problems. What is clinically significant must be determined by the clinician and is based on an individual's environment and culture.

Sixth, a clinician must be able to rule out Factitious Disorder or malingering. Although trust is an important part of the therapeutic relationship, a clinician should not be overly gullible. Some settings, such as prisons, courtrooms, disability hearings, and emergency rooms, provide incentives for individuals to feign symptoms. When a person displays feigned symptoms for external gains (i.e., drugs or the avoidance of punishment), it is called malingering. When an individual displays feigned symptoms not for external gain but to assume the sick role, it qualifies for a diagnosis of Factitious Disorder.

CONDUCTING A MENTAL STATUS EXAMINATION

The counselor may need to do a mental status examination initially. Amchin (1991) argues that all mental health professionals should know how to conduct a mental status examination. Before a word is spoken, the counselor should observe the person's appearance and motor behavior. That is, is the person disheveled, wearing clothes that are inappropriate for the weather, or is the person's gait atypical? As the person speaks, the counselor, sensitive to cultural differences in speech, should listen for some abnormalities in the person's speech. The counselor should assess the content of speech as well as how speech is communicated. That is, is the mood and affect congruence with the content of the speech? Typically, the mood and affect are assessed and then the person's thoughts. Next, a formal assessment of the person's cognitive function is conducted by the use of specific questions designed to evaluate orientation, memory, attention and concentration, and calculations. Last, the counselor assesses the most advanced areas of mental functioning, which consists of the client's abstract ability, intelligence, insight, and judgment. These criteria may be outlined as follows.

1. Appearance
2. Behavior
3. Speech
4. Attitude Toward Interviewer
5. Mood and Affect
6. Thought
   a. Thought process
   b. Thought content
   c. Perceptual disturbance
7. Formal Cognitive Function
   a. Orientation
   b. Memory (immediate, recent, and remote)
   c. Attention and concentration
   d. Calculation
8. Abstraction
9. Intelligence
10. Insight
11. Judgment

Another screening model assesses three overall areas, consisting of appearance, behavior, and cognition. It is referred to as the ABC model for psychiatric screening and is illustrated in Box 4.1.

After a mental status examination, the mental health professional may need to refer the offender to a more skilled practitioner or a psychiatrist for consideration of the need for medication.

CLINICAL ASSESSMENT

As it relates to offenders with substance abuse problems, a clinical assessment involves the collection by a trained professional of detailed information about the offender's substance use, emotional and physical health, social roles, and other factors bearing upon the offender's substance abuse problem. The essential aim of the clinical assessment is to develop a picture of the offender's substance abuse pattern and history, social and psychological functioning, and general treatment needs. From the picture developed, a treatment program can then devise a clinical response. A lesser, but important, aim of the clinical assessment is to begin the treatment process. However, this beginning phase can occur only when the offender earnestly participates in the assessment and recognizes that behavioral changes need to occur.

Box 4.1 ABC Model for Psychiatric Screening

Appearance, Alertness, Affect, and Anxiety

Appearance: General Appearance, Hygiene, Dress
Alertness: Level of Consciousness
Affect: Elation or Depression: Gestures, Facial Expression, Speech
Anxiety: Nervous, Phobic, or Panicky Individual

Behavior

Movements: Rate (Hyperactive, Hypoactive, Abrupt, or Constant?)

Organization: Coherent, Goal-Oriented?
Purpose: Bizarre, Stereotypical, Dangerous, Impulsive
Speech: Rate, Organization, Coherence, Content

Cognition

Orientation: Person, Place, Time, Condition
Calculation: Memory, Simple Tasks
Reasoning: Insight, Judgment, Problem Solving
Coherence: Incoherent Ideas, Delusions, Hallucinations

Though there are several components of the clinical assessment, it can be grouped into three broad domains–the sociobehavioral domain, the psychological domain, and the biomedical domain. The sociobehavioral domain involves an exploration of the offender's social world and behavioral history. This means inquiring about the history of alcohol and other drugs (AOD) abuse, involvement in the criminal justice system, social support and social roles, educational and vocational needs, and spirituality. The psychological domain focuses upon the levels of anxiety and depression; personality disorders; locus of control; level of psychological development; organic brain syndromes; central nervous system function and impairment; history of sexual, emotional, and/or physical abuse; and history of violent behavior. The psychological assessment should identify offenders who are seriously mentally ill and need psychiatric treatment. This treatment may need to occur before an offender can benefit from substance abuse treatment. The biomedical domain pertains to the assessment of an offender's medical problem, including any history of contagious diseases, such as HIV (Inciardi et al, 1994).

Critical information from all three domains should be summarized, and the clinician should make his or her diagnostic impressions regarding the offender and the offender's treatment needs. The summary should discuss the offender's general quality of life and level of functioning. It should also establish priorities for treatment. Such a concluding summary is a requirement for accreditation by the Joint Commission on the Accreditation of Healthcare Organizations (Inciardi, 1994).

CRITICAL ISSUES IN ASSESSMENT

While conducting assessments, some issues stand out that require the consideration of clinicians. Experienced clinicians acknowledge that the DSM-IV leads to overly inclusiveness or false-positives diagnoses, which have a negative effect on some groups (Johnson, 1998). A clinician is urged, for instance, when making an assessment and diagnosis to take into account an adolescent's reaction to his or her immediate social context. However, this recommendation is often neglected with respect to minority adolescents. Externalizing behaviors related to poverty and violence are interpreted as evidence of conduct disorders. Concomitantly, stress among minority adolescents is overlooked as a factor in behavior. As a result, minority adolescents are more likely to be diagnosed as having a conduct disorder (Johnson, 1998). Concerned professionals have observed this overrepresentation of minorities in negative diagnoses and go even further. These professionals state that therapeutic work is made more difficult by diagnoses from the DSM-IV as clinicians seek to identify psychopathological disorders among juvenile delinquents (Brannon, Kunce, Brannon, & Martray, 1990).

Related to this issue, males tend to receive the most negative diagnoses. Kaplan and Sadock (1998) assert that females are underdiagnosed with antisocial personality disorders. No reason was given for this underdiagnosis, but it is likely related to the views that women are not as bad as men.

Although the above discussion refers partly to ethics, another critical issue involves the efficacious use of staff resources. Assessment may be conducted by a clinical interview or self-administered questionnaires, which save time and resources. Questions have been raised about the reliability of self-assessment instruments. Researchers compared the administration of the Brief Background Assessment (BBA) by a clinician and self-administered by probationers for drug offenses. The BBA has sixty-nine items that can be answered mostly as yes or no. It assesses sociodemographic information, employment, family background, psychological and physical health, legal history, alcohol and drug use history, and drug-related problems. The researchers found that considerable concordance occurred between clinicians and probationers, which suggests that offenders can give reliable information through a self-assessment (Broome, Knight, Joe, & Simpson, 1996).

Malingering and Its Detection

Assessing or not assessing malingering has serious implications for offenders. A person who is misclassified as a malinger may suffer from a lack of treatment in the future or suffer legal harm. On the other hand, failing to detect and classify malingering may have negative consequences for the criminal justice system. To avoid such outcomes, a clinician should never base an assessment of malingering on one measure, and a clinician should utilize multiple sources to assess malingering (Rogers, 1998).

Two of the best measures for detecting malingering are the Minnesota Multiple Personality Inventory-2 (MMPI-2) and the Structured Interview of Reported Symptoms (SIRS) (Rogers, 1998). Some of the questions a clinician should ask are whether the MMPI-2 profile is consistent, whether the standard validity indicators are extremely elevated, and if the standard indicators are elevated but not to an extreme level, are specialized indicators extremely elevated. Caution, however, should be used in applying these results to minority populations (i.e., African Americans and Hispanic Americans) because they tend to score higher on the F scale than European Americans (Rogers, 1998).

The SIRS is a structured interview whose validity has been established among clinical, community, and correctional samples. The guidelines for using the SIRS are quite straightforward. A clinician should discern whether any scale is in the definite feigning range, whether three or more scales are in the probable feigning range, and whether the total SIRS score indicates malingering. The use of the SIRS with adolescents and persons with neuropsychological impairment has not been established (Rogers, 1998). It specifically was developed to detect feigning psychopathology and mental disorders, not individuals who feign cognitive impairment (Rogers, 1998).

For the assessment of cognitive impairment, other strategies are used. Feigning cognitive impairment is simpler for an individual than trying to feign a mental disorder. To feign a mental disorder, one must generate believable symptoms and associated features with accompanying data on the onset and course of the mental disorder one is trying to feign. Cognitive impairment is simpler to feign because all one has to do is perform suboptimally in a believable fashion. The detection of feigned cognitive impairment requires consideration of the floor effect, performance curve, symptom validity testing, magnitude of error, psychological sequelae, and inconsistent or atypical presentations. Regarding the floor effect, some malingerers fail on questions that the most cognitively impaired person would not. For instance, asking a person who is older, a mother or her child. A malingerer may get this answer wrong when he or she should not. The performance curve requires a clinical analysis of item difficulty. Often, malingerers do not consider the difficulty of items, and their patterns are markedly dissimilar to the norm for genuine persons.

The Symptom Validity Testing is based on the extent to which a person who is malingering would fail based on probability theory. A performance that is worse than chance is an indicator of possible malingering. Some clinicians examine the magnitude of errors. Though this aspect might be useful, it needs further research. Psychological sequelae involves whether a person feigning cognitive impairment can describe correctly symptoms known to follow particular problems. For instance, depression and anxiety follow certain traumatic events, which some malingerers may not know. Though the data may indicate inconsistent or atypical presentations, these should not necessarily be taken as hard evidence of malingering. A person with genuine neuropsychological impairment may evidence variable performance, and a person with a brain injury may exhibit personality changes. For these reasons, multiple sources of data are needed before concluding that an individual is feigning or malingering (Rogers, 1998).

Another issue is assessment of secondary gain. Three models have been offered as a conceptual basis for understanding secondary gain. These are the psychodynamic model, the behavioral model, and the forensic model. Most relevant to criminal justice is the forensic model. In this model, a motivation for secondary gain is to avoid criminal prosecution (Rogers & Reinhardt, 1998). However, a related issue of secondary gain pertains to offenders who exaggerate, for instance, alcohol and drug problems in order to procure placement in a community-based drug program instead of prison. In addition, a prisoner may enter a treatment program primarily to gain favor with a parole board. Although these ends may suggest disingenuineness, Rogers and Reinhardt (1998) state that assessing secondary gain for clinical purposes should be done cautiously because it has unjustifiably acquired a pejorative meaning. It has come to mean uncooperativeness, manipulative, demanding, treatment-resistant, and fraudulent (Rogers & Reinhardt, 1998).

ASSESSMENT OF OFFENDERS' COMMON PROBLEMS

Assessment of Juvenile and Adult Criminal Attitudes

Assessment of the extent to which offenders hold criminal attitudes is important theoretically, empirically, and practically. However, correctional practitioners have not used this knowledge in their assessment and treatment efforts due to a lack of acceptable measurement tools (Simourd, 1997). Simourd modified and tested two existing scales to fill the void in correctional assessment. One was the Criminal Sentiments Scale-Modified (CSS-M) for adult offenders, and the other was the Pride in Delinquency (PID) scale for juvenile offenders. The CSS-M is a forty-one-item scale with five subscales: attitude toward the law, attitude toward the court, attitude toward the police, tolerance for law violations, and identification with criminal others. The PID is a ten-item scale that measures a juvenile's degree of comfort (i.e., pride versus shame) with committing several criminal behaviors. Partially assisted by the Psychopathy Checklist-Revised and the Minnesota Multiphasic Personality Inventory, the psychometric properties of both the CSS-M and PID were investigated and their construct validity was established. Both the CSS-M and PID were determined to be beneficial tools in assessing adult and juvenile offenders' criminal attitudes (Simourd, 1997).

Adult Substance Abuse Assessment

For substance-abusing adult offenders, the goals of an assessment are to retrieve information from them and describe how the treatment will address their alcohol and other drugs (AOD) problems and the impact of these problems on the offenders' lives. The assessment is both descriptive and prescriptive, identifying the offenders' strengths, weaknesses, and readiness for treatment. Then, the treatment provider plans a course of treatment to meet the offenders' needs (Inciardi et al., 1994).

The goals and purposes of the assessment are

1. To determine the extent and severity of the AOD abuse problem
2. To determine the offender's level of maturation and readiness for treatment
3. To ascertain concomitant problems such as mental illness
4. To determine the type of intervention that will be necessary to address the problems
5. To evaluate the resources the offender can muster to help solve the problem (Typical resources include family support, social support, and personal qualities, such as motivational that the client brings to treatment.)
6. To engage the client in the treatment process

The assessment should be as comprehensive and holistic (i.e., comprehensive, encompassing social, psychological, medical, spiritual, etc.) as possible, and this means a variety of components should be inquired into during this process. This assessment should provide the information needed to make the best treatment plan possible. The areas that would produce such an assessment consist of

1. Archival data on the client, including but not limited to, prior arrests, incarcerations, and previous treatment records
2. Patterns of AOD use
3. Impact of AOD abuse on major life areas such as marriage, family, employment record, and self-concept
4. Risk factors for continued AOD abuse, such as family history of AOD abuse and social problems
5. Available health and medical findings, including emergency medical needs
6. Psychological test findings
7. Educational and vocational background

  8. Suicide, health, or other crisis risk appraisal
  9. Client motivation and readiness for treatment
 10. Client attitudes and behavior during assessment
 11. Tolerance, which indicates an offender has a history of heavy substance abuse
 12. History of physical withdrawal symptoms
 13. Episodes of uncontrolled drug or alcohol use, binges, or overdoses
 14. Use of AOD for self-medication of painful and unpleasant emotions
 15. Attempts to hide use
 16. Physical signs of drug use, such as needle track marks, emaciation, and alcohol odor
 17. Positive drug test results
 18. History of attempts to quit AOD use
 19. Family dysfunction relative to AOD abuse
 20. History and onset of drug use
 21. Drug use behavior, such as using alone, for sex, or to go to work
 22. Method of administration, including injecting, snorting, smoking, or drinking

Furthermore, Mahon (1997) argues that an assessment should include prisoners' use of drugs and sexual activity inside correctional institutions. Mahon notes that needles and makeshift needles exist in prisons and jails. The passing of these unclean instruments around increases the risk of HIV and hepatitis infection. Also, though seldom discussed openly, some prisoners have sex with other prisoners and thereby increase the risk of infection in jails and prisons (Mahon, 1997).

An assessment for substance abuse based on rational emotive therapy, which Ellis, McInerney, DiGiuseppe, and Yeager (1988) say is synonymous with cognitive–behavioral therapy, is different from a traditional assessment with psychometric or psychodiagnostic testing. A rational emotive therapy assessment involves a methodical, clinical process that seeks to understand a substance abuser's self-defeating cycles of thought, feeling, and behavior. It is a continuous process, not a one-time initial session. This assessment constantly formulates hypotheses for testing. As Ellis and colleagues (1988) state, "relevant information is collected by the clinician. Hypotheses are generated about specific dysfunctional ideas and their consequent emotions and behaviors; and then further questions are asked and data collected from the client to confirm or disconfirm these hypotheses. If the clinician's hypotheses are disconfirmed, new ones are formed and the process continues" (p. 45).

A clinician begins the assessment with "what problem would you like help with at this time?" This question should generate a dialogue about the problem—its severity, duration, and dynamics. Rational emotive therapy posits that this dialogue coincides with the building of rapport, reasonable expectations, and therapeutic alliance. The substance abuser sees that the therapist is earnestly trying to understand the problem. It is also the beginning of therapy, showing the substance abuser how logic and information are employed to reveal and test faulty cognition (Ellis et al., 1988).

The clinician uses referral information to generate hypotheses, as well. However, historical information, from a rational emotive perspective, is best collected by self-reports by clients either before the first session or the second session. With this historical information disclosed through a questionnaire, the clinician has more time to generate hypotheses for testing during the sessions (Ellis et al., 1988).

Assessment of Women with Substance Abuse

A group of researchers sought to ascertain empirically stages of change. They tested the utility and psychometric properties of the University of Rhode Island Change Assessment Scale (URICA), an assessment tool for persons who have substance abuse problems, consisting of thirty-two items. The focus of the research was to determine whether URICA identified stages of change among female inmates with recent substance abuse use, whether the research would identify subgroups within the population, and whether female prisoners would differ according to demographics characteristics, drug use patterns, or psychological symptoms. The study was carried out on 257 female inmates from a New York prison, in which 63% were African American.

Factor analysis identified five stages of change subscales. These were Precontemplation, Contemplation, Determination for Action, Action, and Maintenance. In addition, the analysis showed five clusters consisting of denial, uninvolved, ambivalent, decision making, and participation. Women in the five clusters did not differ on demographic variables, drug use, or drug treatment history. However, differences were found based on depression and psychological symptoms. For instance, women who were in denial were less likely to be depressed and report somatic symptoms than women in the uninvolved, ambivalent, decision-making, and participation clusters. Women in the uninvolved and participation clusters were more likely to be depressed than women in the denial, ambivalent, and decision-making clusters. Women in the uninvolved cluster had the highest level of somatic symptoms. Women in the denial cluster had a lower score on the total Brief Symptom Inventory (i.e., somatization, obsessive compulsive, interpersonal sensitivity, depression, anxiety, hostility, phobic anxiety, paranoid ideation, and psychoticism) than women in the other clusters.

These findings have importance for counselors and clinicians. At the individual level, the study suggests that women who are actively involved in change and women who have tried to change are more likely to be depressed, demonstrating a higher degree of psychological distress. This suggests that these women may need more support, services, and treatment. At the program level, the URICA scale may be helpful to counselors in determining discharge planning and matching inmates with drug problems to treatment. Also, the URICA can be useful to counselors in tailoring intervention to inmates' stages of change (El-Bassel, Schilling, Ivanoff, Chen, Hanson, & Bidassie, 1998).

Assessment and Screening of Adolescents
in the Justice System

A large percentage of juveniles entering the juvenile justice system have AOD problems (McLellan & Dembo, 1994). In addition, they present with poor school performance, family dysfunction, physical and sexual abuse, psychological and emotional problem, and presence in a community fraught with violence and poverty. The scope and severity of these psychosocial problems increase the probability of these juveniles continuing drug use and involvement with the juvenile justice system. As a result, a major challenge is presented to a professional staff providing screening, assessment, and treatment (McLellan & Dembo, 1994).

Screening and assessment procedures should occur at different stages of the juvenile justice process—intake, preadjudication, and postadjudication. This continuing process is needed to detect changes in drug use, other problem behaviors, and need for services. It is also needed to identify juveniles who are at risk for drug use but have not had treatment. In that it is difficult to transfer information from one stage to another stage, repeated screening and assessment are necessary (McLellan & Dembo, 1994).

The selection of screening and assessment instruments for juveniles, like all instruments, should be determined by reliability and validity of the instrument, the adolescent population for which the instrument was normed and developed, the type of setting in which it was developed, and the intended purpose of the instrument. Other important factors are the ability to predict criterion measures, such as school performance, performance in treatment, substance abuse relapse, bias possibility, and age appropriateness of the instrument (McLellan & Dembo, 1994).

Five types of screening or assessment should be performed with juveniles—a preliminary screening, risk assessment, drug testing/urinalysis, psychosocial assessment, and a comprehensive assessment. The following areas should be addressed within a specialized abuse screening protocol. This protocol consists of following: (1) motivation to participate in treatment; (2) recognition of an AOD problem; (3) AOD history, including types and modes of substance abuse, quantity and frequency of use, patterns of recent use; (4) HIV risk behaviors associated with AOD abuse; (5) current AOD problem severity and intensity; diagnosis of chemical dependency; and level of AOD treatment services required; (6) the association between AOD abuse and delinquent behavior (offenses committed while under the influence of alcohol or other drugs, and offenses committed to obtain alcohol or other drugs; (7) prior involvement with AOD abuse treatment, including the type and location of services, and responses to treatment (see Table 4.1).

Dual Diagnosis Assessment:
Substance Abuse and Mental Disorders

The psychiatric problems of dual diagnosis offenders can involve a number of mental disorders. Of these many disorders, four mental disorders constitute the majority of cases seen in clinical settings. These top four consist of mood disorders, anxiety disorders, personality disorders, and psychotic disorders. A general assessment is appropriate regardless of the type of mental disorder a person has and a more specific assessment depending upon the type of mental disorder present.

For the general assessment a mental status exam and AOD should be conducted. For the mental status examination, the ABC model for psychiatric screening is recommended. This model consists of assessing the offender's appearance, alertness, affect, and anxiety; behavior; and cognition. A full assessment of dual disorders should be conducted by certified professionals, but professionals not certified can conduct a preliminary assessment using the ABC model. Along with this model, two easily administered screening instruments are useful—CAGE or CAGEAID. The former screens for alcohol and the latter is a modification to screen for alcohol and drugs. Practitioners who see all initial clients should have the skills to conduct a general assessment of dual diagnosis and to recognize when a referral to a specialist is warranted.

Mood Disorders and AOD Assessment for offenders with AOD and mood disorders may be divided into three clinical phases consisting of acute, subacute, and long term. However, inpatient settings are more likely than outpatient settings to see individuals with acute psychiatric symptoms. An acute evaluation requires

Table 4.1 Type of Screening/Assessment for Juvenile Offenders

Initial Screening	Risk Assessment	Drug Testing/Urinalysis	Psychosocial Assessment	Comprehensive Assessment
		Purposes		
To determine emergency needs with respect to supervision, medical, and psychological treatment	To evaluate suicide potential, whether youth will be detained, level of custody/restrictiveness, likelihood of further delinquency or substance use, or degree of compliance with community supervision	To determine the recent use of AOD for detection, monitoring, and supervision	Refers to both psychological and social/environmental aspects of a youth's life	To clarify factors related to onset of problems, describe history and development of problems, assess problem severity, draw diagnostic/treatment implications
		Domains Probed		
(1) Acute intoxication/withdrawal and need for detoxification, (2) suicide risk, (3) potential for violent behavior, or (4) other immediate needs	(1) Demographic variables; (2) offense severity and evidence of AOD abuse; (3) delinquency history, severity of past offenses, disposition of prior charges, prior violations of supervision, escape/absconding, and past involvement in community diversion programs; (4) current legal status; (5) AOD abuse history; (6) psychological functioning and motivation; and (7) any mitigating or aggravating factors	Alcohol, amphetamine, cocaine, cannabinoids, opiates, PCP	(1) Demographic and personal history information; (2) AOD abuse history; (3) history of delinquent and aggressive behavior; (4) medical status, (5) psychological/emotional status; (6) family relationships; (7) peer relationships/social skills; (8) educational status; (9) vocational status; (10) evidence of physical or sexual abuse; (11) specialized substance abuse screening; and (12) detailed personal, family, and peer history of involvement in the juvenile or adult justice systems	(1) AOD abuse history, diagnosis of dependence and dual disorders; (2) delinquent and aggressive behavior; (3) medical status; (4) psychological and emotional status; (5) family relationships; (6) peer relationships and social skills; (7) educational status; (8) vocational status; (9) physical and sexual abuse; (10) other markers of disturbed functioning (e.g., fire setting, cruelty to animals)

Adapted from T. McLellan & R. Dembo, *Screening Assessment of Alcohol and Other Drug-Abusing Adolescents (TIP 3)*. Rockville, MD: Center for Substance Abuse Treatment, p. 42.

assessing whether a person is dangerous to self or others. This assessment focus helps to ascertain if there is a legal duty to protect the individual or others from violence. A screening for suicide should determine whether ideations, if any, are temporary or recurring. To ascertain which condition is present, the clinician should ask about specific suicide plans or intentions and the number of past attempts. In addition, a social assessment, a medical assessment, a substance abuse assessment, and a mood assessment should be conducted (Ries et al, 1994).

Clinicians conducting an AOD using history and psychiatric screening and assessment should expect different responses from different clients. Some persons with AOD disorders may over-stress or under-stress their psychiatric disorder. For example, depressed clients may misrepresent their past psychiatric experiences by exaggerating the frequency and intensity of previous depressive occurrences. Yet, deeply depressed clients may minimize their current and previous depression. They feel that their depression is a normal state, and they deserved to be depressed. They do not realize that depression is a deviation from normal mental health. Some clients feel excessively and inappropriately guilty. Other clients may not recognize or remember previous depression. Because some persons confuse sadness with depression, a clinician should ask specific questions, such as asking whether a client has ever seen a therapist or psychiatrist (Ries, 1994).

Organized by the Center for Substance Abuse Treatment, a group of clinicians developed a treatment assessment protocol for mood disorders. These clinicians prescribe some sample questions for conducting an assessment.

For Depression
1. During the past month, has there been a period of time during which you felt depressed most of the day nearly every day?
2. During this period of time, did you gain or lose any weight?
3. Did you have trouble concentrating?
4. Did you have problems sleeping or did you sleep too much?
5. Did you try to hurt yourself?

For Mania
1. During the past month, have you experienced times during which you felt so hyperactive that you got into trouble or were told by others that your behavior was not normal for you?
2. Have you recently experienced bouts of irritability during which you would yell or fight with others?
3. During this period, did you feel more self-confident than usual?
4. Did you feel pressured to talk a great deal or feel that your thoughts were racing?
5. Did you feel restless and irritable?
6. How much sleep did you need?

Subacute assessment generally occurs in mental health clinics, welfare and social service offices, psychotherapists' offices, and a number of medical facilities. Individuals in this category are not perceived as dangerous to self or others and are appropriate candidates for treatment. Among the areas assessed are functional levels, liabilities, and strengths. The goal of subacute assessment is to develop a treatment plan for the person with AOD and mood disorders. This means a comprehensive assessment of the individual treatment needs.

With this group, assessment is part of the treatment process because the assessment process begins the breaching of the addicted person's denial mechanisms. Simply inquiring about a person's work, relationships, health, and legal problems highlights the impact of AOD use on one's life. If a person's physical symptoms do not correlate with reported use, a toxicology and liver function test should be requested. If the tests show impairment, then this information becomes further evidence of the consequences of AOD use. Besides medical screening, the assessment should consist of psychiatric and addiction screening and a psychosocial assessment. For the psychiatric and addiction screening, a number of assessment instruments are appropriate, including the Brief Psychiatric Rating Scale, the Hamilton Scale, the Addiction Severity Index, and the Beck Scale. Also, the assessing professional may use the DSM-IV or the Structured Clinical Interview from the DSM-IV (SCID).

Anxiety Disorders and AOD A person with an AOD disorder commonly manifests anxiety. An assessment that occurs in the acute phase will, because of the effects of AOD use, show the individual to be either anxious or depressed, but both anxiety and depression may be present. The assessment must take place over time to determine whether the diagnosis should be AOD abuse, anxiety, depression, some combination among the three. Symptoms associated with AOD usually disappear within two to four weeks, but less severe withdrawal symptoms may appear following this period. Anxiety in combination with substance abuse can be dangerous because it can lead to suicide (Ries et al., 1994). Mental health clinicians in jails should be particularly aware of these issues because a significant number of suicides facilitated by the presence of alcohol or drug intoxication, depression, and anxiety occur in jails following some individuals' arrests.

Assessment here may involve acute, subacute, and long term. The acute assessment is determined by the type of drugs to which the person has become tolerant. For instance, a person who complains of something crawling on or under the skin and who do not have any apparent parasites probably has used stimulants. This drug's effect is quite different from PCP, marijuana, and hallucinogens. Regardless of the type of drug, the person may need support, confinement, or medication. The subacute assessment should focus on AOD use, functional level, physical status, and early stages of HIV infection. A psychosocial assessment is needed that searches for psychosocial stressors. The long-term assessment involves possible dissociation.

Personality Disorders and AOD The initial assessment of a person with an antisocial personality disorder involves taking an objective criminal and psychosocial histories. Criminal thinking patterns, which include rationalization and justification for maladaptive and criminal behavior, should be assessed. In addition, the following steps may be useful.

1. Taking a thorough family history
2. Finding out whether or not the patient set fires as a child, abused animals, or was a bed-wetter
3. Taking a thorough sexual history that includes questions about animals and objects

4. Taking a history of the offender's ability to bond with others (This means specifically asking, "Who was your first best friend? When was the last time you saw him or her? Do you know how he or she is? Is there any authority figure who has ever been helpful to you?)
5. Asking questions to find out about possible parasitic relationships and taking a history of exploitation of self and others (In this context, parasitic refers to a relationship in which one person uses and manipulates another until the first has gotten everything he or she wants, then abandons the relationship.)
6. Taking a history of head injuries, fighting, and being hit (It may be useful to perform neuropsychological testing.)
7. Testing urine for recent AOD use
8. HIV testing

Psychotic Disorder and AOD In this area, a typical problem for clinicians is determining whether psychotic symptoms are primary or secondary to AOD use. But this determination is not necessary in the initial assessment period and will likely require a longitudinal assessment process that consists of direct client interviews, collateral data, client observations, and documented history.

The first step in the assessment is to ascertain whether the person has an imminent life-threatening problem. This determination requires assessing three domains—biological or medical risks, psychological risks, and social risks. The medical assessment needs to be conducted by a physician because it could include infections, brain hemorrhage, and endocrine disorders (e.g., diabetes or hyperthyroidism). With respect to the assessment of psychological risk, this would include an assessment of danger to self or others. Individuals should be assessed for specific plans, intent, and means of committing violent acts. A social risk assessment includes determining whether an individual has minimal life support, such as shelter and food. All three areas require a thorough assessment with direct questions.

Assessment of Sexual Victimization

Finkelhor and Browne (1985) state that previous professionals have speculated that childhood sexual abuse is associated with sexual dysfunction, depression, and low self-esteem. But these professionals have not described a clear model that showed how and when sexual abuse resulted in these traumas. Hoping to describe the progression from sexual abuse to psychological difficulty, Finkelhor and Browne depict a model of the impact of sexual abuse on girls and the implication for treatment. Their model posits that sexual abuse can be understood as resulting in four trauma-causing factors. Another name for these factors are *traumagenic dynamics*, which are *traumatic sexualization, betrayal, powerlessness,* and *stigmatization*.

Traumatic sexualization concerns a process in which a child's sexual attitudes and feelings are fashioned inappropriately and dysfunctionally because of the sexual abuse. This outcome can happen in a number of ways. Traumatic sexualization can happen when a child is continuously rewarded by a molester for sexual behavior that is not befitting for the child's level of development. It occurs by the interchange of affection, attention, gifts, or privileges for sexual gratification. The results of this quid pro quo (i.e., something for something) are that the child, reinforced inappropriately for sexual behavior, learns to use sexual behavior to manipulate others. Another way in which traumatic sexualization can occur is when parts of a child's anatomy is eroticized and given distorted meaning. Traumatic sexualization can occur when the child has nightmares or unpleasant memories associated with the sexual abuse.

Betrayal concerns the dynamics that occur when a child has realized that someone to whom they were dependent caused them injury. This, too, occurs in a variety of ways. It occurs when a child has learned that a trusted person has manipulated and used them. This also can occur when a child realizes that she has been treated callously without regard for herself. Betrayal can also occur when family members have chosen not to believe a child's report of abuse. A child who is disbelieved, blamed, or shunned experiences a greater degree of betrayal than a child who has been believed and supported.

Powerlessness pertains to the process of the erosion of power in a child victim. Simply, the child's will, desires, and self-efficacy are destroyed by the sexual assault. Finkelhor and Browne theorize that an elementary form of powerlessness develops when a child's space and body are repeatedly trespassed against the will of the child. It is made worse by an offender's use of coercion and manipulation during the abuse episodes. A child's sense of powerlessness is intensified by her failure to stop the abuse. It is intensified even further when the child feels fear, when the child is unable to convince another adult to intervene, and when the child sees that her minor status prevents escape from the situation.

Stigmatization pertains to the negative messages that are conveyed to the child centered around the abuse, such as badness, shame, and guilt, which then become imbedded in the child's self-image. These negative meanings are conveyed in a number of ways. They come from the abuser who blames her for acting seductively, calls her names, and indicates that she should be ashamed for her conduct. When the abuser, under threats or pressures, demands secrecy, this sends strong messages of shame and guilt. In addition, stigmatization can occur from the comments of others in the family or the community about the deviancy or the taboo of incest. If the abuse is uncovered and negative reactions occur toward the child, further stigmatization occurs.

According to Finklehor and Browne, their model provides clinical and research applications. With respect to the clinical application, it provides an assessment tool for evaluating the impact of the sexual abuse on four dimensions. As advocated by Finkelhor and Browne:

> a clinician might proceed through the model dynamic by dynamic, asking first: How traumatically sexualizing was this experience? Facts about the experience, such as whether intercourse occurred, how long it went on, and the degree to which the child participated, all might contribute to an assessment of the degree of sexualization. Next, a clinician would ask: How stigmatizing was the experience? Factors such as how long it went on, the age of the child, the number of people who knew about it, and the degree to which others blamed the child subsequent to the disclosure would all add to the assessment of this dynamic. Similarly, with regard to the betrayal, facts about the relationship between the victim and the offender, the way in which the offender involved the victim, and the attempts—successful and unsuccessful—of the victim to get assistance and support from other family members would all be taken into account. Finally, the facts about the presence of force, the degree to which coercion was brought to bear, the duration of the abuse, and the circumstances under which the abuse was terminated would be particularly relevant to a determination of the degree to which powerlessness was a major dynamic. (pp. 537–538)

After the assessment of these four dimensions, a clinician should have enough information to conjecture the extent of a victim's concern and the issues for the clinician to address. Intervention strategies, then, can be planned. For instance, if the assessment suggested that betrayal was the chief concern, then strategies to address betrayal would be initiated. Group work may be appropriate or individual counseling to rehabilitate the child's sense of betrayal.

Although Finkelhor and Browne theorize that the abuse is the main traumatic episode in producing the four dimensions, an assessment should be done on the child's experiences before the sexual abuse and after the abuse. Sexual abuse can have differential effects. For instance, a child who has been the victim of emotional abuse may have suffered a lower sense of powerlessness. At the same time, a child who has been forced to undertake an adult-like role of caring for younger siblings may have had an elevated degree of self-efficacy and power. The effect of sexual abuse may be difficult with younger girls, who may experience greater trauma (Finkelhor & Browne, 1985).

Assessment of Juveniles' Sexual Offending

Consisting of a multitude of clinicians and professionals, the National Task Force on Juvenile Sexual Offending (NTFJSO) prepared a comprehensive report on all aspects of intervening with juveniles who sexually molest other individuals. Many agencies that work with juveniles who molest are employed in adolescent psychiatric hospitals and community mental health centers. Often these agencies receive referrals from juvenile or family courts (NTFJSO, 1993). Barbaree and Cortoni (1993) contend that juveniles who have sexually assaulted have a low motivation for treatment and a serious problem with denial and minimization. As a result, the criminal justice system plays a critical role in juveniles' treatment by coercing juveniles into treatment. In working with these adolescents, the NTFJSO recommends preparing a comprehensive assessment that should be conducted before a formal disposition is ordered by the juvenile court judge. This assessment should include the following information and the order of information does not reflect the importance of the information.

1. Victim statements and related reports
2. History (i.e., family, educational, medical, psychosocial, and psychosexual)
3. Evidence of historical progression of sexually aggressive behavior development over time
4. Dynamics/process of victim selection
5. Intensity of sexual arousal, prior to, during, and after offense
6. Use of force, violence, weapons
7. Spectrum of injury to victim (i.e., violation of trust, fear, physical injury)
8. Sadism, animal cruelty, fire setting
9. Ritualistic process
10. Deviant sexual fantasies and interests
11. Deviant nonsexual interests
12. Deviant sexual arousal
13. History of assaultive behaviors against others
14. Chronic/situational factors
15. Sociopathy

16. Extent of childhood mental disorders (i.e., personality disorders, affective disorders, attention deficit, post-traumatic stress)
17. Behavioral warning signs
18. Self-destructive behaviors
19. Identifiable triggers
20. Thinking errors (i.e., irrational thinking)
21. Locus of control
22. Ability to accept responsibility
23. Denial or minimization
24. Understanding of wrongfulness
25. Concern for injury to victim
26. Victim empathy, capacity for empathic thought
27. Substance abuse
28. History of sexual victimization, physical or psychological abuse
29. Gang involvement
30. Family dysfunction
31. Parental separation/loss
32. Masturbatory patterns
33. Impulse control/compulsivity
34. School performance/education level
35. Mental status/retardation/developmental disability
36. Organicity/neuropsychological factors
37. Concurrent psychiatric disorders and/or treatment history

In addition, the family unit should be assessed. This assessment includes

1. Parental response (i.e., denial, minimization, defensiveness)
2. Demonstrated ability and availability of supervision
3. Parental protection for vulnerable family members
4. Family validation of seriousness of abusive behavior
5. Concurrent dysfunctions and stressors, which may impede parental availability, such as substance abuse, depression, unemployment, or spousal conflict
6. The extent of external support systems and social isolation
7. Historical patterns of managing stress and crisis in the home
8. Availability and/or use of pornography in the home
9. Strengths evident in family members and/or system
10. Possibility of involvement of any family members in abusive incidents
11. Unresolved abuse issue from past experiences of family members

Assessment of Juveniles for Alcohol and Other Drugs

According to the Center for Substance Abuse Treatment (1995), any youth referred to juvenile court must be given a comprehensive screening and assessment for AOD. The critical areas that must be explored are as follows.

History of AOD Abuse Questions should be asked regarding use of over-the-counter or prescription drugs, tobacco, caffeine, or psychotropic drugs. If these drugs have been used, the juvenile should be asked how these drugs are administered, age at first use, frequency of use, duration of use, and patterns of use.

Medical History and Physical Examination Questions should be asked about previous illnesses, infectious diseases, sexually transmitted diseases, HIV infection, medical trauma, and pregnancies status if the juvenile is a female.

Developmental Issues Questions should be asked regarding problems related to psychosocial development.

Mental Health History Questions should be posed regarding the youth's extent of depression, suicidal ideation or attempts, the impact of traumatic events such as sexual and physical abuse, the extent of hallucinations that are unrelated to AOD, and a mental status examination should be conducted. If the juveniles have had a history of mental health problems, the written reports should be obtained.

Strengths of Resiliency Factors Questions should be asked to assess the juvenile's level of self-esteem, coping skills, motivation for treatment, support of family, and other community supports.

Family History Questions should be asked to explore the extent of family or legal guardian's history of AOD use and abuse; mental and physical health problems; chronic illnesses; legal involvement and criminal activities that are unknown to law enforcement; traumatic family events; the family's attitude regarding the youth's AOD issues; and the family's cultural, ethnic, and socioeconomic background and child-rearing practices.

School History Questions should be asked regarding the juvenile's academic and behavioral performance, the extent of any learning disabilities, attendance records, and any input from school officials.

Vocational History Questions should be asked regarding the juvenile's work and volunteer history. Further, questions should be asked regarding the juvenile's skills and preemployment development.

Sexual History Questions should be asked to explore the juvenile history of sexual abuse, sexual orientation, and age of first sexual activity.

Peer Relationship Questions should be asked to learn about the juvenile's interpersonal skills, gang involvement, and the quality of the neighborhood environment, such as drug activity on the streets or open drinking on street corners. Additional questions should be posed to learn whether the juvenile has lost any close friends and whether the juvenile has any involvement with other youths in community programs or church.

Juvenile Justice Involvement and Delinquency Questions should be asked to learn the extent and type of delinquency involvement. Also, the juvenile's attitude about these incidents should be explored.

Social Service Agency Program Involvement Questions should be asked to learn the extent of involvement with child welfare, such as any investigations by child

Table 4.2 Selected Assessment Scales for Juveniles and Adults

Instrument	Description of Instrument	Juveniles	Adults
Multidimensional Adolescent Adjustment Scale (MAAS)	MAAS is a self-report measure for adolescents to assess the severity of social functioning, including personal and social functioning, depression, self-esteem problems, problems with mother and father or guardian, personal stress, problems with friends and school, aggression, suicide, confused thinking, disturbed thoughts, alcohol abuse, and drug abuse.	*	*
Symptom Check List (SCL-90)	The SCL-90 is designed to measure nine psychopathology dimensions. These are depression, anxiety, somatization, obsessive-compulsive, and paranoid ideation. It also measures three global indices (global severity, positive symptom distress, and positive symptoms).	* 13+ years	
Addiction Severity Index (ASI)	The ASI is a highly structured clinical instrument designed for trained clinicians to assess the severity of problems in six areas: medical, psychiatric, legal, family and social, employment and support, and use of alcohol and other drugs		
Adolescent Problem Severity Index (APSI)	The APSI is a structured screening interview. It is designed to help identify adolescent problems; it captures seven areas: legal, family relationship, educational/work, medical, psychosocial adjustment, drug/alcohol use, and personal relationships.	*	*
Adolescent Drug Abuse Diagnosis (ADAD)	Patterned after the ASI, this is 150-item instrument to assess adolescents in nine domains: medical, school, employment, social relations, family and background relationships, psychological, legal, alcohol use, and drug use. The ADAD's purpose is to assess substance abuse and other life problems, to assist in treatment planning, and to assess changes in problem areas and severity over time.	*	
Wide Range Achievement Test Revised (WRAT-R)	The WRAT-R is a well-standardized test that is widely used with children, adolescents, and adults to evaluate reading, spelling, and arithmetic skills.	*	*
Structured Clinical Interview for Diagnosis (SCID)	SCID is an instrument for diagnosing substance abuse and dependence.		*
Revised Diagnostic Interview for Children and Adults (DICA-R)	DICA-R is an instrument for adolescents and adults for diagnosis of alcohol or drug abuse and alcohol or drug dependence.	*	*

Personal Experience Inventory (PEI)   The PEI is a comprehensive assessment instrument made up of two parts. One part is a chemical involvement problem severity (CIPS) and the other part is the psychosocial section (PS). Its purpose is to assess the extent of psychological and behavioral issues with alcohol and drug problems; to assess the psychosocial risk factors believed to be associated with teenage chemical involvement; to evaluate the response bias or invalid responding; to screen for the presence of problems other than substance abuse, such as school problems, family problems, psychiatric disorder etc.; and to aid in determining the appropriateness of inpatient or drug outpatient treatment.   *

Symptom Questionnaire (SQ)   This is a 92-item instrument that measures four major aspects of psychopathology—depression, anxiety, somatization, and anger hostility.   *

Beck Depression Inventory   The Beck Depression Inventory is a 21-item scale to asses the intensity of depression in psychiatrically diagnosed individuals.   *   *

Minnesota Multi-Personality Inventory (MMPI)   MMPI is a well-known scale designed to measure a number of areas of psychopathology.   *   *

protection workers or placements in foster care homes. Any activities by child welfare officials regarding the youth, siblings, or family should be included in this assessment.

Leisure Activities Questions should be asked regarding the juvenile's hobbies, interests, recreational activities, or associations with organizations such as Big Brothers or Big Sisters.

SELECTED ASSESSMENT TOOLS

One aid in conducting screening and assessment is with the use of psychological tests. Estimates are that 20,000 new psychological tests are constructed each year (Brouillard, 1998). Every psychometric measure seeks to evaluate an individual's cognitive, emotional, or behavioral functioning. Critically important is that a measure is valid and reliable. Validity refers to the extent to which an instrument measures what it is intended, and reliability refers to the extent to which an instrument repeatedly gives the same or close results. The information gleaned from a psychometric assessment may disclose the etiology of a disorder and ideally should inform or direct treatment (Tarter, Ott, & Mezzich, 1991).

In assessing offenders, a number of psychometric measures are used. Decisions need to be made regarding a measure utility for offender, reliability, and validity (Brouillard, 1998). Below is a selected list of psychometric measures that are used with juvenile and adult offenders. These are by no means exhaustive. An excellent source for finding clinical scales is *Measures for Clinical Practice* (2nd ed.), Volume 1 for Children, and *Measures for Clinical Practice* (2nd ed.), Volume 2 for Adults. Both volumes were assembled by Joel Fisher and Kevin Corcoran.

SUMMARY

This chapter described the Multifactored Assessment Plan, which has been proposed by members of the Ohio legislature for use with adult and juvenile offenders. Discussed next were the Diagnostic and Statistical Manual of Mental Disorders (4th ed.) and related materials to aid in using the DSM-IV. This chapter discussed how to conduct a clinical assessment as well as a mental status examination. Some critical issues in assessment were described. Then the chapter discussed assessing offenders' common problems, involving criminal attitudes, adult substance abuse, dual diagnosis, sexual victimization, juvenile sexual offending, and juvenile alcohol and drug abuse. Last, the chapter listed some commonly used assessment scales for juveniles and adults.

KEY TERMS

Multifactored
  Assessment Plan
Seven primary criminal
  justice interviewing
  skills
*Diagnostic and Statistical
  Manual of Mental
  Disorders* (4th ed.)

Clinical assessment
Multiaxial system
Conduct disorder
Antisocial personality
  disorder
Psychopathy

Structured clinical
  interview for the
  DSM-IV
Mental status
  examination
Malingering
Secondary gain
Traumagenic dynamics

5

Individual Counseling Processes

❈ INTRODUCTION

Providing counseling to offenders is accomplished either in individual or group sessions (Kratcoski, 1994). Certainly, group counseling is preferable for a number of offenders because of the curative dynamics that emanate from a group and the ability to treat more offenders (Lester, 1997). However, individual counseling has several advantages over group counseling. First, individual counseling provides greater confidentiality than group counseling. Although self-help groups, such as Alcoholics Anonymous, strive to protect confidentiality and therapeutic groups require confidentiality, breaches in confidentially still occur. Second, the individualized pace of individual counseling permits the therapist to address clients' needs as they arise, whereas group members' immediate needs may be suborned to the group's need. Third, individual therapy permits more time to an individual's problem than what is allotted in a group. Fourth, individual counseling may be practical for logistical reasons. If treatment is provided in a mental health agency within a rural area, not enough members with a particular disorder may exist to form a group. Also, the time it takes to compose a group might be problematic for an agency. Fifth, individual counseling may be best for addressing a client's needs. For instance, if a client has a problem that is best treated by increasing the bond between therapist and client, individual counseling facilitates that development. Also, some clients simply are unsuitable for groups, such as persons with personality disorders or highly avoidant clients who are extremely resistant to participation in a group (Rounsaville & Carroll, 1997).

Though group counseling is preferred, there is no doubt that counselors in correctional institutions conduct individual counseling with offenders (Alexander, 1997). In addition, counselors in community-based corrections conduct individual counseling with offenders in probation, parole, and halfway houses (Allen & Simonsen, 1998). Because of the wide utility, the aim of this chapter is to discuss individual counseling.

PSYCHOANALYTIC PRINCIPLES AND INDIVIDUAL COUNSELING

Counseling an individual comprises a dyadic relationship involving a counselor and a client (Eisenstein, Levy, & Marmor, 1994). As a dyadic relationship, the dynamics involve the counselor, the client, and the interaction between the two. The psychoanalytic theory, developed by Sigmund Freud and widely adopted by other psychotherapists and the broader society, has been used to explain this dyadic relationship and the processes involved in it. Scenes of clients lying on a couch and talking about their dreams to their therapists suggest that psychoanalysis is applicable to middle-class and upper-class persons (Phares, 1984). A prison counselor or probation officer is unlikely to have a prisoner or probationer in his or her office lying on a couch and discussing recurring dreams (Brandt & Zlotnick, 1988). For this reason, pure psychoanalysis has been considered to be inapplicable in a correctional setting (Aichhorn, 1935; Freud, 1935; Smith & Berlin, 1988).

However, few counselors would deny that aspects of psychoanalytic theory, such as transference, countertransference, and defense mechanisms, have offered explanations to correctional counselors so that they would understand what was going on in the counseling relationship (Hartman, 1978).

During the early development of psychoanalysis, Sigmund Freud wrote that psychoanalysis requires a therapeutic environment consisting of certain psychic structures and a favorable attitude about the psychoanalyst. When these are lacking, such as with adult and juvenile offenders, the psychoanalytic approach must be flexibly applied to these groups (Freud, 1935). Freud's recommendation clearly indicates that pure psychoanalysis is not appropriate for offenders. His recommendation also suggests that an integrative approach is appropriate for counseling offenders and coincides with contemporary counselors.

The consensus among counselors is that no single approach fully explains human behavior and offers the best treatment approach for everyone (Bradley, Parr, & Gould, 1995; Corey, 1991). In the 1980s, several surveys revealed that most counselors considered themselves to be eclectic clinicians (Corey, 1991). Bradley, Parr, and Gould (1995) describe a number of integrative models, but they did not recommend a specific model. Corey (1991), noting that some theoretical approaches were incompatible, describes critical issues that clinicians must consider in developing an integrative or eclectic approach.

For instance, three assumptions have been presented for integrative theory development. One is that it emphasizes the significance of the helping relationship. A second assumption is that the counselor is knowledgeable of appropriate treatment techniques and the correct application to different clients. The third assumption is that the counselor will stay abreast of the literature and revise the integrative theoretical framework as valid, empirical studies suggest (Bradley, Parr, & Gould, 1995).

The therapist's role in an integrative perspective is varied and cannot be confined to one or two. Affecting the role or roles of the counselor are the type of counselor, the counselor's training, the clients to be served, and the setting. As an illustration, Corey reported that he provided training to a hospital treatment staff consisting of psychiatric technicians, psychologists, and social workers who were treating involuntarily committed individuals. The clients consisted of mentally disordered sex offenders and persons diagnosed as psychotic or sociopathic. The treatment team counseled the clients and ultimately determined when the clients were ready to be released from the hospital. To achieve these ends, the counselors functioned as therapists, sponsors, nurses, friends, teachers, parents, administrators, guards, and judges (Corey, 1991). Hence, a counselor with an integrative perspective of treatment functions in a number of roles.

Based on the integrative perspective, this chapter describes a generic framework where a number of interventions may be employed in counseling offenders. This approach is highly appropriate for counseling offenders for a number of reasons. First, the overall framework for this book provides that different treatment approaches are necessary for adults and juveniles and men and women. Adult offenders have different issues from juvenile offenders (McNeece & Daly, 1997; Robertson, 1997), and female offenders have different issues from male offenders (Chandler & Kassebaum, 1997; Walsh, 1997). At the same time, there are some universal principles applicable to all clients, such as offenders' use of defense mechanisms to avoid addressing problems. Second, correctional counseling is provided in a number of settings. It is employed in probation, parole, and institutions (Allen & Simonsen, 1998). Third, a growing number of offenders have severe mental illnesses, and their treatment must be different from offenders who do not have mental illnesses (Alexander, 1992).

For these reasons, an integrative approach is critically important for corrections. As described in this chapter, this generic framework consists of factors in the helping relationship and stages of counseling. In addition, other dyadic counseling relationships, consisting of crisis intervention and case management, are described because they are appropriate for corrections.

THE HELPING RELATIONSHIP

Gross and Capuzzi (1995) state that the process of counseling and psychotherapy depends on establishment of a helping relationship between the client and the counselor. Without a helping relationship, the probability of counseling producing a beneficial result for the client is slim. Counselors and therapists have had multiple terms and definitions for this relationship.

For example, Teyber (1988) calls it the *collaborative relationship*, which is defined as a working alliance with a client. Combs and Avila (1985) refer to structuring the relationship or creating an atmosphere in which the client can ultimately be helped. Rogers (1961) defines a helping relationship as a process in which a counselor furthers the process that aids a client in growth, development, maturity, improved functioning, and better coping skills. Regardless of different terms and definitions, Gross and Capuzzi (1995) list seven definitive characteristics of the helping relationship.

1. Structured initially by the counselor or therapist but open to cooperative restructuring based upon the needs of the client
2. That begins with the initial meeting and continues through termination
3. In which all persons involved perceive the existence of trust, caring, concern, and commitment and act accordingly
4. In which the needs of the client are given priority over the needs of the counselor or therapist
5. That provides for the personal growth of all persons involved
6. That provides for the safety needed for self-exploration of all persons involved
7. That promotes the potential of all persons involved

The application of some of Gross and Capuzzi's characteristics of a helping relationship in the criminal justice system deserves explication. At first glance, emphasizing the needs of the client (criteria one and four) may seem questionable in a prison environment. Most prisons and many of the people who work in them do not place priority on the needs of prisoners. Security takes priority. However, Gross and Capuzzi address the helping relationship, which involves a counselor and a prisoner. Thus, a counselor and prisoner may have established a helping relationship based on an agreed contract when the prisoner experiences a new problem. A restructuring of the original helping relationship to accommodate the needs of the prisoner is not unpractical. Such an accommodation would not be incompatible with prison security. Likewise, the prisoner's need should take priority over the counselor's needs. Ethicists contend that no professional should seek to have his or her own needs met in a counseling relationship. Hence, a prisoner's needs in a helping relationship should take precedence over a counselor's needs. Perhaps more difficult is displaying trust, caring, concern, and commitment for all persons involved. Persons outside the helping relationship, such as prison guards, are not required to demonstrate these qualities. However, the professional who is engaged with an offender should demonstrate trust, caring, concern, and commitment.

The counselor is the primary person responsible for developing the helping relationship, but the client's commitment and involvement are critical. If each person carries out his or her responsibility, the helping relationship emanates and luxuriates (Gross & Capuzzi, 1995).

These characteristics suggest that the helping relationship is predicated upon the presence of several essential counselor-related factors consisting of the provision of empathy, respect or positive regard, genuineness, warmth, immediacy, and cultural awareness (Gross & Capuzzi, 1995). According to Gross and Capuzzi (1995), the first five core conditions were gleaned from the counseling literature. The last, cultural awareness, was added by them because they believe that sensitivity to cultural issues is important in counseling.

However, Gross and Capuzzi (1995) did not include gender awareness and, specifically, sensitivity to women's issues. Of course, a counselor's capacity to communicate empathy would include women's issues, but it should also include cultural or racial issues. Because they rightly include cultural awareness, gender awareness has been added by the author as a core condition in the helping relationship. Including gender issues is important for the number of females, both adult and juvenile, in corrections. In sum, the counselor must have or incorporate empathy, respect or positive regard, genuineness, warmth, immediacy, cultural awareness, and gender awareness in the helping relationship for it to thrive. See Figure 5.1.

Empathy

Rogers (1961) defined *empathy* as a counselor's ability "to sense the client's private world as if it were your own" (p. 284). Empathy is not the same as sympathy because sympathy does not involve identification with the client (Patterson, 1974). A further differentiation between empathy and sympathy is that sympathy is elicited from only a negative emotion. A person is generally sympathetic to hear that another person has had a death in the family. However, a person is not sympathetic to hear that an individual had successful triple-bypass heart surgery (Batson & Coke, 1981). One is not sympathetic to hear that a friend has won a lottery for fifty million dollars or has received a promotion and salary increase. Empathy involves a person's ability to sense another person's private world, regardless of whether the emotion is positive or negative.

Providing a broader context, Batson and Coke (1981) state that empathy involved "an emotional response elicited by and congruent with the perceived welfare of someone else" (p. 169). Cross and Capuzzi (1995) write that empathy is the counselor's capacity to understand a client's feelings, thoughts, ideas, and experiences.

Other clinicians have conceptualized empathy as consisting of two processes. The first is attunement, which refers to the counselor entering the client's frame of reference and viewing this frame of reference from the client's perspective. Attuning also refers to the counselor entering the client's frame of reference and hearing how information comes to the client. Once the information has been initially heard, the counselor follows information moment by moment. Though the counselor is inside the client's frame of reference, the counselor is nonjudgmental. There is no assessment of the truthfulness, appropriateness, or psychopathology of the client's experiences. After the counselor is thoroughly attuned with the client, the second process is implemented, and it is to communicate this attunement to the client and to do so regularly and continually. By communicating empathy, the client feels acceptance by the counselor and feels the counselor's presence in the counseling session (Greenberg, Rice, & Elliott, 1993).

Saying that a counselor should be empathic is easier said than done. Some counselors are unable to be empathic for several reasons. One reason is that some counselors are not empathic during a counseling session because the counselors are not in touch with their own feelings. Another reason is that counselors, like other people, have life difficulties at times and may not be able to show empathy if clients are expressing emotions that the counselors want to avoid or are not ready to address. A final situation is that empathy may be difficult for counselors to convey if their clients have done something that is abhorrent, such as man who has battered his

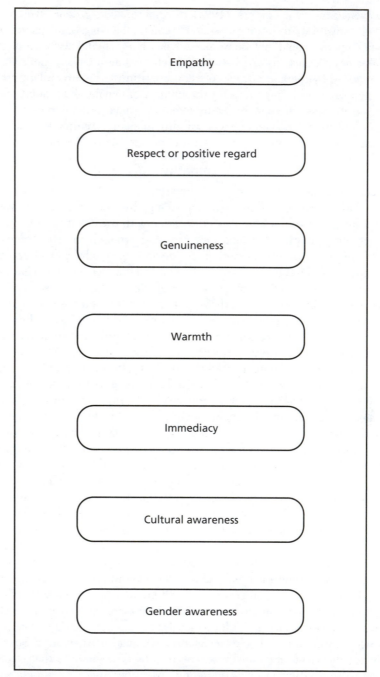

FIGURE 5.1 Core Conditions of the Helping Relationship

spouse (Shulman, 1984). This is especially possible in criminal justice counseling where some offenders have committed very heinous offenses; however, age and experience increase a criminal justice counselor's capacity to communicate empathy (Masters, 1994).

Notwithstanding, a counselor's capacity to demonstrate empathy can be enhanced by means other than the passage of time. Some counselor's attributes and actions can increase the counselor's capacity to convey empathy. These include a counselor acquiring knowledge and sensitivity to the counselor's own values, attitudes, and beliefs and how these values, attitudes, and beliefs affect the counselor's life. A byproduct of this knowledge acquisition is how these factors express themselves in the counseling relationship. Also important is the extent to which the counselors are accepting of their own personal histories and the extent to which they are willing to share some of these histories in the counseling relationship (Gross & Capuzzi, 1995).

Basic empathy can be developed by a counselor's use of attending skills, such as paraphrasing, reflection of feelings, and reflection of meaning (Ivey, 1987). Also, empathy can be conveyed by nonverbal communications, such as trunk lean, eye contact, vocal intonation, and facial expressions (Harrigan & Rosenthal, 1986). The counselor can nod his or her head appropriately to a client's expressions. The counselor could say "Uh-huh" or "Yeah" to the client's expressions. Also, the counselor could indicate that he or she did not get something. As an example, "I didn't quite get that last part, something about being unappreciated." The latter question is empathic because it indicates that the counselor is attempting to hear the client and inviting the client to clarify (Greenberg, Rice, & Elliott, 1993, p. 106).

However, Masters (1994) cautions that counselors should be careful with typical empathic responses in a criminal justice setting and not give canned responses. According to her, offenders are likely to see some counselors as phonies. A criminal justice counselor must know the offender's reality and convey this reality in a manner that the offender can understand.

Respect and Positive Regard

Rogers (1961) describes the concept of *unconditional positive regard*, which means that counselors should accept clients absolutely. Unconditionally, as defined by Carkhuff and Berenson (1967), is the initial suspension by the counselor of possible biased feelings, attitudes, and judgments. However, other counselors understood this concept differently and chose to speak in terms of positive regard, noting that few people are able to unconditionally accept clients (Carkhuff & Berenson, 1967). To illustrate, a counselor should be able to indicate to a client that some behaviors are inappropriate and interfere with the counseling relationship, such as a client who takes off his or her clothing and wants to discuss issues in the nude. A counselor should not unconditionally accept such behaviors when the counselor is uncomfortable by nudity in a counseling session.

Thus, positive regard is respect or concern for a client's feelings, experiences, and potential (Carkhuff & Berenson, 1967). It also has been referred to as the counselor's belief in the innate worth and potentiality of a client and the counselor's ability to convey these feelings to the client. To the extent that the counselor successfully and continuously conveys respect and positive regard to the client, the client is positively reinforced regarding the client's capacity to grow, change, determine goals, and decide personal issues. With the help of the counselor, the client is empowered to take charge and change (Gross & Capuzzi, 1995).

How does the counselor convey respect and positive regard? It can be done in a number of ways because it is totally a task for the counselor. Of course, the counselor can verbally convey to the client his or her utmost respect and regard. However, respect and positive regard can be conveyed without the counselor saying anything. A counselor's patience in allowing a client to come up with answers to expressed dilemmas suggests to the client that the counselor respects the client's ability to find answers without totally relying on the counselor. Also, the counselor can increase his or her capacity to convey respect and positive regard by reexamining himself or herself. To successfully convey respect and positive regard to clients, a counselor must respect himself or herself. The counselor can model those behaviors for clients. The counselor can also be sensitive to his or her own control behaviors, checking these issues so that they do not enter the counseling relationship (Gross & Capuzzi, 1995).

Genuineness

Genuineness refers to the extent to which a counselor is real and unadulterated with a client and the degree to which the counselor is willing to disclose aspects of his or her personality (Carkhuff & Berenson, 1967). Hershenson and Power (1987) add that genuineness is the extent to which the counselor's words are congruent with the counselor's actions. Gross and Capuzzi (1995) advise that a counselor must not indicate that he or she is playing a role and must convey to a client the counselor's authenticity. Notwithstanding, the need to be genuine is not an open invitation to be too frank and honest with a client.

Carkhuff and Berenson (1967) differentiate genuineness from facilitated genuineness. The former refers to the degree to which the counselor is truthful and disclosing. However, genuineness does not mean that the counselor is unfettered in critical comments. Some clients are fragile and cannot handle very critical comments. Thus, facilitated genuineness refers to the above definition of genuineness, which has as its primary end the welfare of the client. In short, facilitated genuineness involves genuineness and tactfulness.

Warmth

The degree to which a counselor conveys warmth and understanding determines the extent to which respect is communicated (Raush & Bordin, 1957). Gross and Capuzzi (1995) stated that warmth is how counselors convey to clients the counselor's caring and concern. A counselor, exhibiting warmth in the therapeutic process, communicates the counselor's embrace of the client, concern for the welfare of the client, and sincerity in helping solve the client's problems (Gross & Capuzzi, 1995). Warmth is communicated by the counselor's commitment, efforts to understand the client, and spontaneity (Raush & Bordin, 1957). It also can be communicated by a smile, touch, tone of voice, and facial expression (Gross & Capuzzi, 1995). However, given the current climate regarding sexual harassment and abuse, no counselor should touch a correctional client.

Concreteness

Concreteness refers to the ability of both the counselor and the client, but mostly the counselor, to express fluently, directly, and completely feelings and experiences (Carkhuff & Berenson, 1967). Stated differently and simply, it "is the ability not only to see the incomplete picture that clients paint with their words, but also to communicate to clients the figures, images, and structures that will complete the picture" (Gross & Capuzzi, 1995, p. 15). Clients' depictions of their problems sometimes are fragmented and partial. Concreteness helps the client to present a whole account. Vague issues are clarified, specific focus is provided, uncertainty is reduced, and judicious expenditure of problem-solving energy occurs when concreteness is utilized (Gross & Capuzzi, 1995).

The quality of concreteness advances three valuable functions. First, the counselor's concreteness addresses and coincides with the client's emotional expressions. Second, concreteness forces the counselor to attend to the client, and any misunderstanding or miscommunications can be corrected. Third, the client is directed to address his or her issues (Carkhuff & Berenson, 1967).

Immediacy

Immediacy refers to the counselor's skills in detecting problems, issues, and distractions as they occur in counseling sessions and bringing these issues immediately to the forefront. As example of some of these impediments are a client's unspoken but obvious anger at the counselor, the counselor's frustrations with the client, and perhaps personal feelings when they have the potential to be barriers to the helping process (Gross & Capuzzi, 1995).

Cultural Awareness

The importance of a counselor's awareness of cultural differences in clients is extremely important. For instance, a Hispanic social worker who worked with gang members observed that differences exist between Asian, African American, and Hispanic gangs. Asian gang members frequently engaged in extortion and home invasion of other Asian members. African American gangs frequently fought other African Americans gangs over drug trafficking. However, Hispanic gangs frequently fought and killed other Hispanics over manhood. According to the social worker, Hispanics have entrenched family values. Support for this contention was provided by an African American adult prisoner who witnessed the closeness of Hispanic prisoners and their families. The prisoner marveled at the loyalty of Hispanic family members in visiting their family members behind bars (Mydans, 1995).

Cross-cultural mental health has become a concern of mental health professionals and an issue in counseling practices. This concern came about when some counselors documented the racism that exists in mental health counseling. Ridley (1995) stated that, compared with white clients, minority clients report more unfavorable experiences in terms of diagnosis, staff assignment, treatment modality, utilization, treatment duration, and attitudes. He described five factors that contributed to racism by counselors. These are a counselor having good intentions but having bad intervention, the counselor's traditional training, cultural tunnel vision, blaming the victim, and either-or thinking (Ridley, 1995). See Figure 5.2.

1. Possessing good intentions but improper interventions

2. Traditional training

3. Cultural tunnel vision

4. Blaming the victim

5. Either-or thinking

FIGURE 5.2 Five Contributing Factors to Counselors' Racism

Criticisms of this nature, as well as acceptance of the significant of past ethnographic studies of different cultures, forced a change in counseling perspective.

As a result, more importance was given to studies on the influence of indigenous, folk-healing practices, psychoanalytic anthropology, and the provision of mental health services to ethnic minorities. The American Psychological Association and American Counseling Association have identified Native Americans, African Americans, Hispanic Americans, and Asian Americans/Pacific Islanders for special attention regarding cultural concerns, observing that a description of all minority groups is arduous (Arciniega & Newlon, 1995).

Early nineteenth-century anthropologists documented folk-healing practices found in different cultures. These early reports included references to psychic healing but failed to indicate confidently the effectiveness of these interventions. Embracing ethnocultural and transcultural psychiatric views, counselors later encouraged consideration of the psychiatric qualities of shamans, curanderos, witch doctors, Yoruba priests, spiritualists, and Navaho healers (Comas-Diaz, 1988). Although these practices were not taken seriously, Griffith and Young (1988) documented the healing power of religious practices.

The second factor in the development of cross-cultural mental health is psychoanalytic anthropology. An early mental health professional, George Devereux, used cultural factors in psychoanalytic therapy with Plains Indians and culturally marginal white patients. Other professionals followed Devereux's lead and used psychoanalytically oriented counseling in a cross-cultural context. A popular research focus from Devereux's perspective considers identity disorders with persons who hold dual cultural memberships. The consideration and inclusion of cultural factors have been called critically important in psychoanalytic counseling (Comas-Diaz, 1988).

The third factor of cross-cultural mental health has been the challenge of the mental health profession to provide effective mental health services to ethnic minorities, such as African Americans, Hispanics, Latinos, Asian Americans and Pacific Islanders, Native Americans, and Native Alaskans. Providing encouragement to the provision of mental health services to these groups were the civil rights movement and the Community Mental Health Act. Because of the mandate provided by these factors, professionals were forced to debate ethnicity and social class factors, minority group membership, dysfunctional versus functional behaviors, counselor and client matching, and culturally relevant treatment (Comas-Diaz, 1988).

Paniagua (1994) recommends general guidelines for assessing and treating multicultural groups. According to him, the development of a helping relationship comprises three levels. The first level is conceptual, which involves the counselor and client's perception of the extent of sincerity, openness, honesty, motivation, empathy, sensitivity, genuine concern, and credibility. The second level is behavioral, which involves the client's belief of the counselor's professional training and competency. The behavioral level also includes the counselor's perception of the client's capacity to carry out the agreed treatment plan. The third level is cultural, which includes either cultural compatibility or universality (Paniagua, 1994).

The cultural compatibility perspective provides that the successfulness of assessing and treating multicultural groups is strengthened by the minimization of ethnic and racial barriers. Ideally, this would involve racial and ethnic matching between the counselor and client. However, research has shown that matching is not associated with outcome (Paniagua, 1994). Further, a racial match may lead to a cultural mismatch. For instance, both a counselor and a client may be Hispanic but may have different ethnicity (i.e., different values and lifestyles). At the same time, a white counselor may be culturally compatible with a highly acculturated Hispanic client (Paniagua, 1994).

The universal approach holds that the assessment and treatment is the same for all minority groups. White counselors, according to the universalistic argument, can be as effective as Hispanic counselors in providing effective counseling to a Hispanic client. The key is that the white counselors must be culturally sensitive by being aware of cultural variables relevant to assessment and treatment. Equally important, the counselor must be culturally competent by taking his or her awareness of culturally relevant variables and behaving in a manner that would lead to effective treatment for the particular minority group being served. A byproduct of the universalistic argument is that a dyad consisting of a counselor and client of the same race may be ineffective provided the counselor does not demonstrate sensitivity and competence (Paniagua, 1994). As an illustration, an African American counselor who comes from a middle or upper class environment can be as ineffective as a middle or upper class white counselor with a lower class African American client if the African American counselor is insensitive and incompetent (Paniagua, 1994).

Regardless of the composition of the dyads, a culturally sensitive counselor possesses certain characteristics (Sue & Sue, 1990). He or she should have an awareness of one's own culture and its influences; an awareness of the narrowness of a single, mainstream perspective; an awareness and appreciation of alternative world views; and a willingness to employ culturally sensitive approaches in diagnosis and intervention (Parsons & Wicks, 1994). The American Psychological Association and the American Counseling Association, concerned by the need for culturally sensitive services, pronounce that a culturally sensitive counselor must be cognizant of the historical, educational, social, political, and economic issues affecting minority groups. In addition, the counselor should be knowledgeable of family factors and values (Arciniega & Newlon, 1995).

Gender Awareness

Gender awareness may be discussed on several levels. One level is to begin with feminist theory. Its central foundation is that "the personal is the political." This phrase means that women's mental health is correlated with the degree to which women are valued in society for their personal qualities and social role performances. Rather than psychic determinism, women are understood from the perspective of the environmental forces that impinge on women. Perceived women's craziness and deviance result from oppressive patriarchally ascribed roles. Feminism rejects psychoanalytic theory because it conveys the notion that women are passive, emotional, and inferior to men. To the extent that women are passive or emotional, they are this way because they are socialized by societal institutions. Essentially, only two theories are congruent with feminism. These are social psychological- and sociological-based theories because they help to explain the learning of roles (Valentich, 1986).

Feminists distinguished sex and gender. Sex describes physiological differences between men and women, whereas gender embodies an individual's status as feminine, masculine, and androgynous. Gender roles represent coerced behaviors, attitudes, and characteristics compatible with gender status. Another changed concept regarding women is the reconceptualization of them not as victims but as survivors.

Comas-Diaz (1988) explains gender issues in cross-cultural counseling. Family and community culture aids individuals in becoming psychologically either male or female. In addition, the normal socialization processes teach and reinforce appropriate behaviors and feelings for each sex. Accordingly, different roles develop for males and females depending upon their culture. These factors, being female and a minority, are significant in cross-cultural counseling. Ethnic differences interact with gender to impact the counseling process and possibly the outcome (Comas-Diaz, 1988). One study found that the probability of misconceptions in counseling is greatest when the counselor is a white male and the client is a minority female (Wilkinson, 1980). Also, women's experiences may be different depending upon the woman's race. Supporting this view, two researchers found that significant differences existed in African American and white incarcerated women regarding mental health issues (Alexander & Nickerson, 1993).

These gender issues help to shape the counseling process. From a feminist perspective, the helping relationship consists of two equals. The counselor does not present herself or himself as an expert. The reason for this stance is that the nonexpert role is not likely to reinforce the counselor as an authority and the woman as subservient to this authority. The nonexpert role also does not impede the growth of the woman and does not make her dependent. The counseling process is demystified and humanized. Techniques that further this equal process is use of first names, self-disclosure by the counselor of both feminist values and personal experiences, an informal and comfortable place for the counseling session, a sliding scale for fees, no or minimal record keeping, permission for clients to have access to their records, development of contracts, input from clients in decisions regarding interventions, and providing a rationale for interactions (Valentich, 1986).

Thomas (1977) surveyed the literature and found five characteristics of feminist practice. These are feminist humanism, feminist consciousness, changes in the traditional relationship between the counselor and client, consciousness raising, and emphasis on the universality of women's experiences.

Drawn from Thomas' survey of the literature, one model of feminist counseling is called *sex fair*. This model is devoid of sex-biased values. Another model provides that skills most needed for a feminist counseling approach are positive evaluation of women, social analysis, encouragement of total development, behavior feedback, and self-disclosure (Valentich, 1986).

These models indicate areas of interventions. Three important interventions of the counselor are counteracting the negative consequences of socialization based on patriarchy, providing support and services to clients that are not available in the client's environment, and treating any problems that emerge in the client's life (Valentich, 1986).

In feminist practice, there are three phases of intervention consisting of exploration, action, and termination. The activities of the counselor in these phases vary. No formal assessment, diagnosis, and treatment are done because these suggest pathology. Feminist counselors stress current concerns in counseling. The past is discussed to provide the client with an understanding of her oppression and its link to the woman's current problems (Valentich, 1986).

To intervene in these areas, certain skills are needed. Thomas (1977) reports that necessary skills for feminist practice are the counselor's encouragement of the woman client to behave nontraditionally, modeling nontraditional behaviors, validation of women's experiences, self-disclosure, making client's aware of sexist social structure, and providing a social structure explanation for problems.

Of course, the feminist perspective discussed here may not be wholly appropriate for corrections. Addressing a counselor by his or her first name may not be appropriate with a probation or parole office. It may not be appropriate either in prison or a halfway house. Also, it may be difficult to focus on female offenders' oppression by a male-dominated society and to attribute her problems to this oppressive environment, while telling an African American male prisoner that he needs to take responsibility for his actions. However, the strength of the feminist model for correction is a focus on women's strengths and less on pathology. Also, referring to women who have been sexually assaulted or girls who have been molested as survivors is ultimately therapeutic. So, feminist's ideology and techniques that empower women are appropriate for the correctional field.

The previously discussed core dimensions of the helping relationship are utilized throughout the counseling process with individuals. Of course, positive regard, empathy, gender awareness, and genuineness should be manifested in the first meeting with the client and all meetings thereafter. So, these core dimensions are not factors that a counselor employs in the first meeting and then forgets about them in the other stages of counseling.

STAGES OF COUNSELING

Therapists and counselors have described a number of stages of therapy or counseling with different terminologies for each stage. For instance, Carkhuff and Berenson (1967) stated that counseling consisted of two stages. Shulman (1984) suggested that there were four stages, calling them preliminary, beginning, work, and ending. Gross and Capuzzi (1995) opined that counseling consisted of four stages. Compton and Galaway (1994) described the stages of counseling as consisting of the contact phase, contract phase, and action phase. Moreover, one counseling professional indicated that there were nine steps in the counseling process.

Regardless of the number of phases and names for specific phases, all seem to encapsulate logical steps in helping individuals with problems. Because this textbook's focus is counseling offenders, a comprehensive model of counseling is needed. Such a model must be adaptable to adolescent females, adult females, juvenile males, and adult males. It must also be useful for counseling mentally ill offenders, whose issues are quite different from offenders who are not mentally ill. It must also be adaptable to community-based and institutional corrections. One model that provides such a comprehensive perspective is Beitman's model (1987), with some minor revisions by the author.

Beitman's (1987) model consists of four stages. These are engagement, pattern search, change, and termination. Additionally, Beitman indicates that each stage has six components consisting of goals, techniques, content, resistance, transference, and counter-transference. Hence, resistance may be reflected during each of the four stages. For instance, while almost all offenders want to get out of prison, some prisoners, fearing failure or experiencing uncertainty, are resistant to leaving prison. In like manner, techniques are utilized to engage the client, assist in identifying pattern search, facilitate change, and effectively terminate counseling. See Figure 5.3. The following sections discuss each stage and the specific component applicable.

Engagement

Beitman (1987) indicates that the goal of engagement is to transform the initial anonymity between the counselor and client into a helping relationship. To this end, engagement consists of four elements—markers, methods, content, and distortions. Markers refer to indicators of engagement, such as trust. Methods involve techniques for enhancing the helping relationship, such as the manifestation of empathy or cultural sensitivity. Content involves clarification and understanding of the clients' problems, psychological pain, and symptoms. Finally, distortions refer to impediments to the process, such as transference, counter-transference, and resistance.

Beitman's first two concepts have been described as core conditions in the discussion of the helping relationship and need not be repeated. Beitman's other two concepts provide a partial framework for describing engagement. Obviously, engagement requires an initial meeting between the client and the counselor; however, Beitman failed to discuss in detail this initial engagement process. For this reason, the author expands upon engagement and tailors it for a correction population.

The Importance of the Initial Correction Interview

The initial meeting or interview with offenders is critically important for several reasons. First, the counselor needs to make an assessment of the offender's psychological state and the reasons for counseling if voluntary on the offender's part. Some institutionalized offenders may want to establish a relationship with a counselor in order to solicit later a parole recommendation. Some offenders are mandated by the legal system for counseling, such as batterers. Because they may be angry, their resistance would need to be addressed early and the counselor should clarify the expectations and goals. Also, more and more mentally ill offenders are sent to prison and an initial meeting is important in order to assess their current mental state. Furthermore, some offenders enter prison at risk for developing mental illness and the

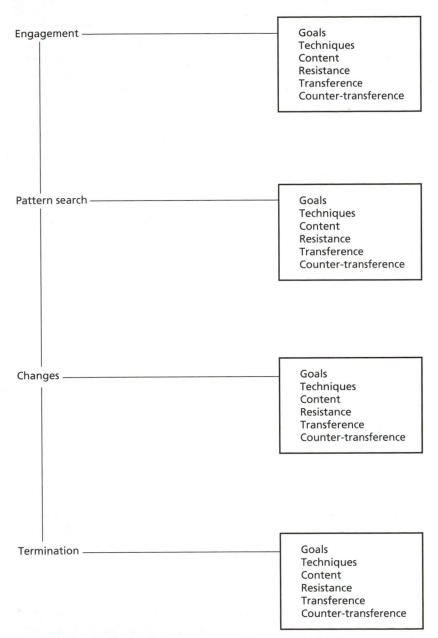

FIGURE 5.3 Beitman's Model
Adapted from *The Structure of Individual Psychotherapy,* B. D. Beitman (New York: The Guilford Press, 1987). © The Guilford Press. Used with permission.

stresses in the prison environment may trigger a psychiatric break, such as a prisoner who is gang-raped or cannot cope with the other violence in the prison environment. So, this part of Beitman's engagement stage is expanded to describe the interview stage and problem identification within the correctional context.

The Initial Interview

Corey (1991), who has worked with involuntary correction clients, states that counselors should begin the counseling relationship by discussing frankly and honestly the nature of their relationship. The counselor should not promise a client anything that cannot be provided, should clarify the extent of confidentiality, and should address any issues that could impinge upon the counseling relationship. Once this foundation has been laid, the counselor should prepare clients for the process. The questions that should be asked are: What is the therapy about? What are the joint responsibilities of each? How might therapy help them get what they want? What can the client do to increase the chances that the therapeutic experience will be positive? What are the potential risks and dangers? What can the client expect in the general course of treatment? The counselor's addressing of these questions reduces involuntary clients' resistance, and failing to raise these questions increases the probability of resistance (Corey, 1991).

The counselor should, along with the client, identify the problems or goals of counseling.

Problem Identification

Patterson (1974) states that behaviorists have made a significant contribution to counseling and psychotherapy by showing the importance of establishing goals in the treatment process. A review of the literature showed that the number and types of goals were extensive. These goals cited included the removal or elimination of symptoms, the unlearning of maladaptive habits and learning of adaptive habits, the reduction of anxiety, relief from suffering, cure or alleviation of a mental disorder, personality reorganization, effective biological and social functioning, and adjustment to the environment. Corey (1991) categorized these goals on a continuum from specific-general to concrete-global. In addition, he called these short-term to long-term goals. Cognitive–behavioral therapies emphasize specific, concrete, and short-term goals, whereas the relationship-oriented therapies emphasize general, global, and long-term goals (Corey, 1991).

With offenders, the goals of counseling are varied, depending upon the type of offender. For juvenile and adult offenders attempting to live in the community, the goals may be the learning of independent living skills or a reduction in dysfunctional behavior. In an institutional setting, the goals may be the adjustment to the prison environment, problematic mental functions, and issues regarding chemical use. For mentally ill prisoners, the goals may be the reduction of symptoms and the learning of social skills. Some specific issues, such as preparing for death, may arise from prisoners suffering from AIDS and prisoners on death row preparing for execution.

Pattern Search

According to Beitman (1987), "the goal of the pattern search is to define patterns of thought, feelings, and/or behavior that are within the client's ability to influence and that, if changed, would lead toward a desirable outcome" (p. 82). Put another way, patterns encompass emotional expression, expectations, major interpersonal styles, intrapsychic conflicts, self-other boundary weakness, and anxiety-producing unconscious materials. Some counselors would refer to this stage as assessment.

The counselor should keep in mind that considerable variability exists among clients, and the beliefs and behaviors have social and cultural basis. For instance, emotional distress may be attributed to unparallelism between the astrological positioning of planets with the client's zodiac signs, ingratitude shown to ancestors and parents, the harmful psychology of the mother when the client was in the womb, and disobedience to the inner voice (Beitman, 1987).

With offenders, emotional distress or problems may be attributable to luck or fate caused by any of several forces including "roots." African Americans reared in the South sometimes seek out "root doctors" when they are experiencing bad luck or physical or emotional distress. Typically, the diagnosis is that someone is working "roots" on the person and thereby causing distress. Problems with the law may be attributable to these forces.

A clear understanding is needed for clients because the content that is communicated to the client is important. Beitman (1987) states that

> many labels may be used to expose and clarify underlying patterns of psychological dysfunction. What is important for psychotherapeutic change is not whether the terms used to explain the problem fit according to a warmly embraced theory, but whether or not the client can understand or use the idea behind it. If the client cannot use the idea, it is not psychotherapeutically effective even if the therapist is convinced of its explanatory power. Therefore, any of a number of contents are potentially able to lead to desired change. This conclusion implies a vision of the human mind in which there are potentially many different handles by which to grasp a maladaptive pattern and to change it. (p. 85)

A number of methods exist for uncovering content. One method is the use of questionnaires or personal logs. Instruments such as the Minnesota Multiphasic Personality Inventory (MMPI) and the Symptom Check List-90 (SCL-90) provide a number of scales that can be used to discern problems or provide a baseline from which to measure future change. Other specific instruments can be used, such as Beck's depression scale, to measure specific mood. In addition, a client may be given a homework assignment consisting of the keeping of a personal log. This is a method for discerning a client's daily activities and when certain problematic behavior tends to occur and at what intensity.

Listening is another method for uncovering content. At times, clients speak in metaphors, allegories, and symbols, which all require interpretation by the counselor. The counselor may be listening to any of three types of speech–symbolic speech, objective speech, and experiential speech. A counselor trained in psychoanalysis may listen attentively for symbolic speech. A counselor trained in behaviorism would take speech at face value while observing that some words may be missing. A counselor trained in humanism strives to experience the feelings emanating from the client. Counselors may listen for any of the three types and may respond differently from one time to another. For instance, a client may tell a story involving a friend, which may be the client. Offenders may use this type of communication, fearing that a frank admission may lead to trouble from a correctional counselor or parole officer. The counselor may listen symbolically or humanistically.

Questioning a client is another method to uncover content. However, questioning may exist in other contexts than only interrogative sentences. In the English language, a person may articulate a declarative, interrogative, exclamatory, or imperative sentence. Obviously, the interrogative is the most frequently used sentence by counselors. Some therapists believe that declarative statements, more than interrogative sentences, may be used. For instance, a counselor, hearing a client's painful story, may respond, "I wonder what feelings you may have had about that," instead of "How did you feel about that?" (Beitman, 1987, p. 123).

Change

Change, called intervention by some clinicians, involves a process consisting of three substages. First, the pattern deemed to be in the problem needing change must eventually be viewed by the client as his or her responsibility. For problematic patterns not created by a client but the client is maintaining them, the client must acknowledge maintenance of the problem. Second, when a client is made aware of his or her responsibility in changing a problem, the client assumes responsibility for changing. The assumption of responsibility marks a new attitude or new behavior. Typically, this desire for change is actuated by emotion (i.e., fear, hope, desire, or guilt). Third, the initial steps toward change, be they a new of acting, thinking, feeling or behavior, must be practiced (Beitman, 1987).

Beitman (1987) recommends some global change techniques (i.e., exhortation, interpretation, and therapist self-disclosure) that could be used in the three stages of change. For instance, he states that exhortation may be used for responsibility awareness, initiation of change, and practice. Clients are exhorted to become aware of their responsibility, their duty to initiate change, and their need to practice new skills. Interpretation, defined as the process of assigning meaning to symptoms, behaviors, emotions, and thoughts, could be employed for responsibility awareness, initiation of change, and practice.

From a psychoanalytic perspective, confrontation, defined as orally holding a mirror before a client, is needed to efface a client's resistance to insight. Confrontation highlights symptomatic behavior and thinking. A number of repeated confrontations may become a clarification. In that the client is involved in the dysfunctional pattern, the counselor encourages overtly and covertly the client to contemplate himself or herself as responsible for the pattern. During this process, the client uncovers his or her responsibility. At the next stage, interpretation reverses the effects of repression, changes superego functioning, and assists the client in functioning independently. During the final stage, repeated interpretations help a client imbibe important information. A client may have had long been affected by unpleasant wishes, fears, fantasies, and memories. The client, by the repeated interpretations, learns that these unpleasant thoughts are unjustified.

The last technique described by Beitman is therapist self-disclosure. At times, a counselor's self-disclosure could be curative in that it could reduce the distance between the counselor and client. Self-disclosure should have a purpose and should further a therapeutic objective. Regarding responsibility awareness, a counselor's self-disclosure may be helpful in furthering a client's awareness of his or her effect on others. A counselor may describe the effect of a client's behavior on him or her and ponder with the client whether others may feel this way. In the initiation of change, a counselor could help a client become more aware of his or her responsibility. It also can become the basis for initiation of change. Regarding practice, a

> Mutually agreed termination
> Client-initiated termination
> Counselor-initiated termination
> Forced termination

FIGURE 5.4 Types of Terminations

counselor's self-disclosure is somewhat limited during the practice phase. A counselor could disclose that he or she had struggled with an issue but persevered until the issue was resolved. This type of self-disclosure entreats the client to copy, match, or identify with the counselor's behavior.

Termination

At some point, a counseling relationship ends. It can end by mutual agreement. It can end when one party, such as the counselor or client, decides to end it. It also can end with external forces, such as probation department or a parole board, terminating the counseling relationship. In some settings, a counseling relationship is open-ended, and termination occurs when both parties intuitively realize that the relationship should come to an end. Several types of terminations exist, such as mutually agreed termination, client-initiated termination, counselor-initiated termination, and forced termination. See Figure 5.4.

Mutually Agreed Termination There may be mutual agreement that more work could be done but they are, in general, satisfied with their accomplishments. Ideally, a counseling relationship should end when previously accepted goals have been achieved. However, with some problems the establishment of rigid goals may be difficult. This is especially true when the issue is a client's personality. Some work may uncover other issues to be addressed. So, a client with an antisocial personality disorder, which is abundant in the prison system, may reveal after some work that other problematic issues exist, such as childhood abuse or negative attitudes toward women.

Client-Initiated Termination Clients terminate counseling for several reasons. For free individuals, clients may terminate for insurance or money-related reasons. However, cost is not a terminating factor with offenders. The reasons that would apply to offenders are demeaning and humiliating situations and an unreadiness to deal with problems. Some clients may not want to deal with certain psychological issues and the counselor's prodding may cause the client to terminate. Clients may terminate when they feel continued counseling is not necessary. Last, a client's death may termite counseling. This cause is quite common when a client has serious mental health problems. It is not uncommon for seriously ill clients to commit suicide or get killed when they wander out in traffic.

Counselor-Initiated Termination A counselor may initiate termination when the client has made adequate improvement but does not want to leave the supportive environment of the counseling relationship. Also, the counselor may feel that an impasse has been reached and termination of the counseling relationship is appropriate. The key issue is determining when is enough or when the client has reached the maximum amount of benefits. However, some situations are easy for counselors to initiate termination. In corrections, there must be rules and some rules are so serious that a counselor may be forced to terminate an offender from treatment, such as fighting or threatening another prisoner's life or the counselor's life.

Forced Termination Counselors can force termination when they leave an agency and another counselor must take over a case load. This occurs frequently with counselors in training or with an organization where change is important for advancement or where change is desired for personal reasons. As an illustration, a prison counselor may transfer from one institution to another, forcing all prisoners to seek out a different counselor or wait for someone new to be hired. Such a move may be for a higher job classification or because the counselor has a conflicting relationship with a supervisor.

Techniques of Termination Counselors take different positions regarding how to terminate. Disagreement exists regarding whether to continue the same frequency of sessions near the end or to taper sessions as a way of weaning clients. Those who favor a continued schedule believe it allows clients to realistically deal with loss. Different views exist regarding terminating at an agreed time or being flexible and extending counseling if deemed necessary. Those who favor adherence to agreed termination are realistic in that life predicaments are unexpected and untimely. Differences exist regarding whether a counselor should maintain his or her professional persona or become more humane at termination. Some counselors believe professionalism should be maintained throughout the counseling relationship, but others feel that counselors should become more sociable or personable.

CRISIS INTERVENTION

From time to time, all people are going to experience a disruption in their lives, and they may not function adequately for a period. However, the level of functioning following a crisis may become more serious. Although all people experience crises in their daily lives and recover from them quickly, some persons do not. Persons suffering from schizophrenia create an abundance of life events that have the potential for creating crises because of their lifestyles and goals. Therefore, they are confronted with crisis-provoking events more than persons without severe mental illnesses (Perris & Skagerlind, 1994).

The criminal justice system has experienced a significant increase in persons with serious mental illnesses, and many of these persons experience crises while they are incarcerated and while they are under supervision by parole and probation officers. Also, mental health professionals state that prisoners who have been sexually assaulted in childhood may suffer a crisis of a limited nature when the assaults occurred. However, some woman prisoners who have been sexually assaulted have long-lasting and potentially severe cognitive, physiological, and behavioral dysfunction, which may trigger a crisis years later (Petretic-Jackson & Jackson, 1990).

This may have happened when a woman prisoner in one of the California prisons experienced a severe reaction to a changed prison policy of having male correctional officers patting down female prisoners (*Jordan v. Gardner*, 1992). The woman prisoner screamed when touched, vomited, and clung to the bars. This type of reaction has been referred by mental health professionals as *post traumatic stress disorder* (Gilliland & James, 1993; Muran & DiGiuseppe, 1994).

Crisis intervention is an extension of brief psychotherapy. At a minimum, the goal is to resolve an individual's psychological distress and to return him or her to the precrisis state. At a maximum, the goal is to enhance the individual's functioning above the precrisis state (Aguilera, 1990). The goal of crisis therapy is to resolve the crisis, change the individual's perception of danger, and restore the individual's functioning (Dixon, 1987).

A person in crisis goes through two and sometimes three stages. The first stage is the impact of the crisis on the individual. Though variation is probable among individuals, a person in crisis typically feels bewildered and confused. The second stage is the coping stage. The individual uses mental and behavioral tasks to resolve the crisis. Most crises are resolved during the second stage. If not, there is a third stage. This is the withdrawal stage. Simply, if none of the techniques employed resolve the crisis, the individual withdraws and ceases trying to resolve the crisis (France, 1990).

Using the contributions of other crisis theorists along with her contributions, Golan (1986) constructed the basic assumptions, hypotheses, and concepts that comprise the principal features of crisis theory. These principle features are

1. Individuals are subjected to periods of increased internal and external stress throughout their normal life span that disturb their customary state of equilibrium with their surrounding environments. Such episodes are usually initiated by some hazardous event that may be a finite external blow or a less-bounded internal pressure that has built up over time. The event may be a single catastrophic occurrence or a series of lesser mishaps that have a cumulative effect.
2. The impact of the hazardous event disturbs individuals' homeostatic balance and puts them into a vulnerable state, marked by heightened tension and anxiety. To regain their equilibrium, they go through a series of predictable phases. First, they try to use their customary repertoire of problem-solving mechanisms to deal with the situation. If this is not successful, their upset increases and they mobilize heretofore-untried emergency methods of coping. However, if the problem continues and cannot be resolved, avoided, or redefined, tension continues until it rises to a peak.
3. At this point, a precipitating factor can bring about a turning point, during which self-righting devices no longer operate and the individual enters a state of active crisis, marked by disequilibrium and disorganization. This is followed by a period of gradual reorganization until a new state of equilibrium is reached.
4. As the crisis situation develops, individuals may perceive the initial and subsequent stressful events primarily as a threat, either to their instinctual needs or to their sense of autonomy and well being; as a loss of a person, an attribute (status or role), or a capacity; or as a challenge to survival, growth, or mastery.
5. Each of these perceptions calls forth a characteristic emotional reaction that reflects the subjective meaning of the event to the individual: threat elicits a

heightened level of anxiety; loss brings about feelings of depression, deprivation, and mourning; challenge stimulates a moderate increase in anxiety plus a kindling of hope and expectation, releasing new energy for problem solving.

6. Although a crisis situation is neither an illness nor a pathological experience and reflects a realistic struggle to deal with the individual's current life situation, it may become linked with earlier unresolved or partially resolved conflicts. This may result in an inappropriate or exaggerated response. Crisis intervention in such situations may provide a multiple opportunity to resolve the present difficulty, to rework the previous difficulties, and/or to break the linkage between them.

7. The total length of time between the initial blow and final resolution of the crisis situation varies widely, depending on the severity of the hazardous event, the characteristic reactions of the person, the nature and complexity of the tasks that have to be accomplished, and the situational supports available. The actual state of active disequilibrium, however, is time-limited, usually lasting four to six weeks.

8. Each particular class of crisis situation (such as the death of a close relative or the experience of being raped) seems to follow a specific sequence of stages that can be predicted and mapped out. Emotional reactions and behavioral responses at each phase can often be anticipated. Fixation and disequilibrium at a particular point may provide the clue as to where the person is "stuck" and what lies behind their inability to do their "crisis work" and master the situation.

9. During the unraveling of the crisis situation, the individual tends to be particularly amenable to help. Customary defense mechanisms have become weakened, usual coping patterns have proved inadequate, and the ego has become more open to outside influence and change. A minimal effort at such time can produce a maximal effect; a small amount of help, appropriately focused, can prove more effective than extensive help at a period of less emotional accessibility.

10. During the reintergration phase, new ego sets may emerge and new adaptive styles may evolve, enabling the person to cope more effectively with other situations in the future. However, if appropriate help is not available during this critical interval, inadequate or maladaptive patterns may be adopted that can result in a weakened ability to function adequately later on (Golan, 1986, pp. 297–298).

Treatment of a Crisis

Treatment of a crisis requires an assessment, establishment of treatment goals, implementation of treatment, and termination. In the assessment phase, five areas must be assessed. These are a hazardous event, the vulnerable state, the precipitating factor, and the state of active crisis, and the extent of reintegration. The hazardous event is a specific-stress–producing internal or external development during a period of stability in an individual's life. The event may be expected and forecast or unexpected and unforeseen. The vulnerable state pertains to the subjective reaction of the individual to the initial occurrence and subsequent reaction. Each individual is different and the response and reactions are going to be different. What is not different is that a parallel effect occurs to each. Threats occasion anxiety; loss occasions depression and mourning; and challenge produces anxiety, hope, excitement, and expectation. Also, a crisis may present shame, guilt, anger, hostility, and cognitive and perceptual confusion. The precipitating factor sparks the stress-provoking happening, bringing tension to a peak and actuating the vulnerable state into a crisis (Golan, 1986).

The state of active crisis refers to the quality of the individual's subjective state after experiencing the cessation of tension, a disruption in the individual's homeostatic condition, and the onset of disequilibrium. This is a key assessment in crisis theory because the assessment determines whether crisis techniques are needed. Persons in active crisis have a common set of reactions, consisting of psychological and physical turmoil. This turmoil may have specific behavioral activities such as disturbances in body functions, mood, mental content, and intellectual functioning (Golan, 1986).

The state of reintegration is a gradual process. As the disequilibrium abates, adjustment will occur. This adjustment may be either adaptive or maladaptive. Cognitive and affective responses occur as a result of the crisis as the individual processes what has happened to him or her. At some point, the individual develops a fresh set of behavioral patterns for coping (Golan, 1986).

Establishing Treatment Goals

Mental health professionals differ regarding the goals of crisis intervention. One professional states that the goal of intervention is to ameliorate the impact of the crisis by providing emotional first aid and to enhance the person's coping and integrative responses. Another professional offers that the goal of crisis intervention is to provide relief of symptoms, restore the precrisis level of functioning, understand the precipitating event and how it affected the person's disequilibrium, identify community resources, understand the nexus between the current crisis and past history, and learn new ways of adapting and coping. Ideally, the latter is preferred because counselors want clients to learn and apply newly learned skills to similar problems in the future (Golan, 1986).

Treatment Implementation

Implementation of treatment involves the identification of persons who are going to carry out tasks. These persons are typically the person undergoing the crisis but may involve the mental health professional or family. Specific treatment varies, depending upon the nature of the crisis. Techniques for addressing a suicidal attempt would be different from death in a person's family. One goal may be the immediate reduction in pressure impinging upon a person, which may be accomplished with the assistance of a family member or a reconception of a problem by an individual with the assistance of a mental health worker (Golan, 1986).

Termination of Crisis Intervention

In crisis intervention, termination carries special importance. In the beginning, the mental health worker is in charge and active, helping the individual to see beyond the crisis and how to get beyond it. In addition, the individual may terminate on his or her own, stating that he or she needs to take charge of his or her life. When this occurs, the mental heath worker becomes less active as the individual becomes more active. When the agreed tasks have been accomplished, the mental health worker and the individual review their progress. The mental health worker stresses the achievement of their goals, the new adaptive patterns learned by the individual, and available resources in the community. The mental health worker reviews future activity by the individual and an intervention plan, if needed, is established (Golan, 1986).

CASE MANAGEMENT

Differentiated from counseling, case management has implications for criminal justice and particularly probation and parole work. Hershenson and Power (1987) wrote that counseling consists of specific processes, including an intervention, whereas case management refers to the monitoring of a client's progress (Marlowe, Marlowe, & Willetts, 1983). Typically, case management consists of assessment, planning, linking, monitoring, and advocacy. In the mental health system, the case manager's job is to facilitate access to services for persons with serious mental illnesses and coordinate such services. These services include assistance in obtaining resources, such as financial, medical, counseling, and vocational services. In addition, the case manager's job is to help protect client's legal rights (Gerhart, 1990). These activities are applicable for helping incarcerated female offenders with minor children who are in foster care and mentally ill offenders who are residing in halfway houses.

Masters (1994), a former parole officer, described fourteen roles that criminal justice counselors assume in providing case management services to offenders, indicating that the counselor performs several roles in a day and alternates among different roles.

Cop/Police Officer

This role reflects a key difference between mental health counseling with the nonoffender population and the offender population. This is a law enforcement role. The cop/police officer role may require the counselor to wear a badge with the power to arrest. To effect an arrest, the counselor (e.g., probation or parole officer) may carry handcuffs, leg and body chains, and a handgun. Assuming the cop/police officer role, counseling experts assert, impedes the counseling relationship. Clients, or offenders in this case, would be reluctant to disclose information that may lead to a revocation of probation or a revocation of parole that will result in incarceration. As a result, trust, a necessary factor in effective counseling, cannot develop and leads to a serious exploration of offenders' issues. Nonetheless, the cop/police officer is a necessary role in working with offenders. For instance, in a correctional institution, a counselor may have to "ticket" an offender for a rule infraction.

Friend

Being a friend to an offender is one of the roles that criminal justice counselors play; however, this role can easily become problematic for the counseling relationship. Considerable similarities exist between the process of friendship and counseling. Both a friend and a counselor are called upon to listen to a person who is disclosing a painful event. The friend and counselor can be supportive, concerned, warm, involved, genuine, caring, sympathetic, and empathetic. In the event the person experiencing a problem becomes depressed and anxious, the friend and counselor can alleviate feelings of isolation and hopelessness.

Yet, major differences exist between being a friend and being a counselor. The first difference involves the degree of objectivity. A counselor working with offenders must be objective in order to render just decisions with respect to the offender. Moreover, one task of the counselor is to help the offender change positively by challenging the offender's antisocial and dysfunctional views. To challenge effectively, the offender requires impartiality on the counselor's part. This requirement differentiates a counselor from a friend. A friend is partial to a friend and may not challenge poor decisions on the friend's part.

A person generally accepts his or her friend unconditionally. When a counselor becomes friends with an offender, making decisions regarding an offender that may lead to imprisonment may be difficult. The effect of such an indecision could jeopardize the public's safety. Also, an offender who believes that a counselor is a friend may try to exploit this friendship.

The extent of privacy with respect to disclosure afforded to a friend and an offender is different. Normally, communications between a counselor and client are privileged and information cannot be divulged by the counselor. An exception, however, is made when a client has communicated a specific threat to a specific person. In a criminal justice setting, the counselor is expected to disclose information involving crimes or threats to a prison's security. Counselors providing help are different from friends providing help by virtue of training. Friends seldom have specialized training. Friends may be helpful in alleviating the symptoms of a friend, but they are not as effective with underlining root issues.

An offender can expect a counselor's undivided attention. The counselor's job is to listen, help, and give. In effect, the relationship is one-way and not reciprocal. With friends, a reciprocal relationship is expected. One friend may be experiencing personal difficulties and the other friend attempts to help. The next month, the friends' roles may be reversed. The friend with the problem last month is now consoling last month's helper.

Confidant

A person to which secrets are confided is called a confidant, which is one of the roles performed by a criminal justice counselor. In some noncriminal justice settings, an offender who confides traumatic secrets to a counselor may receive therapeutic benefits from the disclosure. In a setting, such as a probation office, an officer may be presented with a problem. For instance, a probationer, whom a judge has ordered not to consume any alcohol while on probation, confides to a probation officer that the probationer drank at a baseball game. The probation officer is presented with a dilemma. Should the officer report the violation to the judge? If the probation officer chooses just to reprimand the probationer, the probation officer could incur disciplinary action for failing to report the violation.

Adviser

The consensus among counselors is that giving advice to any client is an ineffective type of communication. Two reasons are generally cited in the literature for the avoidance of giving advice to a client, especially offenders. First, the offender is unlikely to listen attentively and take the advice. The offender may nod his or her head in agreement with the counselor, but internally, the offender rejects the advice. Second, few individuals truly know what is best for another. A third reason, though it is not cited in the literature and comes from Masters' experience with offenders, is that giving advice may serve as an excuse for the offender and permit him or her to blame the counselor for poor, unknowledgeable, or incorrect advice.

However, Masters asserts that abstaining from giving advice is impossible by the counselor. Advice giving is part of counseling and may be direct, coercive, or mandated. It may also be subtle, covert, and veiled. Rather than strongly advising a counselee to take a particular action, the counselor can suggest a course of action. Yet, a situation may call for strong advice, such as telling an offender to avoid and not socialize with someone whom the counselor is sure to lead to problems for the offender. In such a case, a counselor may know that a friend or relative of an offender is being investigated for a crime or is close to being arrested.

Teacher

Occasionally, becoming a teacher is a necessary role for a criminal justice counselor. This role is especially important when an offender is inexperienced in how to apply for a job and how to dress for an interview. The counselor's job is to instruct the offender in what to say or how to act. In fact, the counselor may engage in role-playing with the offender as an aid to providing or improving skills.

Moral Guider

Most persons will agree that counselors should not interject their morals and values in a counseling relationship and force or coerce an offender to adopt the counselor's morals. But while a counselor may strive to refrain from imposing morals or values on offender, it can never be done totally. Writing how difficult it is to refrain from imposing values, Masters recounts an example in which one of her parolees called her to express fears about lesbian feelings. The parolee asked Masters for advice on whether to stop fighting the parolee's feelings toward a woman and whether the parolee should pursue this lesbian relationship.

Masters did not report what she told the parolee. The ideal and politically correct response is to avoid giving advice and tell the parolee that sexual preference is a personal decision based on one's orientation. However, a parole officer can give subtle messages to a parolee by a nonresponse and especially when the parole officer has commented upon less sensitive disclosures. Furthermore, the counselor could prominently wear religious symbols and discuss his or her church activities. Also, the counselor may discuss his or her happiness with a spouse and their children. Last, such a disclosure by telephone or in person may suggest to a parolee what the counselor truly feels despite giving a professionally appropriate response. So, while Masters indicates that being a moral guider is wrong, it may be done unconsciously by a counselor and indirectly serves as one of the roles that a criminal justice counselor performs.

Parent/Nurturer

At times, a criminal justice counselor needs to adopt the role of a parent or nurturer. This role may be especially important when the offender is a juvenile. Most people who are in pain seek care, concern, rapport, and support from other individuals. These desires are present in both nonoffender and offender populations. The person who fills these desires is in the role of a parent/nurturer. In this capacity, though, a parent also should be tough, firm, and set limits, and counselors must do likewise. A counselor can expect to be viewed as authoritarian, and like the rebellion exhibited by children who feel their parents are too strict, the offender may rebel. Another dynamic that comes up in the parent/child relationship is transference and counter-transference.

Change Agent

The change agent role is predicated upon the potentially helpful relationship of the counselor. Simply, the counselor is in a position to effect positive change in the offender and prevent further offending. Yet, the outcome can be the opposite, in that, despite the best efforts of the counselor, the offender commits another crime. But some offenders do change and perhaps some of the change is attribute to the counselor. However, these offenders who have become productive citizens are not going to be on the television or in the newspaper.

Crisis Intervener

Necessitated by an explosion in the number of people handled by all phases of the criminal justice system, much of the counselor work with offenders is crisis intervention. Crisis is characterized by intense emotional reactions to a situation and a dysfunctional manner of coping. Being in a crisis limits some people's abilities to think rationally and function adequately. Providing services to a person in crisis takes considerable energy and is emotionally draining. With offenders, it may also be dangerous because an offender in crisis may respond threateningly to that crisis.

Role Model

By virtue of counselors being in a supervisory role, some offenders see a counselor as a role model. Some offenders imitate the counselor's hairstyle, clothing, makeup, and language style. So long as the counselor meets the expectations of the offender, the counselor will have social influence and power over the offenders. Once the counselor ceases to be a role model, trust dissipates and the relationship is irreparably broken. Then, the counselor's credibility is lost.

Consultant

As a consultant, the counselor listens, observes, collects data, reports observations, teaches, trains, coaches, provides support, challenges, advises, offers suggestions, and advocates. Also, a consultant in the criminal justice field provides specialized information and confers with offenders. By suggesting strategies for specific problems, the counselor acts as a consultant to prisoners.

Social Influencer

In this role, the counselor influences the offender by use of the counselor's power. The counselor isn't put on a pedestal such as when the counselor is viewed as a role model. Instead, the counselor is a person who espouses important opinions that are heeded by the offender. However, the creation of a power base is not easy. The counselor must convince the offender somehow to see the counselor as credible, trustworthy, and competent.

Resource Broker/Advocate

In this role, the criminal justice counselor identifies and locates resources in the community that would be beneficial to the offender. To that end, the counselor, knowledgeable of the offender's problems, matches the most appropriate community resources to the offender. The community is seen as the major provider of treatment services. If the offender needs mental health, educational, or vocational counseling, a referral is made to the appropriate agency. The downside to this role is that the offender may believe that the counselor is pawning the offender off to others, inhibiting the building of trust and damaging the chances that the offender will later come to the counselor in a time of need.

Program Manager

The program manager helps the offender to manage problems effectively so that the offender can live a law-abiding life. The offender is provided with a problem-solving method by the counselor that the offender can use when necessary. The counselor should keep in mind that not all problems can be resolved and should not convey to the offender that all problems are solvable. Some problems and conflicts are not solvable, such as a relative with a serious mental illness that is draining family resources.

The fourteen case management roles that Masters described may be categorized into two roles—law enforcement and social worker (Fulton, Stichman, Travis, & Latessa, 1997). Regardless of the number of roles, fourteen or two, role conflict may occur within probation and parole officers and produce negative and undesirable issues. These are job stress and job burnout. To avoid these mental health hazards, some officers have been advised to abandon the social work role and just adopt the law enforcement role. Yet, this approach produces a type of civil service malaise, boredom, and unfulfilled work (Fulton et al., 1997).

To counter the negative effects, a program in two unspecified cities implemented a training model within an Intensive Supervision Program (ISP) to assist officers in achieving a balanced approach to their jobs. The model consisted of training on such factors as effective intervention, objectives-based case management, and risk/need assessment. In addition, the officers participated in work groups, which intended to teach program components and policies and procedures of the prototypical ISP. To evaluate the effectiveness of ISP, an Officer Attitude Survey was utilized. The survey measured, in part, the extent to which officers developed a balanced approach. The officers rated "terms associated with control or assistance tasks and social worker versus law enforcement roles, and to measure the extent to which they buy in to strategies aimed at promoting long-term behavioral change versus strategies aimed at short-termed offender control" (Fulton et al., 1997, p. 304). The researchers found that officers who had ISP put a stronger emphasis on the rehabilitative function of probation and parole and strategies for offender behavioral change than officers who did not have the training (Fulton et al., 1997).

SUMMARY

This chapter began with the strengths of individual counseling. Then, the chapter described the helping relationship. It described the seven characteristics of a helping relationship. In addition, this chapter listed the core conditions of a helping relationship, which are empathy, respect or positive regard, genuineness, warmth, immediacy, cultural awareness, and gender awareness. Then, the chapter recited the stages of counseling. These stages were engagement, pattern search, changes, and termination. Each stage involves goals, techniques, content, resistance, transference, and counter-transference. The engagement stage was modified slightly to indicate the importance of the initial correction interview, including factors associated with conducting a mental status examination and the identification of problems of offenders.

Next, the chapter described crisis theory and how to treat a person in crisis. This area is important for offenders because much of the work with offenders is of a crisis nature. Last, the chapter described case management, which is a technique used by parole and probation officers. Fourteen roles were depicted that a case manager fulfills. These roles are cop/police officer, friend, confidant, adviser, teacher, moral guider, parent/nurturer, change agent, crisis intervener, role model, consultant, social influencer, resource broker/advocate, and program manager.

KEY TERMS

The helping
   relationship
Core conditions of a
   helping relationship
Cultural awareness
Gender awareness

Factors in counselors'
   racism
Stages of counseling
Markers
Types of terminations
Crisis intervention

Case management
Case management roles
Intensive supervision
   program

6

✻ ✻ ✻

Group Treatment Processes

✻ INTRODUCTION

Group counseling, as a treatment modality, emerged in 1905. At that time, a Boston physician, who was concerned about the depressed state of his tuberculosis patients and who believed that their depression was caused by a lack of information about their disease, summoned his patients for a mass educational session. Once together, the physician learned that the group interaction was therapeutic because patients discussed various aspects of their illness and their lives (Burns, 1983). In 1914, Alfred Adler, impressed with the value of group counseling, recommended group therapy as an efficient way of providing therapy to a number of people (Burns, 1983).

Presently, group counseling is used with an infinite number of problems to alleviate and cure people's suffering (Trotzer, 1989; Whitaker, 1985). The literature reveals that groups have been started to treat parents of murdered children, divorced spouses, children of alcoholic parents, domestic partner violence, noncustodial fathers, people with eating disorders, sexual assault survivors, and cancer survivors (e.g., Clark, 1972; Child & Getzel, 1989; Gainor, 1992; Hetzel & Barton, 1994; Hinkle, 1991; Mahon & Flores, 1992; Mann & Gaertner, 1991; Meador, Solomon, & Bowen, 1972; Milders, Berg, & Deelman, 1995; Proehl, 1995; Scharlach, 1989; Sigafoos, 1994; Thornton & Hogue, 1993). For the most part, these groups provide support, strength, and guidance for those attending (Hall, 1960). Though the issues are different for each group, these groups share a number of commonalties, such as the desire for mutual aid (Vander Kolk, 1985) and the desire to achieve personal goals (Crown & Rosse, 1995).

Another commonality is that the groups cited above are conducted with persons who are not likely under correctional authority. Persons under correctional authority are different by the nature of being in a coercive, negative environment or restricted by social control agents (Rooney, 1992). Garvin (1985) cites five differences between groups for offenders and nonoffenders. First, offenders' membership is mostly involuntary. The courts may order a convicted person to attend group counseling, or a prisoner may be coerced into a group by a parole board or by the hope to influence a parole board. Second, offenders are the objects of society's social control, and the nature of this relationship requires the counselor to reconcile the values of the institution and the counseling profession. Third, social forces in the prison or in the criminal subculture on the street help to maintain deviance. This requires a counselor to understand and address these forces. Fourth, organizational dynamics can positively and negatively affect a group. For instance, the security forces within a prison may not be receptive to prison treatment. Fifth, prisons have an inmate code that provides rules for prisoners. Among these rules is how prisoners should relate to the prison administration and to fellow prisoners.

Walsh (1992) concurs with Garvin regarding the inmate code and explains that the prison environment creates dynamics that affect the correctional staff and prisoners. For instance, prisons are total institutions, which create antagonistic relationships between prisoners and correctional staff. As a result, prisoners have developed a prison code to guide them in their relationships with the prison staff, which includes treatment staff as well (Walsh, 1992).

The inmate code impedes effective institutional counseling. It demands that prisoners mistrust the staff unless there are gains for them. Attendance at counseling or participation in programs is excused by other prisoners, provided there is a chance to make parole or get a reduction in sentence. In group, some inmates are there for these reasons only. For inmates who are not feigning participation, confrontation with other prisoners is to be expected. Despite these impediments and other obstacles, a well-run correctional group can substantially reduce these barriers and be therapeutic (Clagett, 1992; Roberts, Cheek, & Mumm, 1994; Walsh, 1992; Zimpfer, 1992). Thus, prisoners and felons in the community can benefit from group counseling, and groups for offenders share many of the commonalties with group participants in the community. On the other hand, groups for offenders are different from groups for cancer or sexual assault survivors.

The involuntary nature of groups for offenders raises an issue regarding their therapeutic value and effectiveness. Ideally, a counselor should never put someone in a group who does not want to be part of a group. Such a forced move would be counterproductive for the dynamics of the group. Nonetheless, offenders are forced into the group on a regular basis. This fact makes an offender group more difficult to conduct than a typical group in the community where members come based on their free will. Yet, experienced correctional group leaders maintain that therapeutic benefits are derived from an involuntary group, such a mandated group of offenders.

The purpose of this chapter is to discuss the universal components of group counseling for offenders and characteristics that are unique to offenders. The author discusses differences between therapy groups and self-help groups, the benefits of groups, the types of groups, selection of group members, group roles with special emphasis on the group leader, group dynamics, group stages, and last, strategies that may be employed with offenders in a group.

DIFFERENCES BETWEEN THERAPY GROUPS AND SELF-HELP GROUPS

Before discussing the benefits and dynamics of groups, a distinction must be made between therapy groups and self-help groups. The latter constitutes a major modality of addressing a number of individuals' problems, including offenders. Self-help groups emerged as grassroots responses to community problems, such as Alcoholics Anonymous (Galanter, Castaneda, & Franco, 1991). Corey (1995) states that it is incumbent upon counselors to know the differences between self-help and therapy groups so as to know the therapeutic value of each and to make appropriate referrals.

First, self-help groups emphasize a single issue, such as addiction, cancer survivors, or parents of murdered children, whereas therapy groups have more global goals, such as improving mental health or social skills. Second, self-help groups stress persuasion, support, and inspiration, and therapy groups feature reinforcement, self-understanding, and feedback. Third, self-help groups differ from therapy groups in terms of the nature of the problems targeted. Self-help groups are perceived by professionals as appropriate for bereavement, weight control, parenting, addictions, and alcohol abuse. However, these same professionals believe that serious mental health issues, such as suicide and severe depression are more appropriate for therapy groups. Fourth, self-help groups tend to have indigenous leadership, whereas therapy groups do not. Fifth, self-help groups do not have a diversity of members that could generate group dynamics that affect change, such as what occurs in therapy groups. Self-help groups comprise individuals with common life experiences and common identity. Sixth, self-help groups engage in more political strategies to help their members cope with external barriers. For example, self-help groups believe their members suffer from oppression and discrimination and therefore seek to change these conditions. Therapy groups attempt to help members function better despite the obstacles in the environment (Corey, 1995).

Other differences noted are in the leader of the groups and expectations. Therapy groups tend to be led by degreed professionals, such as persons with a bachelor's, master's, or in some instance, doctorate degrees. Self-help groups are more likely to be led by persons with a high school diploma or less (Galanter et al., 1991). Moreover, the group leader of a therapy group maintains adherence to group rules, screens and selects new members, formulates treatment goals, and guides the group through stages of the group. By contrast, the leader of a self-help group provides peer leadership as opposed to professional leadership. In addition, no screening is conducted and new members are regularly added with no limit to the length of membership (Washton, 1992). Members of a therapy group are expected to attend all meetings, be on time, call if they are unable to attend, and give notice if they plan to terminate. In addition, members are expected to bring out-of-group contacts back to the group and in-group activities are addressed. The therapy group focuses more on feelings and learning to communicate these feelings. The past and present experiences are relevant topics to better understand one's life experiences (Vannicelli, 1995).

As far as the therapeutic values of self-help groups and therapy groups, Vannicelli (1995) contends that each can complement the other. A person can attend an AA group as well as a therapy group and derive therapeutic benefits from each. Focusing on hypothesized differences between self-help and therapy groups, one researcher conducted an experiment using a self-help group as the experimental group and the therapy group as the control group in an outpatient psychiatric clinic. The self-help group was surreptitiously led by a social worker but principally assisted by a higher functioning senior patient. The control group was led by two professionals. Both groups were operated simultaneously. The researchers found that retention in the self-help group was 38% higher than in the therapy group, the rate of abstinence from substances was the same for both groups, and social adjustment over a twelve-month follow-up was good. The researchers concluded that the self-help group was less expensive and potentially more effective than a therapy group (Galanter et al., 1991).

BENEFITS OF GROUP COUNSELING

As stated above, a Boston physician unexpectedly learned that patients suffering from tuberculosis benefited therapeutically from being together, and this end was considered a worthy objective for this group. Conversely, the primary goal of providing group treatment to offenders is not to benefit them in a broad therapeutic sense but to reduce or eliminate their recidivism (Fabelo, 1995; DeLeon, Wexler, & Jainchill, 1982; Martin, Butzin, & Inciardi, 1995; Rouse, 1991; Wexler, 1994; 1995; Wexler, Falkin, & Lipton, 1990). However, offenders can benefit in the same manner as tuberculosis patients. For instance, AIDS is a growing problem in the prison community (Haas, 1993; Hogan, 1994; Lachance-McCullough, Tesoriero, Sorin, & Lee, 1993; Lachance-McCullough, Tesoriero, Sorin, & Stern, 1994; Smith & Dailard, 1994). Providing group counseling for a group of prisoners with AIDS or cancer would not be to reduce their recidivism, but to extend to them the same benefits as persons in the free community (Berkman, 1991; Maull, 1991).

Yalom (1985) analyzed the therapeutic benefits of group counseling and identified eleven benefits. These are the instillation of hope, universality, the imparting of information, altruism, the corrective recapitulation of the primary family group, the development of socializing techniques, imitative behavior, interpersonal learning, group cohesiveness, catharsis, and existential factors. These eleven benefits are all applicable to offenders and nonpsychiatric patients. For instance, Siebert and Dorfman (1995) studied the stage of illness, risk group for contracting HIV, and gender on the instillation of hope, universality, and group cohesiveness for HIV and AIDS group patients. In the Siebert and Dorfman's study, three of Yalom's benefits were studied. The section below presents the eleven benefits described by Yalom.

The Instillation of Hope

Instilling and maintaining hope in counselees is important in all treatment. Counselees must have hope to stay in counseling. Believing in treatment is therapeutic in and of itself, as studies involving placebos have shown. Group members are at different stages on the mental health continuum, and hearing a group member who is coping well and has progressed is helpful for another group member who is not coping well.

Universality of Experiences

Persons new to a group counseling experience enter a group thinking that they are alone in their thoughts and feelings. Although individuals believe that they are unique in that others have not shared their specific background and experiences, their disclosures evidence a commonality of experiences, which is clearly apparent to the group.

The Imparting of Information

Information is provided to group members by two sources. First, the group leader provides information to structure the group. He or she explains and clarifies issues, which serve an important therapeutic function. For instance, explanation and clarification are extremely important for severely mentally ill group members who may believe that messages are coming to them from a television. In addition, a leader in group counseling provides information about physical health problems, mental health, mental illness, or psychodynamics. Many persons, following a successful group experience, display a considerable amount of information that they did not have prior to entering the group. Second, the group members receive information from other group members. A group leader or counselor is not likely to possess or know the answers to everything, and information comes also from participants.

Altruism

Often, some persons enter groups feeling that they are worthless and have nothing to contribute to others. By giving help to others, group members receive help. When they see that they have the capacity to assist others, they see that they have value as human beings, which boosts their self-esteem. The literature is replete with examples of how helping someone is immensely therapeutic. Allegedly, a legendary warden at San Quentin Prison stated that the best way to help a prisoner is to permit the prisoner to help you. At religious ceremonies, sick persons will not only pray for themselves, but for others, and doing so allows them to feel that they are unselfish. In AA groups, members who have been sober for years continue to attend meetings because not only can they help struggling new members, but also they can help themselves. Despite the benefits of helping others, nascent group members might resist, holding that the blind is leading the blind. In essence, however, the member is saying that he or she has nothing of value to offer, and a group leader should address this resistance from this perspective by explaining the member's self-evaluation.

The Corrective Recapitulation of the Primary Family Group

The first group to which most people are a member is the family, and for a large number of people this group is dysfunctional. Also, the group comes to resemble a family for some members with family roles and dynamics. For this reason, some groups are led by male and female co-leaders in order to simulate a father and mother. Because of early family experiences and other experiences, a number of patterns emerge. First, a pattern emerges of the helpless, dependent person upon which the group leader is viewed as omnipotent and omniscient. Second, a pattern emerges in which members are defiant of the group leader who is viewed as an impediment to growth and individuality. Third, if the group is led by two leaders, an attempt is made to divide and conquer, which constitutes another pattern. Fourth, competition with group members for attention from the leader emerges. Fifth, strategies emerge with other members to attack the leader. Sixth, a pattern emerges in which members neglect themselves totally to appease or help others.

Given these dynamics, an opportunity is provided to relive or recapitulate family experiences correctly. Growth-inhibiting relationships must be challenged and not permitted to take root. Further, proper limits and ground rules for confronting others must be established. Last, members may work out relationships between leaders and members and thereby resolve issues with parents and siblings.

The Development of Socializing Techniques

Learning basic social skills is a therapeutic technique all groups strive to impart, although variation exists regarding the type of social skills and the subtleness of the teaching. For instance, groups for hospitalized persons who suffer from mental illnesses or delinquent adolescents often focus openly on the learning of social skills. Role-playing is used frequently in these groups so that group members will learn basic skills in relating to others. Also, learning social skills may be subtle for highly educated or mixed race groups, such that members inculcate the norms of other members.

Imitative Behavior

Group members sometimes mimic and imitate the behaviors of the group leader or other members. If the male leader smokes a pipe, other males may take up smoking a pipe, or if the leader smokes a particular brand of tobacco, some members may switch to that brand. A particular manner of dress or speech may be imitated. Group members also can learn by watching others. For instance, a member with a phobia about snakes can learn from watching a group leader handle a snake. This phenomenon is called vicarious or spectator therapy.

Interpersonal Learning

This is an intricate concept consisting of curative factors, such as insight, resolving transference, and the corrective emotional experience. Interpersonal learning occurs when group members, by self-observation and agreed validation, become aware of important facets for their interpersonal behavior, such as their strength, limitation, distortion, and troublesome behaviors that provoke undesired behavior by others. As an illustration, an interpersonal sequence develops by which a maladaptive behavior occurs in the group. The group's feedback and the members' self-observations attend more closely to the behavior and appreciate the effect of the behavior on other's feelings, other's opinions, and one's opinions. After recognizing this sequence, a member becomes aware of his or her personal responsibility for the behavior and that he or she is the only one with the power to change it.

Group Cohesiveness

Cohesion in a group is illustrated by the quality of members' appeal toward each other and the group as a whole. The indicators of a cohesive group are supportiveness by members, a willingness to embrace each other's interests, and willingness to form healthy relationships with group members. High cohesiveness appears to be associated with positive group outcome. Also, there are other positive factors of a cohesive group, such as high attendance, infrequent turnover, self-disclosure, risk taking, and socially approved methods for dealing with conflict.

If members perceive acceptance and understanding from the group, they are more likely to risk disclosure of themselves and to consider seriously the feedback of the group. As a result, a member's self-esteem is increased and reinforced, and the behavior responsible for the esteem of the group transfers to the community.

Catharsis

Catharsis is a component of the interpersonal experience and is related to outcome. However, mere catharsis, such as in a closet, does not provide long-lasting benefits. Its beneficial effects occur when a member discloses strong, emotional material in the group. By doing so, cohesion is strengthened in the group. Without catharsis in a group, the group becomes an animated process. Catharsis, however, is relative and the intensity of it differs from member to member. Some people may cry, scream, or become angry. Others may be calm and stoic.

Existential Factors

From the research conducted by Yalom and his colleagues, a group of issues emerged that were cited by group members and group leaders as critically important but were difficult to categorize by Yalom and others. So, they grouped them together and called them existential factors. These are the recognition that life is sometimes unfair and unjust, that in the end there is no avoiding death or some of life's pains, that regardless of how close one may get to another that some issues must be confronted alone, that ultimately one must abandon trivialities and honestly deal with the issues of life and death, and that one must ultimately take responsibility for one's life regardless of how much support and guidance is provided by friends.

All eleven benefits discussed by Yalom are relevant for a correctional population. As stated previously, Yalom conceptualized these therapeutic benefits by observing his psychiatric patients. Corrections contain an increasing number of prisoners who are seriously mentally ill (Edwards, Morgan, & Faulkner, 1994). For instance, many states have changed their insanity statutes to provide prison sentences for convicted mentally ill defendants (Allen & Simonsen, 1998). This means that instead of some offenders going to mental institutions, they go to prison to serve their sentences while they receive psychiatric treatment for their mental illness. While they may receive medication, group treatment might also be necessary. The goal of treatment is not to reduce their recidivism because some of these offenders may be serving life without parole, but it is to provide legally required mental health treatment.

For prisoners who are in relatively good health and who are likely to return to society, such as prisoners with drug problems, all Yalom's factors are relevant. Prisoners with drug problems need hope, they need to realize the universality of their experiences, they need information, they need to experience altruism, they need to relive or reenact parts of their family experiences, they need functional socializing skills, they need to model functional behaviors, they need interpersonal learning, they need the group to be cohesive, they need to engage in catharsis, they need to understand that life is unfair and unjust to a lot of people, they need to deal with life honestly, and they need to realize that ultimately they are responsible for their lives.

TYPES OF GROUPS

Page, Campbell, and Wilder (1994) listed several types of groups, which included therapy groups, structured groups, encounter groups, consciousness-raising groups, personal growth groups, and marathon groups. They acknowledged that these groups were not appropriate for all populations. Of the groups they listed, therapy, structured, marathon, and encounter groups are more appropriate for offenders, although some of these groups overlapped (Goldberg, 1970). The following section describes these types of groups, and their applicability to treating offenders. See Figure 6.1.

Therapy Groups

These groups address problems of remediation, treatment, and personality reconstruction. Group psychotherapy involves a process of reeducation, focusing on the unconscious, conscious, present, or past. Some therapy groups have as their aim the correction of dysfunctional behavioral and emotional disorders. The aim of treatment, depending upon the theoretical orientation of the group leader, may be minor or major changes in an individual's personality. Given these goals, the treatment tends to be lengthy. Group members are likely to be suffering from severe emotional problems, serious neurotic conflicts, psychosis, or socially deviant behavior (Corey, 1995).

Given these types of issues, therapy groups are most appropriate for drug, sex, mentally ill, or mentally retarded offenders. Describing major changes as a goal, Rich (1994) writes that sex-offender treatment seeks the abolishment of inappropriate sexual behaviors and ideation and reports that clinicians who work with sex offenders in group need broad-based clinical skills. In a similar vein, Sigafoos (1994) relates a treatment modality for working with veterans in prison. According to

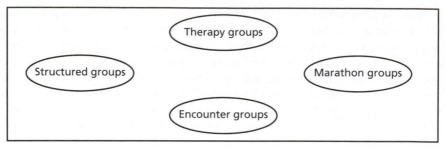

FIGURE 6.1 Groups Appropriate for Offenders

Sigafoos, some incarcerated veterans suffer from Post-Traumatic Stress Disorder (PTSD), and the focus of treatment is stress management; veterans, PTSD, and crime; conflict resolution; handling symptoms of PTSD; and the effects of PTSD on the family.

Structured Groups

Structured groups are groups that are characterized by a main theme. These groups serve a number of aims, including imparting information, sharing common experiences, problem solving, providing support, and assisting individuals in creating their own support systems away from the group. Structured groups have been developed for mid-life transitions, values and life decisions, stress management, depression management, eating disorders, anxiety management, self-esteem problems, and adult female survivors of childhood sexual abuse. The above examples indicate the immenseness of the areas that are addressed in structured groups.

Structured groups seem to have a single or several specific goals. Group members frequently complete a questionnaire at the beginning of treatment and another questionnaire at the end to determine the amount of progress made. The principal activities are structured exercises and homework assignment to teach members new skills. Also, contracts are used to establish goals in and outside the group. Many structured groups use treatment principles from learning theory and behavioral modification (Corey, 1995).

For instance, Marshall, Bryce, Hudson, Ward, and Moth (1996) report the results of a structured group in which incarcerated child molesters are provided group therapy designed to increase their capacity for intimacy and decrease their degree of loneliness. These researchers reported that two loneliness scales were administered before treatment began, and improvements were observed in both intimacy and loneliness (Marshall et al., 1996). Similarly, Davis and Hoffman (1991) used the Minnesota Multiphasic Personality Inventory (MMPI) in a pretest and posttest of incarcerated child molesters. All the prisoners were involved in a group treatment program, and the researchers reported significant decreases and increases in the subscales of the MMPI (Davis & Hoffman, 1991).

Marathon Groups

One of the most frequently studied variables in group research has been the length of time (Stoller, 1972). Because research showed that lengthy treatment had a significant effect on group dynamics, marathon groups developed (Stoller, 1972). Marathon groups are not often conducted in corrections, especially in institutions because of the amount of time it takes and security issues. However, Page, Campbell, and Wilder (1994) reported that a marathon group, consisting of seventeen hours of treatment, was conducted in a Southeastern prison in order to study the relationship among the type of therapeutic level in a group, the type of interactions in the group, and the type of leader behavior. The focus of the study was the variables and not the provision of group treatment, per se. However, other group professionals have discussed the distinguishing features of marathon groups.

Marathon groups may differ in terms of technique or the group leader's theoretical orientation. But the commonality among all marathon groups is the concentration of time together, divorced from other activities. Marathon groups typically last twelve or more hours or may extend to several days (Goldberg, 1970). Gottschalk and Davidson (1972) observed that the purpose of the marathon group is to increase the impact of sensitivity training among members in a short period of time. Proponents of marathon groups have reported that these groups produce a significant increase in emotionality, more expression of negative feelings, a decrease in defensive behaviors because members are fatigued, and more willingness by members to work, again due to the fatigue factor.

As described by Bach (1972), "one of the unique aspects of the marathon technique is an intensification and acceleration of transparency and genuine encounter by a deliberate instigation of the group pressure focused on behavioral change" (p. 142). Marathon groups create a highly elevated amount of emotional tensions that, then, stimulate cognitive reorientation to relieve the tension. Two types of acting, feeling, and being evolve from marathon groups. The first is the transparency of the real self and the second is psychological intimacy.

Encounter Groups

Encounter groups have been used in a variety of settings and populations. They have been used with women (Meador, Solomon, & Bowen, 1972); homosexual males (Clark, 1972), and married couples (Pilder, 1972). They also have been used in correction.

For instance, in 1995, the Ohio Department of Rehabilitation and Correction implemented a long-termed drug treatment program at Ross Correctional Institution, located in Chillicothe, Ohio. The treatment, which was provided through a contract with a private substance abuse treatment agency, was based on the encounter group model (New Life Residential Drug Treatment and Alcohol Treatment Program Handbook, 1997).

An encounter group involves members and staff who are required to sit in a circle in order to confront (i.e., encounter) negative behaviors. A prisoner who is being encountered is required to sit receptively and face the person who is doing the encountering. The encountering person has a number of tools to use to encounter, such as showing compassion, empathy, or projection or using a "karom shot" (i.e., an indirect confrontation in which the a group member gives feedback to another prisoner instead of the prisoner who has exhibited negative behavior; the confrontation develops when the prisoner realizes that the feedback is indeed for him), a "lug" (i.e., an indirect confrontation in which a nontalking prisoner is told to stop talking so much; however, when it is done, it is done lightly and humorously), and "overstating" (i.e., an indirect form of confrontation by exaggerating). The choice of which encounter tool to use is up to the person doing the encountering (New Life Residential Drug Treatment and Alcohol Treatment Program Handbook, 1997).

When the encounter is finished, the floor is opened to other prisoners or counseling staff. Each person is free to support the encounter, provide his or her own perspective, or use a different encounter tool. The prisoner who has been encountered has one acceptable response to having been encountered. The prisoner may share his or her feelings and what is going on with him or her at that moment. He or she cannot offer defenses for this negative behavior, argue with a person who has encountered him or her, or rationalize what was told to him or her (New Life Residential Drug Treatment and Alcohol Treatment Program Handbook, 1997).

The rules of encountering are that there is no ganging up on another prisoner, defending the person being encountered, encountering in retaliation to being encountered, getting out of a seat while being encountered, or interrupting while an encountering is underway. On the other hand, a prisoner can provide feedback after encountering another prisoner, can provide honest feedback when encountering, should sit in front of the prisoner being encountered, and can provide specificity regarding what the encountered prisoner can do to improve. Also, prisoners are advised to attack behaviors and not other prisoners, be honest, use humor, use more than one encounter tool, be patient with the prisoner being encountered, show all their emotions and not only anger, reflect first before speaking when angered, and help other prisoners find a reason to change (New Life Residential Drug Treatment and Alcohol Treatment Program Handbook, 1997).

Probably, the most frequently found groups in correction are therapy groups, encountered groups, and structured groups. However, some groups may have features of all three. Therapy and encounter groups are appropriate for group treatment with offenders who have drug, sexual assault, or battering issues. Structured groups may be used for offenders with specific problems or issues, such as anger control or pre-release employment problems. While marathon groups may be difficult to employ, they are not impossible in institutions, halfway houses, or other community-based programs. Some probationers or community-based offenders may work or be actively searching for employment. However, these requirements do not preclude a marathon group from occurring all day on Sunday.

GROUP SIZE

An important factor in different types of groups is the number of members comprising the groups. The size of the groups can have therapeutic benefits and antitherapeutic effects. For instance, if the group is larger than it should be, group dynamics will be affected. Some members may have a difficult time voicing their feelings given the size of the group and the length of time of the group meeting. If the group is too small, members feel pressured to speak more than they feel comfortable (Jacobs, Harvill, & Masson, 1998).

Other issues in the size of a group are the groups' purpose, length of meeting time, and the extent of the leader's experience. With respect to the therapy groups, Jacobs and colleagues (1998) contend that they should last from one and one-half to three hours, but with adolescents or children the length of time may need to be shorter. As a general rule, education groups should have four to twelve members. Discussion groups should have five to eight members. Therapy groups, personal growth groups, and mutual sharing groups should have from three to fifteen members, but typically they have five to eight members (Jacobs et al., 1998). In correction, however, some groups, because of staffing shortages, may be larger.

SELECTION OF GROUP MEMBERS

Planning is critical to the success of a group. On paper or in the head of the individual planning a group, a number of issues need to be addressed. These issues include the basic purpose of the group, the population that will be assisted, how the group will be publicized, how members will be recruited, what criteria will be used to screen and select members, the desired number in a group, how long the group will last, the frequency of meetings, the duration of each meeting, the group structure and format, the preparation of members for the group, whether the group will be opened or closed for new members at any time, whether the group should be voluntary or involuntary, the extent of follow-up, and the nature of any evaluation (Corey, 1995).

Once these decisions have been made, the next step is the selection of members for the group. Yalom (1985), contemplating working with psychiatric patients, prefers a method of deselection. Patients are excluded from joining a group if they are likely to become deviant, which is defined as the inability to participate in the group tasks. According to Yalom (1985), "in a heterogeneous, interactional group, a deviant is one who cannot or will not examine one's self and one's relationship with others, especially with the other members of the group" (p. 252).

In general, however, no universal criteria exist for group selection. Instead, inclusion in a group is determined by the overall purpose of a group, the goals of members, and the theoretical orientation and practice of the group leader (Parsons & Wicks, 1994). Page (1979) relates the formation of a group in a correctional institution for women. Once the group's availability was made known to the inmate population and its purpose, Page interviewed all women who expressed interest, basing his selection on need and motivation. Garvin (1985) emphasizes the importance of assessment in a social control setting. Despite the view, perhaps, that prisons contain homogenous populations, differences exist with respect to the types of inmates incarcerated. A good assessment helps the group leader to assess the interactional patterns likely to emerge. Such an assessment must be cognizant of value issues and conflicts that correlate with motivation to examine dysfunctional attitude.

GROUP ROLES

All persons initially come to the group as members. As these members interact, they acquire various roles. According to Vander Kolk (1985), a role "refers to behavior and, to some extent, expectations, but specifically to one's typical behavior in relation to a certain set of individuals in a particular context" (p. 137). As a consequence, members may assume facilitative roles, vitalizing and maintenance roles, and anti-group roles. Wilson and Hanna (1990) name thirteen different roles that are played in a group. Group professionals refer to these roles differently, but they all encompass the essence of these roles (Gladding, 1995; Ohlsen, Horne, & Lawe, 1988). For instance, Walsh (1992), focusing on correctional groups, lists the anti-group roles and calls them the *resister*, the *expert*, the *monopolizer*, the *withdrawn member*, the *masochist*, and the *sadist*.

Undoubtedly, the most important role in corrections is that of the leader because he or she is responsible for guiding the group and keeping it on task to achieve the desired end (Kottler, 1994). The leader must have the personal characteristics conducive to facilitating a group, knowledge of group dynamics, and excellent group skills for a successful group.

Leaders' Personal Characteristics

Corey (1995) states that a number of personal characteristics are essential to leading an effective group. These are presence, personal power, courage, willingness to confront oneself, sincerity and authenticity, sense of identity, belief in group process and enthusiasm, and inventiveness and creativity. The following sections expand upon these characteristics.

Presence Presence refers to the capacity of a leader to be affected by the emotions of group members. If a member is sad, the leader should be affected. If a member is happy, the leader should also be affected. Presence also means that the leader is there for members, evidencing genuine caring and a willingness to understand the psyche of members. Presence also means that the leader is in tune with his or her own emotions, comes to the group organized and not consumed with personal issues, and comes to the group attentive to the emotions of the group.

Personal Power Personal power refers to a leader's confidence in himself or herself and in influencing group members. Without a leader's sense of self-power, a leader is unlikely to empower group members to resolve their issues. For sure, a leader cannot impart a quality to someone if that leader does not have that quality. Importantly, power does not involve the subjugation and misuse of members. A leader's recognition of the power that he or she has is used to help the member use the member's untapped power and not to have the member rely on the leader to solve the member's problems. Personal power also does not involve the leader viewing himself or herself as omnipotent. The leader is willing to recognize that a member who risks in a group is exhibiting true power and deserves the majority of credit.

Courage Competent group leaders realize that they must demonstrate courage in their interactions with group members, and their status as the group leader cannot be used as a shield to avoid displaying courage. How does a counselor show courage? He or she shows courage by acknowledging a mistake when made or risking appropriately. Courage is shown by displaying emotions when he or she confronts a member and sharing views about the group process. A group leader can show courage by sharing power with group members. In addition, a leader can show courage by modeling appropriate new behaviors. For instance, group members indicate that abandoning old habits is scary and anxiety-provoking. A leader can assist group members by modeling how to move ahead when feeling anxious about abandoning old habits.

Willingness to Confront Oneself An important task of the group leader is to advance members' self-investigation. If a group leader is unable and unwilling to confront himself or herself, he or she cannot expect members to question themselves critically. The group leader's self-questioning may consist of asking and answering the following internally and externally: Why am I leading groups? What am I getting from this activity? Why do I behave as I do in a group? What impact do my attitudes, values, biases, feelings, and behaviors have on the people in the group? What needs of mine are served by being a group leader? Do I ever use the groups I lead to satisfy my personal needs at the expense of the members' needs? Asking and answering these questions is an ongoing process and a leader is not likely to provide clear answers. But the main factor is that a group leader is willing to explore these questions and react honestly to them.

As a group leader is willing to confront himself or herself, self-awareness follows, and a leader is more likely to be effective. Self-awareness, following from a willingness to confront oneself honestly, means that a group leader is aware of his or her own weaknesses, strengths, unfinished business, and how these factors affect the group process. Also, a self-aware group leader is able to handle therapeutically transference and counter-transference within the group. A group leader does not use the group for his or her own therapy, and being willing to confront oneself and being self-aware make this practice unlikely.

Sincerity and Authenticity A critical quality that a group leader should possess is a sincere desire to see members do well and grow during the group experience. Because being sincere entails being direct, group members will often like a leader's positive comment and dislike negative comments. A group leader must be willing to challenge when appropriate and confront any disingenuous behavior on the part of group members.

Akin to sincerity is authenticity. An authentic group leader is real. He or she does not pretend in the group or hide behind convenient excuses. Authenticity means a group leader is willing to share feelings and interpret the processes in the group. However, authenticity does not mean that a group leader should share every memory, thought, idea, or impression.

Sense of Identity A group leader should know his or her identity before being in a position to help group members discover their identities. This knowledge involves the leader knowing his or her values and living by them. The leader should know his or her strengths, limitations, needs, motivation, fears, and goals. The leader should know his or her capacity, life desires or goals, and the objectives needed to achieve the goals.

A principal task in the group is to help members learn who they are and the identities that they have imbibed and projected to others. When individuals live by consumed identities, their lives lack meaning. An effective group can help members realize that their flawed identities need to be changed. As a result, group members' lives become more meaningful. With the assistance of the group, members can see that their identities are not unchangeable and can be molded anew. The group leader is in position to demonstrate the changing of some meanings.

Belief in Group Process and Enthusiasm The manifestation of the group leader's strong belief in the group process is critical to the success of the group. Members are unlikely to believe in the group if they perceive that the group leader is not a strong believer or is not committed to the process. The enthusiasm shown by the group leader can be contagious to others. If the leader is enthusiastic, the group is not likely to be lifeless. That is not to say a group leader must be a cheerleader. Instead, he or she must demonstrate enjoyment for the work being conducted with the group. A positive association exists for the amount of leader enthusiasm, member enthusiasm, and productive work.

Inventiveness and Creativity A group leader should avoid using stilted techniques and presentations that are lifeless. It may not be possible to bring new ideas to each group. However, inventive and creative leaders welcome different experiences, lifestyles, and values. A key benefit of group is that it provides a multitude of opportunities for being inventive. A group, just by its structure, provides opportunities for creativity. A number of approaches exist to address a variety of problems that are provided by different types of groups.

Besides these eight leader characteristics that Corey identifies, other professionals have discussed additional leader characteristics. For instance, Banawi and Stockton (1993) add that Islamic values are relevant to the role of group leaders. This role is especially important in corrections today because a number of African American prisoners convert to the Islamic faith while they are incarcerated (Abdul-Khaaliq, 1995; Bates-Rudd, 1996; Hassan, 1995; Kaslom, 1996; Saraceno, 1996). The positive aspects of Islamic values on groups are group orientation, leader orientation, group support, expressing emotions, the importance of reflection and pondering, predestination, life experiences, optimism, and accountability. Among the negative aspects of Islamic values are restricted group activities, uneasiness of confrontation, behavioral codes of conduct (e.g., a male group leader should not offer to shake hands with a female Muslim member unless she is comfortable with this type of contact), gender of group leader, and identity and adjustment. The leader should be sensitive to these areas and address them in pre-group preparation. For instance, Muslim prisoners might interact more freely among other Muslim prisoners, such as in group prayers or other activities, but they may be a little inhibited when placed in a group of people with other beliefs. So, the group leader should encourage Muslim group members' participation, reminding them that the Koran encourages an understanding of other cultures. With respect to identity and adjustment, some Muslim, especially those from an Islamic country, may struggle with Americans' treatment interests regarding identity and adjustment (Banawi & Stockton, 1993). Also, some Muslim prisoners who converted while in prison may be struggling with abandoning some of their European values.

In addition, Page, Campbell, and Wilder (1994) studied the role of the group leader in a seventeen-hour-marathon group of drug and alcohol offenders in a correctional institution. They compared the types of leader activity, the types of member activity, and the degree of therapeutic content. While they found that the group was therapeutic with an active group leader, the group was most therapeutic when the leader acted in a less formal way. This study contradicted the drug and alcohol abuse literature, which had indicated that a leader had to be very formal and directive when leading a group of drug and alcohol clients.

GROUP DYNAMICS

Group dynamics emanate whenever individuals come together and interact with each other. Group dynamics involve changes that occur in the life of a group. The interaction of structure, organization, and dynamics affects the group process. The primary structures are boundary and hierarchy. Boundary involves the physical, emotional, or symbolic perimeters of persons inside a group. It also determines what is excluded from a group. Hierarchy determines the distribution of power among group members. It delineates the speaking order of members or who is designated to speak for the group. As such, hierarchy clarifies who is in a leadership role. Boundary determines various alignments within the group—dyad, triad, and larger group assignment (Enos & Southern, 1996).

Enos and Southern (1996) classify three major group dynamics—*cohesiveness, validation,* and *movement.* See Figure 6.2. Cohesiveness represents the shared identity and purpose of a group. It is the group's belief that members are in a given situation together. A group's cohesion is crucial in drawing individuals to the group and keeping attendance and participation. A positive association exists between the extent of cohesiveness and the extent of similar values and goals (Enos & Southern, 1996). If a group has cohesion, the probability of it reaching its goal is high (Enos & Southern, 1996). One factor in facilitating group cohesiveness is a pre-existing commonality among members. For instance, a gang that has had members with similarities in terms of life experiences tends to have extensive cohesiveness. While similarities portend cohesiveness, members who are dissimilar and have different goals can become cohesive. In that case, the group leader has to provide input and promote self-disclosure to establish a shared identity and cohesiveness.

Validation is the development of a shared reality within a group. In physics and chemistry, scientists can agree on universal laws and realities. However, social interactions produce an intricate combination of opinions, prejudices, estimates, and preferences. The result of these combinations is that two individuals can interact and then conclude two totally different views of their encounter. Validation supplies an opportunity for individual reality testing and consensus regarding the reality that the group can adopt. In some groups, some decisions are made by voting, requiring compromise by some members. An effective group will show respect for individual opinions that differ from the group's, while demonstrating the validation of the group's position. Influential group members can substantially impact the validation process of the group.

Movement or locomotion in a group refers to the impact on group members. Movement in the group is essential to the group process. However, not all movement is productive for a group. For movement to be productive and beneficial, the other two dynamics, in addition to proper structure, must be present. Effective

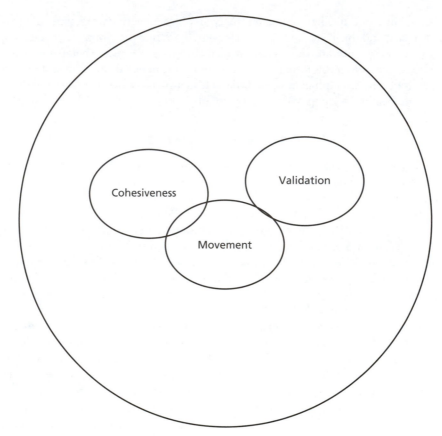

FIGURE 6.2 Three Major Group Dynamics

group counseling is related to sufficient movement within the group in order to change members' attitudes and behaviors. Groups progress from membership, content, alignment, focus, and hierarchy. When groups do not progress, they tend to disintegrate. The group leader must facilitate individual members, dyads, triads, and the group as a whole toward movement. As the group moves, members progress from one position to another, moving toward a more therapeutic position.

An excellent source for evaluating the dynamics and progress of a therapeutic group is the Hill Interaction Matrix (HIM-G). Developed by W. F. Hill, it is an assessment tool that measures two fundamental dimensions of groups—content style and work style. For content style, topic, group, personal, and here-and-now relationships are measured. For work style, conventional, assertive, speculative, and confrontation are measured (Hill, 1965; Hill, 1974). Campbell and Page (1993) utilized the HIM-G in a study of a prison group for drug offenders. For three of the four work styles that were prominent in the group, several curative factors were apparent, including information dissemination, corrective recapitulation of the primary family, development of socializing techniques, imitative behavior, interpersonal learning, group cohesiveness, and catharsis (Campbell & Page, 1993).

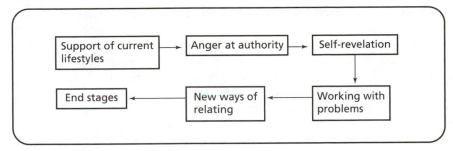

FIGURE 6.3 Six Stages of a Correctional Group

GROUP STAGES

Group theorists and practitioners have reported a number of stages that evolve during the life of a group. Trotzer (1994) indicates that a group undergoes five stages, which are entitled the security stage, the acceptance stage, the responsibility stage, the work stage, and the closing stage. According to Trotzer, he has witnessed these stages in his work with inmates and staff at the Minnesota State Prison, primary school students, college students, youths associated with a church-related retreat, and interracial groups. In a similar manner, Corey (1995) identified four stages—the initial stage, transition stage, working stage, and final stage. Regardless of the number and names of stages that various professionals attest to, the aim here is to focus on the stages identified in a correctional population.

Specifically, Page (1979) illustrates six stages for a group of women prisoners undergoing counseling primarily for drug issues. These were (1) support of current lifestyles, (2) anger at authority, (3) self-revelation, (4) working through problems, (5) new ways of relating, and (6) the ending stages. See Figure 6.3.

Support of Current Lifestyles

Early in the group, women complain about prison and prison rules, recall their drug usage, and extol the lifestyles of drug addicts. Focusing on these issues permits the women to avoid discussing their problems and each other. In addition, focusing on the side issues permits the women to judge the response of the group leader as they discuss their antisocial lifestyles. The group members maintain this level of interaction until they are able to trust the leader and themselves. Page indicates that the best strategy is to avoid siding with the group when the group discusses institutional rules, personnel, or the institution structure. Further, Page states that responses to the group regarding drug talk should not reinforce drug taking or give the members an opportunity to challenge the group leader. Instead, Page would divert discussions about the goodness of taking drugs to other topics, attempt to facilitate members acquiring insight regarding why they take drugs, or focus on the effects of drug taking. The leader should always keep in mind that members in this stage are avoiding discussing their personal issues.

Anger at Authority

During this second stage, the group's trust has increased, but most members still do not discuss their personal feelings. As a result, members look to the group facilitator or leader to mold the group into a constructive and cohesive unit. Used to being told what to do by authority figures, the group becomes angry with the facilitator or leader for not telling them what subjects to discuss in the group. Moreover, this perceived lack of directness from the group leader provides an additional opportunity for members to express their anger at another authority figure, the group facilitator.

When a member evidences anger at the facilitator, the facilitator entreats the member to express directly that anger at the facilitator. The facilitator also encourages the member to express anger that originated from another source to the facilitator. Because of the facilitator's invitations, several beneficial and therapeutic effects occur. Members see that someone in authority listens and understands their anger. They see that the facilitator is capable of handling strong feelings of anger. In addition, their trust of the facilitator increases because they see that someone in authority is being attacked by group members but does not use his or her power to retaliate. As a result, members are more likely to be more objective when assessing the source of their anger and directing their anger more accurately.

Self-Revelation

As members see that they can express themselves without condemnation, they began to disclose their fears, deficiencies, and problems. They may disclose that they had been abusive to their parents and children, or they may disclose that they have been the victims of physical and sexual abuse by their parents. They may also discuss their crimes and how they regret hurting the people that they did. They are also willing during this stage to give positive and negative feedback to other group members, demonstrating their concern for the welfare of other group members. The facilitator's role during this stage is to provide encouragement and support for the group's work.

Working Through Problems

As members disclose their issues, the group assists each other in exploring their feelings and finding workable solutions to their problems. As an illustration, a member might state that living with a parent contributed to the member's drug abuse. So, the group encouraged the member to avoid the parent. Also, the group indicated that a member's planned future action might lead to future problems and that the member did not adequately provide a solution. One member, who had been addicted to heroin, stated that a different method of using would prevent future addiction. However, the group indicated that this perspective was unrealistic. During this stage also, the members discuss their views of other members and the facilitator more than they discuss their own issues. This focus, however, is not problem avoidance and reflects increased trust in the group.

New Ways of Relating

As group members deal with each other more honestly, they come to realize that the members and the facilitator care about them. They listen more carefully as others speak. They become more assertive in addressing each other, giving feedback appropriately. When a member gives feedback inappropriately, the members correct the communication and indicate how to do it correctly. The group and facilitator are regularly praised for their assistance during this stage. The members are willing to change manipulate behavior and demonstrate caring behaviors toward each other.

During this stage, members are more willing to examine seriously their drug usage and their attitudes about drugs and other criminal behavior. Discussions about leading a drug-free lifestyle, and prosocial lifestyles are supported. Members are willing during this stage also to discuss why they use drugs. They also are supportive of members who avoid institutional rule-breaking behaviors.

Ending Stage

The group was open-ended. So, members left the group monthly and new members joined. When members were near terminating, the group assisted the members in formulating their future plans. Members who were not leaving were encouraged to discuss their loss of an important member of the group. Also, the person who was leaving was encouraged to discuss the loss of the group's support. The facilitator also disclosed his or her views regarding the loss and used this occasion to discuss loss in everyday life and how to respond to it.

GROUP STRATEGIES

Every correction group has an ultimate aim to achieve, such as decreasing recidivism, promoting positive institutional adjustment, or providing legally mandated treatment. Achieving these ends requires tasks and strategies that are implemented in the group. Some strategies are implemented to facilitate the group, and others are implemented to promote significant attitudinal and behavioral changes. The next section discusses a number of strategies to use with correction groups. The first section describes some pre-group strategies and the second describes ways to facilitate group dynamics. The third section provides some specific strategies for changing offenders and some discussion topics for promoting group discussions.

Pre-Group Strategies

Couch (1995) notes that an ethical and effective group requires adequate screening. Some methods used are individual interviews, group interviews, and questionnaires. Of these methods, the personal interview is the most efficacious. He proposes a four-step process for this personal interview. In the first step, the interviewer should identify members' needs, expectations, and commitment. During the second step, the interviewer should challenge myths and misconceptions about groups and group participation. The third step involves conveying information, such as the importance of confidentiality, admission processes, anticipated duration, purpose of the group, stages of the group process, and the role of the leader and members. During the fourth stage, the interviewer actually does the screening, deciding whether an interviewee is appropriate for the particular group planned (Couch, 1995).

To focus the group initially and prepare them to work, Friedman and Fanger (1991) recommend pre-group introduction exercises. First, group members are given a set of questions to answer in writing and to be presented at the first group meeting. Among the questions are: What do you want to have happen as a result of being in this group? In what way specifically do you want your life to be different at the end of the group? How will you know explicitly when you have reached your goals? What stops you from having this outcome now? The purpose of this initial assignment is to help the individuals realize small objectives needed to achieve larger goals. As each member describes his or her goals, the counselor helps the member to formulate concrete, behavioral outcomes. This initial process also helps to actuate the group process as members began to see similarities among themselves (Friedman & Fanger, 1991).

In addition, a pre-group strategy in prison should explore the motivation of prisoners. Similar to students who join college groups or take specific classes for future rewards, some prisoners may join a treatment group for making a stronger case for the parole board. Also, convicted offenders may be ordered to group treatment in lieu of prison. So, prisoners and probationers' secondary or primary gains should be discussed in pre-group, and probationers' involuntary status and their feelings regarding mandated treatment should be explored too.

Strategies to Facilitate Group Dynamics

Miller (1993) developed a strategy to illustrate to members the power of the group, illustrated by promoting self-disclosure, group cohesion, and group members' feedback. Miller called this strategy *lifeline*. It is a direct, elementary strategy that is aimed at helping individuals with the reality of their lives and death. Specifically, it helps individuals examine meaningful episodes in their lives and evaluate the positive and negative impacts of these episodes.

Lifeline involves giving members a five-by-seven-inch index card and asking members to draw a line from near the edge of the left to near the edge of the right side. At each end, members are asked to place a dot. The left dot represents a person's birth and the right dot the person's death. Each member is asked to indicate on the line where she is now along this continuum. Members are instructed to write their most positive, happy, or rewarding experiences, with the dots on the lines indicating such periods in chronological order. Below the line, members are instructed to do similarly; however, these events are the most negative, unhappy, or painful (Figure 6.4). Because the exercise has the potential to nudge members into psychologically sensitive areas, the leader should provide structure in the beginning and end. The leader asks a member to share, in five minutes, one of their positive experiences. Hopefully, everyone shares a positive experience. The group leader's task is to comment upon the similarities and differences among members in terms of their positive experiences. The goal is to "break the ice," facilitate group identification, and provide humor.

Then members are asked to share one of their negative experiences. The leader tells members about the strength that it takes to risk. Also, the leader stresses the

FIGURE 6.4 Lifeline

importance of confidentiality. At the end of these admonitions, the leader compliments and reinforces members' sharing. Then, the leader queries whether someone
would like to discuss a painful or disappointing event in more detail or discuss something that was not written down. Lifeline provides a springboard to understanding
group issues, such as the homogeneous and heterogeneous qualities of the group.
Members also realize that other members have similar life experiences and begin to
acquire a clearer understanding of their values, mood states, needs, desires, sense of
self, cause-and-effect relationships, and manner of solving problems. The lifeline
strategy is flexible and usable, with some modifications, with children, adolescents,
and adults. It also can be used with different cultural and racial groups, students
with disabilities, and individuals from different socioeconomic classes (Miller,
1993).

Higgs (1992) offers strategies for how to deal with resistance in a group, observing that it is an important phenomenon affecting group dynamics. Resistance takes
many forms and can be illustrated by consistent silence, telling jokes, falling asleep,
excessive talking, or intellectualizing. The reasons for resistance are varied and may
be because members fear being seen by others as stupid, abnormal, or weak. Also,
members may be afraid to disclose information because they fear being attacked or
rejected. In general, Higgs suggests that leaders should not label members who evidenced resistance. No one should be labeled as the "silent one" or "the talker." Instead, the focus should be on the behaviors. Repetitive silence should be explored
for the meaning for it, which is directed at the individual who is silent and other
members in the group. Excessive or inappropriate laughter may be addressed in several ways. The leader could comment or speculate about the meaning, such as seeking to avoid group work or impede the group. Other comments are that the laughter
may be a mechanism for the group to communicate. Excessive talking, especially
about extraneous issues, may elicit the observation that the group needs to focus on
present issues involving the group. One who monopolizes could be checked by asking the group why it permits a member to monopolize. Intellectualizing is characterized by preference for focusing on intellectual aspects of issue and avoiding the
affective. Here, members may be confronted about the avoidance of affective issues.
A related resistant facet is generalizing, such as the use of "people," "everyone," or
"them" to avoid specificity. The leader could ask, who are those people and are you
one of them?

Strategies to Change Offenders

Evans and Kane (1996) propose an intervention technique for working with offenders in a group. They observe that offenders have a private logic that justifies
their offending. Containing three psychological processes, private logic includes the
long-range goals of the offender's lifestyle, the immediate goals in a given situation,
and the covert justification or hidden reasons for their behaviors and thoughts. In
group, offenders say what he or she thinks the leader wants to hear. So, they will su-
perficially ventilate their feelings, disclose the bad upbringing, discuss their past,
and show insight, but "how they process the world around them is not changed"
(Evans & Kane, 1996, p. 111).

These hidden reasons are not generally shared. So, Evans and Kane developed a
group technique called *sophistry* to uncover offenders' hidden reasons. Sophistry,

aided by group dynamics, "creates interactions revealing hidden reasons found in the offender's private logic" (p. 112). The group is used to manifest offenders' fallacious reasoning. Sophistry consists of six elements—warm-up, paradoxical intention, cognitive click, mirroring, hidden reasons, and reorientation.

Warm-Up

The counselor administers twelve hidden reasons in a brief questionnaire and instructs the group members to respond on a five-point scale—1 "Absolutely True" to 5 "Absolutely False." The statements are (a) Money will solve all my problems; (b) If treated unfairly, I have the right to be unfair back; (c) A strong person demands respect from others; (d) I am to be admired and made to feel important despite what I do; (e) My childhood experiences control my current behavior and emotions; (f) An important person has power and control; (g) I have the right to be dependent and others will enjoy taking care of me; (h) People should accept me despite my past behavior (I am a changed person); (i) I must avoid difficulties rather than face them (My life should be trouble free); (j) Because I have been treated poorly, I am not responsible for my actions; (k) Honest people are really dishonest (lawyers, judges, ministers); and (l) Everyone thinks this way.

The purpose of this assignment is to serve as a warm-up and to focus the offenders on how they think. Later, this questionnaire is administered a second time to learn whether there have been any changes in the offenders' thinking at the end of the group.

Paradoxical Intention

A paradoxical intention is a clinical tool that, if successful, will produce the opposite of what the counselor, on the face, insinuates. The use of paradoxes stems power struggles between group members and the counselor. Also, paradoxes are used for deep-rooted and repetitive problems that do not respond to logical or rational queries. The counselor begins this technique by highlighting one of the offenders' beliefs. The leader, then, encourages the group not to change, but to relate how they actually think. The leader joins the members, recognizing, praising, and exaggerating their deep-rooted thoughts and beliefs. The aim is to carry their views to the extreme so that they can see how ridiculous some of their thoughts are.

Cognitive Click

Sophistry centers around the use of a stimulus that is called a cognitive click. It "is a dramatic moment at which the client must face the evidence and begin drastic revision of his or her cognition and related attitudes and beliefs" (p. 112). The basis for centering sophistry around the cognitive click is the recognition that offenders act according to their private logic, but they have the capacity to accept their common sense. Often, offenders contradict themselves in group by proclaiming that they will change (i.e., common sense), but their behaviors suggest otherwise (i.e., private logic). A cognitive click is needed to gain entry into the offender's private sense. This is done with the use of the twelve hidden reasons and the division of the group into two teams. One team argues for the first six statements while the other team argues against them. According to Evans and Kane, "the team arguing against the idea begins each round and concludes each round with a rebuttal to the arguments supporting the statement made by the team going second. This is done so that the rounds end by pointing out the flawed logic of each statement" (p. 112). The group leader facilitates movement but does not provide answers. The leader urges members to express how they think. Each member gets a chance to argue for and against each statement and to hear others' statements for and against. The cognitive click is the debate among the group. Offenders are forced to present their private logic and have them challenged by other group members.

Mirroring

As stated, offenders say what they believed that the counselor wants to hear. To help draw them out, mirroring, a technique used in psychodrama, is employed. The cognitive click that emerges from the debate permits members to mirror other members' behaviors and thinking. Mirroring permits self-confrontation of each group member in that he or she can see other members display his or her behaviors. Ideally, these sessions should be videotaped because videotaping can provide another mirroring effect. Members can see themselves and others discuss their hidden reasons and differentiate between them and common sense.

Hidden Reasons

Offenders' private logic causes maladaptive behaviors and leads to difficulties in their personal and social lives. Evans and Kane interviewed a number of offenders and found twelve frequently used hidden reasons. They facilitate the faulty thinking that offenders have that lead them to commit crimes. So, the use of these hidden reasons constitute the fifth technique. This use is done by administering the questionnaire again to determine if there have been any changes from the warm-up assessment.

Reorientation

After the debate, the leader strives to help reorient group members. The effectiveness of reorientation determines the success of sophistry. The main goal of this stage is to help offenders align their views with common sense. This end is achieved through group discussions, utilizing pre- and post-questionnaires, the debate, and the videotape. Members assist each other's new thinking that uses alternative perceptions, interpretations, and self-statements. A critical task of the group leader is to provide encouragement and to facilitate other members to provide encouragement to each other. As far as how to encourage effectively, the leader is free to use whatever will support new ways of thinking. Without encouragement, ultimate change is difficult.

A common strategy in working with offenders is to teach them social skills (De-Lange, Barton, & Lanham, 1981; Kempf, 1994; Segal & Marshall, 1985; Spence, 1981; Stermac & Quinsey, 1986; Wright, 1995). The following section describes the components of social skills training.

SOCIAL SKILLS TECHNIQUES

Shean (1985) presents a group of psychoeducational strategies, or social skills, that were used with rehabilitation groups. Rehabilitation or social skills groups are premised on the theory that many psychological problems emanate from inadequate or deviant social learning patterns, buttressed perhaps by biological factors. These deviant social learning patterns create faulty patterns of thinking, feelings, and behaviors. According to Shean, "the purpose of skills training is to identify and prioritize those inadequate or inappropriate action patterns that interfere with the client's psychological and social adjustment, and to create structured learning opportunities in which more adequate or appropriate patterns of interpersonal behavior can be understood, practiced, learned, applied, and generalized to everyday life" (p. 24).

In applying social skills training, a counselor can address a variety of topics in groups and is limited only by his or her imagination. However, the counselor should have a specific goal or goals in mind to achieve. Shean identified six skills training techniques for counselors' use. These are modeling, role-playing, learning techniques, prompting, homework, and feedback. See Figure 6.5.

Modeling

Modeling involves the demonstration by the group leader of skills pertinent to a group discussion. The group leader, correctly and naturally, performs the skills so the group members can emulate the skill. Ideally, the leader should practice the skills or be sure that he or she can demonstrate them well before illustrating them to the group. Researching the literature, Shean reports that three stages of learning occurred by modeling. First, the leader should be cognizant of the group's attention, which is required before learning is achieved. The leader should ensure that his or her modeling is specific to phases that should be learned because the leader does not want undesirable behaviors to be adopted. Extraneous and irrelevant statements cause members' attention to drift. Second, the leader helps members to recall the modeled behavior, and this is aided by role-playing. Third, the leader encourages members to actually use the behaviors in interactions. The likelihood of members using the behavior, though, is determined by interest, motivation, social support, and reward. So, groups that engage in worthwhile topics receive adequate social reinforcement, and secure opportunities for success are more likely to increase its members' motivation and anticipatory reward.

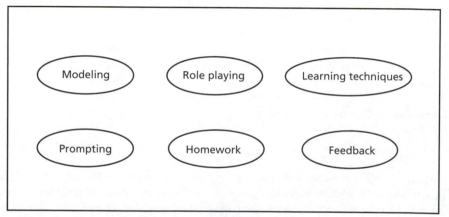

FIGURE 6.5 Skills Components

Role-Playing

Role-playing is a technique that is significant for a social skill group. It involves at least two persons with the leader often acting as the director. As the director, the leader should set the scene and inform the members of the aspects that should be demonstrated. Role-playing involves learning by doing, and repetitive doing aids learning. It is a situation in which a group member performs a role that is the focus of a group exercise.

Prompting

Prompting should be done when needed, such as a member engaged in role-playing and not making eye contact. The group should be instructed by the leader, and the leader should have modeled eye contact before prompting a member. Prompting may be needed also for a member forgetting to say thank you when it is socially required.

Homework

Homework, properly provided, meets the goal of stimulus and response generalization by guiding members when they first attempt a new skill and preparing them for a lack of success. Homework should not be given until a skill has been practiced several times in a group. Also, the leader should prepare group members for disappointment and unrehearsed or unexpected responses from the public.

Feedback

Feedback should be given but it should not be negative feedback. The focus should be on achievement and improvement, and positive reinforcement should be provided for these achievements and improvement. If a member has made partial improvement, he or she should be praised for this improvement and not criticized for incomplete goal attainment.

Other strategies have been developed for working with offenders. Roberts, Cheek, and Mumm (1994) studied the effects of community building upon prisoners' reading scores. While their findings were important in that a group that had community building and a reading program performed better than two other groups, an important aspect of their study was the technique of creating community building. The goal of community building is to create a "true community." A *true community* is characterized by respect for differences among group members, shared leadership, spontaneity, quietness, joy, respectful conflict, commitment to accepting painful life experiences, and a heightened awareness of the well being of the group. However, members are not told what a true community is. The intent is to permit the group to learn what it is through experience. Only a few basic rules are established, such as the responsibility of each member to help achieve success; displeasure must be presented in group; the group must commit to staying in the group even when they are frustrated, angry, depressed, or have doubts about the efficacy of the group; and the group must be committed to confidentiality. In addition, other norms were addressed by the facilitators, such as being punctual, wearing name tags, stating one's name before speaking, and cautioning that the greatest impediment to communication is to talk without reasons and to not talk when there are reasons to

The Rabbi's Gift involves a story about a dying monastery that had lost its influence among the people. The house was decaying and it looked physically in ruin. Only four monks and the Abbot (the leader) remained in the monastery, and all were over seventy years of age. Near the monastery, in nearby woods, was a hut that a Rabbi used as a hermitage. The Abbot and the other monks could tell when the Rabbi was in the hut, and they speculated whether the Rabbi could advise them on how to revive the monastery and attract people back to the area. The Abbot went to the Rabbi's hut, telling him of the decaying conditions of the monastery and how people were shunning it. The Rabbi commiserated with the Abbot and told him the synagogues were in a similar state. The Rabbi told the Abbot that he did not have any advice for him. So, they prayed together and discussed religious and philosophical issues. As the Abbot was leaving, the Rabbi told him that the Messiah was one of them. Upon telling the monks that the Rabbi did not have any advice for them but stated that the Messiah was one of them, they all pondered what the Rabbi meant. Then they began to speculate who was or could be the Messiah. Because they did not know, they began to treat each other with more respect on the chance that this person could be Messiah and was worthy of respect. They also began to treat themselves with more respect on the chance that they were the Messiah. While the monastery was dying, a few people always came by to picnic on nearby grounds and to meditate in the dilapidated chapel. As people came by, they noticed the difference among the monks and the Abbot and the radiant manner that emanated from them. An appealing and attractive aura had developed. People began to return to the picnic area and the chapel and brought their friends with them. Their friends brought other friends, and soon younger persons were inquiring about how to join the monastery. Within a few years, the monastery had been transformed into a thriving spiritual center. This transformation was wholly due to the Rabbi's gift.

FIGURE 6.6 The Rabbi's Gift

talk. Following these rules and admonitions, the group is told a story, such as "The Rabbi's Gift" (Figure 6.6), which is described in the community-building model (Peck, 1987).

Following the story, the group remains silent for three minutes. Then the community-building process starts, using a story to inspire interpretations and the nature of the group at that moment. The group proceeds through a pseudocommunity, chaos, emptiness, and then becomes a true community (Roberts, Cheek, & Mumm, 1994).

Walsh (1992) recommends an exercise that he used with property offenders in a group. He states that offenders believe that crime pays and that the benefits of stealing outweigh the cost of punishment. This exercise is designed to challenge this view. With a burglary suspect, Walsh asks him or her to list actual and fenced values for all his or her burglaries, those in which he or she was charged and not charged. According to the prisoner's total, he or she had stolen goods that netted $1,025. The burglar had served forty months in prison. So, the offender earned $25.62 a month, 82 cents a day, and 10 cents per hour. Prisoners are sometimes amazed at how much property crimes really pay. This exercise can be enhanced by further calculating how much they would have earned with a job that paid only minimum wage for forty months. Working only ten hours a week at minimum wage would have netted this prisoner during this time about $7,000. While this amount would not make prisoners financially sufficient, it beats $1,025. So, an issue for the group to discuss is the sensibility of working for $7,000 and being free compared with $1,025 and imprisoned.

Gibbs (1993) provides an invention strategy that is designed to increase institutionalized juvenile delinquents' moral reasoning. Drawn from cognitive-structural theory, a group of juveniles are presented with a story involving two brothers. The older brother tells his younger brother that he, the older brother, is selling a dangerous drug on the streets. The drug has the potential to cause lung and brain damage, and, under some circumstances, could kill. The younger brother asks his older brother to stop, but the older brother, saying the family needs the money, extracts a promise to keep the drug dealing a secret.

Four questions are presented to the group to spur their thinking and challenge their values. The goal is to achieve a consensus on the best decision for the best reason. The first question is whether the younger brother should tell on his older brother. This question raises several important issues, juxtaposing the law, life, affiliation, property, and contract. Second, the group is asked what if the younger brother finds out that the older brother is selling drugs to small kids. Should the younger brother tell then? The third question is whether it is ever right to tell a secret after promising not to tell. Finally, the group is asked what if the younger brother finds out that the older brother is not helping out the family financially and instead is buying clothes and gambling. While the strategies above involve specific examples used with offenders, a number of strategies exist in the literature, and many of them are adaptive for group work with offenders (Goodstein & Pfeiffer, 1985; Jones & Pfeiffer, 1981; Pfeiffer, 1987; Pfeiffer & Goodstein, 1986; Pfeiffer & Jones, 1980).

Group Discussion Topics

Scott (1993) reported the result of a study of three groups of mentally and emotionally disturbed prisoners. One group consisted of prisoners who were lower functioning in terms of their IQ, had difficulty in expressing themselves, had an extensive criminal record, had little personal pride, had minimal psychological inquiry, had frequent periods of psychosis, and needed direction. The second group consisted of prisoners who were verbal, young, bright, unit leaders, anxious to solve other prisoners' problems, and had a borderline personality disorder. The third group consisted of promising treatment members, some with the ability to engage in self-observation, capacity to reciprocate, and the capacity to examine their crimes. Scott reported some changes with group members, but provided no statistical support for his conclusions. However, he contributes to working with offenders in groups by listing discussion topics that he uses in his groups. Below are statements Scott used.

1. Once an offender, always an offender.
2. An offender can't be trusted.
3. All offenders are alike.
4. Offenders hate.

5. Crime is exciting.
6. Evil—what is it?
7. Most offenders want all the attention or no attention: A split group.
8. Can a "solid con" be mentally ill?
9. The person I love most is _____.
10. Do we have too many offenders?
11. How can an attitude be changed?
12. Your earliest memory is _____.
13. "Sour grapes" versus "the grass is greener elsewhere." Which one is your attitude?
14. What was your happiest event and what was your saddest event? Which one was "deeper" or more meaningful?
15. An offender can line up everyone's ducks, but not his own.
16. Is today's world a mental hospital or a prison?
17. When I can laugh at myself as much as at others, I'm on the road to maturity.
18. "When he opened the book, he closed his mind." What does that mean? Apply it to group therapy.
19. Offenders can't really talk; they gossip, argue, and fight but cannot discuss issues.
20. Offenders don't know themselves.
21. Offenders make poor choices.
22. Crime has a lot of benefits. Name some.
23. "Love me, love my dog means love me, love my crime, and love my excuses."
24. How do offenders mourn a loss?
25. Most offenders wouldn't have committed a crime if not on alcohol or drugs. (Love my excuses.)
26. You made me angry.
27. Six different ways to commit a crime.
28. Six different ways not to commit crime.
29. What does this mean: He was brain dead but sexually active.
30. The only time most offenders are in the fast lane is when they're going in the wrong direction.
31. Stay in your own head, get out of other people's heads; it's worse than breaking into a house.
32. Old hatred can keep you alive, but it's not much of a life.
33. Would you tell "the man" if you knew a member of the unit was going to get shanked?
34. Mental illness is worse than being an offender.
35. Do you tell the group the real story of your life and the part you played?
36. "The devil made me do it." Explain.
37. What is a professional victim?
38. What does the offender mean when he says, "I've learned my lesson"?

Group versus Individual Counseling

As stated in the previous chapter, individual counseling provides some advantages over group counseling, and as stated in this chapter, group counseling provides a number of therapeutic benefits. One can complement the other and neither can be thought of as being better than the other. Though not looking at which was better in terms of rehabilitation, Towberman (1993) examines the impact of group versus individual counseling among incarcerated female juvenile offenders on perceptions of the treatment environment. The type of treatment was the independent variable and the perception of the environment as measured by the Correctional Institutions Environment Scale (CIES), was the dependent variable. The CIES measures three environmental dimensions—the treatment program, the degree of interpersonal relationships, and the degree of emphasis on institutional order and control within the correctional environment. Those females who were in group counseling gave higher ratings on perceptions of interpersonal relationships and the treatment program than those females who were in individual counseling (Towberman, 1993). The researcher speculates that these higher ratings may be attributed to the curative benefits of group counseling (Towberman, 1993).

SUMMARY

This chapter has discussed the various aspects of group counseling. First, the benefits of counseling, as discussed by Yalom (1985), were presented. Though these benefits were originally discussed in reference to psychiatric patients, the author showed that these benefits are also applicable to the offender population. Next, the author described the types of groups that are commonly used with offenders. Then, the author described the selection of group members, group roles and especially the role of the group leader, and group dynamics. Then, stages of group were presented. Finally, a list of strategies was described for various stages of the group process.

KEY TERMS

Self-help groups
Therapy groups
Cohesiveness
Validation
Movement
Curative factors

Encounter groups
Marathon groups
Structured groups
Group roles
Group dynamics
Group stages

Sophistry
Private logic
Cognitive click
Hidden reasons
Lifeline

7

※ ※ ※

Treating Female
Juvenile Offenders

※ INTRODUCTION

Female adolescents are far less delinquent than male adolescents (Siegal & Senna, 1997). Their ratio to male juveniles for index crimes is one to fifteen for murder, one to ten for robbery, one to four for assault, one to nine for burglary, one to two for larceny, one to five for auto theft, one to seven for arson (Siegel & Senna, 1997). As the numbers suggest, males are more criminogenic, but on rare occasions, some females are charged with violent crimes. For instance, a twelve-year-old girl in Peoria, Illinois, was held responsible for killing her two-month-old brother. She twisted the child's neck until he was dead and put the cord of a laundry bag around the baby's neck to make it appear as an accident. The girl was given seven years of probation, which she was to serve in a home for troubled children. There, she was expected to get psychiatric counseling and educational instructions ("Girl Gets Probation," 1998). Much of females' troubles, however, involve status offenses (i.e., running away and family problems), risk-taking behaviors (Shapiro, Siegal, Scovill, & Hays, 1998), and sex offenses (Miller, Fejes-Mendoza, & Eggleston, 1997).

Adolescent females differ from adolescent males also in that they are three times more likely than males to be the victims of sexual abuse (Sickmund, Snyder, & Poe-Yamagata, 1997). Furthermore, some professionals attribute female adolescents' sexual victimization to much of their delinquency (Hoyt & Scherer, 1998). As an illustration, Higgs, Canavan, and Meyer (1992) reported a case study of a juvenile sex offender who they named Carol. Carol, then seven years old, was sexually molested by a seventeen-year-old relative. Carol and her twelve-year-old brother began to have sex, and this behavior continued for several years until Carol was a teenager. When it was discovered, Carol, her brother, and the parents underwent counseling. During counseling, Carol and her brother contracted with the therapist not to engage in sex, but they still would continue to have sexual intercourse. Carol became promiscuous with other boys at school and later in a residential treatment program. Carol developed mental health problems and began to cut her wrists. Later, Carol was discovered forcing her seven-year-old cousin to have sex with her (Higgs, Canavan, & Meyer, 1992). Apparently, Carol's victimization as a seven year old traumatized her and distorted her sexual development. Because of her distorted development, she developed an unhealthy view of sex and its purpose. This case study reveals how sexual victimization as a child can later lead to sexual offending as a juvenile. It also shows how counseling and treatment may not be promptly effective in terminating offending behaviors.

THE CONTEXT OF TREATING FEMALE JUVENILE OFFENDERS

In treating female juvenile offenders, as well as all the other offenders discussed in subsequent chapters, context is consequential. Morrison (1994) states that

> understanding the context in which practice takes place is vital. It enables the practitioner to take proper account of the wide-ranging set of influences which bear upon their [sic] ability to be effective, including societal attitudes, legislation and organisational [sic] factors. Some, probably the majority, of these influences lie beyond the control of the practitioner, not least the acute resource shortages in health and welfare agencies. Nonetheless, if practitioners do not take such factors into account, intervention and treatment plans may be unrealistic and inappropriate, leading to failure and disillusionment. (p. 25)

The consideration of the contextual nature of treatment and intervention has particular importance for adolescent female offenders. For instance, the author's barber related that she was having problems with her twelve-year-old daughter, prompting her to call the juvenile authorities. Allegedly, the daughter became under the influence of a friend, who reportedly was rebellious, and influenced the daughter to be rebellious, too. Her daughter was put in detention for a few days and given counseling, which the mother later said was therapeutic and helped her daughter. This illustration shows how the juvenile justice system may get involved in conflict between a mother and her daughter. While the mother believes that juvenile court intervention was justified, other conflicts between girls and their parents may be dubious and present an ethical dilemma for clinicians.

As stated earlier, a number of juvenile offenders are diagnosed as having conduct disorder or oppositional defiant disorders. Girls are more likely than boys to be diagnosed as having an oppositional defiant disorder (Kaplan & Sadock, 1998). As shown by the barber's daughter, this disorder may be treated as a juvenile justice problem, but it is typically viewed as a mental health issue. Viewed as a mental health issue, some girls are hospitalized in psychiatric hospitals. The author worked in an adolescent unit of a psychiatric hospital and observed the records of one girl who had been hospitalized with a diagnosis of oppositional defiant disorder. The source of the family conflict was that the girl, who was white, had an African American boyfriend. The parents tried to break up this relationship. Failing, they sought out the psychiatrists to help them make their daughter less defiant and more obedient in accepting family rules.

This issue raises ethical question about the coerced treatment of adolescents. Some adolescents' problems may be of a lesser nature than the parents', but because of the power and rights of the parents, the adolescents' rights might be secondary to the parents (Morrison, 1986). Clinicians need to ponder the ethics of treating adolescents when parental rules and standards do not involve criminal or harmful behaviors.

Silber and Silber (1996) describe this dilemma as a primary moral issue in treating adolescents, involving the conflict between autonomy and beneficence. Adults, which include clinicians, want to protect adolescents. However, this paternalism conflicts with adolescents' need to make autonomous decisions. Further, if an adolescent does decide autonomously to consent to treatment for substance abuse, this carries a right to confidential counseling. In sum, the ethical issues involve autonomy, beneficence, paternalism, guidance, confidentiality, and consent (Silber & Silber, 1996). To ethically resolve many of these ethical issues, Sapsford (1997), who counsels girls on probation through a private practice, requires girls to interview her and hire her before she will take them as clients.

Besides the ethical issues, other issues involving female juvenile offenders are paramount. A counselor should be sensitive to several issues involved in the treatment of juvenile female offenders. Reitsma-Street and Offord (1991), for instance, challenge the notion that delinquent and nondelinquent girls are different, and, as a result, counselors should look at delinquent girls differently. They came to this conclusion following a study of the development of delinquency in siblings. They focused on girls who met the criteria of little age differences, shared early upbringing, and delinquency discordance. They identified twenty-six sister pairs for analysis by qualitative means of their similarities and differences. Previous quantitative analysis examined 235 variables and found fifty-five variables that statistically differentiated the sister pairs, which means that 180 (76.6%) variables did not differentiate the sisters.

Examining the issue further, they state that delinquent and nondelinquent sisters were similar in terms of relationships with significant others; were similar in school, work, and recreational activities; were similar in health and reproductivity; and were similar in their feminine identities. These commonalties have costs in terms of relationship, the future, invisible reproductive problems (e.g., infertility, pregnancy, miscarriages), and feminine identity. All girls, according to Reitsma-Street and Offord, pay very high costs consisting of abusive and violent relationships with males, inadequate future preparation, burdensome consequences of sexual activity, and a feminine identity that guarantees second-class citizenship.

Reitsma-Street and Offord urge moving beyond differences and a recognition of similarities. Professionals should be looking for the characteristics that tie females together rather than characteristics that tell them apart. Doing so "helps to break open the static, restrictive stereotypes of what is a girl delinquent, a woman offender, a normal female, and appropriate social work practice" (p. 22). Rejecting differences based on standards of normalcy or goodness helps individuals concerned about females to minimize the use of labels or stereotypes. For instance, in one of the case files of the sisters studied, a counselor described a client as an "unsocialized, egocentric, sexually promiscuous girl" (p. 22).

This type of labeling would not occur if counselors were not bent on focusing on differences among females. Also, counselors and policy makers would be less likely to blame the victim or look to imprisonment as a solution. The development of empathy, genuine interest, and creative problem solving occurs when girl delinquents, social workers, and correctional personnel concentrate on the core characteristics of females' lives that tie them together. As stated by Reitsma-Street and Offord (1991), "attention to commonalties, however, goes beyond deeper empathy and reduction of stereotypes. The questions and priorities change. For instance, rather than predicting and treating the social or psychological characteristics of females who shoplift, use drugs, or sell sex, the emphasis veers towards understanding the common characteristics that maintain or transform the pervasive economic vulnerability faced by both delinquent and non-delinquent females, female clients and professionals" (p. 22).

Similarly, Miller, Fejes-Mendoza, and Eggleston (1997) contend that no evidence exists suggesting that programming for female juvenile delinquents need to be different from intervention efforts for adolescent females in general who have problems. The programs developed should focus on girls' strengths instead of perceived deficits that need to be fixed, girls' involvement in planning and implementation of programming, creation of a supportive network among girls and between girls and woman staff members, and creation of an environment in which girls feel free to speak up without censoring, belittling, or interruption (Miller, Fejes-Mendoza, & Eggleston, 1997).

Another issue raised is how society contributes to the delinquency of girls (Chesney-Lind & Shelden, 1998) and mental health problems (Sands, 1998; Solomon, 1994). Chesney-Lind and Shelden (1998) argue that despite the women's movement, gender differences exist in socialization processes. Girls are taught early what the expectations are for their gender, and these expectations are enforced by parents, schools, and other institutions. At the same time, many of the behaviors expected of girls are not valued by the larger society and affect girls' self-esteem. In addition, these institutions put more effort in preventing girls from sexual experimentation. As stated by Chesney-Lind and Shelden (1998), "girls' plummeting self-esteem is likely tied, particularly among white girls, to the overemphasis on physical attractiveness and unhealthy eating habits. For girls of color, problems with invisibility within a school system that ignores or belittles you, as well as violence in your neighborhood, produce different problems" (p. 122).

The experiences of white girls and girls of color contribute to their delinquency. While the control exerted by institutions reduces delinquency in some girls, it causes delinquency in other girls who rebel against perceived unfair control. Girls of color and working-class girls are not freed from standards of beauty established for white girls. Moreover, they must compete in a hostile school environment and deal

with the violence in their communities. These girls of color must find their own solutions to their predicament, which may entail delinquent behavior. Furthermore,
all girls are at risk for sexual violence, which may contribute to delinquency problems (Chesney-Lind & Shelden, 1998).

Issues of Minority Females

African American Partly supporting Chesney-Lind and Shelden's (1998) observations of different experiences of girls of color, Stevens (1997) states certain imper-
fect attributes are ascribed to minority groups, and females experience issues unique
to their gender. For instance, females know that they are expected to separate and
disconnect somewhat from their families during the emergence of adolescence, and
this process produces "normative relational crisis" (p. 149). African American females experience this same crisis but have the added pressures from their cultural
group. Stevens contends, therefore, that African American adolescent females have
an identity formation that is multidimensional and intricate. They must synthesize
coherent meaning systems from three socialization experiences. First, they must
deal with the expectations from mainstream society that emphasizes a Eurocentric
worldview. Second, they must address a devalued social status that is produced by
the convergence of their race and gender. Third, they must respond to their cultural
reference group that involves the experiences interpreted from an Afrocentric
world view (Stevens, 1997). Traditional counseling models fail to take these experiences into account (Stevenson, 1998).

Hispanic Adolescents Flores, Eyre, and Millstein (1998), surveying the literature
regarding Mexican American culture and its relationship to adolescent sexual activity and partner selection, stated that these activities take place in a culture that
emphasizes specific values of the Mexican American community. Among these are
familism (which accentuates the primacy of the family, traditional roles for women,
and the valuing of children), *simpatia* (which requires agreeable and harmonious interpersonal relationships), *personalismo* (which involves maintaining a close tie to
extended family and friends), *respeto* (which means respecting traditional sex roles,
elders, and community), *marianism* (which, for females, means observing traditional
values of virginity, chastity, virtue, obeying significant males in their lives, spiritual
strength, and assuming the role of central caregiver for the family and community).
See Figure 7.1.

Familism

Simpatia

Personalismo

Respeto

Marianism

FIGURE 7.1 Mexican American Values

Minorities in the United States, such as Mexican Americans and Hispanics, must frequently take into account the interaction of their cultural values and the assimilation with the dominant culture and its values (Brook, Whiteman, Balka, Win, & Gursen, 1998; Flores et al., 1998; Fraser, Piancentini, Van Rossen, Hien, & Rotheram-Borus, 1998). Fraser and associates (1998) studied the influence of sociocultural influences on mental health problems and substance abuse of suicidal Hispanic female adolescents. Sociocultural influences involved the extent of acculturation and biculturalism. The findings were mixed. When acculturation was measured multidimensionally, biculturalism was associated with sexual activity. But strong identification with the mainstream culture was not associated with sexual activity. There was no association between being bicultural and substance use. But more acculturated Hispanic girls were more likely to use drugs than less acculturated Hispanic girls. Moreover, their study reveals positive associations between substance use and anxiety disorder, affective disorder, disruptive disorder, and suicidal ideation. The data further reveal that the more Hispanic girls were acculturated, the more likely they were to be suicidal (Fraser et al., 1998).

Findings from Fraser and colleagues' study may have implications for treatment. On one hand, it might suggest that Hispanic adolescents in correctional institutions who become suicidal might be helped by strengthening their identification with their culture. But if a counselor does recommend strategies to increase one's knowledge about her culture, it may reinforce principles that are rejected by feminist principles. For instance, feminist theory rejects patriarchal structures, but reconnecting a Hispanic adolescent to her culture might mean being subservient to males and adhering to traditional female sex roles.

In addition to these issues and considerations, factors related to the juvenile justice system are also important. Several issues are critical in providing services to female juvenile offenders. First, school programs must address issues of gender bias in classrooms. Second, all residential programs must address the lack of adequate medical services for girls. Third, programs that offer pregnancy prevention and sex education must delve into the numerous reasons why girls have sex and get pregnant, instead of emphasizing just the biological nature. Fourth, all programs must address the high rate of girls referred to the juvenile justice system who have been sexually abused (Maniglia, 1996).

Also, within the juvenile justice system, adolescents with alcohol and drug problems may receive insufficient drug treatment because of fiscal, philosophical, and systemic factors. Little money exists to fund comprehensive services, key personnel believe juveniles need to be punished, and components of the system are fragmented (Schonberg et al., 1993).

The Center for Substance Abuse Treatment recommends guidelines for the treatment of juveniles with substance abuse problems within the juvenile justice system. Among the guidelines are juvenile justice officials recognizing that juveniles have a right to treatment, coordinating of all juvenile services, providing training to treatment professionals to integrate services, utilizing contractual service, involving the community, and implementing all recommendations so as to provide the best treatment possible. Moreover, if all juvenile justice personnel endorse the concept of a juvenile's right to treatment, then treatment would occur in the least restrictive, short-term confinement facilities and detention centers. Instead, the juvenile court judges would select as an alternative setting for treatment intensive community supervision, report centers, day treatment, evening and weekend programs, electronic monitoring, home detention, community service, or volunteer programs (Schnonberg et al., 1993).

TECHNIQUES AND PROCEDURES OF TREATING FEMALE JUVENILE OFFENDERS

Treatment for Sexual Victimization

As stated earlier, females are more likely to be sexually abused than males, which may lead to subsequent juvenile justice problems or mental health difficulties for these females. Deblinger and Heflin (1996) recommend cognitive–behavioral intervention techniques with adolescents who have been sexually abused. Effective techniques are coping skills training, gradual exposure, affective and cognitive processing, education about sexual abuse, and healthy sexuality. Principal among these are gradual exposure and affective and cognitive processing. At first, gradual exposure is used to help sexually abused adolescents to uncouple the associations between their emotional distress and memories, thoughts, discussions, and other remembrances connected to the sexual abuse. This is done in a safe, therapeutic environment. According to Deblinger and Heflin (1996), "with repeated exposures, children's emotional responses diminish through a process referred to as habituation. When this occurs, relaxed or neutral responses may become connected with previously feared abuse-related memories and/or discussion. The resulting overall reduction in emotional distress free sexually abused children to process their abusive experiences cognitively and affectively" (p. 50).

When gradual exposure has been successfully accomplished, counselors are in position to help the adolescent understand what happened, clarify misconceptions, and place the abuse in perspective. Also, the counselor can help the adolescent process the experience effectively. Adolescents are encouraged to systematize their feelings about the experience and the offender, seeking emotional equilibrium.

Deblinger and Heflin (1996) promote a number of cognitive techniques to use in counseling. For instance, they illustrate how to convey to adolescents that different thoughts may result in different emotions. For instance, they tell girls a story of two girls receiving the same grade, 52, on a math examination. One girl declares that she will receive an F in the class and will fail the fourth grade. The adolescent in treatment is invited to indicate how this girl would feel. The other girl who also receives the same grade concludes that she did not study for it and realizes that she needs to put in more work to pass. This girl also tells herself that she now knows how the teacher tests and is confident that she will do much better the next time. The adolescent is invited to describe how this second girl feels.

In another cognitive technique, Deblinger and Heflin reveal how to dispute a negative thought and thereby assist an adolescent who ascribes negative thoughts to unclear situations. They relate another case in which a girl goes through a lunch line and sits alone in the corner. Two of her friends go through the line and sit elsewhere. The girl sitting alone begins to tell herself that she is unpopular and her friends now dislike her. The adolescent is invited to assess this situation in another manner. If the adolescent is unable, the counselor relates that the girl could have said to herself that her friends did not see her and it is hard to see someone in the corner. As a result, the girl tells herself to go over to her friends and sit with them.

Finally, Deblinger and Heflin reveal how to help an adolescent who has been sexually abused from feeling guilty. In the example they relate, a twelve-year-old girl was sexually abused by her seventeen-year-old brother. The girl felt guilty about experiencing pleasurable feelings during the abuse. The counselor reminded the adolescent about previous lectures on sexuality and why humans biologically feel pleasure during sexual activity. Particularly, the adolescent is reminded that sensitive nerves exist in some parts of the body and that it is healthy to feel sensations when these parts are stimulated. In short, the aim is to let the adolescent know that they are not bad because they felt sensations during abuse (Deblinger & Heflin, 1996).

Treatment for Adolescents Who Run Away

Females are more likely to run away than males (Siegal & Senna, 1997). An adolescent's running away may invite the intervention of the juvenile justice system. This involvement may be increased if the adolescent runs away from a treatment program when this placement is court ordered. Some adolescents run away from abusive homes, and other adolescents run to the streets because it is perceived to be more exciting than home. A topology on runaways, developed by Orten and Soll (1980), classifies runaways by degrees. First-degree runaways involve those juveniles who are the least estranged from their families. Second-degree runaways are those juveniles who have some street experience and who are uncertain about returning home. Third-degree runaways are those juveniles who identify with the street and have no desire to return home or to accept treatment (Orten & Soll, 1980).

The topology and clinical experiences of professionals who work with female runaways provide a number of treatment strategies, as enumerated by Miller, Eggertson, and Quigg (1990).

1. Residential treatment should not be undertaken when running away is identified as a presenting problem until an agreement is reached among the youth, family, and professionals regarding house rules. The juvenile must agree to the placement conditions before a treatment agreement is achievable.
2. Once the juvenile has agreed to the house rules, a treatment agreement should be struck among the youth, family, and professionals. If the runaways are third-degree runners, it is extremely important to coordinate treatment goals, strategies, and solutions with other professionals, such as the juvenile probation officials.
3. If running away continues to be predominant pattern, a new commitment should be renegotiated rather than focusing on the running away. The purpose of this renegotiation is that the problem is ambivalence, no direction, little progress in treatment, or some other problem.
4. The factors that precede running away should be assessed because running away may be a solution or a problem and may vary from time to time. In this manner, treatment can be appropriately focused.
5. The degree of severity of runaway behavior should be assessed initially, and if the running away is ongoing, a continuous assessment should be made. For

first-degree runners, the primary focus should be the family. For second-degree runners, a variety of treatment modalities are important, including individual counseling, group counseling, and family counseling. For third-degree runners, the primary goal is to help them prepare for independent living with whatever treatment modality is helpful.

6. The treatment focus will differ depending upon whether the juvenile is running away from home or residential care. If the juvenile is running away from home, family work is appropriate. But if the juvenile is running away from residential care, a good assessment is warranted to determine why and determine the function of the running away.

7. Clinicians should seek consultation when they feel stuck and out of solutions.

Adolescent Drug Treatment

A clinician working with adolescents who abuse drugs needs to be aware of a group of special characteristics unique to adolescents. First, instead of showing signs of drug abuse, adolescents abusing drugs exhibit problem behaviors. More times than not, these problem behaviors involve school or home problems. Adolescents have a quicker progression to chemical dependency than adults (Margolis, 1995). Second, for adults, first use to dependency takes from two to seven years, but for adolescents, the progression takes from six to eighteen months (Margolis, 1995). Third, adolescents, while having a favorite drug, abuse more then one drug. Fourth, because adolescents have not had a longer period of negative consequences, they engage in denial longer than adults, not connecting their school or home problem to drug use. Fifth, adolescents' peers reinforce drug use more intensely than adults. Among adolescents who use drugs, drug use is universally accepted. Sixth, when adolescents use drugs, their development is slowed. Socially, these adolescents fall behind their age group in academics, impulse control, social skills development, and ability to delay gratification. These delays must be taken into account, for addressing them is critical in providing successful treatment (Margolis, 1995). Seventh, adolescents have a more difficult time internalizing values, ideas, and concepts that are based on abstract thinking. As a result they may not easily embrace treatment concepts (Kaminer, 1991). As a result of these special characteristics, treatment for adolescents may take longer and may need to be more intense than treatment for adults (Margolis, 1995).

Within adolescents with substance abuse problems, gender differences exist as well (Senay, 1998). Among adolescents who report drug use, girls report a higher level of depression and use of mental health services than boys (Cole & Weissberg, 1994). In treatment, girls in a co-ed group are reluctant to discuss some issues openly with boys present and may not discuss some issues even in an all-girl group, requiring individual counseling in conjunction with group counseling (Rickel & Becker-Lausen, 1994).

To appropriately treat juveniles with substance abuse dependency, the U.S. Department of Health and Human Services Office for Treatment Improvement recommends that substance abuse programs broadly have program structure and administration and clinical interventions. More specifically, Ross (1994) maintains that substance abuse programs for adolescents must include eight essential components. These are (1) a thoughtful rationale for diagnosis and treatment; (2) pertinent screening, assessment, and diagnostic procedure; (3) a continuum of care; (4) a treatment environment conducive to treatment; (5) effective treatment strategies; (6) active family involvement; (7) competent staff; and (8) efficacy and efficiency of treatment.

Ross (1994) begins with the contention that four plateaus of recovery exist when working with adolescent substance abusers. These plateaus are (1) admitting, (2) submitting, (3) committing, and (4) transmitting. Admitting is the stage when the adolescent admits that he or she has a drug problem. The length of such admittance is variable, and some adolescents may never achieve it. Goals must be established that address the denial mechanisms that sustain dishonesty and prevent adolescents from acknowledging their drug problem. The challenge for the counselor is "to break through a well-rehearsed cognitive structure that maintains the two outer layers of the emerging personality of the teenager substance abuser: psychological/physiological addiction and denial of feelings and actions" (p. 55).

Submitting involves getting an adolescent to submit to a treatment process after he or she admits to a problem. The major obstacle at this point is refusal. Some adolescents voice statements of indifference, self-sufficiency, self-righteous, rejection, and defiance. Individual counseling tends to be ineffective at this point. Group counseling is more advantageous here. A well-structured cognitive–behavioral group process helps to challenge an adolescent's irrational belief. Committing involves the juvenile committing to a new set of functional beliefs. The fourth plateau involves the realization of an adolescent that a drug-free lifestyle requires repeated daily rehearsal.

Ross states three objectives for the admitting and submitting plateaus. These are enhancing awareness, managing feelings, and changing processes. For enhancing awareness, some treatment strategies are using the awareness wheel (e.g., sensations, thoughts, feelings, intentions, and actions); feeling log (e.g., documentation of feelings at specific times of the day and the situations that brought on these feelings); ABCDEs of emotion and behavior (i.e., A Event or Situation, B thoughts about A, C Feelings or one's emotional response to A, D Thoughts about C, and E Behavioral response to A); daily moral inventory (i.e., a modification of the tenth step of Alcoholics Anonymous); developing a life plan, rebel-without-a-cause syndrome (i.e., helping adolescents to see that they have a choice rather than some force being used against them); steps one, two, and three of Alcoholics Anonymous; styles of manipulation and actualization; and searching and fearless moral inventory (i.e., a tool to help adolescents identify and confront character defects) (Ross, 1994).

For managing feelings, effective strategies are using the three signs (i.e., think, think, think; first things first; easy does it), serenity prayer, and discussions of the fallible and correctable human being. For changing processes, a counselor may use the five steps to change (e.g., awareness, commitment, identification of irrational thought patterns, substitution of rational thought patterns, and practice-dissonance), law of the harvest (i.e., a biblical story that says that we reap what we plant, we reap in a different season what we plant, and we cannot change the harvest from last year), and getting straight (i.e., lectures that indicate what getting straight is not, what getting straight is, what getting straight requires, and the rewards of getting straight) (Ross, 1994).

The committing and transmitting plateaus have three overall purposes, which are to identify self-defeating self-talk, to change self-talk, and to learn relapse prevention. To identify self-defeating self-talk, five treatment strategies are appropriate. These are the five criteria for rational thinking (e.g., Is my thinking based on fact? Does my thinking help protect my life and health? Does my thinking help me achieve the goals now and in the future? Does my thinking help me prevent unwanted and unnecessary conflict with others? and Does my thinking help me feel the way I need to feel?), styles of irrational or dysfunctional thinking (e.g., absolutes, what-ifing, have to–got to–must, should and ought, awfulizing, good people–bad people, hard and easy, trying versus doing, can't, yes-but, the double bind, romanticizing, abuse of generalities, selective listening, and thinking in vivid images) self-downing and self-acceptance cycle (i.e., failing to complete a task and concluding with a view of worthlessness, which is replaced with views of being capable, doing my best, and choosing a course of action), language of anger and resentment (e.g., a tool to help adolescents reduce the frequency of anger and resentment by challenging thinking errors, such as should and damning others, that produce anger and resentment, secondary virginity (e.g., a tool to help adolescents realize that after being sexually active that it is possible to stop or be more responsible) (Ross, 1994).

To change self-talk, some strategies are using steps five, six, and seven of Alcoholics Anonymous, seven steps to a happy FACE, recovery scripts, changing dislike behaviors, and the Lord's Prayers. FACE is a technique modified by Ross that helps adolescents develop more functional automatic emotional and behavioral responses. Specifically, it involves teaching adolescents to (1) describe factually events, (2) identify self-talk, (3) identify feelings and behaviors, (4) critique self-talk, (5) create new self-talk, (6) create script that leads to new feelings and behaviors, and (7) practice script. Recovery scripts are an application of the seven steps of FACE to a self-defeating response to a situation. It is in a story form for the adolescent to discuss and then read throughout the day. To be effective, the script must describe the pain or uncomfortableness and a decision to behave more positively and feelings from such a positive decision. Altering dislike behavior is a cognitive–behavior technique to help adolescents enumerate their disliked behaviors and how they reinforce these behaviors.

For relapse prevention, several strategies are useful, including steps eight, nine, eleven, and twelve of Alcoholics Anonymous. A counselor can identify the ten common causes of failure (i.e., blaming others, blaming oneself, having no goals, choosing the wrong goals, taking the short cut, taking the long road, neglecting little things, quitting too soon, burden of the past, and illusion of success), relapse signs and symptoms list (i.e., becoming overconfident during recovery, frequenting old places and friends associated with substances, overreacting to stressful events), and goal setting. For goal setting, the adolescent is asked to state a minimum of three six-month goals in nine life activities. These goals must be concrete, believable, and desirable. The nine life activities are physical self-improvement, emotional self-improvement, spiritual self-improvement, family relationships, education and vocation, leisure time, drug-free friendships, service, and financial planning (Ross, 1994).

Treatment for Sex-Related Problems Associated with Drugs and Alcohol

For some adolescents with alcohol and drug problems, their substance use may lead to other problems. Prostitution, which can be engaged by girls and boys, is intermixed with alcohol and drugs. Some adolescents, particularly homeless or marginally domiciled, may engage in "survival sex," where they engage in sex to buy food and pay rent. Also, some chemically addicted adolescents may engage in sex in exchange for drugs. Even if the adolescent is not exchanging sex for drugs, the use of drugs and alcohol may lead to an adolescent making poor choices regarding sex. For instance, an adolescent may say no to sex when sober but may say yes when under the influence of substances.

Indiscriminate and unprotected sex may not only lead to the contraction of sexually transmitted diseases and HIV infection but also unplanned pregnancy for females. Some adolescents continue to abuse substances while pregnant, putting their fetuses at risk. According to some clinicians, treatment for pregnant, substance-abusing adolescents may be implemented in the same program as pregnant, substance-abusing adult women. In one study, adolescents differed primarily in terms of type of drugs and their administration. Pregnant women are more likely to use opiates and inject the drugs than pregnant adolescents (Farrow, Watts, Krohn, & Olson, 1999). They were similar, however, in terms of psychological and treatment history profiles (Farrow, Watts, Krohn, & Olson, 1999).

In accordance with the contention that pregnant adolescents and women are similar, the following intervention model is described. It was developed for the Center for Substance Abuse Treatment by a group that has had involvement with pregnant, substance-abusing females (Mitchell et al., 1993). The group contends that pregnant, substance-abusing females require a continuum of treatment for an extended time. A continuum of services is needed because of the multiple roles that pregnant females perform, including a person in recovery, parent-to-be, partner, and probably single head of a household.

To serve these multiple roles, case management provides a vital function in securing a connection to needed services. Ideally, case management should be commenced prenatally and should continue throughout the postpartum period for all pregnant, substance-abusing females. The case manager should shepherd and support the client to address issues involving her substance abuse, psychosocial and parenting skills, and survival needs (Mitchell et al., 1993).

Hence, the case manager has several key functions, which include the following:

1. A review and assessment
   a. Covering physical and mental health history
   b. Covering psychosocial status, including family history, parenting skills and knowledge, and potential parenting problems (e.g., a history of sexual abuse)
   c. Alcohol and other drug use, treatment, and recovery status
   d. Support system available to and used by the family, including sources of primary and emergency care
   e. Nutritional status of the mother and fetus
   f. Status of any unresolved legal issues, including outstanding warrants, domestic violence, child custody, adoption, foster care, and divorce

    g. Environmental circumstances, including financial status and needs, condition of housing, and availability of transportation

    h. Educational and vocational competencies

    i. Involvement with other social service agencies

2. An individual case plan developed with input from the client and other service providers. At a minimum, the case plan should include the areas enumerated above. Depending upon the client, it may include plans for the baby once born.

3. Discussion of the plan with the client and other involved participants. When all have agreed, the case manager should begin scheduling the services or putting aspects of the plan in motion.

4. Referral to other agencies, groups, or institutions as needed by the client.

5. Monitoring of the client's progress in the programs. If appointments are missed, the case manager should find out why and try to correct whatever problems have cropped up.

6. Ongoing case management support at regularly scheduled periods until an agreed termination. Success should be determined on an individual basis, allowing the client to become adjusted to being drug free, to achieve self-sufficiency, and to feel comfortable with parenting skills.

7. A review of the client's individual care plan with revisions as appropriate during the recovery process.

These case management activities should be provided in conjunction with a comprehensive service delivery program, postpartum. These comprehensive services constitute five areas with thirty-four described activities. The list below indicates the five areas with a limited number of activities for each area to give a flavor of what the services are.

1. Health care services
   a. Comprehensive, high-risk obstetrical care
   b. Family planning
   c. Counseling for postpartum depression and guilt over drug use effect on fetus
2. Alcohol and other drug treatment success
   a. Ongoing alcohol and other treatment that is gender, ethnically, and culturally sensitive
   b. Connection to community groups, such as AA or NA
3. Survival-related services
   a. Legal services if needed for domestic violence, child custody, or adoption
   b. Procurement of safe housing
4. Psychosocial services
   a. Personal care, issues of sexuality, and image enhancement
   b. Stress management; assertiveness; issues of sexism, racism, and class bias
5. Parenting and family services
   a. Counseling for reunification
   b. Education about nutritional needs
   c. Education about child growth and development
   d. Education about nonabusive discipline

SPECIFIC PROGRAMS FOR JUVENILE FEMALES

INTERVENTION PROGRAMS RESEARCHED

Adolescent Mothers Who Use Drugs

Considerable attention has been given to and several treatment programs have been developed for females who use drugs while pregnant. Most of these programs involve adult mothers. Little has been said about adolescent mothers with drug problems. Field and colleagues (1998) sought to replicate a successful school-based program for nonsubstance-using adolescent mothers with a group of substance-using adolescent mothers in Miami, Florida. In this program for nonsubstance-using adolescent mothers, which Field was involved in, the intervention consisted of parent training, job training, and minimum-wage jobs for the teenage mothers. Primarily the employment involved the mothers being teacher aide trainees in a nursery used by a medical school faculty and staff. The on-the-job training lasted for six months and was provided during the hours when the mothers were not in school. The adolescent mothers received training in infant stimulation tasks and exposure to proper parenting and child-care techniques. The nursery provided caregiving for the adolescent mothers' children and other children. When the mothers' infants were one year old, they had had increased weight, interactions, and motor skills. For the adolescent mothers, the benefits of the intervention were an increased rate of employment or return to school and their pregnancy rate was lower. Because of the program's success, Field and associates (1998) wanted to know if a similar program for adolescent mothers who were poly-drug users could be effective too.

The research sample consisted of 126 young mothers who were assigned to three groups—nondrug, drug control, and drug intervention. These groups were based on urine screens of both the mothers and their infants. Racially, 64% were African American, 27% were Hispanic, and 10% were non-Hispanic white. A number of outcome measures were used, and measurement occurred at three, six, and twelve months. The mothers were instructed to pretend that they were at home and playing with their babies. These were videotaped at three and six months and subsequently assessed. At twelve months, the Early Social Communication Scales, Bayley Scales of Infant Development, and physical measurements were taken.

The intervention program lasted for four months and included of a number of components. These were drug and social rehabilitation, parenting and vocational classes, and relaxation therapy. The relaxation therapy consisted of aerobics, progressive muscle relaxation, music mood induction, and massage therapy. Specific treatment components were determined after each participant was given evaluations involving drug abuse, psychiatric, social, educational, and vocational assessments from which treatment plans were created. The intervention was provided in the afternoon in the high schools in which the mothers attended. In the morning, the mothers were in school or in GED classes. Some of the mothers worked in the nursery under the supervision of a teacher.

The drug rehabilitation aspect used an outpatient drug rehabilitation curriculum. It involved group counseling, psychoeducational sessions, urine monitoring, self-help group sessions that consisted of NA and AA facets, and individual and drug counseling. During the group counseling focus was given to drug use denial, problem-solving skills, coping skills, lifestyle changes, and the twelve-step principles. The psychoeducational sessions consisted of presentations on theories of addiction; medical problems arising from drug addiction; family relationships; male and female interactions; interaction skills; communications skills; assertiveness training; empowerment; HIV and AIDS; sex education; contraception information; sexually transmitted diseases; twelve-step programs; spirituality; and securing social, health, and vocational services.

The results of the intervention were mostly positive. Initially, the infants who were exposed to drugs, more than the control group, evinced habituation deficits, orientation deficits, abnormal reflexes, general irritability, and power regulatory capacity. Moreover, they had a lesser amount of quiet sleep, more crying, and heightened stress. At three months, the treatment group began to look more like the control group; and by six months, they were similar on almost every measure. At the twelve-month follow-up, the treatment group infants scored higher than the control group on the Early Social Communication Scale and the Bayley Mental Scale. Also at twelve months, the treated group had more head circumference and fewer pediatric problems than the control group. The mothers had lower drug use, repeat pregnancy, more educational achievements, and job placement (Field et al., 1998).

Treatment of Sexually Abused Girls

Employing a multiple baseline design, Farrell, Hains, and Davies (1998) report the effectiveness of cognitive–behavioral interventions with three sexually abused girls who showed signs of posttraumatic syndrome disorder (PTSD). Farrell and associates did not clearly define the characteristics of PTSD. According to the *Diagnostic and Statistical Manual* (4th ed.) (DSM-IV), PTSD is characterized by symptoms that occur after a traumatic event. For girls, the traumatic event may be reflected in repetitive play, frightening dreams without recognizable content, and reenactment of trauma-specific events. The person may have trouble falling or staying asleep, irritability or outbursts of anger, difficulty concentrating, hypervigilance, or exaggerated startle responses. These behaviors may occur shortly after the traumatic events or years later (American Psychiatric Association, 1994).

The intervention consisted of the conceptualization phase, skill acquisition and rehearsal phase, and application phase. The conceptualization phase consisted of two sessions. The first session consisted of rapport building, discussing therapy goals, and imparting the framework for cognitive–behavioral therapy. Both functional and unpleasant situations were identified and their accompanying thoughts and feelings. This was done by homework assignments, which were rewarded with stickers. In the second session, the girl was required to identify feelings. Drawings were used to depict how the girl felt during stressful situations and how the girl saw stressful situations. Role-playing was utilized for feelings and affective indicators (Farrell et al., 1998).

The skill acquisition and rehearsal phase involved learning how a girl responded to affect-provoking situations. The girl was given audio tapes that described relaxation training, deep-breathing exercises, progressive muscle relaxation, and relaxing imagery scenes. The girl was taught how to recognize negative self-talk and change them to positive thoughts. Cartoons were used with thought bubbles to represent different affect-provoking situations and the girl filled in the thought bubbles. Homework was given in which a girl cut out pictures, pasted them on paper, and completed thought bubbles. Cognitive restructuring was utilized to deal with maladaptive thoughts (Farrell et al., 1998).

The application phase consisted of practicing responses to future stressful events. Emphasized were relaxation skills, contemplation of the thoughts associated with the anticipated event, and role-playing of positive responses. Homework was assigned regarding how to respond to unpleasant future events and to log responses. Other future anxiety-provoking events were brainstormed and how to respond to them. Previously learned skills were reviewed and applied to these future situations. Last, the girls' feelings and thoughts surrounding termination were addressed (Farrell et al., 1998).

As stated, the researchers used a multiple baseline design, with outcome measures involving PTSD, affect, and an anxiety scale. Measures were taken at baseline, intervention, and follow-up phases. Decreases were found in all areas (Farrell et al., 1998). Because the baseline was longer for different girls and the decreases did not start until the intervention began, the multiple baseline design provided strong evidence of the effectiveness of cognitive behavioral intervention for girls who had been sexually abused (Farrell et al., 1998).

Treatment for Delinquent Females

A private not-for-profit facility in Duluth, Minnesota, operates a treatment program for delinquent girls. Called the Laker group, this program involves an open-ended group of twelve girls utilizing principles from Erik Erikson's development model and Positive Peer Culture. According to Erickson, adolescence is a time for youths to develop a healthy identity. Youths must harmonize the physical changes that their bodies are undergoing and the emotional, intellectual, spiritual, and social changes that are occurring as they undergo these changes. However, gender differences exist, and females find that their sense of self is determined by their relationships with others. As a result, girls have a crisis of intimacy, which they must resolve as they establish their identities. Because of societal pressures and entices of contemporary society, such as insufficient role models, weakened communities, promiscuous sex, and freely available drugs, the task of developing a healthy identity and a connection with others is arduous. Yet, girls, because of how they are socialized and because of the unique developmental needs, are exceptional candidates for Positive Peer Culture.

Positive Peer Culture "uses the power of a positive peer group to establish connections and rekindle a positive sense of self that may have been lost in young women as a result of trauma, antisocial behavior, or association with a negative peer group" (Quigley & Steiner, 1996, p. 103). A positive peer culture emphasizes that group members are responsible for themselves as well as others. Moreover, they are taught that they are the catalyst for helping others and advancing the group. It uses girls' inherent desire to help others and to be a part of others' lives.

A positive peer culture must initially be created by the staff. The staff must be positive role models who show genuine concern for the girls in their care. Staff is responsible for helping to create a safe environment in which girls are free to express themselves and risk their vulnerable states. Once established, issues and problems can be discussed and addressed. These may involve conflicts in their families, schools, and the communities. Utilization of "everyday problems are vehicles for teaching youth about errors in their thinking process so they can replace their hurting behaviors with pro-social ones" (p. 104). Moreover, a positive peer culture requires that girls look at the broader community, such as demonstrating their care about the facility, the environment surrounding the facility, and nearby residential communities. This means the Laker group was involved in community service projects, such as assisting the elderly and developmentally disabled persons in a nearby town.

Researching the impact of the program, Quigley and Steiner (1996) reported outcomes for the Laker group. While not saying so, they used a discrepancy model of evaluation. A discrepancy model of evaluation involves using the literature to ascertain the range of recidivism or successful treatment for a group. Then, the researchers compared their findings or outcomes to this range. Accordingly, Quigley and Steiner aver that residential programs for adolescents in Minnesota have a success rate of 69% and the Laker group had a success rate of 93% from 1991 to 1995. They also compared the girls' behavior prior to entering the facility and during treatment. According to them, 57% of the girls had presenting problems for running away, but during treatment, only 6% ran away. Also, 37% of the girls had presenting problems of physical aggression, but during treatment only 15% were physically aggressive (Quigley & Steiner, 1996).

Examining another program for incarcerated delinquent females, criminal justice professionals noticed that incarcerated delinquent girls gave regular social reinforcement for other girls who broke institution rules and voiced antisocial ideas. In addition, these girls punished other girls who engaged in institutionally and socially appropriate behaviors. Other observations were that staff was ineffective in producing appropriate behaviors because they punished behaviors capriciously and arbitrarily. As a consequence, these professionals concluded that correctional institutions tend to be environments where negative behaviors are learned rather than environments where socially appropriate behaviors are taught.

To change such a negative environment, a group of professionals decided to target girls' peer groups in an attempt to modify a correctional environment in a girls' institution. Specifically, they were interested in testing whether self-recording with token reinforcement would change delinquent girls' peer interaction. They also wanted to increase the girls' prosocial comments and the girls' positive attention to prosocial comments. This program and study were implemented at the Nyandi Treatment and Research Centre for Adolescents in Perth, Western Australia. This institution maintained three units within its grounds. One was a short-stay maximum-security unit, a second was an opened cottage unit, and the third was a community-based unit. The program was implemented within the maximum-security unit and consisted of Caucasian girls, Australian Aborigine girls, and one Asian girl. Twelve girls were participants in this study and they averaged five offenses and all had been in the institution before.

A multiple baseline design was used. The three dependent variables were the percentage of prosocial comments, antisocial comments, and positive attention within a ten-second time sampling period. The intervention program was implemented in four phases. First, baseline data were gathered for ten days. Second, the girls were given training in the program and their comments solicited. The girls were told that the researcher was there to teach them how to relate to other girls and the staff, and later in the community. They were told that prosocial comments and positive attention were important in helping to get along better with others. The girls participated in defining these two behaviors, which were renamed *helpful plans* and *caring comments*. A free discussion occurred in which a staff member operated a cueing light. Whenever a girl made a helpful plan or caring comment, the staff member operated the cueing light. Each girl's desk had a cueing light and the girl was asked to operate the light herself when she made a helpful plan or caring comment. A staff member recorded on a blackboard each girl's name and specific points for correct recognition. The exercise became a game for the girls. This was meant to give the girls feedback with no actual reinforcers being provided. During the second session, a similar game was played. Points were assigned to each girl for appropriate comments and recognition of appropriate comments. In this manner, this provided a transition from passive recognition to active performance. In the second phase, self-recording was introduced. They practiced self-recording by listening to a tape and recording their recognition of helpful plans and caring comments on that tape. Next, they used the cards to record their own thoughts. Finally, the girls were told to record behavior in the same way in their living area within the institution. They were told that they would be given tokens for their records. The tokens were used to buy privileges, such as earning swimming privileges, television time, and items from the commissary. The third phase consisted of self-recording in interaction with the staff instead of peers. The fourth and final phase consisted of fading, which meant the number of tokens that were given were reduced.

The multiple baseline design showed significant increases in prosocial comments and attention to prosocial comments. Also, the numerical data and analyses showed that there was a decrease in antisocial comments and attention. Sanson-Fisher and associates (1978) concluded that the research demonstrated that an intervention program could change delinquent girls' interaction so as to be consistent with rehabilitation objectives. Other effects of the intervention were that arguments between girls were decreased, use of profanity decreased, and when it did occur, the girls reprimanded the offender's use of inappropriate language.

INTERVENTION PROGRAMS NOT RESEARCHED

Treating Adolescents Who Have Been Sexually Abused

A pilot treatment program was developed for girls who had been sexually abused based on Finklehor and Browne's Model. It was called the Stuart House and was part of the Rape Treatment Center at Santa Monica Hospital Medical Center. According to Finklehor and Browne, sexually abused girls suffer from traumatic sexualization, betrayal, powerlessness, and stigmatization. Stuart House sought to ameliorate these traumagenic dynamics through group counseling.

Referrals came from counselors within the Rape Treatment Center who concluded that their clients were ready to address their sexual abuse within a group setting. The girls were then prescreened and told about the group composition, structure, rules regarding confidentiality, and goals. The group met for ninety minutes weekly for seven months. The group process consisted of several modules, consisting of (1) the promotion of group cohesiveness, (2) discussion of sexual abuse experiences, (3) new coping strategies, (4) sexuality, (5) prevention of future victimization, and (6) termination.

Before the girls could discuss fully and freely their sexual victimization, they needed a safe environment. To this end, the development of group cohesiveness was necessary. A number of techniques were used to create this group dynamic. For instance, the first group meeting consisted of a game in which members could interview each other for a mock newspaper, *Stuart House News*. This gave the therapist an opportunity to emphasize similarities among the girls. Warm-up exercises were conducted in which members wrote their names using different body parts (e.g., with their noses, elbows, big toes, and index fingers). The purpose of this exercise was to incur humor in the group and to sensitize the girls to nonverbal communication.

Promotion of abuse experiences was done with a game called the "Hat Game." Questions regarding sexual abuse experiences were written by the therapist and put in a hat. Some of the questions were, "Do you think your body has changed since you were molested? How has it changed?" "What would you say to someone who has been molested?" "Who knows that you were molested and how did they act when they found out?" Each member would get chance to answer a question. The girls enjoyed the Hat Game so much that they eagerly asked to play it. It was modified and the girls wrote questions. Their questions were, "Have you felt like killing yourself?" "Did you like how he molested you?" "Do you think it was your fault that you were molested?" "Have you ever felt real crazy?" (Zaidi & Gutierrez-Kovner, 1995, p. 219). This game and questions proved to be less threatening than direct questions. In addition, the girls used Ken and Barbie dolls to discuss their abuse and to role-play the abuse. These experiences, especially the Hat Game, were designed to address distorted images that the girls might have had regarding their bodies and to help them overcome feelings of powerlessness by role-playing their abuses.

Discussion and games regarding sexuality were designed to address sexualized behaviors associated with being female. For instance, the girls were given a large piece of paper that was divided in half. One side was for the girls to indicate what it means to be a female and what it means to be a male. They were given newspapers and magazines. The girls were instructed to cut out words and pictures and paste them on each side of the paper to indicate females and males. For female roles, the girls cut out images involving lingerie, makeup, and jewelry. This exercise provided an opportunity to discuss sex roles.

Finally, the girls discussed coping strategies and how to prevent future victimization. For coping strategies, they learned how to relax, engaged in deep-breathing exercises, and stress reduction. They engaged in games to discuss how they would prevent future victimization. This was entitled "What would you do if …?" The topics included inappropriate sexual overtures, physical abuse, decisions regarding birth control, drug use, and gang involvement. Termination was planned in conjunction with the girls and the therapist presented group members with a gift to symbolize the group experiences. In this group, it was a stuffed bear to symbolize "the Teddy Bear Group" (Zaidi & Gutierrez-Kovner, 1995).

Intervention with Females with
General Delinquency Problems

One criminal justice professional depicts three programs for female delinquents that was called model programs for female delinquents (Maniglia, 1996). These programs were called models because they included three components considered vital for working with delinquent girls. The first component is that school programs must address issues of gender bias. The second aspect is that residential programs must address the inadequate medical services for girls. The third aspect is that programs that provide sex education must present more than biological explanation and delve into why girls have sex and get pregnant. The fourth aspect is that programs must address the high rate of girls referred to the juvenile justice system that have been sexually abused.

The first program is called the Practical and Cultural Education (PACE) Center for girls in Jacksonville, Florida. This program was created as an alternative to placing girls in detention centers. Because of its purported success, it has spread to other Florida cities. Its purpose is to provide day-treatment services that are gender sensitive for delinquent females. The program is voluntary, serving girls from the ages of twelve to eighteen, and the average stay is six to eight months. All the PACE programs provide a core academic curriculum that is accredited as a dropout prevention program. The girls can earn their high school diploma or earn credits that qualify for a General Equivalency Diploma (GED). These classes are small with emphasis on experiential learning and teacher interaction. In addition, courses in life skills, vocational training, and health are provided. The girls participate in community service projects. A social worker meets with the families monthly and makes referrals for services as necessary. At termination, girls are expected to complete their individual treatment plans that have goals such as achieving a 92% attendance rate, completing two gender-specific classes such as self-defense or sex education, and achieving one or two grade levels. Assistance is provided in securing employment or returning to school. PACE provides a three-year follow-up to provide continuing support.

The second program described by Maniglia is a program in Chicago, Illinois, for girls with chemical dependency problems who have had extensive involvement with the juvenile justice system. The program was called "City Girls" and implemented by a program called Intervention. City Girls operates under the assumption that chemical dependency among delinquent girls masks other issues in these girls' lives. These issues include being a school dropout or performing less than adequately in school. Typically, they present a history of sexual abuse and lack of adequate parenting. Some girls have been forced out of the home due to their chemical dependency or pregnancies. The girls suffer from depression, low self-esteem, suicidal ideation, and feelings of worthlessness. To address these issues, City Girls provide girls-only self-help and support groups. A "culture of recovery" is created in which girls learn that they have choices in their lives. City Girls offer vocational and educational training as well as sex education, AIDS awareness, nutrition, and exercise instruction. Family counseling and opportunities are provided to learn functional coping skills in an extensive therapeutic recreational program.

The third program was developed within the Maryland Department of Juvenile Services. A task force on female offenders studied the circumstances of juvenile female offenders and their needs. Like other assessments of females, the study revealed that most incarcerated female offenders come from single-parent homes, were more likely to be African American, and were between the ages of fifteen and seventeen. Many were teen parents, had health issues, and a history of abuse. Typically, they had been incarcerated for assault or property offenses. To address these characteristics, the Maryland Department of Juvenile Services created the Female Intervention Team (FIT) probation unit, with the goal to prevent the incarceration of girls and work with them in the community. The probation officers volunteered to have only girls on their caseload. The probation officers received specialized training in handling issues that female juvenile offenders have, such as sexual abuse, teen parenting, drug and alcohol abuse, and low self-esteem. In addition, Maryland's only secure institution, Cheltenham Young Women Facility, was totally redesigned based on adolescent female development.

For institutionalized delinquents in the state of Washington, a cognitive–behavioral program was developed by correctional officials. Developed for females and males within the institution, the problem-solving program was called WISER, which is an acronym for wait, identify, solution, evaluate, and reinforce (DeLange, Barton, & Lanham, 1981). DeLange, Barton, and Lanham (1981) describe reports from some of the female delinquents and how they felt the WISER program had helped them. For this reason, WISER is discussed in this chapter.

Responding to the criticisms that some social skills programs lacked assessment tools and problem situations tailored to a juvenile population, WISER created situations specific to the population within its institution. For instance, some juveniles have a problem being told no, but no problem with phasing a proper request. For other juveniles, the problem may be reversed or may involve other problems. For this reason, specific situations were created through the following process. First, sixty female and male delinquents were in groups to generate problematic situations. One hundred seventy-five situations were created from this initial process. Second, these 175 situations were refined and grouped into ten categories. Program administrators then took the six most frequent categories. Third, their six categories were used to prepare program materials and videotaped situations. The videotapes consisted of peer models who were taught specific skills and who role-played specific situations. Some of the situations were specific to female delinquents and the others were more general.

The treatment was delivered in the following manner. Small groups of delinquents were created. The group met during school time for seven one-hour sessions. Each session was divided into twenty-minute segments in which three situations representing one problem were presented. So, three different problems would be presented during the hour. The videotape depicted the peer models demonstrating an aggressive, unassertive, and effective response to a problem. The groups were led by graduate social work students who had received training in group dynamics and cognitive–behavioral techniques. In addition, the group leaders were given a therapist manual that outlined how the sessions should be conducted, what introduction remarks should be given, coaching comments, and a transcript of the videotaped sessions.

The procedures for each session followed these steps.

1. The group was shown a videotape of a specific problem and the inappropriate stimulus line.
2. The group leader would ask what members were thinking in a similar situation. The group leader would also ask what would you do or say, emphasizing the connection between thoughts and subsequent behaviors.
3. The group was given an opportunity to apply the WISER techniques and practice each step in the problem-solving model.
4. The group leader coached members on the tasks to be completed.
5. A repeat viewing of the peer models using the WISER method was conducted. As it was shown, the group leader pointed out pertinent and critical points in the video, such as the juvenile's overt response and covert self-reinforcement.
6. The group discussed the peer model use of WISER and group members' reactions to it.
7. The group leader engaged in recoaching, with the group leader pointing out what made the peer model's response effective while acknowledging that other responses may be equally effective.
8. The group was given time to practice WISER and self-verbalization.
9. The group engaged in behavior rehearsal with members role-playing a stimulus line and a response.
10. Group members were given opportunity for positive self-statements for assertive responses.
11. Group members were given opportunities for self-evaluation.
12. Group members evaluated other responses, suggesting more appropriate responses.
13. If the group leaders saw a need, repetition of steps eight through twelve were provided.
14. If the group leaders saw a need, repetition of steps eight through thirteen with a second group member was provided.

Throughout the process, the group leaders emphasized the dynamics of verbal and nonverbal aspects of effective communication, such as eye contact, body language, and voice tone. While no empirical evaluation was reported on the program, the authors repeated that one young woman reported that the intervention was valuable for her. She stated that a staff member asked her to mop the floor. Before WISER, she would have responded aggressively to the staff member's request, but did not after receiving training in WISER (DeLange et al., 1982).

SUMMARY

This chapter began with statistics showing differences between females and males. It showed the progression of a girl's sexual victimization to that of an abuser. Socialization issues were discussed regarding white, African American, and Hispanic girls. Then, it discussed techniques and procedures for treating girls who have been sexually victimized, who have running away problems, who have alcohol and drug problems, and who have sex-related drug and alcohol problems. Then, specific researched programs were discussed for adolescent mothers who use drugs, treatment for girls who have been sexually abused, and treatment for incarcerated delinquent girls. Unresearched programs involving sexual abuse and delinquent girls were then described.

KEY TERMS

Familism

Simpatia

Personalismo

Marianism

Respeto

Traumatic sexualization

First-degree runaways

Second-degree runaways

Third-degree runaways

Admitting

Submitting

Transmitting

Awareness wheel

Culture of recovery

Positive peer culture

WISER

8

Treating Male Juvenile Offenders

⠶ INTRODUCTION

Among adolescents, male juveniles alarm society the most ("A Nation Stunned," 1998; Loeber & Hay, 1997). Because of their offending, most theories that have been developed to explain juvenile delinquency, and concomitant intervention strategies, focused on males (Siegel & Senna, 1997; Smith, 1998). This concern and alarm that society has regarding juvenile offenders has intensified because some juveniles have committed heinous crimes, incurring the wrath of legislatures (Lesher, 1998). Exacerbating these cases, sometimes, is the race of offenders. Particularly, African American and Latino males tend to concern society the most ("Psychiatric Tests on Minority Kids," 1998), and many of them are handled by the adult criminal justice system (National Prison Project, 1990). This chapter describes the context of treating male juvenile offenders, techniques and procedures of treating male juvenile offenders, and researched and unreasearched intervention programs for male juveniles.

THE CONTEXT OF TREATING
MALE JUVENILE OFFENDERS

The criminal behaviors of male juveniles that cause the most concerns are violent offenses (Tate, Reppucci, & Mulvey, 1995) and drug offenses (Fagan, 1992). This means juveniles who have been involved in murder (Cornell, Benedek & Benedek, 1987), aggravated assaults (Goldstein & Glick, 1996), sexual assaults (Breer, 1996; Ferrara & McDonald, 1996; Marshall & Eccles, 1993), and drug possession and use (Fagan, 1992; Peterson & Harrell, 1992). Many of these serious juvenile offenders have diagnoses of conduct disorders (Adam & Livington, 1995; France & Hudson, 1993; Kazdin, 1995; Metzner & Ryan, 1995), making treatment more difficult. Juveniles who are involved in lesser criminal offenses also are of some concern, such as juveniles who run away from home, steal, or engage in prostitution (Sholevar & Sholevar, 1995).

In terms of the most serious offenses that a juvenile can commit, most of them are handled by the adult criminal justice system. A juvenile who kills someone while in the commission of a felony, such as robbery, burglary, and sexual assault, is likely to be transferred to adult court for trial. Punishment, not treatment or rehabilitation, is the primary objective, and these juveniles may be sentenced to life without parole or a lengthy time of imprisonment before parole is considered. (See Case Illustration below.)

The case study referred to above involves a young African American male. Because of their overrepresentation among the serious categories, African American juveniles have been the focus of considerable study, commentary, and intervention (Gorman-Smith, Tolan, Zelli, & Huesmann, 1996; Welsh, Harris, & Jenkins, 1996). Reddington and Sapp (1997), having surveyed several adult correctional institutions that incarcerated juveniles, report that correctional officials indicate that these juveniles should receive family counseling, career training, prison survival, and other programming. Some counseling professionals feel that African American juveniles present special needs (Hudley & Graham, 1993) and require unique services from the justice system. For instance, some professionals contend that African American juveniles would benefit more from treatment and intervention that is based on an Afrocentric framework (Harvey & Coleman, 1997; King, 1997). However, many of the African American juveniles who are serving lengthy sentences, such as life without parole, may die in prison unless clemency is given. This scenario de-emphasizes rehabilitation.

But some juveniles who kill as the result of a dispute with relatives or a peer may be kept in the juvenile justice system. Treatment professionals contend that this latter group is more amenable to treatment and the chances of successfully rehabilitating them is greater (Cornell, Benedek, & Benedek, 1987).

Surveying 755 juvenile and sex offender treatment programs, Knopp, Freeman-Longo, and Stevenson (1992) state that the most frequently used treatment models for adolescent sex offenders are the Behavioral–Cognitive Model (41%), Psycho-Socio-Educational Model (25%), the Relapse Prevention Model (16%), the Psychotherapeutic Model (11%), the Family Systems Model (2%), the Addiction Model (2%), the Behavioral Model (1%), and other Models (2%). While the name of the treatment models differ, often these models utilize the same treatment modalities. For instance, 97% of all treatment programs use techniques to increase victim

Nathan Riley, an African American male, was born on June 17, 1978, in Philadelphia, Pennsylvania. His parents separated when he was six years old and he had infrequent contact with his father. During this period, there was considerable conflict between the mother and father. When Nathan was about ten years old, he was taken from his mother and placed in foster care because of physical abuse by his mother's boyfriend. He was in an emergency home at the Northern Home for Boys for a year. Nathan had to stay in placement because his mother and siblings had moved into a shelter and his biological father was on drugs and unable to care for him. While in placement, Nathan was referred for psychiatric evaluation due to a series of problems with staff and other boys. He was diagnosed as having a conduct disorder.

Nathan was able to return to the Philadelphia area and began to get into trouble in the neighborhood. When he was fifteen years old, Nathan, along with three others, entered a jewelry store to rob it. Armed with a pistol, Nathan shot the owner in the neck, which caused him to die. At trial, Nathan's defense was that he was coerced to commit the crime by an older man in the neighborhood who was a major crack dealer. Besides selling drugs for this individual, Nathan was gambling with him. When his debts were considerable, he was ordered to commit the robbery, panicked, and shot the jewelry-store owner. Rejecting his defense of duress, the jury convicted Nathan and he is serving a life sentence without parole in a maximum-security prison for adults.

CASE 8.1 Case Illustration

empathy, 91% of all treatment programs use techniques to address anger or aggression management, and 91% use sex education techniques. Other techniques are communication, cognitive distortions, assertiveness training, relapse prevention plans, personal victimization or trauma, relapse cycle, and conflict resolution.

Juveniles who use drugs and alcohol manifest a serious threat to their well-being and the well-being of their families. Their use of these substances also is a precursor to involvement in more serious crimes. Traditional treatment programs for juveniles have been based on a willingness of the juvenile and the family to want treatment. Juveniles who have serious behavioral and emotional problems, combined with substance abuse issues, need treatment that is configured differently than what has traditionally existed for voluntary youths and their families. In addition, juveniles require a different core treatment service than adults, which must focus on age-appropriate skill development. Many treatment professionals who have been involved with juveniles connected to the juvenile justice system contend that treatment has not been highly effective because the model of treatment has been inadequate (McPhail & Wiest, 1995).

For this reason, professionals, consisting of researchers, program managers, and treatment professionals, have developed treatment improvement protocols (TIP) for juveniles with substance abuse problems and who are involved in the juvenile justice system. The development of TIP involved a three-staged process consisting of various professionals for each stage. The aim was to obtain a consensus for a state-of-the-art treatment strategy. The final TIP "spells out a strategy for diverting youth with substance abuse problems from further penetration into the juvenile justice system. Members of the consensus panel have defined a process for communities to use in building new linkages and partnerships among treatment programs, community health and social services, and the juvenile court to plan juvenile AOD" (i.e., alcohol and other drugs) interventions (McPhail & Wiest, 1995, p. v).

TECHNIQUES AND PROCEDURES OF TREATING MALE JUVENILE OFFENDERS

Treating Juveniles Who Commit Homicides

Applicable to juveniles who kill following a dispute or family conflict, several treatment issues need to be considered in treating juvenile murderers. First, a treating professional needs to determine what is the best setting for treatment and whether there are any options for each forensic disposition. Second, the treating professional needs to know the safest and most effective treatment that would decrease the juvenile's violent impulses. Third, the treating professional needs to know which systems may need to be brought into the process, such as the family. Fourth, the treating professional needs to know appropriate interventions for co-morbid conditions and whether these interventions can be applied in the setting in which the juvenile resides (Adam & Livington, 1995).

Juvenile murderers do not constitute a homogeneous group. Cornell and associates (1987) propose a typology for classifying juvenile murderers. As stated, juvenile murderers fall into three categories—psychotic, conflict, and crime. (See Figure 8.1.) Juveniles in the psychotic category have killed because of obvious, major psychiatric problems. Juveniles in the conflict category have killed because of conflict with another person. This may include disputes with gangs, associates, or parents. Juveniles in the crime category include juveniles who have killed as a result of a another felony, such as burglary, armed robbery, or sexual assault. Cornell and colleagues (1987) state that the group that is most amenable to treatment is juveniles who have killed as a result of conflict.

Because juvenile murderers are different, individualized treatment is appropriate. Some clinicians recommend hospitalization. The goals for treating in this setting are the redirection of homicidal impulses, strengthening ego functioning, and decreasing conflict between the juvenile and the family. Specific treatment modalities include individual, group, and family therapy. As a matter of course, and especially

> Psychotic murderers
> Conflict murderers
> Crime (felony) murderers

FIGURE 8.1 Types of Juvenile Murderers

if hospitalization is long termed, a juvenile should receive schooling. Moreover, medication may be appropriate to help control a juvenile's aggression. When hospitalization is not an option, long-termed residential treatment is preferable. This type of setting is needed in order to shield the juvenile from society's loathe, assist the juvenile in understanding the seriousness of the behavior, and teach new coping skills for stress and anger. Finally, treating professionals believe that juvenile murders, though they constitute only a small percentage of all murders, can be reduced. Particularly, juveniles who have conduct disorders and who have demonstrated an insensitivity to the rights of others are at risk for homicidal behavior. Also, juveniles who aggress against others as a problem-solving technique are at risk and their behavior may escalate to murder. Hence, it behooves professionals to address aggressive behaviors by juveniles before these behaviors escalate to homicides.

Treating Aggressive Juveniles

Delinquent juveniles are very skilled in fighting, bullying, intimidating, and manipulating other individuals. They engage in these types of socially disapproving behaviors because they are unskilled in more socially approved behaviors, such as negotiation, compromising, and responding appropriately to accusations. In addition, these juveniles do not know how to respond appropriately to failure, teasing, rejection, and anger. The cognitive processes that are targets for change are perceptions, self-statements, attributions, expectations, strategies, and problem-solving skills (Kazdin, 1985). To address these adolescent deficits, Goldstein and Glick have developed a treatment program that they called Aggression Replacement Training (ART). ART was developed for professionals who worked with aggressive children, such as teachers, counselors, social workers, and child-care workers.

ART consists of three components—skillstreaming, anger control, and moral education—that are each taught weekly. Skillstreaming involves the teaching of fifty skills characteristic of prosocial behaviors to highly aggressive juveniles. The fifty skills spring from six areas. These are (1) elementary social skills, such as how to initiate a conversation, introduce yourself, and give a compliment; (2) advanced social skills, such as asking for help, apologizing, and giving instructions; (3) skills needed to address emotions, such as how to respond to someone's anger, display affection, and respond to fear; (4) skills for demonstrating alternatives to aggression, consisting of negotiation, helping others, and responding nonaggressively to teasing; (5) skills for handling stress, such as how to react at being left out of a situation, responding to an accusation, and planning for stressful conversation; and (6) planning skills, such as how to set goals, set priorities, and use decision-making steps.

These skills are taught in group counseling. Ideally, the group should contain about six to eight juveniles. The group leader conveys these skills through modeling, role-playing, performance feedback, and transfer training. The group leader shows the juveniles how to give a compliment, how to introduce oneself, and how to respond to a verbal attack. The group leader also gives the juveniles opportunities to practice these skills and give appropriate feedback on how the juveniles are doing. Finally, the group leader gives the juveniles suggestions for how to take the group activities into the juveniles' communities (Goldstein & Glick, 1996).

Anger-control techniques were developed by other professionals, and Goldstein and Glick included them as a part of ART. The anger-control training component

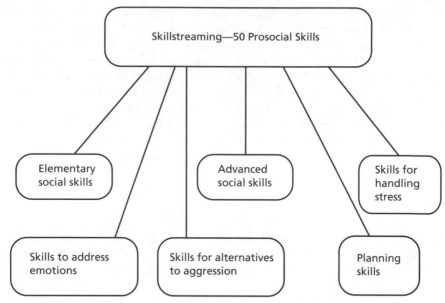

FIGURE 8.2 Aggression Replacement Training

consists of requiring a juvenile to log anger-evoking experiences (e.g., situations in which the juvenile felt hassled) and bring these recorded experiences to the group. For ten weeks, the juveniles are counseled to respond to these anger-provoking incidents by engaging in the following steps. First, they should identify the triggers, which could be external or internal. Second, they should identify the physical cues that indicate their rising anger. Third, they are urged to use reminders or self-statements to restrain themselves, such as "stay calm," "chill out," or "calm down." Fourth, they are counseled to use reducers, such as deep breathing, counting backward, imaging a calm and peaceful situation, or considering the long-term consequences of a violent response. Fifth, they are counseled to use self-evaluation by processing how they proceeded through each of the first four steps and praising themselves for appropriate responses.

Moral education involves teaching juveniles through techniques and procedures so that they will have an increased sense of justice, fairness, and concern for others' rights. According to Goldstein and Glick, previous professionals who have worked in the area of moral development have reported that exercises in which juveniles were given a situation involving a moral dilemma and working through it can increase juveniles' sense of moral reasoning. However, Goldstein and Glick doubt that moral education in and of itself can decrease aggressive behavior. They see the utility in adding moral education to ART due to aggressive juveniles' lack of prosocial skills. Moral education gives juveniles a reason or provides a compass for prosocial behavior. Combining skills with moral reasoning is more likely to decrease juveniles' aggressive behaviors.

Structuring the treatment of aggressive juveniles a little differently, Varley (1984) states that treatment for aggressive behavior involves the planned use of techniques for accelerating and decelerating behaviors and elevating interactive skills. Techniques to accelerate prosocial behaviors rest on the application of positive and negative reinforcement. Techniques to decelerate antisocial behavior rest on the application of punishments. One punishment is based on aversive stimulation and the removal of positive stimulation. The other type of punishment is based upon extinction. These techniques, which have been discussed in Chapter 3, are the principal tools in treating individual aggression and managing group aggression.

Treating Juvenile Sex Offenders

A significant difficulty in treating juvenile sex offender is determining what sexual behaviors are normal, unsettling, and problematic. To this end, O'Callaghan and Print (1994) offer a typology for male juvenile sex offenders. Before describing their topology, O'Callaghan and Print state that two core concepts form the basis for their typology. The first is consent. It requires that any interpersonal sexual behavior that does not involve consenting individuals is abusive. Consent demands (1) an understanding of a proposal; (2) knowing the standard of that behavior, or put differently knowing the legal requirement; (3) knowledge of the possible consequences of engaging in sex; and (4) knowing that a refusal to engage in sex should be respected. The other core concept is power. Power involves the coercing of one person to engage in sex and thereby denying the free will of the desired participant. Some variables that affect power are age, gender, race and culture, physical size or strength, significant differences in cognitive levels, invested authority, self-image differences, and arbitrary labels. Using the core concepts of consent and power, a typology for defining adolescent sexual behaviors is made possible (O'Callaghan & Print, 1994).

Normal Male Juvenile Sexual Behaviors (No Treatment Required)
Explicit sexual discussion among peers, use of sexual swear words, obscene jokes
Interest in erotic materials and their use in masturbation
Expression through sexual innuendo, flirtations, and courtship behaviors
Mutual consenting noncoital sexual behavior, such as kissing or fondling
Mutual consensual masturbation
Mutual consensual sexual intercourse

Sexual Behaviors that Suggest Monitoring, Limited Responses, or Assessment
Sexual preoccupation or anxiety
Use of hard-core pornography
Indiscriminate sexuality activity/intercourse
Combining sexuality and aggression
Sexual graffiti involving individuals or with a disturbing content
Single incidents of exposure, peeping, frottage, or obscene telephone calls

Behaviors that Suggest Assessment and Intervention
Chronic or public masturbation
Persistent or aggressive attempts to expose others' genitals
Chronic use of pornography with a sadistic or violent theme
Sexually explicit conversations with significantly younger children
Touching another's genitals without permission
Sexually explicit threats

Behaviors that Require a Legal Response, Assessment, and Treatment
   Persistent obscene telephone calls, voyeurism, exhibitionism, or frottage
   Sexual contact with significantly younger children
   Forced sexual assault and rape
   Inflicting genital injury
   Sexual contact with animals

With a topology as a guiding framework, the next step is what issues need to be addressed. According to the National Task Force on Juvenile Sexual Offending (NTFJSO) (1993), the issues that need to be addressed in treating juvenile sex offenders are the acceptance of responsibility for behavior without minimization or externalizing blame; identification of pattern or cycle of abusive behavior; resolution of victimization in the history of the abusive juvenile; development of victim awareness; development of internal sense of mastery and control; understanding the role of sexual arousal in sexually abusive behavior; development of a positive sexual identity; understanding the consequences of offending behavior for self, the victim, and the family; recognition of the triggers for offending behaviors; identification and expression of feelings; and development of prosocial relationship skills (NTFJSO, 1993). Ultimately, the goals of treatment are (1) to stop all sexually abusive behavior, (2) to protect members of society from further sexual victimization, (3) to prevent other aggressive or abusive behavior that the youth may manifest, and (4) to assist the youth in developing more functional relationship skills (NTFJSO, 1993).

Models of Treatment
The Eclectic Model Proposed by the NTFJSO, a series of methods and techniques have been combined to provide an eclectic model for dealing with adolescents who sexually molest. These methods and techniques may not be used in every treatment program or with every adolescent. Many of these techniques are well known among counselors and therapists, but some are not known well outside of corrections. These methods and techniques involve activities to address accountability, cycle, history, victim empathy, arousal and fantasy, power and control, consequences of sexually abusive behavior, family dysfunction, denial and minimization, cognitive distortions, addiction/compulsion, positive prosocial sexuality, sexual identity and gender issues, impulse control, developmental deficits, attachment disorders, and skill deficits and educational deficits.

Accountability Legal accountability begins with the reporting of sexual abuse by an adolescent to the police, prosecution, and adjudication by the courts. It extends from a deposition to a mental health agency, probation, and parole or aftercare. Personal accountability is emphasized regularly during treatment. During treatment, an adolescent is required to waive confidentiality, which entails abandoning secrets and reinforces his need to be accountable for his behavior. In waiving confidentiality, a juvenile is free to self-disclose, self-monitor, and participate fully in his treatment. The juvenile is pressed to be accountable for his behavior and thinking. The juvenile's thinking and behavior are monitored through journals, self-reports, behavioral observations, and reports from staff. Irresponsible behavior is confronted and irrational thinking is reconstructed. Accountability, a continuing theme, is stressed whenever irresponsible thoughts, action, and fantasies manifest themselves. Written and verbal contracts are used to ensure a juvenile's compliance with treatment requirements and activities. Other tools used to assist in accountability are polygraph testing and surveillant procedures or equipment.

Cycle A clinician uses the sexual abuse cycle as a theoretical framework for understanding the connections among situations, thoughts, feelings, and behaviors that precipitate sexual molestations. (See Figure 8.3.) Situations that provide opportunities for abuse are identified as risks. When these risks are identified, the juvenile is provided with information that should alert him of the need to avoid these situations or use a strategy to deal with these situations differently. Thinking errors are eliminated, feelings are labeled correctly, and new and nonexploitive behaviors are taught. Covert sensitization is employed to counter harmful fantasies. The sexual abuse cycle is also used to sensitize a juvenile and help him learn how to disrupt this cycle.

History A juvenile's current level of functioning is revealed through the clinician gathering psychosocial, familial, sexual, and behavioral histories. These histories expose the juvenile's view of the world, behaviors, attitudes, self-image, and degree of empathy for the victim or victims. Particularly, the childhood history may show an elevation of dysfunctional thinking, antisocial behavior, and exploitive behavioral patterns. Also, any trauma that the juvenile has experienced, such as physical or sexual abuse, abandonment, rejection, or loss, may reveal the juvenile's view of

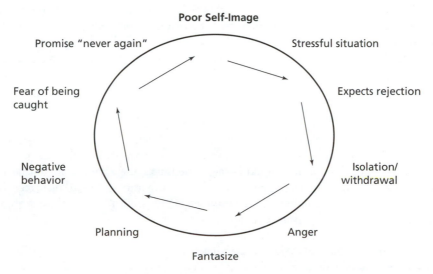

Cognitive distortions occur throughout the cycle.

FIGURE 8.3 Offense Cycle

self and others, values, relationships, and communication style. A family history may disclose dysfunctional child rearing, reversal of parent and child roles, and the degree of denial and minimization habits. If a juvenile is to benefit from treatment, he must be willing to give up his and familial secrets and resolve treatment issues. Only then will he be able to reevaluate his functioning and acquire a degree of normative development.

Victim Empathy Juveniles, like adult offenders, commit crimes for a variety of reasons. One of the factors that permits juveniles to offend sexually is the lack of empathy for victims. Therefore, in counseling, techniques need to be employed to instill empathy for victims. This is done by several techniques. One technique is to refer to victims by names, having the juvenile to play the role of the molested victim, relating the victim's perspective while being aware of the nuances in behavior and thinking that objectifies and exploits others. Juveniles who molest frequently have not had significant others to empathize with them; therefore, the counselor models empathy in working with juveniles. For juveniles who have been sexually molested themselves, they acquire empathy for others generally as they work through their own victimization. However, the counselor should not excuse or permit the juvenile to excuse his behavior by what was done to him.

Arousal and Fantasy Unclear in juvenile sexual offending is the role of arousal and fantasy. This must be explored in order to learn the juvenile's sexual interests. A counselor should not take for granted that the victim is the source of arousal. Juveniles may become aroused after viewing materials or from their fantasies. Irrational and distorted thinking may empower a juvenile to act out a harmless fantasy in an abusive situation or perform a harmless act while engaging in a deviant fantasy. Deviant fantasies may be reinforced during masturbation. All juveniles who have molested should explore the role that fantasy and arousal play in their offending. A number of methods are used to assist in this end. During an interview, the juvenile could be asked about his sexual interests. A plethsmograph may be used to gage the extent of a juvenile's arousal to various stimuli. Also, a card-sort that depicts various situations from nonerotic to erotic could be shown and the juvenile asked to reveal his impressions of these cards.

Power and Control A juvenile's perception regarding a situation that results in him feeling without control and helpless can lead to a sexual assault. According to sexual assault cycle, a juvenile counteracts his feeling of helplessness and a lack of control by taking control of another person. Accordingly, a juvenile's feelings of helplessness and no control should be addressed, and the juvenile should be redirected to control only his behavior. Cognitive restructuring is used to correct the errors in a juvenile's thinking. The juvenile is taught to regain control through rational thinking and respectful behavior.

Consequences of Sexually Abusive Behavior A number of negative consequences for individuals develop as a result of sexual abuse. Among the persons affected are the victims, perpetrators, and families of both. These systems incur difficulty personally, socially, psychologically, economically, and legally. Obviously, the legal system meets out its consequences, but individual consequences for the juvenile can also occur through the development of victim empathy and self-esteem building. Covert sensitization serves the juvenile's need to contemplate the negative consequences of his sexual assault. Hopefully, this processing will serve as a deterrent and prevent a relapse.

Family Dysfunction If family dysfunction exists, leaving it untreated can impede and set back the juvenile's treatment. Thus, it is imperative to identify any family dysfunctional pattern that facilitates, supports, or excuses a juvenile's sexual offending. This is especially needed if the juvenile is residing at home while under some probationary conditions. Parents who maintain households with unclear role boundaries, power imbalances, twisted attachments, inadequate communication, improper sexual boundaries, and denial and minimization must be recognized and addressed. It may be necessary to conduct extensive family therapy rather than individual counseling with the juvenile. This, however, is not to say that all families are dysfunctional because one of its member has sexually offended. Healthy families may have a son who has abused another person. When the family is adequate and functional and has a son who has sexually offended, the family can be of critical importance in the treatment process.

Denial and Minimization To combat a juvenile's or his family's denial and minimization, a counselor frequently uses confrontation. A common misconception about confrontation is that it is delivered in an intense and combative manner. Confrontation should be direct, firm, and responsible while being supportive. It should never be delivered in a condescending, derogatory, or humiliating fashion. It should be used strategically to challenge a juvenile or his family's minimization or denial. For instance, a police and victim report may be used to challenge a juvenile's version of events. Also, daily reports from the juvenile may be used to confront irrational thinking and inappropriate behavior.

Cognitive Distortions A juvenile's illogical and rationalizing thought processes that facilitate sexual victimization are called cognitive distortion or thinking errors. The counselor uses cognitive restructuring to circumvent irrational thinking. Hopefully, the juvenile's irrational thinking will be replaced with rational thinking.

Addiction/Compulsion Appropriate and inappropriate sexual behavior is reinforced by psychological and physiological rewards. Over time, sexual behavior can become strongly reinforced or become addictive. Treatment is geared at abating the addictive and compulsive character of the juvenile's sexually abusive behavior.

Positive/Prosocial Sexuality Juveniles with a pattern of sexually abusive behavior typically have not undergone normal sexual development. Thus, if juveniles are redirected to complete normal sexual development, there is less of a chance of returning to illicit and deviant sexual behavior. The counselor imparts prosocial information regarding sex education and sexual identity issues. Harmful sexual fantasies are explored and redirected through restructuring to buttress positive sexuality.

Sexual Identity and Gender Issues The counselor, acknowledging the diversity of sexuality, approaches gender confusion without bias or prejudice. Any confusion regarding homosexual issues is addressed and homophobia is challenged.

Impulse Control A number of cognitive approaches are used to help a juvenile develop internal control. Support for a juvenile acquiring internal control comes from the monitoring of thought, learning problem-solving skills, stress management, and taking responsibility for choices and decisions. A number of cognitive approaches are used to help a juvenile develop internal controls. External control, provided by counselors and the legal system, is employed until the juvenile is able to demonstrate regularly internal control.

Developmental Deficits A counselor should be sensitive to a juvenile with developmental deficits. A juvenile who has grown up in a dysfunctional family may have experienced developmental delays. Trust, autonomy, and psychosocial competence, all necessary for successful human functioning, are impaired. Programming should be compatible with any developmental deficits that the juvenile has.

Attachment Disorders Abusive relationships are associated with dysfunctional boundaries, and dysfunctional boundaries are associated with distorted attachment. These distorted attachments may be enmeshed, unattached, or sexualized. Patterns of attachment are learned early in a child's life. Counselors, to combat distorted attachments, should model respectful boundaries and bonding. A counselor also works with the family to create healthier attachments and appropriate boundaries.

Skill Deficits and Educational Deficits A counselor should develop programming to address dating skills, assertiveness training, social skills, communication, problem-solving skills, expression of feelings, anger management, stress management, values clarification, sex role stereotyping, and academic classes.

Cognitive–Behavioral Approach Becker and Kaplan (1993) describe a sexual treatment program for juveniles that they provide at the Sexual Behavior Clinic, which is located within the New York State Psychiatric Institute. When a referral is made, the following records are examined: victim statement, hospital records, police records, and any psychological or psychiatric reports. In the assessment process, both juveniles and parents are interviewed and both must sign consent forms. If either or both refused, no assessment is conducted. If both agree, the assessment consists of three factors. There are a clinical interview, psychometric testing, and physiological evaluation. The clinical interview gathers information that includes demographic characteristics, family background, criminal history, social history, drug and alcohol history, a complete sexual history, and a history of any physical or sexual abuse.

The psychometric testings involve a number of self-reports. Among them were the Beck Depression Inventory; Adolescent Sexual Interest Card-Sort, which is a sixty-four–item measure of sexual interest; the Adolescent Cognitions Scale, a thirty-two–item exam to learn the extent of distorted cognition regarding sex; the

Math Tech Sex Test, a scale that measures sexual knowledge and attitudes and values; and the Matson Evaluation of Social Skills, a sixty-two–item scale that measures five areas consisting of (1) appropriate social skills, (2) inappropriate assertiveness, (3) impulsive-recalcitrant traits, (4) overconfidence, and (5) jealousy withdrawal.

Following these tests, an assessment is conducted and a treatment plan is formulated. Becker and Kaplan (1988) initially patterned treatment after an adult treatment model but found that modifications had to be made for juveniles. Juveniles differ cognitively, emotionally, and developmentally from adults. The program begins with verbal satiation, which is a modified technique for repeated masturbation. The juvenile is shown several nude slides, which are comparable to the juvenile's victim. For example, if the juvenile assaulted a child, he is shown nude slides of children who are close to the age of the victim. As the juvenile views the slides, he is requested to describe over a thirty-minutes period what he said to the victim. If the juvenile is unable to recall saying anything, the therapist selects phrases for him that would be similar to what he might have said or thought. For instance, a juvenile who has molested a child might be requested to say the following while viewing a slide:

"I'm feeling this girl all over."
"This little girl wants me."
"Me and this girl are going to have fun."

A juvenile who has raped an adult woman would be requested to say the following repeatedly:

"I'm ripping her clothes off."
"I'm beating this woman up."
"I want to rape this woman."

Following verbal satiation for eight sessions, the juvenile enters a forty-week closed group treatment that is led by male and female cotherapists. Because of juveniles' generally lower attention span, a maximum of an hour of group was deemed best. During the early session, juveniles are presented the group rules, such as no shouting or yelling, one person speaks at a time, no leaving one's seat, and no putting down other group members. For juveniles in treatment as a result of a juvenile court judge order, they are told the consequences of dropping out of the group and treatment. Then, each juvenile is asked to describe the characteristics of his offense and victim, such as telling the age and sex of the child, whether he and the child were related, and the number of times the offense occurred.

Following the introduction, the group activity focuses on modifying cognitive distortions, and this segment of treatment goes on for five weeks. The modification of juveniles' cognitive distortions occurs with therapists performing the role of the molester. The therapist performs the role of the molester, and the juveniles perform the role of the therapist, court personnel, judge, or a psychiatrist. When role-play is completed, the juveniles either agree or disagree with the performed molester's rationalization and a group discussion follows. Further, other situations are role-played, such as child molestation, incest, date rape, non–date rape, voyeurism, exhibitionism, and frotteurism. In addition, juveniles are provided with information regarding consent, and specifically that a child cannot legally consent to sex, a woman who is intoxicated and unconscious cannot legally consent, and a woman who is severely developmentally disabled cannot legally consent.

During the next stage of the group process, juveniles are asked to write down their thoughts when they engaged in sexually deviant behavior. Often, these writings reveal a lack of empathy, objectification of females, viewing sex selfishly, lack of remorse, and endorsement of violence. Juveniles acquire these beliefs through personal violence, negative role models at home and in the community, association with antisocial peers, unflattering presentations of females, and acceptance of violence. Group exercises are developed to address these problem areas.

Next, juveniles receive counseling on developing and using covert sensitization techniques. The aim of these techniques is to educate juveniles regarding the thoughts and behaviors that place them at risk for sexually abusing others. These at-risk thoughts and behaviors are juxtaposed with the consequences of the behavior. For instance, a juvenile would recognize the following risk, *Risk:* "I see a child who is wearing a short dress playing in the yard. No one seems to be around. I think I will go down and see if she wants to do it." *Consequences:* "I'm in the detention center and scared because I don't know what is going to happen to me. This occurred because I went over to that little girl."

The next part of the group counseling involves helping juveniles to develop assertiveness skills and learning to control their anger. Some juveniles have a problem identifying and curbing their aggressive impulses. As a result, they use aggression to solve problems. The aim of this particular focus is to help juveniles discriminate among passive, assertive, and aggressive behaviors. Also, they receive instructions in anger management and appropriate, alternative responses. Other emotions are also addressed. For instance, they are told that anger often hides other emotions, such as frustrations and resentment. By way of illustration, a juvenile, whose father has remarried, is angry with his new step-sister for getting all the attention in the family. The juvenile is also angry with his father for remarrying and molests his step-sister out of anger.

Hennepin County Home School's Model Fay Honey Knopp, Director of the Safer Society Program, visited the Juvenile Sex-Offender Program (JSOP) at the Hennepin County Home School in Minnetonka, Minnesota. The Hennepin County Home School is a correctional residential treatment facility for adjudicated delinquent juveniles court-ordered for treatment. Focusing upon graduates residing in Minnesota, Knopp relates that a one-year follow-up reveals that 93% of juveniles had not reoffended, and an examination from 1979, the opening of the facility, to about 1986 reveals that the annual success rate ranges from 93% to 97% (Knopp, 1987). The treatment consists of nine stages, which have been described in detail in a treatment manual written by the treatment staff (Heinz, Gargaro & Kelly, 1987). Table 8.1 depicts for each of the nine steps the behaviors manifested by juveniles in the program, programs goals, and treatment strategies.

Table 8.1 Hennepin County Home School's Juvenile Sex Offender Program Model

Stage 1: Orientation

Behavior Manifested	Program Goals	Treatment Strategies
1. Extremes in behavior; aggression to passivity 2. Loneliness 3. Fear 4. Feelings of separation and anxiety around family	1. Assess the juvenile's tendencies toward violence 2. Facilitate peer relationships 3. Teach the juvenile about the structure of the program 4. Assess the juvenile's personal and social style	1. Use "noncookbook" methods and consequences to fit the offender's behavior 2. Promote group responsibility for the juvenile's adjustment, through the group 3. Utilize the group to establish beginning of inner control of the youth

Stage 2: Power and Passivity

Behavior Manifested	Program Goals	Treatment Strategies

1. Do nothing (overt denial)
2. Over-adaptation
3. Agitation
4. Violence
	1. Raise the juvenile's anxiety
	2. Strip defenses
	3. Help the juvenile realize that what he is doing is not meeting his needs
		1. Respond to do-nothing behavior by
		  a. Doing something
		  b. Remaining in the here and now
		  c. Confronting reality
		  d. Writing or acting out offense
		  e. Engaging in intense verbal confrontation
		2. Respond to over-adaptation behavior by exaggerating demands or making conflicting demands
		3. Respond to agitation by
		  a. De-escalating
		  b. Escalating
		  c. Maintaining
		4. Respond to violence by offering safety

Stage 3: Confusion and Frustration

Behavior Manifested	Program Goals	Treatment Strategies

1. Anger acting out; intimidation
2. Withdrawal—physically and/or emotionally
3. Panic/desperation
4. Possible suicidal attempts or gestures
	1. Ensure safety of the juveniles
	2. Provide support
	3. Build self-esteem
	4. Make juvenile aware of need to ask for help
		1. Safety
		  a. Surveillance
		  b. Being there
		2. Support
		  a. Nurturing
		  b. Loving
		  c. Hugging
		  d. Rocking
		3. Esteem building
		  a. Compliment game and lifts
		  b. Handicapped riding

continued

Table 8.1 Hennepin County Home School's Juvenile Sex Offender Program Model, *cont'd*

Stage 3: Confusion and Frustration, *cont'd*

	c. Recreation
	d. Tutoring
	4. The juvenile asks for help
	a. Victim role
	b. Assertiveness
	c. Problem solving

Stage 4: Bonding

Behavior Manifested	Program Goals	Treatment Strategies
1. Seeking out adults	1. Help the juvenile develop trusting relationships	1. Individual attention and counseling
2. Wanting to develop relationships	2. Help the juvenile general-ize trust	2. Teaching—experiential and concrete
3. Lot of testing of limits	3. Help the juvenile learn about feeling	a. Sex education curriculum
	4. Help the juvenile learn new ways of meeting needs	b. Feelings and emotions
		c. Fantasies—sexual and nonsexual
		d. Sexual abuse/victims
		e. Homosexuality
		f. Elimination of self-defeating behaviors
		g. Grief
		h. Sex roles
		i. Assertiveness
		j. Psychological defenses

Stage 5: The Offender as Victim

Behavior Manifested	Program Goals	Treatment Strategies
1. Regression to earlier stages	1. Help the juvenile to stop blaming himself and to work through his shame	1. Listening to other victims
2. Bizarre or psychotic behaviors	2. Help the juvenile to ac-cept care and love	2. Writing about victimization
a. Incapacitation	3. Help the juvenile to stop taking hurt and anger out on others	3. Talking and role-playing the incident, re-enacting the as-sault but winning
b. Hallucination	4. Help the juvenile to un-derstand his offense	4. Anger-work
c. Disturbing dreams	5. Help the juvenile to for-give the perpetrator	5. After discharging anger and pain, getting lots of hugs
3. Self-pity		6. Referrals to psychiatrist for possible medication
4. Anger and pain		
5. Lack of trust		
6. Suicide ideation		

Stage 6: Integration

Behavior Manifested	Program Goals	Treatment Strategies
1. Regression into a help-less state	1. To redirect responsibility back to the juvenile	Through group process and re-lationships, the following techniques are used to reteach learned behavior
2. Shame/codependent relationships	2. To promote the juvenile's ability to learn and make better choices	1. Fantasies
3. Reoccurring irritating behavior	3. To help the juvenile for-give himself and others	2. Imagery
4. Lack of real boundaries		3. Large and small group process
5. Sexualized feelings		

Table 8.1 Hennepin County Home School's Juvenile Sex Offender Program Model, *cont'd*

Stage 6: Integration, *cont'd*

6. Disengagement from relationships	4. Re-enacting old trauma to gain new ways of taking care of self
	5. Forgiveness ceremonies

Stage 7: Honesty about Feelings and Victims

Behavior Manifested	*Program Goals*	*Treatment Strategies*
1. Anxiety level rises	1. To know everything about the juvenile's sexual acting out	1. Write down sexual history
2. Acting out increases		2. Write details of offense
3. Asking for more time in groups	2. To obtain help for all new victims identified	3. Role-play offense
	3. To clean up the legal aspects of the newly admitted offenses	4. Talk about other victims
	4. To help the juvenile forgive himself	5. Fantasies: understanding fantasies in general and sexual fantasies specifically, and learning how these fantasies fit into sexual acting out
	5. To help the juvenile trust others	
	6. To help the juvenile know himself and let others in	
	7. To help the juvenile accept unconditional love	

Stage 8: Developing Empathy

Behavior Manifested	*Program Goals*	*Treatment Strategies*
1. Regression to Stage 5—the offender as a victim	1. Help the juvenile accept responsibility	1. Identify blockages to feeling empathy
2. Sharing and caring for others	2. Help the juvenile to forgive himself	2. Structure positions of responsibility
3. Wanting to please	3. Help the juvenile develop victim empathy	3. Observe how the juvenile meets his needs with peers, parents, and siblings
		4. Engage in victim work
		5. Facilitate writing of victim paper
		6. Enable juvenile to forgive himself

Stage 9: Reintegration

Behavior Manifested	*Program Goals*	*Treatment Strategies*
1. Not wanting to disengage from the program (codependency)	1. To gently disengage the juvenile	1. Issues to be discussed in group
2. Some fear, apprehension, regression to earlier stages	2. To make him responsible for his behavioral choices	a. How hard it is to leave
	3. To encourage his leadership	b. What the juvenile has to offer
		c. How relationships will change and people can meet the juvenile's needs

continued

Table 8.1 Hennepin County Home School's Juvenile Sex Offender Program Model, *cont'd*

Stage 9: Reintegration, *cont'd*

3. Modeling leadership, nurturing others
4. Excitement and joy
	4. To engage staff in reviewing and learning from this individual's treatment	2. Moves toward greater independence
		  a. Getting increased space from residents and staff
		  b. Making longer home visits
		  c. Job hunting
		  d. Participating in independent community activities
		3. Ways group continues to take care of the juvenile
		  a. Preplacements
		  b. Community supports
		  c. Aftercare
		4. Structured leadership
		  a. Sports
		  b. Work with other residents around treatment, pain, and anger issues
		5. Individual work
		  a. Planning and coordinating services
		  b. School liaison
		  c. Meet with school
		6. Exit interview
		  a. Psychological testing
		  b. Staff meetings
		  c. Staff review of release plans

Treating Juveniles with Alcohol and Drug Problems

The Center for Substance Abuse recommends a full continuum of services. The continuum of services should include prevention services, early intervention services, outpatient services, intensive outpatient treatment services, and residential services. Depending upon the needs of the juvenile, this continuum would provide low-intensity services for juveniles in the initial stages of substance abuse to high-intensity services for juveniles with severe substance abuse (McPhail & Wiest, 1995).

Juveniles should be matched according to their needs and the type of service. Treatment should consist of a variety of behavioral, cognitive, and family therapies. Treatment would also provide plans for preventing relapse, continuing care, and the development of independent living skills. Services may include specialized education, pre-employment training, health maintenance, transportation, leisure activities, and mentoring. Because relapse holds significant consequences for a juvenile who is involved with the juvenile justice system, an initial case conference should be held. This conference should include the juvenile, the juvenile's parents, treatment official, and the juvenile's probation officer. This conference is needed to assess the juvenile's progress to-date and to reinforce the legal consequences for resuming drug use.

Furthermore, successful treatment requires that the family and community be part of the intervention efforts. While occasionally being less than ideal, families are one of juveniles' essential primary groups and remain part of those units. Treatment must go beyond informational and self-help and include the family and peer group. Family treatment, thus, is critical. It is needed to help parents in establishing and maintaining house rules and communication and enforcing consequences consistently. Treatment for the parents also would include addressing any issues they have that impinge negatively on the family unit and the juvenile. They also are provided skills by which they could assist in successful treatment. If the juvenile has a network of familial support, such as grandparents, uncles, and aunts, they may be employed to assist in achieving a successful outcome.

Treating a Disruptive, Dually Diagnosed Adolescent

Treating adolescents with substance abuse dependency in residential settings is made more difficult when they suffer from a mental disorder, such as attention deficit hyperactivity disorder (ADHD). The behavioral indicators of ADHD are rapid breathing, rapid speech, picking nails, knuckle cracking, pulling or twisting hair, silliness, clenched fists, muscle tension, poor concentration, bouncing legs, pacing, increased voice volume, decreased ability to follow directions, heavy smoking, poking or kicking with hands and feet, increased caffeine intake, disrupted sleep, jumping on beds, spinning, poor anger control, and swinging from door jambs. If they are out of control, some of the behaviors manifested are inability to sit, inability to sleep, driven speech, lack of insight, anger or frustration, and physically and verbally acting out. Because of these behaviors, the adolescents are unable to accept help or examine their own behaviors. They also interfere with the treatment of other adolescents. Sometimes, these highly disruptive adolescents may be dismissed from the program (Stratton & Gailfus, 1998).

Sensory treatment theory, and its accompanying treatment techniques, was applied to adolescents with a substance abuse disorder and ADHD. The theory is based on neurodevelopmental processes or stimuli. Stimuli within an individual need to be synchronously organized. Normally, this organization takes place naturally. But in some individuals this process may be impeded during development, causing them to be "overwhelmed by stimuli in the tactile (touch), auditory, olfactory, visual, and vestibular (movement) sensory realms" (p. 91). Adolescents so affected are incapable of functioning in a healthy, productive manner (Stratton & Gailfus, 1998).

Employed by a trained occupational therapist, sensory integration techniques include the following.

1. Brushing program involves the tactile system and consists of using a soft surgical scrub brush to brush the arms, back, and legs every two to four hours, which is followed by joint compression.
2. Joint compression is the application of ten compressions of the arms and ten head compressions.

3. Rolling in a blanket focuses on the proprioceptive and tactile systems. It is similar to swaddling a baby.
4. Swinging is directed at the vestibular system. It is a cocoon swing suspended from a ceiling that rotates in a variety of directions.
5. Rocking is directed at the vestibular, proprioceptive, and tactile systems. It is similar to rocking a baby.
6. Playing with putty focuses on the tactile and proprioceptive systems. It is an orthopedic hand strengthener. The putty also is used to increase attention and increase self-calm.
7. Rolling on a large ball addresses the vestibular, proprioceptive, and tactile systems. The person lies on the ball, and it is gently rolled. The aim is to position the head in a variety of directions.
8. Jumping on trampoline affects the proprioceptive and vestibular systems. This reorganizes systems and is self-stimulating.
9. Scooter boards are similar to skateboards, but squarer. This focuses on the tactile, vestibular, and proprioceptive systems.
10. Massage is used to calm the individual, alleviate stress, muscle tension, and fatigue. This technique focuses on the proprioceptive and tactile systems.

The adolescent and occupational therapist decide which of these techniques is best for him. Sensory integration was used with a sixteen-year-old male with a history of ADHD, which was diagnosed when he was nine. Prior to entering treatment, the sixteen year old was in juvenile detention for assault. Since he was twelve years old, he was a regular user of cannabis, which he claimed decreased tension and calmed him down. Hence, the goal of treatment is to relieve the adolescent's tension and increase his calmness. By achieving these goals, an adolescent is more receptive to treatment and able to more attend to clinicians and his peer treatment group. The sixteen year old demonstrated significantly improved behaviors after application of some of the sensory integration techniques, and more scientific study is underway (Stratton & Gailfus, 1998).

RESEARCHED INTERVENTION PROGRAMS

Treating Delinquent Behavior

For a number of years, group programs for antisocial juveniles have been implemented in residential programs and schools with inconsistent results. One explanation given by treatment professionals for these inconsistent results was that some groups had members who did not know how or did not have the skills to help themselves or others. The premise of these professionals was that juveniles would be able to help others and themselves when they were equipped with required techniques and skills. Accordingly, these professionals developed a program that they called EQUIP (Gibbs, Potter, & Goldstein, 1995).

EQUIP was developed to address three limitations of antisocial juveniles in a group setting. These are social skill deficiencies, social developmental delays, and social cognitive distortions. Antisocial juveniles simply do not possess the social skills to address some problems. A juvenile may respond angrily and violently to social situations and thereby cause himself more difficulty. For example, a juvenile in a room with other juveniles may ask for permission to engage in playing a game. An adult, planning to initiate a group activity, may respond, "Not at the moment." The juvenile then shouts some profanity and storms off. Antisocial juveniles are developmentally delayed because they exhibit immature or superficial moral judgment and obvious egocentric bias. The latter is reflected in the above example. A juvenile who reacts angrily and violently to a response is indicating that what he wants is the most important factor and other issues are significantly less important. Antisocial juveniles possess a number of primary and secondary distortions. Among the distortions are self-centeredness, assuming the worst, blaming others, and minimizing and mislabeling (Gibbs et al., 1995).

EQUIP corrects skill deficiencies, social developmental delays, and social cognitive distortions. It requires juveniles to relate their cognitive distortions or thinking errors. The cognitive distortions, along with sociomoral developmental delays and social skill deficiencies, are discussed in meetings that are called *equipment meetings*. After the group jells a little and becomes more of a mutual-help group, the equipment meetings are initiated. Equipment meetings follow a coordinated curriculum plan and consist of strategies to address moral education, anger management, cognitive distortions, and social skills (Gibbs et al., 1995).

Testing Gibbs' theory, Leeman (1991) reported the results of an experiment designed to determine the effectiveness of an intervention program based on cognitive–behavioral and moral reasoning approaches. The name of the program was "Identify It/Own It/Replace It: Equipping Youth to Help One Another," or IOR for short. This program is a combination of Goldstein and Glick's (1987) ART and Vorrath and Brendtro's Positive Peer Culture (PPC). The IOR lasted about six months and was provided to juveniles who were living on a unit that was designed as the IOR unit. Juveniles were randomly assigned to an experimental group, motivational control group, and simple control group. There were eighteen in the experimental group, which received the IOR intervention, seventeen in the motivational group, and nineteen in the control group. The juveniles had been incarcerated for such crimes as burglary, arson, breaking and entering, receiving stolen property, armed robbery, felonious assault, and rape.

The researcher concluded that the IOR had a powerful effect on the juveniles who received the intervention. Qualitative reports from institutional staff reported that the juveniles on the IOR unit were much easier to manage than other juveniles in the facility. Moreover, the IOR juveniles had fewer fights, less verbal abuse, less attempts at escaping, and less defiance of the staff. Though there was not a significant difference among the three groups in terms of recidivism, the experimental group's recidivism was almost half of the control group's at six months, and a little less than half at twelve months. The researcher speculated that more intensive treatment might improve the recidivism rates more and increase the moral judgment of juveniles (Leeman, 1991).

Treatment for Violent Delinquents

Multisystemic Treatment (MST) was developed from principles of system theory and causal models of delinquency based on integrated theory. It views delinquents as being nested within a ring of other systems, including the family, peers, and schools. Intervention may be directed at the delinquent or at one or more of the

other systems. In addition, MST recognizes child development variables and intervention drawn from behavioral theory (Henggeler, 1994).

Program-wise, MST is delivered in approximately thirty hours of direct contact
over a three-month period. The last two or three weeks of treatment is less intensive and monitors the maintenance of therapeutic gains. The length of session
varies and ranges from ninety minutes to fifteen minutes. Depending upon the
needs of the family and delinquent, treatment may be every day or once a week.
Also, the MST counselors are available twenty-four hours a day, seven days a
week. It is not unusual for MST counselors to see families late in the evenings or on
weekends. However, to facilitate empowering families, sessions after 10 P.M. are discouraged unless a significant emergency has arisen that requires a session. These sessions are conducted either within the family's home or within a community setting.
The caseload for each counselor is four to six families (Henggeler, 1994).

A principal aim of MST is to promote behavioral change in the delinquent's natural environment. Particularly, the goals are aimed at family problems, family empowerment, juvenile, peers, school, and the court and juvenile justice system.
During the initial session with the delinquent and family, a counselor assesses the
strengths and weaknesses of each system. The counselor also assesses the transactions with other systems, such as the delinquent's peers, friends, school, and the
parental workplace. When problems are identified, the counselor uses the strength
of the systems to facilitate behavioral change. Although, in general, families differ
regarding their strengths and weaknesses, seriously delinquent juveniles have families with common problems (Henggeler, 1994).

Intervention with delinquent juveniles is geared at the juveniles' social
perspective-taking skills, belief systems, and motivational systems. One factor that
exacerbates the behavioral problems of delinquents is their attitudinal biases. These
youths frequently believe that others are out to get them and the manner in which
they respond furthers problems. Delinquents need to learn that body postures, voice
tone, and combative gestures play a role in the cycle of hostility. To assist a delinquent youth who had challenged a teacher's authority in class, the counselor might
ask the youth to understand the position of the teacher. Specific questions might be,
"What is the role of the teacher?" "How do you think the teacher felt about your
challenge?" "How would you respond if you were a teacher and a student said what
you did?" Some delinquents' problems may occur because of skill deficits. Simply,
these youths do not know how to interact with adults, to interact with the opposite
sex, to handle peer pressure, and to handle aggressive behaviors of others. The
counselor's task is to assist the delinquent in learning these skills. For instance, a juvenile who has been told to "go to hell" by another juvenile may feel it is necessary
to fight, which could escalate into a serious injury. The counselor can offer other alternative responses and instruct the juvenile on how to deal with internal and external pressures to respond aggressively (Henggeler & Borduin, 1990).

Delinquent youths tend to come from families in which there is considerable
conflict and little affection for each other. Parents in these homes tend to disagree
regarding discipline and other conflicts between parents negatively affect parenting.
The goal of familial intervention is to help the parents acquire the resources to parent more effectively, increase family structure, and develop family cohesion. Specific techniques are geared toward helping parents to institute systematic rewards

and discipline, improving communication between parents regarding the delinquents' problems, and perfecting everyday problem-solving skills (Henggeler, 1994).

Family empowerment is a key task of the counselor and represents an overriding goal of MST. The counselor strives to empower both parents and youths. Parents need to be empowered to deal independently with the problems of rearing teenagers. The counselor's task is to be supportive and teach parents. If a parent does not have support in his or her environment, a goal of the counselor is to help establish this support. This might mean helping to bridge problems with other relatives. Delinquent youths also need to be empowered to deal with school, peers, and neighborhood problems (Henggeler, 1994).

Delinquent youths tend to have peers who are supportive of delinquent behaviors. A key intervention is to curtail the youth's involvement with delinquent peers and the promotion of association with peers who are prosocial. However, this intervention is ideally provided by the parents with support from the counselor. Similarly, the parents are instrumental in addressing school issues. At the urging and support of the counselor, the parents establish contact with their child's teachers and restructure the youth's evening so that the youth will have an increased chance of experiencing academic success. While the focus is on system change, some intervention may be directed at the delinquent. Intervention emphasizes on social perspective taking, belief system, motivational system, and assertive skills to address negative peers (Henggeler, 1994).

The final systematic intervention involves the juvenile justice system. This means that the counselor develops and maintains positive and cooperate relationships with juvenile justice officials. A counselor attends sessions in juvenile court and juvenile court staffing involving the juvenile with which the counselor is working. Families are asked to sign releases so that the counselor may communicate information to juvenile justice officials as needed. Working closely with agents of the juvenile justice system is critical to the success of MST (Henggeler, 1994).

Borduin and colleagues (1995) tested the effectiveness of MST and the longterm effects of MST with seriously delinquent youths who were in the Missouri Delinquency Project. They interviewed 200 families who were referred by the juvenile justice system. Twenty-four families refused to participate, leaving 176 families. Using a pretest-posttest control group design, they randomly assigned families with seriously delinquent juveniles to MST and individual therapy. After treatment commenced, some families in both groups dropped out, creating two additional groups for analyses. The studied groups consisted of MST completers ($n = 77$), MST dropouts ($n = 15$), IT completers ($n = 63$), IT dropouts ($n = 21$), and treatment refusers ($n = 24$).

Consistent with the theoretical basis for MST, the outcome measures involved individual adjustment, family relations, peer relations, and criminal activity. Specifically, Symptom Checklist and the Global Severity Index were used to measure individual functioning of parents and the delinquent. Moreover, the juvenile behavior problems were measured by the Behavior Problem Checklist, according to parental reports. Family relations were measured by Family Adaptability and Cohesion Evaluation Scales. Also, the families were videotaped as they answered nine items from the Unrevealed Differences Questionnaires to assess family interactions, consisting of supportiveness, verbal activity, and conflict hostility. Peer relations were measured by the Missouri Peer Relations Inventory as determined by parents and teachers. This inventory measures emotional bonding, aggression, and social maturity. Criminal activity was measured by subsequent arrests following termination from treatment.

Borduin and associates (1995) found a number of significant differences between the MST and IT groups. In terms of individual adjustment, both mothers and fathers in the MST group, compared with the IT group, showed significant decreases in symptoms at posttest. Also, mothers in the MST group reported a significant decrease in juveniles' behavior problems compared to the IT group. In terms of family functioning, the MST showed significant improved cohesion and adaptability at posttest (Borduin et al., 1995).

The ultimate outcome was arrest, and the MST group showed several significant differences. Juveniles in the MST were significantly less likely to be arrested compared to the IT group. Particularly, at the end of four years, 26.1% of the MST completers group had been arrested compared to 46.6% of the MST dropouts, 71.4% of the IT group, 71.4% for the IT dropouts, 87.5% for the treatment refusers. Also, the MST completers had a lower risk of arrests than IT completers, MST dropouts, IT dropouts, and treatment refusers. MST dropouts had a lower risk of arrests than treatment refusers and IT dropouts. When the MST group did get arrested, they were less likely than the IT group to be arrested for a serious offense. Also, the analysis showed that the treatment effects were independent of race, gender, age, and social class. The only unexpected finding regarding the impact of MST was that there were no differences regarding the peer relations among the different groups (Borduin et al., 1995).

Boot Camps

Boot camps were implemented in 1983, and much of the studies of them have involved adult offenders. In 1995, the Office of Juvenile Justice and Delinquency Prevention (OJJDP) convened a round table of criminal justice professionals to discuss the development and research of boot camps for juvenile offenders. The panel identified six essential components of an effective juvenile boot camp. These six components include (1) education, job training, and placement; (2) community service; (3) substance abuse counseling and treatment; (4) health and mental health care; (5) continuous, individualized case management; and (6) intensive aftercare services that are fully integrated with the boot camp program. The overall goal of these components is to rehabilitate the juvenile offenders, which contrasted with adult boot camps, which emphasize deterrence, incapacitation, rehabilitation, punishment, and cost control (OJJDP, 1997a).

Given these parameters, OJJDP in 1990 solicited proposals to develop and test a juvenile boot camp program that emphasized discipline, treatment, and work. The winning proposals consisted of three public-private partnerships in Cleveland, Ohio; Denver, Colorado; and Mobile, Alabama. Each site proposed to use random assignment to treatment and control groups. The three sites provided different activities in both residential treatment and aftercare services. For example, the Cleveland site had a greater emphasis on treatment with the military aspects secondary. The Denver site had a greater emphasis on the military aspects with treatment services secondary. The Mobile site had the greatest emphasis on education with some attention given to environmental awareness and outdoor activities. At the Mobile site, there was competing emphasis on military and treatment. In a somewhat similar manner, the three sites offered different proposed services during aftercare (OJJDP, 1997a).

The researchers found that in Cleveland, 72% of the participants in the treatment group had a subsequent arrest compared to 50% of the control group. In Denver, 39% of the treatment group had an arrest compared to 36% of the control group. In Mobile, 28% of the treatment group experienced an arrest compared to 31% of the control group. In short, the boot camps did not reduce recidivism. According to the researchers, "none of the three sites was able to implement the OJJDP boot camp program model fully. Each of the programs experienced considerable instability and staff turnover [and]... none of the experimental programs was able to implement and sustain stable, well-developed aftercare services. None of the programs was prepared for the difficulties of reintegrating juvenile offenders into families, neighborhoods, and schools after release from boot camp" (OJJDP, 1997, p. 25).

UNRESEARCHED PROGRAMS AND INTERVENTIONS

Treatment for Juvenile Probationers

Illustrating an example of an intervention program that looks laudable but lacks empirical support, Goodman (1997) describes the development of a cognitive–behavior group-counseling program for offenders in a major urban area. The program was a collaborate effort between a graduate school of social work and a probation department. The probation department approached the school of social work to solicit its assistance in training probation officers to do group work. It evolved into a much larger project involving the design of specialized cognitive restructuring groups for different offenders. One group was for male offenders between the ages of sixteen and twenty who were at risk for rearrests involving violence. Closely tying the program to the literature, the program was brief and intensive, meeting twice a week for eighteen weeks. Group leaders (i.e., probation officers) followed a written protocol that concentrated on exposing and confronting faculty thinking.

The program was structured in the following manner. For any offender who was assigned to the cognitive restructuring group, participation was involuntary. Early in the group, the format was predetermined, with little influence by group members. For instance, the topics were determined by the probation officer. As the group developed, it became less structured. Then, group members could suggest topics for discussion. Issues were prioritized such that the areas thought to be critical for offenders were discussed early in the group. Homework was given, and one such homework assignment was creating a "Thought Record." Personal goals were established, such as registering for a GED program, finding a job training program, and improving family relationships.

Goodman reported that the group delved into other issues. As Goodman stated,

> The structured nature of the group experience helped members organize their personal lives, taught them to follow routines and provided tools for meeting pro-social objectives. Simple expectations, such as arriving on time for the groups, bringing materials

and preparing assignments between group meetings paralleled the expectations that the participants would encounter in the community to keep a job or stay in school. Group content enhanced critical thinking and interpersonal problem solving capacity. The group leaders, and ultimately other group members, confronted and challenged thinking that would lead the probationers to behave in ways that would derail them from meeting their self-identified goals. Any attempt to alter behavior required a parallel effort to change entrenched thinking that rationalized antisocial behavior or placed offenders at-risk of victimization. (p. 56)

The cognitive techniques used by the probation officers were linked to some of the homework assignments and real-life problems. For instance, one offender went on a job interview and was told by one interviewer that he had a good chance at getting the job. Upon a second interview, another interviewer said that he would not hire the offender because the offender wore braids. The offender stated that the interviewer did not say if he (the interviewer) would hire the offender if the offender changed his hair. The offender was very angry about this incident and declared in group that he would not go on any more interviews. This real-life situation provided a number of issues for the group to discuss. Also, members carried cards with messages designed to help them think and respond appropriately to avoid impulsive behaviors. These cards were called SODAS, which Goodman did not explain but were designed to aid in anger management. Other cards were developed for issues involving peer relationships, false pride and true pride, and intimate relationships. The latter was important because a number of offenders had problems with objectifying females as sex objects. In conclusion, Goodman reported that the program was a success and that "neither the probation officers nor the administration anticipated the important impact these groups could have on the thinking and behavior of probationers" (p. 61).

Wilderness Camps

Clagett (1992a) described the joining of principles from reality therapy in a wilderness camp for emotionally disturbed and delinquent boys. He referred to this combination as the Group-Integrated Reality Therapy (GIRT). First, Clagett described the seven principles of reality therapy, which consisted of the following:

1. Involvement
2. Acquiring awareness of client's current behavior
3. Client evaluates his behavior
4. Planning responsible behavior
5. Commitment of clients
6. Counselors accept no excuses
7. Punishment is not employed

Clagett discussed how these principles were integrated into a treatment program for delinquent boys in a wilderness camp program in East Texas, called the Hope Center Wilderness Camp. Located in the Davey Crockett National Forest, the Wilderness Camp is located on about 125 acres of land. This program utilizes group therapy to correct dysfunctional behaviors of boys. There are a maximum of ten to twelve boys in the group with three counselors assigned to each group. Each group has its own name and campsite, which consists of the Eagles, Rangers, Woodsmen, Tonkawas, and Pioneers. The groups live in their campsites and eat their meals in a building called the Chuck Wagon, except for two days a week in which the groups cook and eat their meals in campsites. The Wilderness Camp provided the following treatment activities:

Plan of service (i.e., treatment plan)
Plan of service review (review every ninety days of treatment plan)
Planning (group decision making)
Discipline (no punishment but natural consequences allowed)
Schooling
Religious services
Weekend cookouts
Homesday (four days a month in which campers go home)
Homesday staff meeting
Parents' meeting (held in Houston the first Thursday after the end of homesday)
Huddle-up (called group session to resolve problems)
Pow wow (pre-bedtime in which each member evaluates his day)
Aftertalk (discussions of various topics by counselor after evening meal and a brief report by each group of its activities that day)
Terminal service review process (a called group meeting when a camper believes he is ready to leave the program, with other campers and counselors providing their opinions)
Aftercare (six months of services and support by a caseworker after a camper has been discharged from the camp)

Afrocentric Programming

Using an Afrocentric perspective, King (1997) explains violence among African American youths and recommends a different approach to address it. An Afrocentric perspective takes into account violence from slavery, violence to maintain white supremacy following slavery, and discrimination directed at African American males. King, then, discusses the impact on the African American community and African American youth psychosocial development as a result of the environment imposed on them.

King notes that when white national scholars and politicians discuss the causes of youth violence and insinuate that African American youth are the prime culprits, they never discuss the violent nature of slavery and brutality directed against African American males, institutional racism, and intransigent poverty and economic deprivation. He observes that no other group has endured what African Americans have endured in this country. According to King, "the Afrocentric paradigm overcomes Eurocentric social sciences theories' inability to adequately and fairly explain the worldview, culture, psychology, and behaviors of African Americans" (King, 1997, p. 81).

When African American males become ten to thirteen years of age, they know that the doors of opportunities have closed on most adult males in their community. African American boys know that society has little concern for them unless they can shoot a basketball, run a football, hit a baseball, sing, dance, or do stand-up comedy. Even with or without these talents, hopelessness is widespread. Then, exacerbating this condition are large numbers of stores that sell powerful malt liquor and omnipresent employers for crack and other drug selling. On top of these factors is the American society and its glorification of violence.

King finds that "striving to mature under these social conditions often leads to unimaginable levels of confusion, personal frustration, and emotional pain. More important, these conditions destroy, albeit ever so slowly, the moral character and conscience of many young men and boys. The emotional upheaval that they endure all too often leads to an obvious sense of personal devaluation, degradation, and a disrespect for their lives and the lives of their peers" (King, 1997, p. 89).

In sum, African American youths have self-destructive attitudes, perceptions, and psychosocial states. Particularly, they display behaviors indicative of low self-worth that is caused by a lack of nurturing. They do not have a sense of purpose and direction. They do not possess the social, educational, and vocational skills necessary to flourish in an unfriendly outer community and broader racist society. They do not have a semblance of connectedness with themselves and the African American community. They do not have a culturally specific and appropriate worldview and ethos that would provide a foundation for interactions with peers, the community, and society. Stated differently, they "lack a worldview and belief system that would help them overcome the ravages of economic deprivation, institutional racism and discrimination, and the despair and hopelessness that accompany these problems" (King, 1997, p. 93).

King avers that violence-prevention programs designed to address violence among African American males must address their psychosocial needs. These programs must be Afrocentric in nature so African American males can develop healthy frames of mind. King stresses that violence-prevention programs and Afrocentric programs must focus on African American males in correctional institutions. According to King, "these are the young people who will eventually have the greatest influence on teenagers who have yet to shoot, stab, or rob their first victim. If the African American community, social workers, and other human service professionals can help incarcerated African American males develop a sense of hope and self-respect and equip them with the skills required to survive and thrive in a hostile environment, then they will leave adult and juvenile correctional institutions and return to their communities willing and capable of assuming the responsibilities African men have assumed for thousands of years" (King, 1997, p. 94).

Based on views similar to King (1997), several Afrocentric programs have been developed for juvenile offenders. For instance, Harvey and Coleman (1997) describe a specific Afrocentric program for African American juveniles who have involvement with the juvenile justice system. The program was delivered by the MAAT Center for Human and Organizational Enhancement, an organization in the District of Columbia that serves children, youths, and families using an Afrocentric framework. MAAT, a word from the Egyptian culture, means living a virtuous and moral life. The program receives referrals from the mental health system and juvenile justice system. Most of the youths referred for treatment have issues regarding abuse and neglect, mental health difficulties, problems in school, and delinquent behavior.

The MAAT Center created a Rites of Passage program to treat African American males and their families who were involved in the juvenile justice system. The Rites of Passage program strives to teach youths and their families how to create and nurture character, unity, and self-esteem. Specifically, the program involves three components: in-home family and individual counseling, adolescent after-school groups, and family enhancement and empowerment intervention.

In-home family and individual counseling is critical to the Afrocentric perspective. In-home counseling is important because people are more relaxed in their homes, it facilitates access to services, and it establishes more quickly the credibility of the counselors. Buttressing these reasons, it is provided in the evenings and weekends. Family counseling emphasizes problem solving, decision making, awareness and identification of feelings and emotions, ameliorating communication, conflict resolution, and understanding and cherishing other family members. Also, family counseling strives to help parents gain effective control of their children and use effective disciplinary practices, create positive self-concept and high self-esteem, increase the ability to handle stress, create positive parent-child relationships, create family ties, and refrain from alcohol and other drugs. If the family is able to internalize these principles, it is in a better position to assist a delinquent son in rejecting gang involvement and crime and to feel better about himself, his families, and his community.

Individual counseling focuses on developing character, self-esteem, and pride by imbibing the principles of collectivity and spirituality as crucial values. Spirituality consists of living one's life virtuously and morally. Collectivity refers to demonstrating behaviors that strengthen one's group of origin. A juvenile is assisted to imbibe these principles by realizing his strengths and learning that he can achieve goals without violence and crime. He examines his feelings and emotions to acquire a positive sense of his internal control and self-worth. Next, the emphasis is on strengthening the juvenile's internal locus of control and eliminating gang activity and crime involvement that define the juvenile's self-worth. The counselor helps the juvenile to acquire problem-solving and decision-making skills. The juvenile examines the choices he has made, differentiating the ones that have had positive and negative outcomes. He works with the counselor "to use a cognitive and behavioral worldview in making appropriate life choices" (Harvey & Coleman, 1997, p. 202). Counseling for the juvenile continues until he shows attitudinal and behavior lifestyles changes.

The after-school group provides an adolescent with the opportunity to strengthen skills by participating in a group. In this group, the focus is on strengthening lifestyle changes by nurturing constructive interpersonal skills, promoting new relationships, and creating positive self-esteem rooted in personal and cultural strength. The aim of this group is to use the dynamics of the group to make a positive transition from adolescence to manhood and to foster positive friendships. Particular attention is given to helping juveniles acquire knowledge and positive behaviors that are going to help them successfully resist gangs and negative peer pressure. Attention is also given to changing erroneous perceptions of the African American race and culture; eliminating distorted views of manhood, fatherhood, and male-female relationships; abating acts of violence and crime; eliminating drug use; giving up delinquent behavior; and changing low educational and occupational beliefs.

The group consists of ten to fifteen boys who meet once a week for two hours. Nguzo Saba is used to teach juveniles the principles of spirituality, culture, family, education, economics, community, and adolescent activities to aid them in learning about themselves, others, and the world. Each group session consists of mastering specific modules. These modules are

African American culture and heritage
Principles and guides for living
African American lifestyles
Oppression and racism
Adolescent stages of development
Male physical development
Female physical development
Birth control
Fatherhood/marriage
Physical health
Diet and exercise
HIV/AIDS and other sexually transmitted diseases
Drugs and other harmful substances
Entrepreneurial development
Win-win relationships
Mediation as a means to self-development and self-control

Upon completion of each module, the boys receive a certificate, and upon completion of all modules, the boys participate in a formal Rites of Passage ceremony. This ceremony is planned by the boys with help from the counselors, and the parents, along with community members, are invited to witness the ceremony. Food is served and music is played. In addition, the boys are asked to demonstrate some of the skills that they have learned in the program.

The family enhancement and empowerment is a supplement to the in-house family therapy and consists of two parts. The first is the monthly Parent Training Seminars, and the second is the Semiannual Family Therapy Retreat. The overall objectives of both parts are to increase the quality of parents' relationship with their children so as to strengthen family bonding and to increase parents' competence to advocate for their family and community. In addition, the family enhancement and empowerment emphasizes increasing parents' abilities to control their children, adequate parenting skills, correct knowledge about adolescent development, parent-child relationship, family ties, communication skills, and adequate individual and group strategies for coping with various systems. In addition, teaching parents how to contend with community problems, such as gangs, drug dealers and users, neighborhood crime, and school problems, is provided.

The Monthly Parent Training is held once a month for two hours in a church community family center. Child care and transportation are provided so as to facilitate attendance. The aim of this group is to illustrate that parents share common problems and build group solidarity among them. The Semiannual Family Therapy Retreat is held on the weekends during the fall and spring. Again, child care and transportation are provided. The goals are to increase the bonding between and within families and to increase spiritual growth. The emphasis is on the Afrocentric belief of tribalism, which means that one should be faithful to one's racial group.

SUMMARY

This chapter discussed the context of treating male juveniles, noting that males concern society the most. Males are more aggressive and are more likely to engage in violent offenses, including murder, aggravated assault, and sexual assault. Minority male juveniles are of some concern to society and many of them are tried in the adult criminal justice system. This chapter discussed how to treat male juveniles who have committed homicide, aggression against persons, sexual assaults, and alcohol and drug offenses. Included in the latter group is treatment for a dually diagnosed adolescent with a diagnosis of substance abuse dependency and attention-deficit hyperactivity disorder. The chapter ended with a discussion of three programs for juvenile delinquents in which experimental research was conducted—a program for institutionalized delinquents in Ohio, violent juvenile probationers in Missouri, and boot camp programs. Only the boot camp programs failed to show positive results; however, they were not implemented as planned. Then, several unreseached programs were described, including one involving juveniles in Maryland, a wilderness camp program, and Afrocentric programs.

KEY TERMS

Types of juvenile
  murderers
Typology of adolescent
  sexual behaviors
Sexual abuse cycle
Aggressive replacement
  training
Skillstreaming

Treatment improvement
  protocol
Attention-deficit
  hyperactivity
  disorder (ADHD)
Sensory integration
EQUIP
Multisystemic treatment

Boot camps
Wilderness camp
Group-integrated reality
  therapy (GIRT)
Family enhancement
  and empowerment
Rites of passage
Nguzo Saba

9

✷ ✷ ✷

Treating Female
Adult Offenders

✼ INTRODUCTION

Adult women offend considerably less than men, and their criminal offenses tend to be property and drug related (Hay & Stirling, 1998; Jolin, 1997; Rierden, 1997). Just as women tend to commit different offenses than men, women have different issues that have implications for treatment and intervention (Alexander & Nickerson, 1993; Jones, 1993; Simmons, Sack, & Miller, 1996). Females are more likely to be sexually abused as children (Daley & Argeriou, 1997), causing them to have mental health, drug, and criminal issues (Heney & Kristiansen, 1997; Jantzen, Ball, Leventhal, & Schottenfeld, 1998; Wenninger & Ehlers, 1998). In addition, some women enter the criminal justice system pregnant and have child custody issues (Boudin, 1997; Corse & Smith, 1998; Johnston, 1995; Klein & Bahr, 1996; Uziel-Miller, Lyons, Kissiel, & Love, 1998). For many of these issues (e.g., drugs and children issues), women of color constitute the majority of those affected

(Alexander, Butler, & Sias, 1993; Covington, 1997; McQuaide & Ehrenreich, 1998; Smith, 1993).

Currently, the primary problem for woman offenders centers around drug addiction (Green, Fullilove, & Fullilove, 1998; Sanders, McNeill, Rienzi, & DeLouth, 1997; Uziel-Miller et al., 1998). Although middle-class and upper-class women may be addicted to prescribed medications, they are not the focus of the criminal justice system. The focus of the criminal justice system is women who abuse illegal substances. This means that the focus is on crack cocaine and other illegal drugs. This means also that African American women, Hispanic, and lower-class white women predominate the attention of the criminal justice system. For instance, a judge in Franklin County, Ohio, had before him a twenty-three-year-old white woman who had been charged with armed robbery. Upon going to jail, she learned that she was one month pregnant. The judge reduced the charge against her and sent her to Amethyst, a residential program that treats female drug addicts with children. After a year at Amethyst, the woman had kicked her alcohol and heroin addiction and gave birth to a daughter (Thomas, 1996).

There has been a tremendous growth of literature regarding how to treat woman substance abusers and factors believed associated with successful outcomes (Center for Substance Abuse Treatment, 1994; Kelly et al., 1995; Kropp et al., 1996). Kelly (1995), for instance, states that women's sobriety following participation in a treatment program is explained by program variables, such as participation in an aftercare component and vocational and educational training. Looking at individual characteristics, Kropp (1996) reports that women's sobriety following treatment is related to women's medical and income status. Particularly, women are more likely to stay sober if they have an affiliation with Alcoholics Anonymous, have income, and are in poor health. Being in poor health is interpreted as a motivation for treatment and abstinence (Kropp et al., 1996).

THE CONTEXT OF TREATING FEMALE ADULT OFFENDERS

Before developing services for woman offenders, need assessments have been conducted. A group of researchers surveyed, nationally, community-based programs for woman offenders to determine how these programs assessed needs for services and the extent to which services were provided for these needs. They found a number of problems. First, programs inadequately determined the needs of woman drug-abusing offenders. Second, they learned that a number of women had dependent children, which made it difficult to enter treatment because child care was not available. Third, they found that women needed comprehensive services, which often were not provided (Wellisch, Prendergast, & Anglin, 1996).

Promising programs for women in order of importance, according to some criminal justice professionals, were those programs that provide substance abuse education, substance abuse treatment, parenting skills, life skills, relationships, and basic education. Lesser important programs are transition services, alternative to violence, aftercare, vocational interest, vocational preparation, prior sexual abuse, HIV and health status, high-risk pregnancy, sexuality and love, and mental health (Koons, Burrow, Morash, & Bynum, 1997).

Besides these specific areas, promising programs target several areas because women's problems are complex and intertwined. Thus, treatment models have to be holistic and target a minimum of five areas. By holistic, professionals mean that treatment should address the whole person and all the person's problems that need intervention. As an illustration, a probation and parole department, because of women's multiple needs, implemented a case management system in which it referred woman offenders to a variety of services. In addition to meeting women's complex needs, promising programs were characterized by effective program staff, program participation, individualized and structured programs, technology and resources, program environment, victimization services, cohesive administrative and treatment staff, support from outside the agency, and the learning of needed skills (Koons et al., 1997).

Looking at the needs of African American women and their children, Uziel-Miller and colleagues (1998) contend that African American women are the most impacted group among substance-abusing women. African American women with substance abuse problems are worsened by poor education, little money, and living in high-crime neighborhoods. To determine the needs of these women, researchers administered the Addiction Severity Index to a group of African American women in treatment for substance abuse in the inner city of Chicago, Illinois. They conclude that these women had significant, multidimensional treatment needs. Many of the women had participated in treatment programs in the past but had failed to achieve their treatment goals. Most women had sparse work and educational histories. Most were single parents with several children and had involvement with Children Protection Services. They had little social support available to them. While they did not have significant participation in violent crimes, a number of women had charges against them for child abuse and neglect (Uziel-Miller et al., 1998).

Indeed, African American women suffer problems that are different from other woman offenders (Brewer, 1995; Dickerson, 1995; Hemmons, 1995). For instance, crack cocaine has had a major impact on African American women, particularly those who maintained single-headed households and were on Aid to Families with Dependent Children (AFDC). Before the introduction of crack, these women's lives centered around smoking marijuana, drinking beer, and watching soap operas. When crack came on the scene, it forced women to leave the home to get additional income to pay for crack. This meant stealing and prostituting to earn additional income. Sometimes, they exchanged sex for drugs. These women also put themselves in danger of assaults and homicide by stealing drugs or money from male substance-abusing partners (Hamid, 1992).

Showing both how African American women succumb to crack and how the criminal justice system focuses on African American women, South Carolina has prosecuted more than forty women for using drugs while pregnant and almost all of them were African Americans (Levinson, 1998). Levinson discussed the case of an African American woman named Ms. Cornelia Whitner in Easley, South Carolina. Ms. Whitner was the last of six children born to her parents. Her parents separated shortly after she was born. Ms. Whitner's mother died when she was forty-two and Ms. Whitner was fourteen years old. She and some of her siblings were taken in by relatives. Ms. Whitner began to drink and use drugs despite the strict rules by her legal guardian. At sixteen, Ms. Whitner had a child and moved out on her own.

Then, she became hooked on crack cocaine. She stole and prostituted herself to buy crack. She had another son, and both were taken from her by social services and placed with other relatives. She, pregnant with a third child, was charged with neglect and pled guilty. She was placed on probation with the condition that she not use any substances. A violation of this condition would mean ten years in prison. There was a night drug program in her county, but it did not provide child care or transportation. When her third child was born, she tested positive for cocaine and Ms. Whitner was arrested. Saying he was tired of "these bastard crack babies," the judge sent her to prison. She served nineteen months before another judge freed her, ruling that the law did not apply to fetuses. However, the state appealed to the South Carolina Supreme Court and it ruled that the law did apply to fetuses. Ms. Whitner was returned to prison. If she does not make parole or the U.S. Supreme Court does not reversed the South Carolina Supreme Court, she will leave prison on March 9, 2001 (Levison, 1998).

While many clinicians may recommend traditional services, such as AA or NA, for women like Ms. Whitner, other clinicians disagree. Rhodes and Johnson (1997) criticize the medical model of addiction and twelve steps as they apply to African American women with substance abuse issues. These models, according to Rhodes and Johnson, deny the experiences of African American women. In their place, Rhodes and Johnson propose a feminist model and explain how this model would address issues that African American women have. Above all, a feminist model appreciates the full context of women's lives and takes into account that successful intervention requires a holistic approach. This requires looking at the impact of domestic violence on substance use. The feminist model grasps that race and gender oppression affect addiction and must be addressed in counseling. Because the personal is political, the race of the therapist and client must be considered and dealt with in counseling. For instance, one of the byproducts of racism is that some people benefit from it, including white women counselors. As stated by Rhodes and Johnson, "while an examination of how white women benefit from racism is a painful process, without such personal confrontation, the unacknowledged racism will be infused into the therapeutic relationship" (p. 33).

Because of economics, some communities have inpatient, substance programs that are coed. Males live in one area and women in another area, with socialization permitted in common areas. These types of programs may present additional issues because of the inclusion of males in the milieu and how males affect group dynamics. Welle and associates (1998) studied several coed programs to learn how these programs dealt with the issues that arose and how women's needs were addressed. With males around, clinicians in one substance abuse program established rules against gender-specific behaviors and street behaviors. For instance, one rule was that men could not create a "posse" (i.e., congregating with a group of women) or "pimp" (i.e., sitting with one or two favorite women on a regular basis). Also, in the women's dormitory, women were discouraged from issuing personalized insults to other women or disrespecting other women. Violations of these rules were addressed in encounter groups.

Shifting to the structures of these programs to address women's needs, Welle and colleagues found several patterns. The staff tended to be former users and prisoners. Also, most of the staff had dealt with similar women's issues, such as problems with child welfare. Besides using recovered ex-offenders as staff, programs used a modified confrontational intervention. Traditional confrontation often is perceived as a reenactment of abuse from women's past. Instead, one program utilized women-only encounter groups in which the group highlighted problem behaviors within a context of "care and concern." When confrontation was used, it was seen as an effective technique in preventing violence, threats, rule breaking, sexual contact, and secret-keeping by the women in treatment (Welle et al., 1998).

With the staff's support and expectations, women gradually divulged and discussed freely their drug use in group. Popular themes that emerged in groups were the effect on one's mental health of prostituting oneself for drugs and physical and sexual abuse by fellow drug users, family members, and intimate partners. Other topics discussed were the consequences of drug use in general, such as HIV infection, memory problems, estranged family relationships, contemptible body image, and adverse parent-child relationships. Further, unresolved problems that were covered up by drug use surfaced in groups, such as depression, learning disabilities, sexual orientation, and eating disorders and were addressed in individual counseling (Welle et al., 1998).

Programs differ regarding treating women's criminality. In one of the East Coast programs, criminality is viewed as a part of the street culture where individuals commit crimes in order to get money to buy drugs. Viewed in this manner, criminality is treated through a number of interventions within the overall drug treatment program. However, one West Coast program viewed women's criminality differently. There, criminality is seen as occurring as result of cognitive deficits, which need to be treated separately from the drug problem. Thus, intervening with women's criminal thinking is a prerequisite to addressing women's criminality. This is done through a cognitive restructuring model. The counseling staff helps residents to recognize thought patterns that they use to justify criminal activity and other rule-breaking behaviors. The staff focuses upon consequential thinking so that women can prevent both drug use and criminality (Welle et al., 1998).

Specialized programs for woman offenders incorporate women's victimization as a part of their treatment for drug use and criminal behavior. However, differences exist regarding whether women's victimization should be of primary or secondary concern. Differences exist within programs and among women. Some women want to hear more about drug addiction and relapse and are critical of programs that emphasize victimization. At the same time in another program, other women criticize what they perceive as a lack of sufficient attention to victimization. As a result, some women refer to themselves as recovering drug users and others as survivors of abuse. Whether victimization is made primary or secondary, it involves women relating in group being victimized by significant others. Almost all are angry that their abusers were not held accountable by the criminal justice system, but women are held responsible (Welle et al., 1998).

A number of researchers examined the effects of a therapeutic community on women's personality characteristics. At admission to the therapeutic community, the Beck Depression Inventory, the Hamilton Anxiety Scale, and the Million Clinical Multiaxial Inventory were administered to the women and again at twelve months following discharge from the therapeutic community. These researchers found that the therapeutic community helped women to decrease depression; anxiety; avoidant, dependent, self-defeating behaviors; and borderline behavioral characteristics. However, the therapeutic community did not positively affect women who had antisocial and passive-aggressive personalities (Schinka et al., 1999).

The last contextual issue involves woman sexual offenders—one of the more unreported and undiscussed topics (Sgroi & Sargent, 1993). A few females have been initially included in studies of sex offenders, but they typically were discarded from analysis because of their low numbers (Muram, 1996). Another reason for this topic not being discussed is that feminists have focused on male sexual abusers and have limited discussions regarding females as abusers (Young, 1993). Yet, other feminists believe this topic should be discussed openly (K. A. Holmes, 1996). Furthering the discussion of woman sex offenders is the case of Mary LeTourneau, the thirty-five-year-old teacher who conceived two children from one of her students and who served a brief time in prison (Peterson, 1998).

Most professionals agree that female sexual abusers are much easier to treat than male abusers, but their treatment must include some issues that are generally not addressed in treating males (Lane & Lobanov-Rostovsky, 1997). Matthews (1994), who has worked clinically with female sex abusers, states that female and male sexual abusers differ. First, woman abusers take longer to forgive themselves than males. Second, woman abusers take longer to reach the stage of shame and guilt, delaying their healing. Third, woman offenders have more internal anger over abusing others. Fourth, woman offenders develop empathy toward their victims quicker than male offenders. Fifth, woman offenders tend to be less pathological than male offenders. The latter difference makes their prognosis for treatment better than males.

TECHNIQUES AND PROCEDURES OF TREATING FEMALE ADULT OFFENDERS

Strategies in the Treatment of Female Substance Abusers

A Cognitive–Behavioral Treatment Model for Cocaine Abuse Under the auspices of the National Institute of Drug Abuse, a manual has been prepared for teaching clinicians how to use cognitive–behavioral treatment for cocaine addiction (Carroll, 1998). Several reasons have been offered for why cognitive–behavioral treatment is effective with individuals suffering from cocaine addiction. First, it is short term and suited to most clinical programs. Second, it has been extensively tested and has substantial empirical support. Third, it is structured, goal oriented, and focused on an individual's present problem in controlling addiction. Fourth, it is flexible, accommodating inpatient or outpatient treatment as well as applicable to group or individual counseling. Fifth, it is in accordance with other treatments, such as pharmacotherapy. Sixth, its broad approach concurs with tasks viewed as important in successful substance abuse treatment (Carroll, 1998).

Cognitive–behavioral therapy has two critical parts—functional analysis and skill training. Functional analysis refers to the process of a client and substance abuse counselor analyzing each instance of cocaine use during treatment, which is likely to occur, especially in an outpatient setting. This means identifying the client's thoughts, feelings, and circumstances before and after the cocaine use. In the beginning of treatment, functional analysis plays a critical role in understanding why a person would use cocaine, such as interpersonal difficulties or to experience a sense of euphoria. As treatment progresses, functional analysis identifies areas that are still problematic for the client.

Skills training involves helping the cocaine abuser to unlearn behaviors tied to cocaine abuse and learn more functional habits and behaviors. When a person enters treatment, she is likely to be using cocaine as her sole means of dealing with a wide range of problems. This style of problem solving occurs, perhaps, because the individual, having used since adolescence, has never learned effective coping strategies. Another reason is that the individual learned some strategies for dealing with personal problems, but these strategies, or skills, have been eroded by continual use of cocaine. A final reason is that the individual's ability to use effective coping strategies have been severely compromised by a severe mental disorder, such as schizophrenia (Carroll, 1998).

Bolstered by these two critical components, the key interventions for cognitive–behavioral treatment to address cocaine addictions, as stated by Carroll (1998), are illustrated below.

Key Interventions

History and Relationship Building During the first interview, the clinician should spend a sufficient amount of time getting to know the client. The clinician wants to know the client's history, substance use, degree of motivation, and the circumstances of the client seeking treatment at that time. A number of open-ended questions may be asked to acquire this information, such as "Have you ever been in treatment for cocaine before?" (history), "How did your cocaine use get started?" (history), and "How do you get cocaine?" (current pattern).

Enhance Motivation As the client reports history and current practice, the clinician should listen empathetically and listen for why the client is seeking treatment at this time. The clinician should elicit self-motivational statements on the part of the client. The enhancement motivation literature recommends questions like, "What bothers you most about your cocaine use?" "It sounds like, from what you've told me, that your parents and your probation officer are worried about your cocaine use, but I was wondering how you feel about it?" To demonstrate empathy, use empathic statements, such as "You feel like you want to stop, but you're are worried because you've tried treatment before and you've gone back to cocaine use each time." The clinician should accept resistance by possibly responding that the clinician understands that the client does not see a problem and it is the client's life to live. At this point, a bit of confrontation might be therapeutic. For instance, the clinician might say that "you state that you don't have a problem but people who care about you, such as your family, are concerned and you were given a choice of either entering treatment or going to prison." The clinician should clarify that it is up to the client to change and the program cannot change the client. Then, the clinician can help the client to process what stopping cocaine use will do and what continuing cocaine use is likely to bring.

Negotiate Treatment Goals Keeping in mind that abstinence is the goal of treatment, the clinician should negotiate other treatment goals with a client. Unlike some problems, a significant reduction is not good, such as reducing outbursts from three times a day to once every two weeks. Cocaine has significant health and legal risks. Clients, sometimes, are ambivalent about stopping cocaine use altogether. Others may want only to cut down, believing that they can regain control over their lives by reducing cocaine use. However, the goal should be abstinence. Often, cocaine use may be associated with other problems, which can be negotiated with the client in terms of priority. The client may have a problem with depression, marital discord, or the legal system. These can be prioritized with the client, and significant improvement in some areas may be desirable and beneficial. However, a client's goal should not be to smoke crack cocaine "every now and then."

Present the Cognitive–Behavioral Model The clinician should present the cognitive–behavioral model, informing the client that cocaine use is viewed as learned behavior. Also, the client should be told that over time, cocaine use can affect how a person thinks, feels, and behaves. If a client understands and accepts this theoretical framework, she is more likely to believe that she can learn new habits that are functional.

Establish Treatment Ground Rules Establishing clear expectations and obligations of everyone involved is extremely important. The client should be told what is expected of her, such as attendance, collection of urine samples, and coming to treatment sober. If treatment consists of group counseling, the client should have some preliminary understanding of what the group rules are.

Introduce Functional Analysis The client should be introduced to what a functional analysis is. First, she should be told and then an illustration should be provided. For instance, the clinician would say the following. "To get an idea of how all this works, let's go through an example. Tell me all you can about the last time you used cocaine. Where were you and what were you doing? What happened before? How were you feeling? When was the first time you were aware of wanting to use? What was the high like at the beginning? What was it like later? Can you think of anything positive that happened as a result of using? What about negative consequence?" (Carroll, 1998, p. 45).

Drug Courts One of the recent changes in the handling of offenders who are addicted to drugs is the creation of drug courts. These courts and the programs that they provide, however, are not available to every defendant. Accused who have been charged with very serious criminal offenses are not likely to be processed through the drug courts. Chemically addicted accused who have been charged with drug offenses or with property crimes may find themselves in a drug court. This type of intervention would seem suitable for woman offenders given many of them come into the criminal justice system with chemical addiction problems and property or economic charges.

Drug courts are simply courts that have connected drug assessment services with alcohol and drug treatment services. The courts use their power over defendants to encourage them to participate in treatment. If the individual chooses not to participate or drops out of treatment, she is handled or processed like typical offenders

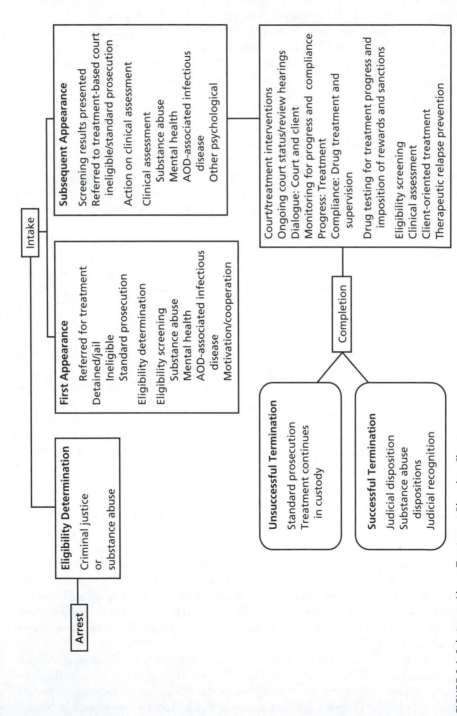

FIGURE 9.1 Substance Abuse Treatment Planning Chart

through the criminal justice system. Messalle (1997) depicts a flow chart indicating how an offender would enter the system and how she would leave. Figure 9.1 is a modified version of the system.

Pregnant Women with Drug Problems The Center of Substance Abuse Treatment recognizes that drug treatment programs must be gender specific (McPhail & Wiest, 1995). Treatment programs that serve pregnant women, and some adolescents who may be living independently, should include the following services:

1. Comprehensive inpatient and outpatient treatment on demand.
2. Comprehensive medical services.
3. Gender-specific services that are ethically and culturally sensitive. These services must respond to women's needs regarding reproductive health, sexuality, relationships, and all forms of victimization. Services must be offered in a non-judgmental manner and in a supportive environment.
4. Transportation services, including cab vouchers, bus tokens, and alternatives for women who live in communities where public transportation is cumbersome, unreliable, and unsafe.
5. Child care, baby-sitting, and therapeutic day care services for children.
6. Counseling services, including individual, group, and family therapy.
7. Vocational and educational services leading to training for meaningful employment, the General Equivalency Diploma (GED), and higher education.
8. Drug-free, safe housing.
9. Financial support services.
10. Case management services.
11. Pediatric follow-up and early intervention services.
12. Services that recognize the unique needs of pregnant, adolescent substance abusers.

Developmental Model of Recovery Many drug treatment professionals indicate that recovery is a process that develops over time. This process consists of six stages, involving the transitional stage, the stabilization period, early recovery period, middle recovery period, late recovery period, and maintenance stage. For treatment to be successful, each stage requires the completion of tasks and skills to be learned. According to Gorski and Kelley (1996), the following are the stages and the tasks and skills needed for each stage.

Transition Stage The first time an individual experiences an alcohol or drug-related problem starts the transition stage. The progression of addiction causes an individual to try several strategies to control use. Failing, the individual recognizes that safe use of alcohol or drugs is not possible. The struggle by the individual to control use reflects a conflict over personal identity. Individuals who use alcohol and drugs begin this phase thinking that their use is within normal boundaries. As the addiction worsens and control dissipates, the individual must acknowledge that she is addicted and is incapable of controlled use.

During the transition stage, addicted individuals try to stop or control their use. This is an effort to prove to themselves and others that they can use safely; however, they are doomed to fail. They will certainly fail if they are associating with other individuals who are also using and are involved in criminal activities. Drug and alcohol use in such an environment is considered normal behavior, and thus each person is reinforcing the other.

A key conclusion is that, "The major cause of inability to abstain during the transition stage is the belief that there is a way to control use."

Stabilization Period For addicted persons, the stabilization period encompasses a host of experiences. Persons experience physical withdrawal and other medical problems, learn to reduce the psychological dependency, stabilize the crisis that forced them to seek or get treatment, and learn to identify and manage symptoms of brain dysfunction. These skills prepare addicted persons for the processes of rehabilitation. Traditional treatment does not address these issues, choosing instead to focus on detoxification only. As a result, addicted persons cannot cope with the stresses and find no support in the treatment environment. They begin to use substances to cope with the stresses. With adequate treatment, mastery of these experiences takes from six weeks to six months.

A key conclusion is "The major cause of inability to abstain during the stabilization period is the lack of stabilization management skills."

Early Recovery Period This period is characterized by individuals' desire to establish a lifestyle free of drugs and alcohol. Individuals must learn about the effects of drugs and the recovery process. To break free of drugs and alcohol, addicted persons must abandon old friends and establish new friends who support a drug-free lifestyle. This could be extremely difficult for persons in the criminal justice system, who often have many associates who drink and use drugs. Still, individuals must overcome this difficulty and learn recovery-based values, thinking, feelings, and behaviors to supersede old values, thinking, feelings, and behaviors. The old behaviors and thinking make participation in a treatment program difficult. Individuals will need major intervention to learn skills necessary to lead a drug-free lifestyle. This stage lasts between one and two years.

A key conclusion is "The primary cause of relapse during the early recovery period is the lack of effective social and recovery skills necessary to build a sobriety-based lifestyle."

Middle Recovery Period Middle recovery is characterized by the emergence of an evened lifestyle. Recovering individuals, during this period, learn to mend social and personal relationships. The recovery program is modified to permit offenders to reestablish relationships, develop new friends, and set new vocational goals. Individuals begin to move from the safety and protection of the group into the mainstream to establish a new lifestyle. This period is marked by a heightened amount of stress as individuals attempt to use newly learned skills with the real-life problems.

The key conclusion is "The major cause of relapse during the middle recovery period is the stress of real-life problems."

Late Recovery Period During this stage, individuals make personality changes that would allow them to achieve more life satisfaction. This stage is akin to being self-actualized in psychotherapy. Particularly, in this late recovery period, individuals examine the values and goals that they learned in their environment. The individuals make conscious decisions about appropriate values. In normal, healthy, drug-free persons, this developmental stage occurs in their mid-twenties. In persons with drug problems and in recovery, this developmental stage occurs three to five years after individuals enter treatment regardless of the age of the individuals. As stated by Gorski and Kelley (1996), "for criminal offenders, this is the time when they learn to change self-defeating behaviors that may trigger a return to alcohol or drug use. These self-defeating behaviors often come from psychological issues starting in childhood, such as childhood physical or sexual abuse, abandonment, or cultural barriers to personal growth" (p 8).

The key conclusion is "The major cause of relapse during the late recovery period is either the inability to cope with the stress of unresolved childhood issues or an invasion of the need to develop a functional personality style."

Maintenance Stage The maintenance stage is achieved when individuals evidence continued growth and development. They cope with everyday life problems and transition without drugs and sensitize themselves to relapse. The physiology of addiction remains with individuals all their lives and any use of drugs or alcohol will rekindle the physiological, psychological, and social progression of the disease of addiction.

The key conclusion is "the major causes of relapse during the maintenance stage are the failure to maintain a recovery program and encountering major life transition."

Treating Female Sex Offenders

A theoretical basis for sexual offending that is applicable for women has been described by Saradjian (1996). Saradjian, drawing upon the proposition that a symptom is a personal solution to a problem, theorizes that an offender's sexually abusive behavior is a symptom of a problem or problems. Sexual offending represents a solution to one or more of a person's constellation of needs. These needs are power and control needs, affiliation needs, esteem needs, social needs, or physiological needs. The aim of therapy is to determine what problem or problems the sexual abuse of a child solves for the offender and to help the offender solve the problem without offending. A counselor's task is to determine which needs of the offender are satisfied by sexual offending and what internal or external processes led the offender to believe these needs could be met in an offending manner. In addition, the counselor should address the psychological defenses that rationalize offending behavior, such as distorted thinking and emotional denial and blockage. Finally, attention should be directed to societal messages that support abuse, such as adults owning children (Saradjian, 1996).

Establishing an effective therapeutic relationship with a woman sex offender is important. Women have issues with power and power imbalances. The counseling relationship represents another power situation and must be managed professionally. To address this area, Saradjian advocated forming a working alliance by use of a metaphor. Therapy is equated to a woman writing her life story. The woman has written a significant portion of the life story but has gotten stuck. Moreover, she has dropped previously completed chapters, scattering and mixing up the pages. As a result of being stuck and mixing up the pages, the woman is unsure about the plots and subplots in her story. The role of the counselor is to assist the woman in organizing the pages and help her determine how she got where she is. Also, the counselor helps the woman to determine what options she has, which helps her to finish the rest of her life story.

Once the working relationship has been established and a contract agreed on, specific areas need to be addressed in therapy. These areas are

1. The issue of the woman offender accepting that she has sexually violated a child or children and taking responsibility for her behavior
2. The issue of understanding the woman's pattern of behaviors, including distinguishing triggers that led to the offending, beliefs that led to the offending, the manner in which the woman selected her victim, and the role of sexual fantasy employed by the woman
3. The issue of the woman abuser, if any, as a child or as a woman
4. The issue of identifying and reattributing emotional feelings
5. The issue of acquiring intellectual and emotional empathy
6. The issue of relationship difficulties with partners, parents, peers, and children
7. The issue of self-esteem
8. The issue of developing an ability to develop emotionally intimate relationships
9. The issue of social skills and social network development
10. The issue of relapse prevention

In addition, other therapeutic issues need to be addressed. One issue involves the overcoming of a woman's resistance to engaging in therapy. As resistance is overcome, a counselor should be cognizant and deal with the feelings that arise from a therapeutic relationship. Particularly, the therapist should have supervision and support. The therapist should be mindful of maintaining boundaries, transference, and counter-transference. For offenders, one of the common transference issues is the offender viewing the therapist as a sexual object and interpreting the therapist's behavior as a come-on. Another issue is the viewing of the therapist as a parent figure from the past who intends to punish and berate. For the therapist, a common counter-transference issue is the over-identification with the woman offender, especially if the woman offender has been sexually or physically abused. Another issue is the feeling of intense anger toward the woman offender (Sardjian, 1996).

RESEARCHED PROGRAMS AND INTERVENTIONS

Drug Treatment for Female Prisoners and Parolees

Woman prisoners and parolees who participated in the Forever Free Substance Abuse Program, a 120-bed drug treatment program at the California Institution for Women were examined by several researchers. The program consisted of four months of treatment during a woman's last six months of confinement and six months of residential treatment while she was on parole. The six months of treatment was voluntary, but strongly recommended by the treatment staff. The aim of the program was to reduce drug use and to improve a woman's behavior both in the institution and in the community on parole. Specifically, the program included individual substance abuse counseling, specialized workshops, educational services, twelve steps programs, parole planning, family counseling, vocational/rehabilitation counseling, recreational and social activities, and urine testing (Prendergast, Wellishch, & Wong, 1996).

The researchers examined three groups of women: (1) women who completed Forever Free and stayed in the community-based residential programs for at least thirty days, (2) women who completed Forever Free but did not choose to go into the community-based residential treatment, and (3) women who volunteered for Forever Free but who did not get in. In examining parole outcome, the researchers found a significant difference. About 68.4% of the women in the residential treatment had favorable parole outcomes compared to 52.2% of the women who completed the program but did not go into the community-based program and 27.2% of the women who did not get into the treatment program (Prendergast et al., 1996). In addition, they found that when women were returned to prison, the women who had the combined treatment had the lowest rate for new criminal offenses, 33.3%. This was in contrast to the women who had just Forever Free (45.5%) and the women who did not get into the program at all (50.0%) (Prendergast et al., 1996). A reasonable conclusion drawn from this program is that a holistic, substance abuse programs for woman prisoners, combined with community support on parole, are significantly rehabilitative.

Treating Dually Diagnosed Females

Discovering that little empirical evidence existed for women with a dual diagnosis of substance abuse and posttraumatic disorder, Najavits, Weiss, Shaw, and Muenz (1998) sought a developmental grant to study the effectiveness of treatment. The treatment was cognitive–behavioral and was delivered during twenty-four structured sessions. It was equally divided among cognitive, behavioral, and interpersonal coping skills. All the sessions focused on issues relevant to this population, including asking for help, self-care, setting boundaries, self-nurturing, resisting triggers, and HIV risk. The program was called "Seeking Safety," which refers to the overriding creed of the treatment program. Safety places essential priority on both posttraumatic disorder and drug dependency. Specifically, it means abstaining from all substances, reducing self-destructive behavior, creating a network of support, and protecting oneself from the dangers of both disorders, such as HIV risks and domestic violence.

The program designers strove to make treatment engaging and obtainable in order to increase participants' involvement. Strategies to achieve this end included beginning each session with an inspirational quote or maxim, illustrations, practice exercises, and use of simple language. For instance, instead of therapists discussing cognitive restructuring, the therapists used rethinking. The therapists used repeatedly a few core principles throughout treatment, such as "help from others is essential." They also used memory exercises to help participants remember important objectives. The therapists' tone was current focused, compassionate, and optimistic. To keep the therapists' focused and adhered to treatment principles, they were provided with a guide for each session, handouts for participants to guide skill rehearsal, and a feedback sheet for participants. In addition, therapists were given extensive background materials, such as a literature review on women with substance abuse and mental health problems, use of praise and accountability with treatment clients, and how to recognize and manage counter-transference.

Najavits and colleagues (1998) evaluated the effectiveness of the above-described treatment. Particularly, they were interested in client retention, client satisfaction, therapist adherence to treatment principles, and comparison of completers and dropouts at pretest and posttest. They were not able to use an experimental design or quasi-experimental design, an acknowledged limitation of their research. They used instead a pretest and posttest design with a three-month follow-up. They found that 63% were completers and 37% were dropouts. Participants who completed were fairly satisfied with the program. The mean was 3.03 on a scale from one to four, with four being very satisfied. Therapist adherence to treatment, the group process, and competence was good. A comparison of completers and dropouts showed surprisingly that completers were more impaired than dropouts. In terms of outcome, there was a significant decrease in substance use. This was measured by self-reports with use of urinalysis and alcohol breath tests for corroboration. A decrease was found in post traumatic stress disorder and trauma-related symptoms. Also, significant improvement was found in cognitive, behavioral, and interpersonal domains (Najavits et al., 1998). Though limited in the research design, the program had a positive effect on women.

Treating Pregnant Substance-Abusing Females

Several researchers studied whether contingency management interventions would be effective in treating cocaine-dependent pregnant women. To be eligible for the study, the women had to have used cocaine during their current pregnancy but ceased use more than thirty days before entering the study. The women were referred to the program by self, court, and probation and parole. These categories were stratified and then randomly assigned to treatment and control groups. Women in the treatment group received contingency management interventions, which were intended to reinforce both cocaine abstinence and compliance with prenatal care. Particularly, women earned monetary reinforcers of $18 for each cocaine-free urine sample. For three required drug-free urine samples and attendance at required prenatal visits, the women were eligible for a $20 bonus. The researchers examined six outcome measures—retention in treatment, percentage of cocaine-free urine samples, percentage of other drug use, compliance with prenatal visits, occurrence of any of four adverse prenatal outcomes associated with cocaine use and/or poor prenatal care, and changes in the Addiction Severity Index. Of these outcome measures, there were significant differences in the percentage of compliance with prenatal visits and the number of women who experienced adverse perinatal outcomes, such that women in the treatment group performed better than the women in the control group (Elk, Mangus, Rhoades, Andres, & Grabowski, 1998).

In another program for pregnant women, Corse and Smith (1998) reported the results of a program for substance-abusing pregnant women in Philadelphia, Pennsylvania. The program was called ANGELS, but the authors did not state what ANGELS is an acronym for. The ANGELS program had two aims: lessen substance abuse among pregnant women and improve birth outcome by facilitating prenatal care and addiction-related services. ANGELS was provided in an outpatient prenatal care unit of a hospital. Most of the women serviced were Medicaid recipients and about 70% of them were white.

ANGELS was developed from a holistic philosophy built around an expanded role of nurse-midwifery. Instead of just conducting standard screening and referrals, the nurse conducted regular assessment, education, intervention, and referral. The nurse-midwife concentrated on developing trusting relationships with the pregnant women and addressed substance abuse issues as they came within the provision of prenatal care.

The ANGELS program included several components that were geared toward reducing substance use and increase visits for prenatal care. First, there was a routine or standard intervention that was provided to all pregnant women. These services consisted of (1) assignment to a certified midwife who provided continuity of care, (2) longer appointment times when meeting with pregnant women to allow a full discussion of psychosocial concerns and substance abuse issues, (3) assessment of substance use by the certified midwife, (4) initial urine screen, (5) preventive education during prenatal appointments and pregnancy classes, (6) follow-up on all substance abuse issues during each visit, and (7) increased visits for women with substance abuse during pregnancy.

The second component involved specialized interventions, which were provided for all pregnant women with substance abuse problems. The services provided were (1) on-site individual and group counseling with master's level counselors, (2) referrals to intensive alcohol and drug counseling or social services, (3) home visits for women who consistently miss appointments, (4) child care whenever women are participating in programming, and (5) transportation vouchers.

Corse and Smith evaluated ANGELS. One area of interest was the continuity of care. The researchers found that the likelihood of seeing the same certified nurse midwife increased from 20% before implementation of ANGELS to 80% after implementation. For women with substance abuse problems the increase was 84%. They used the level of change in substance abuse as one key variable and found that 51% of the women abstained from substances during pregnancy, 35% of the women had reduced their use of substances, and 14% showed no change in use. They, then, sought to determine which variables differentiated use among these three categories of women. They found that the discriminating variables were the severity of cannabis use, severity of cocaine use, severity of psychosocial problems, the number of weeks of gestation at intake, and participation by a certified midwife coordinator and addiction counselor (Corse & Smith, 1998).

Treating Substance-Abusing Parents

The Coalition on Addiction, Pregnancy, and Parenting (CAPP) of Boston, Massachusetts, received a grant from the Center for Substance Abuse Prevention for a demonstration project. The project consisted of several components, including a parenting component. Delivered at two long-term residential substance abuse treatment programs for women in Boston, the parenting component involved specialized individual and group counseling for both mothers and children (Camp & Finkelstein, 1997).

The individual counseling consisted of parenting concerns, a child, or the parent-child dyad. The group counseling consisted of a parenting skills group, a child development group, and a mothers' support group, all led by CAPP counselors. Of these three groups, the most structured group was the parenting skills group. It utilized the *Nurturing Program for Parents of Children Birth to Five Years Old*, which was developed by Dr. Stephen J. Bavolek. The curriculum required a two-and-one-half-hour session a week for twenty-three weeks. Bavolek's curriculum addressed parenting skills and behaviors. Specifically, it emphasized four areas of parental behavior associated with abusive and neglectful parenting behaviors—inappropriate expectations, lack of empathy, corporal punishment, and role reversal. In addition, information was provided about child development and parenting issues. Skill development consisted of teaching parent behavior management, communication, and developing play activities for children. Group sessions focused on discussing the inception and effectiveness of parenting behaviors and changing attitudes, values, and beliefs. The nurturing program was modified to serve the needs of clients and the program. Role-playing and participatory exercises were experiential techniques used to help parents learn (Camp & Finkelstein, 1997).

The other two groups were not as structured as the parenting skill group. The child development group offered specialized information about children's developmental stages, skills, and abilities from birth to three years of age. The mothers' support group provided parents the opportunity to share daily experiences and to receive support in parenting efforts. Following completion of the program, pregnant women received aftercare services consisting of home visits, counseling, and case management services (Camp & Finkelstein, 1997).

Camp and Finkelstein (1997) evaluated the demonstration project. The aim of the evaluation was to determine whether the demonstration project met its goals and whether it has a positive impact on participants. The researchers used a quasi-experimental design comparing one program to another program. They referred to these programs as Program A and Program B. Program A had seventy-nine women and Program B had ninety-one. Program A was for pregnant women, and Program B was for women who were parents. They used five instruments to measure the parenting skills and self-esteem. These instruments were the Intake Interview, the Adult-Adolescent Parenting Inventory, the Hudson Self-Esteem Index, the Nursing Child Assessment Satellite Training Feeding Scale, and the Participant Evaluation of the Parenting Program. Some of these instruments were administered three times. The first measurement occurred at admission to the nurturing program. The second measurement occurred three months after admission or at discharge if participants left before three months. The third measurement occurred at completion of the parenting skill training or discharge from treatment if it occurred. The aim was to make comparisons among Time 1, Time 2, and Time 3 (Camp & Finkelstein, 1997).

The results were that almost 80% of the participants were African Americans. Most of the women were poly-drug users with 92% using alcohol, 91% using crack, and 84% using marijuana. In terms of self-esteem, there were significant differences from admission to discharge. The range for the Hudson Scale of Self Esteem is 0 to 100, with higher scores meaning lower self-esteem. Thirty is the cutoff score, so that scores above 30 are an indication of significant self-esteem problems. For Program A, at admission or Time 1, the mean score was 51, for Time 2 the mean score was 42, and for Time 3, the mean score was 35. These scores show a steady decline but with some problem at discharge. For Program B, the mean score at Time 1 was 43, for Time 2 it was 37, and for Time 3 the mean score was 29. All comparisons (i.e., Time 1 with Time 3, Time 1 with Time 2, and Time 2 with Time 3) for both programs were statistically significant (Camp & Finkelstein, 1997).

With respect to the Adult-Adolescent Parenting Inventory, the scores for it ranged from 1 to 10. Scores 1 and 2 indicate significant deficiency in parenting behavior, and scores of 5 or 6 are average. Seven to 10 indicate very appropriate parenting skills. For Program A, Inappropriate Expectations increase from 6.1 to 7.3, Lack of Empathy from 4.9 to 6.4, Belief in Corporal Punishment from 7.0 to 8.2, and Role Reversal from 5.9 to 7.7. The measures for these four areas were statistically significant from Time 1 to Time 3; however, for Inappropriate Expectations, there was an initial decrease from Time 1 to Time 2. For Program B, there were significant differences in two areas, Lack of Empathy and Role Reversal. From Time 1 to Time 3, Lack of Empathy increased from 3.6 to 5.0, and Role Reversal from 5.5 to 6.2. For Inappropriate Expectations there was a decrease in Time 2 from Time 1, but Time 3 revealed a rebound. The same pattern was found for Corporal Punishment, a decrease in Time 2, but a rebound in Time 3. The rebound, however, was not great enough to be statistically significant (Camp & Finkelstein, 1997).

For the feeding scale, researchers noted that racial and educational factors of the mother and the age of the child affected the assessment of this scale. The researchers' analysis was that there was improvement in interactional patterns between mothers and children. Finally, participants in the program reported favorable assessment of the programs. More parents indicated that they were giving more praises for appropriate behavior than punishment for inappropriate behavior. They also reported that they were spending more positive time with the children (Camp & Finkelstein, 1997).

Treating Traumatized Female Prisoners

As the literature indicates, some women had traumatizing experiences prior to imprisonment. Valentine (1998) tested the effectiveness of an intervention called traumatic incident reduction (TIR) on traumatized female inmates at the Federal Correction Institute in Tallahassee, Florida. The theoretical basis of TIR is broad. TIR is informed partly by psychodynamic theory, behavior theory, cognitive theory, and cathartic theory. The intervention derived from these theories, TIR, is brief. Similar to imaginal flooding, it is delivered usually in one session that is a memory-based intervention. A memory-based intervention, such as TIR, suggests that symptoms that female inmates have are related to past events, and an effective resolution of those symptoms requires targeting the memory. Specifically, the aim of the research was to examine the effectiveness of TIR on depression, anxiety, low self-efficacy, and symptoms of posttraumatic syndrome disorder (PTSD), such as intrusion, avoidance, and arousal.

At the Federal Correction Institute, 148 women met the criteria of having experienced trauma and were willing to participate in the study. These women were randomly assigned to treatment and control groups. Measures were taken at pretest, posttest, and three months after the posttest. Inmates in the experimental group had significant decreases in depression, anxiety, and symptoms of PTSD. Furthermore, inmates in the experimental group had a significant increase in self-efficacy compared with the control group (Valentine, 1998).

UNRESEARCHED PROGRAMS
AND INTERVENTIONS

Afrocentric Drug Programs

According to some treatment professionals, an intervention is more likely to be successful if the intervention is culturally congruent. By culturally congruent, they mean that the intervention is tailored toward the minority group being served (Longshore, Grills, Annon, & Grady, 1998; Kalichman, Kelly, Hunter, Murphy, & Tyler, 1993). One Afrocentric program believed to be appropriate for African American women is called the Engagement Project (Longshore et al., 1998).

The Engagement Project aims to connect the client with counseling in the first session. The belief is that the first session is critical, and if the first session is positive and viewed as beneficial, the client is mostly likely to continue. During the first session, the client is seen by a counselor and a former drug user. The former drug user assumes the role of a peer and assists in making the connection to the process. The three sit for a traditional African American meal while they watch a fifteen-minute video on the causes of drug use and the road to recovery. After the meal and video, the three talk, using the video as a spark for discussions. Among the questions posed are "What issues in the video did the client find most interesting and personally relevant? What aspects of his or her own drug use raise feelings of guilt or ambivalence? What does the client want to do about these feelings?" (Longshore et al., 1998, p. 320). The aim is to guide the client toward a decision to proceed further into the recovery process. This next step could be cognitive, such as reconsidering the negative and positive aspects of drug use, or could be behavioral, such as deciding to enter a self-help program or get further treatment.

The entire treatment approach (i.e., the conceptual basis, intervention goals, and intervention techniques) for the Engagement Project is based on Afrocentric principles. The conceptual basis for the Engagement Project is based on Nguzo Saba, which are seven desired values in African and African American culture. According to Karenga (1988), the values are

> *Umoja* (unity in the family, community, nation, and race)
> *Kujichagulia* (self-determination in all areas)
> *Ujima* (collective work and responsibility for community problems)
> *Ujamaa* (cooperative economics in the community)
> *Nia* (purpose in resurrection the great African past)
> *Kuumba* (creativity in community life)
> *Imani* (faith in other Africans and justness of our struggle)

Central to these seven principles is the idea of communalism or collective support. Themes from these seven values are imbued in the fifteen-minute video and counseling sessions. For instance, drug addiction is presented as an individual problem and as a community problem exacerbated by uneven power differentials between African American and white communities. Also, the road to recovery is suggested as the acquiring of power in terms of knowledge, spiritual insight, and community health. Recovery is not only seen as beneficial to the individual but also for the family and the larger community.

The intervention goals were drawn from the transtheoretical stages of change model. This model posits that individuals with behavior problems experience several conditions. Some are eager to change, some are indecisive about change, and some are not ready to change. A successful intervention is more likely to occur if the strategy is geared toward the stage of the client. Modified for drug intervention, the transtheoretical stages, seemingly patterned after Prochaska, DiCemente, and Norcross's (1992) readiness to change process stages, are

Precontemplation: This stage consists of a person who uses drugs, does not recognize a problem, and is not contemplating change.
Contemplation: This stage consists of a person who recognizes a problem with drugs and is contemplating change.
Preparation: This stage consists of a person who is earnestly considering changing behavior.
Action: This stage consists of a person who has made an apparent behavior change, which involves ceasing drug use temporarily or entering a treatment program.
Maintenance: This stage consists of a person who uses drugs who labors to avert relapse and fortifies steps performed in the action stage.

The Engagement Project assumes that its clients are individuals from the early stages. Hence, the intervention is designed to move clients from the precontemplation and contemplation stages to the preparation and action stages. The affected processes are conscious raising, self-revaluation, dramatic relief, and environmental reevaluation. According to Longshores and associates (1998)

> to maintain cultural congruence, we articulated these processes in terms consistent with the Nguzo Saba. For example, we sought to raise user's consciousness about the consequences of drug use in language congruent with the principle of purpose (nia). We reviewed the effects of racism on personal behavior and traced the effects of each person's behavior on the wider community. As another example, we attempted to stimulate a process of self-reevaluation in terms congruent with the principle of self-determination (kujichagulia). In the video and counseling session, we encouraged users to consider their drug use as a barrier to personal accountability and to developing their full potential. Finally, to tap emotional aspects of change (dramatic relief), we included in the video several highly charged scenes involving the consequences of drug use for self, loved ones, and the community. (pp. 323–324)

A number of interventions were utilized in the Engagement Project. First, brief intervention was used. The counseling literature reveals that brief intervention is effective. It consists of minimal counseling, viewing a video, or receipt of self-help manuals. Moreover, its effectiveness has been reported as due to six elements— feedback, advice, responsibility, a menu of alternative strategy, empathy, and self-efficacy. These elements are utilized by counselors in the Engagement Project. Second, focused dyadic counseling is employed as an intervention because it has been shown to be effective in working with African American clients. Third, motivational interviewing is employed and is critical when clients are in the early stages. It consists of expressing empathy, demonstrating discrepancy between current behavior and goals, avoiding arguments, rolling with resistance, and supporting self-efficacy (Longshore et al., 1998).

Endorsing these principles also, Jackson (1995), observing that African American women increasingly are involved in the criminal justice system for drug offenses and noting that a number of drug-involved women do not successfully complete treatment, extols the utility of an Afrocentric drug treatment program for African American women and their children. According to Jackson, the Center for Substance Abuse Treatment has underwritten a residential treatment program that principally espoused an Afrocentric perspective. This program is called *Iwo San,* which is a Swahili word for "House of Healing." This program provides a multistage treatment program for women and their children. When the residential stage is completed, the women return to Iwo San for aftercare, consisting of individual counseling, group counseling, and other needed services.

Incorporating the writings of African American scholars, the Afrocentric perspective involves a continuous process that stresses a powerful sense of spirituality, deep respect for tradition, harmony with nature, the centrality of community, life as a series of passages, the significance of elders, and the creation of self-identity. Iwo San, however, emphasizes spirituality, community, respect for tradition, harmony with nature, and the creation of self-identity and dignity.

Specifically, in Iwo San, spirituality does not mean God, but that spirit is in everything—people, the wind, and trees. Attention is given to helping women understand and acknowledge their power. Emphasis is placed on women's strengths and accomplishments, and these factors are part of the spiritual universe. Harmony with nature refers to the accordance of the spiritual, mental, and physical aspects. When a woman uses drugs, however, harmony is disrupted. The importance of community involves participation of the community in the treatment. They come to programs and craft exhibits. Moreover, the community participates in the treatment. In the Afrocentric program, efforts are made to eliminate the notion that the community or nonclients cannot know or participate in treatment. Breach of confidentiality is a nonissue. Deep respect for tradition involves both clients and treatment staff undergoing rites of passages. More effective counseling occurs when client and staff eliminate the distance between them.

The rites of passage ceremony involves learning about responsibility for one's self, one's affinity group, and one's village or community. The Council of Elders evolves from the rites of passage. Traditionally, elders were selected because of their sex, age, recognition, and standing in the community. In Iwo San, elderhood is determined by the degree of esteem and perceived wisdom as determined by fellow residents and staff. The creation of self-identity and dignity is important. Self-identity comes from learning about oneself and one's cultural identity. Dignity comes from knowing about the link to historical past and ancestors and knowing that one is not responsible only for oneself but others within Iwo San.

While these factors are essential to Afrocentric treatment, other issues are important from an Afrocentric perspective. There are the issues of drug abuse, length of treatment, and discharge. Drug abuse is viewed as a means of forming a meaningful and worthwhile self-concept, although it may be considered deviant and dysfunctional by some professionals. Therefore, the question is not, are drugs bad, but what societal factors lead African American women to adopt drug abuse as a viable option. Participation in treatment, it is hoped, helps a woman to develop different roles other than drug user. Therapy, or the length of treatment, is variable and depends upon the woman. Women have different issues and helping to resolve these issues take different lengths of time. Discharge is determined by elders, according to the treatment policy. However, clients who violate rules or relapse are given a sabbatical, but they are permitted to return (Jackson, 1995).

The Iwo San program is delivered in four phases. During the first phase, an intensive rites of passage is provided for both staff and clients. In the second phase, program administrators identify and establish a council of elders. During the third phase, an integration of Afrocentric programming and treatment activities is accomplished. During the fourth phase, staff and researchers conduct a study of the effectiveness of the program that is in process (Jackson, Stephens, & Smith, 1997).

In a final Afrocentric program, Poitier, Niliwaanbieni, and Rowe (1997) describe what they called an innovative program for drug-addicted African American women and mothers. Employing Afrocentric principles, the aim was to treat and restore the family. Principally, it uses the rites of passage, which combines four central principles. These are restraint, respect, responsibility, and reciprocity. Poitier, Niliwaanbieni, and Rowe contend that if embodied into a drug treatment program, these four principles "can inspire participants and their family members to make personal life changes and to grow mentally, spiritually, and physically healthy" (p. 174).

The program is designed around transition through various rite stages. A *rite* is a ceremony marked by cultural and sometimes religious formal activities. A rite is scheduled at important cultural points to symbolize both an individual's passage from one state to another and others' recognition of the individual's undergoing the passage. According to Poitier and colleagues, there are five major rites of passage in African experiences. There are rite of birth, rite of puberty, rite of marriage and parenthood, rite of eldership, and rite of death.

The intervention program prepares an individual for the rite of passage within a collective framework. This means that the family, children, and close relatives are viewed as one unit or system. The family rite of passage aspect is carried out in four phases or stages of treatment. There are Genesis, Initiation, Passage/Transformation, and Sande Society. Each phase is integrated with the four basic principles discussed above. Accordingly, the Genesis phase is linked with restraint, the Initiation phase is linked with respect, the Passage/Transformation phase is linked to responsibility, and the Sande Society phase is linked to reciprocity. These phases and principles are not sequential but overlapped and intertwined.

This program is best provided in an environment that entails communal living. Ideally, it should consist of residential treatment with quarters for a woman and her children. Space should be available for a communal group meeting, child care center, officers for recreational, vocational, medical, and treatment staff (Poitier et al., 1997).

Phase One: Genesis Lasting about four months, the Genesis Phase focuses on the ethical principal of restraint. The woman is required to begin addressing the forces that precipitated her abuse of drugs. A woman's addressing these forces successfully is important because "only then can she learn to live without abusive substances, and only then, can she learn what restraint means to a female individual within a family and within the larger communities of which she is a part" (Poiter et al., 1997,

p. 183). Restraint means refraining from doing one's own thing and one's rights must be balanced against the group (i.e., the family and community). During Genesis, focus is placed on a woman's personal development within the context of group participating and bonding. Furthermore, attention is directed at detoxification, regular exercise, nutrition, training in parenting skills, daily living skills, and problem-solving skills. A woman's readiness to move to the next phase is made by the staff and women in Phase Four, the Sande Society women.

Phase Two: Initiation Also lasting about four months, the Initiation Phase focuses on the ethical principle of respect. This means respecting oneself, respecting one's family, respecting staff members, respecting rules, and respecting the community. There is a continuation from Phase One of the structured daily schedule, daily living skills, communal living, and collective responsibility for maintaining clean living quarters. Also, emphasis is placed upon individual counseling. Womanhood, sisterhood, and motherhood are paramount in this phase as well. Activities are provided to increase the women's cognizance of their personal developmental needs. Accordingly, the women are provided spiritual counseling, academic testing, and the development of parental skills. For women with children, considerable emphasis is devoted to stressing that their needs and desires must be subordinated to the children's development and nurturing. Mothers are taught that a child's development depends on their guidance, nurturance, and direction. Besides providing a child with guidance, nurturance, and direction, emphasis is placed on the parent-child relationship. The staff teaches ways to lessen the "diminution of frenzy," which is the condition of responding as if enraged. Mothers are given skills to diminish the strength of negative reactions to their children. In its place, they are taught more positive and purposeful responses. To assist reunification with their children, women in Phase Two are required to partake in bonding activities by working in the child care unit. Children also are counseled because they may have come to believe that their mothers do not want them. As a way of helping to build community, children refer to every woman as *Mama*. So, a woman in the residential program may be Mama Cora, Mama Betty, Mama Mildred, and a staff member may be Mama Thelma.

Phase Three: Passage/Transformation The third phase emphasizes the ethical principle of responsibility. Also, there is a continuation of activities from the Phase Two with less supervision by the staff. The aim is for women to become more self-directed and more independent. They learn how to ask for help. They learn more about African history and culture in this phase. The theory is that substance abuse occurs, in part, because of a lack of self-knowledge and values. Their conditions, lack of self-knowledge and values, come from their ignorance about their culture and history. Furthermore, addiction is likened to slavery, and succumbing to addiction is a type of enslavement. The last aspect of this stage is volunteer employment and the aim is to develop a work ethic and show their children that they can function in the community and can, potentially, take care of them financially.

Phase Four: The Sande Society The Sande Society is the last phase of the treatment program and centers on the ethical principle of reciprocity. Taken from the

Bundu society in Sierra Leone, the Sande Society represents a rite of passage for adolescent females into the role of adult woman capable of full societal participation. Entrance into Sande Society occurs in a private ceremony attended by the woman aspirant, her grandmother if available, female staff members, and the Sande Society Council members. After the private ceremony, a public ceremony that is attended by women in Phases One, Two, and Three, as well as family and friends occurs. At this public ceremony, the woman receives an African name and Sande Society beads. The beads recognize each year of participation in the program and recovery. Also, the woman is reminded of the challenges of life as she is received into the Sande Society. This occasion is festive, marked by speeches and African dances. As a member of Sande Society, a woman is expected to demonstrate considerable responsibility. She is expected to assist in program planning and to assist the women in the other three phases, which demonstrate their reciprocity.

Solution-Focused Intervention for Alcohol-Dependent Mothers

As stated earlier in this chapter, some substance-abusing women encounter problems with the criminal justice system due to charges of child abuse and neglect. A significant number of single parents experience problems with parenting when they have substance abuse issues. The problem is often exacerbated by the family structure that exists in many single-parent homes. Older children are often "parentified," which means that they have been thrust in the roles of mini-parents. Often, a boy becomes the man of the house, and a girl becomes the mother's confidant. As a single parent with an alcohol dependency problem struggles with recovery, taking the role of a functioning parent is made more difficult because of the structure of the family. To intervene in such situations, solution-focused therapy has been recommended for the parent and her children (Juhnke & Coker, 1997).

While many therapies targets deficits, weaknesses, and limitations, solution-focused therapy stresses competencies, strengths, and possibilities. Clients are deemed to have personal resources with which, with some guidance and assistance by a counselor, they are capable of solving many of their own problems. As averred by Juhnke and Coker (1997), "when using solution-focused counseling with recovering, alcohol-dependent, single parent mothers and their children, emphasis is placed on creating solutions and identifying successful behaviors that establish functional family dynamics and healthy hierarchical structures" (p. 78). As such, the term *solution-focused* is used here in the context of family therapy with the children being viewed as clients, too.

The solution-focused intervention model consists of several components—taking a history, identifying and establishing family goals, implementing successful interactions, and identifying progress. Before the beginning of family therapy, the therapist should meet with the parent individually. The purpose is to learn more about the mother's addiction and recovery experiences. Learning about the issues leading to the mother's addiction, the types of drugs used, the frequency of use, treatment history, relapse history, and the reasons for seeking treatment at that point are vitally important.

Further, during this history taking, the clinician elicits information that reveals the mother's perceived parenting strengths and resources. For instance, if the mother states that she does not engage in a particular activity in her children's presence or terminated a relationship with a man who did not like her children, this type of revelation would be reframed as strengths. The clinician could emphasize the mother's desire to protect her children or the mother evidencing that she cares about her children being accepted. Then, the clinician can ask about other efforts to protect her children or the mother's sensitivity to her children being accepted.

Family treatment goals are established, then. One type of goal is a specific goal, such as establishing the accomplishment of a specific task in six weeks. Another beneficial practice is to establish session goals. In other words, the family establishes goals or a goal for each session. If the mother and children have difficulty expressing specific or session goals, one technique is to ask a "miracle" question or a "fast-forward" question. A miracle question is phrased this way. "If a miracle happened tonight and you awoke tomorrow morning noting that things had improved as you expect they will by the end of our eighth counseling session, what would be the first behavior you noticed yourself doing differently within this family?" "If a miracle happened just before you got into the arguments you have with your daughter and instead of arguing you found yourself enjoying a conversation with her, what would be the first thing you would notice yourself doing differently?" An example of a fast-forward question is "If I were to make a videotape of your family today and fast forward to the end of our counseling sessions eight weeks into the future, and make another videotape of this family, what would I be seeing this family do differently?" "What will your family members be doing in the second videotape that they weren't doing in the first?" (Juhnke & Coker, 1997, p. 81). These are just some of the questions that can be used to prod goal settings.

As counseling continues, the clinician should review with the family progress made in achieving goals. If some goals have been achieved, the family is more likely to continue working on other goals. As stated by Juhnke and Coker, "we have used the described solution-focused counseling intervention with over 180 recovering, alcohol-dependent, single-parent mothers and their children. These mothers have generally indicated that the described intervention increased parenting confidence, increased parental satisfaction, and contribute to their alcohol abstinence. It seemed particularly important to these mothers to understand that they were capable of using existing strengths and resources to create positive personal and familial changes. Most children who participated in the described intervention reported a noticeable increase in family harmony and greater family order" (Juhnke & Coker, 1997, p. 86).

SUMMARY

This chapter describes the treatment needs of women with substance abuse problems, including the needs of African American women. A substance abuse treatment-planning chart was presented. Next, this chapter described a recovery model that consisted of six stages. A neglected area in the treatment of sex offenders is that of woman offenders. This chapter discussed issues related to the treatment of such offenders. A discussion of researched and unresearched programs for woman offenders was presented.

KEY TERMS

Drug courts
Center for substance
  abuse treatment
University of Rhode
  Island Change
  Assessment Scale
  (URICA)

Functional analysis
Holistic treatment
Developmental model
  of recovery
Traumatic incident
  reduction (TIR)
Family rites of passage

Parentified
Solution-focused
  intervention
"Miracle" questions

10

※ ※ ※

Treating Male Adult Offenders

※ INTRODUCTION

Like juvenile males who break the law, adult males who break the law are of considerable concern to society. Juvenile and adult males commit many of the same offenses, but adults commit more of them (Bureau of Justice Statistics, 1997). Murders, robberies, and sexual assaults most often are committed by adult males (Bureau of Justice Statistics, 1997; Hageman & Sigler, 1998). In addition, adult males are charged with domestic violence. Criminal justice policy makers have concluded that many persons in prisons have substance abuse problems, which exacerbate their criminality (Wexler, 1995). As a consequence, treatment has been advocated, and sometimes mandated, for offenders with drug problems, as well as offenders who have engaged in random violence, sexual assaults, and domestic violence (Alexander, 1998). For instance, often many persons charged with assault or domestic violence are mandated for anger management counseling (Tolman, Edleson, & Fendrich, 1996).

In addition, a major focus of policy makers is treating substance abuse among male adult offenders (Milas, 1997; Siegal & Cole, 1993). As an illustration, the Texas legislature passed a bill authorizing the creation of substance abuse treatment facilities. The purpose of this bill is to provide community-based treatment for probationers with drug and alcohol problems. One such facility has been created in Dallas County and is called the Dallas County Judicial Treatment Center (DCJTC). DCJTC provided a 300-bed residential treatment program based on a twelve-step model. Two hundred beds are designated for primary care, and 100 beds for aftercare, which is called Phase IV. Phase IV is essentially for probationers who do not have support systems in the community, and this part of treatment lasts for three months. In addition, graduates of primary treatment and Phase IV are mandated to participate in outpatient treatment for up to six months. The actual treatment consists of a continuum of care, involving life-skills training, drug education, and group counseling (Knight & Hiller, 1997).

Sometimes, substance-abusing offenders are treated in boot camps. In Texas, the Harris County Adult Probation Department created a program that it called the Court Regimented Intensive Probation Program (CRIPP). This program is a ninety-day program that is designed to be an intermediary program between regular probation and prison. Participants are sentenced to the program by a judge. The probationers are assigned probation officers who work with the offenders while they are in the boot camp.

The services provided are geared to meet probationers' medical, vocational, physical, and social needs. In addition, drug and alcohol counseling is provided to improve probationers' coping and life skills (Anderson & Dyson, 1996).

Anger management counseling has been viewed as vital in working with offenders (Beck & Fernandez, 1998; Sappington, 1996; Valliant & Raven, 1994; Valliant, Ennis, & Raven-Brooks, 1995). It is believed critical because of the link between poor anger control and violent, assaultive behaviors. For instance, a person with poor anger control may engage in an aggravated assault, sexual assault, or domestic violence. In correctional institutions, poor anger control is linked to assault by prisoners on other prisoners and staff (Ward & Baldwin, 1997). While anger management programs have been developed for prisoners, most of the development has involved systems management (Ward & Baldwin, 1997).

THE CONTEXT OF TREATING
MALE ADULT OFFENDERS

On a given day, 234,000 offenders convicted of rape or sexual assaults are under the care, custody, or control of corrections agencies (Greenfeld, 1997). Approximately, 60% of this total is supervised in the community (Greenfeld, 1997). The violent sex offender tends to be male, white, and in his thirties (Greenfeld, 1997). Victims of sex offenders are more likely to be female, and the female tends to know the offender, who is usually a family member, intimate, or acquaintance (Greenfeld, 1997).

Echoing other clinicians, Perkins (1991) maintains that "the context in which treatment occurs can be as important in determining outcome as the therapy itself, and yet its influence is often overlooked in formal accounts of treatment" (p. 152). With respect to sex offenders in secure settings, these central issues are denial, motivation to change, and sincere investment in the process of treatment (Perkins, 1991). These issues are especially important because a growing number of states are transferring, by civil commitment, sex offenders who are incarcerated in prison systems and nearing release to mental hospitals for involuntary treatment (Alexander, 2000), adversely affecting their motivation for treatment and active participation in treatment. Furthermore, the prison system fosters denial in that sex offenders, and especially child sex offenders, are despised by the general prison population. Sometimes, child molesters are assaulted by other prisoners. If the sex offender is small in stature and relatively young, he may be sexually assaulted himself. As a consequence, denying one is guilty and attributing one's imprisonment to a lying child and the child's vindictive mother is protective in nature. If accepted by other inmates, the sex offender may be spared from attacks.

A number of professionals have discussed the context surrounding battering. In a comprehensive review, Brandl (1990) identifies four areas of concerns, including ending violent, abusive, and controlling behavior; holding batterers accountable for their behavior; the effects on battered women; and community interaction and social action. She describes the philosophies of various programs, such as insight, system theory, cognitive–behavioral, and sociopolitical. Then she specifies the treatment methods used, which are individual, couples, and group counseling. She recites the orientations, which are social service, grassroots, and coordinated community response. Brandl asks whether programs for batterers are effective. From these areas, several elements relevant to counseling and criminal justice emerge.

First, the most frequently used method is group counseling and is used within the context of the Duluth Model. Widely adopted by a number of batterers' programs nationwide, the Duluth model is considered an educational intervention that was developed by Michael Paymar and Ellen Pence. It examines eight themes consisting of intimidation, emotional abuse, isolation, minimizing, denying and blaming, using children, using male privilege, economic abuse, and coercion and threats. During the first week, the men learn about abusive behavior through videotapes. In the second week, the emphasis is on how individual group members abuse and control their mates. During the third week, the members learn and practice nonviolent alternatives and behaviors.

With respect to the effectiveness of battering programs, Brandl (1990) reviews first the issues for determining whether programs for batterers are successful. She examined limitations for programs that strove to educate abusers, recidivism, attribution rates, types of abusers, and special population (e.g., men of color, older men, gay men, female batterers, and lesbian batterers). Brandl concludes that the research was limited due to methodological problems, including the lack of attention to other variables in explaining abusers' behaviors.

Edleson (1995), noting the complexity of the problem, contends that one cannot say yes or no to the question of whether batterers' programs work. A central problem is the criteria for success. Differences exist regarding success. Some argue that an elimination of physical violence is success, but others include mental violence and efforts to eradicate women's relationship oppression as the criteria for success. Critics of the latter position contend that it is unfair to require or legally mandate that some men, mostly minority and lower class, give up power and control tactics in their relationships while other men, wealthy and privileged, do not. Simply, poor and powerless men are compelled to achieve perfect, egalitarian relationships (Edleson, 1996).

Though the rate of drug-abusing offenders has increased faster for some groups more than others, without a doubt, the group with the greatest volume of drug-abusing offenders is males. For instance, Ohio operates more than twenty-two correctional institutions. It has one maximum-security prison and two prerelease centers for women. The remaining institutions are designated as male prisons with the largest prison having over 4,000 prisoners. Thus, in terms of sheer numbers, male prisoners consume a very large proportion of all correctional dollars. Given that sometimes the building of new prisons has not kept up with the demand and given the advocacy of some criminal justice professionals, intermediate sanctions that are less expensive than prisons have increased considerably. Hence, more offenders reside in the community than in prisons. They are found on probation and parole and in a variety of community programs (Aukerman & McGarry et al., 1994).

Intermediate sanctions are any correctional sanction sandwiched between regular probation and prison. This could include fines, community service, restitution, day reporting centers, house arrest, special probation (i.e., intensive or specific offender-related supervision such as sex offenders or domestic abuse), outpatient or residential alcohol and other drug abuse treatment centers, halfway houses, and boot camps (Aukerman & McGarry et al., 1994). Pertaining to substance abuse treatment, a number of levels and types of treatment have been provided. These may be grouped into pretreatment services, outpatient treatment, and inpatient treatment. Further, each group has specific services provided (Aukerman & McGarry et al., 1994). See Table 10.1.

Taking both intermediate criminal justice sanctions and types and levels of substance abuse treatment, a panel of experts has expressed that successful merger of these mixtures of components requires sufficient and flexible services, good information, well-informed collaboration, and mutual understanding (Aukerman & McGarry et al., 1994). The panel further contends that successful collaboration demands that treatment providers understand the intent of sentencing for each offender, that to avoid turf fights the scope and responsibilities of each system must be

Table 10.1 Levels and Types of Substance Abuse Treatment

Pretreatment Services	Outpatient Treatment	Inpatient Treatment
Primary Prevention	Nonintensive	Medically Monitored
Early Intervention	Intensive	Medically Managed
	Methadone Maintenance	Short-Term Nonhospital Intensive
	Day Treatment or Partial	Residential
	Hospitalization	Psychosocial Residential Care
		Therapeutic Community
		Halfway House
		Group Home Living

clearly understood, that each system understands the other's system view of the offender, that clear guidelines are understood for addressing offenders' rule violating, that an agreement is obtained for each offender's case plan, and that effective communication occurs (Aukerman & McGarry et al., 1994). Finally, the panel states that the treatment provider must be knowledgeable of certain critical information, such as the length of time the offender is to be in treatment, the exact terms of the court order or probation and parole conditions, the nature of the offender's accountability and to whom the offender is accountable, and the consequences of behavior (Aukerman & McGarry et al., 1994).

TECHNIQUES AND PROCEDURES OF TREATING MALE ADULT OFFENDERS

Treating Anger in Males

Most anger management programs include the same techniques—use of an anger diary, awareness of arousal cues, and coping skills (Ward & Baldwin, 1997). These techniques have been said to come from the seminal work of Raymond W. Novaco (1975). Many of these techniques have been incorporated in a workbook on anger control for prisoners (Cullen, 1992).

For some offender groups, anger management is more difficult. Serin and Kuriychuk (1994) utilize a theoretical model and discuss the implications for treatment of violent offenders who have social and cognitive processing deficits. This group of offenders was identified by Serin and Kuriychuk as psychopaths. They noted that whereas nonpsychopathic offenders have deficits or impulsivity or attribution of hostile intent, psychopaths have extreme deficits in both areas. They depicted a model with cognitive schema in the middle. On one end, it has a reciprocal relationship with arousal and impulsivity. On the other end, it has a reciprocal relationship with external events and attention cues. Below the cognitive schema is a reciprocal relationship with aggression. The treatment continuum based on this model is hierarchical with the mastering of techniques at the lower behavioral levels being necessary before the learning of the next skill. For instance, from bottom to top are (1) definition of anger, (2) stress inoculation/arousal reduction, (3) cognitive distortion, (4) impulse control, (5) communication skills, (6) assertiveness training, (7) cognitive processing, (8) and empathy/moral reasoning. An offender must master cognitive distortions before being able to acquire impulse control. Also, the offender must be able to acquire impulse control before developing communication skills.

Treatment based on this conceptualization has been provided in individual and group formats. Serin and Kuriychuk (1994) propose that most sessions do not extend beyond twenty sessions, and a monthly booster is valuable. The first session should consist of a review of group rules, including the limits of confidentiality. In subsequent sessions, a session is devoted to content with a subsequent session devoted to review, rehearsal, and role-playing. An advantage of this format is that it doubles offenders' exposures to content. Ideally, two counselors should lead the group, with one leader being female. Her role is critically important when role-playing heterogeneous relationships and situations.

Treating Sex Offenders

One theoretician contends that incest offenders have four types of cognitions. The first type is cognition related to sociocultural factors. These factors consist of beliefs that offenders have regarding societal responses to incest. For instance, some offenders believe that cases of incest are hard to prove, and punishment tends to be slight. Another sociocultural factor is that some offenders believe that they can attribute their behavior, if uncovered, to alcohol. The second type is cognition that is used to overcome fear of disclosure, involving using problems between the daughter and mother as a basis for believing that the daughter would not report the abuse. If the daughter did report the abuse, the mother would not believe her. The third type involves cognition employed to diminish responsibility. This entails the offenders telling themselves that the abuse is harmless because it does not involve intercourse. The offender may use the context of the abuse as justification. For instance, he may say that they were playing when the abuse occurred and it was not premeditated. Also, the offender may use the child's behavior as justification for the abuse. As an illustration, the child may not have protested and the offender views this behavior as encouragement. The fourth type is cognition related to permission seeking. Offenders sometimes ask permission or interpret the child's behavior as giving permission. These cognitions may overlap some, and a cognition may be used to moderate fear and responsibility. Accordingly, these types of cognitions have implications for treatment. Simply, in treating sex offenders, therapists must do cognitive restructuring (Hartley, 1998).

In another theoretical perspective, Laws and Marshall (1990) depict a conditioning and social learning model of deviant sexual practices. Specifically, this model provides that deviant sexual preferences and cognitions are acquired by the same processes in which individuals learn conventional sexual ideations and practices. Represented by thirteen general principles and fourteen derived propositions, the model consists of two stages—acquisition processes and maintenance processes. The acquisition stage involves Pavlovian conditioning, operant conditioning, and social learning. The maintenance stage consists primarily of intermittent reinforcement. Treatment principles are derived from the fourteen propositions and social learning principles (Laws & Marshall, 1990). Before treatment begins, however, an assessment should be conducted.

In evaluating a child molester, a clinician should conduct a clinical interview and psychological test. In some cases, additional tests may include a phallometric assessment and polygraph test. In the interview, questions should be asked regarding an offender's paraphilia and nonparaphilia sexual behavior. In addition, data should be gathered on the extent of an offender's sexual and physical victimization; social history; alcohol and substance abuse; and medical, employment, and criminal justice history (Quinsey & Lalumiere, 1996). A clinician should have access to an offender's criminal history, using it as a check of the offender's honesty. A clinician should gather further information regarding behaviors for which the offenders may have not been referred to the justice system. Offenders tend to be reluctant to disclose fully their sexual activity. Therefore, a clinician should specifically ask about other types of paraphilia, such as exhibitionism, fetishism, frottage, public masturbation, rape, sadism, masochism, and obscene phone calls. In exploring these areas, a clinician should not use clinical terms and should consider the educational and social status of the offender. Specific behaviors should be queried and the offender asked whether he has engaged in these behaviors. In terms of tests, a number may be employed, such as multiphasic sex inventory, the sexual interest card-sort, or the Abel and Becker cognition scale (Quinsey & Laumiere, 1996).

A final model has been created to treat men who sexually abused children. Framed in terms of a typology, Rencken's conceptualization contends that sex offenders differ in terms of taxonomy or classification. Some are *pedophiles*. Defined by the DSM-IV, pedophiles are adults who prefer sexual gratification with children. A second type is the *rapist*, whose key sexual pattern is the infliction of violence. The dynamics surrounding a rapist may be power, anger, or sadism. *Symptomatic* refers to offenders whose sexual behavior is symptomatic of some other principal mental disorder. Such principal disorders may be schizophrenia, substance abuse, or mental retardation. *Addictive/compulsive* involves those offenders who manifest a compulsion or addiction to sexual behavior, such as compulsive masturbation, voyeurism, exhibitionism, dependence on prostitution, or pornography. The last is *regressed*, which refers to offenders who are not sexually attracted to children during the offender's sexual development but exhibits this type of offending later. The etiology of the regression may differ but may include power issues, severe stress, substance abuse, marital dysfunction, or some combination of issues. The regressed sex offender makes up the largest proportion of offenders and includes intrafamilial and extrafamilial sexual abuse (Rencken, 1989).

Writing for the American Association for Counseling and Development, Rencken (1989) lays out treatment planning, treatment goals, and intervention strategies for regressed sex offenders. These approaches assume that the treatment is legally mandated and long term. Treatment planning begins when the legal system opts for psychiatric treatment instead of long-term imprisonment. The counselor, then, becomes a critical part of the treatment planning process, receiving input from the probation department and likely Child Protection Services. Treatment has a better chance at being successful when it is multimodal and involves more than one therapist. A team approach to therapy limits controlling and manipulating behaviors by the offender and the offender's family (Rencken, 1989).

Goals for offenders will vary, but some goals are uniform regardless of the modality and intervention. Overall, these goals are responsibility, power, control, affective awareness, communication, and interpersonal relationships. Rencken articulates these overall goals and subgoals as follows.

Responsibility
The offender will
   Clearly accept the responsibility for the pedosexual contact without reservation or rationalization
   Clearly acknowledge the actual and potential harm to the victim, himself, and the family
   Accept the ongoing responsibility for support and protection of the family regardless of reunification decisions
   Demonstrate responsibility in employment, finances, and similar areas
   Demonstrate responsibility in attendance and utilization of therapy opportunities

Accept and adhere to conditions of probation and other directives of the criminal justice and child protection systems

Differentiate between responsibility and guilt

Power
The offender will
Acknowledge the inappropriate power relationship inherent in the pedosexual contact

Identify and correct inappropriate power relationships in the family

Identify areas of individual powerlessness and plans for change

Assist in empowering the victim

Demonstrate ability to share power in the marital, familial, or work situation

Control
The offender will
Demonstrate control over sexual arousal, behavior, and fantasy

Acknowledge disinhibitors and plans for controlling them

Describe the "set-up" for the pedosexual contact and plans for controlling these (relapse prevention)

Demonstrate general impulse control, including control over "temper" and substance abuse

Demonstrate control over day-to-day decision making for himself

Understand and resolve issues regarding need for control over others and relinquish this need

Affective Awareness
The offender will
Identify the full range of his feelings consistently with understanding

Express the range of feelings and clarify these to the counselor and the family

Demonstrate ability to understand, clarify, and take appropriate action on others' feelings

Specifically, demonstrate ability to appropriately express anger

Communication
The offender will
Demonstrate ability to use "I" messages and active listening

Demonstrate ability to express and receive thoughts, feelings, opinion, and beliefs

Develop effective extrafamilial communication (work, social, etc.)

Demonstrate improved parenting skills

Interpersonal Relationships
The offender will
Demonstrate improved relationship with spouse or significant other

Demonstrate awareness of intimacy needs within relationships

Show appropriate sexual relationship(s) with adult partner(s)

Demonstrate improved socialization skills and reduced isolation (Rencken, 1989, p 97–99)

With sexual abuse within a family, the offender may be at risk for suicide when the abuse becomes known to the family and the criminal justice system. This requires crisis intervention strategies by the counselor. Considerable confusion, fear, and questions may arise in the family. Will the offender go to prison? Will Children Protection Services remove siblings or the victim from the family? How will the offense affect the family and relatives? At this point, the therapists should not promise anything, acknowledging that the family is powerless to control these events. Reframing, the therapists can emphasize what the family can control. The offender, for self-protection, is likely to deny or minimize the offense. Without minimizing the offender's responsibility, the therapist can demonstrate unconditional positive regard and a belief that the offender is treatable. Requiring the offender to take responsibility for the offense is paramount, but it should be stressed in a positive fashion.

Following the crisis work, the apology sessions begin. The offender is expected to initiate the first session by taking total responsibility and apologizing for the sexual contact. As part of an early session, the victim is given an opportunity to express whatever feelings he or she has and to ask any questions of the offender about the abuse. The offender is expected to accept whatever feelings the victim expresses. Other apology sessions should emphasize the harm to other family members.

Pattern analysis is the major treatment task. It involves an understanding of the offender, system dynamics, history, disinhibition, arousal patterns, and affective awareness. These pieces resemble a puzzle, requiring that it be put together by the therapist and offender. To this end, the first step in understanding the puzzle is to recognize and group the pieces. Examined are time of the sexual abuse, place where the abuse occurred, frequency of the abuse, duration of the abuse, and pattern of the abuse. Also, the tactics that the offender used to manipulate or control the victim are explored. Also, the offender's arousal dynamics are discussed in detail. Once these factors are determined, the disinhibiting factors should be discussed. Disinhibiting factors are those factors that facilitate offending, including alcohol and the myriad of rationalizations (Rencken, 1989).

Empowerment is the process of empowering an offender to achieve an equitable power balance within the family. A strategy is needed to empower the offender for the following reason. For a combination of reasons, the offender feels powerless while perceiving the victim as powerful. Fighting fire with fire, the offender uses sex as a power tool. Also, empowerment coincides with control issues. Developing independence and assertiveness can occur through decision making, the exploration of options, and negotiating skills. Empowerment may involve also employment issues. Offenders, as a result of an arrest, may lose their jobs and, as a result, need to take initiatives to change careers or lines of work.

Although termination on the surface may seem simply the end of therapy, the termination of therapy with sex offenders is more complex. To some extent, termination occurs at various times. Child Protection Services may terminate supervision of the case and close it. The offender may have his probation terminated. The separation of the family may terminate supervision. Then, there is termination from treatment. Because treatment is mandated by the courts, termination may involve more than the completion of treatment goals. The treatment team might have to unanimously agree that the offender achieved his goals. Also, an independent evaluation may need to be completed, consisting of a clinical or psychophysiological examination. Finally, termination may include the assessment of risk for reoffending and a conclusion that the risk is minimal (Rencken, 1989).

Regardless of the theoretical orientation of a program, the ultimate goal of sex offender treatment is for the offender to cease offending. If the goal is to help a sex offender better manage deviant sexual interests, a number of techniques may be employed. For instance, one intervention for deviant sexual interest is aversion therapy, which entails pairing the deviant images or thoughts with unpleasant consequences, such as electric shock or unpleasant smells. Another intervention is covert sensitization, which involves pairing contemplation of a deviant act with negative consequences, such as going to jail. Orgasmic reconditioning might be employed in which deviant fantasies are replaced with masturbation fantasies. A final technique for deviant sexual practices is castration and anti-libidinal medication (Perkins, 1991). (Perkins resides in the United Kingdom. However, the Cruel and Unusual Punishment Clause from the Eighth Amendment of the United States Constitution and its development may prevent castration in this country. Even a choice of castration or a long sentence may be legally suspect.)

Focusing on therapeutically engaging sex offenders in treatment, Perkins (1991) maintains that persuasion and contingency management are highly effective and advises that a number of issues are meaningful in effective persuasion and contingency management. For effective persuasion, the clinician should

1. Establish common goals with the client: Starting from there the client is prepared to accept change, even if this means accepting a lesser level of commitment or insight than is ideal.
2. Always keep the purpose of intervention in mind: guide interview with "open" questions (who, what, when, where, why, how), but pin down facts with "closed" questions. Accept that not all facts will be elicited at once; be prepared to come back to potentially threatening topics.
3. Clarify, but do not challenge the offender's beliefs too early; positively reinforce rather than punish revelations. Pick the right time to challenge offense-related thinking once data gathering has been carried out.
4. Reference to likely offense scenarios. Doing this can help unblock offenders too anxious to describe details; for example, "There are often two main reasons why people have committed your sort of offense" (spell this out with example as appropriate—e.g., sexual deviance versus social inadequacy explanations). "Which do you think most applies to you?" Sometimes offenders will give clues to which might apply in their verbal and nonverbal responses to these descriptions.
5. Use a casual approach to potentially threatening closed questions. This can be helpful, for example, an off-the-cuff, low-key style of questioning, perhaps while looking away from the offender can sometimes work; subsequently, reflect back, question, and if rapport will allow, challenge inconsistencies in the client's attitudes or behavior, perhaps with a style conveying genuine but good-natured incredulity at offense-related thinking.
6. Never persist with advice to argumentative or rationalizing clients. Rather, attempt to place them in the position of making suggestions for therapy, and reinforce good suggestions.

7. Make sure that any particularly uncooperative client attributes as many good therapeutic ideas as possible to himself rather than to the therapist. The therapist can facilitate this by making reference to, for example, "Your good idea from last week's session," even if it was not quite all the offender's own idea.

8. Stress the "togetherness" of therapy with cooperative clients. Use of terms such as *we could* rather than *I think* and *you should* can help with this. However, be careful to avoid assuming personal responsibility for the offender's problems (Perkins, 1991, p. 171).

For effective contingency management, a clinician should

1. Provide the client with information relevant to the process of becoming committed to behavior change, for example, types of treatment options available, and the consequences of no treatment.

2. Make the client aware of reinforcement contingencies operating outside the therapy situation (e.g., the likelihood of further imprisonment, divorce, and loss of contact with children if offending continues).

3. Capitalize on the principle of "cognitive dissonance" by encouraging the client to believe that he is undertaking treatment with the minimum of external pressure. In this way, genuine attitude change at the end of treatment is likely to be maximized.

4. Capitalize on any short-term external reinforcers to treatment that might be available, for example, improving relationships with relevant others in the institution or community and taking time out from a boring routine in prison (Perkins, 1991, pp. 171–172).

Treating Substance Abuse

In Chapter 3, we discussed Ivan Pavlov's experiments with a dog and stated that Pavlov's research had implications for understanding emotions and thus counseling. Robak (1991), applying Pavlov's behavioral findings and knowledge of the importance of cognition, explains a model for treating substance abuse. In this approach, the clinician first instructs the client to do a functional analysis, which involves three activities. Utilizing a diary, the client writes down each episode of the problem behavior. Documentation is made regarding the circumstances or stimuli surrounding the behavior. This would include the day, time, and place of the behavior. Second, the client documents all facets of the behavior, including the thoughts and feelings that occurred. Third, the client writes down the results, or possible reinforcers, following the behavior. This includes the client's reaction as well as others' reactions.

With a well-documented log, an analysis is conducted by the clinician and client that examines (1) the stimuli for the behaviors, (2) the behaviors themselves including the thoughts and feelings that go with the actions, and (3) the reinforcers following the behaviors. Having thoroughly analyzed these factors, the clinician and client are in position to develop specific strategies. The strategies employed are determined by the functional analysis and whether a behavior is a stimulus, behavior, or reinforcer.

For stimuli, some strategies are to avoid stimuli that trigger habits. In the world of the substance addict, this would be people, places, and things. Recovering persons strive "to avoid anyone who was part of their drug-abusing lifestyle; avoid any places where their pattern of substance-abusing behaviors was strong (that means stopping even the thought of driving in the direction of the neighborhood or bar where they typically bought drugs); and staying away from anything that triggered any substance abuse. That could be anything from a song on the radio to a glass of beer" (Robak, 1991, p. 87). Another strategy is to restrict the stimuli field. This means that in the event the recovering person cannot avoid some areas, the next best strategy is to restrict oneself to certain environments. Though it is preferable to avoid a triggering environment, limiting oneself is the second best strategy. Another strategy is stimuli control. A functional analysis directly reveals negative and indirectly reveals positive environments. Stimuli control involves putting oneself in positive environments because just avoiding negative environments is not enough. For example, attendance for substance abusers at an Alcoholics Anonymous and Narcotic Anonymous meeting is stimulus control.

Strategies for behavior involve shaping one's own behavior. An example of shaping one's behavior is establishing several achievable objectives related to a significant goal. Recovery is a goal, but it cannot be achieved in one step. It takes a series of smaller steps. Another strategy is developing competing responses. This involves engaging in positive behaviors during times that one normally engages in negative behaviors in the past. For instance, if one had a practice of drinking Friday and Saturday nights, then one would do other things on those days at those times. A final strategy for behavior is to break the chain of the undesirable behavior. Bad habits entail a number of smaller behaviors in a chain-like fashion. A certain mood might be the beginning of a substance-using problem. The next step might be talking to substance-using associates. Once they start talking, the subject of getting high comes up. Then, they decide to get together, obtain some money, and buy some drugs. Hence, the chain needs to be broken.

Strategies aimed at self-reinforcement involve reinforcing good behavior. Remembering that behavior is a function of its consequences, one should be aware that this includes also self-reinforcement. A person who goes regularly to Narcotics Anonymous meetings should reward oneself for each attendance. Another strategy is punishing bad behaviors. An example of such a strategy is to set up a system for punishing missed meetings. This can be a situation in which money is given to a friend in recovery. For each missed meeting, a previously agreed sum is donated to charity. Practicing covert reinforcement is another strategy. This strategy consists of creating positive, rewarding images, such as being strong, competent, positive, or even heroic. These images are used whenever a person is feeling down or feeling incompetent. The last strategy is to practice covert sensitization. It involves telling oneself of all the negative possibilities for relapsing. For some individuals, this might be losing one's family or job, or returning to prison.

RESEARCHED PROGRAMS
AND INTERVENTIONS

Domestic Violence

Seeking to ascertain the most efficacious treatment, Edleson and Syers (1990) experimentally studied batterers who were being treated in six different groups. They examined the recidivism of batterers six months after treatment. The study involved three models of treatment—a self-help group, an education group, and a combination of self-help and education. The self-help group was led by a former abuser who had not been abusive for a year. He received training in how to run a self-help group and had a consultant available to him. The group determined the topics and focuses of each meeting; however, over the course of the group, the men had to discuss four themes, which were (1) personal responsibility for violent behavior, (2) development of an individual plan to be nonviolent, (3) use of time-outs, and (4) the cycle of violence (Edleson & Syers, 1990).

The educational model included the four themes described above, too. In addition, presentations included lectures on abuse, videotaped and role-playing demonstrations, and group discussions. Group leaders utilized several modules that had a workbook for each module. The modules were introduction, abuse and how it happens, the impact of abuse on people in my life, why abuse is a part of my life, and how to change abusive behavioral patterns. Focus was maintained on the materials, and personal stories were politely and professionally discouraged.

Each of the three groups was provided in twelve and thirty-two sessions. In effect, there were six groups to which men were randomly assigned. The twelve-session groups met weekly for two hours and fifteen minutes, whereas the thirty-two-session groups met twice a week for two hours and fifteen minutes for sixteen weeks. No significant differences were found for whether men were violent after treatment and the length or type of group. They found that shorter treatment was as effective as longer treatment. Also, they found that in all groups, men were less violent and used fewer threats after treatment (Edleson & Syers, 1990).

Later, Edleson and Syers (1991), examining essentially the same set of data, reported the results at twelve months and at eighteen months. At the eighteen-month follow-up, there was no relationship between whether men were violent and the type of group the men had participated in. The results of this subsequent study also suggest that short-term treatment was as effective as more intense, long-term treatment. Of interest to criminal justice, men who had court involvement were less violent at eighteen months compared with six months (Edleson & Syers, 1991). This conclusion suggests that long-term court involvement is important in reducing domestic violence.

In another program for batterers, Saunders (1996) studied feminist cognitive–behavioral intervention and process-psychodynamic intervention for men who battered their partners. Feminist cognitive–behavioral therapy is characterized by skills training and gender role resocialization in a highly structured format. It uses brief lectures, demonstration role-plays, behavioral rehearsal, and homework as the primary intervention methods. The feminist model of cognitive–behavioral therapy posits that men who are violent towards their partners have skill deficits that cause men to be unable to state their needs and feelings. These men also have cognitive skills deficits that produce anger, distortions, and negative self-talk. Finally, cultural norms that promote male dominance exist (Saunders, 1996).

A process-psychodynamic understanding of men who are violent to partners and the intervention derived from it indicate that violence occurs as a result of men's childhood when men, as children, witnessed violence. The anger formed by witnessing this violence is carried over to their adult relationships. The focus of intervention, which is less structured, is to provide a supportive environment in which men can reexamine and reexperience childhood trauma, grieve their losses, forsake control over others, and learn to be more empathic (Saunders, 1996).

Each intervention use a close-ended group that meets for about two and one-half hours once a week, for twenty weeks. As previously stated, the feminist cognitive–behavioral model was structured. Each session had an agenda and homework. Each session had a didactic section on communication, cognitive skills, relaxation/desensitization training, consciousness raising about sex roles, woman violence, and behavioral or cognitive rehearsal. The process-psychodynamic intervention did not use an agenda, but there were repeated tasks to create trust and a safe environment for disclosing intimate information. When a trusting environment had been created, the group leader helped members in uncovering childhood trauma, reconnecting to these traumatic events, developing mutual support, creating awareness of hurt and fear, developing awareness of alienation from self and others, transferring lessons about reactions to abuse to current relationship, and handling termination.

Saunders hypothesized that there would not be any significant differences between the two interventions; however, he hypothesized that the personality of the men would determine the effectiveness of each intervention. Particularly, some men are more appropriate for feminist cognitive–behavioral therapy, and some men are more appropriate for process-psychodynamic intervention. To test these hypotheses, Saunders randomly assigned eligible men to the two types of groups. A number of measures were used for men's behaviors, including Millon Clinical Multiaxial Inventory, relationship satisfaction, beliefs about woman abuse, self-esteem, general hostility, traditional views of women's roles, democratic decisions making, level of conflict, anger toward partner, jealousy, depression, adjustments for social desirable, and level of abuse that was determined by partners' reports and offenders' arrests. As hypothesized, there was no difference in the level of violence between the men who had feminist cognitive–behavioral therapy and men who had process-psychodynamic intervention. Further, personality styles and disorder interacted with the two types of interventions. Particularly, men with antisocial traits were less likely to be violent when treated with feminist cognitive–behavioral counseling, and men who had dependent traits were less likely to be violent when they were treated with a process-psychodynamic intervention (Saunders, 1996). These findings suggest that clinicians should assess batterers and match them to either a process-psychodynamic intervention or a cognitive–behavioral intervention.

Anger Management with Offenders

A violent prisoner serving a life sentence agreed to undergo cognitive–behavioral counseling to control his violence (Daniel, 1992). The prisoner agreed to undergo several ninety-minute sessions over a two-month period. The first session consisted of a detailed ABC (i.e., antecedents, behaviors, and consequences) analyses of the prisoner's violent behavior during the previous twelve months. In addition, the prisoner completed a self-assessment regarding his anger. This self-assessment was amalgamated with a stress inoculation procedure for the clinician to develop a "personalized bibliotherapy." The purpose of the combination was to provide the prisoner with a set of coping skills or cognitive and behavioral skills for handling stressful situations and for controlling personal stress reactions. The cognitive–behavior skills were tailored to address the prisoner's violent behavior. The personalized bibliotherapy consisted of relaxation therapy for personalized triggers, instructions to use coping self-statements, cognitive rehearsal, and anger diaries (Daniel, 1992).

The clinical intervention consisted of individual counseling and was provided in six weekly sessions. Each session consisted of three stages. During the first stage, the clinician and prisoner discussed a part of the manual (i.e., the personalized bibliotherapy) with the prisoner's experiences. The second stage involved the two parties discussing the daily record of anger-arousing situations. These situations were used to supplement, exemplify, or amplify manual. During the third stage, the prisoner and clinician concluded the session with the anger-arousing situations that were described in the second stage. They, then, agreed that relaxation exercises would be used for these situations.

To evaluate the effectiveness of this intervention, Daniel used the Profile of Mood States (PMS). The PMS measures six bipolar areas consisting of anxiety, hostility, depression, confidence, clear-headedness, and tired versus energetic. Each area is measured as a positive and negative polarity. The scale was administered one week before treatment began, before each session began, one week after treatment ended, and six months after treatment. In addition, as a more direct measure, Daniel examined the number of disciplinary reports six months before treatment and six months after treatment. Finally, Daniel collected some qualitative data from the prisoner.

An examination of these data revealed that before the intervention, the prisoner had eighteen disciplinary reports with fifteen of those being for aggressive behavior. During treatment, the prisoner had one disciplinary report and this was for aggression. Six months after treatment, the prisoner had five disciplinary reports and four were for aggression. All the scales regarding PMS were in the positive direction, and the prisoner reported positive feelings about the intervention. Nonetheless, Daniel concludes that few interventions are likely to be permanent and that a booster treatment is needed periodically.

In a treatment strategy similar to Daniel's, an anger management workshop was provided to eighteen male prisoners chosen randomly from the population at Utah State Prison. The workshops consisted of a two-hour session that was provided on three consecutive Fridays. All total, the intervention consisted of six hours. The program had four objectives—present common symptoms of anger, relate why some individuals get angry, describe how anger can be effectively controlled, and assist offenders in using these skills in the prison environment (Smith & Beckner, 1993).

During the three sessions, the following tasks were provided. In the first session, the researchers provided an introduction of the program and its objectives. Next, the prisoners were administered the Novaco Anger Scale to obtain a pretest score. After the administration of the scale, the workshop presenters discussed the symptoms of anger according to the *Diagnostic Statistical Manual*. Particularly, a lecture was given on the emotional, physical, cognitive, and behavioral manifestation of anger. At the end of the session, the prisoners were given a homework assignment of rating their anger in a log. They were asked to document the symptoms and events that occurred when they were very angry (Smith & Beckner, 1993).

In the second session, a review session was conducted on the homework assignment. In particular, the prisoners were asked to discuss their anger evaluations, the symptoms that led them to make the evaluations that they did, the events that precipitated the anger, and recognition of the cues that indicated that the anger had reached a critical level. Following this discussion, the presenter described the ways in which anger can be controlled, such as walking away, counting to ten, deep breathing, relaxation exercises, physical activity, and cognitive processing. The prisoners were asked to continue with their logs and to record the use of an anger management strategy (Smith & Beckner, 1993).

The third session consisted of a review of the homework assignment and how well the technique helped in alleviating the anger episode. The presenters discussed the strategies used to alleviate anger and what strategies seemed to be the most effective. Another review, then, is conducted summarizing what was presented and learned. Finally, the prisoners completed the Novaco Anger Scale again.

The Novaco Anger Scale ranged from 0 to 100 with 100 being highest anger. On pretest, the prisoners scored a mean of 64.6 and at the posttest, their score was 55.7, a statistically significant reduction. Because the sample was small, the researchers were able to examine individual change. They reported that two prisoners who had high scores had experienced anger-provoking episodes. One had been denied parole and the other had his commissary privileges taken away after a confrontation with a correctional officer. Both prisoners recorded significant reduction, and both reported that the skills learned in the workshop had helped them to deal with these negative episodes (Smith & Beckner, 1993).

Treating High-Risk Probationers

In Canada, criminal justice professionals were challenged to develop an effective program for working with high-risk probationers. These professionals developed a program that was delivered in six stages. In Stage 1, a review of the literature in North America was conducted. A number of studies from 1973 to 1978 showed impressive results with respect to recidivism, lasting from three to fifteen years. Stage 2 involved a close scrutiny or comparison of what worked and what did not work. The successful programs shared a common theme. That is, all impacted offenders' thinking. These successful programs not only targeted behaviors, feelings, and vocational and interpersonal skills, but also cognition, self-evaluation, expectations, values, and offenders' assessment of the world. Stage 3 consisted of further review of the literature and the discovery that offenders have developmental delays in learning new skills necessary for social adaptation. Stage 4 involved a component analysis that revealed that effective programs targeted offenders' cognitive deficits and that cognitive training was essential for effective programs. Stage 5 consisted of identification and refinement of cognitive training procedures, practices, and techniques (Ross, Fabiano, & Ewles, 1988).

Stage 6 was the development of the program, which was called Reasoning and Rehabilitation and which was to be tested by an experimental research design. Some old techniques were refined and new techniques developed. Reasoning and Rehabilitation consists of several modified techniques.

1. Structured learning therapy to teach social skills
2. Lateral thinking to teach creative problem solving
3. Critical thinking to teach logical, rational thinking

4. Values education to teach values and concern for others
5. Assertiveness training to teach nonaggressive, socially appropriate ways to meet needs
6. Negotiation skill training to teach alternatives to belligerent or violent behaviors in interpersonal conflict situations
7. Interpersonal cognitive problem solving to teach the thinking skills needed to deal with interpersonal conflict
8. Social perspective training to teach how to recognize and understand others' feelings
9. Role-playing and modeling to demonstrate appropriate social behavior

These techniques and skills were aided and facilitated by audio and visual presentations, reasoning exercises, games, and group counseling (Ross et al., 1988). The aim of these techniques was to modify "the impulsive, egocentric, illogical and rigid thinking of the offenders and teaching them to stop and think before acting, to consider the consequences of their behaviour, to conceptualize alternative ways of responding to interpersonal problems and to consider the impact of their behaviour on other people, particularly the victim" (Ross et al., p. 31). Reasoning and Rehabilitation was delivered by trained probation officers working with four to six probationers for eighty hours.

To evaluate Reasoning and Rehabilitation, Ross and associates (1988) randomly assigned probationers to three groups, consisting of regular probation, regular probation and life skills training, and regular probation and cognitive training. The first group was to be a control group. The life skills group was an attention control group and the members were provided with life skills, such as money management, use of leisure time, family law, employment-seeking skills, and alcohol and drug education. The aim was to give them the same amount of time as the experimental group. After nine months following treatment, the recidivism rate for the regular probation was 69.5%, for the life skills group it was 47.5%, and for the cognitive group it was 18.1%. Other analyses revealed that the regular probation group had 30% of their members to be incarcerated, life skills had 11%, and the cognitive group had 0% (Ross et al., 1988).

Following the success of the Reasoning and Rehabilitation in Canada, Britain created a similar program in Mid Glamorgan that it called the Straight Thinking on Probation (STOP). STOP was modeled after Reasoning and Rehabilitation with some minor twists (Raynor, 1998; Raynor & Vanstone, 1996). One of the changes was STOP involved thirty-five two-hour groups (Raynor & Vanstone, 1996). Other differences were that STOP was changed slightly to fit better with the local cultural and lifestyle and was delivered by two probation officers (Raynor, personal communication, June 17, 1998). Along with the creation of the STOP program, criminal justice professionals believed that a new assessment tool needed to be developed to determine the impact of probation services besides the extent of recidivism. Accordingly, a group of researchers and criminal justice professionals worked together to create such an instrument, which was called CRIME-PICS.

CRIME-PICS is an assessment tool that measures seven areas: C measures an offender's awareness of the costs of crime, R measures the degree to which an offender accepts responsibility, I measures an offender's degree of impulsiveness, M measures an offender's degree of moral attitude about crime, and E measures the extent of an offender's awareness of the effect of crime on a victim. These measures formed a CRIME index and measured the extent to which an offender's attitude supported criminality. The other part of the assessment tool involves a problem inventory: P measures the degree that an offender rated himself on fifteen problems (e.g., money, relationships, employment, getting into trouble, needing excitement, family problems, health and fitness, boredom, housing, alcohol and drugs, gambling, feeling depressed, feelings about self, lack of confidence, and lots of worries), IC measures an offender's degree of identity as a criminal, and S measures the degree of an offender's self-prediction about offending again. CRIME-PICS was revised and another version, CRIME-PICS II, was developed. However, STOP was evaluated with the original version (Raynor, 1998).

As reported by Raynor (1998), STOP was compared to other probationers and offenders sentenced to community service. The original version CRIME-PICS scores the Crime Index in a manner such that an increased score reflected less crime-prone attitudes, but self-reported problems had an opposite scoring such that a reduction in the score means a reduction in self-identified problems. (This was part of the reason for revising the instruments and CRIME-PICS II has a different scoring system with respect to the Crime Index.) With respect to the Crime Index, STOP, using a pretest and posttest design, had an increase from 27.2 to 28.3; other probation had an increase from 26.8 to 28.8; and community service had a slight decrease from 26.9 to 26.5. On the other hand, STOP had a reduction in problems from 3.1 to 2.4; other probation had a slight decrease from 2.3 to 2.0; and community service showed no change from 1.9 at pretest to 1.9 at posttest (Raynor, 1998). While many of these comparisons were not statistically significant except for the reduction in problems for the STOP group, Raynor states that the trend was in the positive direction. Further, Raynor concludes that, "although the STOP programme does not aim to sort people's problems for them, it does make a systematic attempt to help people to acquire the cognitive skills and attitudes necessary for more effective problem-solving" (Raynor, 1998, p. 11).

Treating General Offenders

In 1988, the Vermont Department of Correction, concerned about the rising criminal population in its state, created a pilot treatment program for its offenders at the Northwest State Correctional Facility. The program was based on the literature that reported that offenders have cognitive thinking errors that supported criminal behavior. These thinking errors are represented by the minimization of an offense (e.g., stealing a car is not as bad as robbing), assuming the role of victim (e.g., I deserve some money after what I have undergone), or denial of responsibility (e.g., he should not have worn the Rolex if he did not want someone to take it). Thus, the program was called the Cognitive Self-Change (CSC) (Henning & Frueh, 1996).

Entrance into the CSC program was made possible by a referral from a caseworker. After the referral, the prisoner was interviewed by a staff member and the program was explained to him. To be accepted into the program, the prisoner had to have six months or less to serve and an opening had to be available. If the treatment staff accepted the prisoner, the prisoner had the final say on whether to participate in treatment.

The actual CSC program was housed in a twenty-five-bed residential unit within the prison. New prisoners to the unit underwent an eight-week orientation. During this orientation, they were informed of the theory of the program. They were also told how to recognize frequent cognitive distortions and how to develop skills needed for cognitive–behavioral self-monitoring. After the initial phase, the offenders were assigned to a group, which consisted of between five and ten prisoners and several members of the treatment staff.

The groups met three to five times a week. During each group session, a designated prisoner was required to present a "thinking report" to the group. This report revealed prior acts of criminal behavior and current acts of antisocial behaviors. Typically, the prisoner provided an objective description of the criminal or antisocial behavior. Next, he would describe all the thoughts and feelings he had prior to, during, and after the crime or act. After the report, the group assisted the prisoner in identifying the cognitive distortions accompanying the behavior. Sometimes, the group engaged in role-playing to clarify its points. When prisoners learned their criminogenic thoughts, strategies were developed to block these thoughts from occurring. Of the cognitive strategies used, some were challenging one's cognition and cognitive redirection. Behaviorally, a strategy could be avoiding high-risk situations or discussions of cognitions and feelings.

Participants were required to give two reports a month. In addition, they completed homework that pertained to a thinking report on deviant behavior and kept journals. The treatment staff inspected the journals so as to give each prisoner regular feedback. Because the prisoners had to have six months or less to enter the program, treatment length reflected this condition.

To evaluate this treatment program, Henning and Frueh (1996) used a quasi-experimental design to test the effects of the CSC program. Prisoners who received treatment were compared with prisoners who had not taken the program. The outcome variable of interest was the amount of recidivism. According to their results, 50% of the prisoners who received the treatment engaged in recidivism compared to 70.8% of the prisoners who had not. This difference was statistically significant. Using a different statistical analysis, the researchers found that participation in CSC was a significant predictor of failure rate, such that at one year, CSC had a failure rate of 25%, two years 38%, and three years 46%, whereas the comparison group had a failure rate at one year of 46%, two years 67%, and three years 75% (Henning & Frueh, 1996).

Treating Clinically Depressed Prisoners

Some prisoners become clinically depressed while serving their sentences. Wilson (1990) studied the effectiveness of a group cognitive intervention for significantly depressed prisoners. He utilized a supportive, nondirective treatment approach as a comparison group, which had been shown in previous studies to be beneficial. The prisoners in the cognitive group treatment, during the first session, introduced themselves and discussed their concerns and goals. After establishment of the group rules, the group discussed the pamphlet Coping with Depression and the assignment of homework. In the subsequent thirteen sessions, the group focused on specific techniques (e.g., recording dysfunctional and functional thoughts, creating activity schedules, and completing rating scales) and group processes (e.g., modeling, attentiveness to group dynamics, and focusing on cognitions). Specifically, the prisoners were counseled to distinguish, challenge, and change dysfunctional thoughts. Also, they were encouraged to imbibe positive self-statements and envision pleasant activities. As far as the individual supportive group, the prisoners received a general therapy format, which focused on clarifying, through reflections, problematic issues. These prisoners were encouraged to discuss their moods, current functioning, and personal concerns with a counselor.

Assessments were done at pretreatment, midtreatment (i.e., six weeks after the first treatment session), and posttreatment. The outcome measures used were the Beck Depression Scale, the Multiple Affect Adjective Check List, the Hopelessness Scale, the Minnesota Multiphasic Personality Inventory (MMPI) D Scale, a Daily Mood Rating Scale, and a Consumer Satisfaction Questionnaire. Significant differences were found for the Beck Depression Scale and the MMPI D scale from pretest to midtest, and posttest. Particularly, prisoners who had cognitive group treatment experienced about a 50% reduction in the depression score compared to about a 25% reduction for individual supportive therapy (Wilson, 1990).

Treating Sex Offenders

Within the offender population, probably the most difficult offenders to treat are sex offenders (Furby, Weinrott, & Blackshaw, 1989). However, one longitudinal study showed some relatively positive preliminary results. The study was of the Sex Offender Treatment and Evaluation Project (SOTEP), which was operated by the California Department of Mental Health. SOTEP had two primary goals. One goal was to create and operate an innovative treatment program. The second goal was to perform a rigorous evaluation of the program.

Admittance into SOTEP required that an offender be convicted of rape or child molestation. Offenders who had participated in gang rapes or incest were excluded. Admittees had to have fourteen to thirty months to serve before release. In addition, there were some other requirements, such as they had to be between eighteen years old and sixty years old, they had to speak English, they had to have a maximum of two felony convictions, they had to have an IQ over eighty, they had to be free from any psychotic or organic impairment, they had to free from serious behavioral problems in prison, they had to be relatively physically fit so as not to require the services of a skilled nursing facility, they had to have no felony holds, and they had to admit their offenses.

After the initial screening and group assignment, prisoners accepted for the program were transferred to the Atascadero State Hospital. The average stay was about two years. When released from Atascadero, they spent a year in an aftercare program. The aftercare program was called the Sex Offender Aftercare Program (SOAP). Participation in SOAP is made as a condition of parole, and failure to participate can result in a return to prison. Then the men were tracked for a minimum of five years. Each man was interviewed annually to collect information about personal and social controls, coping styles, their degree of commitment to abstinence, self-efficacy, and self-report of deviant behavior. However, these data were additional information that was made possible by the National Institute of Mental Health.

The primary intent of the treatment program, however, was to treat the men's sexual offending and whether they sexually offended again was the primary outcome measure. To treat the sexual offending, a comprehensive cognitive–behavioral program was developed. It helps offenders to understand situations that place them at risk and to develop coping responses. It uses a relapse prevention framework. From the beginning to the end of the treatment program, prisoners attend a core relapse prevention group for four and one-half hours per week. During this group, the primary relapse prevention concepts were described so that prisoners could confront the personal, social, and sexual problems that place them at risk for reoffending. Additionally, the prisoners are seen in individual counseling for one hour each week by their primary therapist who was a clinical psychologist or clinical social worker. They also are seen for two hours by a member of the nursing staff.

All prisoners take a variety of specialty groups. These groups involve a number of groups that focus on relaxation training, sex education, human sexuality, social skills training, stress management, anger management, and relapse planning. Moreover, prisoners with a serious history of substance abuse were required to participate in substance abuse counseling. As part of the initial assessment, the prisoners take a psychophysiological assessment to ascertain their degree of arousal for deviant stimuli. For prisoners who manifest a deviant sexual arousal pattern, they are required to participate in behavioral reconditioning. To ensure the integrity of treatment in light of personnel changes and time, treatment staff is required to follow a manual that spelled out the goals and techniques for each session.

As mandated by the California legislature, SOTEP had to be evaluated by an experimental design. Accordingly, sex offenders were randomly assigned to SOTEP and to a no-treatment control group. In addition, the researchers created another comparison group that consisted of a nonvolunteered comparison group. The primary variable of interest was the amount of recidivism for the three groups. The treatment group had a lower risk of reoffending than the two comparison groups, although it was not quite statistically significant, ($p < .07$) (Marques, Day, Nelson, & West, 1994).

In another program for sex offenders, Pithers (1994) used a predesign and postdesign to determine if incarcerated sex offenders could increase their level of empathy for victims. The sex offenders were pedophiles and rapists and represented two groups. He used a structured cognitive intervention, which was delivered in five stages. During the first stage, offenders were required to relate to the group a detailed description of their offenses. In the second stage, offenders were required to read passages from several prominent books written by women who had been sexually abused about what these assaults did to them. They had to prepare a report describing the factual and emotional content of the readings and discuss how their victims may have had similar experiences. During the third stage, which lasted about four to eight weeks, the offenders reviewed videotapes. They also listened to audiotapes where sexual abuse victims described their victimization and the healing process. During the fourth stage, the offenders wrote narrative from the victim's perspective of the abuse they experienced. Role-playing was used with the offender recounting from the narrative and responding to questions from group members. In the last stage, more role-playing was used. The offender role-played the perpetrator and another member the victim. Then, these roles were reversed. During role-plays, the offender, using the first-person perspective, related the thoughts, feelings, and fantasies surrounding the abuse. These role-playing situations were videotaped for further discussion and analysis.

The measures used to evaluate the program were the interpersonal reactivity index, Abel's cognitive distortions scale, Burt's rape myth acceptance scale, a generalized expectancy for success scale, selfism scale, and the splitting scale. Each of these scales was administered at pretest and posttest for the pedophiles and rapists. According to Pithers, the cognitive–behavioral intervention had a positive effect on both groups and increased their levels of empathy. The results showed that the intervention increased empathic skills, decreased acceptance of cognitive distortions that facilitate child sexual abuse and rape, decreased expectation of being able to obtain one's goals, and decreased narcissistic defenses (Pithers, 1994). Pithers (1994) entertains the possibility that prisoners gave exaggerated responses in order to show improvement but rejects this possibility. An examination of all the scales showed genuine improvement in empathy (Pithers, 1994).

A final study involving a sex offender was conducted by Horley (1990). Using a single case design, he relates the apparent successful intervention with cognitive–behavioral therapy with an exhibitionist serving time in prison. Called T.C., the client was a thirty-four-year-old male who had a long history of exposing his genitalia to women and masturbating. T.C. reported that this behavior began when he was about sixteen years old. During this eighteen-year career, he had five convictions for committing indecent acts and three convictions for assault (i.e., touching a victim) while masturbating. T.C.'s assessment revealed that his offenses tended to occur when he felt negative emotions, such as anxiety, depression, and anger. Often, these negative emotions would emerge following some type of family conflict. Compounding these negative emotions, he had deviant sexual fantasies that he satisfied by masturbating.

The intervention for T.C. was implemented in two phases. The first phase consisted of relapse prevention, which was provided in twelve weekly sessions. Among the areas covered during this individual counseling were the role of negative emotion in sexual offending, victim impact, forming helping networks, informed decision making, and averting high-risk situations. The second phase emphasized inappropriate sexual fantasies and deviant sexual responses. An assessment of these targeted areas was determined by phallometric measurement. With data from the phallometric assessment, the client and therapist had an intensive session for one hour per day for two weeks. During these intense sessions, both would monitor penile responses to audio depictions of consenting and nonconsenting sexual encounters. Covert sensitization was used to treat deviant fantasies, and appropriate fantasies were reinforced with verbal acknowledgment and imaging. Included in the second phase also were more discussions about negative emotions, family relations, and communications within a sexual relationship.

With respect to the evaluation of T.C., the pretest measurement of the Phallometric test showed that appropriate arousal increased from 12.0 at pretest to 20.4 at posttest. Inappropriate arousal decreased from 13.0 at pretest to 6.3 at posttest. With respect to recidivism, T.C., after being released from prison had no arrests for sixteen months, which was the longest period that T.C. had undergone without an offense in about fifteen years (Horley, 1995).

Treating Prisoners with Substance Abuse Problems

In Delaware, a drug treatment program consisting of three phases was created for prisoners in the Delaware Correctional System. The program consisted of a

therapeutic community within one of the prisons that was called KEY and a work release program that was called CREST. KEY was Phase One and CREST was Phase
Two. KEY consisted of twelve months in a therapeutic community within the prison.
CREST consists of six months in a residential program. In Phase Three, they receive
an additional six months of individual and group counseling after they were released
and while they were on parole or other supervised release. In all phases, the emphasis was on correcting negative patterns of thinking, feelings, and behaving that promoted drug use. They also learn to take responsibility for their behavior and acquire
positive social attitudes and behaviors that would lead to a drug-free lifestyle. While
not stated, this emphasis espouses a cognitive–behavioral treatment approach.

Inciardi researched the effectiveness of the KEY/CREST program. He compared
four groups consisting of offenders who participated in KEY only, CREST only, both
KEY and CREST, and a no-treatment comparison group. The initial evaluation occurred six months after treatment and consisted of a total of 457 offenders. The outcome measures were whether the offenders were drug free and whether they were
arrest free. The research showed that of the offenders that participated in both KEY
and CREST, 95% of them were drug free and 97% were arrest free six months after
treatment. Eighteen months after treatment, 76% of the offenders in both KEY and
CREST were drug free, compared to 45% of the CREST only group, 30% of the
KEY only group, and 19% of the comparison group. With respect to arrests, 71% of
the offenders who were involved in both KEY and CREST were arrest free, compared to 65% of those offenders who were in CREST only, 48% who were in KEY
only, and 30% who were in the comparison group. These results showed that an effective treatment program must consist of initial treatment in prison and a follow-
up treatment program in the community. Hoping to evaluate the long-term effects
of the program, the researcher planned to conduct subsequent follow-up at forty-
two and fifty-four months after treatment (Mathias, 1995).

Martin, Butzin, and Inciardi (1995) conducted additional, multivariate analyses
on the data involving the therapeutic community in the Delaware prison. The outcome measures of interest were whether released offenders were drug free, arrest
free, injection free, and risky-sex free (e.g., were using condoms). They coded the
type of treatment (i.e., KEY, CREST, KEY/CREST, and the comparison group) and
entered them in a logistic regression. Participation in CREST and KEY/CREST
was a significant predictor in being drug free and arrest free. Participation in CREST
was a significant predictor in being injection free, and participation in KEY/
CREST was a significant predictor in being risky-sex free. Martin and associates
controlled for other variables and found that participation in KEY, CREST, and
KEY/CREST were all significant predictors in being drug free and arrest free.

UNRESEARCHED PROGRAMS
AND INTERVENTIONS

Drug Programs

A Federal Program Torres (1997), a retired federal probation officer and current
university professor, rejects the medical model in providing a framework for intervening with substance-abusing offenders. Instead, he espouses a view that individuals choose to use drugs and have free will. The most effective strategy for

probation officers who work with drug offenders is to establish explicit limits, to tell probationers and parolees of the consequences of not following the rules, and to be prepared to enforce consequences for rule violations. According to Torres, "the preferred course of action for many, if not most, users is placement in a therapeutic community, with credible threats and coercion if necessary. If the probation officer concludes that such placement in not needed, then a system of graduated sanctions or consequences is appropriate for techniques violations, such as dirty tests" (p. 38). In short, an effective strategy is surveillance through frequent drug testing and treatment.

This philosophy was established in the 1980s as a policy directive in the Central District of California (CDC) and adopted by federal probation officers. As indicated by a position statement, one does not volunteer to be addicted and one's volition plays a critical role in addiction. The CDC does not support the belief that addiction is a disease or a medical problem. Drug abuse that leads to negative results or a physical disease, such as liver disease, is not in and of itself a disease. Diseases do not disappear simply because one wants them to go away, such as a heart disease or cancer. In terms of substance abuse addiction, it will not cease until a person decides to end it. The cause or cure for a disease is never a decision. As a result, drug use is not a disease.

The CDC acknowledges that some social problems, such as unemployment, dysfunctional families, and drug-infested neighborhoods, exacerbate drug use. However, there is no direct link between these social problems and drug use. A number of people experience various social pressures and do not use drugs. People initially use because of social influence, the desire to change one's state of mind, and availability. They continue to use because it becomes psychological, socially, and physically reinforcing. In the CDC, the use of drugs is approached from a legal perspective. It is violation of the law and a violation of conditions of probation and parole. An addicted offender cannot benefit from other services, such as employment training or counseling, until he or she is free of an addiction.

The CDC has a total abstinence policy for the protection of the community and the offender. The reasons for this goal are to reduce crimes stemming from drug abuse and assist the offender by helping him or her to stay out of the criminal justice system and reduce the likelihood of the offender dying from drugs or incurring serious mental and physical disabilities. These goals can be achieved in the following manner. The first goal is to help the offender make the decision to not use drugs. The second goal is to place the offender in a treatment program. The third goal is to return the offender to a correctional institution if use continues. The successful accomplishment of these goals is to provide regularly a sophisticated drug-use detection process, which employs urine drug testing and physical examination. The purpose is to communicate to the offender that he or she cannot use without being detected, and if detected, graduated sanctions are employed, including a return to prison. A number of offenders will get the message and develop motivation to not use. Offenders who do not get the message experience the consequences of their behavior, such as a return to prison. At some point, perhaps after repeated returns to prison, the offenders learn that if they want to stay free, they must stop using. When offenders have stopped, the probation officer can assist the offenders with other problems that they have.

The above position statement produces a number of implications for caseload management and casework implementation for federal probation officers in the CDC. These are

1. The probation officer does not discharge from offenders the responsibility for their drug use. The policy of the Probation Office is to take action on every illegal drug use by offenders.
2. By rejecting the medical model, the Probation Office says to offenders that their ability to not use and the Probation Office's expectation for their success.
3. The probation officer shall impress upon offenders the total abstinence policy and structure offenders to that end. This policy forces offenders to decide whether they will remain drug free in the community, a residential program, or in prison.
4. Frequent testing and quick detection permit probation officers to react promptly to offenders' drug use. This is in the best interests of both offenders and the community.
5. A total abstinence policy decreases the chance of offenders associating with other drug users and provides reinforcement and companionship for them.

Given this philosophy, Torres reports how these principles are implemented. As stated, surveillance is a critical part of the CDC approach. The degree of surveillance is determined by the level of offender risk. The U.S. Probation Office has specialized officers who handle substance-abuse offenders. When an officer receives a file of a drug offender, the officer reviews the file and determines the degree of risk. Guidelines are provided to determine the degree of risk. The high-risk category involves offenders with a documented history of substance abuse, gang membership within the past ten years, or a criminal history consisting of violence. On the other hand, low-risk offenders are those offenders who have no significant substance abuse within the past five years.

Based on the risk, phases of surveillance are implemented and the level of risk determined how long an offender remains in each phase. Phase I requires the most intense surveillance. It requires a minimum of six urine collections a month but normally eight are done. This translates to twice a week and is done randomly. Therefore, an offender might be tested on Monday and Thursday one week and tested Tuesday and Wednesday the following week. All offenders are placed in Phase I. High-risk offenders remain in Phase I for four months and low-risk offenders for two months. Phase II requires a minimum of four random tests each month, but five are usually done. High-risk offenders have to be in Phase II for at least four months and low-risk offenders for at least two months. Phase III requires at least two random tests each month. All offenders have to remain in Phase III for at least four months. Then, offenders enter phases of suspension of testing or a tapering off. Phase IV requires at least one test each month. High-risk offenders have to be in this phase for at least four months and low-risk offenders for at least two months. Phase V requires one test per quarter. High-risk offenders remain for the balance of the supervision and low-risk for at least six months. Phase VI is the last phase of suspended testing and testing is done as needed. High-risk offenders are not eligible for this phase, and low-risk offenders might be placed in this phase at any time for the balance of supervision.

Intervention in a Community-Based
Therapeutic Community

Serenity Street Foundation Modeled after Delancey Street, Serenity Street Foundation, located in Columbus, Ohio, is a community-based, transitional program that assists recovering alcoholics, drug addicts, and ex-offenders. Serenity Street operates businesses for residents to work in and earn money and provides a structured living environment in which programming is provided. Programming consists of mandatory participation in a twelve-step program, education classes, employment, community involvement, peer counseling, involvement with a sponsor, and life skill classes. Life skill classes aim to give residents the tools to participate lawfully in society. It consists of stress management, anger management, interpersonal skills, basic health care, spirituality, criminal thinking, parenting, self-esteem, social skills, time management, HIV/AIDS/STD awareness, self-empowerment, domestic violence, and how to establish or reestablish credit.

The program appears to be based on a community model. Residents in the house meet for community meetings. Besides ensuring that the house is properly maintained, the community meets to discipline other members who have violated house rules. The community can vote to expel members who consistently violate rules, such as curfew violations, smoking in a restricted area, having unauthorized visitors on the second floor or the bedroom, or disrespecting others' rights and property. Immediate expulsion occurs whenever someone has violated a cardinal rule. These are no drugs or alcohol, no physical violence or threats to cause physical violence, no stealing, and no unauthorized overnight stays.

Residents transit through four phases after orientation.

Phase One

1. Attend a minimum of ninety days and a minimum of seven AA meetings per week
2. Maintain a sponsoring relationship with a sponsor
3. Have employment either at serenity street or in the community
4. Complete all house chores
5. Attend all house meetings
6. Have a positive attitude and behavior
7. Work on Step 1
8. Meet one-on-one with staff

Phase Two

1. Attend a minimum of five AA meetings per week
2. Have a sponsor
3. Work for forty hours a week
4. Complete all house chores
5. Attend all house meetings
6. Complete Step 1 and work on Steps 2 and 3
7. Have a positive attitude and behavior
8. Meet one-on-one with staff

9. Work on short-term goals
10. Step-up plan for long-term goals
11. Complete all homework assignments
12. Follow all house guidelines

Phase Three

1. Attend a minimum of five AA meetings per week
2. Have a sponsor
3. Work forty hours a week
4. Complete all house chores
5. Attend all house meetings
6. Have a positive attitude and behavior
7. Must have Steps 2 and 3 completed and work on Steps 4 and 5
8. Meet one-on-one with staff
9. Work on short-term goals
10. Plan for long-term goals
11. Complete all homework assignments
12. Follow all house guidelines

Phase Four

1. Attend a minimum of four AA meetings per week
2. Continue working with a sponsor
3. Work forty hours a week
4. Complete all house chores
5. Attend all house meetings
6. Have a positive attitude and behavior
7. Continue working on steps
8. Meet one-on-one with staff
9. Work on short-term goals
10. Work on move-out plans
11. Complete all homework assignments
12. Follow all house guidelines

An Afrocentric Intervention for Prisoners

In one of the South Carolina correctional institutions for adult offenders, an Afrocentric group program has been developed for African American males. It is called the Manning Cultural Awareness Program. Its aim is to enhance social and cultural identities, help the group members negotiate the process of self-knowledge and personal growth, and reconnect the participants with their African American ethos of family and community. The program has seven goals.

1. To increase prisoners' knowledge about their historical social and cultural heritage and identities
2. To strengthen prisoners' self-esteem, social competence, and sense of harmony, balance, and spirituality

3. To strengthen prisoners' ability to communicate with other African American males respectfully
4. To give prisoners a healthy environment in which each person could receive support and enhance their manhood
5. To assist prisoners in developing a sense of community with other males, their families, and neighbors
6. To assist prisoners in developing a culturally relevant perspective that would lead to optimal growth and finding a purpose in life
7. To assist prisoners in bettering their literacy and problem-solving skills

To achieve these goals, a number of activities are provided to the prisoners. These include inviting experts in the areas of African and African American culture, history, psychology, art, music, and philosophy to the program. These areas are enhanced through celebrations. Books and reading materials about African American and African history and culture are available to the prisoners. Some of the group sessions are centered around discussions of various topics and issues from the readings (King, 1994).

SUMMARY

This chapter described facets of anger and how it is linked to a multitude of adult males' offending, such as sexual assault, aggravated assault, and domestic violence. It discussed techniques and procedures for treating anger, domestic violence, sex offenders, and substance abuse. Then, a variety of treatment and intervention programs were described for male offenders. Among them were treatment programs for batterers, angry prisoners, general prisoners, depressed prisoners, sex offenders, and substance abuse offenders. The chapter concluded with a discussion of an invention program for federal drug probationers, a community-based therapeutic community, and an Afrocentric program for prisoners.

KEY TERMS

CRIPP
Duluth model
Regressed sex offenders
Personalized
    bibliotherapy

Reasoning and
    rehabilitation
STOP
CRIME-PICS
Cognitive self-change
SOTEP

SOAP
STOP
KEY/CREST
Serenity Street
    Foundation

11

❊ ❊ ❊

Treating and Intervention with Special Offender Populations

❊ INTRODUCTION

This chapter discusses counseling and interventions with a number of special offenders, involving jail detainees, gangs, developmentally disabled offenders, mentally ill offenders, elderly prisoners, and death row prisoners. These groups present special considerations for correctional policy makers and mental health professionals. Beginning the process of legal confinement, jails contain different offenders (i.e., men, women, and sometimes juveniles) with a multitude of problems, such as mental illnesses, substance abuse, suicide and suicide attempts, and pregnancy. Related to the issue of offenders having multiple problems is the issue of dual diagnosis, a major concern to clinicians (Breeder & Millman, 1992; Pestle, Card, & Menditto, 1998). Typically, the issue of dual diagnosis involves an individual with a substance abuse diagnosis and a mental disorder, such as antisocial personality disorder, schizophrenia, or mood disorders.

This chapter also discusses gangs, which consist of juveniles and adults and males and females. Interventions applicable to offenders with mental retardation and mental illness are provided. In addition, interventions applicable to elderly offenders follow. Finally, this chapter discusses prisoners on death row and counseling strategies for them. The justification for including death row prisoners is that, from time to time, mental health issues emerge with this group. For instance, a few years ago, a Florida death row prisoner reportedly had become insane and mental health professionals were requested to assess his competency to be executed. Even if competency to be executed is not an issue, they may legally require mental health counseling if they seriously deteriorate on death row, or correctional practices may permit mental health counseling in preparation for death.

CONTEXT OF JAIL DETAINEES

Jails differ from prisons in that jails are administered locally, hold unsentenced persons, and hold some persons who are serving sentences of twelve months or less (Harlow, 1998). Moreover, jails hold accused and convicted felons and misdemeanants, males and females, and adults and juveniles (Harlow, 1998). As a matter of public policy, some jails provide alcohol and drug treatment to detainees, but it is not legally required. Because of the shorter length of time that many detainees serve, treatment has been said to be more difficult in jails than in prisons (Mahon, 1997).

With respect to treatment, jails are similar to prisons in that jails are legally required to provide medical treatment to detainees, such as detainees who are severely mentally ill (Diamont, 1992) and detainees with medical problems (El-Bassel et al., 1995; National Commission on Correctional Health Care, 1995; Rosenblum, 1996; *Women Prisoners v. District of Columbia*, 1994). Also, detainees who are in crises have a legal right to mental health intervention to prevent them from committing suicide (National Commission on Correctional Health Care, 1995). Detainees undergoing severe withdrawal from substance abuse that has life-threatening implications have a right to medical attention (National Commission on Correctional Health Care, 1995). Failure to provide constitutionally required treatment results in many cases of civil liability for counties and mental health professionals (Gaura, 1995; Meyer & Deitsch, 1996).

A number of professionals have complained of the inadequacies of mental health services in jails (Belcher, 1988; Briar, 1983; Morales, 1978; Steiner, 1984) and have recommended changes in public policy (Hairston, 1991; Singer, Bussey, Song, & Lunghofer, 1995). Steadman and Veysey (1997), surveying 1,053 jails, observed that deficiencies still existed in jails, and "few jails, regardless of size, offered case management services to link [mentally ill] detainees leaving jails to community services" (p. 3).

Sensitive to the deficiencies in jails and legal concerns, the American Psychiatric Association (APA) Task Force on Psychiatric Services in Jails and Prisons (hereafter referred to as "The Task Force") has made specific recommendations for adequate mental health services in jails. The Task Force lists four core elements of adequate mental health services: (1) mental health screening and evaluation, (2) crisis intervention, (3) treatment, and (4) discharge and transfer planning (American Psychiatric Association, 1989).

Referencing these recommendations, Steadman and Veysey (1997) identify six core elements of competent jail mental health services: (1) screening, evaluation, and classification procedures; (2) crisis intervention and short-term treatment; (3) discharge planning mechanisms; (4) court liaison mechanisms; (5) diversion practices; and (6) contracting procedures. Seemingly, Steadman and Veysey's first five elements are a modification of the four core elements by the Task Force, and they include a sixth core element that involves contracting (American Psychiatric Association, 1989).

Interventions with Jail Detainees

The Hillsborough County Sheriff's Office, located in Tampa, Florida, created a substance abuse treatment for detainees in its jail. This program was one of three demonstration programs funded by the Bureau of Justice within the U.S. Department of Justice. The initial aim of the program was to serve the treatment needs of pretrial detainees, but as the program progressed, judges used it as a sentencing option. If the judge used it as a sentencing option, it was coupled with a period of probation following completion of treatment (Peters, Strozier, Murrin, & Kearns, 1997).

The in-jail program served males and females in two forty-eight-bed units. The male unit was always at capacity, but the female unit was not. The female unit averaged about twelve women receiving services. The other thirty-six beds were used by females not involved in the treatment program. All participants in the program were detoxified before admission. Individuals who were accused of violent offenses, were suicidal, or were psychotic were not admitted to the program. The treatment program lasted six weeks. It focused on cognitive–behavioral interventions, relapse prevention, and coping skills. Additionally, the treatment provided educational and vocational training, AIDS prevention, twelve steps, aftercare planning, and case management (Peters et al., 1997).

Based on the findings of a study of the program, Peters and colleagues (1997) underscore the treatment implications for female detainees regarding several areas. They contend that treatment intervention for female inmates should help female detainees recognize antecedents of alcohol abuse, such as trauma from past sexual abuse or familial substance abuse. Moreover, female detainees should understand the effect of abuse on psychosocial functioning, understand relapse prevention, and engage the use of an alcohol-related peer recovery groups.

Peters and associates (1997) also offer some other observations regarding specific treatment for woman detainees. They state that mental health and substance abuse screening should be done at booking, pretrial intervention, presentencing, and at the time of admission to a jail substance abuse program. This screening should explore whether depression or sexual abuse is an issue, and jail staff members should have training in recognizing these issues. When problems are validated, specific treatment interventions should focus on women's strengths rather than twelve steps because some professionals contended that twelve steps promoted dependency. Group treatment should be utilized so that women would feel free to discuss past issues of abuse, and women counselors should be used in order to facilitate disclosure. Last, the treatment program should help to establish linkages to community services for female detainees.

Deemed a model program that other jails have copied, the Orange County, Florida, Jail Educational and Vocational Programs provide a comprehensive intervention for detainees in its jail (Figure 11.1). This jail has beds for 3,300 detainees,

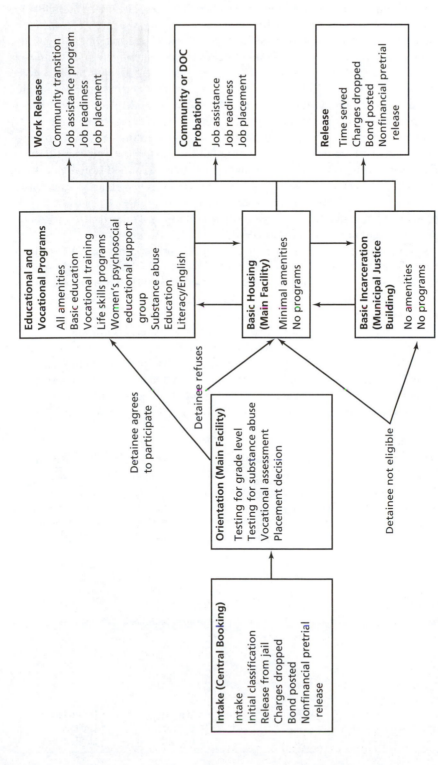

FIGURE 11.1 Flow Chart for the Orange County, Florida, Jail Educational and Vocational Programs

and most of the detainees are provided treatment services. Detainees ineligible for the programs are those who are mentally ill, have maximum-security classification, and have less than sixty days to serve. Each arrestee is assessed for eligibility to the program. If found to be eligible, a series of assessments are conducted, including educational, vocational, and substance abuse. If eligible, the detainees have a choice of whether to participate. If they refuse, they are housed in one of two jails that provides only a minimum of amenities (e.g., limited visits and telephone privileges, limited recreational activities, and limited commissary privileges). (See Table 11.1.) Agreement to participate entitles the detainees to be placed in one of five programs. These detainees are entitled to all amenities and privileges (i.e., air conditioning, nondormitory living, coed option, contact visits, television, additional gain time, secure personal lockers, newspapers, visits and telephone use, recreational activities, and commissary privileges). A detainee who initially refuses to participate can change his or her mind, and a detainee who violates the rules of the program is transferred to the no-frill jails (Finn, 1997).

The program consists of five types of courses: (1) basic education; (2) vocational training; (3) life skills development, each of which entails six hours of classes, five days a week; (4) women's psychoeducation support group, which meets daily for two hours; and (5) substance abuse education. Basic education consists of classes geared toward detainees receiving their GEDs. Vocational training offers auto maintenance, desktop publishing, carpentry, culinary arts, warehousing, and electrical wiring. In addition, the detainees receive instruction in resume writing and interviewing. Life skills consists of parenting and relationship skills, money management, and job search techniques. The women's psychoeducational support group promotes self-esteem, sober living, anger management, and basic life skills. The substance abuse counseling consists of a program called Moral Reconation Therapy,

Table 11.1 Quality of Life in Jail Facilities

Amenities/Privileges	Educational and Vocational Programs (Genesis, Horizon, Phoenix, Whitcomb, and Zenith Facilities)	Basic Housing (Main Facility)	Basic Incarceration (Municipal Justice Building)
Direct Supervision	*		
Air Conditioning	*		
Nondormitory Living	*		
Coed Option	*		
Contact Visits	*		
Television	*		
Additional Gain Time	*		
Secure Personal Lockers	*		
Newspapers	*		
Library Services	*		
Visits and Telephone Use	*	* Limited	* Limited
Recreation Activities	*	* Limited	* Limited
Commissary Privileges	*	* Limited	* Limited

which is a nontraditional approach for substance abusers, batterers, and detainees with "resistant" personalities. Geared to change how individuals act by changing the way they think, the Moral Reconation Therapy utilizes a workbook with exercises to address individuals' behavioral and social behaviors and their moral reasoning. An evaluation of the program found financial savings in operations, less use of force by correctional staff, low rate of violence, educational improvement for the detainees, and lower recidivism (Finn, 1997).

CONTEXT OF GANG MEMBERS

Gangs have changed considerably within recent years (Howell, 1998). Years ago, gangs were essentially juveniles who tended to leave gangs as they approached the end of their teen years (Thornberry, 1998). Gangs have changed in that some members are not leaving gangs and carry their gang affiliation long into adulthood (Riposa & Dersch, 1995). Provided that they are not killed as juveniles, contemporary gangs have members who are in their late twenties and thirties (Evans, 1998; Leland, 1998). As an illustration, Columbus, Ohio, similar to several Midwestern cities, has a problem with a gang that is based in Gary, Indiana, and that is a significant seller of crack cocaine in Columbus. This gang calls itself the G.I. Boys. A Columbus federal jury convicted several members of the G.I. Boys, and their ages were thirty, twenty-six, and twenty-eight (Ruth, 1998). Also, some gangs have adult women who consider themselves to be gang members (Brotherton, 1996; Wing & Willis, 1997).

Intervention for Female Gang Members

Five strategies are used by social control agents for dealing with gangs. These are suppression, social intervention, social opportunities, community mobilization, and organizational development or change. Of these five, the favorite strategy of police and prosecutors is suppression. Suppression involves gang sweeps in which police arrest gang members. It also can consist of prosecution offices establishing gang units within their offices. Prosecutors in these offices use vertical suppression, which involves the same prosecutor or prosecutors handling a case from the beginning to the end. This strategy provides more knowledgeable prosecutors handling a case and the gang member is not permitted to "slip through the cracks" because of a new prosecutor coming into the case later. To aid prosecutors, new laws have been passed such as California's Street Terrorism Enforcement and Protection (STEP), which makes it a crime to be members of a gang and which provides penalty enhancements for gang-related offenses. Also, the 1994 Violent Crime Control and Law Enforcement Act provides suppression tools for gang involvement in the federal criminal justice system (Wing & Willis, 1997).

Noting the ineffectiveness of suppression techniques, Wing and Willis (1997) propose a broad, macro approach for addressing gangs based on a critical race and feminist approach. This approach places the African American female at the center of intervention initiatives rather than on the fringes. According to Wing and Willis, African American females need to be at the focus because as inner city residents they are at risk for gang involvement. Also, African American women need to be at the center because they occupy multiple roles, consisting of mother, sister, and daughter and potentially have considerable influence on African American male gang members. Hence, a critical race and feminist approach accommodates the multiple roles and perspectives of African American females.

In line with this approach, Wing and Willis (1997) aver that "such solutions and the resulting programs must be targeted at improving the status of Black women in all their roles" (p.173). In part, this means that adolescent African American females must be furnished with educational and employment opportunities to decrease their probability of joining a gang. For African American adults, services should be provided that decrease the oppressive environment of poverty-stricken neighborhoods and improve the quality of life for single-parent families. This approach means comprehensive programs aimed at child care, health care and employment must be drastically improved.

Intervention Approaches with Adolescent Gangs

Adolescent Female Gangs Garland (1996), a social worker and former gang member in Philadelphia, Pennsylvania, describes his knowledge and experiences with female adolescent gang members. He states that girls join gangs to gain a sense of family, security, love, and respect. Girls leave gangs when they are given options or alternatives. Linked to them leaving are their realization that males use them and their desire to create a better life for themselves and their children if they have any. Garland contends that caring adults can have influence with female gang members. Being caring, consistent, trustworthy, and keeping commitments are invaluable qualities in intervening with female gang members.

Using information from a qualitative study of incarcerated gang members, Molidor (1996) identifies several contextual areas, consisting of education, family and neighborhood life, gang initiation, reasons for joining a gang, fear and paranoia, physical and sexual abuse, and criminal behavior (Molidor, 1996). Given the themes and contexts, Molidor further recites several implications for social work practice with females who are at risk for gang involvement. Molidor urges social workers to encouraged school-based programs where girls could get involved with programs that provide the same lure that gangs do. Such programs would include sports, art, and educational groups where girls could develop their identity, satisfy their social needs, and enhance opportunities for peers' recognition and acceptance. Social workers also should start intervention programs when girls are younger, acknowledging that targeting high school girls is too late. Recognizing the dysfunction in the family, parent intervention should be developed whereby the resolution of some parents' problems could have a positive effect on daughters. Finally, communities should recognize the need to restrict the availability of firearms to juveniles (Molidor, 1996).

Adolescent Male Gangs A group of law enforcement personnel from several large cities convened to formulate strategies for dealing with gangs (Spergel et al., 1996). Universal among the tactics used are suppression activities. However, some representatives state that they also work with community-based agencies. They list a number of community activities that they think are promising. These include

1. In-school anti-gang education programs that alert grade school youth to the consequences of gang membership and encourage their participation in positive alternative activities.
2. Social agency crisis intervention teams to mediate disagreements between gangs. These teams work closely with police and probation officers to identify potential trouble spots, prevent gang retaliations, or resolve gang problems without violence.
3. Alternative education programs to teach young people basic skills that they may not have mastered while in school, and to prepare them for a GED or, where possible, higher education.
4. Vocational training and job placement for gang members supported their efforts to hold jobs.
5. Pairing of gang members with local businessmen (some of whom belonged to gangs at one time). These businessmen provide support and guidance as well as a positive role model to the gang member to channel energies into positive activities.
6. Parent education classes and other programs that promote the family as a strong unit capable of providing young people with emotional support and supervision as well as clothing, food, and shelter.
7. Instruction to school personnel, community residents, agency staff members, as well as criminal justice personnel and others on gang activities and their impact, signs and symbols, and the way to counter gang influence.

Spergel and associates (1996) conclude that none of these activities has been systematically researched, but the belief is that suppression and social interventions are critical in stopping gang violence, enticing members away from gangs, and giving them alternatives.

A therapist in a mental health clinic, Branch (1997), espouses a mental health approach for working with gangs. First, he states that a mental health clinician must have a well-grounded clinical answer to several questions, and failure to obtain answers will result in obstacles to treatment. One question is who is making the referral. A second question is what conditions led to the referral. Another important question is whether mental health counseling is being sought because everything else has failed. If counseling has been previously tried, a second referral to a mental health clinic means the first counseling attempt failed. This means that the gang member is likely to be resentful, distrustful, and angry. The same feelings would hold for parents if they were actively involved in the intervention. If the parents were not involved in the first counseling experience, they may be puzzled and confused regarding why they were asked to participate in a second counseling attempt. Answers need to be readied for all these questions.

Then, Branch enumerates a number of clinical issues involving interventions with adolescent gang members. First, he urges that the mental health clinician attempt to get as many family members involved as possible. This doesn't mean that it is easy because some adolescents have destroyed or severely strained relationships within the family system. Also, some families have become splintered due to long unresolved problems. A number of gang members come from single-parent family homes where the father resides elsewhere. Yet, an adolescent in trouble may help begin the resolution of familial problems. Also, fathers who have been mostly absent from their sons' lives have responded to legal initiatives that required parental participation.

Other clinical issues involve providing the family with information regarding the psychotherapeutic process. Branch suggests sending parents a letter before the first appointment to explain the process. Another issue is deciding the setting in which therapy is to take place. Branch recommends that some sessions be held in the homes of the families, and some in offices. Having some sessions in the home provides an opportunity for the clinician to get a better handle on the level of family functioning. With these issues as a backdrop, Branch proposes a model for working with gangs and their families. This project, located in Denver, Colorado, is called the Family Intervention Project (FIP).

The FIP model is supported by a rationale and several assumptions. The rationale or theoretical base recognizes that the family of origin is the first place in which children are socialized. The family provides a foundation on which other teachings lie. Children learn basic skills and develop the aptitude for future learning from their family of origin. Contrary to popular beliefs regarding gangs and their pathological nature, gang members really have fairly normal socialization until their behavior becomes dysfunctional and antisocial. They then seek out or are attracted to gangs in order to get their psychological needs met.

Many family members demonstrate a lack of knowledge and unrealistic thinking regarding an offspring in a gang. Many parents will deny that their child is in a gang despite irrefutable evidence to the contrary. These parents also tend to distance themselves from reality, rather than confront the situation (Branch, 1997). They may be distancing themselves in preparation for their child's death or imprisonment.

As Branch stresses,

> The FIP is predicated on the idea that gang adolescents and their families share many commonalties that are often dormant. By having the family reunite in a safe, supportive environment, it is felt that they can engage in an introspective process, with assistance from clinicians. More important, it is believed that families need to rediscover their shared values and develop actions to accomplish meeting their needs as individuals and as families. Early experience with the FIP suggested that families are more responsive to other families with shared dilemmas than to professional clinicians, resulting in the design of multiple-family groupings. It appears that families are more apt to consider their adolescents' needs when they view other families, whom they perceive to be like themselves, struggling with adolescents around a similar dilemma. A major goal of the FIP is to create situations in which families can interact with other families and engage in community problem-solving around the misbehavior of adolescents. (p. 187)

A number of clinical assumptions are apparent in the FIP model. One assumption is that juveniles who are involved in gangs and their families possess the capacity to make significant changes. A second assumption is that the conveying of the first assumption to juveniles and families is therapeutic. It conveys the message that the family unit has the power to make things better. A third assumption is that families want their situations to be better. A fourth assumption is that the juvenile is a system and a juvenile's misbehaviors are symptomatic of dysfunctional family dynamics (Branch, 1997).

Specifically, FIP is provided in an all-day workshop that begins at 8:30 A.M. and ends at 4:30 P.M., consisting of orientation, several exercises for parents and juveniles to do, lunch, and scheduled breaks. Orientation begins with parents having the opportunity to share whatever they would like to share with other parents. More times than not, some parents express resentment and anger about being compelled to participate in their children's intervention. The mental health clinician should acknowledge the parents' feelings and urge them to give the program a try. Then, the exercises begin.

The first exercise is called "Why Are We Here?" It is intended to assist in substantiating the goals and objectives for that day. In addition, it gives the clinician an understanding of what the participants expect and gives insights into the parents' cognitions. Apparent are cognitive slippage, loose associations, cognitive intrusions, and other kinds of cognitive problems. Though challenges by the parents and gang members are likely to occur, this exercise provides an opportunity for the mental health clinician to summarize and reframe parents' reasons into the FIP goals and objectives.

The other exercise is called the "Black Delinquent Gang Youth Values" exercise. Branch, with some modification, utilized it with a mixed group consisting of Latino and African American parents. Probably, with other racial gangs, this exercise should be revised to reflect the ethnic nature of the gang. All participants, both parents and juveniles, were given a copy of the exercise with the following instructions:

> The following list of 13 images were given to a large sample of individual Black delinquent gang youth. They were asked to rank these images in the order in which they valued them, with most valued at number 1 and least valued at number 13. Your task is to rank these images as you predict the Black [or Latino] delinquent gang youth did. Place a number 1 by the highest valued image, number 2 by the next, and so on to number 13. (p. 191)

The items on the list were as follows:

_____Sticks by his friends in a fight
_____Has a steady job washing and greasing cars
_____Saves his money
_____Is a good fighter with a tough reputation
_____Knows where to sell what he steals
_____Gets his kicks by using drugs
_____Stays cool and keeps to himself
_____Works for good grades at school
_____Has good connections to avoid trouble with the law
_____Likes to read good books
_____Likes to spend his spare time hanging on the corner with his friends
_____Makes money by pimping and other illegal hustles
_____Shares his money with his friends

After completion of this exercise, the parents and juveniles are separated. Discussions ensue about the exercise. Principally, it gives insights into juveniles and parents' perceptions and what is important to them. Other possibilities with this exercise are that parents can be asked how they come to make the choices that they do. According to Branch, "a second layer of analysis to this exercise has to do with group members reconstructing and verbalizing the psychological dimensions of their participation in the group consensus exercise" (p. 194).

The afternoon portion of the workshop consists of communication skills practices. Conflictual relationships often lead to incomplete or inadequate communication. When the speaker does not communicate well, the listener makes poor decisions because he or she is hearing something other than what the speaker intended. The aim of teaching satisfactory communication skills is to avoid miscommunication and unproductive decisions. Parents are given the five rules of good communication, which are

Rule 1: Offer ownership for our own statements. Use "I" statements to show personal responsibility for what is said.

Rule 2: Never make statements for a person who is not available to state his or her position.

Rule 3: Keep focused on the issue at hand.

Rule 4: Only one person speaks at a time.

Rule 5: Make certain if you are the sender of the message that the receiver understands exactly what you mean.

Parents are given index cards on which to write the rules, and they are later asked to read them back. The clinician should help any parent who does not correctly remember these rules. Parents role-play with a juvenile other than their own child. The clinician gives a hypothetical situation and asks the dyads to solve it using the rules. Some parents or juveniles generally balk that the exercise is not real, which the clinician agrees. The clinician, then, asks them to solve a real problem. The parent is reunited with his or her child and is asked to discuss a real family problem.

At the conclusion of FIP, the families are given an assessment by the clinician. A follow-up plan is made in conjunction with the probation officer. Some of the possible recommendations might be a recommendation for family therapy, a drug assessment, more psychological testing, and out-of-home placement if the juvenile is at risk for abuse (Branch, 1997).

Branch declares the effectiveness of FIP but admits that there are no formal studies of it. However, he notes that the agencies that have used FIP have reported favorable results. Among the reports are that it is economical, it provides an observation of a family in seminatural environment, it provides an opportunity for families to try to be functioning families again, it provides a screening tool for probation officers, and it provides a different way of serving juveniles in gangs and their families (Branch, 1997).

CONTEXT OF DEVELOPMENTALLY DISABLED OFFENDERS

In California, which operates one of the largest prison systems in the country, estimates are that its correctional institutions handle over 22,000 offenders with mental retardation or developmental disabilities (Petersilia, 1997). In prison, these inmates are more likely to be beaten by other prisoners and sexually assaulted (Petersilia, 1997). Because of the treatment of developmentally disabled prisoners in California prisons, a class action lawsuit has been filed against the California prison system. One of the allegations against California prison administrators is that officials have violated the Americans with Disabilities Act (ADA) with respect to developmentally disabled offenders. As Petersilia (1997) contends, the ADA requires screening and rehabilitation for developmentally disabled offenders.

Another issue related to persons with developmental disability is that professionals do not recognize that this population may have mental health issues (Prout & Strohmer, 1998). According to Prout and Strohmer (1998), discrimination exists in the treatment of persons with mental illnesses and persons with mental retardation. Professionals who work with each group prefer not to work with the other group. Moreover, some professionals fail to believe that a person with mental retardation can have some psychopathology. As a consequence, intervention for persons with mental retardation tends to be unidimensional, such as offering only behavioral modification. Some professionals fail to recognize that some persons with mental retardation, for instance, suffer from depression or other mental disturbances, requiring a wide range of mental health services (Prout & Strohmer, 1998).

Intervention Applicable to Mentally Retarded Offenders

Several researchers tested the efficacy of treating persons with severe and profound mental retardation (Matson, Smalls, Hampff, Smiroldo, & Anderson, 1998), which has applicability to offenders. Residents in a facility for persons with severe mental retardation were randomly assigned to the treatment and control groups. The intervention consisted of staff training and edible reinforcement. Staff were trained in how to implement a strategy for getting residents to perform a task. They were given instruction in the rationale for the program, modeling the teaching procedures to use, and role-playing. The procedure called for prompting, modeling, guidance, and documentation of completion of each step. The control group received the normal procedure, which was prompting, modeling, guidance, and documentation of completion of each step. The tasks that each group was to perform included residents washing their hands and turning on a television set. Statistical analysis showed that the experimental control outperformed the control group (Matson et al., 1998).

Although the research participants in Matson and colleagues' study were not offenders, this study had implications for developmentally disabled offenders. It shows that staff training and reinforcements are critical in getting low-functioning individuals to perform some tasks. If severely disabled persons are incarcerated, the Matson and associate study shows that correctional officers need training and offenders are more likely to complete tasks with reinforcements. For an incarcerated offender population, a determination must be made about what the reinforcement may be. Candy bars may or may not be appropriate reinforcements in a prison setting. But some offenders with developmental disabilities are treated in the community in their own residence.

For instance, Smeltzer (1998) describes a residential program in Franklin County, Ohio, for developmentally disabled offenders who have sexually offended. The program is called Mi Casa, which means *my home*. Mi Casa owns three apartment buildings where about ten offenders reside. Each offender has his or her own apartment. Residents pay rent, buy food, pay utilities, and work in sheltered programs in the community. Treatment is primarily individual with behavioral modification principles. Treatment is provided one-on-one, twenty-four hours a day, seven days a week. It teaches residents to recognize their own warning signs that put them at risk for offending. They earn points for power control, empathy, responsibility, impulse control, obligations, anger control, and social skills.

CONTEXT OF MENTALLY ILL OFFENDERS

According to the General Accounting Office (1991), the percentage of prisoners with serious mentally illness is between 6% and 14%. These percentages may be on the increase. Laws have been changed, such as Guilty but Mentally Ill (GBMI), in which mentally ill offenders following convictions are imprisoned in correctional institutions instead of being committed to a mental institution (Arrigo, 1996). Then, some prisoners, adversely affected by overcrowding and violence, deteriorate while incarcerated and need mental health services (National Commission on Correctional Health Care, 1995). Among the diagnoses of prisoners include schizophrenia, bipolar disorder, depression, and antisocial personality disorder (National Commission on Correctional Health Care, 1995). Furthermore, some of these prisoners have problems with substance abuse, which then give them a label of having a dual diagnosis (Edens, Peters, & Hills, 1997). Moreover, some professionals contend that female prisoners have a greater problem with mental health issues and dual diagnosis than male prisoners (Cherry, 1995).

Some general treatment considerations for inpatient dual diagnosis patients should be observed by clinicians. First, staff must coordinate their efforts in working with dually diagnosed clients. The therapist must have knowledge of psychiatric illness, and the psychiatrist must have knowledge of addiction. Second, addiction must not be seen as secondary to mental illness or justified by mental illness. If it were, abstinence would be hard to achieve. Psychopharmacological therapy should be viewed as treatment for mental illness, not addiction. Third, when a patient has been detoxified, the prescribing of addictive drugs should cease. Further, psychotropic medications should be prescribed only when spontaneous remission has been ruled out. This admonition is so because behaviors associated with addiction can mimic psychiatric symptoms. Fourth, individual counseling is a critical factor of inpatient treatment. This counseling, targeting the addiction, should be more active and confrontive than psychotherapy with psychiatric patients. The goal is abstinence, not insight. The therapist should explain and address the major resistances to accepting treatment. Further, the therapist should stress principles of AA and NA, such as the recognition of powerlessness over addiction and control issues (Dackis & Gold, 1992).

Interventions Applicable to Mentally Ill Offenders

A major symptom of severely mentally ill persons is paranoid delusions. They see something routine and begin interpreting this activity as something sinister or harmful. Increasing medications may not be appropriate. Instead, conducting psychotherapy may be more appropriate. To this end, Levine, Barak, and Granek (1998) conducted an experiment to learn if inducing cognitive dissonance would alter psychotic paranoid ideation in persons who had been diagnosed with paranoid schizophrenia. Cognitive dissonance refers to the condition of having two dissonant beliefs at the same time. When it occurs, an individual feels tension and uneasiness. Levine, Barak, and Granek (1998) hypothesized that treatment that induced cognitive dissonance systematically would enable "patients who accepted the axiom to be gradually exposed to neutral, low and finally highly emotion-laden paranoid ideation in such a way that they eventually began to question the very existence of the paranoid system" (p. 11).

Twelve persons who had been diagnosed as paranoid schizophrenia were randomly assigned to two groups. To be included in the study, individuals had to meet six conditions: have a diagnosis according to the *Diagnostic Statistical Manual-IV*, be between the ages of twenty and forty-five, have had the disease for at least five years, have had eight years or more of school, have an active delusional system, and have had no change in antipsychotic drugs within the past three months. The control group met weekly for six weeks and then had a final session four weeks after the sixth meeting. The therapists, one male and one female, focused on coping with everyday life, avoiding treating delusional content, and concentrating upon enhancing extant defenses.

Before entering the cognitive-dissonance group and preparing individuals for it, individuals are brought into an office singularly with two therapists. One therapist posed a question to the other—what may cause a traffic jam? The other therapist gave several plausible reasons, such as a car being out of gas, engine trouble, a driver having a medical problem like a heart attack, traffic light out of order, accidents, and construction work. Then, the individual with mental illness is asked a similar question. The therapists are careful to select neutral questions. The individuals give several alternative answers and practiced giving answers until he or she is proficient in providing alternative answers. Then, towards the end, the therapist declares, "It is axiomatic that any event has several alternative explanations perceived by the keen observer" (p. 6). This axiom is put on a piece of paper, and the two therapists and the individual with the mental illness sign it. Research had shown that highly functioning persons, which in this case were the therapists, can influence lower functioning persons and a group's norms. After this exercise is done for each individual for the cognitive-dissonance group, therapists are ready to begin the group.

The group meets for six sessions for fifty minutes each session. A follow-up meeting occurs four weeks after the sixth meeting. At the first meeting, introductions are made for the therapists, one male and one female, and members of the group. Then, everyone repeats the axiom that each signed. The group is told that the purpose of the group is to be a working group to understand life situations. They are told that homework is assigned to be discussed at the next meeting. Rehearsals then occur of alternative explanations for neutral events. Individuals are given two typed neutral situations, and they, for this first homework assignment, are to write two alternative explanations. Upon seeing the situations, if a group member gives a delusional explanation, the therapists do not contradict the group member. Instead, they say that the response is one of many and to consider other possibilities.

In the second session, the homework is reviewed and discussed. Then, individuals are asked to develop three alternative explanations and these are practiced in the group. In addition, group members are encouraged to pose their own questions for other group members to come up with alternative explanations. As some members struggled with coming up with answers, other members of the group assist. For homework this time, members have to give three plausible answers to a typed neutral situation.

During the third session, the homework is discussed. Then, members are asked about situations in their lives that have the potential for stimulating paranoid ideation. Typically, there are everyday situations that lead many seriously ill persons to become delusional, such as a telephone repair person working on a line. The homework is to give explanations for such a situation. The question was "what may explain a scene where two people force a pedestrian into a car and drive off?" (p. 6).

The fourth session begins with discussions of the homework assignment. The session focuses on explaining alternative issues of insanity and eccentricity. For instance, members are asked to give several alternative reasons for thought insertions and involuntary hospitalization. When members give delusional explanations, the answers are treated as one of several possibilities. Homework is restricted to general issues of psychosis.

The fifth session consists of reviewing homework again. Members are asked to describe their delusions, provide alternative explanations, and to consider explanations offered by others. Homework is customized individually for each member's particular delusion, and each member has to develop three alternative explanations.

The sixth session is similar to the fifth. Also, each member is asked to give several explanations for their hospitalizations and psychiatric treatment. For example, one patient states that his hospitalization is due to a vindictive psychiatrist. The therapist asks could there be a more overriding issue for his hospitalization. When the man says no, the therapist asks the group if there is an event with only one explanation. The group is asked to give several possible explanations. At the end, they are told that the working group has given them a powerful tool for understanding their inner experiences with the axiom that they had learned and practiced. The follow-up session focuses on reinforcement of the sixth session.

The researchers used the Positive and Negative Syndrome Scale (PANSS) to assess participants in both groups at baseline, two weeks, four weeks, six weeks, and ten weeks (i.e., the follow-up). The PANSS was scored by an independent, board certified senior psychiatrist who was blind to which group the participants were treated in. For positive symptoms, the researchers found significant differences between the experimental and control group at week four, week six, and follow-up (Levine et al., 1998). In effect, the cognitive-dissonance group had lower scores than the control group. For the negative subscale, significant differences were found for the experimental group at week six and follow-up. Using the subscale of the PANSS, they computed a thought disturbance score for each participant and found significant differences between the experimental and control group at week four, week six, and follow-up. Again, the experimental group scored lower than the control group (Levine et al., 1998). Also, the experimental group had significantly less psychopathology than the control group at week six and follow-up (Levine et al., 1998).

Treating Dually Diagnosed Offenders

Some prisoners with mental illnesses also have another major diagnosis. Edens, Peters, and Hills (1997) studied seven state and federal treatment programs to learn how these programs served prisoners with dual diagnoses. The overall goal of Edens, Peters, and Hills (1997) was, following the review, to develop guidelines for developing a dual diagnosis treatment program for prisoners. From the seven federal and state programs, they identified commonalties among the programs and innovative strategies for working with this population. To these two ends, they studied each program's admission procedures, treatment strategies, staffing, coordination and linkage with other correctional service or community programming, and evaluation.

The seven programs represent a varied group throughout the nation. First, there is the Dual Diagnosis Unit of the Ventress Correctional Facility in Alabama. This is a sixty-two-bed program for male prisoners within a prison that is designed specially for inmates with substance abuse problems. Most of the prisoners, 60% to 70%, had been diagnosed with chronic depressive disorders, about 10% were diagnosed with schizophrenia, and 15% were diagnosed with bipolar disorders. The prisoners on the unit receive twenty-five to thirty hours of treatment each week for fifteen weeks. Specific treatment includes group counseling using twelve-step principles, psychoeducational groups, and relapse prevention. The prisoners on the Dual Diagnosis Unit receive the same core services provided to prisoners who have just a substance abuse problem, but the prisoners on the Dual Diagnosis Unit receive supplemental treatment geared toward their dual diagnosis. For instance, some of the prisoners on the Dual Diagnosis Unit are on medication and the staff receives additional training in dual diagnosis and the importance of medication compliance.

The second program is the Crisis Care Unit of the Sussex Correctional Institution in Delaware. It is a forty-bed unit located in a maximum-security institution. This unit initially began as a unit for prisoners with mental illness and mental retardation, but later was redesigned as a dual diagnosis unit because more and more prisoners had substance abuse issues. About 75% of the prisoners on the unit had a diagnosis of schizophrenia and substance abuse. Treatment lasts about two or three months. It includes comprehensive psychosocial assessment, individual counseling, group counseling, medication compliance, psychoeducational group, relapse prevention, recreational therapy, and case management. In addition, the unit operates on a level system, whereby progression to higher levels, by the achievement goals and adhering to unit rules, entitles prisoners to more privileges.

The third program is the Turning Point Alcohol and Drug Program of the Columbia River Correctional Institution in Oregon. This program, a fifty-bed therapeutic community for woman prisoners, consists of five phases that lasts from six to fifteen months. This program began as a substance abuse program and later became a dual diagnosis unit after the discovery that dropouts occurred because a number of women had mental disorders. Some of the disorders were post traumatic stress disorder, depression, and bipolar disorder. A minimum of thirty hours of treatment is provided each week, and this treatment consists of group counseling involving substance abuse and sexual and physical abuse. Also, the women are provided life skills classes and relapse prevention.

The fourth program is the Dual Diagnosis Track of the Lexington Federal Medical Center in Kentucky. It is a sixteen-bed subunit within a 120-bed substance abuse unit. The entire prison is for federal prisoners with medical problems. In the Dual Diagnosis Unit, the majority of prisoners have a major mood disorder or psychotic-spectrum disorders. The prisoners receive about twenty hours of treatment a week, delivered in three twelve-weeks phases over nine months. Treatment is based on a biopsychosocial model of recovery. Specifically, it entails psychoeducational, cognitive, and relapse prevention groups. In addition, activities are provided to address the prisoners' mental illness, including individual counseling and medication compliance strategies.

The fifth program is the Substance Abuse Felony Punishment Facility in the Estelle Unit in Texas. It is a rather large unit consisting of 130 beds. About 60% of the prisoners have a major mental disorder, and most of the disorders are schizophrenia. The program is delivered in three phases over a nine- to twelve-month period. Treatment is provided mainly through groups, involving substance abuse and relapse prevention. The substance abuse component is based on the twelve-step principles.

The sixth program is the Substance Abuse Felony Punishment Facility in the Hackberry Unit in Texas. It is a 288-bed program for women prisoners with substance abuse disorders with about 55% of the women on the unit having major mental disorders. In order, 22% were major depression, 16% were bipolar disorder, 13% were psychotic-spectrum, and 5% were anxiety disorders. Women with dual diagnosis are treated in three phases over a nine- to twelve-month period. It is based on a modified therapeutic community that consists of psychoeducational programs, women issues, AA, process groups, and relapse prevention. In addition, individual counseling is available for women.

The seventh program is the Dual Diagnosis Unit of the San Carlos Correctional Facility in Colorado. This is a thirty-two-bed unit within a 250-bed prison. About 40% of the men on the unit have a psychotic-spectrum disorder and about 50% of them have a major depressive disorder. It is based on a modified therapeutic community, providing psychoeducational, life skills, and cognitive–behavioral treatment. The prisoners on the unit have eight hours of treatment each day, and it lasts about a year. Release decisions are made by the Parole Board.

Based on their review of these programs, Edens and associates (1997) conclude that referrals to a dual diagnosis unit occur by one of three ways—after symptoms developed while the prisoner is in the general population, after screening in a reception center, and a referral from either a substance abuse program or a mental health program. Admissions are based on diagnoses according to DSM-IV. Treatment, while differing somewhat philosophically, is universal in activities. They all embrace a therapeutic community approach, incorporating psychoeducational, twelve steps, cognitive–behavioral, and relapse prevention treatments. In addition, the goals are quite similar in that they provide structured treatment, destigmatizing mental illness, striving for management rather than curing prisoners, education, changing prisoners' thinking errors, life skills, and problem-solving skills. The common method for delivering treatment is through group counseling. The programs for woman offenders include groups for sexual abuse, trauma, parenting, and relationships. Research on dual diagnosis treatment has been sparse. Some preliminary studies report that, for instance, treatment for woman prisoners in Oregon are less likely to be arrested than woman prisoners from the general population (Edens et al., 1997).

An Intervention Model of Chemical Dependency and Antisocial Personality Disorder Clinically informed by over twenty years of direct experience, Dr. Gary G.

Forrest (1994) formulated a general treatment model for persons with diagnoses of substance abuse and antisocial personality disorder. This model is geared primarily to the diagnosis of antisocial personality disorder with secondary importance afforded to the substance abuse diagnosis and can be used in either an inpatient or outpatient setting. Forrest's model consists of (1) detoxification, (2) long-term treatment, (3) commitment to total abstinence, (4) intensive cognitive–behaviorally oriented treatment, (5) structure, and (6) holistic and individualized care.

Detoxification is necessary because engaging in therapy with clients under the influence is ineffectual. Most individuals can be detoxified in three to seven days; however, some drugs, such as marijuana, remain in the brain several weeks after ceasing use. Some individuals may experience acute withdrawal symptom, but less than 5% experience this condition. If severe withdrawal symptoms emerge, hospitalization and close medical care are needed. Detoxification is the initial phase.

Long-term treatment is needed for persons with diagnoses of chemical dependency and antisocial personality disorder. Social and systemic factors force agencies and therapists to prefer short-term or brief treatment—twenty-one to sixty days. However, this length of treatment is inadequate for this population. If this brief treatment is used, it needs to be the beginning, followed by an intensive phase in a halfway house for eighteen to sixty months. Forrest argues that persons with antisocial personality disorders and substance abuse "find it easy to placate and 'get over' on counselors and treatment program personnel in brief treatment settings. Extended treatment relationships and programs force these patients to actualize and maintain long-term patterns of cognitive, behavioral, affective, and interpersonal change. Therapists also become progressively more aware, sensitive, tactically skilled, and effective when they are able to work with these patients within the context of a long-term psychotherapeutic relationship" (p. 164).

This population must have as a goal total abstinence from all substance use leading to dysfunctional and unlawful behaviors. Assault, homicide, incest and rape, and vehicle homicide occur when this group is under the influence of substances. While it may be unrealistic to extract a promise to never drink again, the therapist can remind a client to make a daily commitment to total abstinence. Taking one day at a time, such as the step utilized in AA, is therapeutic. As a person achieves accumulated daily abstinence and successes, then the probability of total abstinence becomes more probable.

The most efficacious therapy in working with substance abusers and antisocial personality disorder is cognitive–behavioral therapy. This therapy focuses on the here and now, instead of the past or future. It stresses the importance of rational thinking, reality, effective choice making and decision making, expressing and recognizing different feeling states, developing alternative courses of action, behaving responsibly, accepting responsibility for one's behavior, and effective problem solving. For effective treatment and rehabilitation, the client's cognitive style must be changed. Cognitive–behavioral therapy is ideally suited to change this faulty and maladaptive style of thinking, behaving, and emoting that sustains antisocial personality disorder and substance abuse dependency.

Structure is an important part of the program developed to treat individuals with antisocial personality disorder and substance dependency diagnoses. In the beginning, rules, standards, and expectations need to be established. Among the areas that need to be covered are (1) the type of treatment offered, (2) the need and reason for treatment, (3) therapist-client responsibilities and relationship, (4) treatment goals, (5) probable length of treatment, (6) alternative placements, (7) use of psychotropic medication, (8) relapse, (9) motivation to change and commitment to treatment, and (10) termination of the treatment process.

Because even among individuals with antisocial personality disorder and substance abuse diagnoses differences exist, a holistic and individualized treatment focus is needed. Holistic therapy addresses the needs of the whole person, attending the psychological, social, physical, and spiritual needs of the person in treatment. Single-focused programs do not work. Further, individualized care is needed because some, despite the dual diagnoses, differences exist. Some persons may respond to Antabuse, while some persons may need residential treatment more than once. Some individuals may have diabetes and need special dietary care (Forrest, 1994).

Intervention with Psychopaths

Clinicians agree that psychopaths are the most difficult offenders to treat, and some interventions make them worse (Hare, 1996; Rice 1997). They are more likely to be repeat offenders and these offenses tend to be quite violent (Blackburn, 1993; Hare, 1996; Rice, 1997). Nonetheless, Hare (1996) was commissioned by the Canadian government to design a treatment program for incarcerated psychopaths. Though the program was not implemented, Hare, aided by other clinical experts, used everything that they knew about psychopathy and psychopaths to design a treatment program.

Hare proposes "relapse-prevention techniques be integrated with elements of the best available cognitive–behavioral correctional programs" (Hare, 1996, p. 42). Such a program would deemphasize the development of empathy, conscience, or personality changes. Instead, the focus would be on convincing the offenders that only they are responsible for their behavior. Furthermore, these offenders have stressed to them that they can learn functional and prosocial means of utilizing their strengths and abilities to fulfill their needs and desires. The program would be tightly controlled in the institution, and the offenders would be closely supervised in the community. Hare could not promise that this program would be effective. It represents the best thinking of clinicians regarding psychopaths. To determine the successfulness of the program, Hare proposed a sophisticated experimental research design, in which randomization would be used and modules created to determine what works best for which type of psychopath. As stated, this program was developed by Hare but was not implemented by prison officials and remained just a proposal (Hare, 1996).

CONTEXT OF ELDERLY OFFENDERS

The proportion of elderly prisoners has increased in recent years (Chaneles, 1987). This increase is attributed to a couple of factors. First, there has been an increase in the number of elderly persons committing some offenses (Alday, 1994; Vito & Wilson, 1985) and mandatory sentences might make them ineligible for probation or early parole (Walsh, 1989). As an illustration of the former, a nearly fifty-year-old man murdered his wife around 1962. In 1997, he was the oldest prisoner in the Michigan prison system, eighty-four ("Wife's Killing Years Ago Locks Elderly," 1997). Second, changes in sentencing laws, such as life without parole or a lengthy period before parole eligibility comes, have resulted in prisoners staying incarcerated longer and dying in prison. Many of the elderly in prison are mostly male and mostly minority males (Gilliard & Beck, 1998). Recent statistics reveal that the rate of sentenced prisoners fifty-five and older under state and federal jurisdiction are ninety-six per 100,000 for white males, 505 per 100,000 for African American males, 413 per 100,000 for Hispanic males. For women, the rate is three per 100,000 for white, eighteen per 100,000 for African American, and nine per 100,000 for Hispanic (Gilliard & Beck, 1998).

A number of professionals report that elderly prisoners present a number of problems for correction (Booth, 1989; Goetting, 1983; Moore, 1989; Silfen, Ben David, Kliger, Eshel, Helchel, & Lehman, 1977). They are the most costly prisoners, needing frequent medical and nursing care and special devices to aid them in seeing, hearing, and walking. Alday (1994) surveyed all fifty states and the District of Columbia. Only seven states reported that there were no pressing problems in responding to the needs of elderly prisoners. Most of the other states reported that their most pressing problem is the rising costs of medical services for them and their chronic health problems (Alday, 1994).

Interventions Applicable to Elderly Offenders

A number of professionals have described the problems and issues of older persons (Parkinson & Howard, 1996; Rosen & Persky, 1997). These discussions have implications for treating elderly offenders. For instance, Brown and Romanchuck (1994) portray how existential social work practice and logotherapy may be used with the elderly. Existentialism involves the problems and problem resolution of individuals. These problems are problems of living, such as loneliness, self-consciousness, choice, decision, and death and dying. As Brown and Romanchuk explain it, "in existential counseling, the individual is viewed as a free agent who achieves meaning in life through the choice s/he makes and the stance s/he takes toward life circumstances. The meetings held between the client and the social worker are viewed as encounters. These encounters consists of two or more persons, usually the social worker and the client who meet in a series of encounters, characterized by a sharing, a caring concern and active dialogues between the participants" (p. 51).

The relationship between the social worker and the client is the essence of existential counseling. Also looming in the background is the realization that people live in three worlds—the natural, the interpersonal, and the private, personal environment. These three spheres of living are interconnected. The objectives of logotherapy with the elderly are to activate the elderly's capacity to accept responsibility and to make decisions about those conditions that confront them. A social worker using existential practice must have knowledge about the aging process, a conceptual framework, traditional social work knowledge, skills, and values.

For instance, a sixty-six-year-old man lived an isolated life in a residential hotel, causing the manager to ask for a social worker to intervene. Forced to leave a previous home involuntarily because of road construction, the man, who had lost a leg and refused to use a crutch, stayed in his room and refused to talk with other residents. Encounters revealed that the man had retired from the Navy, had been married, and had a son whom he did not see. His wife had divorced him because of a reputed dislike of living the life of a Navy family and the man's refusal to leave the Navy. Recounting happier times in his life, the man stated that he enjoyed gambling and going to the race tracks. The social worker offered to accompany the man to the race tracks. Thereupon, the man began to review the racing newsletter, studying the horses, their jockeys, and their wins. He used his crutch and the outing was successful because the man taught the social worker about racing and selecting winners. At the hotel, the man organized poker games with other residents and convinced them to join him at the tracks. The social worker maintained periodic contact with the man until the man's death and attended his funeral (Brown & Romanchuk, 1994).

An analysis of this case reveals that this elderly person had the view that life had no or little meaning for him. He was in existential crisis as a result of life's changes. As a consequence, isolation from others occurred and his suffering increased. The social worker did not attempt to tell the clients what their purposes in life were but to assist them in finding those purposes. A paramount aspect of existential counseling with the elderly is to focus on the present and future. A goal is to help the person determine what to do with his or her remaining time. Within a social work framework, "the client is always accepted as a responsible individual. The acceptance of this responsibility in making choices can lead to a modification of existing attitudes and diminishing of irrational beliefs; it can also lead to some cognitive restructuring which enhance the client's coping and problem-solving capacities" (p. 63).

Many professionals focus on the elderly's weaknesses as a basis for practice. However, Perkins and Tice (1995) recommend a focus on the elderly's forte through "a strength perspective for working with older people with mental health challenges by building on the common thread of survivorship, and examining how people live, and sometimes thrive, in an oppressive environment" (p. 84). A strength perspective utilizes several key concepts. These concepts are empowerment, suspension of disbelief, dialogue and collaboration, membership, synergy, and regeneration. Empowerment, in its usual meaning, consists of aiding disenfranchised or silenced clients to find their voices. Encompassing this deficit also is that a social worker or counselor must relinquish some of his or her power as a furtherance to clients finding their voices. In the strength model, pursing empowerment means the social worker must observe and learn how people in diverse communities were addressing their problems.

Suspension of disbelief involves a social worker rejecting the notion that clients are unknowledgeable about their problems or have misinterpretations. For counseling to be effective, clients must believe in the process, themselves, and the counselor. However, in the past, positions have been taken that degreed professionals know everything about problem assessments and solutions and clients know nothing. Suspension of disbelief increases individuals' personal power, reconfigures the role of the professional, and concedes that individuals may know best how to solve their problems.

Dialogue and collaboration are necessary processes if clients are to be helped. Dialogue is important if two parties are to maintain a collaborative process. An important element of dialogue is client-centeredness or starting where the client is. In this process, the social worker is not a passive agent but seeks to help the client in his or her immediate situation. Dialogue around the present leads to assessments that are verifiable, reconsideration, and change by the client and social worker.

Membership involves developing other relationships with others besides the social worker. As the professional relationship is strengthened, other relationships and networks may be renewed and initiated. As these other relationships, especially between client and the community, are developed synergy is created. Synergy occurs when the combination between the individual and the community produce benefits greater than what the individual acting alone can. Recognition of the community as a resource occurs when synergy is realized. Regeneration is the idea that individuals have the capacity to change and can become self-motivated to find solutions to their problems.

Perkins and Tice illustrated the strength model and the application of the concepts described. A seventy-six-year-old woman had insomnia, eating problems, and suicidal ideations. The woman declared that she had no reason to live, her daughter had been raised, her health was poor, and she was alone. Recognition of the woman's empowerment was aided by the social worker suspending the belief about elderly people's lack of resiliency and inability to change in later life. During the early stage of dialogue and collaboration, the elderly woman was "centered" and the social worker accepted her where she was as a woman who was scared, alone, and had no will to live. As the dialogue continued, discussion about her family and social networks occurred. The dialogues focused on the relationships and previous life experiences rather than specific problems. This led to conversations about her former work as a legal secretary, leisure activities, and past marriage. She was asked later about what she wanted to accomplish in the next year using three-month intervals. The woman responded that she wanted to do something that made her feel that she belonged, increase her activities, and sleep better. The woman remembered that her church had been a source of strength and support for her and that she could renew her attendance, which had waned in the past years. This also led to her involvement in a widow/widower support group. As a result of these changes, synergy and membership were created and the concept of regeneration was realized (Perkins & Tice, 1995).

Occasionally, aggressive elderly residents exhibit behaviors that are problematic for other residents, administrators, and staff. These problem behaviors consist of yelling, cursing, shouting, destruction of property, combativeness, and belligerency. Some institutions respond by the use of just medications or restraints. Cox (1993), using an ecological perspective that posits that behaviors are caused by internal and external factors, recommends a comprehensive perspective for intervening with aggressive elderly individuals. This approach may involve the use of medication and restraints, but other interventions are examined as possible remedial techniques. The ecological perspective posits that problems emanate from transactions between the individual and the environment. Particularly, these transactions produce stresses that impinge upon an individual's adjustment. Moreover, the sources for these problems may be from life transitions, stresses from the environment, and maladaptive individual responses.

In trying to understand any problem, a social worker begins with an assessment. Among the areas assessed are physical and cognitive causes, multidimensional factors in the environment, such as staff attitudes and social relations, life transitions, environmental stress, and maladaptive processes. To help in the assessment process, a social worker may use the results from a mental status examination, observational rating scales, and personal observations.

Following the assessment, interventions are developed. The goal is to reduce the intensity, frequency, duration, or presence of the aggressive behavior. Hence, interventions may involve supportive therapy and counseling, behavioral approaches, environment alternatives or changes, operant conditioning, reality orientation, physical restraints, or medication. Cox (1993) indicates that use of physical restraints and medication should be used sparingly and never as the sole intervention without attempt to use less intrusive methods of intervention.

Berman-Rossi (1994) illustrates group work with the institutionalized elderly. Her activities are grounded by five principles reported to be central for social workers in operating a group to solve a problem based on mutual aid (Schwartz, 1961). The tasks are (1) searching out the common ground, (2) detecting and challenging the obstacles, (3) contributing data, (4) lending a vision, and (5) establishing the bounds and limits of the working relationship between the group and the group leader. The issue that the group and Berman-Rossi addressed involved dietary. Berman-Rossi recognized that the dietary area was sensitive to residents' opinions, but residents believed that their opinions were unimportant to the dietary staff. This recognition by Berman-Rossi was that the residents did not know how to voice a complaint, which Berman-Rossi coaxed them into making a decision without specifically telling residents what to do. Berman-Rossi had to indicate regularly that change was possible whenever residents questioned whether they could influence the dietary director. Berman-Rossi made it clear that she would not tell residents what to do and would perform tasks only if these tasks indeed were too hard for residents.

Berman-Rossi was guided by the belief that a mutual aid group was an effective means of addressing problems of older, institutionalized persons. Guided by this belief, "the social worker's practice in groups with older institutionalized people is influenced by (1) the meaning of institutionalization, (2) the high degree of uncertainty, unpredictability, and loss experience, (3) the existential nature of life, and (4) the need to continue a meaningful life in the face of loss and ongoing uncertainty. Older people, like people in all ages, possess the ability to work on issues of importance in their lives" (p. 407). Although Berman-Rossi's description of a mutual aid group focused on elderly persons in an institution for senior citizens, it is easily adaptable to the prison environment.

CONTEXT OF PRISONERS ON DEATH ROW

Recent statistics reveal that there are 3,219 men and women under death sentences in 1996 (Bureau of Justice Statistics, 1998). One of the Justices of the United States Supreme Court expressed concern about the lengthy confinement of some persons on death row ("Justice Questions Lengthy Delays," 1998), perhaps inducing more executions. Individuals on death row have issues that are germane to mental health professionals and counselors (Showalter, 1992). Some mental health professionals are charged with determining whether some condemned persons are competent to be executed (Kermani & Drob, 1988). Moreover, some condemned persons deteriorate mentally on death row (Gallemore, Panton, & Kaufman, 1972), and when they do, they are entitled to mental health counseling for serious psychological problems like other prisoners (Pellegrino, 1993). Then, some condemned persons, nearing imminent execution, need some type of intervention (Miller & Radelet, 1993). For instance, some states offer prisoners a mild sedative just before an execution. Almost all states permit pastoral counselors or spiritual advisors to attend to the condemned before an execution. This section focuses on counseling in preparation for execution.

Intervention for Prisoners on Death Row

Searching for a theoretical framework, a few professionals with knowledge of the culture of death row have applied Kubler-Ross's Model of Dying to the condemned (Johnson, 1979). Developed to explain the experiences of ordinary individuals facing death, Kubler-Ross' s Model posit five stages of death—denial, isolation, anger, bargaining, depression, and acceptance. In 1979, the warden of a Florida prison, David Brierton, had read Kubler-Ross's book to help him understand what occurred with men on death row. At one point, the warden commented that John Spenkelink, who was nearing execution and who indeed was shortly executed, was in the anger phase (Von Drehle, 1995).

Kubler-Ross (1980) briefly portrays the conducting of therapy with terminally ill and elderly persons. These groups of person have special needs that can be partially satisfied, provided a counselor was willing to sit and hear the concerns. A vital task for all counselors is to let the individual know that they are willing to share some of the individuals' concerns. Getting an individual to share his or her concerns requires a "door-opening interview." This type of interview is simply a period in which two people can communicate without fear or anxiety. As indicated by Kubler-Ross, "the therapist—doctor, chaplain, or whoever takes this role—will attempt to let the patient know in his own words or actions that he is not going to run away if the word cancer or dying is mentioned. The patient will then pick up this cue and open up, or he may let the interviewer know that he appreciates the message though the time is not right. The patient will let such a person know when he is ready to share his concerns, and the therapist will reassure him of his return at an opportune time" (Kubler-Ross, 1980, p. 197).

Shneidman (1980) argues that a clinical thanatologist, whether he or she is a physician, psychologist, nurse, or social worker, does more than just talk. Any person in this role is a therapist because he or she is trying to help a dying person achieve a more psychologically relaxed death. Shneidman relates thoughts about conducting therapy with dying persons that appear to be more applicable to persons on death row. According to Shneidman, "from the psychosocial point of view, the primary task of helping the dying person is to focus on the person—not the biochemistry or pathology of the diseased organs, but a human being who is a living beehive of emotions, including (and especially) anxiety, the fight for control, and terror. And, with a dying person, there is another grim omnipresent fact in the picture: time is finite. The situation is dramatic, unlike that of psychotherapy with an essentially physically healthy person, where time seems 'endless' and there is no push by the pages of the calendar" (p. 202).

In accordance with this assessment, Shneidman specifies several types of human exchanges. One is ordinary talk or conversations such as that between two relative strangers discussing the weather or traffic. A second is a hierarchical exchange, which is illustrated by directives from an executive director to a secretary. The third is a professional exchange, such as a counselor who is treating a client. Finally, there is a thanatological exchange, which occurs between a helping professional and a dying person. Being in the role of a thanatologist is different from all the other exchanges because the several unique aspects of thanatological work. These aspects, pared from thirteen to nine, have implications for counseling prisoners on death row.

1. Goals are more definable because time is short. The primary goal is the psychological comfort of the person dying.
2. Because death is near, rules are different. The ordinary rules for psychotherapy may be modified. For instance, issues surrounding transference and countertransference may be different for a client who is dying and a client who is not. Moreover, a counselor may disclose personal information about himself or herself with a dying client but not a client who is not dying.
3. Working with the dying may involve elements of psychotherapy but it may not. The work may consist of rapport building, interview, conservation, history taking, plain talk, or communicative silence. What occurs depends largely upon the dying person's shifting needs, moods, control efforts, or traverse into denial.
4. In thanatological work, the focus is benign intervention. There is little concern about transgressing on the rights and liberties of dying persons. Intervention can be active, as long as it is in the dying person's interests. Intervention can take the form of interpretation, suggestion, requested advice, or interacting with institutional staff.
5. No one has to die after achieving psychoanalytically nirvana. Counselors must adjust their desire to achieve success. Shneidman maintains that "few individuals die right on psychological target with all their complexes and neuroses beautifully worked through. The therapist needs to be able to tolerate incompleteness and lack of closure. Patients never untangle all the varied issues of their intrapsychic and interpersonal life; to the last second there are psychic creations and recreations that require new resolutions. Total insight is an abstraction; there is no golden mental homeostasis" (p. 210).
6. Working through issues may not be achievable. Some people die with unresolved issues. A person who is dying can be helped to put his or her affairs in order, however, everyone dies, psychologically speaking, more or less intestate.
7. The dying individual establishes the speed of movement. Focus is on the process and the thanatologist's continued presence. Death does not need to be mentioned by the thanologist. Different individuals acknowledge an impending death or illness, with different moments of frankness. Anytime is okay provided it is comfortable for the person who is facing death.
8. Denial is present but it is not a stage. It is an expected part of the dying process, occurring or not occurring at various points. It is human for a person to forget about the end and ponder future events. A counselor should wait out this temporary denial, for the dying person, seeing the counselor's patience, will return to the present moment.
9. Achieving an enhanced psychological comfort is the goal. This may be achieved by visiting, plain talk, advice, interpretation, or listening. The achievement of

psychological comfort is the only measure of effectiveness. While hope should not be abandoned, a counselor should not be Pollyannaish or Cassandraish.

SUMMARY

This chapter began by discussing jail detainees and the counseling issues that some detainees have. Some detainees are mentally ill, have substance abuse problems, are in crisis, and are pregnant and give birth in jail. Gangs were discussed and how they have changed through the years. Intervention for female gangs was briefly described because little literature exists for illustrating how to intervene with them. One intervention for male adolescent gang members, the Family Intervention Project, was described in detail. This chapter also presented several interventions that were applicable to developmentally disabled and mentally ill offenders. Discussions occurred about interventions for elderly prisoners and prisoners on death row.

KEY TERMS

Detainees
Core elements of jail
    mental health
    services
Gang intervention
    strategies
Family Intervention
    Project

Cognitive dissonance
Dual diagnosis
Psychopaths
Existentialism
Strength perspective
Suspension of disbelief
Synergy
Regeneration

Ecological perspective
Types of human
    communication
    exchanges
Thanatology

REFERENCES

Abbott, A. A. (1995). Substance abuse and the feminist practice. In N. Van Den Bergh (Ed.), *Feminist practice in the 21st century* (pp. 258-277). Washington, DC: NASW Press.

Abdul-Khaaliq, R. (1995, July 21). Women behind the iron walls. *Muslim Journal, 6*, 3.

Adam, B. S., & Livingston, R. (1995). Homicidal behavior. In G. P. Sholevar (Ed.), *Conduct disorders in children and adolescents* (pp. 95-117). Washington, DC: American Psychiatric Press.

Addict has chance to kick habit. (1997, December 17). *Columbus Dispatch*, p. 4B.

Aguilera, D. C. (1990). *Crisis intervention: Theory and methodology.* St. Louis, MO: Mosby.

Aichorn, A. (1935). *Wayward youth.* New York: Viking.

Alcoholics Anonymous World Services, Inc. (1957). *Alcoholics anonymous comes of age: A brief history of A.A.* New York: Author.

Alday, R. H. (1994). Golden years behind bars: Special programs and facilities for elderly inmates. *Federal Probation, 58*, 47-54.

Alexander, R., Jr. (1988). Mental health treatment refusal in correctional institutions: A sociological and legal analysis. *Journal of Sociology and Social Welfare, 15*, 83-99.

Alexander, R., Jr. (1989). The right to treatment in mental and correctional institutions. *Social Work, 34*, 109-112.

Alexander, R., Jr. (1990). The Mapp, Escobedo, and Miranda decisions: Do they serve a liberal or conservative agenda? *Criminal Justice Policy Review, 4*, 39-52.

Alexander, R., Jr. (1991). The United States Supreme Court and an inmate's right to refuse mental health treatment. *Criminal Justice Policy Review, 5*, 225-240.

Alexander, R., Jr. (1992). Determining appropriate criteria in the evaluation of correctional mental health treatment for inmates. *Journal of Offender Rehabilitation, 18*, 119-134.

Alexander, R., Jr. (1992a). The demise of state prisoners' access to federal habeas corpus. *Criminal Justice Policy Review, 6*, 55-70.

Alexander, R., Jr. (1992b). Cruel and unusual punishment: A slowly metamorphosing concept. *Criminal Justice Policy Review, 6*, 123-135.

Alexander, R., Jr. (1993). Slamming the federal courthouse door on inmates. *Journal of Criminal Justice, 21*, 103-116.

Alexander, R., Jr. (1994a, March). *Sex discrimination in west coast prisons: A woman's prerogative.* Paper presented at the Annual Meeting of the Academy of Criminal Justice Sciences, Chicago, IL.

Alexander, R., Jr. (1994b). Hands-off, hands-on, hands-semi-off: A discussion of the current legal test used by the United States Supreme Court to decide inmates' rights. *Journal of Crime and Justice, 17*, 103-128.

Alexander, R., Jr. (1995a). Incarcerated juvenile offenders' right to rehabilitation. *Criminal Justice Policy Review, 7*, 202-213.

Alexander, R., Jr. (1995b). Employing the mental health system to control sex offenders after penal incarceration. *Law and Policy, 17*, 113-130.

Alexander, R., Jr. (1995c). Involuntary medication of mentally ill and pretrial detainees. *Journal of Crime and Justice, 18*, 3-20.

Alexander, R., Jr. (1996). African American youths and drugs: A time to pursue a mental health approach. *Journal of Black Psychology, 22*, 374-387.

Alexander, R., Jr. (1997). Juvenile delinquency and social work practice. In C. A. McNeece, & A. R. Roberts (Eds.), *Policy and practice in the justice system* (pp. 181-197). Chicago: Nelson-Hall.

Alexander, R., Jr. (1998). *A preliminary evaluation of the substance abuse treatment program at Ross Correctional Institution.* Unpublished report.

Alexander, R., Jr. (2000). Civil commitment of sex offenders to mental institutions: Should the standard be based on serious mental illness or mental disorder? *Journal of Health & Social Policy, 11,* 67–78.

Alexander, R., Jr., Butler, L., & Sias, P. (1993). Women offenders incarcerated at the Ohio penitentiary for men and the Ohio reformatory for women from 1913-1923. *Journal of Sociology and Social Welfare, 20,* 61-79.

Alexander, R., Jr., & Nickerson, N. (1993). Predictors and nonpredictors of female recidivism. *Free Inquiry in Creative Sociology, 21,* 141-148.

Allan, E. F. (1979). Psychoanlytic theory. In F. J. Turner (Ed.), *Social work treatment: Interlocking theoretical approaches* (2nd ed.)(13-32). New York: The Free Press.

Allen, B., & Brekke, K. E. (1996). Transference and counter-transference in treating incarcerated sex offenders. *Journal of Offender Rehabilitation, 23,* 99-109.

Allen, H. E., & Simonsen, C. E. (1995). *Corrections in America: An introduction* (7th ed.). Englewood Cliffs, NJ: Prentice-Hall.

Allen, H. E., & Simonsen, C. E. (1998). *Corrections in America* (8th ed.). Upper Saddle River, NJ: Prentice-Hall.

Amchin, J. (1991). *Psychiatric diagnosis: A biopsychosocial approach using DSM-III-R.* Washington, DC: American Psychiatric Press.

American Psychiatric Association (1989). *Psychiatric services in jails and prisons.* Washington, DC: Author.

American Psychiatric Association (1994). *Diagnostic and statistical manual of mental disorders (4th ed.).* Washington, DC: Author.

American Psychological Association's Ethical Principles of Psychologists and Code of Conduct. (1998). In G. P. Koocher, J. C. Norcross, & S. S. Hill III (Eds.). *Psychologists' desk reference* (pp. 413-434). New York: Oxford University Press.

Anderson, J. F., & Dyson, L. (1996). A tracking investigation to determine boot camp success and offender risk assessment for CRIPP participants. *Journal of Crime & Justice, 19,* 179-190.

Anderson, R. D., Gibeau, D., & D'Amora, D. A. (1995). The sex offender treatment rating scale: Initial reliability data. *Sexual Abuse Journal of Research and Treatment, 7,* 221-227.

Andreae, D. (1996). Systems theory and social work practice. In F. J. Turner (Ed.), *Social work treatment: Interlocking theoretical perspectives* (4th ed.). (pp. 601-616). New York: The Free Press.

Annon, J. S. (1996). Treatment programs for sex offenders. *American Journal of Forensic Psychology, 14,* 49-54.

Antony, M. A., Meadows, E. A., Brown, T. A., & Barlow, D. H. (1994). Cardiac awareness before and after cogntive-behavioral treatment for panic disorder. *Journal of Anxiety Disorder, 8,* 341-350.

Applebome, P. (1992, November 14). Jailers charged with sex abuse of 119 women. *New York Times,* p. A1.

Arciniega, G. M., & Newlon, B. J. (1995). Counseling and psychotherapy: Multicultural considerations. In D. Capuzzi & D. R. Gross (Eds.), *Helping relationships in counseling and psychotherapy* (pp. 558-587). Columbus, OH: Merrill.

Arden-Smith, T. H. (1995, June 20). P.G. teacher charged in fire, sex abuse. *Washington Post,* p. B5.

Armstrong, R., & Altschuler, D. (1994). Recent developments in programming of high-risk juvenile parolees. In A. R. Roberts (Ed.), *Critical issues in crime and justice* (pp. 189-213). San Francisco: Sage.

Arrigo, B. A. (1996). The behavior of law and psychiatry: Rethinking knowledge construction and the guilty but mentally ill. *Criminal Justice and Behavior, 23,* 572-592.

Atkinson, P. (1996, December 31). Jeff deputy is fired in inmate sex case. *Times-Picayune,* p. B1.

Aukerman, R. B., & McGarry et al. (1994). *Combing substance abuse treatment with intermediate sanctions for adults in the criminal justice system.* Rockville, MD: Center for Substance Abuse Treatment.

Bach, G. R. (1972). The marathon group: Intensive practice of intimate interaction. In H. I. Kaplan & B. J. Sadock (Eds.), *Sensitivity through encounter and marathon* (pp.142-148). New York: E. P. Dutton.

Balla v. Idaho State Bd of Corrections, 869 F.2d 461 (9th Cir. 1984).

Banawi, R., & Stockton, R. (1993). Islamic values relevant to group work, with practical applications for the group leader. *Journal for Specialists in Group Work, 18*, 151-160.

Barbaree, H. E., & Cortoni, F. A. (1993). Treatment of the juvenile sex offender within the criminal justice and mental health systems. In H. E. Barbaree, W. L. Marshall, & S. M. Hudson (Eds.), *The juvenile sex offender* (pp. 243-263). New York: The Guilford Press.

Barker, J. A. (1993). Professional-client sex: Is criminal liability an appropriate mean of enforcing professional responsibility? *UCLA Law Review, 40*, 1275-1340.

Barratt, E. S., Stanford, M. S., Kent, T. A., & Felthous, A. (1997). Neuropsychological and cognitive psychophysiological substrates of impulsive aggression. *Biological Psychiatry, 41*, 1045-1061.

Barrett, C. L., & Meyer, R. G. (1993). Cognitive therapy of alcoholism. In J. H. Wright, M. E. Thase, A. T. Beck, & J. W. Ludgate (Eds.), *Cognitive therapy with inpatients: Developing a cognitive milieu* (pp. 315-336). New York: The Guilford Press.

Basco, M. R., & Rush, A. J. (1996). *Cognitive-behavioral therapy for bipolar disorder*. New York: The Guilford Press.

Bass, A. (1995, June 22). Woman sues, says she was molested by nun. *Boston Globe*, p. 26-1.

Bassin, A. (1976a). Reality therapy and corrections: Introduction. In A. Bassin, T. E. Bratter, & R. L. Rachin (Eds.), *The reality therapy reader* (pp. 484-489). New York: Harper & Row.

Bassin, A. (1976b). Reality therapy at Daytop Village. In A. Bassin, T. E. Bratter, & R. L. Rachin (Eds.), *The reality therapy reader* (pp. 543-559). New York: Harper & Row.

Bates-Rudd, R. (1996, April 17). Minister unchains hearts, lifts spirits of prisoners. *Detroit News*, p. K,1.

Batson, C. D., & Coke, J. S. (1981). Empathy: A source of altruistic motivation for helping? In J. P. Rushton & R. M. Sorrentino (Eds.), *Altruism and helping behavior: Social, personality, and developmental perspectives* (pp. 167-187). Hillsdale, NJ: Lawrence Erlbaum Associate.

Beck, A. T. (1976). *Cognitive therapy and the emotional disorders*. New York: New American Library.

Beck, A. T., & Freeman, A. (1990). *Cognitive therapy of personality disorders*. New York: The Guilford Press.

Beck, A. T., Wright, F. D., Newman, C. F., & Liese, B. S. (1993). *Cognitive therapy of substance abuse*. New York: The Guilford Press.

Beck, J. S. (1995). *Cognitive therapy: Basics and beyond*. New York: The Guilford Press.

Beck, R., & Fernandez, E. (1998). Cognitive-behavioral therapy in the treatment of anger: A meta-analysis. *Cognitive Therapy and Research, 22*, 63-74.

Becker, J. V., & Kaplan, M. S. (1993). Cognitive behavioral treatment of the juvenile sex offender. In H. E. Barbaree, W. L. Marshall, & S. M. Hudson (Eds.), *The juvenile sex offender* (pp. 264-277). New York: The Guilford Press.

Becker, R. J. (1980). A criticism of the juvenile offender's right to treatment: The recognition of a local problem. *Loyola Law Review, 26*, 379-388.

Beitman, B. D. (1987). *The structure of individual psychotherapy*. New York: The Guilford Press.

Belcher, J. R. (1988). Are jails replacing the mental health system for the homeless mentally ill. *Community Mental Health Journal, 24*, 185-195.

Bentley, K. J. (1994). The right of psychiatric patients to refuse medication: Where should social workers stand? *Social Work, 38*, 101-106.

Berkman, A. (1991). Prisoner/patient struggles: A view from the inside. *Humanity and Society, 15*, 417-421.

Berkson, L. C. (1975). *The concept of cruel and unusual punishment*. Lexington, MA: D. C. Heath.

Berman-Rossi, T. (1994). The fight against hopelessness and despair: Institutionalized aged. In A. Gitterman & L. Shulman (Eds.), *Mutual aid groups, vulnerable populations and the life cycle* (2nd ed.). (pp. 385-409). New York: Columbia University Press.

Bingham, J. E., Turner, B. W., & Piotrowski, C. (1995). Treatment of sexual offenders in a outpatient community-based program. *Psychological Reports, 76*, 1195-1200.

Black's Law Dictionary (1990). St. Paul, MN: West.

Blackburn, R. (1993). Clincial programmes with psychopaths. In K. Howells & C. R. Hollin (Eds.), *Clinical approaches to the mentally disordered offender* (pp. 179-208). Chichester, England: John Wiley & Sons.

Blasko, M. L. (1985). Saving the child: Rejuvenating a dying right to rehabilitation. *New England Journal on Criminal & Civil Confinement, 11*, 123-158.

Blodgett v. Minnesota, 115 S. Ct. 146 (1994).

Booth, D. E. (1989). Health status of the incarcerated elderly: Issues and concerns. *Journal of Offender Counseling, Services, & Rehabilitation, 13(2)*, 193-213.

Borduin, C. M., Cone, L. T., Mann, B. J., Henggeler, S. W., Fucci, B. R., Blaske, D. M., & Williams, R. A. (1995). Multisystemic treatment of serious juvenile offenders: Long-term prevention of criminality and violence. *Journal of Consulting and Clinical Psychology, 63*, 569-578.

Borruso, M. T. (1991). Sexual abuse by psychotherapists: The call for a uniform criminal statute. *American Journal of Law and Medicine, 17*, 289-311.

Borys, D. S., & Pope, K. S. (1989). Dual relationship between therapist and client: A national survey of psychologists, psychiatrists, and social workers. *Professional Psychology: Research and Practice, 20*, 283-293.

Boudin, K. (1997). Lessons from a mother's program in prison: A psychosocial approach supports women and their children. *Women & Therapy, 21*, 103-125

Bowring v. Godwin, 551 F.2d 44 (4th Cir. 1977).

Boyd v. Coughlin, 914 F. Supp. 828 (N.D.N.Y. 1996).

Bradley, L. J., Parr, G., & Gould, L. J. (1995). Counseling and psychotherapy: An integrative perspective. In D. R. Gross & D. Capuzzi (Eds.), *Helping relationships in counseling and psychotherapy* (pp. 589-614). Columbus, OH: Merrill.

Branch, C. W. (1997). *Clinical interventions with gang adolescents and their families.* Boulder, CO: Westview Press.

Brandl, B. (1990). *Programs for batterers: A discussion paper.* http://comnet.org/bisc/brandl.html.

Brandt, D. E., & Zlotnick, S. J. (1988). *The psychology and treatment of the youthful offender.* Springfield, IL: Charles C. Thomas.

Brannon, M. E., Kunce, J. T., Brannon, J. M., & Martray, C. (1990). Toward the nonpathological assessment of behavioral and conduct disordered adolescents. *Journal of Addictions and Offender Counseling, 11*, 20-30.

Bratter, T. E. (1976). Group reality therapy with drug abusers. In A. Bassin, T. E. Bratter, & R. L. Rachin (Eds.), *The reality therapy reader* (pp. 588-599). New York: Harper & Row.

Breaking news (1999, February 8). *White house outlines anti-drug plan.* Associated Press.

Breeder, A. B., & Millman, R. B. (1992). Treatment of patients with psychopathology and substance abuse. In J. H. Lowinson, P. Ruiz, R. B. Millman, & J. G. Langrod (Eds.), *Substance abuse: A comprehensive textbook* (3rd ed.). (pp. 675-690). Baltimore, MD: Williams & Wilkins.

Breer, W. (1996). *The adolescent molester* (2nd ed.). Springfield, IL: Charles C. Thomas.

Breiling, J. (1992, October 31). *Summary overview of Mark Lipsey's meta analysis of delinquency interventions.* Overview presented at the NIMH meeting for Potential Applicants for Research to Prevent Youth Violence, Bethesda, MD.

Brewer, R. M. (1995). Gender, poverty, culture, and economy: Theorizing female-led families. In B. J. Dickerson (Ed.), *African American single mothers: Understanding their lives and families* (pp. 164-178). Thousand Oaks, CA: Sage.

Briar, K. H. (1983). Jails: Neglected asylums. *Social Casework, 64*, 387-393.

Bricker, D., Young, J. E., & Flanagan, C. M. (1993). Schema-focused cognitive therapy: A comprehensive framework for characterological problems. In K. T. Kuehwein & H. Rosen (Eds.), *Cognitive therapies in action: Evolving innovative practices* (pp. 88-125). San Francisco: Jossey-Bass.

Brill, H. (1959). Historical background of the therapeutic community. In H. C. B. Denber (Ed.), *Therapeutic community* (pp. 3-16). Springfield, IL: Charles C. Thomas.

Brochu, S., Guyon, L., & Desjardins, L. (1999). Comparative profiles of addicted adult populations in rehabilitation and correctional services. *Journal of Substance Abuse Treatment, 16*, 173-182.

Brodsky, S. L. (1998). Psychotherapy with reluctant and involuntary clients. In G. P. Koocher, J. C. Norcross, & S. S. Hill III (Eds.). *Psychologists' desk reference* (pp. 306-310). New York: Oxford University Press.

Brok, A. J. (1997). A modified Cognitive-behavioral approach to group therapy with the elderly. *Group, 21*, 115-134.

Brook, J. S., Whiteman, M., Balka, E. B., Win, P. T., & Gursen, M. D. (1998). Drug use among Puerto Ricans: Ethnic identity as a protective factor. *Hispanic Journal of Behavioral Sciences, 20*, 241-254.

Broome, K. M., Knight, K., Joe, G. W., & Simpson, D. D. (1996). Evaluating the drug-abusing probationer: Clinical interview versus self-administered assessment. *Criminal Justice and Behavior, 23*, 593-606.

Brotherton, D. C. (1996). Smartness, toughness, and autonomy: Drug use in the context of gang female delinquency. *Journal of Drug Issues, 26*, 216-277.

Brouillard, P. (1998). Popular psychological tests. In G. P. Koocher, J. C. Norcross, & S. S. Hill III (Eds.). *Psychologists' desk reference* (pp. 176-181). New York: Oxford University Press.

Brown, D. T., & Prout, H. T. (1989). Behavioral approaches. In D. T. Brown & H. T. Prout (Eds.), *Counseling and psychotherapy with children and adolescents: Theory and practice for school and clinic settings* (2nd ed.). (pp. 235-300). Brandon, VT: Clinical Psychology Publishing Company.

Brown, J. A., & Romanchuk, B. J. (1994). Existential social work practice with the aged: Theory and practice. *Journal of Gerontological Social Work, 23*, 49-65.

Brown, P. (1984). The right to refuse treatment an the movement for mental health reform. *Journal of Health Politic, Policy and Law, 9*, 291-313.

Brown, T. A., & Barlow, D. H. (1995). Long-term outcome in cognitive-behavioral treatment of panic disorder: Clinical predictors and alternative strategies for assessment. *Journal of Consulting and Clinical Psychology, 63*, 754-765.

Buchanan, J. (1991). Enabling dependent drug users: A cognitive behavioural assessment. *Practice, 5*, 34-46.

Bukhari v. Hutto, 487 F. Supp. 1162 (E.D. Va. 1980).

Bureau of Justice Statistics (1997). *Correctional populations in the United States, 1995*. Washington, DC: Office of Justice Programs.

Bureau of Justice Statistics (1998). *Capital punishment statistics*. Washington, DC: U. S. Department of Justice.

Burns, R. B. (1983). *Counselling [sic] and therapy: An introductory survey*. Boston: MTP Press Limited.

Camp, B. H., & Thyer, B. A. (1993). Treatment of adolescent sex offenders: A review of empirical research. *Journal of Applied Social Sciences, 17*, 191-206.

Camp, J. M., & Finkelstein, N. (1997). Parenting training for women in residential substance abuse treatment: Results of a demonstration project. *Journal of Substance Abuse Treatment, 14*, 411-422.

Campbell, L., & Page, R. (1993). The therapeutic effects of group process on the behavioral patterns of a drug-addicted group. *Journal of Addictions and Offender Counseling, 13*, 34-45.

Campbell, R. J. (1996). *Psychiatric dictionary* (7th ed.). New York: Oxford University Press.

Cannizaro, S. (1993, April 2). Convictions returned in court-martial. *Times-Picayune*, p. B8.

Carkhuff, R. R., & Beresnson, B. G. (1967). *Beyond counseling and therapy*. New York: Holt, Rinehart and Winston.

Carroll, K. M. (1998). *A cognitive-behavioral approach: Treating cocaine addiction*. Rockville, MD: National Institutes of Health.

Cavior, H. E., & Schmidt, A. (1978). A test of the effectiveness of a differential treatment strategy at the Robert F. Kennedy Center. *Criminal Justice and Behavior, 5*, 131-139.

Center for Substance Abuse Treatment. (1994). *Practical approaches in the treatment of women who abuse alcohol and other drugs*. Rockville, MD: Author.

Chacon, R. (1995, May 25). Therapist gets 2 years for sexual assault. *Boston Globe*, p. 74.

Chadwick, P., & Birchwood, M. (1996). Cognitive therapy for voices. In G. Haddock & P. D. Slade (Eds.), *Cognitive-behavioural interventions with psychotic disorders* (pp. 71-85). London: Routledge.

Chambliss, W. J. (1997). Toward a political economy of crime. In J. Muncie, E. McLaughlin, & M. Langan (Eds.), *Criminological perspectives: A reader* (pp. 224-231). London: Sage.

Champion, D. J. (1998). *Corrections in the United States: A contemporary perspective* (2nd ed.). Upper Saddle River, NJ: Prentice-Hall.

Chandler, S. M., & Kassenbaum, G. (1997). Meeting the needs of female offenders. In C. A. McNeece & A. R. Roberts (Eds.), *Policy and practice in the justice system* (pp. 159-180). Chicago: Nelson-Hall.

Chaneles, S. (1987). Growing old behind bars. *Psychology Today, 21,* 46-51.

Chemtob, C. M. (1997). Cognitive-behavioral treatment for severe anger in posttraumatic stress disorder. *Journal of Consulting and Clinical Psychology, 65,* 184-189.

Cherry, R. A. (1995, October 5). *Programming and treatment of mentally ill women offenders in the United States.* Paper presented at the Annual Meeting of Midwestern Criminal Justice Association, Chicago, IL.

Chesney-Lind, M. & Shelden, R. G. (1998). *Girls, delinquency and juvenile justice* (2nd ed.). Belmont, CA: West/Wadsworth.

Chesney-Lind, M. (1995). Girls' crime and woman's place: Toward a feminist model of female delinquency. In P. M. Sharp & B. W. Hancock (Eds.), *Juvenile delinquency: Historical, theoretical, and societal reactions to youth* (pp. 157-172). Englewood Cliffs, NJ: Prentice-Hall.

Chesney-Lind, M., & Shelden, R. G (1992). *Girls, delinquency and juvenile justice.* Belmont, CA: Wadsworth.

Chesney-Lind, M., & Shelden, R. G. (1992). *Girls, delinquency, and juvenile delinquency.* Belmont, CA: Wadsworth.

Chick, J. (1998). Treatment of alcoholic violent offenders: ethics and efficacy. *Alcohol & Alcoholism, 33,* 20-25.

Child, R., & Getzel, G. S. (1989). Group work with inner city persons with AIDS. *Social Work With Groups, 12,* 65-80.

Clagett, A. F. (1992a). Group-integrated reality therapy in a wilderness camp. *Journal of Offender Rehabilitation, 17,* 1-18.

Clagett, A. F. (1992b). Group-integrated reality therapy: Functional relations to rehabilitating felons. *International Review of Modern Sociology, 22,* 1-12.

Clark, D. (1972). Homosexual encounter in all male groups. In L. N. Solomon & B. Berz (Eds.), *New perspectives on encounter groups* (pp. 368-382). San Francisco: Jossey-Bass.

Cohen, B. Z., & Sordo, I. (1984). Using reality therapy with adult offenders. *Journal of Offender Counseling Services and Rehabilitation, 8,* 25-39.

Cole, P. S., & Weissberg, R. P. (1994). Substance use and abuse among urban adolescents. In T. P. Gullotta, G. R. Adams, & R. Montemayor (Eds.), *Substance misuse in adolescence* (pp. 92-122). Thousands Oak, CA: Sage.

Comas-Diaz, L. (1988). Cross-cultural mental health treatment. In L. Comas-Diaz & E. E. H. Griffith (Eds.), *Clinical guidelines in cross-cultural mental health* (pp. 337-361). New York: John Wiley & Sons.

Combs, A. W., & Avila, D. L. (1985). *Helping relationships: Basic concepts for the helping professions* (3rd ed.). Boston: Allyn and Bacon.

Committee on the Practice of Psychotherapy (1996). *Resource document on medical psychotherapy.* Washington, DC: American Psychiatric Association.

Compton, B. R., & Galaway, B. (1994). *Social work processes* (5th ed.). Pacific Grove, CA: Brooks/Cole.

Conarton, S., & Silverman, L. K. (1988). Feminine development through the life cycle. In M. A. Dutton-Douglas & L. E. Walker (Eds.), *Feminist psychotherapies: Integration of therapeutic and feminist systems* (pp. 37-67). Norwood, NJ: Ablex.

Cook, R. (1992a, December 17). Prison scandal continues as rookie guard is fired. *Atlanta Constitution,* p. E6.

Cook, R. (1992b, September 18). Former inmate sues state, guard over sex abuse. *Atlanta Constitution,* p. G2.

Cook, R. (1992c, August 12). Fired prison official re-hired. *Atlanta Constitution,* p. D3.

Corey, G. (1991). *Theory and practice of counseling and psychotherapy* (3rd ed.). Pacific Grove, CA: Brooks/Cole.

Corey, G. (1995). *Theory and practice of group counseling* (4th ed.). Pacific Grove, CA: Brooks/Cole.

Cornell, D. G., Benedek, E. P., & Benedek, D. M. (1987). Juvenile homicide: Prior adjustment and a proposed typology. *American Journal of Orthopsychiatry, 57,* 383-393.

Corse, S. J., & Smith, M. (1998). Reducing substance abuse during pregnancy: Discriminating among levels of response in a prenatal setting. *Journal of Substance Abuse Treatment, 15,* 457-467.

Couch, R. D. (1995). Four steps for conducting a pregroup screening interview. *Journal for Specialist in Group Work, 20,* 18-25.

Courchaine, K. E., & Dowd, E. T. (1994). Group approaches. In F. M. Dattilio & A. Freeman (Eds.), *Cognitive-behavioral strategies in crisis intervention* (pp. 221-237). New York: The Guilford Press.

Covington, S. S. (1997). Women in prison: Approaches in the treatment of our most invisible population. *Women & Therapy, 21,* 141-155.

Cox, C. (1993). Dealing with the aggressive nursing home resident. *Journal of Gerontological Social Work, 19,* 179-192.

Crouch, B. M., & Marquart, J. W. (1989). *An appeal to justice: Litigated reform of Texas prisons.* Austin, TX: University of Texas Press.

Crowe, A. H., & Reeves, R. (1994). *Treatment for Alcohol and Other Drug Abuse: Opportunities for Coordination.* Rockville, MD: Center for Substance Abust Treatment.

Crown, D. F., & Rosse, J G. (1995). Yours, mine, and ours: Facilitating group productivity though the integration of individual and group goals. *Organizational Behavior and Human Decision Processes, 64,* 138-150.

Crumbaugh, J. C. (1973). Everything to gain: A guide to self-fulfillment through logoanalysis. Chicago: Nelson-Hall.

Cullen, M. (1992). *Cage your rage: An inmate's guide to anger control.* Baltimore: American Correctional Association.

Czajkoski, E. (1976). Reality therapy with offenders. In A. Bassin, T. E. Bratter, & R. L. Rachin (Eds.), *The reality therapy reader* (pp. 560-567). New York: Harper & Row.

Dackis, C. A., & Gold, M. S. (1992). Psychiatric hospitals for treatment of dual diagnosis. In J. H. Lowinson, P. Ruiz, R. B. Millman, & J. G. Langrod (Eds.), *Substance abuse: A comprehensive textbook* (3rd ed.). (pp. 467-485). Baltimore: Williams & Wilkins.

Daley, M., & Argeriou, M. (1997). Characteristics and treatment needs of sexually abused pregnant women in drug rehabilitation: The Massachusetts MOTHERS project. *Journal of Substance Abuse Treatment, 14,* 191-196.

Daniel, C. (1992). Anger control bibliotherapy with a convicted murderer under life sentence: A clinical report. *Journal of Offender Rehabilitation, 18,* 91-100.

Darke, S., Kaye, S., & Finlay-Jones, R. (1998). Antisocial personality disorder, psychopathy and infecting heroin use. *Drug and Alcohol, 52,* 63-69.

Davis, G. L., & Hoffman, R. G. (1991). MMPI and CPI scores of child molesters before and after incarceration for treatment. *Journal of Offender Rehabilitation, 17,* 77-85.

Davis, P. (1993, October 16). Woman gets 30 days for having sex with student. *Washington Post,* p. B1.

Deblinger, E., & Heflin, A. H. (1996). *Treating sexually abused children and their nonoffending parents: A cognitive behavioral approach.* Thousand Oaks, CA: Sage.

Deep, S. (1994, August 19). Dispute's over: DNA tests on 8-week-old baby leads to her dad. *Detroit News,* p. B3.

del Carmen, R. V. (1992). Legal issues and liabilities in community corrections. In T. Ellsworth (Ed.), *Contemporary community corrections* (pp. 383-407). Prospect Heights, IL: Waveland.

DeLange, J. M., Barton, J. A., & Lanham, S. L. (1981). The wiser way: A cognitive-behavioral model for group social skills training with juvenile delinquents. *Social Work with Groups, 4,* 37-48.

DeLeon, G. (1988). The therapeutic community and behavioral science. In B. A. Ray (Ed.), *Learning factors in substance abuse* (pp. 74-99). Rockville, MD: National Institute on Drug Abuse.

Deleon, G., Wexler, H. K., & Jainchill, N. (1982). The therapeutic community: Success and improvement rates 5 years after treatment. *International Journal of the Addictions, 17,* 703-747.

Denoff, M. S. (1987). Cognitive appraisal in three forms of adolescent maladjustment. *Social Casework, 68,* 579-588.

Deputy is charged with raping teen-ager. (1996, January 11). *New York Times,* p. A20.

Dettweiler, L. E., Acker, M. A., Guthrie, B. F., & Gregory, C. (1972). Toward a community approach to behavior modification with emotionally disturbed children. In T. Thompson & W. S. Dockens III (Eds.), *Applications of behavior modification* (pp. 265-284). New York: Academic Press.

Diamant, A. (1992, September 10). Jails are holding thousands of mentally ill, study says. *Boston Globe,* p 8:1.

Dickerson, B. J. (1995). Centering studies of African American single mothers and their families. In B. J. Dickerson (Ed.), *African American single mothers: Understanding their lives and families* (pp. 1-20). Thousand Oaks, CA: Sage.

Diclemente, C. C. (1998). Treating matching in substance abuse. In G. P. Koocher, J. C. Norcross, & S. S. Hill III (Eds.). *Psychologists' desk reference* (pp. 311-315). New York: Oxford University Press.

DiGiuseppe, R. (1988). A cognitive-behavioral approach to the treatment of conduct disorder children and adolescents. In N. Epstein, S. E. Schlesinger, & W. Dryden (Eds.), *Cognitive-behavioral therapy with families* (pp. 183-214). New York: Brunner/Mazel.

Dixon, S. L. (1987). *Working with people in crisis: Theory and practice* (2nd ed.). Columbus, OH: Merrill.

Doty v. County of Lassen, 37 F.3d 540 (9th Cir. 1994).

Dowdy, Z. R. (1996, October 30). Guard fired for improper contact with inmate. *Boston Globe*, p. B3.

Doyle, K. (1998). Confidentiality revisited: A response to Manhal-Baugus. *Journal of Addictions & Offender Counseling, 19*, 2-6.

Dryden, W. (1987). *Counselling individuals: The rational-emotive approach.* London: Taylor & Francis.

Dryden, W. (1990). *The essential Albert Ellis: Seminal writings on psychotherapy.* New York: Springer

Dryden, W. (1996). *Inquiries rational emotive behaviour therapy.* Thousands Oaks, CA: Sage.

Duchschere, K. (1993, June 9). Two social workers disciplined, lose licenses to practice in Minnesota. *Star Tribune*, p. A9.

Dutton-Douglas, M. A., & Walker, L. E. A. (1988). Introduction to feminist therapies. In M. A. Dutton-Douglas & L. E. Walker (Eds.), *Feminist psychotherapies: Integration of therapeutic and feminist systems* (pp. 3-11). Norwood, NJ: Ablex.

Edens, J. F., Peters, R. H., & Hills, H. A. (1997). Treating prison inmates with co-occurring disorders: An integrative review of existing programs. *Behavioral Sciences & the Law, 15*, 439-457.

Edleson, J. L. (1996). Controversy and change in batterers' program. In J. L. Edleson & Z. C. Eisikovits (Eds.), *Future interventions with battered women and their families* (pp. 154-169). Thousand Oaks, CA: Sage.

Edleson, J. L. (1996). Controversy and change in batterers' program. In J. L. Edleson & Z. C. Eisikovits (Eds.), *Future interventions with battered women and their families* (pp. 154-169). Thousand Oaks, CA: Sage.

Edleson, J. L., & Syers, M. (1990). The relative effectiveness of group treatments for men who battter. *Social Work Research and Abstracts, 26(2)*, 10-17.

Edleson, J. L., & Syers, M. (1991). The effects of group treatment for men who batter: An 18-month follow-up study.

Research on Social Work Practice, 1, 227-243.

Edwards, A. C., Morgan, D. W., & Faulkner, L. R. (1994). Prison inmates with a history of inpatient psychiatric treatment. *Hospital and Community Psychiatry, 45*, 172-174.

Eisenstein, S., Levy, N. A., & Marmor, J. (1994). *The dyadic transaction: An investigation into the nature of the psychotherapeutic process.* New Brunswick, NJ: Transaction.

El-Bassel, N., Ivanoff, A., Schilling, R. F., Gilbert, L., Borne, D., & Chen, D. R. (1995). Preventing HIV/AIDS in drug-abusing incarcerated women through skills building and social support enhancement: Preliminary outcomes. *Social Work Research, 19*, 131-141.

El-Bassel, N., Schilling, R. F., Ivanoff, A., Chen, D., Hanson, M., & Bidassie, B. (1998). Stages of change profiles among incarcerated drug-using women. *Addictive Behavior, 23*, 389-394.

Elk, R., Mangus, L., Rhoades, H., Andres, R., & Grabowski, J. (1998). Cessation of cocaine use during pregnancy: Effects of contingency management interventions on maintaining abstinence and complying with prenatal care. *Addictive Behaviors, 23*, 57-64.

Ellis, A. (1985). Love and its problems. In A. Ellis & M. E. Bernard (Eds.), *Clinical applications of rational-emotive therapy* (pp. 32-53). New York: Plenum Press.

Ellis, A. (1986a). Application of rational-emotive therapy to love problems. In A. Ellis & R. M. Grieger (Eds.), *Handbook of rational emotive therapy*, Vol 2 (pp. 162-182). New York: Springer.

Ellis, A. (1986b). Rational-emotive therapy and cognitive behavior therapy: Similarities and differences. In A. Ellis & R. M. Grieger (Eds.), *Handbook of rational emotive therapy*, Vol 2 (pp. 31-45). New York: Springer.

Ellis, A. (1994). *Reason and emotion in psychotherapy: Revised and updated.* New York: Birch Lane Press Book.

Ellis, A., & Dryden, W. (1987). *The practice of rational-emotive therapy (RET).* New York: Springer.

Ellis, A., & Dryden, W. (1997). *The practice of rational emotive behavior therapy* (2nd ed.). New York: Springer.

Ellis, A., McInerney, J. F., DiGiuseppe, R., & Yeager, R. J. (1988). *Rational-emotive therapy with alcoholics and substance abusers.* New York: Pergamon Press.

Ellis, R. (1994, June 21). Sentencing ends child abuse ordeal. *Atlanta Constitution,* p. E4.

Ellis, T. E. (1996). Cognitive-behavioral 911. [Review of the book *Cognitive-behavioral strategies in crisis intervention*]. *Contemporary Psychology, 41,* 349-350.

Emery, G. (1993). Radical cognitive therapy. In K. T. Kuehlwein & H. Rosen (Eds.), *Cognitive therapies in action: Evolving innovative practices* (pp. 301-325). San Francisco: Jossey-Bass.

Empey, L. T. (1969). *Contemporary programs for convicted juvenile offenders: Problems of theory, practice, and research.* Washington, DC: U. S. Governmental Printing Office.

Enos, R., & Southern, S. (1996). *Correctional case management.* Cincinnati, OH: Anderson.

Enstad, R. (1992, March 26). Ex-lake counselor indicted in sexual abuse. *Chicago Tribune,* p. 2C3.

Enstad, R. (1993, November 15). Coach conviction called a vindication of Grayslake sex victim's story. *Chicago Tribune,* p. C3.

Erlinder, C. P. (1993). Minnesota's gulag: Involuntary treatment for the politically ill. *William Mitchell Law Review, 19,* 99-159.

Estelle v. Gamble, 429 U.S. 97 (1976).

Eth, S., & Robb, J. W. (1986). Informed consent: The problem. In D. K. Kentsmith, S. A. Salladay, & P. A. Miya (Eds.), *Ethics in mental health practice* (pp. 83-109). Orlanda, FL. Grune & Stratton.

Evans, P. F. (1998, June 1). Cops, crime and clergy: Boston's commish on how the new alliance between police and preachers work. *Newsweek,* p. 25.

Evans, T. D., & Kane, D. P. (1996). Sophistry: A promising group technique for the involuntary client. *Journal for Specialist in Group Work, 21,* 110-117.

Everson v. Board of Education, 330 U.S. 1 (1947).

Ex-judge jailed for trading sex for ruling. (1994, April 20). *New York Times,* p. B11.

Fabelo, T. (1995). What is recidivism? How do you measure it? What can it tell policy makers? *Bulletin from the Executive Director,* Number 19. Austin, TX: Criminal Justice Policy Council.

Fagan, J. (1992). Drug selling and licit income in distressed neighborhoods: The economic lives of street-level drug users and dealers. In A. V. Harrell & G. E. Peterson (Eds.), *Drugs, crime, and social isolation: Barriers to urban opportunity* (pp. 99-146). Washington, DC: The Urban Institute Press.

Farabee, D., Simpson, D. D., Danserequ, D., & Knight, K. (1995). Cognitive inductions into treatment among drug users on probation. *Journal of Drug Issues, 25,* 669-682.

Farrell, S. P., Hains, A. A., & Davies, W. H. (1998). Cognitive behavioral interventions for sexually abused children exhibiting PTSD Symptomatology. *Behavior Therapy, 29,* 241-255.

Farrow, J. A., Watts, D. H., Krohn, M., & Olson, H. C. (1999). Pregnant adolescents in chemical dependency treatment: Description and outcomes. *Journal of Substance abuse treatment, 16,* 157-161.

Ferrara, M. L., & McDonald, S. (1996). *Treatment of the juvenile sex offender: Neurological and psychiatric impairments.* Northvale, NJ: Jason Aronson.

Feske, U. & Chambless, D. L. (1995). Cognitive behavioral versus exposure only treatment for social phobia: A meta-analysis. *Behavior Therapy, 26,* 695-720.

Field, T. M., Scafidi, F., Pickens, J., Prodromidis, M., Pelaez-Nogueras, M., Torquati, J., Wilcox, H., Malphurs, J., Schanberg, S., & Kuhn, C. (1998). Poly-using adolescent mothers and their infants receiving early interventions. *Adolescence, 33,* 117-141.

Finkelhor, D., & Browne, A. (1985). The traumatic impact of child sexual abuse: A conceptualization. *American Journal of Orthopsychiatry, 55,* 530-541.

Finn, P. (1995). Do sex offender treatment programs work? *Judicature, 78,* 250-252.

Finn, R. (1997). *The Orange County, Florida, jail educational and vocational programs.* Washington, DC. National Institute of Justice.

Fishbein, D. H. (1994). Psychological correlates of frequency and type of drug use among jail inmates. *Addictive Behaviors, 19,* 583-598.

Fisher, E. M., Helfrich, J. C., Niedzialkowski, C., Colburn, J., & Kaiser, J. (1995). A single site treatment evaluation study of a military outpatient drug and alcohol program. *Alcoholism Treatment Quarterly, 12,* 89-95.

Fisher, J., & Corcoran (1994). *Measure for clinical practice: A Sourcebook* Volume 2

Adults (2nd ed.). New York: The Free Press.

Fisher, J., & Corcoran (1994). *Measure for clinical practice: A Sourcebook* Volume 2 Children (2nd ed.). New York: The Free Press.

Flores, E., Eyre, S. L., & Millstein, S. G. (1998). Sociocultural beliefs related to sex among Mexican American adolescents. *Hispanic Journal of Behavioral Sciences, 20,* 60-82.

Fodor, I. G. (1988). Cognitive behavior therapy: Evaluation of theory and practice for addressing women's issues. In M. A. Dutton-Douglas & L. E. Walker (Eds.), *Feminist psychotherapies: Integration of therapeutic and feminist systems* (pp. 91-117). Norwood, NJ: Ablex.

Forrest, G. G. (1994). *Chemical dependency and antisocial personality disorder: Psychotherapy and assessment strategies.* New York: The Haworth Press.

Foucha v. Louisiana, 112 S. Ct. 1780 (1992).

France, K. (1990). *Crisis intervention: A handbook of immediate person-to-person help* (2nd ed.). Springfield, IL: Charles C. Thomas.

France, K. G., & Hudson, S. M. (1993). The conduct disorders and the juvenile sex offender. In H. E. Barbaree, W. L. Marshall, & S. M. Hudson (Eds.), *The juvenile sex offender* (pp. 225-234). New York: The Guilford Press.

Frances, A., & Ross, R. (1996). *DSM-IV case studies: A clinical guide to differential diagnosis.* Washington, DC: American Psychiatric Press.

Francis, G., & Hart, K. J. (1992). Depression and suicide. In V. B. Van Hasselt & D. J. Kolko (Eds.), *Inpatient behavior therapy for children and adolescents* (pp. 93-111). New York: Plenum Press.

Frankl, V. E. (1963). *Man's search for meaning: An introduction to logotherapy.* New York: Pocket Books.

Fraser, D., Piacentini, J., Van Rossem, R., Hien, D., Rotheram-Borus, M. J. (1998). Effects of acculturation and psychopathology on sexual behavior and substance abuse of suicidal Hispanic adolescents. *Hispanic Journal of Behavioral Sciences, 20,* 83-101.

Fraser, M. W., Hawkins, J. D., & Howard, M. O. (1988). Parent training for delinquency prevention. *Child and Youth Services, 11,* 93-125.

Freeman, A. (1983). Cognitive therapy: An overview. In A. Freeman (Ed.), *Cognitive therapy with couples and groups* (pp. 1-9). New York: Plenum Press.

Freeman, A., Schrodt, G. R., Jr., Gilson, M., & Ludgate, J. W. (1993). Group cognitive therapy with inpatients. In J. H. Wright, M. E. Thase, A. T. Beck, & J. W. Ludgate (Eds.), *Cognitive therapy with inpatients: Developing a cognitive milieu* (pp. 121-153). New York: The Guilford Press.

Freud, S. (1935). Foreword. In A. Aichhorn (Ed.). *Wayward youth* (pp. v-vii). New York: Viking.

Frick, P. J., O'Brien, B. S., Wootton, J. M., & McBurnett, K. (1994). Psychopathy and conduct problems in children. *Journal of Abnormal Psychology, 103,* 700-707.

Friedberg, R. D. (1996). [A Review of the book *Cognitive-behavioral therapy of schizophrenia*]. *Journal of Cognitive Psychotherapy, 10,* 153-155.

Friedman, S., & Fanger, M. T. (1991). *Expanding therapeutic possibilities: Getting results in brief psychotherapy.* Lexington, MA: D. C. Health.

Fujimoto, B. K.(1993). Sexual violence, sanity, and safety: Constitutional parameters for involuntary civil commitment of sex offenders. *University of Puget Sound Law Review, 15,* 879-911.

Fulton, B., Stichman, A., Travis, L., & Latessa, E. (1997). Moderating probation and parole officer attitudes to achieve desired outcomes. *The Prison Journal, 77,* 295-312.

Furby, L., Weinrott, M. R., & Blackshaw, L. (1989). Sex offender recidivism: A review. *Psychological Bulletin, 105,* 3-30.

Gainor, K. A. (1992). Internalized oppression as a barrier to effective group work with Black women. *Journal for Specialist in Group Work, 17,* 235-242.

Galanter, M., Castaneda, R., & Franco, H. (1991). Group therapy and self-help groups. In R. J. Francis & S. I. Miller (Eds.), *Clinical textbook of addictive disorders* (pp. 431-451). New York: The Guilford Press.

Gallemore, J. L., Panton, J. H., & Kaufman, E. (1972). Inmate response to lengthy death row confinement. *American Journal of Psychiatry, 129,* 167-172.

Gardner, M. R. (1989). The right of juveniles to be punished: Some implications of treating kids as persons. *Nebraska Law Review, 68,* 182-215.

Garland, R. (1996). Gangs and girls in the hood. *Reclaiming Children and Youth, 5,* 74-75.

Garrett, P. W., & MacCormick, A. H. (Eds.).(1929). *Handbook of American prisons and reformatories*. New York: National Society of Penal Information.

Garvin, C. D. (1985). Resocialization: Group work in social control and correctional settings. In R. K. Conyne (Ed.), *The group workers' handbook: Varieties of group experience* (pp. 113-134). Springfield, IL: Charles C. Thomas.

Gary H. v. Hegstrom, 831 F.2d 1430 (9th Cir. 1987).

Gaura, M. A. (1995, December 14). Family of injured inmate given 1.7 million. *San Francisco Chronicle*, p. A16.

Gavin, D. R., Sobell, L. C., & Sobell, M. B. (1998). Evaluation of the readiness to change questionnaire with problem drinkers in treatment. *Journal of Substance Abuse, 10*, 53-58.

Gendreau, P. (1996). Offender rehabilitation: What we know and what needs to be done. *Criminal Justice and Behavior, 23*, 144-161.

General Accounting Office (1991). *Mentally ill inmates: Better data would help determine protection and advocacy needs*. Washington, DC: Author.

Gerhart, U. C. (1990). *Caring for the chronic mentally ill*. Itasca, IL: F. E. Peacock.

Gibbs, J. C. (1993). Moral-cognitive interventions. In A. P. Goldstein & C. R. Huff (Eds.), *The gang intervention handbook*, (pp. 159-185). Champaign, IL: Research Press.

Gibbs, J. C., Potter, G. B., & Goldstein, A. P. (1995). *The EQUIP program: Teaching youth to think and act responsibly through a peer-helping approach*. Champaign, IL: Research Press.

Gilliard, D. K., & Beck, A. J. (1998). *Prisoners in 1997*. Washington, DC: Bureau of Justice Statistics.

Gilliland, B. E., & James, R. K. (1993). *Crisis intervention strategies* (2nd ed.). Pacific Grove, CA: Brooks/Cole.

Girl gets probation for killing her brother. (1998, February 1). *Columbus Dispatch*, p. 7a.

Gladding, S. T. (1995). *Group work: A counseling specialty* (2nd ed.). Columbus, OH: Merrill.

Glantz, M. D., & McCourt, W. (1983). Cognitive therapy in groups with alcoholics. In Freeman (Ed.), *Cognitive therapy with couples and groups* (pp. 157-182). New York: Plenum Press.

Glaser, D. (1975). Achieving better questions: A half century's progress in correctional research. *Federal Probation, 39*, 3-9.

Glasser, W. (1965). *Reality therapy: A new approach to psychiatry*. New York: Harper & Row.

Glover v. Johnson, 478 F. Supp. 1075 (E.D. Mich. 1979).

Glover v. Johnson, 75 F.3d 264 (6th Cir. 1996).

Goetting, A. (1983). The elderly in prison: Issues and perspectives. *Journal of Research in Crime & Delinquency, 20*, 291-309.

Golan, N. (1986). Crisis theory. In F. J. Turner (Ed.), *Social work treatment: Interlocking theoretical approaches* (3rd ed.). (pp. 296-340). New York: The Free Press.

Goldapple, G. C., & Montgomery, D. (1993). Evaluating a behaviorally based intervention to improve client retention in therapeutic community treatment for drug dependency. *Research on Social Work Practice, 3*, 21-39.

Goldberg, C. (1970). *Encounter: Group sensitivity training experience*. New York: Science House.

Goldberg, C. (1995, May 21). Betraying a trust: Teacher-student sex is not unusual, experts say. *New York Times*, p. 37.

Goldstein, A. P., & Glick, B. (1996). Aggression replacement training: Methods and outcomes. In C. R. Hollin & K. Howells (Eds.), *Clinical approaches to working with young offenders* (pp. 151-179). Chichester, England: John Wiley & Sons.

Goldstein, M. J. (1996). Treating the person with schizophrenia as a person [Review of the books *Innovations in psychological management of schizophrenia: Assessment, treatment and services; Cognitive-behavioral therapy of schizophrenia*]. *Contemporary Psychology, 41*, 256-258.

Goldston, R. B. (1997). [A review of the book *Cognitive-behavioral therapy with bipolar disorder*]. *Child & Family Behavior Therapy, 19*, 29-31.

Goldyn v. Angelone, No. 94-15128, 1994 U.S. App. LEXIS 27145.

Goodman, H. (1997). Social group work in community corrections. *Social Work With Groups, 20*, 51-64.

Goodstein, L. D., & Pfeiffer, J. W. (Eds.) (1985). *The 1985 annual: Developing human resources*. San Diego, CA: University Associates.

Goodstein, L., Mackenzie, D. L., & Shotland, R. L. (1984). Personal control and inmate adjustment to prison. *Criminology, 22,* 343-369.

Gorman-Smith, D., Tolan, P. H., Zelli, A., & Huesmann, L. R. (1996). The relation of family functioning to violence among inner-city minority youths. *Journal of Family Psychology, 10,* 115-129.

Gorski, T. T., & Kelley, J. M. (1996). *Counselor's manual for relapse prevention with chemically dependent criminal offenders.* Rockville, MD: Center for Substance Abuse Treatment.

Gorski, T. T., Kelley, J. M., Havens, L., & Peters, R. H. (1995). *Relapse prevention and the substance-abusing criminal offender: An executive briefing.* Rockville, MD: Center for Substance Abuse Treatment.

Gottschalk, L. A., & Davidson, R. S. (1972). Sensitivity groups, encounter groups, training groups, marathon groups, and the laboratory movement. In H. I. Kaplan and B. J. Sadock (Eds.), *Sensitivity through encounter and marathon* (pp. 59-94). New York: E. P. Dutton.

Grabow, R. W., & Burkhart, B. R. (1986). Social skill and depression: A test of cognitive and behavioral hypotheses. *Journal of Clinical Psychology, 42,* 21-27.

Greason v. Kemp, 891 F.2d 829 (11th Cir. 1990).

Green, L. L., Fullilove, M. T., & Fullilove, R. E. (1998). Stories of spiritual awakening: The nature of spirituality in recovery. *Journal of Substance Abuse Treatment, 15,* 325-331.

Greenberg, L. S., Rice, L. N., & Elliott, R. (1993). *Facilitating emotional change: The moment-by-moment process.* New York: The Guilford Press.

Greenfeld, L. A. (1997). *Sex offenses and offenders: An analysis of data on rape and sexual assault.* Washington, DC: Bureau of Justice Statistics.

Greenwood, V. (1985). RET and substance abuse. In A. Ellis & M. E. Bernard (Eds.), *Clinical applications of rational-emotive therapy* (pp. 209-235). New York: Plenum Press.

Gregg v. Georgia, 342 U.S. 153 (1976).

Grieger, R. M. (1986). Anger problems. In A. Ellis & R. M. Grieger (Eds.), *Handbook of rational emotive therapy* (Vol 2) (pp. 121-140). New York: Springer.

Griffith, E. E. H., & Young, J. L. (1988). A cross-cultural introduction to the therapeutic aspects of Christian religious ritual. In L. Comas-Diaz & E. E. H. Griffith (Eds.), *Clinical guidelines in cross-cultural*

mental health (pp. 69-89). New York: John Wiley & Sons.

Griffith, J. (1984). Evidence of unidimensionality of locus of control in women prisoners. Implications for prisoner rehabilitation. *Journal of Offender, Services, & Rehabilitation, 9,* 57-69.

Gropper, M., Liraz, Z., Portowicz, D., & Schindler, M. (1995). Computer integrated drug prevention: A new approach to teach lower socioeconomic 5th and 6th grade Israeli children to say no to drugs. *Social Work in Health Care, 22,* 87-103.

Gross, D. R., & Capuzzi, D. (1995). Helping relationships in counseling and psychotherapy. In D. Capuzzi & D. R. Gross (Eds.), *Counseling and psychotherapy: Theories and interventions,* (pp. 5-27). Columbus, OH: Merrill.

Grumman, C. (1995, July 20). Jailor allegedly harassed inmates for sexual favors. *Chicago Tribune,* p. 2C8.

Grummett v. Rushen, 779 F.2d 491 (9th Cir. 1985).

H. C. by Hewett v. Jarrard, 786 F.2d 1080 (11th Cir. 1986).

Haas, K, C. (1993). Constitutional challenges to the compulsory HIV testing of prisoners and the mandatory segregation of HIV-positive prisoners. *Prison Journal, 73,* 391-422.

Haddock, G., Bentall, R. P., & P. D. Slade (1996). Psychological treatment of auditory hallucinations: Focusing or distraction. In G. Haddock & P. D. Slade (Eds.), *Cognitive-behavioural interventions with psychotic disorders* (pp. 45-70). London: Routledge.

Hageman, J. T., & Sigler, R. T. (1998). An evaluation of the implementation of a specialized treatment of sexual offenders program. *International Journal of Offender Therapy and Comparative Criminology, 42,* 198-209.

Hairston, C. F. (1991). Mothers in jail: Parent-child separation and jail visitation. *Affilia, 6,* 9-27.

Hales, R. E., Yudofsky, S. C., & Talbott, J. A. (Eds.). (1994). *Textbook of psychiatry* (2nd ed.). Washington, DC: American Psychiatric Press.

Hall, D. M. (1960). *Dynamics of group action* (2nd ed.). Danville, IL: The Interstate.

Hall, G., & Nagayama, C. (1995). Sexual offender recidivism revisted: A meta-analysis of recent treatment studies. *Journal of Consulting and Clinical Psychology, 63,* 802-809.

Hamid, A. (1990). The political economy of crack-related violence. *Contemporary Drug Problems, 17,* 31-78.

Hamid, A. (1992). Drugs and patterns of opportunity in the inner city: The case of middle-aged, middle-income cocaine smokers. In A. V. Harrell & G. E. Peterson (Eds.), *Drugs, crime, and social isolation: Barriers to urban opportunity* (pp. 209-239). Washington, DC: The Urban Institute Press.

Hardy, A. (1994, December 21). Former teacher charged with sexually assaulting student. *Houston Post,* p. A23.

Hare, R. D. (1996). Psychopathy: A clinical construct whose time has come. *Criminal Justice and Behavior, 23,* 25-54.

Hare, R. D., Strachan, C. E., & Forth, A. E. (1993). Psychopathy and crime: A review. In K. Howells & C. R. Hollin (Eds.), *Clinical approaches to the mentally disordered offender* (pp. 165-178). Chichester, England: John Wiley & Sons.

Harlow, C. W. (1998). *Profile of jail inmates 1996.* Bureau of Justice Statistics Special Report: Washington, DC: U. S. Department of Justice.

Harmelin v. Michigan, 111 S. Ct. 2680 (1991).

Harper v. the State of Washington, 110 Wn. 873 (1988).

Harrigan, J. A., & Rosenthal, R. (1986). Nonverbal aspects of empathy and rapport in physician-patient interaction. In P. D. Blanck, Buck, R., & R. Rosenthal (Eds.), *Nonverbal communication in the clinical context* (pp. 36-73). University Park, PA: The Pennsylvania State University Press.

Harris, P. M. (1995). Prison-based sex offender treatment programs in the post sexual psychopath era. *Journal of Psychiatry and Law, 23,* 555-581.

Harris v. Thigpen, 941 F.2d 1495 (11th Cir. 1991).

Hartley, C. C. (1998). How incest offenders overcome internal inhibitions through the use of cognitions and cognitive distortion. *Journal of Interpersonal Violence, 13,* 25-39.

Hartman, H. L. (1978). *Basic psychiatry for corrections workers.* Springfield, IL: Charles C. Thomas.

Harvey, A. R., & Coleman, A. A. (1997). An afrocentric program for African American males in the juvenile justice system. *Child Welfare, 76,* 197-211.

Hassan, R. A. (1995, July 7). Prison ministry revolution. *Muslim Journal, 3:*1.

Hay, A., & Stirling, A. (1998). Women need women. *Probation Journal, 45,* 36-39.

Hearn, G. (1979). General systems theory and social work. In F. J. Turner (Ed.), *Social work treatment: Interlocking theoretical approaches* (2nd ed.). (pp. 333-359). New York: The Free Press.

Heinz, J. W., Gargaro, S., & Kelly, K. G. (1987). *A model residential juvenile sex-offender treatment program: The Hennepin county home school.* Syracuse, NY: Safer Society Press.

Hemmons, W. M. (1995). The impact of the law on single mothers and the innocent. In B. J. Dickerson (Ed.), *African American single mothers: Understanding their lives and families* (pp. 94-116). Thousand Oaks, CA: Sage.

Henderson, M. C. & Kalichman, S. C. (1990). Sexually deviant behavior and schizotypy: A theoretical perspective with supportive data. *Psychiatric Quarterly, 61,* 655-703.

Heney, J., & Kristiansen, C. M. (1997). An analysis of the impact of prison on women survivors of childhood sexual abuse. *Women & Therapy, 20,* 29-44.

Henggeler, S. W. (1994). *Family preservation using multisystemic treatment: A cost-savings strategy for reducing recidivism and institutionalization of serious juvenile offenders.* Charleston, SC: Department of Psychiatry and Behavioral Sciences.

Henggeler, S. W., & Borduin, C. M. (1990). *Family therapy and beyond: A mutisystemic approach to treating the behavior problems of children and adolescents.* Pacific Grove, CA: Brooks/Cole.

Henning, K. R., & Frueh, B. C. (1996). Cognitive-behavioral treatment of incarcerated offenders: An evaluation of the Vermont Department of Corrections' cognitive self-change program. *Criminal Justice and Behavior, 23,* 523-541.

Herbert, R. (1985). Women's prisons: An equal protection evaluation. *Yale Law Journal, 94,* 1182-1206.

Hershenson, D. B., & Power, P. W. (1987). *Mental health counseling: Theory and practice.* New York: Pergamon Press.

Hetzel, R. D., Barton, D. A., Davenport, D. S. (1994). Helping men change: A group counseling model for male clients. *Journal of Specialists in Group Work, 19,* 52-64.

Heugle, R. L., Jr. (1980). The right to treatment for juvenile offenders. *Loyola Law Review, 26*, 360-378.

Higgs, D. C., Canavan, M. M., & Meyer, W. J. III (1992). Moving from defense to offense: The Development of an adolescent female sex offender. *The Journal of Sex Research, 29*, 131-139.

Higgs, J. A. (1992). Dealing with resistance: Strategies for effective group. *Journal for Specialists in Group Work, 17*, 67-73.

Hill, W. F. (1965). *HIM: Hill Interaction Matrix*. Los Angeles: Youth Study Center, University of California.

Hill, W. F. (1974). Systematic group development—SGD therapy. In A. Jacobs & W. Spradlin (Eds.), *The group as agent of change* (pp. 252-271). New York: Behavioral Publications.

Hinkle, J. S. (1991). Support group counseling for caregivers of Alzheimer's disease. *Journal for Specialists in Group Work, 16*, 185-190.

Hirschi, T. (1969). *Causes of delinquency.* Berkerly, CA: University of California.

Hirschi, T. (1995). A control theory of delinquency. In P. M. Sharp & B. W. Hancock (Eds.), *Juvenile delinquency: Historical, theoretical, and societal reactions to youth* (pp. 112-118). Englewood Cliffs, NJ: Prentice-Hall.

Hodgins, S. & Cote, G. (1993). Major mental disorder and antisocial personality disorder: A criminal combination. *Bulletin of the American Academy of Psychiatry and the Law, 21*, 155-160.

Hodgins, S., & Cote, G. (1993). Major mental disorder and antisocial personality disorder: A criminal combination. *Bulletin of the American Academy of Psychiatry and the Law, 21*, 155-160.

Hogan, N. L. (1994). HIV education for inmates: Uncovering strategies for program selection. *Prison Journal, 74*, 220-243.

Holleman, J. (1995, June 30). Guard says he helped three women escape. *St. Louis Post-Dispatch*, p. A1.

Holmes, K. A. (1996). Boos reviews [Review of the book *Female sexual abuse of children*]. *Families in Society, 77*, 639-640.

Holmes, S. A. (1996, December 27). With more women in prison, sexual abuse by guards become greater concern. *New York Times*, p. A18.

Hooper, R. M., Lockwood, D., & Inciardi, J. A. (1993). Treatment techniques in corrections-based therapeutic communities. *Prison Journal, 73*, 290-306.

Hoptowit v. Ray, 682 F.2d 1237 (9th Cir. 1982).

Hoptowit v. Ray, No. 79-359 (E.D. Wash. 1980).

Horley, J. (1995). Cognitive-behavioral therapy with an incarcerated exhibitionist. *International Journal of Offender Therapy and Comparative Criminology, 39*, 335-339.

Howell, J. C. (1998). Promising programs for youth gang violence prevention and intervention. In P. Loeber & D. P. Farrington (Eds.), *Serious & violent juvenile offenders: Risk factors and successful interventions* (pp. 284-312). Thousand Oaks, CA: Sage.

Hoyt, S., & Scherer, D. G. (1998). Female juvenile delinquency: Misunderstood by the juvenile justice system, neglected by social science. *Law and Human Behavior, 22*, 81-107.

Hudley, C., & Graham, S. (1993). An attributional intervention to reduce peer-directed aggression among African-American boys. *Child Development, 64*, 124-138.

Hudson, S. M., Marshall, W. L., Ward, T., Johnston, & P. W. (1995). Kia marama: A cognitive behavioural program for incarcerated child molesters. *Behaviour Change, 12*, 69-80.

Huff, C. R. (1980). The discovery of prisoners' rights: A sociological analysis. In G. P. Alpert (Ed.), *Legal rights of prisoners* (pp. 47-65). Beverly Hills, CA: Sage.

Hulsman, L. H. C. (1997). Critical criminology and the concept of crime. In J. Muncie, E. McLaughlin, & M. Langan (Eds.), *Criminological perspectives: A reader* (pp. 299-303). London: Sage.

In re Blodgett, 510 N.W.2d 910 (Minn. 1994).

In re Winship, 397 U.S. 358 (1970).

In re Young, 857 P.2d 989 (Wash. 1993).

Inciardi, J. A. et al. (1994). *Screening and assessment for alcohol and other drugs among adults in the criminal justice system.* (TIP 7). Rockville, MD: Center for Substance Abuse Treatment.

Isenhart, C. E., & Krevelen, S. V. (1998). Relationship between readiness for and processes of change in a sample of alcohol dependent males. *Journal of Substance Abuse, 10*, 175-184.

Ivey, A. E. (1987). *Intentional interviewing and counseling: Facilitating client development* (2nd ed.). Pacific Grove, CA: Brooks/Cole.

Jackson v. Indiana, 406 U.S. 715 (1972).

Jackson, M. S. (1995). Afrocentric treatment of African American women and their children in a residential chemical dependency program. *Journal of Black Studies, 26,* 17-30.

Jackson, M. S., Stephens, R. C., & Smith, R. L. (1997). Afrocentric treatment in residential substance abuse care. *Journal of Substance Abuse Treatment, 14,* 87-92.

Jacobs, E. E., Harvill, R. L., & Masson, R. L. (1998). *Group counseling: Strategies and skills* (3rd ed.). Pacific Grove, CA: Brooks/Cole.

Jantzen, K., Ball, S. A., Leventhal, J. M., & Schottenfeld, R. S. (1998). Types of abuse and cocaine use in pregnant women. *Journal of Substance Abuse Treatment, 15,* 319-323.

Jeldness v. Pearce, 30 F.3d 1220 (9th Cir. 1994).

Jenson, J. M., Wells, E. A., Plotnick, R. D., Hawkins, J. D., & Catalano, R. F. (1993). The effects of skills and intentions to use drugs on posttreatment drug use of adolescents. *American Journal of Drug and Alcohol Abuse, 19,* 1-18.

Johnson, R. (1979). Under sentence of death: The psychology of death row confinement. *Law & Psychology Review, 5,* 141-192.

Johnson, R. (1998). Clinical assessment of ethnic minority children using the DSM-IV. In G. P. Koocher, J. C. Norcross, & S. S. Hill III (Eds.). *Psychologists' desk reference* (pp. 103-108). New York: Oxford University Press.

Johnston, D. (1995). Child custody issues of women prisoners: A preliminary report from the CHICAS project. *The Prison Journal, 75,* 222-239.

Jolin, A. (1997). *An evaluation of the WICS-Lifeskills program for women at the Columbia River Correctional Institution: Preliminary results.* Unpublished manuscript.

Jones, C. (1998, April 8). Old enough to pay the ultimate penalty: The upcoming execution of a Texas man for a murder committed when he was 17 stokes debate over capital punishment and juvenile crime. *USA Today,* p. 10a, 11a.

Jones, J. E., & Pfeiffer, J. W. (Eds.). (1981). *The 1981 annual handbook for group facilitators.* San Diego, CA: University Associates.

Jones, M. (1979). The therapeutic community, social learning and social change. In R. D. Hinshelwood & Manning, N. (Eds.), *Therapeutic communities: Reflections and progress* (pp. 1-9). London: Routledge & Kegan Paul.

Jones, R. S. (1993). Coping with separation: Adaptive responses of women prisoners. *Women & Criminal Justice, 5,* 71-97.

Jordan v. Gardner, 968 F.2d 984 (9th Cir. 1992).

Jordan v. Gardner, 986 F.2d 1521 (9th Cir. 1993).

Jordan, B. K., Schlenger, W. E., & Caddell, J. (1997). Etiological factors in a sample of convicted women felons in North Carolina. In M. C. Zanarini (Ed.), *Role of sexual abuse in the etiology of borderline personality disorder* (pp. 45-69). Washington, DC: American Psychiatric Press.

Josi, D. A., & Sechrest, D. K. (1996). Treatment versus security: Adversarial relationship between treatment facilitators and correctional officers. *Journal of Offender Rehabilitation, 23,* 167-184.

Judge asked to halt sex offender program. (1995, August 26). *Columbus Dispatch,* p. 5A.

Juhnke, G. A., & Coker, J. K. (1997). A solution-focused intervention with recovering, alcohol-dependent, single parent mothers and their children. *Journal of Addictions and Offender Counseling, 17,* 77-87.

Justice questions lengthy delays in carrying out death sentences. (1998, October 14). *Columbus Dispatch,* p. 3A.

Kalichman, S. C., Kelly, J. A., Hunter, T. L., Murphy, D. A., & Tyler, R. (1993). Culturally-tailored AIDS risk-reduction messages targeted to African-American urban women: Impact on risk sensitization and risk reduction. *Journal of Counseling and Clinical Psychology, 61,* 291-295.

Kaminer, Y. (1991). Adolescent substance abuse. In R. J. Frances & S. I. Miller (Eds.), *Clinical textbook of addictive disorders* (pp. 320-346). New York: The Guilford Press.

Kaminer, Y., & Bukstein, O. G. (1992). Inpatient behavioral and cognitive therapy for substance abuse in adolescents. In V. B. Van Hasselt, & D. J. Kolko (Eds.), *Inpatient behavior therapy for children and adolescents* (pp. 313-339). New York: Plenum Press.

Kanfer, F. H., Phillips, J. S. (1970). *Learning foundation of behavior therapy.* New York: John Wiley & Sons.

Kansas v. Hendricks, 117 S. Ct. 2022 (1997).

Kaplan, H. I., & Sadock, B. J. (1991). *Synopsis of psychiatry: Behavioral sciences clinical psychiatry* (6th ed.). Baltimore: Williams & Wilkins.

Kaplan, H. I., & Sadock, B. J. (1998). *Synopsis of psychiatry: Behavioral sciences/clinical psychiatry* (8th ed.). Baltimore: Williams & Wilkins.

Kaplan, S. J. (1986). *The private practice of behavior therapy: A guide for behavioral practitioners*. New York: Plenum

Karenga, M. (1988). *The African American holiday of Kwanzaa: A celebration of family, community, and culture*. Los Angeles: University of Sankore Press.

Kaslow, A. (1996, May 20). Nation of Islam extends its reach behind prison walls. *Christian Science Monitor*, 9:1.

Kassebaum, G., Ward, D., & Wilner, D. (1971). *Prison treatment and parole survival: An empirical assessment*. New York: John Wiley & Sons.

Katz, J. (1998, February 4). Texas executes born-again woman after appeal fails, Death penalty: Convicted pickax killer Tucker's death by injection caps high-profile capital punishment debate. *Los Angles Times*, p. A1.

Kazdin, A. E. (1985). *Treatment of antisocial behavior in children and adolescents*. Homewood, IL: The Dorsey Press.

Kazdin, A. E. (1995). *Conduct disorders in childhood and adolescence* (2nd ed.). Thousand Oaks, CA: Sage.

Keefe, F. J., & Van Horn, Y. (1993). Cognitive behavioral treatment of rheumatoid arthritis pain: Maintaining treatment gains. *Arthritis Care and Research, 6,* 213-222.

Keevan v. Smith, 100 F.3d 644 (8th Cir. 1996).

Kelly, V. A., Kropp, F. B., & Manhal-Baugus, M. (1995). The association of program-related variables to length of sobriety: A pilot study of chemically dependent women. *Journal of Addictions and Offender Counseling, 15,* 42-50.

Kempf, J. L. (1994). The effects of a social skills intervention on the sexually intrusive thoughts of male adult child molesters. *Dissertation Abstracts International, 55 (3-A),* 472.

Kendall, P. C., & Braswell, L. (1985). *Cognitive-behavioral therapy for impulsive children*. New York: The Guilford Press.

Kennard, D. (1983). *An introduction to therapeutic communities*. London: Routledge & Kegan Paul.

Kent v. U.S. 383 U.S. 541 (1966).

Kentucky Revised Statute § 335.150.

Kermani, E. J., & Drob, S. L. (1988). Psychiatry and the death penalty: Dilemma for mental health professionals. *Psychiatric Quarterly, 59,* 193-212.

Kerr v. Farrey, 95 F.3d 472 (7th Cir. 1996).

King, A. E. O. (1994). An Afrocentric cultural awareness program for incarcerated African-American males. *Journal of Multicultural Social Work, 3,* 17-28.

King, A. E. O. (1997). Understanding violence among young African American males: An afrocentric perspective. *Journal of Black Studies, 28,* 79–96.

Kingdon, D. G., & Turkington, D. (1994). *Cognitive-behavioral therapy of schizophrenia*. New York: The Guilford Press.

Kleber, H. D. (1992). Federal role in substance abuse. In J. H. Lowinson, P. Ruiz, R. B. Millman, & J. G. Langrod (Eds.), *Substance abuse: A comprehensive textbook* (pp. 32-38). Baltimore: Williams & Wilkins.

Klein, S. R., & Bahr, S. J. (1996). An evaluation of a family-centered cognitive skills program for prison inmates. *International Journal of Therapy and Comparative Criminology, 40,* 334-346.

Kleinig, J., & Smith, M. L. (1997). The development of criminal justice ethics education. In J. Kleinig & M. L. Smith (Eds.), *Teaching criminal justice ethics: Strategic issues* (pp. vii-xix). Cincinnati, OH: Andeson.

Klinger v. Department of Corrections, 107 F.3d 609 (8th Cir. 1997).

Klinger v. Nebraska Department of Corrections, 31 F.3d 727 (9th Cir. 1994).

Klinger v. Nebraska Department of Correctional Services, 824 F. Supp. 1374 (D. Neb. 1993).

Knecht v. Gillman, 488 F.2d 1136 (8th Cir. 1973).

Knight, K., & Hiller, M. L. (1997). Community-based substance abuse treatment: A 1-year outcome evaluation of the Dallas County judicial treatment center. *Federal Probation, 61(2),* 61-68.

Knopp, F. H., Freeman-Longo, R., & Stevenson, W. F. (1992). *Nationwide survey of juvenile & adult sex-offender treatment programs & models*. Orwell, VT: The Safer Society Program.

Knopp, K. H. (1987). Introduction. In J. W. Heinz, S. Gargaro, & K. G. Kelly (Eds.), *A model residential juvenile sex-offender treatment program: The Hennepin county home school*. Syracuse, NY: Safer Society Press.

Knox, K. S. (1995). Effectiveness of cognitive behavioral therapy: Evaluating self-instructional training with adolescent sex offenders. *Dissertation Abstracts International, 56,* 705-A.

Koons, B. A., Burrow, J. D., Morash, M., & Bynum, T. (1997). Expert and offender perceptions of program elements linked to successful outcomes for incarcerated women. *Crime & Delinquency, 43,* 512-532.

Kooyman, M. (1993). *The therapeutic community for addicts: Intimacy, parent involvement, and treatment success.* Amsterdam: Swets & Zeitlinger.

Kottler, J. A. (1994). *Advanced group leadership.* Pacific Grove, CA: Brooks/Cole.

Krasner, L. (1982). Behavioral therapy: On roots, contexts, and growth. In G. T. Wilson & C. M. Franks (Eds.), *Contemporary behavior therapy: Conceptual and empirical foundations* (pp. 11-62). New York: The Guilford Press.

Kratcoski, P. C. (Ed.). (1994). *Correctional counseling and treatment* (3rd ed.). Prospect Heights, IL: Waveland.

Krause, M. S. (1966). A cognitive theory of motivation for treatment. *Journal of General Psychology, 75,* 9-19.

Kroese, B. S. (1997). Cognitive-behavioral therapy for people with learning disabilities: Conceptual and contextual issues. In B. S. Kroese, D. Dagnan, & K. Loumidis (Eds.), *Behaviour therapy for people with learning disabilities* (pp. 1-15). New York: Routledge.

Kropp, F. B., Manhal-Baugus, M., & Kelly, V. A. (1996). The asociation of personal-related variables to length of sobriety: A pilot study of chemically dependent women. *Journal of Addictions and Offender Counseling, 17,* 21-34.

Kubler-Ross, E. (1969). *On death and dying.* New York: Macmillan.

Kubler-Ross, E. (1980). Therapy with the terminally ill. In E.S. Shneidman (Ed.), *Death: Current perspectives* (2nd ed.). (pp. 196-201). Palo Alto, CA: Mayfield.

Kuehlwein, K. T. (1993). A survey and update of cognitive therapy systems. In K. T. Kuehwein & H. Rosen (Eds.), *Cognitive therapies in action: Evolving innovative practices* (pp. 1-32). San Francisco: Jossey-Bass.

Kuhner, C., Angermeyer, M. C., & Veiel, H. O. F. (1996). Cognitive-behavioral group intervention as means of tertiary prevention in depressed patients: Acceptance and short-term efficacy. *Cognitive Therapy and Research, 20,* 391- 409.

Lachance-McCullough, M. L., Tesoriero, J. M. Sorin, M. D., & Stern, A. (1994). HIV infection among New York state female inmates: Preliminary results of a voluntary counseling and testing program. *Prison Journal, 74,* 198-219.

Lachance-McCullough, M. L., Tesoriero, J. M., Sorin, M. D., & Lee, C. (1993). Correlates of HIV Seroprevalence among male New York state prison inmates: Results from the New York state AIDS institute criminal justice initiative. *Journal of Prison and Jail Health, 12,* 103-134.

LaFond, J. Q. (1992). Washington's sexually violent predator law: A deliberate misuse of the therapeutic state for social control. *University of Puget Sound Law Review, 15,* 655-703

Lakin, M. (1991). *Coping with ethical dilemmas in psychotherapy.* New York: Pergamon Press.

Lane, S., & Lobanov-Rostovsky, C. (1997). Children, females, the developmentally disabled, and violent youth. In G. Ryan & S. Lane (Eds.), *Juvenile sexual offending: Causes, consequences, and correction* (pp. 322-359). San Francisco: Jossey-Bass.

Lantz, J. (1997). *Existential psychotherapy, logotherapy and existential analysis.* Unpublished manuscript.

Laws, D. R., & Marshall, W. L. (1990). A conditioning theory of the etiology and maintenance of deviant sexual preference and behavior. In W. L. Marshall, D. R. Laws, & H. E. Barbaree (Eds.), *Handbook of sexual assault: Issues, theories, and treatment of the offender* (pp. 209-229). New York: Plenum Press.

Lay v. Norris, 876 F.2d 104 (6th Cir. 1989).

Lee, J. K. P., Proeve, M. J., & Lancaster, M., & Jackson, H. J. (1996). An evaluation and 1-year follow-up study of a community-based treatment program for sex offenders. *Australian Psychologist, 31,* 147-152.

Leeman, L. W. (1991). *Evaluation of a multicomponent treatment program for juvenile delinquents.* Unpublished master's thesis, The Ohio State University.

Leland, J. (1998, June 1). Savior of the street. *Newsweek,* p. 20-25.

Leonhardt, D. (1995, March 16). Arundel teacher is fired in sex-with-student case. *Washington Post,* p. C6.

Lesher, D. (1998, February 4). California and the West: Governor vows showdown on juvenile crime bills. *Los Angeles Times*, p. A3.

Lester, D. (1997). Group and milieu therapy. In P. V. Voorhis, M. Braswell, & D. Lester (Eds.), *Correctional counseling and rehabilitation* (3rd ed.). (pp. 189-217). Cincinnati, OH: Anderson.

Levine, J., Barak, Y., & Granek, I. (1998). Cogntive group therapy for paranoid schizophrenics: Applying cognitive dissonance. *Journal of Cognitive Psychotherapy, 12*, 3-12.

Levine, R. S. (1980). Disaffirmance of the right to treatment doctrine: A new juncture in juvenile justice. *University of Pittsburgh Law Review, 41*, 159-204.

Levinson, A. (1998, March 15). Crack mom: Addict or criminal. *Columbus Dispatch*, p. 4B.

Levinson, B. (Executive Producer). (1997). *Oz*. New York: Home Box Office.

Liebrum, J. (1995, December 15). Ex-Aldine teacher indicted over affair with teen student. *Houston Chronicle*, p. A37.

Liese, B.S., & Larson, M.W. (1995). Coping with life-threatening ilness: A cognitive therapy perspective. *Journal of Cognitive Psychotherapy International Quarterly, 9*, 19-34.

Lipsey, M. W. (1992, October 31). *The effects of treatment on juvenile delinquents: Results from meta-analysis*. Paper presented at the NIMH meeting for Potential Applicants for Research to Prevent Youth Violence. Bethesda, MD.

Lipton, D. S., Falkin, G. P., & Wexler, H. K. (1992). Correctional drug abuse treatment in the United States: An overview. In C. G. Leukefeld & F. M. Tims (Eds), *Drug abuse treatment in prisons and jails* (pp. 8-30). Rockville, MD: National Institute on Drug Abuse.

Lochman, J. E., & Wells, K. C. (1996). A social-cognitive intervention with aggressive children: Prevention effects and contextual implementation issues. In R. Dev. Peters & R. J. McMahon (Eds.), *Preventing childhood disorders, substance abuse, and delinquency* (pp. 111-143). Thousand Oaks, CA: Sage.

Lochman, J. E., White, K. J., Curry, J. F., Rummer, R. R. (1995). Antisocial behavior. In V. B. Van Hasselt & D. J. Kolko (Eds.), *Inpatient behavior therapy for children and adolescents* (pp. 277-312). New York: Plenum Press.

Loeber, R., & Hay, D. (1997). Key issues in the development of aggression and violence from childhood to early adulthood. *Annual Review of Psychology, 48*, 371-410.

Longshore, D., Grills, C., Annon, K., & Grady, R. (1998). Promoting recovery from drug abuse: An Africentric intervention. *Journal of Black Studies, 28*, 319-333.

Lord, A., & Barnes, C. (1996). Family liaison work with adolescents in a sex offender treatment programme. *Journal of Sexual Aggression, 2*, 112-121.

Lovejoy, M., Rosenblum, A., Magura, S., Foote, J., Handelsman, L., & Stimmel, B. (1995). Patients' perspective on the process of change in substance abuse treatment. *Journal of Substance Abuse Treatment, 12*, 269-282.

Ludgate, J. W., Wright, J. H., Bowers, W., & Camp, G. F. (1993). Individual cognitive therapy with inpatient. In J. H. Wright, M. E. Thase, A. T. Beck, & J. W. Ludgate (Eds.), *Cognitive therapy with inpatients: Developing a cognitive milieu* (pp. 91-120). New York: The Guilford Press.

Lukins, R., Davan, I. G. P., & Drummond, P. D. (1997). A cognitive behavioral approach to preventing anxiety during magnetic resonance imaging. *Journal of Behavior Therapy and Experimental Psychiatry, 28*, 97-104.

Lutgendorf, S. K., Antoni, M. H., Ironson, G., Kilmas, N., Kumar, M., Starr, K., McCabe, P., Cleven, K., Fletcher, M. A., & Schneiderman, N. (1997). Cognitive-behavioral stress management decreases dysphoric mood and herpes simplex virus-type 2 antibody titers in symptomatic HIV-seropositive gay men. *Journal of Consulting and Clinical Psychology, 65*, 31-43.

MacKenzie, D. L. (1997). Criminal justice and crime prevention. In L. W. Sherman, D. Gottfredson, D. Mackenzie, J. Eck, P. Reuter, & S. Bushway (Eds.), *Preventing crime: What works, what doesn't, what's promising*. Washington, DC: National Institute of Justice (http://www.ncjrs.org/works/).

Mackey v. Procunier, 477 F.2d 877 (9th Cir. 1973).

Madden, R. G. (1998). *Legal issues in social work, counseling, and mental health: Guidelines for clinical practice in psychotherapy*. Thousand Oaks, CA: Sage.

Maden, T., Swinton, M., & Gunn, J. (1994). Psychiatric disorder in women serving a prison sentence. *British Journal of Psychiatry, 164*, 44-54.

Mahon, L., & Flores, P. (1992). Group psychotherapy as the treatment of choice for individuals who grew up with alcoholic parents: A theoretical review. *Alcoholism Treatment Quarterly, 9*, 113-125.

Mahon, N. (1997). Treatment is prisons and jails. In J. H. Lowinson, P. Ruiz, R. B. Millman, & J. G. Langrod (Eds.), *Substance abuse: A comprehensive textbook* (3rd ed.). (pp. 455-458). Baltimore: Williams & Wilkins.

Makeig, J. (1993, March 13). Jailer is fired after indictment on sex charges. *Houston Chronicle*, p. A33.

Makela, K. (1996). *Alcoholics anonymous as a mutual self help movement: A study in eight societies.* Madison, WI: The University of Wisconsin Press.

Malott, R. W., Whaley, D. L., & Malott, M. E. (1993). *Elementary principles of behavior* (2nd ed.). Englewood Cliffs, NJ: Prentice Hall.

Manhal-Baugus, M. (1996). Confidentiality: The legal and ethical issues for chemical dependency counselors. *Journal of Addictions & Offender Counseling, 17*, 3-11.

Maniglia, R. (1996) New directions for young women in the juvenile justice system. *Reclaiming Children and Youth, 5*, 96-101.

Mann, J. A., & Gaertner, S. L. (1991). Support for the use of force in war: The effect of procedural rule violations and group membership. *Journal of Applied Social Psychology, 21*, 1793-1809.

Marcotte, D. (1997). Treating depression in adolescence: A review of the effectiveness of cognitive-behavioral treatments. *Journal of Youth and Adolescence, 26*, 273-283.

Marcus-Mendoza, S. T., Klein-Saffran, J., & Lutze, F. (1997). A feminist examination of boot camp prison programs for women. *Women & Therapy, 21*, 173-185.

Margolis, R. (1995). Adolescent chemical dependency: Assessment, treatment, and management. In A. M. Washton (Ed.), *Psychotherapy and substance abuse: A practitioner's handbook* (pp. 394-412). New York: The Guilford Press.

Marlowe, H. A., Jr., Marlowe, J. L., & Willetts, R. (1983). The mental health counselor as case manager: Implications for working with the chronically mentally ill. *AMHCA Journal, 5*, 184-191.

Marques, J. K., Day, D. M., Nelson, C., & West, M. A. (1994). Effects of cognitive-behavioral treatment on sex offender recidivism: Preliminary results of a longitudinal study. *Criminal Justice and Behavior, 21*, 28-54.

Marsh, R. L., & Walsh, A. (1995). Physiological and psychosocial assessment and treatment of sex offenders: A comprehensive victim-oriented program. *Journal of Offender Rehabilitation, 22*, 77-95.

Marshall, I. H. (1981). Correctional treatment processes: Rehabilitation reconsidered. In R. R. Roberg & V. J. Webb (Eds.), *Critical issues in corrections: Problems, trends, and prospects* (pp. 14-46). St. Paul, MN: West.

Marshall, W. L., & Eccles, A. (1993). Pavlovian conditioning processes in adolescent sex offenders. In H. E. Barbaree, W. L. Marshall, & S. M. Hudson (Eds.), *The juvenile sex offender* (pp. 118-142). New York: The Guilford Press.

Marshall, W. L., Bryce, P., Hudson, S. M., Ward, T., & Moth, B. (1996). The enhancement of intimacy and the reduction of loneliness among child molesters. *Journal of Family Violence, 11*, 219-235.

Martarella v. Kelley, 349 F. Supp. 575 (S.D.N.Y. 1972).

Martin, G., & Pear, J. (1992). *Behavior modification: What it is and how to do it* (4th ed.). Englewood Cliffs, NJ: Prentice Hall.

Martin, S. E., Sechrest, L. B., & Redner, R. (Eds.). (1981). *New directions in the rehabilitation of criminal offenders.* Washington, DC: National Academy Press.

Martin, S. S., Butzin, C. A., & Inciardi, J. A. (1995). Assessment of a multistage therapeutic community for drug-involved offenders. *Journal of Psychoactive Drugs, 27*, 109-116.

Martinson, R. (1974). What works?—questions and answers about prison report. *The Public Interest, 35*, 22-54.

Masters, R. E. (1994). *Counseling criminal justice offender.* Thousand Oaks, CA: Sage.

Mathias, R. (1995). Correctional treatment helps offenders stay drug and arrest free. *NIDA Notes, 10*, 10-11.

Matson, J. L., Smalls, Y., Hampff, A. Smiroldo, B. B., & Anderson, S. J. (1998). A comparison of behavioral techniques to teach functional independent-living skills to individuals with severe and profound mental retardation. *Behavior Modification, 22,* 298-306.

Matthews, J. K. (1994). Working with female sexual abusers. In M. Elliott (Ed.), *Female sexual abuse of children* (pp. 57-73). New York: Guiford.

Maull, F. (1991). Dying in prison: Sociocultural and psychosocial dynamics. *Hospice Journal, 7,* 127-142.

Maurer, R. J. (1995). Ohio psychotherapist civil liability for sexual relations with former patients. *The University of Toledo Law Review, 26,* 547-574.

Mayer, C. (1989). Survey of case law establishing constitutional minima for the provision of mental health services to psychiatrically involved inmates. *New England Journal on Criminal and Civil Confinement, 15,* 243-275.

McCray v. Sullivan, 509 F.2d 1332 (5th Cir. 1975).

McKibben, G. (1993, May 4). No sex-assault charges set for former jail guard. *Denver Post,* p. B3.

McLellan, T., & Dembo, R. (1993). *Screening and assessment of alcohol- and other drug-abusing adolescents.* Rockville, MD: Center for Substance Abuse Treatment.

McNeece, C. A., & Daly, C. M. (1997). Treatment and intervention with chemically involved adult system. In C. A. McNeece & A. R. Roberts (Eds.), *Policy and practice in the justice system* (pp. 69-86). Chicago: Nelson-Hall.

McPhail, M. W., & Wiest, B. M. (1995). *Combining alcohol and other drug abuse treatment with diversion for juveniles in the justice system.* Rockville, MD: Center for Substance Abuse Treatment.

McQuaide, S., & Ehrenreich, J. H. (1998). Women in prison: Approaches to understanding the lives of a forgotten population. *Affilia, 13,* 233-246.

Meador, B., Solomon, E., & Bowen, M. (1972). Encounter groups for women only. In L. N. Solomon & B. Berz, (Eds.), *New perspectives on encounter groups* (pp. 335-348). San Francisco: Jossey-Bass.

Meichenbaum, G., & Camera, R. (1982). Cognitive-behavior therapy. In G. T. Wilson & C. M. Franks (Eds.), *Contemporary behavior therapy: Conceptual and empirical foundations* (pp. 310-338). New York: The Guilford Press.

Meloy, J. R. (1988). *The psychopathic mind: Origins, dynamics, and treatment.* Northvale, NJ: Jason Aronson.

Meloy, J. R. (1996). Antisocial personality disorder. In G. O. Gabbard, S. D. Atkinson, (Eds.), *Synopsis of treatments of psychiatric disorders (2nd ed.).* (pp. 959-967). Washington, DC: American Psychiatric Press.

Messalle, R. (1997). *Planning chart treatment-based drug courts.* Washington, DC: Center for Substance Abuse Treatment.

Metzner, J. L., & Ryan, G. D. (1995). Sexual abuse perpetration. In G. P. Sholevar (Ed.), *Conduct disorders in children and adolescents* (pp. 119-144). Washington, DC: American Psychiatric Press.

Meyer, R. G., & Deitsch, S. E. (1996). *The clinician's handbook: Integrated diagnostics, assessment, and intervention in adult and adolescent psychopathology* (4th ed.). Boston: Allyn and Bacon.

Michaels, K. W., & Green, R. H. (1979). A child welfare agency project: Therapy for families of status offenders. *Child Welfare, 58,* 216-220.

Michelson, L. (1987). Cognitive-behavioral strategies in the prevention and treatment of antisocial disorders in children and adolescents. In J. D. Burchard & S. N. Burchard (Eds.), *Prevention of delinquent behavior* (pp. 275-310). Newbury Park, CA: Sage.

Michenfelder v. Sumner, 860 F.2d 328 (9th Cir. 1988).

Milas, B. (1997). *Similarities and differences of prisoners who were screened for drug and alcohol use and who participated in a discipline and rehabilitation center.* Unpublished master's thesis, The Ohio State University, Columbus, Ohio.

Milders, M. V., Berg, I. J., Deelman, B. G. (1995). Four-year follow-up of a controlled memory training study in closed head injured patients. *Neuropsychological Rehabilitation, 5,* 223-238.

Miller, A. T., Eggertson-Tacon, C., & Quigg, B. (1990). Patterns of runaway behavior within a larger systems context: The road to empowerment. *Adolescence, 25,* 271-289.

Miller, D., Fejes-Mendoza, K., & Eggleston, C. (1997). Reclaiming 'fallen angels': Values and skills for delinquent girls. *Reclaiming Children and Youth, 5,* 231-234.

Miller, F. G., & Miller, G. A. (1998). Mandated addiction services: Potential ethical dilemmas. In R. F. Small & L. R. Barnhill (Eds.), *Practicing in the new mental health marketplace: Ethical, legal, and moral issues* (pp. 169-183). Washington, DC: American Psychological Association.

Miller, J. G. (1955). Toward a general theory of the behavioral sciences. *American Psychologist, 10,* 513-531.

Miller, K. S., & Radelet, M. L. (1993). *Executing the mentally ill: The criminal justice system and the case of Alvin Ford.* Newbury Park, CA: Sage.

Miller, M. J. (1993). The lifeline: A qualitative method to promote group dynamics. *Journal for Specialists in Group Work, 18,* 51-54.

Miller, W. R., & Rollnick, S. (1991). *Motivational interviewing: Preparing people to change addictive behavior.* New York: The Guilford Press.

Mitchell, J. L. et al. (1993). *Pregnant, substance-using women.* Rockville, MD: Center for Substance Abuse Treatment.

Mitford, J. (1973). *Kind and usual punishment: The prison business.* New York: Alfred A. Knopf.

Molidor, C. E. (1996). Female gang members: A profile of aggression and victimization. *Social Work, 41,* 251-257.

Moone, J. (1997). *States at a glance: Juveniles in public facilities, 1995.* Washington, DC: Office Juvenile Justice and Delinquency Prevention.

Moore, B. E., & Fine, B. D. (1990). *Psychoanalytic terms and concepts.* New Haven, CONN: The American Psychoanalytic Association and Yale University Press.

Moore, E. O. (1989). Prison environments and their impact on older citizens. *Journal of Offender Counseling, Services, & Rehabilitation, 13(2),* 175-191.

Morales v. Turman, 383 F. Supp. 53 (E.D. Tx. 1974).

Morales, A. (1978). Institutional racism in mental health and criminal justice. *Social Casework, 59,* 387-395.

Morenz, B., & Becker, J. (1995). The treatment of youthful sexual offenders. *Applied and Preventive Psychology, 4,* 247-256.

Morgan v. Sproat, 432 F. Supp. 1130 (S.D. Miss. 1977).

Morgan, O. J., Toloczko, A. M., & Comly, E. (1997). Graduate training of counselors in the addictions: A study of CACREP approved programs. *Journal of Addictions and Offender Counseling, 17,* 66-76.

Morrison, H. L. (1986). Ethics and values in the evaluation and treatment of children: A clinician's viewpoint. In D. K. Kentsmith, S. A., Salladay, & P. A. Miya (Eds.), *Ethics in mental health practice* (pp. 123-132). Orlando, FL: Grune & Stratton.

Morrison, R. L. (1985). Social skills training. In A. S. Bellack & M. Hersen (Eds.), *Dictionary of behavior therapy techniques* (pp. 206-209). New York: Pergamon Press.

Morrison, T. (1994). Context, constraints and considerations for practice. In T. Morrison & M. Erroga, & R. C. Beckett (Eds.), *Sexual offending against children: Assessment and treatment of male abusers* (pp. 25-54). London: Routledge.

Muram, D. (1996). Book review [Review of the book *Female sexual abuse of children*]. *Journal of Family Violence, 11,* 307-308.

Muran, E. M., DiGiuseppe, R. (1994). Rape. In F. M. Sattilio & A. Freeman (Eds.), *Cognitive-behavioral strategies in crisis intervention* (pp. 161-176). New York: The Guilford Press.

Mydans, S. (1995, September 11). Hispanic gang members keep strong family ties. *New York Times,* pp. A1, A8.

Myers, L. J. (1988). *Understanding an Afrocentric worldview: Introduction to an optimal psychology.* Dubuque, IA: Kendall/ Hunt.

Nace, E. P. (1992). Alcoholics anonymous. In J. H. Lowinson, P. Ruiz, R. B. Millman, & J. G. Langrod (Eds.), *Substance abuse: A comprehensive textbook* (2nd ed.). (pp. 486-495). Baltimore: Williams & Wilkins.

Nagel, W. G. (1985). Hands off, hands on, hands off: An editorial. *The Prison Journal, 65,* i-iii.

Najavits, L. M., Weiss, R. D., Shaw, S. R., & Muenz, & L. R. (1998). "Seeking safety": Outcome of a new cognitive-behavioral psychotherapy for women with posttraumatic stress disorder and substance dependence. *Journal of Traumatic Stress, 11,* 437-456.

National Commission on Correctional Health Care (1995). Position statement: Mental health services in correctional settings. *Journal of Correctional Health Care, 2,* 85-91.

National Prison Project (1990). Juvenile justice: Is there a better way? *National Prison Project Journal, 5,* 1.

National Task Force on Juvenile Sexual Offending (1993). The revised report from the national task force on juvenile sexual offending, 1993 of the national adolescent perpetrator network. *Juvenile & Family Court Journal, 44(4),* 5-120.

(A) nation stunned by school mayhem searches for answers. *USA Today*, (1998, March 26), p. A 14.

Neergaard, L. (1992, November 14). 14 are indicted in Georgia prison sexual abuse case. *Boston Globe*, p. 3.

Negreiros, J. (1994). Theoretical orientations in drug abuse prevention research. *Drugs: Education, Prevention and Policy, 1*, 135-142.

Nelson v. Heyne, 355 F. Supp. 451 (N.D. Ind. 1972).

Nelson v. Heyne, 417 U.S. 976 (1974).

Nelson v. Heyne, 491 F.2d 352 (7th Cir. 1974).

Nes, J. A., & Iadicola, P. (1989). Toward a definition of feminist social work: A comparison of liberal, radical, and socialist models. *Social Work, 34*, 12-21.

New life residential drug and alcohol treatment program handbook (1997). Chillicothe, OH: New Life Residential Drug and Alcohol Treatment Program.

Newman v. Alabama, 559 F.2d 283 (5th Cir. 1977).

Newman, M. G., Kenardy, J., Herman, S., Taylor, C., & Barr, C. (1997). Comparison of palmtop-computer-assisted brief cognitive-behavioral treatment to cognitive-behavioral treatment for panic disorder. *Journal of Consulting and Clinical Psychology, 65*, 178-183.

Nixon, S. J., Tivis, R., & Parsons, O. A. (1995). Behavioral dysfunction and cognitive efficiency in male and female alcoholics. *Alcoholism Clinical and Experimental Research, 19*, 577-581.

Novaco, R. W. (1975). *Anger control: The development and evaluation of an experimental treatment*. Lexington, MA: Lexington Books.

O'Callaghan, D., & Print, B. (1994). Adolescent sexual abusers: Research, assessment and treatment. In T. Morrison, M. Erroga, & R. C. Beckett (Eds.), *Sexual offending against children: Assessment and treatment of male abusers* (pp. 147-177). London: Routledge

O'Connor v. California, 855 F. Supp. 303 (C.D. Cal. 1994).

O'Connor v. Donaldson, 422 U.S. 563 (1975).

Office of Juvenile Justice and Delinquency Prevention (1997). *Boot camps for juvenile offenders*. Washington, DC: Author.

Office of Juvenile Justice and Delinquency Prevention (1997). *Juveniles in private*

facilities, 1991-1995. Washington, DC: Author.

Ohio Jur. 3d [460], Family Law 359.

Ohio Jur. 3d [460], Family Law 361.

Ohio Legislative Service Commission (1999). *House Bill 121*. Author.

Ohio Revised Code Annotated 4757.02 (1998).

Ohio Revised Code Annotated 4757.36 (1998).

Ohio Revised Code Annotated, Title 51 Public Welfare, 5139.07.

Ohio Revised Code Annotated, Title 51 Public Welfare, 5139.13.

Ohlinger v. Watson, 652 F.2d 775 (9th Cir. 1980).

Ohlsen, M. M., Horne, A. M., & Lawe, C. F. (1988). *Group counseling* (3rd ed.). New York: Holt, Rinehart and Winston.

Orten, J. D., & Soll, S. K. (1980). Runaway children and their families: A treatment typology. *Journal of Family Issues, 1*, 249-261.

Overholser, J. C. (1996). Cognitive-behavioral treatment of depression, part V: Enhancing self-esteem and self control. *Journal of Contemporary Psychotherapy, 26*, 337-360.

Page, J. D. (1989). Cruel and unusual punishment and sodomy statutes: The breakdown of the *Solem v. Helm* test. *University of Chicago Law Review, 56*, 367-396.

Page, R. C. (1979). Developmental stages of unstructured counseling groups with prisoners. *Small Group Behavior, 10*, 271-278.

Page, R. C., Campbell, L., & Wilder, D. C. (1994). Role of the leader in therapy groups conducted with illicit drug abusers: How directive does the leader have to be? *Journal of Addictions and Offender Counseling, 14*, 57-66.

Palmer, T. (1975). Martinson revisited. *Journal of Research of Crime and Delinquency, 12*, 133-152.

Palmer, T. (1978). *Correctional intervention and research: Current issues and future prospects*. Lexington, MA: Lexington Books.

Palmer, T. (1983). The effectiveness issue today: An overview. *Federal Probation, 47(2)*, 3-10.

Palmer, T. (1992). *The re-emergence of correctional intervention*. Newbury Park, CA: Sage.

Paniagua, F. A. (1994). *Assessing and treating culturally diverse clients: A practical guide*. Thousand Oaks, CA: Sage.

Parkinson, C. B., & Howard, M. (1996). Older persons with mental retardation/developmental disabilities. *Journal of Gerontological Social Work, 25,* 91-103.

Parsons, R. D., & Wicks, R. J. (1994). *Counseling strategies and intervention techniques for the human services* (4th ed.). Boston, MA: Allyn and Bacon.

Patterson, C. H. (1974). *Relationship counseling and psychotherapy.* New York: Harper & Row.

Payne, D. (1995, April 29). Officer charged with having sex with one of his parolees. *Atlanta Constitution,* p. C6.

Peck, M. S. (1987). *The different drum: Community making and peace.* New York: Simon & Schuster.

Pellegrino, E. D. (1993). Societal duty and moral complicity: The physician's dilemma of divided loyalty. *International Journal of Law & Psychiatry, 16,* 371-391.

Pepinsky, (1991). Forword. In M. C. Braswell, B. R McCarthy, & B. J. Mc-Carthy (Eds.), *Justice, crime and ethics* (pp. ix-xi). Cincinnati, OH: Anderson.

Perkins, D. (1991). Clinical work with sex offenders in secure settins. In C. R. Hollin & K. Howells (Eds.), *Clinical approaches to sex offenders and their victims* (pp. 151-177). Chichester, England: John Wiley & Sons.

Perkins, K., & Tice, C. (1995). A strengths perspective in practice: Older people and mental health challenges. *Journal of Gerontological Social Work, 23,* 83-97.

Perris, C., & Skagerlind, L. (1994). Schizophrenia. In F.M. Dattilio & A. Freeman (Eds.), *Cognitive-behavioral strategies in crisis intervention* (pp. 104-118). New York: The Guilford Press.

Perris, C., Ingelsson, U., & Jonsson, P. (1993). Cognitive therapy as a general framework in the treatment of psychotic patients. In K. T. Kuehlwein & H. Rosen (Eds.), *Cognitive therapies in action: Evolving innovative practice* (pp. 379-402). San Francisco: Jossey-Bass.

Perry v. Louisiana, 110 S. Ct. 1317 (1990).

Pestle, K., Card, J., & Menditto, A. (1998). Therapeutic recreation in a social-learning program: Effect over time on appropriate behaviors of residents with schizophrenia. *Therapeutic Recreation Journal, 32,* 28-41.

Peters, R. H., Strozier, A. L., Murrin, M. R., & Kearns, W. D. (1997). Treatment of substance-abusing jail inmates: Examination of gender differences. *Journal of Substance Abuse Treatment, 14,* 339-349.

Petersilia, J. (1997). Justice for all?: Offenders with mental retardation and the California corrections system. *The Prison Journal, 77,* 358-380.

Peterson, G. E., & Harrell, A. V. (1992). Introduction: Inner-city isolation and opportunity. In A. V. Harrell & G. E. Peterson (Eds.), *Drugs, crime, and social isolation: Barriers to urban opportunity* (pp. 1-26). Washington, DC: The Urban Institute Press.

Peterson, K. S. (1998). Woman's obsession for boy crosses many lines. *USA Today,* p. 4D.

Petretic-Jackson, P., & Jackson, T. (1990). Assessment and crisis intervention with rape and incest victims: Strategies, techniques, and case illustrations. In A. R. Robert (Ed.), *Crisis intervention handbook: Assessment, treatment and research.* Belmont, CA: Wadsworth.

Petrila, J., Otto, R. K., & Poythress, N. G. (1994). Violence, mental disorder, and the law. In M. Costanzo & Oskamp, S. (Eds.), *Violence and the law* (pp. 161-180). Thousand Oaks, CA: Sage.

Peyrot, M., Yen, S., & Baldassano, C. A. (1994). Short-term substance abuse prevention in jail: A cognitive behavioral approach. *Journal of Drug Education, 24,* 33-47.

Pfeiffer, J. W. (Ed.). (1987). *The 1987 annual: Developing human resources.* San Diego, CA: University Associates.

Pfeiffer, J. W., & Goodstein, L. D. (Eds.) (1986). *The 1986 annual: Developing human resources.* San Diego, CA: University Associates.

Pfeiffer, J. W., Jones, J. E. (Eds.). (1980). *The 1980 annual handbook for group facilitators.* San Diego, CA: University Associates.

Phares, E. J. (1984). *Clinical psychology: Concepts, methods, and profession.* Homewood, IL: The Dorsey Press.

Pilder, R. (1972). Encounter groups for married couples. *New perspectives on encounter groups* (pp. 303-312). San Francisco: Jossey-Bass.

Pisciotta, A. W. (1994). *Benevolent repression: Social control and the American reformatory–prison movement.* New York: New York University Press.

Pithers, W. D. (1994). Process evaluation of a group therapy component designed to enhance sex offenders' empathy for sexual abuse survivors. *Behaviour Research and Therapy, 32,* 565-570.

Plummer, D. (1995, July 20). Officer accused of having sex with probationer. *Atlanta Constitution,* p. D10.

Poe-Yamagata, M. S. (1997). *Detention and delinquency cases, 1985-1994.* Washington, DC: Office Juvenile Justice and Delinquency Prevention.

Poitier, V. L., Niliwaambieni, M., & Rowe, C. L. (1997). A rite of passage approach designed to preserve the families of substance-abusing African American women. *Child Welfare, 76,* 173-195.

Poythress, N. G., & Miller, R. D. (1991). The treatment of forensic patients: Major issues. In S. Shah & B. Sales (Eds.), *Law and mental health: Major developments and research needs* (pp. 81-113). Bethesda, MD: National Institute of Mental Health.

Prendergast, M. L., Wellisch, J., & Wong, M. M. (1996). Residential treatment for women parolees following prison-based drug treatment: Treatment experiences, needs and services, outcomes. *The Prison Journal, 76,* 253-274.

Price, R. (1997, September 18). No trial for Hall in fireworks blaze. *Columbus Dispatch,* pp. 1A, 2A.

Prinz, R. J. (1995). Behavior therapy. In G. P. Sholevar (Ed.), *Conduct disorders in children and adolescents* (pp. 251-267). Washington, DC: American Psychiatric Association.

Prochaska, J. O., DiClemente, C. C., & Norcross, J. C. (1992). In search of how people change: Applications to addictive behaviors. *American Psychologist, 47,* 1102-1114.

Procunier v. Martinez, 94 S. Ct. 1800 (1974).

Proehl, R. A. (1995). Groups in career development: An added advantage. *Journal of Career Development, 21,* 249-261.

Prout, H. T., & Strohmer, D. C. (1998). Issues in mental health counseling with persons with mental retardation. *Journal of Mental Health Counseling, 20,* 112-121.

Psychiatric tests on minority kids draw complaints (1998, April 18). *Columbus Dispatch,* p. 3A.

Pugh, D. N. (1993). The effects of problem-solving ability and locus of control on prisoner adjustment. *International Journal of Offender Therapy and Comparative Criminology, 37,* 163-176.

Quigley, R., & Steiner, M. E. (1996). Unleashing the power of young women

through peer helping groups. *Reclaiming Children and Youth, 5,* 102-106.

Quinsey, V. L., & Lalumiere, M. L. (1996). *Assessment of sexual offenders against children.* Thousand Oaks, CA: Sage.

Rankin, B. (1991, October 9). Counselor sentenced to 15 years for abuse. *Atlanta Constitution,* p. D6.

Raush, H., & Bordin, E. S. (1957). Warmth in personality development and in psychotherapy. *Psychiatry, 20,* 351-363.

Raynor, P. & Vanstone, M. (1996). Reasoning and rehabilitation in Britain: The results of the straight thinking on probation (STOP) programme. *Journal of Offender Therapy and Comparative Criminology, 40,* 272-284.

Raynor, P. (1998). Attitudes, social problems and reconvictions in the 'STOP' probation experiment. *The Howard Journal of Criminal Justice, 37,* 1-15.

Reardon, J. D. (1992). Sexual predators: Mental illness or abnormality? A psychiatrist's perspective. *University of Puget Sound Law Review, 15,* 849-853.

Reddington, F. P., & Sapp, A. D. (1997). Juveniles in adult prisons: Problems and prospects. *Journal of Crime and Justice, 20,* 139-152.

Reed, W. L., & Tachman, M. A. (1979). Evaluation of a counseling program for probationers and parolees. *Offender Rehabilitation, 3,* 299-317.

Reid, W. H., & Wise, M. G. (1995). *DSM-IV training guide.* New York: Brunner/ Mazel.

Reisner, R. (1985). *Law and the mental health system: Civil and criminal cases.* St. Paul, MN: West.

Reitsma-Street, M., & Offord, D. R. (1991). Girl delinquents and their sisters: A challenge for practice. *Canadian Social Work Review, 8,* 11-27.

Rencken, R. H. (1989). *Intervention strategies for sexual abuse.* Alexandria, VA: American Association for Counseling and Development.

Rhoden, N. K. (1980). The right to refuse psychotropic drugs. *Harvard Civil Rights-Civil Liberties Law Review, 15,* 363-413.

Rhodes, R., & Johnson, A. (1997). A feminist approach to treating alcohol and drug-addicted African-American women. *Women & Therapy, 20,* 23-35.

Rice, M. E. (1997). Violent offender research and implications for the criminal justice system. *American Psychologist, 52,* 414-423.

Rich, K. D. (1994). Outpatient group therapy with adult male sex offenders: Clinical issues and concerns. *Journal of Specialists in Group Work, 19,* 120-128.

Rickel, A. U., & Becker-Lausen, E. (1994). Treating the adolescent drug misuser. In T. P. Gullotta, G. R. Adams, R. Montemayor (Eds.), *Substance misuse in adolescence* (pp. 92-122). Thousands Oaks, CA: Sage.

Riddle v. Mondragon, 83 F.3d 1197 (10th Cir. 1996).

Ridley, C. R. (1995). *Overcoming unintentional racism in counseling and therapy: A practitioner's guide to intentional intervention.* Thousand Oaks, CA: Sage.

Rierden, A. (1997). *The farm: Life inside a women's prison.* Amherst, MA: University of Massachusetts Press.

Ries, R. et al. (1994). *Assessment and treatment of patient with coexisting mental illness and alcohol and other drug abuse TIP 9.* Rockville, MD: Center for Substance Abuse Treatment.

Riggins v. Nevada, 112 S. Ct. 1810 (1992).

Riggins v. Nevada, 860 P.2d 705 (Nev. 1993).

Rimm, D. C., & Masters, & J. C. (1979). *Behavior therapy: Techniques and empirical findings* (2nd ed.). New York: Academic Press.

Riposa, G., & Dersch, C. (1995). The nature of gang violence. *Journal of Crime and Justice, 18(2),* 31-46.

Roach v. City of Evansville, 111 F.3d 544 (7th Cir. 1997).

Robak, R. (1991). *A primer for today's substance abuse counselor.* New York: Lexington Books.

Roberts, R. E., Cheek, E. H., & Mumm, R. S. (1994). Group intervention and reading performance in a medium-security prison facility. *Journal of Offender Rehabilitation, 20,* 97-116.

Robertson, G., & Taylor, P. J. (1985). Some cognitive correltates of schizophrenic illnesses. *Psychological Medicine, 15,* 81-98.

Robertson, J. G. (1997). Using the criminal justice system to prevent adolescent drug abuse. In C. A. McNeece & A. R. Roberts (Eds.), *Policy and practice in the justice system* (pp. 87-123). Chicago: Nelson-Hall.

Robinson v. California, 370 U.S. 660 (1962).

Rogers, C. R. (1961). *On becoming a person: A therapist's view of psychotherapy.* Boston: Houghton Mifflin.

Rogers, R. (1998). Assessment of malingering on psychological measures: A synopsis. In G. P. Koocher, J. C. Norcross, & S. S. Hill III (Eds.), *Psychologists' desk reference* (pp. 53-57). New York: Oxford University Press.

Rogers, R., & Reinhardt, V. R. (1998). Conceptualization and assessment of secondary gain. In G. P. Koocher, J. C. Norcross, & S. S. Hill III (Eds.), *Psychologists' desk reference* (pp. 57-62). New York: Oxford University Press.

Rollnick, S., & Morgan, M. (1995). Motivational interviewing: Increasing readiness for change. In A. M. Washton (Ed.), *Psychotherapy and substance abuse: A practitioner's handbook* (pp. 179-191). New York: The Guilford Press.

Romeo v. Youngblood, 457 U.S. 660 (1962).

Rooney, R. H. (1992). *Strategies for work with involuntary clients.* New York: Columbia University Press.

Rose, S. D. (1977). *Group therapy: A behavioral approach.* Englewood Cliffs, NJ: Prentice-Hall.

Rosen, A., & Persky, T. (1997). Meeting mental health needs of older people: Policy and practice issues in social work. *Journal of Gerontological Social Work, 27,* 45-54.

Rosen, R. C., & Leiblum, S. R. (1995). Treatment of sexual disorders in the 1990s: An integrated approach. *Journal of Consulting and Clinical Psychology, 63,* 877-890.

Rosenblum, N. (Producer and Director). (1996). *Lock-up: The prisoners of Rikers Island.* New York: A Home Box Office Production.

Rosenson, M. K. (1994). Social work and the right of psychiatric patients to refuse medication: A family advocate's response. *Social Work, 38,* 107-112.

Rosewater, L. B. (1988). Feminist therapies with women. In M. A. Dutton-Douglas & L. E. Walker (Eds.), *Feminist psychotherapies: Integration of therapeutic and feminist systems* (pp. 137-155). Norwood, NJ: Ablex.

Ross, G. R. (1994). *Treating adolescent substance abuse: Understanding the fundamental elements.* Boston: Allyn and Bacon.

Ross, R. R., & McKay, H. B. (1978). Behavioural approaches to treatment in corrections: Requiem for a panacea. *Canadian Journal of Criminology and Corrections, 20,* 279-295.

Ross, R. R., Fabiano, E. A., & Ewles, C. D. (1988). Reasoning and rehabilitation. *Journal of Offender Therapy and Comparative Criminology, 32,* 29-35.

Roth, A. D. (1985). An examination of whether incarcerated juveniles are entitled by the Constitution to rehabilitative treatment. *Michigan Law Review, 84,* 286-307.

Rothman, C. (1997, September 30). Search for meaning leads Kirk Douglas to Judaism. *USA Today,* p. 8D.

Rotman, E. (1986). Do criminal offenders have a constitutional right to rehabilitation? *Journal of Criminal Law & Criminology, 77,* 1023-1068.

Rounsaville, B. J., & Carroll, K. M. (1997). Individual psychotherapy. In J. H. Lowinson, P. Ruiz, R. B. Millman, & J. G. Langrod (Eds.), *Substance abuse: A comprehensive textbook* (3rd ed.). (pp. 430-439). Baltimore: Williams & Wilkins.

Rouse v. Cameron, 373 F.2d 451 (D.C. Cir. 1966).

Rouse, J. J. (1991). Evaluation research on prison-based treatment programs and some policy implications. *International Journal of the Addictions, 26,* 29-44.

Russell, M. N. (1984). *Skills in counseling women: The feminist approach.* Springfield, IL: Charles C. Thomas.

Ruth, R. (1998, May 30). Four gang members guilty of drug crimes. *Columbus Dispatch,* p. 3B.

Safley v. Turner, 777 F.2d 1307 (8th Cir. 1985).

Sanders, J. F., McNeill, K. F., Rienzi, B. M., & DeLouth, T.N.B. (1997). The incarcerated female felon and substance abuse: Demographics, needs assessment, and program planning for a neglected population. *Journal of Addictions & Offender Counseling, 18,* 41-51.

Sands, T. (1998). Feminist counseling and female adolescents: Treatment strategies for depression. *Journal of Mental Health Counseling, 20,* 42-54.

Sanson-Fisher, B., Seymour, F., Montgomery, W., & Stokes, T. (1978). Modifying delinquents' conversation using token reinforcement or self-recorded behavior. *Journal of Behavioral Therapy & Experiential Psychiatry, 9,* 163-168.

Santana v. Collazo, 533 F. Supp. 966 (1982).

Santana v. Collazo, 714 F.2d 1172 (1st Cir. 1983).

Sappington, A. A. (1996). Relationships among prison adjustment, beliefs, and cognitive coping style. *International Journal of Offender Therapy and Comparative Criminology, 40,* 54-62.

Sapsford, L. (1997). Strengthening voices: A soulful approach to working with adolescent girls. *Women & Therapy, 20,* 75-87.

Saraceno, J. (1996, March 15). Tyson fighting to find himself, regain crown. *USA Today,* p. C1.

Saradjian, J. (1996). *Women who sexually abuse children: From research to clinical practice.* Chichester, Englanad: John Wiley & Sons.

Saunders, D. G. (1996). Feminist-cognitive-behavioral and process-psychodynamics treatments for men who batter: Interaction of abuser traits and treatment models. *Violence and Victims, 11,* 393-414.

Scarnati, R. A. (1992). Prison psychiatrist's role in a residential treatment unit of dangerous psychiatric inmates. *Forensic Reports, 5,* 367-384.

Scarpino v. Grosshiem, 852 F. Supp. 798 (S.D. Iowa 1994).

Scharlach, A. E. (1989). Social group work with the elderly: A role theory perspective. *Social Work With Groups, 12,* 33-46.

Schiele, J. H. (1997). An afrocentric perspective on social welfare philosophy and policy. *Journal of Sociology and Social Welfare, 24,* 21-39

Schinka, J. A., Hughes, P. H., Doletti, S. D., Hamilton, N. L., Renard, C. G., Urmann, C. F., & Neri, R. L. (1999). Changes in personality characteristics in women treated in a therapeutic community. *Journal of Substance Abuse Treatment, 16,* 137-142.

Schonberg, S. K. et al. (1993). *Guidelines for the treatment of alcohol- and other drug-abusing adolescents (TIP 4).* Rockville, MD: Center for Substance Abuse Treatment.

Schrodt, G. R., Jr. (1993). Adolescent inpatient treatment. In J. H. Wright, M. E. Thase, A. T. Beck, & J. W. Ludgate (Eds.), *Cognitive therapy with inpatients: Developing a cognitive milieu* (pp. 273-294). New York: The Guilford Press.

Schwartz, W. (1961). *The social worker in the group.* New York: Columbia University Press.

Scott, E. (1993). Prison group therapy with mentally and emotionally disturbed offenders. *International Journal of Offender*

Therapy and Comparative Criminology, *37*, 131-145.

Sechrest, L., White, S. O., & Brown, E. D. (1979). *The rehabilitation of criminal offenders: Problems and prospects*. Washington, DC: National Academy of Sciences.

Segal, Z. V., & Marshall, W. L. (1985). Heterosexual social skills in a population of rapists and child molesters. *Journal of Consulting & Clinical Psychology*, *53*, 55-63.

Senay, E. C. (1998). *Substance abuse disorders in clinical practice* (2nd ed.). New York: W. W. Norton & Company.

Serin, R. C., & Kuriychuk, M. (1994). Social and cognitive processing deficits in violent offenders: Implications for treatment. *International Journal of Law and Psychiatry*, *17*, 431-441.

Sex ban upheld in LA. Prisons. (1997, January 16). *Times-Picayune*, p. B8.

Sex predator law ruled unconstitutional (1995, August 1995). *Columbus Dispatch*, p. 4A.

Sgroi, S. M., & Sargent, N. M. (1993). Impact and treatment issues for victims of childhood sexual abuse by female perpetrators. In M. Elliott (Ed.), *Female sexual abuse of children* (pp. 14-36). New York: The Guilford Press.

Shapiro, D. (1997). Reduction in drug requirements for hypertension by means of a cognitive-behavioral intervention. *American Journal of Hypertension*, *10*, 9-17.

Shapiro, M. H. (1974). Legislating the control of behavior control: Autonomy and the coercive use of organic therapies. *Southern California Law Review*, *47*, 237-356.

Shapiro, R., Siegal, A. W., Scovill, L. C., & Hays, J. (1998). Risk-taking patterns of female adolescents: What they do and why. *Journal of Adolescent*, *21*, 143-159.

Shaw, T. A., Herkov, M. J., & Greer, R. A. (1995). Examination of treatment completion and predictive outcome among incarcerated sex offenders. *Bulletin of the American Academy of Psychiatry and the Law*, *23*, 35-41.

Shean, G. D. (1985). Rehabilitation: Social skills groups. In R. K. Conyne (Ed.), *The group workers' handbook: Varieties of group experience* (pp. 23-41). Springfield, IL: Charles C. Thomas.

Shearer, R. A. (1993). *Interviewing in criminal justice* (2nd ed.). Acton, MA: Copley.

Sheldon, B. (1995). *Cognitive-behavioural therapy: Research, practice and philosophy*. London: Routledge.

Shepherd, R. E., Jr. (1977). Challenging the rehabilitation justification for indeterminate sentencing in the juvenile justice system: The right to punishment. *Saint Louis University Law Review*, *21*, 12-21.

Sherman, L. W. (1982). *Ethics in criminal justice education*. New York: Institute of Society, Ethics and the Life Sciences, The Hastings Center.

Shneidman, E. S. (1980). Some aspects of psychotherapy with dying persons. In E. S. Shneidman (Ed.), *Death: Current perspectives* (2nd ed.). (pp. 202-213). Palo Alto, CA: Mayfield.

Shobat, S. (1985). Pathway through the psychotropic jungle: The right to refuse psychotropic drugs in Illinois. *The John Marshall Law Review*, *18*, 407-443.

Sholevar, G. P., & Sholevar, E. H. (1995). Overview. In G. P. Sholevar (Ed.), *Conduct disorders in children and adolescents* (pp. 3-26). Washington, DC: American Psychiatric Press.

Showalter, R. C. (1992). Death row inmates: Evaluation and treatment. In R. I. Simon (Ed.), *American psychiatric review of clinical psychiatry and the law* (Vol. 3). (pp. 173-181). Washington, DC: American Psychiatric Press.

Shulman, L. (1984). *The skills of helping: Individuals and groups* (2nd ed.). Itasca, IL: Peacock.

Sickmund, M. (1997). *The juvenile delinquency probation caseload, 1985-1994*. Washington, DC: Office of Juvenile Justice and Delinquency Prevention.

Sickmund, M., Snyder, H. N., Poe-Yamagata, E. (1997). *Juvenile offenders and victims: 1997 update on violence*. Washington, DC: Office of Juvenile Justice and Delinquency Prevention.

Siebert, M. J., & Dorfman, W. L. (1995). Group composition and its impact on effective group treatment of HIV and AIDS patients. *Journal of Developmental and Physical Disabilities*, *7*, 317-334.

Siegal, H. A., & Cole, P. A. (1993). Enhancing criminal justice based treatment through the application of the intervention approach. *Journal of Drug Issues*, *23*, 131-142.

Siegel, L. J., & Senna, J. J. (1997). *Juvenile delinquency* (6th ed.). St. Paul, MN: West.

Sigafoos, C. E. (1994). A PSTD treatment program for combat (Vietnam) veterans in prison. *International Journal of Offender Therapy and Comparative Criminology, 38,* 117-130.

Silber, T. J., & Silber, D. (1996). Ethical issues in counseling adolescents who abuse alcohol and drugs (pp. 175-196). In J. Lonsdale (Ed.), *Treating substance abuse* Part II. New York: Hatherleigh Press.

Silfen, P., Ben David, S., Kliger, D., Eshel, R., Heichel, H., & Lehman, D. (1977). The adaptation of the older prisoner in Israel. *International Journal of Offender Therapy & Comparative Criminology, 21,* 57-65.

Silk, M. (1995, December 8). Schoolteacher sentenced for student affair. *Atlanta Constitution,* p. F2.

Simmons, K. P., Sack, T., & Miller, G. (1996). Sexual abuse and chemical dependency: Implications for women in recovery. *Women & Therapy, 19,* 17-30.

Simourd, D. J. (1997). The criminal sentiments scale-modified and pride in delinquency scale: Psychometric properties and construct validity of two measures of criminal attitudes. *Criminal Justice and Behavior, 24,* 52-70.

Singer, M. I., Bussey, J., Song, L., & Lunghofer, L. (1995). The psychosocial issues of women serving time in jail. *Social Work, 40,* 103-113.

Slade, P. D., & Haddock, G. (1996). A historical overview of psychological treatments for psychotic symptoms. In G. Haddock & P. D. Slade (Eds.), *Cognitive-behavioural interventions with psychotic disorders* (pp. 28-42). London: Routledge.

Slaiken, K. A. (1973). Evaluation studies on group treatment of juvenile and adult offenders in correctional institutions: A review of the literature. *Journal of Research in Crime and Delinquency, 10,* 87-100.

Smeltzer, N. J. (1998). Program helps treat mentally retarded sexual offenders. *Columbus Dispatch,* p. 4E.

Smith v. Schneckloth, 414 F.2d 680 (9th Cir. 1969).

Smith, A. B., & Berlin, L. (1988). *Treating the criminal offender* (3rd ed.). New York: Plenum Press.

Smith, B. V. (1993, Spring). Special needs of women in the criminal justice system. *TIE Communique.* Rockville, MD: U.S. Department of Health and Human Services.

Smith, B. V., & Dailard, C. (1994). Female prisoners and AIDS: On the margins of public health and social justice. *AIDS and Public Policy Journal, 9,* 78-85.

Smith, H. (1998). Save our sons: Wrong to say violence strictly home-grown. *Houston Chronicle,* p. C1.

Smith, J. C. (1990). *Cognitive-behavioral relaxation training: A new system of strategies for treatment and assessment.* New York: Springer.

Smith, L. L., & Beckner, B. M. (1993). An anger management workshop for inmates in a medium security facility. *Journal of Offender Rehabilitation, 19(3/4),* 103-111.

Snyder, H. N. (1997). *Juvenile arrests 1996.* Washington, DC: Office of Juvenile Justice and Delinquency Prevention.

Solomon, H. (1996). Girls in day treatment: A different flavor of sugar and spice. *Reclaiming Children and Youth, 5,* 90-95.

Somerson, M. D. (1999, January 10). AMA gives immortality to sex-scandal reporter. *Columbus Dispatch,* p. 7B.

Souryal, S. S. (1992). *Ethics in criminal justice: In search of the truth.* Cincinnati, OH: Anderson.

Spence, S. H. (1981). Differences in social skills performance between institutionalized juvenile male offenders and a comparable group of boys without offense records. *British Journal of Clinical Psychology, 20,* 163-171.

Spergel, I, Curry, D., Chance, R., Kane, C., Ross, R., Alexander, A., Simmons, E., & Oh, S. (1996). *Gang suppression and intervention: Problem and response.* Washington, DC: Office of Juvenile Justice and Delinquency Prevention.

Stacey, J. (1993). Untangling feminist theory. In D. Richardson & V. Robinson (Eds.), *Thinking feminist: Key concepts in women's studies* (pp. 49-73). New York: Guilford Press.

Steadman, H. J., & Veysey, B. M. (1997). *Providing services for jail inmates with mental disorders.* National Institute of Justice Research in Brief. Washington, DC: U. S. Department of Justice.

Steiner, J. (1984). Group counseling with retarded offenders. *Social Work, 29,* 181-185.

Stere, L. (1986). A reformist perspective on feminist practice. In M. Bricker-Jenkins & N. R. Hooyman (Eds.), *Not for women only: Social work practice for a feminist future* (pp. 40-47). Silver Spring, MD: National Association of Social Workers.

Stermac, L. E., & Quinsey, V. L. (1986). Social competence among rapists. *Behavioral Assessment, 8,* 171-185.

Stevens, D. J. (1994). The depth of imprisonment and prisonization: Levels of security and prisoners' anticipation of future violence. *Howard Journal of Criminal Justice, 33,* 137-157.

Stevens, G. F. (1994). Prison clinician's perceptions of antisocial personality disorder as a formal diagnosis. *Journal of Offender Rehabilitation, 20,* 159-185.

Stevens, J. W. (1997). African American female adolescent identity development: A three-dimensional perspective. *Child Welfare, 76,* 145-172.

Stevenson, H. C. (1998). Raising safe villages: Cultural-ecological factors that influence the emotional adjustment of adolescents. *Journal of Black Psychology, 24,* 44-59.

Stoller, F. H. (1972). Marathon groups: Toward a conceptual model. *New perspectives on encounter groups* (pp. 171-187). San Francisco: Jossey-Bass.

Stratton, J., & Gailfus, D. (1998). A new approach to substance abuse treatment: Adolescents and adults with ADHD. *Journal of Substance Abuse Treatment, 15,* 89-94.

Strean, H. (1996). Psychoanalytic theory and social work practice. In F. J. Turner (Ed.). *Social work treatment: Interlocking theoretical approaches* (2nd ed.).(pp. 523-554). New York: The Free Press.

Sue, D. W., & Sue, D. (1990). *Counseling the culturally different: Theory and practice* (2nd ed.). New York: John Wiley & Sons.

Sundel, S. S., & Sundel, M. (1993). *Behavior modification in the human services: A systematic introduction to concepts and applications* (3rd ed.): Newbury, CA: Sage.

Surati, M. (1989). Pyschotherapy with addicts. *Indian Journal of Social Work, 50,* 69-80.

Sutphen, R. D., Thyer, B. A., & Kurtz, P. D. (1995). Multisystemic treatment of high-risk juvenile offenders. *International Journal of Offender Therapy and Comparative Criminology, 39,* 327-334.

Swenson, L. C. (1993). *Psychology and the law for the helping professions.* Pacific Grove, CA: Brooks/Cole.

Sykes, G. M., & Matza, D. (1991). Techniques of neutralization: A theory of delinquency. In W. E. Thompson & J. E. Bynum (Eds.), *Juvenile delinquency: Classic and contemporary readings* (pp. 219-226). Boston: Allyn and Bacon.

Tarter, R. E., Ott, P. J., & Mezzich, A. C. (1991). Psychometric assessment. In R. J. Frances & S. I. Miller (Eds.), *Clinical textbook of addictive disorders* (pp. 237-267). New York: The Guilford Press.

Tate, D. C., Reppucci, N. D., & Mulvey, E. P. (1995). Violent juvenile delinquents: Treatment effectiveness and implications for future action. *American Psychologist, 50,* 777-781.

Tennessee Code Annotated § 41-21-241 (1998).

Texas Human Resources Code § 141.061 (1998).

Texas Revised Civil Statutes Article 4512g (1998).

Teyber, E. (1988). *Interpersonal process in psychotherapy: A guide for clinical training.* Chicago: The Dorsey Press.

Thomas, A. (1996, June 9). Referrals rise for troubled moms-to-be: ADAMH treating more women for addictions. *Columbus Dispatch,* p. 4C.

Thomas, S. A. (1977). Theory and practice in feminist therapy. *Social Work, 22,* 447-454.

Thompson, L. W. (1996). Cognitive-behavioral therapy and treatment for late-life depression. *Journal of Clinical Psychiatry, 57,* 29-37.

Thornberry, T. P. (1998). Membership in youth gangs and involvement in serious and violent offending. In P. Loeber & D. P. Farrington (Eds.), *Serious & violent juvenile offenders: Risk factors and successful interventions* (pp. 147-166). Thousand Oaks, CA: Sage.

Thornton, D., & Hogue, T. (1993). The large-scale provision of programmes for imprisoned sex offenders: Issues, dilemmas and progress. *Criminal Behaviour and Mental Health, 3,* 371-380.

Timm v. Gunter, 917 F.2d 1093 (8th Cir. 1990).

Tims, F. M., & Leukefeld, C. G. (1992). The challenge of drug abuse treatment in prisons and jails. In C. G. Leukefeld & F. M. Tims (Eds), *Drug abuse treatment in prisons and jails* (pp. 1-7). Rockville, MD: National Institute on Drug Abuse

Tipton, V. (1991, September 7). Female guards suspended at Chesterfield county jail. *St. Louis Post-Dispatch,* p.A3.

Title 42 U.S.C. Section 1983 (1871).

Tolman, R. M., Edleson, J. L., & Fendrich, M. (1996). The applicability of the theory of planned behavior to abusive men's cessation of violent behavior. *Violence and Victims, 11*, 341-354.

Toneatto, A., Sobell, L. C., Sobell, M. B., & Kozlowski, L. T. (1995). Effect of cigarette smoking on alcohol treatment outcome. *Journal of Substance Abuse, 7,* 245-252.

Toneatto, T. (1995). The regulation of cognitive states: A cognitive model of psychoactive substance abuse. *Journal of Cognitive Psychotherapy, 9,* 93-104.

Torraco v. Maloney, 923 F.2d 231 (1st Cir. 1991).

Torres, S. (1997). An effective supervision strategy for substance-abusing offenders. *Federal Probation, 61(2),* 38-44.

Towberman, D. B. (1993). Group vs. individual counseling: Treatment mode and the client's perception of the treatment environment. *Journal of Group Psychotherapy, Psychodrama, and Sociometry, 45,* 163-174.

Trad, P. V. (1994). Developmental vicissitudes that promote drug abuse in adolescents. *American Journal of Drug and Alcohol Abuse, 20,* 459-481.

Trop v. Dulles, 356 U.S. 86 (1959).

Trotzer, J. P. (1989). *The counselor and the group: Integrating theory, training, and practice* (2nd ed.). Muncie, IN: Accelerated Development.

Trotzer, J. P. (1994). The process of group counseling. In P. C. Dratcoski (Ed.), *Correctional counseling & treatment* (pp. 333-359). Prospect Heights, IL: Waveland.

Turner v. Safley, 107 S. Ct. 2254 (1987).

Tyson, A. S. (1996, December 9). Sexual abuse rises as more women do time. *Christian Science Monitor,* p1.

U. S. Department of Justice (1997a). *Nation's jail and prison incarceration rate almost doubled during last decade.* [Press Release] Internet Address: http://www.ojp.usdoj.gov/bjs/pub/press/pjimy96.pr.

U. S. Department of Justice (1997b). *Nation's prison population increased 5 percent last year.* [Press Release] Internet Address: http://www.ojp.usdoj.gov/bjs/pub/press/p96.pr.

U. S. Department of Justice (1997d). *Nation's probation and parole population reached almost 3.9 million last year.* [Press Release] Internet Address: http://www.ojp.usdoj.gov/bjs/pub/press/propar94.pr.

U. S. Department of Justice (1997e). *Nearly three-quarters of all probationers had some recent contact with their probation officers.* [Press Release] Internet Address: http://www.ojp.usdoj.gov/bjs/pub/press/cap95.pr.

Uziel-Miller, N. D., Lyons, J. S., Kissiel, C., & Love, S. (1998). Treatment needs and initial outcomes of a residential recovery program for African American women and their children. *The American Journal of Addictions, 7,* 43-50.

Valentich, M. (1986). Feminism and social work practice. In F. J. Turner & K. A. Kendall (Eds.), *Social work treatment: Interlocking theoretical approaches* (3rd ed.), (pp. 564-589). New York: The Free Press.

Valentine, P. V. (1998). Traumatic incident reduction: Brief treatment of trauma-related symptoms in incarcerated females. *Proceedings of the Tenth National Symposium on Doctoral Research in Social Work.* Columbus, OH: College of Social Work, The Ohio State University.

Valliant, P. M., Ennis, L. P., & Raven-Brooks, L. (1995). A cognitive-behavior therapy model for anger management with adult offenders. *Journal of Offender Rehabilitation, 22(3/4),* 77-93.

Valliant, P. M., & Raven, L. M. (1994). Management of anger and its effect on incarcerated assaultive and nonassaultive offenders. *Psychological Reports, 75,* 275-278.

Vander Kolk, C. J. (1985). *Introduction to group counseling and psychotherapy.* Columbus, OH: Merrill.

Vannicelli, M. (1995). Group psychotherapy with substance abusers and family members. In A. M. Washton (Ed.), *Psychotherapy and substance abuse: A practitioner's handbook* (pp. 337-356). New York: The Guilford Press.

Varley, W. H (1984). Behavior modification approaches to the aggressive adolescent. In C. R. Keith (Ed.), *The aggressive adolescent: Clinical perspectives* (pp. 268-298). New York: The Free Press.

Vitek v. Jones, 445 U.S. 480 (1979).

Vito, G. R., & Wilson, D. G. (1985). Forgotten people: Elderly inmates. *Federal Probation, 49,* 18-24.

Von Drehle, D. (1995). *Among the lowest of the dead: The culture of death row.* New York: Times Books.

Walen, S. R., DiGiuseppe, R., & Dryden, W. (1992). *A practitioner's guide to rational-emotive therapy* (2nd ed.). New York: Oxford University Press.

Wallace, B. C. (1995). Women and minorities in treatment. In A. M. Washton (Ed.), *Psychotherapy and substance abuse: A practitioner's handbook* (pp. 480-492). New York: The Guilford Press.

Walrond-Skinner, S. (1986). *A dictionary of psychotherapy*. London: Routledge & Kegan Paul.

Walsh, A. (1992). *Correctional assessment, casework, and counseling*. Laurel, MD: American Correctional Association.

Walsh, C. E. (1989). The older and long term inmate growing old in the New Jersey prison system. *Journal of Offender Counseling, Services, & Rehabilitation, 13(2)*, 215-248.

Walsh, T. C. (1997). Alcoholic offenders: Survey data suggesting auxiliary treatment interventions. *The Prison Journal, 77*, 58-76.

Walston, C. (1989, July 7). Counselor gets 7 years on sodomy, drug charges. *Atlanta Constitution*, p. C2.

Ward, A., & Baldwin, S. (1997). Anger and violence management programs in correctional services: An annotated bibliography. *The Prison Journal, 77*, 472-488.

Warner v. Orange County Dept. of Probation, 870 F. Supp. 69 (S.D.N.Y. 1994).

Washington Statute, 71.09.060.

Washington v. Harper, 110 S. Ct. 1028 (1990).

Washton, A. M. (1995). Clinical assessment of psychoactive substance use. In A. M. Washton (Ed.), *Psychotherapy and substance abuse: A practitioner's handbook* (pp. 23-54). New York: The Guilford Press.

Wastell, C. A. (1996). Feminist developmental theory: implications for counseling. *Journal of Counseling & Development, 74*, 575-581.

Weems v. U.S., 217 U.S. 349 (1910).

Welle, D., Falkin, G. P., & Jainchill, N. (1998). Current approaches to drug treatment for women offenders: Project WORTH. *Journal of Substance Abuse Treatment, 15*, 151-163.

Wellisch, J., Prendergast, M. L., & Anglin, M. D. (1996). Needs assessment and services for drug-abusing women offenders: Results from a national survey of community-based treatment programs. *Women & Criminal Justice, 8*, 27-60.

Wells, E. A., Peterson, P. L., Gainey, R. R., Hawkins, J. D., & Catalano, R. F. (1994). Outpatient treatment for cocaine abuse: A controlled comparison of relapse prevention and twelve-step approaches. *American Journal of Drug and Alcohol Abuse, 20*, 1-17.

Welsh, W. N., Harris, P. W., Jenkins, P. H. (1996). Reducing overrepresentation of minorities in juvenile justice: Development of community-based programs in Pennsylvania. *Crime & Delinquency, 42*, 76-98.

Wenninger, K., & Ehlers, A. (1998). Dysfunctional cognitions and adult psychological functioning in child sexual abuse survivors. *Journal of Traumatic Stress, 11*, 281-301.

Wessler, R. L. (1993). Cognitive appraisal therapy and disorders of personality. In K. T. Kuehlwein & H. Rosen (Eds.), *Cognitive therapies in action: Evolving innovative practices* (pp. 240-267). San Francisco: Jossey-Bass.

West v. Virginia Dept. of Corrections, 847 F. Supp. 402 (W.D. Va. 1994).

Wettstein, R. M. (1992). A psychiatric perspective on Washington's sexually violent predator statutes. *University of Puget Sound Law Review, 15*, 597-633.

Wexler, H. K. (1994). Progress in prison substance abuse treatment: A five year report. *Journal of Drug Issues, 24*, 349-360.

Wexler, H. K. (1995). The success of therapeutic communities for substance abusers in American prisons. *Journal of Psychoactive Drugs, 27*, 57-66.

Wexler, H. K., & Love, C. T. (1994). Therapeutic communities in prison. In F. M. Tims, DeLeon, G., & Jainchill, N. (Eds.), *Therapeutic community: Advances in research and application* (pp. 181-208). Rockville, MD: National Institute of Drug Abuse.

Wexler, H. K., Falkin, G. P., & Lipton, D. S. (1990). Outcome evaluation of a prison therapeutic community for substance abuse treatment. *Criminal Justice and Behavior, 17*, 71-92.

Whiddon, M. F. (1983). Logotherapy in prison. *Logotherapy: Journal of Search for Meaning, 6*, 34-39.

Whitaker, D. S. (1985). *Using groups to help people*. London: Routledge & Kegan Paul.

White v. Napolean, 897 F.2d 103 (3rd Cir. 1990).

Whitehead, J. T. (1991). Ethical issues in probation and parole. In M. C. Brawell, B. R. McCarthy, & B. J. McCarthy (Eds.), *Justice, crime and ethics* (pp. 253-275). Cincinnati, OH: Anderson.

Wife's killing years ago locks elderly inmate into a confined existence. (1997, December 4). *Detroit News*, p. C8.

Wilde, J. (1996). *Treating anger, anxiety, and depression in children and adolescents: A cognitive-behavioral perspective*. Washington, DC: Accelerated Development.

Wilkinson, D. Y. (1980). Minority women: Socio-cultural issues. In A. Brodsky & R. Hare-Mustin (Eds.), *Women and psychotherapy: An assessment of research and practice* (pp. 285-304). New York: Guilford.

Williams, J. B. W. (1994). Psychiatric classification. In R. E. Hales, S. C. Yudofsky, & J. A. Talbott (Eds.), *Textbook of psychiatry* (2nd ed.). (pp. 221-246). Washington, DC: American Psychiatric Press.

Wilson, G. L. (1990). Psychotherapy with depressed incarcerated felons: A comparative evaluation of treatments. *Psychological Reports, 67*, 1027-1041.

Wilson, G. L., & Hanna, M. S. (1990). *Groups in context: Leadership and participation in small groups* (2nd ed.). New York: McGraw-Hill.

Wilson, J. G., & Pescor, M. J. (1939). *Problems in prison psychiatry*. Caldwell, ID: Caxton Printers.

Wilson, J. R., & Wikson, J. A. (1992). *Addictionary: A primer of recovery terms and concepts from abstinence to withdrawal*. New York: Simon & Schuster.

Wing, A. K., & Willis, C. A. (1997). Critical race feminism: Black women and gangs. *Journal of Gender, Race and Justice, 1*, 141-175.

Winick, B. J. (1997). *The right to refuse mental health treatment*. Washington, DC: American Psychological Association.

Winn, M. E. (1996). The strategic and systematic management of denial in the cognitive/behavioral treatment of sexual offenders. *Sexual Abuse Journal of Research and Treatment, 8*, 25-36.

Witt, P. H., Rambus, E., & Bosley, T. (1996). Current developments in psychotherapy for child molesters. *Sexual and Marital Therapy, 11*, 173-185.

Wolf, Y., Friedlander, M., Addad, M., & Silfan, P. (1993). Moral judgement of borderline and antisocial personality. *Israel Journal of Psychology, 7*, 135-143.

Wolf, Y., Katz, S., & Nachson, I. (1995). Meaning of life as perceived by drug abusing people. *International Journal of Offender Therapy and Comparative Criminology, 39*, 121-137.

Wolfgang, M. E. (1988). The medical model versus the just deserts model. *Bulletin American Academy Psychiatry and Law, 16(2)*, 111-121.

Wolk, J. L., & Hartmann, D. J. (1996). Process evaluation in corrections-based substance abuse treatment. *Journal of Offender Rehabilitation, 23*, 67-78.

Women Prisoners of the Dist. of Columbia Dept. of Corrections v. District of Columbia, 93 F.3d 910 (DDC. 1996).

Worell, J., & Remer, P. (1992). *Feminist perspectives in therapy: An empowerment model for women*. New York: John Wiley & Sons.

World-wide: a drill sergeant in Missouri. (1996, November 14). *Wall Street Journal*, p A1.

Wowk, M. (1993, January 22). Reader opinions not guarded on inmates' charges. *Detroit News*, p. B4S.

Wright, N. A. (1995). Social skills training for conduct-disordered boys in residential treatment: A promising approach. *Residential Treatment for Children & Youth, 12*, 15-28.

Yablonsky, L. (1989). *The therapeutic community: A successful approach for treating substance abusers*. New York: Gardner Press.

Yalom, I. D. (1985). *The theory and practice of group psychotherapy* (3rd ed.). New York: BasicBooks.

Young, V. (1993). Women abusers—a feminist view. In M. Elliott (Ed.), *Female sexual abuse of children* (pp. 100-112). New York: The Guilford Press.

Youngberg v. Romeo, 457 U.S. 307 (1982).

Zaidi, L. Y., & Gutierrez-Kovner, V. M. (1995). Group treatment of sexually abused latency-age girls. *Journal of Interpersonal Violence, 10*, 215-227.

Zimpfer, D. G. (1992). Group work with juvenile delinquents. *Journal for Specialists in Group Work, 17*, 116-126.

INDEX